THE
CHIEF
EXECUTIVE

THIRD EDITION

THE
CHIEF
EXECUTIVE

THIRD EDITION

LOUIS W. KOENIG
New York University

HARCOURT BRACE JOVANOVICH, INC.
New York   Chicago   San Francisco   Atlanta

To Juliana, Fred, and David

ISBN: 0-15-506672-2

Library of Congress Catalog Card Number: 74-33005

Printed in the United States of America

PREFACE

This is the third edition of a book that was first published in 1964. The previous versions of *The Chief Executive* advocated a strong Presidency as a source of good works, as a force for betterment in domestic society and in the world at large. My argument for a strong Presidency included a tacit assumption, encouraged by the historic record, that the office, despite its substantial power, was readily compatible with democracy.

Watergate, Richard Nixon's relinquishment of the Presidency forced by his imminent impeachment, and aspects of the Indochina war have disclosed dramatically that the office can be misused to the point at which democracy itself is threatened. These untoward developments have forced me, in this new edition, to articulate what had been unexplored in the earlier editions, that is, how, and to what degree, a Presidency of strength can be reconciled with democratic values and processes.

I still contend that the United States and humankind need a strong Presidency to deal sufficiently with a lengthy agenda of problems—inflation, unemployment, food, energy, health, housing, poverty, arms control. In this edition, however, I also attempt to develop a proviso to my contention: that the Presidency must be constrained by other forces and institutions—Congress, the courts, political parties, the news media, interest groups, and by a sturdy democratic socialization of the President. In essence, the book focuses on the problem of establishing and maintaining equilibrium between the strong Presidency and democratic counterforces, a problem that must be resolved for the sake of human liberty and happiness. The task is similar to that which engaged the makers of the Declaration of Independence, and by interesting coincidence reemerges to the forefront of political concerns as the nation nears the two-hundredth anniversary of its founding.

This third edition has been revised to encompass the considerable body of new scholarship on the Presidency, particularly that relating to personality, socialization, public opinion, and contemporary constitutional questions concerning war, impoundment of funds, executive privilege, and the power to pardon. I have added a chapter on the President's role as a conflict manager and another on Presidential leadership and its links to the varieties of constituency. I have also enlarged and reordered the bibliography in ways that should make it more useful to the reader.

It is a pleasure to acknowledge my gratitude to James David Barber of Duke University for his thoughtful reading of the manuscript, and to many users of the previous editions who generously have offered fruitful suggestions. At Harcourt Brace Jovanovich the book has benefited from the careful editing of Peter Kaldheim and the helpfulness of Harrison C. Griffin, Thomas A. Williamson, and Everett M. Sims. My views on the Chief Executive have continued to gain from the perceptive comments of students in my university classes on the American Presidency and from participants in the Executive Seminar Center of the United States Civil Service Commission at Kings Point, New York. To my wife Eleanor and daughter Juliana, my gratitude continues—unrevised.

LOUIS W. KOENIG

CONTENTS

Preface   v

1
Perspectives on Presidential Power   1

Excesses of Presidential   The Need for a Strong
  Power   2   Presidency   9
The Sun King Complex   3   The Imperiled Presidency   10
Nixon as Radical   5   Practical Politics   12
Democratic Ground Rules   8   Presidential Types   14

2
Beginnings   18

The New York Governor   19   Structural Concepts   27
The Philadelphia Convention   20   The Presidency Begins   29
Decisions at Philadelphia   22   Presidential Strength:
Drafting the Presidential   George Washington   30
  Article   25   Presidential Weakness:
Makers of the Presidency   26   John Adams   33

3
Selection   35

The Preconvention Struggle   36   The Electoral College   54
Preconvention Strategies   38   Defects of the Electoral College 56
The National Nominating   Alternatives to the Electoral
  Convention   40   College   58
The Convention Decides   44   The Future Presidency   61

4
Tenure   63

Resignation   65   Handling Disability:
Impeachment   66   The Twenty-fifth Amendment 81
The President and Legal   Succession   84
  Processes   73   Presidential Transitions   86
Disability   76   The Future Presidency   89

5
Publics   92

The President and Public   The President-Constituency
  Opinion   92   Influence Process   98
Constituencies   95   Roles   102

vii

The Mass Media 103
Communications Experts 104
The News Conference 105
The Art of News Management 108
The President as Consensus
  Leader 111
The Majoritarian President 112
The Future Presidency 113

6
Party Chief 115

The President and His Party 115
The Presidential Nominee 119
Winning Renomination 121
The Congressional Party 123
The Jeffersonian Success Model 126
Those Who Failed 129
Franklin Roosevelt as Party
  Leader 131
Eisenhower as a Bipartisan 135
Kennedy and the Urban Era 138
Johnson the Consensus Leader 141
Nixon and the New American
  Majority 144
The Future Presidency 146

7
Legislative Leader 150

The Good Legislative Years 151
Congress and the President:
  An Imbalance? 153
Congress and the President:
  Basic Differences 158
Inside Congress 159
Congressional Majorities 161
Open and Closed Politics 164
Approaches to Legislative
  Leadership 168
The Future Presidency 176

8
Administrative Chief 181

Congress as Administrator 183
The Bureaucracy 184
The Presidential Staff 185
Roosevelt as Administrator 189
Eisenhower's Staff System 192
Kennedy's Personal Management 196
Johnson's Consensus Method 200
Nixonian Centralism 202
Ford: Centralism Diminished 208
The Future Presidency 210

9
Chief Diplomat 213

The Two Presidencies 213
Constitutional Limitations 215
Presidential War 217
Cooperation with Congress 220
The Foreign Aid Program 221
The Secretary of State 222
The President's Staff 224
Foreign Leaders 229
Summit Conferences 231
Alliances 233
The United Nations 235
The Future Presidency 236

10
Commander-in-Chief 239

Limitations on Presidential Power	239	Communist War-making	253
The Defense Department	240	Alliances	254
The President and the Generals	242	Nuclear Weaponry	256
Sources of Authority	245	The Scientific Community	259
The Courts	248	The Future Presidency	261

11
The Economy 264

The President as Friend of Business	265	Business's Weapons	277
Winning Business Confidence	267	Labor Leaders and the President	279
Frictions	270	How Presidents Are Useful to Labor	283
How Presidents Fight Business	271	Labor-Management Disputes	288
The "New Economics"	274	The Future Presidency	291

12
Social Justice 293

A Historical View	294	Early Efforts for Civil Rights	314
The President as Social Critic	299	John Kennedy and Civil Rights	315
The Limitations of Politics	301	Lyndon Johnson and Civil Rights	319
The President Keeps the Balance	303	Richard Nixon and the Black	
Reform as Legislation	305	Community	319
The Executive Branch	309	A Ford Is Not a Lincoln	320
How Presidents Resist Social		Limitations of Power	322
Programs	312	An Overview	324

13
Political Personality 326

Values	327	What Kind of Strong President Is	
Goals	331	Most Compatible with Democracy?	339
Style	333	Views of the Presidency	340
High-Democracy and Low-		An Overview	341
Democracy Presidential Types	336		

14
Decision-Making 343

Varieties of Decision	343	Consequences	356
The Environment	346	Pathologies of Decision-Making:	
The Alternatives	348	The Case of the Vietnam War	357
Choice-Making	351	An Overview	358
Making the Decision Known	354		

15
Conflict   360

Types of Conflict   361   Gradients of Conflict   365
The President as Conflict Generator   362   Conflict-Solving   368
Conflict as Political Exchange   363   Crisis   369

16
The Presidency Compared   381

The Governor   381   The British Prime Minister   395
The Mayor   385   The Parliamentary System Evaluated   398
Foreign Executives: Selection   The Administrative State   400
  and Tenure   388   Decision-Making Compared   403
Succession Compared   391   The Presidency Abroad   405
The British Parliamentary System   394

Epilogue: The Future of the American Presidency   407

Notes   411

Presidents of the United States   425

Constitutional Provisions Relating to the Presidency   426

Sources   431

Index   440

THE
CHIEF
EXECUTIVE

THIRD EDITION

1

PERSPECTIVES ON PRESIDENTIAL POWER

The Presidency was contrived by the hands of men who had their fingers crossed. The cause of their doubt became clear, as never before, near the advent of the two hundredth anniversary of American independence, when the Presidency was beset by abuses of power on a greater scale and more ominous than anything in any previous incumbency. The Watergate and related scandals and their aftermath of relentless cover-up led a British commentator to conclude that a standard of values was operative in the White House "formerly associated only with the presidential palaces of Latin-American banana republics, by comparison with which the conduct of the Mafia is made to seem positively dignified and salubrious." [1]

Are these sudden afflictions, which Gerald Ford termed a "national nightmare," to be attributed wholly to the President and his administration, that is, to Richard Nixon—to defects in his values and untoward facets of his character? To none of the thirty-five other Presidents has criminality been imputed, nor the commission of unconstitutional acts of such scope and force. Was Nixon an aberration, the single one in the history of the office? If so, with his departure, the Presidency should revert to a more normal course, free of recent stress and upheaval, in the incumbency of a successor whose behavior reflects the generally established and more acceptable patterns of Presidential conduct. Is the nightmare really "over" as Ford asserted in his inaugural address? And can its repetition be avoided simply by firm adherence to his pledge "to follow my instincts of openness and candor"? [2]

Or are the Nixonian malfeasances part of a continuum of excessive power in the Presidency, long moving in ever widening abuse? Seldom do historic disruptions spring from a single force, personality, or event; normally there are many contributors and causality ranges over an extended time-span. Thus the issue: Is it a single transgressor—Nixon—or is he the culmination of errancies by many Presidential predecessors, including some who sparkle as heroes in the

1

nation's memories? If it is the latter, it suggests a long-developing impairment of the resonance between forces external to the President—such as public opinion, Congress, the parties, the courts, and his personality—that together set in motion the dynamic of the Presidency.[3] Abuse extending over a number of Presidencies implies that these external forces are performing less than adequately in holding the President to acceptable conduct.

All this is preliminary to a larger and more basic issue: whether a Presidency of strong power, which, it will be argued, is needed today, can be arranged to function in the larger political system in ways that are compatible with democracy.

Excesses of Presidential Power

The case for the second view, that of continuous, enlarging abuse, focuses less upon the malpractices of the Nixon White House than upon the phenomenon of Presidential war, the initiation of war solely by executive decision, while Congress, which the Constitution empowers to declare war, is either shut out or permitted to exercise only negligible influence. The formulator of this Presidency in the modern era was Franklin Roosevelt. In the months before Pearl Harbor and following the conquest of France (June 1940–December 1941) that left Britain alone and threatened, and faced with Congressional and public opinion closely divided between isolationism and intervention, Roosevelt committed warlike acts on his own initiative and discretion. Among other things, he ordered the Navy to shoot Axis naval craft on sight, which it did on several occasions, and he dispatched American forces to occupy Greenland and Iceland, whose mother country, Denmark, the Germans had seized.[4]

After the Second World War, the phenomenon of Presidential war unfolded in its broadest proportions. It was then that the Presidency pursued an absorbing mission of containing Communist expansion around the globe. More and more the Presidency, largely by autonomous decisions, assumed the role of policeman to the world, reacting to real or imagined upsurges of danger with commitments of armaments and combat forces. The freest indulgers in independent power were Johnson and Nixon during the Indo-China War.[5] Johnson ordered American troops into combat and vastly multiplied their numbers by a sequence of decisions, until, compounding the more limited involvements of earlier Presidents, a war resulted that lasted longer than any other in American history and cost more money than any except the Second World War. When Johnson committed American troops to active hostilities, he ordered what Roosevelt never dared consider prior to Pearl Harbor. Unlike the Cuban missile crisis that confronted Kennedy, Johnson faced no sudden threat to the United States mainland by which he could justify secret and autonomous decisions, nor did he seek empowerment from external authority, as Truman did from the UN in the Korean War and Kennedy from the Organization of American States in the Cuban missile crisis. Prior to his more major war-making decisions, Johnson induced Congress to enact the Gulf of Tonkin resolution, though he made it clear at the time that he would confine himself only to seeking, as he said, "the opinion of Congress." The resolution was later discounted and seen as the progeny of misinformation supplied by the executive, an act—some have argued—of calculated deception.

Johnson's autonomous actions were directed only at North Vietnam, with which the United States was already engaged in de facto war. It remained for Richard Nixon to sweep beyond that confinement and invade neutral Cambodia and bomb neutral Laos, without consulting Congress. William Rehnquist, the then Assistant Attorney General, tried to justify Nixon's decisions by contending that the Commander-in-Chief clause of the Constitution was "a grant of substantive authority" that empowered Presidents throughout American history to send troops "into conflict with foreign powers on their own initiative." According to Rehnquist, this endowment of power enabled the President to carry the war into Cambodia to destroy sanctuaries of the North Vietnamese enemy as a step toward assuring the safety of American forces in adjacent South Vietnam. Nixon's move was "precisely the sort of tactical decision traditionally confided to the Commander-in-Chief in the conduct of armed conflict." [6]

The Nixon-Rehnquist argument, however, could cite no previous occasion when a President initiated a grand-scale invasion of a neutral country to protect American troops in a third country. The endangerment of American troops at the time of the Cambodian decision was less than it had been in prior years, and there was no suggestion that American forces were engaged in "hot pursuit" of the enemy on a route that led across Cambodia's borders. The argument's logic was open-ended, acknowledging no limitation, and by its terms it was conceivable that the President could order American forces to storm Moscow and Peking to safeguard their compatriots in Vietnam.

The Sun King Complex

The excessive Presidency has a monarchic dimension. In his insightful study, *The Twilight of the Presidency*, George Reedy, a former aide to President Johnson, observed that "the life of the White House is the life of a court," its endeavor committed to a single purpose—"to serve the material needs and the desires of a single man." [7] To the sundry attendants of this regal enterprise, the President appears engrossed in problems of the most enormous consequence, and, that he might concentrate his efforts fully upon them, he is spared the distractions and vexations that buffet the average citizen. Upon the President is lavished every facility to ease the travail of daily living and to assist his encounters with the "great issues." If the President himself lags in donning monarchic trappings, others will put them on him. Kennedy's modesty and ready self-depreciation did not deter the press from creating a modern Camelot by likening the White House to the valorous Arthurian court, an absurdity that the President himself would have laughingly derided. And Gerald Ford, whose middle-American demeanor causes him to be likened more to Babbitt than to royalty, was fawned over by the press in his early tenure, with his photograph a steady feature of the newspapers, and with minutiae such as his self-reliance and his eating habits at breakfast meticulously reported. The news media make the confident assumption that the President's countrymen are eager to assign him the role of father-figure.

Those inside the White House also contribute to the monarchic tendency. The President is surrounded and served by the human appurtenances of the monarch—by clerks, aides, and courtiers, who do not speak unless spoken to first. Like kings of old, the President abides not in one "castle," but migrates regularly between several. Of all Presidents, the most blessed in this regard was Richard Nixon, who regularly peregrinated to Camp David in Maryland and to his respective private estates in Florida and California. These retreats featured such luxuries as an electrical heating system installed to replace a gas system, a special ice machine to cope with the discovery that "the President does not like ice cubes with holes in them," and a three-hole golf course, built by gifts from admiring businessmen. In a Boeing 707 jet, "The Spirit of '76," Nixon journeyed to his estates, followed by a back-up plane and preceded by a Secret Service plane. When the Presidential jet was en route, the Air Force regularly sent out sorties of fighter planes to assure the President's security from attack.[8] One day a staff sergeant, seeing Lyndon Johnson, who was similarly favored with aircraft, start off toward the wrong helicopter, called, pointing, "Mr. President, *that* is your helicopter over there." The big Texan hugged the sergeant and explained, "Son, they are *all* my helicopters." [9]

Gone is the simplicity of Thomas Jefferson, who walked from his boarding house to the Capitol for his inaugural and returned the same way. That evening, at dinner, he found every seat in the dining room taken. No one chose to interrupt his repast to offer the new President of the United States his place, until finally the wife of Senator John Brown of Kentucky rose to yield hers at the preferred end of the table. Jefferson graciously declined her kindness.

Potentially, the most costly feature of the monarchic Presidency is its tendency to wall off the incumbent Chief Executive from contact with reality.[10] Those faithful tools for comprehending reality—caution, introspection, and humility—are inundated by the distracting activity of ceremonies and heavy workloads and the automatic acquiescence of courtiers, whose numbers are constantly multiplied by the unrelenting growth of the White House staff. The President's insulation from reality is reinforced by the trappings of power, the endless attentions and comforts, and the inhibiting awe generated by the White House itself, where hallowed figures—Jefferson, Jackson, Lincoln—have dwelt. To a degree, some contemporary Presidents have fought against their euphoric imprisonment. Johnson consulted a wide circle of acquaintances and authorities outside the White House, kept three television sets and three wire service teletypes running in the Oval Office, and each morning leafed avidly through newspapers and the *Congressional Record* to gauge his status according to external opinion.

Not as attentive as Johnson to sentiment in the outside world, Richard Nixon most fulfills the monarchic configuration of the Chief Executive, secluded and shielded from reality. His White House aides were tough and uncompromising gatekeepers who barred the access even of senators, governors, and cabinet secretaries, and when they complained publicly or angrily resigned there was still not the slightest change in the system. Withdrawal helped Nixon to preserve his "coolness," his pride in being "the coolest person in the room," a tranquility more easily attained by avoiding entanglement in criticism and argument. Nixon, an aide noted, "abhors confrontations, most particularly those based on philosophical convictions." The White House staff grew as never before, the television sets vanished from the Oval Office, the critical press was assailed, and the traditional Presidential news conferences became a rarity. Unreality was hoisted to a new pinnacle.

"The more a President sits surrounded only by his own views and those of his personal advisers," observed Senator Charles Mathias (R., Maryland), "the more he lives in a house of mirrors in which all views and ideas tend to reflect and reinforce his own." [11] By withdrawing from external reality, Nixon could more easily impose upon his immediate environment his own sense of what was real, and also attempt to impose that same sense on the nation. One of his more remarkable sorties was a radio address in which he announced that the urban crisis was over, that crime was on the run, and that the air was becoming breathable again. "The hour of crisis," he proclaimed, "has passed." [12]

Even Gerald Ford, who had ample cause to distinguish his Presidency from that of his predecessor, soon lapsed into the regal style. More in the fashion of Louis XIV and Richard Nixon than in the spirit of his promised open Presidency, he indulged in over-reaching executive power by proclaiming, "The ethical tone will be what I make it." [13] Again, in blocking the workings of the judicial process by pardoning Nixon before he could be tried, Ford declared, approximating Louis XIV, "My conscience says it is my duty." [14]

Nixon as Radical

To the solitude of his seclusive White House, Nixon, despite his conventional appearance, brought the stuff of radical, if not revolutionary, dreams. Nixon was a radical in the literal, derivative sense of the word, possessed with a hyper-readiness to destroy the established political order by pulling up its roots, to break with the past, whether with the nation's traditional policies and democratic polity or with his own public record and utterances. Ironically, he was more radical than most of the war protesters and peace marchers who would gather near the White House. Many of these dissidents misperceived Nixon as the granitic exponent of the status quo, and yet, better than most of his vilifiers, he was able to accomplish his purposes.

After an early career in which he championed anti-Communism, and often alleged that his opponents were soft on Communism, he proudly worked to-ward rapprochement with China and the Soviet Union. With greater breast-beating than any other Presidential candidate, save perhaps Governor George Wallace, he rallied to the banner of law and order, while his White House became the launching pad of criminal acts that, had they remained undetected, as they almost did, could have crippled the democratic system and its cardinal principle, the rule of law. According to public opinion polls, a large majority of the American public believed that Nixon himself committed crimes, and a fed-eral grand jury would have recommended his indictment had he not been Presi-dent—shadows that have darkened the reputation of no other Chief Executive. Though graft and corruption bedevilled the administrations of Grant, Harding, and Truman, the misdeeds were committed by subordinates and no flicker of suspicion touched the Presidents.

In essence, Nixon's radicalism meant the overturn of democracy, the hand-cuffing of its institutions, and the stifling of its processes. Several basic thrusts comprised the Nixon attack. In his administration's contentions, national secu-rity was posed as a superordinate value, and it was deemed so susceptible to harm in domestic affairs that for its sake civil liberties must be curtailed and illegal acts committed. In justifying the operation in which White House hire-lings burglarized the office of Daniel Ellsberg's psychiatrist, Nixon's aide John Ehrlichman declared that the venture was "well within the President's inherent constitutional power," a view, he said, with which the President had expressed total agreement.[15]

Likewise, for the sake of national security Nixon approved in 1970 a general scheme for maintaining internal security prepared by a working group that in-cluded representatives from the CIA, the FBI, and a White House aide. The scheme called for intensified electronic surveillance of domestic security threats, monitoring of American citizens using international communications facilities, increased mail surveillance, more informants on college campuses, and breaking and entering certain categories of targets in situations relating to national security. Though Nixon approved the plan, it eventually was stalled when FBI Director J. Edgar Hoover objected that "the civil liberties people may become upset. . . ." Nevertheless, the CIA conducted massive illegal domestic intelligence operations against antiwar and other dissident groups, with break-ins, wiretapping, and surreptitious inspections of mail.[16]

Nixon's radicalism led to studied assaults on the principal organs of govern-ment to foster their denigration and disutility. A coterie of Presidential house-hold guards wielded power and made decisions in lieu of the departments and the cabinet, whose members increasingly were individuals without political force or stature. Nixon was contemptuous toward Congress, to the point of ig-noring or defying its enactments. He impounded funds it had appropriated, on a scale that made the few slender precedents buckle. Again, carrying modest his-toric practice to virtually unbounded extremes, his administration at times claimed executive privilege to withhold from the scrutiny of Congress virtually any information of the executive branch that the President chose. Nor did the "law and order" President spare the courts. He demeaned the Supreme Court with substandard nominations and characterized as "soft-headed" judges who disagreed with his beliefs.

Toward the further range of supportive institutions and processes of the democratic order he also unloosed threats and thunderbolts. Almost continuously the administration was at war with the news media, particularly television, in what, the Watergate papers make clear, was an orchestrated effort to pressure the networks into adopting a sympathetic attitude toward the Nixon Presidency. A White House aide condemned the "ideological plugola" of TV newsmen and warned that those concerned would "be held fully accountable . . . at license renewal time." [17] Interest groups, whose freedom and variety are the fiber of American democracy, were manipulated by governmental decisions and favors, such as price controls, import quotas, tax relief, and grain deals with the Soviet Union. Politically sympathetic groups and economic enterprizes were rewarded, while recalcitrants were penalized. The sorry tale unfolds to reveal acts of sabotage and espionage during the 1972 elections, extortion and other illegalities in campaign fund raising, and ominous lists of "enemies"— citizens from many walks of life whose conduct displeased the White House. In all, Nixon seemed to claim an indefinite power to modify or even set aside the democratic order in such emergencies as he might select and define by the free play of his rampant suspicions.

Is Nixon thus unique in Presidential history, a solitary radical who gained incumbency? Have not other Presidents also transgressed the democratic order? To cope with the Civil War, Lincoln claimed authority to set aside normal governmental processes. But Lincoln was wrestling with the most frightening crisis the nation has ever faced, far beyond the wildest imaginings of the Nixon camp. What of other Presidencies? Certainly one of the most devastating assaults on civil liberties came during World War II, when Franklin Roosevelt uprooted thousands of Japanese-American and Japanese aliens from the west coast and removed them to inland internment camps encircled by barbed wire, police dogs, and armed guards. No single act or collection of acts of the Nixon Presidency visited so much actual hardship on so many persons. Is not, then, the characterization of Nixon as a radical and revolutionary overstated?

What distinguishes the Nixon Presidency's pattern of malfeasance is its breadth and integration, its attack across the board of governmental processes: all the branches of government, the elections, the press, interest groups, individual freedoms—nothing escapes. The Lincoln and Roosevelt transgressions were prompted by specific emergencies that the Presidents themselves defined, not alone, but in conjunction with sources outside themselves—Congress, public opinion, and, eventually, the courts. For Nixon, emergency was to be the monopoly of Presidential discovery, maintained by domination over other political institutions and processes. Thereby, Nixon could avoid any possible disturbance of a Presidentially defined order by these external elements.

Democratic Ground Rules

In its lengthy experience of nearly two centuries, the Presidency has pursued ideals and followed ground rules that support and even extend democratic government. Without that commitment, the Presidency would long ago have fallen into place as another variant in a long line of dictatorships that has cursed humanity since earliest times. A number of ground rules can be identified whereby the Presidency simultaneously exercises imposing powers while abiding by democratic constraints. What are the principal of these ground rules that the historic Presidency has observed and the Nixon Presidency violated or threatened?

1. The power of the Presidency must be wielded by constitutional means. The incumbent must observe the civil liberties incorporated in the Bill of Rights and respect the processes of the other two great branches, Congress and the courts.

A DeGaulle-like contempt for the legislature is the antithesis of this norm. The constitutional Presidency does not continuously subordinate its commitment to the fundamental law to other values—values, such as Nixon's open-ended commitment to "national security," to which it accords expansive and ephemeral definition. As Egil Krogh, Jr., the White House aide who directed the break-in at the office of Daniel Ellsberg's psychiatrist, noted, the use of "national security" as an all-purpose justification "served to block critical analysis." Eventually Krogh perceived that individual rights cannot be sacrificed "to the mere assertion of national security." [18]

2. The Presidency must respect the capacity of the public to distinguish between good electoral candidates and bad, between wise men and fools. A Presidency that becomes distrustful of public judgment and moves paternalistically to substitute its own has travelled well down the road to antidemocratic behavior. A springboard into malfeasance for the Nixon men was their judgment that the American public could not be counted on to reject George McGovern, who was perceived by the Presidential entourage as a muddle-headed and dangerous candidate whose rejection at the polls they must assure by hook and crook.

3. The Presidency must observe the rights of the opposition to criticize, to challenge, and possibly to overthrow its incumbency in a free election. The perpetration of "dirty tricks" and the employ of trunkloads of "dirty money" defeats the purpose of democratic elections. To compile lists of enemies and to harass those "enemies" by subjecting their income tax returns to extra scrutiny and by other heavy-handed tactics is to negate the democratic politics of free debate, party competition, and open elections. This is not politics, but war. The special kind of war that the CIA wages against the nation's foreign enemies was levied at the President's domestic opponents. The motive force was not democratic, but self-righteous and fearful—a hybrid of political-ideological hatred. [19]

4. The ethical behavior on which democracy is predicated extends to the President himself. At the very least, he ought to satisfy the obligations of good citizenship and comply with its elementals—pay his taxes and obey the laws. He falls well short of providing an example to the rest of the nation if, as an individual of substantial income, he pays a tax appropriate to a low income by dint of the ministrations of talented accountants and lawyers whose fees are beyond the means of the average citizen.

5. Democracy and its public offices, including the Presidency, require an ethical base in society. Appropriate ethical standards are less likely to govern the Presidency if society itself is riddled with seamy practice. If the prevailing morality is that anything goes provided you can get away with it, if work is shoddy, if products are misrepresented, and if cheating is rampant, the President has little spur to set his ethical sights any higher than expediency dictates. Much of the unacceptable behavior of the Nixon Presidency has counterparts in the ruthless competition of the private sector of American society—spying on competitors, stretching to one's advantage the rules of the game, the cold mapping of strategies that allow no compassion to rivals and look only for their destruction.[20] "Winning isn't everything; it's the only thing," proclaimed Vince Lombardi, the eminent football coach. This ethic of professional sports, so glorified in contemporary America, is a poor guide for democratic behavior. If evidence be necessary, Lombardi's maxim was emblazoned on a banner high in the Situation Room of the Committee for the Reelection of the President, a hatchery of misdeeds that spawned some of the worst misdeeds of the Nixon Presidency.

The Need for a Strong Presidency

For all of the lamentation concerning the contemporary Chief Executive, the United States and the world need a Presidency that is both strong and responsive to democratic constraints. In the nearly two centuries of the office's existence such a Presidency has appeared intermittently, and its presence has fortunately coincided with the nation's more severe trials. The launching of the new government of 1789 was entrusted to the capable hands and impeccable character of the first President, Washington. In the Jefferson and Jackson eras, the republic became transformed into a more popular government. The successful emergence of the nation from the test of the Civil War was managed chiefly by the Presidency.

The office also has led in the rigorous adjustments of the twentieth century. The Presidency brought the nation out of its nineteenth-century isolation and onto the world stage, where it became a force for peace as well as the conductor of major wars. Some of these wars, especially the two World Wars, protected democracy. The Presidency has diminished the crudities and oppressiveness of industry, provided indispensable succor to labor in its struggles to organize and defend itself, and helped the farmer through endless sequences of lean years. Presidents have championed racial justice against local repression and have protected natural resources against private exploitation. In the sweep of history, the Presidency clearly exceeds the other governmental branches as a force for enhancing civil liberties and the workings of distributive justice.

If the contemporary movements for consumer rights and environmental protection are to become consequential, they will require the indispensable ingredients of Presidential commitment and support. The urban crisis, the energy crisis that commenced in the seventies, and other crises that are predictable for coming decades—water and air pollution, disposal of solid waste, noise pollution, dwindling open space, food shortages and hunger on an international scale—will be coped with, to the extent that they can be, largely through Presidential leadership.

More than the other branches, the Presidency possesses the capacity for action, for achieving specific results in the shortest possible time—valuable traits in a political system that is diffuse and characteristically slow moving. Its capacities and resources embrace the power of decision and command, vast stores of information, legions of experts, huge sums to spend. The burden for action falls readily on the President. The need for a strong Presidency also derives from the limitations, inherent and self-imposed, of the other organs of government. On matters which are controversial and politically hazardous, Congress often prefers not to act, but to delegate unwanted responsibility to the Chief Executive. In its initial major response to the energy crisis, for instance, Congress authorized the President to exercise enormous, scarcely limited discretion even though the incumbent, Richard Nixon, was sustaining some of the most severe of his castigations and talk flowed freely of his impeachment. Even so constrained a President as Calvin Coolidge noted another potent phenomenon contributing to legislative reticence and executive assertion: "It is because in their hours of timidity the Congress becomes subservient to the importunities of organized minorities that the President comes more and more to stand as the champion of the rights of the whole country." [21] Likewise, the inability and disinclination of the bureaucracies of the Executive Branch to respond to the evolving problems of the industrial and social orders foisted upon the Presidency the task of developing initiatives. While performing tolerably well at policy and program maintenance, the bureaucracies exhibit mulelike reticence toward adjusting to emerging problems. It is hardly rash to predict that bureaucratic inertia will persist. If the burdens of creative public policy are to be picked up, the Presidency is most apt to do it.

The Imperilled Presidency

The contemporary Presidency can be perceived not only in terms of gross or excessive power but in opposing terms, as an office of uncertain power, a vessel readily prey to failure and futility, despite the unstinting commitment of its resources and the incumbent's political skill and prestige. Each of three most recent Presidencies was overwhelmed by events, sustained serious, and sometimes disastrous, losses of power, and resulted in abnormal personal damage to the incumbent. John Kennedy was murdered, a victim of occupational hazard; Lyndon Johnson was driven from office by social dissension and his inability to master events; and Richard Nixon, unable to master himself and his hold on the office slipping badly, surrendered power to a degree rarely known in history. The Presidency can devour Presidents.

It is necessary to distinguish between *the imagined Presidency* and *the real Presidency*. Often in its history the Presidency has been imagined to have more power than it really has. The real Presidency is what the Presidency effectively is in the present, what it can do in a given situation. The imagined Presidency is a euphoric impression of its past, present, and future and is grounded partly in reality and partly in fancy. It exaggerates the office's strength, encouraged by the substantial power the Presidency actually possesses, the prestige built in its past, and the pomp that surrounds it. If the Presidency seems enormously powerful in foreign affairs (which it is), its weaknesses in domestic policy (which are grave) are overlooked. The imagined Presidency underestimates the limitations of power and environment that the office suffers and the shrinkages of power that can be engendered by defects in the incumbent's character and political skill. It equates past Presidential success, the nation's might, and expectations of how the world should go with available Presidential power.

Instead of an excessively powerful Presidency, the nation may witness Presidents lacking in important power. Most nineteenth-century Presidents did, and the twentieth century too provides its illustrations: Truman was almost wholly balked on his Fair Deal program of domestic legislation; and John Kennedy, despite solemn promises, during his 1960 campaign, of future civil rights legislation, was unable to wrest it from Congress during his lifetime. The most recent experience of executive enfeeblement is the Nixon post-Watergate Presidency. As a step toward fending off his possible impeachment, Nixon made an extraordinary concession when he agreed to appoint an independent special prosecutor, Archibald Cox, in order to secure the confirmation of Elliot Richardson as Attorney General. Though Cox was an employee of the Executive Branch, the President was apparently to assert no control over him whatever. Since his appointment had been forced by the Democratic Senate, he was in effect the emissary plenipotentiary of the Democratic Congress. Nixon became the first President in history to abandon, or promise to abandon, the right to fire a top policy-making official in the Executive Branch.

This huge concession led to another, which, until Nixon, no other President had made. Nixon promised Cox access not merely to certain records of the Presidency, but to all tapes, documents, or private papers relevant to his prosecutorial task. Ultimately, Nixon reneged on the agreement and fired Cox, but in the torrential criticism that followed, Nixon concluded that he had no choice but to reinstitute the agreement through the appointment of Leon Jaworski as Cox's successor. In effect, Nixon is the first President to surrender control of the Justice Department, and he yielded, as again no other President has done, the right to absolute confidentiality in discussions with his executive subordinates.[22] In Nixon's enfeeblement the term "Chief Executive" was not altogether appropriate. The post-Watergate Presidency suffered other losses of power: the sagging morale of top officials, the absorption of the President and his chief advisers in Watergate problems, the slowing of important decisions, the diminished standing of the President and his office in public regard.[23] Enfeeblement persisted in the Presidency of Nixon's successor, Gerald Ford.

A major historic strength of the Presidency is its foundation of general, vaguely defined powers, a quality that has facilitated the office's adjustment to sharp changes in the environment of governmental problems at home and abroad. Nixon damaged the office's traditionally flexible and adaptive qualities by abusing the heritage of power and by embarking on legal confrontations that forced the courts and, in some instances, Congress to delineate more precisely the boundaries of Presidential power. Impoundment, an historic practice that rested on comity between Congress and the President, was pushed by Nixon to extremes that no predecessor ever dreamed of and into the courts, resulting in a string of rulings against the President. By asserting outrageous claims of executive privilege, Nixon was forced to make huge retreats and yield documents to public scrutiny to a degree that no predecessor would have indulged. Impeachment has been a sleeping dog with sharp teeth, previously aroused only once in Presidential history, in the case of Andrew Johnson, who narrowly escaped. Inevitably, and fortunately for democracy, that dog has been aroused again by Nixon's misconduct, and he eluded its fatal bite only by resigning. Nixon has demonstrated that after a century of dormancy, impeachment is not a remote, but a ready and practical weapon to threaten or eradicate an unwanted Presidency. One can imagine future Presidents gazing on Nixon's portrait with thankless remembrance of the vulnerabilities to which he exposed the office.

In the seventies other weakening factors are visible on the political landscape. The Nixon malfeasances raised proposals that the Presidency be abolished or drastically modified. Some thoughtful critics have suggested that the single President be replaced by an executive committee in the fashion of the Swiss executive.[24] Eugene McCarthy and George McGovern, among others, have called for reduced Presidential power and expanded roles for the cabinet and Congress, in effect an approximation of Nixon's post-Watergate Presidency. Such a Presidency amply demonstrated its susceptibility to leaderlessness, its easy tendency to leave serious national problems to drift.

Practical Politics

The presence or absence of the strong Presidency depends crucially upon how well a particular President fares in the political marketplace. Consequently, a quest for a strong and effective Presidency that performs in balanced accord with democratic constraints leads to the world of practical politics in which every President lives and functions.

Impressed by his own full and intimate knowledge of the limitations the Chief Executive toils under, Harry S. Truman once observed, "The principle power that the President has is to bring people in and try to persuade them to do what they ought to do without persuasion. That's what I spend my time doing. That's what the powers of the President amount to." [25] Given the interdependence of its powers, the Presidency is an intensive experience in practical politics. To lead, to win support, to achieve, the President must practice with skill and ardor the arts of political persuasion. Woodrow Wilson noted before taking up the Presidency, "We have all been the disciples of Montesquieu, but we have also been practical politicians." [26] The President must woo party leaders, legislators, and chieftains of veto groups. He must bring the several parts of government, the private groups, and public opinion into harmonious effort to accomplish shared objectives.

George Washington discovered the necessity for practical politics promptly upon taking up the Presidential office. The new government, he wrote, was to be one "of accommodation as well as a government of laws." [27] The President's political means run a wide gamut: blandishments, favors, bargains, compromises, and the application, when necessary, of naked pressure. Herbert Hoover, aiming to secure tariff reform legislation, met with the legislative leaders and made public appeals. When these proved unavailing, he granted a rare recognition by entertaining Senator William E. Borah alone at dinner to woo him, and, varying his attack, dispatched a sharp message to Senator Reed Smoot, who was guiding the bill in the Senate: "No flexible tariff, no tariff bill." Again, failure on both counts, whereupon Hoover entertained all the Republican leaders at breakfast, but without success. When he learned that the House-Senate conference committee had watered down the flexible provisions nearly to the point of drowning them, Hoover responded with equal ferocity. "I wrote out the provision I wanted," he said, "I sent word that unless my formula was adopted the bill would be vetoed. The result was a complete victory." [28]

To get his controversial measures enacted, whether in foreign or domestic affairs, the President, because of the unreliability of his own party, must build a special coalition for his purpose from both major parties. Lyndon Johnson, this is to say, could not have secured civil rights legislation in 1964 and 1965 without Republican support. The coalitions keep forming and breaking up as their purpose is achieved. Moving on to new objectives, the President must develop a new combination of support. To make his way, the President must know when to spend and when to hoard his influence and how to build it. He must realize, as Richard Neustadt has suggested, that the essence of his persuasive task is to convince the legislators whose support he courts "that what the White House wants of them is what they ought to do for their sake and on their authority." [29] In playing the political game, the President occupies certain of the best vantage points in the political system. His power of publicity, his veto, his power over budget and expenditure, his power of appointment are means that exist nowhere else in the political structure. For all the limits upon his power, he is the major unifying force in a diffuse political system and pluralistic society. He, better than anyone else, can act affirmatively and flexibly.

But the President, if he shall write his name large on the pages of history, must do more than excel at practical politics. He must use political power to advance great ends. His shining hours occur in the Fourteen Points of Wilson, in the social purposes of Lincoln and the Roosevelts, and in the assertion of principle by Grover Cleveland against the test of events. He must rise to moments as Cleveland did when pressing the House Speaker to support an administration measure; Cleveland found him hesitant and fearful of the consequences to his future. "Mr. Speaker," Cleveland exclaimed, "what is your political future weighed in the balance against the fortunes of the country? Who are you and I compared with the welfare of the whole American people?" [30] The Speaker surrendered. But the President who, like Cleveland, chooses to enter the roaring furnace where political necessity and principle converge subjects himself to the burning anguish that reaches its highest intensity in the Presidency itself. One day Cleveland invited a visitor, Dr. Wilton M. Smith, to listen to the draft of a speech. Cleveland, as he read on, worked up into a high pitch of emotion. He exclaimed, turning suddenly on his visitor,

> Doctor, I suppose at times you won't approve of many things I do, but I want you to know that I am trying to do what is right. . . . Sometimes the pressure is most overwhelming, and a President cannot always get at the exact truth; but I want you to know that I am trying to do what is right. *I am trying to do what is right.* [31]

Tears welled in the big President's eyes; he blew his nose hard and paced the room.

Presidential Types

Without undue violence to history, it is possible to divide the Presidents the United States has had into three recurrent types with a view to assessing their suitability as models for the contemporary Chief Executive who is both strong and responsive to democratic constraints.

The most numerous type is one that might be styled a "literalist" President. Madison, Buchanan, Taft, and, to a degree, Eisenhower are of this school. The mark of the literalist President, as his title suggests, is close obedience to the letter of the Constitution. If anything, he is apt to veer too far toward the democratic end of the spectrum and permit the undue sacrifice of power and strength. Taft, who, with Buchanan, was the most literal of the Presidents, formulated the operative belief of the literalists:

> The true view of the Executive function is . . . that the President can exercise no power which cannot be fairly and reasonably traced to some specific grant of

power or justly implied and included within such express grant as proper and necessary to its exercise. Such specific grant must be either in the Federal Constitution or in an act of Congress passed in pursuance thereof. There is no undefined residuum of power which he can exercise because it seems to him to be in the public interest.[32]

The Taft-like President tends also to live by the Whig assumption that the legislative power is popular and the executive monarchical. He is respectful, even deferential, to Congress. "My duty," James Buchanan was prone to say, "is to execute the laws . . . and not my individual opinions." [33] When Congress did nothing in the face of gathering rebellion, Buchanan too did nothing. In a later day, President Eisenhower is reported sometimes to have remarked privately to his aides that he felt called upon to "restore" to Congress powers that Franklin Roosevelt had "usurped." In public pronouncement and personal act, Eisenhower was respectful of Congressional prerogative and the doctrine of separation of powers. "Our very form of Government," he declared to the Convention of the National Young Republican Organization in 1953, "is in peril unless each branch willingly accepts and discharges its own clear responsibilities—and respects the rights and responsibilities of the others." [34]

The Taft-like President makes little use of his independent powers or prerogative (his powers, for example, as Commander-in-Chief and as implied in the executive power clause). He exerts political pressure sparingly. Symptomatic of his approach is James Bryce's observation that the typical nineteenth-century President's communications to Congress were so perfunctory that "the expression of his wishes . . . in messages has not necessarily any more effect on Congress than an article in a prominent party newspaper." [35]

The literalist President has little taste for innovation in social policy. He is nostalgic for the past and urges it be used as a blueprint for the future. He feels, as Taft did, that the bane of government is "ill-digested legislation" and that "real progress in government must be by slow stages." [36] It is a view that Theodore Roosevelt found upheld in society by "most able lawyers who are past middle age" and "large numbers of well-meaning, respectable citizens." [37]

The Presidency in the manner of Taft and Buchanan is, on its face, inadequate for the necessities of the contemporary Presidency faced with grave social and environmental problems at home and the dynamics of foreign affairs, with opportunities of detente with old opponents in order to provide good offices for building peace among warring nations, for disarmament and expanded trade. The past, which the literalist Presidency venerates, can be only a partial and imperfect guide to the present and future. It excessively neglects the President's independent powers, which again and again have been a constructive force in times of crisis and change. Its neglect of politics abdicates action to passivity and, as the experience of many nineteenth-century Presidents proves, can thoroughly reduce the President from leader to clerk. The best proof of the inadequacy of the literalist model is the abandonment of its key concepts by Presidents who once had taken them up. Cleveland at first proposed to be a literalist

President, spurning to use patronage and pressure upon Congress and declaring, "I did not come here to legislate." [38] But when Congress blocked the bills he was driven to sponsor, his attitude changed, and he went furiously to work to win votes by promising jobs. Dwight Eisenhower, for all his professed deference to Congress and distaste for politics, in time did push his legislative program, and his campaigning in Congressional elections was on a scale comparable to Franklin Roosevelt's.

At the opposite end of the spectrum from the literalist President is the "strong" President, typified by Washington, Jackson, Lincoln, Wilson, and the Roosevelts. He generally, although not exclusively, flourishes in times of crisis and change—during a war or a depression—and when political movements such as progressivism are at their crests. He interprets his powers with liberality; he is a precedent-maker and precedent-breaker to the point where the legality of his acts is questioned or disproved. His bible is the "stewardship theory" of Theodore Roosevelt, who felt that it was the President's "duty to do anything that the needs of the nation demanded unless such action was forbidden by the Constitution or by the laws." "I acted for the public welfare," Roosevelt said. "I acted for the common well-being of all our people." [39] But the peril of the strong Presidency, as recent experience unfortunately illuminates, is its penchant for straying into illegality, its thrust beyond normal constraints, its excessive infringement of democratic values and processes. The march of its logic is toward the dictatorial, and the effort to keep it within acceptable democratic bounds imposes extra strains on the vigor and competence of surrogate institutions—Congress, the courts, the parties, interest groups, and organized opinion.

In his most fruitful moments, the strong President provides leadership, in Franklin Roosevelt's words, "alert and sensitive to change," which in the Jefferson-Jackson tradition means that the government must act positively in promoting a good life, and in the Wilson tradition means that the nation cannot shun or escape its obligations of world leadership. His orientation is less to the past than to the future, which he approaches with hope and plan. He is skillful politically and is concerned more with substance than with form. When necessary, he resorts to bold action, whether economic, social, diplomatic, or military, which he does not avoid for the sake of containing the national debt. He accepts and abides a strong Congress but purposefully uses the lawmaking process. He has the gift of inspiring and rallying the people with messages that mix practicality and prophecy. In his view, the President as a person must dominate the Presidency as an institution. He, a fleeting political figure, must bend, divert, and lead the cumbrous bureaucratic executive branch according to his purpose. But he must walk a tightrope in order not to slip into behavior that violates or jeopardizes democratic processes.

Between the strong and literalist Presidents is a middle ground that many Chief Executives have occupied; it unites elements of both extremes. This middle ground need not now detain us. The magnitude of problems and opportunities at home and abroad makes clear that only one of the three available Presidential types is suitable for the future. For the United States to best cope with problems and capitalize on opportunities requires a Presidency that is continuously strong, rather than intermittently, as a major source of constructive accomplishment to deal positively with society's problems and to bring the greatest good to the greatest number of people. On the other hand, as the Watergate experience and the excesses of Presidential war-making illuminate in clearest hieroglyphics, that all may understand, the strong Presidency bears the risk of antidemocratic behavior. The risk must be managed and overcome by the enhancement of democratic safeguards capable of containing substantial Presidential power within limits compatible with a free society. Most of the Framers of the Constitution—though not all—were confident that they had mastered the problem of the strong Presidency coexisting harmoniously with human liberty. Since their time, the adequacy of their solution has sometimes come into question, especially after the Watergate tragedy. In the 1970s and beyond, a central problem of American politics and political science, if not *the* central problem, is the coupling of the strong Presidency with the institutions and processes of democracy in ways that are enduring and safe for liberty. This book is addressed to that problem.

2

BEGINNINGS

$\mathbf{A}$ year before the Constitutional Convention of 1787, John Jay, in a letter to George Washington recounting the inadequacies of the existing government, moved boldly to the inevitable question: "Shall we have a king?" [1] It was indeed a question stirring in many influential minds, but few men dared ask it openly. The propagandists of the Revolution had done their work too well in portraying that enterprise as a struggle against a tyrannical monarch, although their description of that monarch was much more appropriate for the earlier James I or Charles I than for the monarch of their day, the unfortunate, ineffective George III. The general revulsion from monarchy had produced in the states a prevailing pattern of the weak executive and in the Articles of Confederation almost no executive at all. But the weak executive was maintained at a high price. The event that drove Jay to his writing desk was Shays's Rebellion in Massachusetts, an upheaval exposing the impotence of government and foreshadowing for the young nation a desperate existence of anarchy, confiscation of property, possible military dictatorship, and foreign intervention.

Hard questions pounded like hailstones upon responsible men's thoughts. How could the strong executive that circumstances required be best provided? Should there be a monarch, as Jay suggested? Or could some other form of strong executive be discovered or created, untainted with the tyranny that the country dreaded yet endowed with sufficient authority? In the interlude before the Convention, men carried on the search, and at Philadelphia they struggled with it under the pressure of decision.

The states, and before them the colonies, provided the major domestic experience with executive power. The colonial governor initially was a strong executive: commander-in-chief of the provincial forces and representative of the crown, embodying the several kingly prerogatives. He was the fountain of honor and privilege and thus created offices and filled them. With little exception he shared power with a council, usually of twelve members appointed by the crown at the governor's recommendation. The council functioned as the legislative upper house, advised and influenced the governor, and was his ally in local political struggles. [2]

As relations with the mother country deteriorated, the governorship passed under the increasing influence and direction of the assembly, the lower and more popular legislative house. Particularly in the French and Indian War, when the governor was constantly in need of money for the army, the assembly employed its control over supplies to pare down the governor's power. The American view of George III as the tyrant over Parliament spurred the hostility against his agent, the local governor.

The animus against executive power carried into the early state constitutions of the Revolutionary period. Power rushed to the legislature. The governor, or president as he was called in several states, was reduced almost to a cipher. His term was for one year, except in South Carolina where it was two and in Delaware where it was three. His reeligibility was strictly limited. He was chosen by, and was therefore the creature of, the legislature. The executive branch was deliberately disunified. The governor was saddled with a council chosen by the legislature, except in Pennsylvania. Most of the enumerated executive powers and functions were subject to council control. In Maryland the council was a "board" in which the executive had one vote "for the transacting of business." In Virginia Governor Edmund Randolph viewed himself as "a member of the executive." [3] The power that the legislature did not have by direct grant it could get by bold assertion against the other branches, which were endowed with little power to defend themselves. Thomas Jefferson observed of the Virginia as he might have of most state constitutions, "All the powers of government, legislative, executive and judiciary, result to the legislative body." [4]

The governor's drab plight was relieved only in Massachusetts, where he possessed the veto power (subject to overriding by two-thirds of the legislature) and was indefinitely reeligible, and in New York, where he could fairly be termed a strong executive.

The New York Governor

The New York constitution was established late, in 1777, sometime after the creation of other state constitutions, and it profited from their imperfections. The folly of the weak chief executive characteristic of those constitutions was daily revealed in the urgencies of the Revolution, which demanded the summoning of effective executive power. New York's situation, exceedingly roughened by the onmarching British, made strong executive power imperative. The state convention that drafted the constitution was literally chased up the state by the British army. It was a convention on the run, which moved from Harlem to Kingsbridge and then successively to Philipse Manor, Fishkill, Poughkeepsie, and finally Kingston, as the British pressed relentlessly northward.

The New York constitution rejected the ascendancy that the legislature enjoyed in other state constitutions. In language instilled in the future federal Constitution "the supreme executive power and authority of the state" was vested in the governor. The New York governor, in contrast to the governors of other states, served a substantial term—three years—with no limit upon his reeligibility. He was chosen not by the legislature, the prevailing pattern else-where, but by a constitutionally identified electorate, a popular suffrage that for the time was generously defined. His electoral independence from the legislature was a giant step toward making the governor the strongest officer of his kind in the Confederation.

His further powers all foreshadowed the Presidency. The governor was commander-in-chief and admiral of the navy; he could convene the legislature on extraordinary occasions; and he could grant reprieves and pardons. His duty was to inform the legislature of the condition of the state, recommend matters for their consideration, and take care that the laws were faithfully executed. He did not escape altogether the restraints commonly imposed upon other governors. His power of appointment was shared with a Council of Appointment of four senators elected by the assembly from each of the four senatorial districts. The governor was president of the council and possessed a casting vote. The governor shared his otherwise strong veto power with a Council of Revision, consisting of the governor, the chancellor, and the judges of the Supreme Court. They, or any three of them, always including the governor, could veto legislative measures inconsistent with the spirit of the constitution or the public good. A two-thirds vote in both houses could override the veto.[5]

But the offices a constitution creates cannot live on the written document alone. They thrive upon skilled and vigorous incumbents. The New York governorship, by rare good fortune, had as its first occupant a skillful and coura-geous chief executive, George Clinton. Clinton's reign was rich and memora-ble; Clinton used fully his store of power and became the dominant political figure of his state. Particularly impressive to the federal Founding Fathers was Clinton's ability, as a strong executive, to maintain public order. He put down the severe Doctors' Riots in New York City with the militia and routed out the remnants of Shays's men who fled to New York after springing their rebellion in Massachusetts.[6] The New York governorship's influence was further assured by the circumstance that a Founding Father who was to be most influential in creating the Presidency was a principal draftsman of the New York constitu-tion; Gouverneur Morris engaged in this double enterprise.

The Philadelphia Convention

The Constitution-makers who gathered in Philadelphia in 1787, hailed by Thomas Jefferson as "an assembly of demi-gods," organized themselves by electing George Washington their "president" and Major William Jackson their secretary. Rules of procedure were adopted and precautions taken to keep the proceedings secret. In the weeks of lengthy, intense, and often dis-heartening deliberations, no single problem was more perplexing in building the new government than the office of President. The President must be en-dowed with impressive powers yet must not appear to the people, nor in fact be, another king and incipient tyrant. He must have sufficient but not excessive independence. He must be dependent but not, as state governors commonly were, the mere creature of the legislature.

The Convention began its hard grapple with specifics when it resolved itself on May 29 into a Committee of the Whole to consider several competing plans and proposals submitted by state delegations and individual members. Each plan dealt with the whole structure of a federal government, including the question of executive power.

The Virginia plan, which had been prepared chiefly by James Madison before the Convention assembled, called for a "national executive" to be chosen by the "National Legislature." The executive would be eligible only for a single term, and "besides a general authority to execute the National laws, [he] ought to enjoy the Executive rights vested in Congress by the Confederation." The Committee of the Whole at the Convention added certain features to the Virginia plan: The term of the executive would be seven years, he could make appointments "in cases not otherwise provided for," and he would be removable "on impeachment and conviction of malpractice, or neglect of duty." He could "negative" any legislative act unless overridden "by two third parts" of each branch of the legislature. With certain "members" of the judiciary, he could exercise the veto power. The Virginia plan was bold in conception. Instead of simply revising or altering the Articles, it aimed to enlarge them and proposed a national executive, legislature, and judiciary to do what was done, or should have been done, by the Continental Congress.[7]

The New Jersey plan, offered by William Paterson on June 15, was the response of the small states to the power of the large states that would have resulted from the Virginia plan. Whereas the Virginia plan undertook to replace the Articles with a document for a truly national government, the New Jersey plan merely revised them. It would endow the central government with powers to levy import duties and regulate foreign and domestic trade. The states were to collect taxes, but Congress could act if the states defaulted. The New Jersey plan called for a plural executive chosen by Congress, removable on the application of a majority of the state executives, ineligible for a second term, and empowered to direct all military operations though in no case to take command in the field.[8]

In addition to the rival plans of the large and small states, comprehensive plans of two Convention members dealt with the executive. One plan, by Alexander Hamilton, presented in a five-hour speech on June 18, was the most extreme proposal to be offered at the Convention for a strong executive and central government. Hamilton announced himself as "unfriendly" to both the Virginia and the New Jersey plans, terming the former, the stronger of the two, "pork still, with a little change of the sauce." The severity of the crisis required a central government of highest competence. "The general power whatever be its form if it preserves itself, must swallow up the State powers, otherwise it will be swallowed up by them." For the substance of the new government, Hamilton's probing gaze fell upon the British structure, "the best in the world"; he doubted "whether any thing short of it would do for America."

Monarchy and Parliament he unreservedly admired. No good government could exist without a good executive, and no good executive could ever be established "on Republican principles." The hereditary monarch, endowed with great wealth, was above corruption from abroad and was "both sufficiently independent and sufficiently controlled, to answer the purpose of the institution at home."

The Hamilton plan called for a monarch and nobles, a single executive and a Senate for life or good behavior, and an inferior popular house. The states would have no powers except over local affairs. So extreme was the plan that it was supported by no other delegate and was not even discussed. Days later, on June 29, Hamilton left Philadelphia, despairing that the Convention would fail to recommend a strong central government and would "let slip the golden opportunity of rescuing the American empire from disunion, anarchy, and misery. No motley or feeble measure can answer the end or will finally receive the public support." The Virginia plan was "motley" and the New Jersey plan "feeble." [9]

Still another plan was advanced by Charles Pinckney of South Carolina, member of a congressional committee charged with recommending amendments to the Articles. His plan, most of it now lost, seems from its several surviving parts to have attempted to revise the Articles rather than supplant them. In drawing his executive, Pinckney relied heavily upon the New York constitution. The powers and duties of the executive and the contingencies of his death and removal all followed the New York arrangement. His election and term, however, did not. Pinckney's executive would be elected by Congress annually.[10]

Decisions at Philadelphia

The Committee of the Whole debated the several plans with their conflicting conceptions. The issue of Virginia's proposed single executive versus New Jersey's plural executive quickly came to a head when James Wilson of Pennsylvania moved and Charles Pinckney seconded that the executive consist of one person. In the debate the principal argument made against the single executive was that it would constitute a standing invitation to the very kind of monarchy that the Revolution was intended to overcome. Randolph typified this opinion, according to Madison's *Journal,* when he "strongly opposed a unity in the Executive magistracy. He regarded it as the foetus of monarchy. We had, he said, no motive to be governed by the British Government as our prototype." Randolph also objected that a single magistrate could never evoke confidence and that the appointment would generally be in favor of some inhabitant near the "center of the Community," and the "remote parts" consequently "would not be on an equal footing." He preferred an executive department of three persons "drawn from different portions of the Country." [11]

James Wilson answered. Randolph, he contended, was less concerned with merit than with the popularity of the Convention's handiwork. Wilson, for his part, believed that the people well knew that "a single magistrate is not a King." All thirteen states, although agreeing upon almost nothing else in their constitutions, had established a single head as governor or president. "The idea of three heads," which promised neither "vigor" nor "tranquillity," "has taken place in none." Other Framers viewed the single executive not as an "absolute" monarch like the propagandized image of George III but as a kind of "limited" monarch, the most desirable of all executives. "A firm Executive," as John Dickinson of Delaware put it, "could only exist in a limited monarchy." [12] While the Convention analyzed the monarchy, stories circulated in the world outside that the Framers, in their love for that brand of executive, were bent upon importing a Hanoverian bishop to be king of the United States. Fortunately, the stories quickly subsided. [13]

A lengthy struggle centered upon two further questions, viewed as inseparable: the source of the executive's election and the length of his term. Three major types of election were advanced. James Wilson and Gouverneur Morris, friends of a strong executive, urged election, as Morris put it, "by the people at large, by the freeholders of the Country." When practical administrative difficulties were cited, Morris retorted that these had been overcome in New York and could be likewise in other states. The people, the doubters said, would be uninformed and misled by designing men. Morris preferred to be optimistic: "If the people should elect, they will never fail to prefer some man of distinguished character, or services; some man, if he might so speak, of continental reputation." [14] A second method was election by the legislature. That body's handling of the task, Morris contended, would be the work "of intrigue, of cabal, of faction." The final method, and the one ultimately adopted, was choice by electors. Advocates of an electoral system felt that it would best give effect to the dominant popular choice whose direct expression was barred for practical reasons. Many Fathers feared that citizens would blindly favor local candidates and would be ignorant of able men in other states.

Linked with method of choice were the questions of length of term and reeligibility. Elbridge Gerry of Massachusetts argued that the longer the term the less would the executive depend upon the legislature that chose him. Oliver Ellsworth of Connecticut likewise proposed a long term of six years. If elections were too frequent, the executive would not "be firm enough." (He said, "There must be duties which will make him unpopular for the moment.") Without a long term (seven years), Hugh Williamson of North Carolina argued, "The best men will not undertake the service and those of an inferior character will be liable to be corrupted." [15]

Proposals of six- or seven-year terms were predicated upon the assumption that the legislature would choose the President. A long term plus ineligibility for reelection, a common feature of such proposals, appeared the best means to safeguard executive independence of the legislature. Reeligibility would prompt the executive to court the legislature to win another term. The alternative of a shorter term and reeligibility came to the fore when selection by electors was ultimately settled upon.

The Fathers considered long and anxiously the question of annexing a council to the chief executive. A council would diminish the monarchical tendency and the danger of tyranny. Collective advice was deemed safer and more competent than the assorted individual advice that might befall the President. Various kinds of councils were proposed. The Pinckney plan vested in the executive "a Right to advise with the Heads of the different Departments as his Council." Ellsworth, rather fearful of personal government, would add to the council the President of the Senate and the Chief Justice. George Mason preferred a council representative of the chief sections of the country, the East, the Middle States, and the South. James Madison, a strong exponent of the council, proposed that it possess initiative to advise the President and to record its sentiments. But the floor discussion proved inconclusive, and ultimately the council idea was dropped.[16] The prospect that the venerated Washington would serve as first President drained much of the interest from the council proposal. Indeed many Fathers feared that a council of some power might harass the position of future President Washington.

In its final draft the Constitution not only failed to provide a council, it did not even call for the "cabinet" that appeared early in Washington's Presidency. The Constitution merely specified that the Chief Executive could require the "opinions of the heads of his departments in writing." Hamilton, for one, considered even this provision redundant as the right "would result of itself from the office." Other critics were haunted to the very end by monarchical fears. George Mason, crying doom, warned that a Presidency without a council was an "experiment" that even "the most despotic governments" had never undertaken. Benjamin Franklin, ordinarily optimistic, beheld a melancholy prospect, seeing only "caprice, the intrigues of favorites and mistresses, etc." in the absence of a council.[17]

The Fathers debated a score of issues in establishing the substantive powers of the executive. These were resolved with a tendency toward generosity to the executive, sparked by the prospect that Washington would become President. The veto power, remembered as an arbitrary instrument of the royal governors, was critically scrutinized. The Declaration of Independence's first indictment of George III was his refusal to "Assent to Laws, the most wholesome and necessary for the public good." But excesses by the state legislatures since Revolutionary days made the Fathers receptive to a strong veto power. The Virginia plan's coupling of the judiciary with the executive in the veto was dropped. The variant proposals for a Council of Revision met a like fate, and the President emerged as the solitary executive possessor of the veto power.

The appointing power was one of the knottier issues. James Wilson, constant friend of a strong Presidency, opposed the eventual arrangement, a power shared between the President and the Senate. "There can be no good Executive," he argued, "without a responsible appointment of officers to execute." Responsibility was impaired by involving the Senate. Wilson's view was respected to a degree when the President was given an exclusive appointing power "in all cases not otherwise provided for."[18]

Treaty and war powers and the President's pay, removal, and disability also evoked considerable discussion. "What is the extent of the term 'disability' and who is to be the judge of it?" Dickinson asked, questions that the Framers were never able to resolve definitively. Debate waxed over the respective powers of Congress and the executive to "declare" and to "make" war.[19] When the dust of debate had settled, it did seem clear that the Convention did not want either to deny the President the power to respond to surprise attack or to give the President broad power to initiate hostilities. One motion on the subject shocked Gerry, who "never expected" to hear in a republic a proposal to empower the executive alone to declare war. Madison contended that the war power could not be safely entrusted to the President or the Senate. He was for "clogging" rather than "facilitating" war.[20]

Drafting the Presidential Article

The work of the Committee of the Whole was supplemented by two drafting committees, the Committee of Detail and the Committee of Style. After discussion lasting some weeks, the Convention established the Committee of Detail—the members being Edward Rutledge (South Carolina), Randolph (Virginia), Nathaniel Gorham (Massachusetts), Ellsworth (Connecticut), and Wilson (Pennsylvania)—to reduce the delegates' ponderings to a systematic Constitution draft. The work of the Committee of Detail, a long stride toward the strong Presidency, was aided by Convention-adopted resolutions providing for a single executive empowered to execute national laws, to veto national legislation, and to appoint to offices in cases not otherwise provided for. The executive was also made subject to impeachment. The Committee of Detail adapted these resolutions to its draft and, with an eye on the New York constitution, further elaborated the President's powers. The committee made it the President's duty to give information to the legislature, to recommend measures, to convene Congress into extraordinary session, and, in disagreement between the two houses on the subject, to adjourn them. The President would also receive ambassadors, grant pardons and reprieves, and act as Commander-in-Chief.[21]

The Convention debated intensively for five weeks, section by section, the draft of the Committee of Detail. On September 8 a Committee of Style headed by Gouverneur Morris was appointed to "revise the style and arrange the articles which had been agreed to by the house." This committee too was innovative. It installed the plan for choosing the President through electors and empowered him to make treaties, provided two-thirds of the Senators present concurred, and to nominate and, with the advice and consent of the Senate, appoint ambassadors, other public ministers and consuls, and justices of the Supreme Court. The President's term was put at four years with indefinite reeligibility. The Presidential Article II began with a sentence, attributed to Morris, of vast future significance: "The executive Power shall be vested in a President of the United States of America."

On September 13 the Committee of Style presented a draft of the Constitution to the Convention in the handwriting of Gouverneur Morris. Two days later the Constitution was adopted, and in another two days the Convention adjourned. The Presidency, as it finally emerged, mirrored the ideal of a strong but responsible Chief Executive. The President would be a single, not a plural, executive, with no council but presumably heads of departments, although these were not specifically provided for. His election and identity were distinct and separate from Congress. His term of four years was longer than the state governors', and he was reeligible for an indefinite number of terms. His powers were generous and both specific and general. The opening language of Article II, "The executive Power shall be vested in a President," was clearly broader than the investiture of Article I, "All legislative Powers herein granted shall be vested in a Congress," or Article III, "The judicial Power shall extend to all cases, in Law and Equity, arising under this Constitution, the Laws of the United States, and Treaties." [22]

Makers of the Presidency

In any listing of Founding Fathers who played a heroic part in creating a strong Chief Executive tempered by constraints, the name of James Wilson of Pennsylvania would take an honored place. Forty-five years of age at the time of the Convention, Wilson was a Scotsman by birth and education, tall, large-featured, and afflicted with nearsightedness, which with his glasses added a touch of sternness to his appearance. Endowed with a tough, perceptive mind, Wilson contributed more than anyone else to the concept of the strong but responsible Presidency. He laid it persuasively before the Convention and was an instrumental member of the Committee of Detail that worked out the final revision. Wilson's success, although impressive, was not total. His chief defeat was the rejection of his proposal that the executive be chosen by the people.

Gouverneur Morris, chairman of the committee that wrote the final draft of the Constitution, is another hero. Draftsman of the New York constitution, member of the Continental Congress, and hardy *bon vivant,* he illuminated the Convention's deliberations with insights from the instructive New York experience. Eloquent, caustic, dynamic, and aggressive, Morris steadily championed the strong executive who would also be responsible and democratic. In Morris's eyes, the executive must be the advocate and defender of "the people, even of the lower classes," against legislative "tyranny," against "the great and the wealthy who, in the course of things, will compose the legislature." [23] Madison, too, stands among the heroes. He began conservatively on the question of executive power but gradually came around to Wilson's views.

The indispensable presence at the Convention was the presiding officer, the nation's future first Chief Executive, George Washington. Elected unanimously to his Convention post, his tall, heavy, ruddy presence, grave mien, his very embodiment of the young country's agony and triumph, marked him as the most conspicuous and the most influential delegate. Although he spoke but once, his commitment to strong central government was well known. "My wish is," he wrote to Madison, prior to Philadelphia, "that the convention may adopt no temporizing expedients, but probe the defects of the constitution to the bottom, and provide a radical cure, whether they are agreed to or not." [24] The prevailing assumption, candidly articulated in the Convention, was that he would become the first President. Pierce Butler of South Carolina expressed Washington's significance in the creation of the Presidency when he wrote, "Entre nous, I do [not] believe they [the executive powers] would have been so great had not many members cast their eyes toward General Washington as President; and shaped their Ideas of the Powers to be given the President, by their opinions of his Virtue." [25]

But there were also prestigious voices that spoke of inherent dangers in the strong Chief Executive. Upon hearing of the necessity of secrecy, vigor, and dispatch in the discharge of public business, and the uniqueness of the executive in embodying those attributes, the perspicacious John Dickinson of Pennsylvania reminded his colleagues that, important as these qualities were, "that of responsibility is more so . . . ." [26] Pierce Butler of South Carolina warned, "But why might not a Cataline or a Cromwell arise in this Country as well as in others?" [27] Benjamin Franklin, the Convention's worldly sage, illuminated a theme, widely embraced by his colleagues, that the transformation of executive power into tyranny, was, at bottom, the consequence of the evil lurking in human nature. Who, normally, would strive to possess the offices of government? Franklin's answer was knowing and confident: "the bold and violent, the men of strong passions and indefatigable activity in their selfish pursuits. These will thrust themselves into your Government and be your rulers." [28]

Observations like these spurred the Framers to search for means to forestall the abuses of that most dangerous combination, imperfect human nature coupled with substantial power.

Structural Concepts

The making of the Presidency adhered to two overarching structural concepts: the separation of powers and checks and balances. Mutually contradictory, even though directed toward the same ends, one posed division and independence, the other interaction and dependence.

The separation of powers was a basic principle in the works of several major political writers well known to the Framers. Although the writers differed in the ways these powers should be separated, they shared a common view of the nature and purpose of separated powers. John Locke's *Two Treatises of Govern-*

ment, probably the most powerful philosophic influence at the Convention, Montesquieu's *Esprit des lois,* and William Blackstone's *Commentaries on the Laws of England* all viewed the concentration of power as an invitation to tyranny. Liberty was best preserved if power were distributed between several branches. Locke, for instance, divided governmental power between the legislative or lawmaking power, the executive or law-enforcing power, and the "federative" power of war and peace, leagues and alliances, and other foreign relations. Locke did not specify the judicial power but presumably intended to safeguard its independency by the Act of Settlement.

Although the Founding Fathers repeatedly and reverently invoked separation of powers, the doctrine fared unevenly at their hands. As Charles C. Thach has rightly observed, few governments exceed the functional overlapping of that created by the American Constitution.[29] Lawmaking is shared between the two-house Congress and the President, treaty-making and appointments between the President and the Senate, and so on. The Fathers did meticulously observe the doctrine in the sense of arranging a personal separation of powers in contrast to functional separation. The memberships of the three branches—executive, legislative, and judicial—were separated. An officer of one could not serve in another, except for the Vice President, who had minor duties in the Senate but a general identity with the executive.

Checks and balances, the second overarching doctrine for making the strong executive responsible and free of temptation to lapse into tyrannical ways, was also well articulated by influential writers. The theory of balanced government reached back to the Greeks and enjoyed vogue in the eighteenth century among English and continental writers. Montesquieu and Blackstone interpreted the English constitution as a complex of checks: the Lords against the Commons and both against the crown. Government was viewed not as a cooperative enterprise between its several parts but as an enduring conflict of opposite interests.

The leading American exponent of balanced government was John Adams, whose *Defence of the Constitutions of the United States of America Against the Attack of Mr. Turgot* was well known to the Founding Fathers. For liberty to be preserved and property safeguarded, Adams argued, government must be poised in an equilibrium. Governments, like the populations they govern, divide into three distinct entities: the one, the few, and the many; or the leader, the aristocracy of birth or property, and the mass of people. Each part is capable of abuse—of jealousy, encroachment, and folly. The wellspring of disequilibrium, in the words of Thucydides, is "thirst of power, from rapacious and ambitious passions." The art of constitution-making, as Adams perceived it, was the establishment of "a multitude of curious and ingenious inventions to balance in their turn, all those powers [legislative, executive, and judicial], to check the passions peculiar to them, and to control them from rushing into the exorbitancies to which they are most addicted." The stability and purposes of a government, in a word, were best achieved by a delicate balance between more or less equal powers vitalized by mutual jealousies.

The Founding Fathers were much preoccupied with the problem of balance. "It is [the] most difficult of all rightly to balance the Executive," Gouverneur Morris observed: "Make him too weak: the Legislature will usurp his power. Make him too strong: he will usurp on the Legislature." The leading analyst of balanced power was Madison, whose views are most fully stated in the *Federalist* paper Number 51. "The great security against a gradual concentration of the several powers in the same department," he wrote, "consists in giving to those who administer each department the necessary constitutional means and personal motives to resist encroachments of the others. Ambition must be made to counteract ambition."

The Presidency Begins

The final phase of the creation of the Presidency was Washington's nearly impeccable workmanship as the office's first incumbent. His strong and good hands imparted to the Presidency a form and substance that have forever remained with it. In confronting his duties, Washington knew well that what he did possessed both present and future significance, that his every act was a potential precedent, and that the body of his conduct was creating an entire executive system.

On Inauguration Day, April 30, 1789, the joint inaugural committee of Congress arrived at the President-elect's temporary residence in New York to escort him to Federal Hall. Shortly after midday the general started out in a grand coach drawn by four horses, preceded by troops and the Senators of the joint committee and followed by his secretaries, the Representatives of the committee, Chancellor Robert Livingston, who would administer the oath, the heads of the federal departments, and a handful of eminent citizens. When the procession reached Federal Hall, Washington passed with simple dignity into the building and mounted the stairs to the Senate chamber, where members of the two houses of Congress, foreign diplomats, and other dignitaries had assembled. The general passed through an arched central door leading onto a small, half-enclosed portico overlooking Wall and Broad Streets. Cheers rolled up from the vast multitude below. Samuel Otis, Secretary of the Senate, lifted the Bible reposing on a red cushion on a small table. Washington placed his hand on the Bible, Livingston pronounced the oath, and Washington repeated it and kissed the Book. "It is done," Livingston declared, and, turning to the crowd, made a broad sweep with his hand and shouted, "Long live George Washington, President of the United States." The crowd roared back Livingston's words and "God bless our President"; church bells rang, the flag was run up in the cupola of Federal Hall, and guns were fired from the Battery and a Spanish sloop of war in the harbor. The Presidency was now in being.[30]

Presidential Strength: George Washington

In two terms of office Washington launched the Presidency on a high note of success. Weathering times that were full of crisis, he left the republic stronger, more purposeful, and more confident than when he had begun his task. A string of measures, highly impressive by twentieth-century standards in their number and scope, steadily emerged from the Washington administration: a national currency was issued and the Bank of the United States was established to provide credit; manufacture and trade were fostered by tariffs and bounties; inventions were protected by patent and copyright laws; neutrality was preserved in the face of an enlarging European war; and the national security was enhanced by reorganization of the army and navy, the founding of West Point, and the building of fortifications in the East and West.

Washington exercised the powers of his office in a fashion that permitted vigorous and innovative administration, but he respected the necessities of legitimacy and responsibility. Midway in his term Washington wrote,

> The powers of the Executive of the United States are more definite, and better understood perhaps than those of almost any other Country; and my aim has been and will continue to be, neither to stretch nor relax from them in any instance whatever, unless imperious circumstances should render the measure indispensable.[31]

Where authority was clearly his, Washington maintained his mastery. He truly dominated the executive branch. He was not long in office when he requested the heads of departments to provide "a full, precise and general *idea*" of the work entrusted to them.[32] With few exceptions he prescribed the duties of his department heads and kept abreast of daily detail. He read incoming and outgoing communications of the executive branch and passed upon important plans and actions that the departments submitted in writing. All loan and debt transactions were subject to his approval. Each use of the seal of the United States required his consent. No lighthouse keeper, customs collector, or captain of a cutter could be appointed without his consideration. So confident was he of his mastery that he brought into the leading posts of his administration two of the most gifted department heads the nation has ever known, Thomas Jefferson as Secretary of State and Alexander Hamilton as Secretary of the Treasury.

Washington triumphed in an area where many of his successors have floundered: relationships with Congress. He converted his popularity into major laws without tarnishing his prestige in the inevitable struggle. In his deportment toward Congress he was the essence of constitutional propriety. He stayed officially aloof from most major struggles, leaving the heat and dust of battle to his subordinates, chiefly Hamilton.

Washington was careful to respect Congress. Following his Annual or State of the Union Address, the Senate and House prepared addresses in response. The great throng of lawmakers of both chambers, led by the Speaker and the bearer of the mace, symbol of Congressional authority, gathered before the President. The Vice President and the Speaker spoke for their respective houses. The President, for his part, was also attentive to Congress with social and ceremonial gesture. Shortly before the inauguration, he visited the members of Congress, and his manner was agreeable. "He made us complaisant bows," Senator William Maclay of Pennsylvania noted, "one as he mounted and the other as he went away on horseback." [33] He regularly tendered dinners with a dozen and more guests from the Senate, the House, and his own administration.

The close work of researching and drafting legislative proposals and the chores of advocating them, rallying votes, and working out compromises were left to his lieutenant, Alexander Hamilton, Secretary of the Treasury and field leader of the Federalist party. Hamilton drafted the Great Reports, presenting with detail and justification the major legislation of the administration: public credit, the Bank, manufactures, and the like. Washington engaged in no public advocacy of these measures. He seems, however, to have been a behind-the-scenes influence when Jefferson and Hamilton arranged their famous compromise, the location of the future capital in Washington in exchange for federal assumption of state debts. The observant Senator Maclay confided to his diary, "The President of the United States has (in my opinion) had a great influence in this business. The game was played by him and his adherents . . . his name goes to wipe away blame and silence all murmuring." [34]

Washington was a resolute defender of the integrity of Presidential power against all trespass, even when Congress was the offender. A most momentous challenge was the call by the Republican-controlled House of Representatives for the instructions and pertinent papers of John Jay's mission to negotiate the treaty bearing his name. The House's bold intrusion into an enterprise allotted by the Constitution to the President and Senate gripped the capital with tension. "Anxiety is on the tiptoe. . . . our galleries have been crowded," Representative Francis Preston of Virginia noted. Washington's response was strong and forthright. Foreign relations by their very nature, the President wrote, required secrecy; disclosure of the requested papers would be "impolitic" and "a dangerous precedent." The fundamental law did not require the House's assent to a treaty. "A just regard to the Constitution and to the duty of my Office . . . forbids a compliance with your request." The House opposition thundered and maneuvered, but all in vain, "What firmness does this great man display!" Senator William Plumer rejoiced. [35]

But another time, when the House of Representatives, investigating the failure of General St.Clair's expedition against northwest Indian tribes, requested from the executive "such persons, papers and records as may be necessary" to its inquiry, Washington readily acknowledged the propriety of the request. The House was rightfully conducting an "inquest" and, consequently, could make a general call for papers. But he also could anticipate that "there might be papers of so secret a nature, as that they ought not to be given up," and his executive colleagues agreed that such papers must be withheld "as would injure the public." [36] Concerning St.Clair, there were none, and Washington, complying fully with the House request, demonstrated that the strong President could also be accountable and responsible.

Washington, the President of strength, was no slave to literal constitutional prescription but a resourceful innovator. The Constitution said little of how the President might secure advice in the daily business of decision- and policy-making. Washington exploited the freedom this silence permitted and instituted practices that Presidents since his time have followed. He founded the cabinet. In the autumn of 1791 he began bringing his department Secretaries—Jefferson, Hamilton, his Secretary of War Henry Knox, and his Attorney General Edmund Randolph—together for a joint consideration of policy. The cabinet meeting was a timesaver over individual consultation with the Secretaries and permitted the testing of the opinions of his counselors in the presence of their peers. The responsible Chief Executive, Washington believed, responded not merely to external constraints such as Congress and public opinion. He felt that responsibility could be nurtured by internal executive processes. The cabinet harmonized with these perceptions and with Washington's belief that advice should be competitive, that one individual's views should be checked against other sources. Repeatedly he ranged beyond the cabinet for counsel, to Congressman James Madison, for example, and Chief Justice John Jay, from whom he invited "ideas . . . not confined to matters judicial, but extended to all other topics which have occurred, or may occur to you, as fit subjects for general or private communications." [37] Washington also believed that advice should be broadly representative. He recruited his cabinet from the three principal sections of the country, the North, the South, and the Middle States. A close student of grass-roots opinion, he maintained correspondents in all the sections and instituted the grand tour, traveling the length and breadth of the republic to gather impressions firsthand.

But for Washington's Presidency all was not serenity and assurance. His mind was often the battleground for conflicts that flared between the ideal of the strong Presidency and the ideal of the responsible Presidency. Often the line between them was blurred and therefore discoverable only by experience. Within the cabinet were redoubtable exponents of each kind of Presidency— Hamilton articulated the energetic, assertive Presidency and Jefferson the limited, accountable executive. One of their more dramatic clashes erupted when Washington unilaterally issued a proclamation of American neutrality in the Franco-British war. As justification, Hamilton argued that since foreign policy was by nature an executive function, the powers to declare war and approve treaties accorded the legislature in the Constitution were "exceptions out of the general 'executive power' vested in the President" and therefore were "to be construed strictly, and ought to be extended no futher than is essential to their execution." While Congress might declare war, the President was empowered to preserve peace prior to the declaration, as a concomitant of the "executive power" to do whatever the law of nations requires the United States to do in relations with other powers. Though executive action might "affect the exercise of the power of the legislature to declare war," that was insufficient reason, Hamilton argued, for the executive not to use his authority.

Disturbed by Hamilton's expansive interpretation of Presidential power, Jefferson implored Madison to "select the most striking heresies and cut him to pieces in face of the public." A reluctant Madison denied that the power to make wars or treaties was inherently executive. Indeed, this "vicious" doctrine was patently borrowed from Britain, he claimed, and the fact that these were royal British prerogatives did not make them Presidential prerogatives. Only Congress could judge whether the United States must declare war, a judgment that could not be foreclosed by Presidential proclamations of neutrality or by other executive actions creating "an antecedent state of things." As for Hamilton's suggestion of concurrent Presidential and Congressional authority, Madison cited an inherent absurdity: What if the President proclaimed neutrality and Congress declared war? [38] Although he went along with Hamilton, Washington quickly responded to the Madisonian interpretation when grand juries refused to indict offenders, since no neutrality law existed to violate. Accordingly, Washington was driven to recommend that Congress legislate, and, ever since, neutrality has remained the province of Congress.

As part of his conception of the strong Presidency, Washington prized and jealously maintained the intrinsic dignity of the Presidential office. He wanted, he said, to make the Presidency "respectable." His natural taste for regal display was freely indulged.

But, more importantly, the Presidency was sustained by the unfailing magnificence of Washington's character. Judgment, vision, skill in managing men, integrity, infinite patience, self-discipline—all were his marks. "His integrity was most pure," Thomas Jefferson observed, "his justice the most inflexible I have ever known. . . . He was indeed, in every sense of the words, a wise, a good and a great man. . . ." [39]

Presidential Weakness: John Adams

But the Presidency was not all strength, achievement, and glory; it also harbored weakness. Ironically, it was the leading American theoretician of checks and balances, the second President of the United States, who provided the earliest illustration of the weakness his ideas had helped create. John Adams was not long in the Presidency when he demonstrated where the provision for the strong executive left off. He proved by his own experience the far depths of trouble in which the President can wallow as party chief, as legislative leader, and as general manager of the executive branch. For the first of these the Founding Fathers had made no provision; for the others, very little. The Presidency was in several large particulars an unfinished office.

Adams the President was only the nominal leader of his Federalist party; its real leader was an outsider who held no public office at the time, the talented, driving, ubiquitous Alexander Hamilton. The contrast was exaggerated by a growing break between the two men. Thomas Jefferson, leader of the Anti-

Federalists, noted that the Congressional Federalists were only "a little less hostile" to the President than to himself. The Jefferson men and disaffected legislative Federalists were unstinting in demonstrating the President's weakness as legislative leader. When relations with France crumbled and war threatened, Adams, anxious to maintain peace, recommended to Congress a defensive policy based upon expanded naval power. Hamilton, the covert influence, reputedly eager to drive the French out of North America, instructed his Congressional followers to vote appropriations for an expanded army, which they did. Congress, in another defiance of Presidential leadership, passed in succession the Alien and Sedition Acts, which empowered the President to deport undesirable aliens and made it a crime to criticize the federal government or its officials. Adams neither requested nor wanted either law.

But Adams drank his bitterest draft as chief administrator of the civil and military affairs of the executive branch. Yielding to Congress's enthusiasm for an army in an act designed to win the popular acclaim he so badly lacked, he drew George Washington out of retirement to command the provisional forces. This seemingly splendid triumph was suddenly jeopardized when Washington requested the appointment as his generals of the following in order of rank: Hamilton, Pinckney, and Knox. Adams disputed the order, holding that Knox rightfully should come first, followed by Pinckney and then Hamilton. Ironically, Washington, creator of the strong Presidency, now became the agent of its degradation. In a forceful letter to Adams he insisted upon his listing; otherwise, he strongly implied, he would resign. The President, in all his political feebleness, could hardly afford the storm of Washington's resignation. The Commander-in-Chief yielded to his commanding general. Adams staggered on through a full agenda of woe. When upon his own initiative he nominated W. Vans Murray to be minister to the French Republic, his cabinet displayed unconcealed resentment at his failure to consult it. Other times the cabinet concentrated upon its major preoccupation of leaking secrets to Hamilton to assist his campaign against the President. Adams, the man of large talents and rich public experience, ultimately crowned his failure and abandoned his misery by sustaining defeat for reelection.

The Founding Fathers, the Washington-Adams experience reveals, had created a Presidency of both strength and weakness. The first two Presidencies were the beginning of a continuing dilemma in American history between the people's fear of executive power and their confidence in its necessity and capacity for good.

3

SELECTION

The American Presidency can be no better or stronger than the caliber of its incumbents. Being a highly personal office, it is foredoomed to an interlude of mediocrity if the Chief Executive who fills it can boast no more than middling talents. Being an intensely political office, it faces deadlock and futility, unless the processes of selecting its holders can screen out individuals lacking in the high order of political talent required to function successfully in a governmental system where power is much divided. In the modern era, the incumbent needs to be both a man of action and a man of thought, one who "can get things done" and one who is alert to new ideas, one who is adept at the practical politics of getting bills through Congress and one who can engage in dialogue with the universities and other incubators of thought, all to the end of producing policies of depth and sophistication, fit for times of technical complexity and grand-scale change.

The processes of selection that will somehow produce this human paragon must make the widest possible search. If Presidential hopefuls are heavily concentrated in the wealthy classes or dependent upon them for support, the recruiting base is obviously and practically too narrow, and it violates the democratic ideal of a widely available citizenry for office-holding. The selection outcome must be suffused with legitimacy. It cannot be if the victor perpetrates repeated acts of espionage and sabotage, if his campaign is woven with deceit, if it exploits fears and prejudices, if it is a flood of words and images that say little about issues, or if it is a noncampaign of withdrawal and silence. Rational debate is the essence of democratic politics, to the point that political power, as it is normally exercised in the American system, is the power to persuade. Democracy requires elections that are free, honest, and serious. Above all, selection must produce candidates who are democratic animals, who comprehend the bounds of constitutional government, who consort with a diversity of citizens, mighty and humble. The supreme function of the selection process is the production of candidates who comprehend and value democracy. If the process produces a candidate who deliberately and systematically violates democratic practice, it has committed a grievous lapse and unloosed a threat to democracy itself. Upon the electorate falls a heavy burden of assessing the democratic fitness of candidates, a task that is complicated by the media's capacity to exaggerate and mystify the qualities of Presidential contenders.

There can be no strong President if the selection process fails to produce or reflect a social and political consensus that will sustain a constructive program for major public problems. Thus, the function of the selection process is not only to choose the incumbent but to build political union among disparate interests and sections. And ideally, to assure that the selection process will produce a Chief Executive who is democracy oriented, the voter should be able to penetrate the smokescreen of the candidate's imagery and probe his earlier, formative years that produced his present political personality and provide the basis of predicting how he will perform in the Presidency. Such a scrutiny would focus on the candidate as a child, a boy, and as a young man, and on his earlier campaigning and office-holding.

It is not altogether clear when the selection of a President actually begins. Often candidacies are launched two or even three years before the election itself. The long duration of the race and the lavish investment of effort and money it requires militate against the production of candidates who will treat the office with the modesty appropriate to democracy. Thus a dilemma is posed between the prodigious exertion that winning the office requires and the modesty of demeanor that becomes democracy. Still another dilemma hovers in the circumstance that no set of democratic standards can control the selection process from beginning to end. In a sense, the President selects himself; in a sense the party selects him; in a sense—and here the final decision lies—the people do the selecting themselves. To win the Presidency, the aspirant must travel a long, hard, treacherous road abounding in bumps and quicksand and divisible into three distinct segments: the preconvention buildup, the national nominating convention, and the postconvention electoral campaign.

The Preconvention Struggle

The preconvention phase is the longest, often the severest, part of the journey, and it may engage the candidate in fiercer struggles with his rival contenders for the nomination than his later race with the opposing nominee. Competition for the nomination, by contributing to voter choice, may or may not contribute to the bread-and-butter desideratum, party victory. According to a study, when harmony attends the nominating process for the party controlling the Presidency, its chances of winning are good. But conflict leading to factional victory in the nomination renders the chances of the in-party poor. The opposite propositions hold for the out-party—less chance of capturing the Presidency if the nomination is harmonious, and a better chance if factional strife flares.[1] In this initial phase of the campaign struggles, the candidate surrounds himself with an entourage of helpers of assorted skills. The entourage has expanded from less than a handful in the nineteenth century to well-nigh a score for the serious modern candidate such as John Kennedy. His preconvention staff included his brother Robert, as general manager of operations, and Lawrence F. O'Brien, congenial, sagacious, and hard-working, as commander of the organizational base, a phalanx of young men who had done their political teething in the Senator's home state of Massachusetts. Kenneth O'Donnell, a taciturn former Harvard football captain and veteran of Kennedy's Massachusetts wars, was the candidate's link with the organization and transmitted Kennedy's reflections and directives to O'Brien. Theodore C. Sorensen was an "idea man" and star draftsman—"my intellectual blood bank," [2] Kennedy called him. Stephen Smith, a brother-in-law, discreet and business-trained, opened the Washington headquarters for the Kennedy staff and eventually became the general manager in charge of mobilizing scores of thousands of volunteers and employees. Pierre Salinger, a former California newspaperman, Congressional investigator, and a big-cigar man, presided with joviality and shrewdness over press relations. Louis Harris, public opinion analyst and market research entrepreneur, was the candidate's personal polltaker. His findings were the basis of key campaign decisions. John Bailey, Connecticut Democratic chairman, coordinated the Northeastern bosses.

On the preconvention landscape are several other standard political types. Not the least important, of course, are the several species of opposing candidates: the serious contenders, the dark horses, and the favorite sons. For the 1976 race, Gerald Ford, promptly upon assuming the Presidency, disclosed that he expected to run for the office in 1976, a move that insulated him from a lame-duck role in dealing with Congress and his party. And, as early as 1973, Democratic candidates were afield, making speeches, issuing high-minded pronouncements, and courting support from influentials—Jackson, Muskie, Humphrey, Bentsen, McGovern and, for a time, Kennedy, Mondale, and others among the Democrats.

The landscape is also dotted with prestigious political figures who are not candidates but whose support is cherished and whose favor is courted: governors, Senators, Congressmen, party patriarchs, and labor, business, nationality, and racial leaders. Beyond Washington and into the American hinterland stretches the intricate continental tangle of party machinery, manned by a varied body of functionaries, known collectively as "organization politicians," the state and local party officialdom. Many a Presidential aspirant has run aground from want of support from the organization politicians. A formidable obstacle to Wilson's 1912 candidacy was his cold rejection by the generality of organization politicians. "They have an impression of you," Wilson's manager, William F. McCombs, wrote with frankness, "in a large degree that you are austere and dictatorial and that you will not have a due appreciation of what is to be done for you. . . . Another thing I hear much of, particularly throughout the East, is that you are unreliable." [3]

But contemporary seekers of the Presidential nomination, particularly since the later 1960s, have become less dependent on state and local party organizations. In recent elections, the path to the White House is more worn through the Senate than through that conduit of yesteryear, the governor's mansion. Contemporary national issues in foreign and domestic policy are alien to the customary concerns of state and county chairmen and district leaders. Presidential aspirants base their quest for the nomination increasingly on television, public relations techniques, and personalized financing, and markedly less than their forebears on precinct work and traditional party fund-raising.

Not the least importance of the traditional organization politicians and the incumbents of the reformed party structures of the 1970s is their large hand in selecting the delegates, the official decision-makers, of the future convention.

Preconvention Strategies

The preconvention campaign, the struggle to win delegates by the contending aspirants for the nomination, is a time of hard choices between alternative strategies. Franklin Roosevelt and his managers at the outset of his preconvention candidacy perceived a choice between two major and opposite courses. They could sit back and conduct a passive campaign, limited to building friendly contacts and issuing press statements extolling Roosevelt's virtues. The risk of antagonizing the rather numerous favorite son candidates would be avoided, at least until the campaign began in earnest. Or the pressure could be turned on immediately, Roosevelt's candidacy announced, and the job begun of rounding up delegates to clinch the nomination. History provided not a few grisly illustrations of the outstanding candidate who declared early and subsequently was trampled into the dust by opponents who ganged up on him. Democratic candidates in Roosevelt's day, because of the party's convention rule requiring a two-thirds vote to nominate, were highly susceptible to the deadly danger. Another risk was that a candidacy begun too early might wither and die from public apathy. This species of political blight is known in the trade as the "morning-glory" candidacy. Roosevelt ultimately decided to run early and to run fast, notwithstanding the risks. Candidates as a rule back away from the Roosevelt pattern by carefully avoiding any announcement of their candidacy for as long as possible, all the while, however, pursuing the grail with might and main.

Tours, visits, and speeches—the chief preconvention activities—involve basic strategic and tactical choices. They also lead the candidate onto some of the most treacherous terrain of his preconvention effort—taking a stand on issues. Worst of all is the unavoidable issue on which any position the candidate takes will alienate support he needs. Franklin Roosevelt in 1932 was bedeviled by a momentous question he could not avoid—his attitude toward United States membership in the League of Nations. William Randolph Hearst in his transcontinental newspaper chain attacked the candidate unmercifully as an "internationalist," quoting abundantly in front-page editorials Roosevelt's pro-League statements in his Vice-Presidential campaign of 1920.

In a carefully devised release Roosevelt acknowledged that in 1920 he had worked for American participation in the League. He said,

> But the League of Nations today is not the League conceived by Woodrow Wilson. . . . Too often through these years its major function has been not the broad overwhelming purpose of world peace, but rather a mere meeting place for the

political discussion of strictly European political national difficulties. . . . Because of these facts, therefore, I do not favor American participation.[4]

Fortunately for Roosevelt, the statement accomplished its immediate purpose. Hearst ceased his attacks. But there were costs, which presumably the candidate and his managers had anticipated and weighed. The statement stretched to the uttermost the loyalty of the Wilsonians, a compact and powerful band of associates of the last Democratic President. Colonel Edward N. House, Wilson's former confidant, wrote to Farley that Roosevelt's position "created something akin to panic among the devoted Wilson followers." Intellectuals of the school of Walter Lippmann were sorely distressed. Roosevelt swabbed the disgruntled with a remedy that his secretary Louis Howe called "soothing syrup." One body of opinion Roosevelt could not allay was the cynics, a not uncommon breed among political professionals. Senator William E. Borah, eying Roosevelt's statement, muttered sarcastically, "Repent ye, for the kingdom of heaven is at hand." [5]

The candidate in the preconvention period is confronted with the possibility, and sometimes the necessity, of "deals" on issues and offices. The deals presumably will strengthen his chances for the nomination if, on balance, they gain more support than they lose. In the fall of 1895, with the future convention well in sight, Mark Hanna sat down with two great political dictators of the day, Senator Matt Quay of Pennsylvania and former Senator Tom ("Boss") Platt of New York. Both ruled their respective state machines absolutely and were grand masters of the arts of venality. Hanna met with the dark, cynical Quay and the scrawny, secretive Platt to bargain for the huge electoral votes of their respective states. With these William McKinley's nomination would be assured. The bosses' terms came high. Probably more than one cabinet seat was involved, and Platt wanted the Secretaryship of the Treasury for himself, in writing, please. Hanna rushed back to Ohio to report the terms of incipient victory to the candidate. He fortified McKinley first with a choice cigar. As Hanna spoke, McKinley listened in silence, pulled on his cigar, got up, and paced the floor. "There are some things in this world that come too high," he said at last. "If I cannot be President without promising to make Tom Platt Secretary of the Treasury, I will never be President." McKinley thus took a long stride toward sainthood.[6]

PRIMARIES The candidate makes a major strategic decision in choosing among the several Presidential primaries in which to make his race. In the 1972 elections, primaries, held in 23 states, were the crucial battlegrounds in which two-thirds of the delegates were chosen. Consequently, after a long, indifferent history, Presidential primaries have acquired a new democratic dimension as a potential instrument of popular determination of the Presidential nomination. With most delegates chosen by primaries for the first time in 1972, the tactic used by Hubert Humphrey in 1968 was precluded. Humphrey gained the support of key people, avoided the primaries, and won the nomination. In the 1970s, candidates for the Democratic nomination must win in the primaries, and for a Republican candidate, unless he is a solidly established Presidential incumbent, the primaries are a gauntlet to be run with possibly fatal consequences. It is no longer enough to gain the favor of party leaders and other would-be kingmakers. A possible exception to this seemingly democratic scenario is that if a succession of primaries produces a hodgepodge of winners, the kingmakers can roll up their sleeves and determine the outcome. Primaries sometimes stumble on the obstacle of low voter participation and expose the hollowness of their democratic pretensions. Although, typically, Presidential primaries exceed other primaries in voter turnout, the turnout in the Presidential election often exceeds by thirty points the rate for the primary.

Presidential contenders rightly complain of the inhuman strain upon their endurance caused by existing primaries that force them to wage full-scale campaigns in a succession of states. Late in February 1972, for example, Edmund Muskie, then the front-running candidate, left Washington on a Thursday morning, spoke in Chicago that day and attended a reception, flew to Florida that night for a luncheon and two receptions on Friday, and then flew to New Hampshire that night. On Saturday, he conducted a television interview, a walking tour, appeared at dogsled races, and then flew to Hartford, Connecticut, for an evening speech.[7] For officeholders such as governors, primaries, with their weeks of intensive effort, mean neglect of official duties. As well, primaries present endlessly varied formats, with each state brewing its own version of rules and procedures that bewilder both voters and candidates. As Congressman Morris Udall (D., Arizona) put it, "a candidate's future is in the hands of a hodge-podge of laws, regulations, and faceless officials over which he has no recourse." In primaries with many contestants—the Democrats in 1972—a candidate such as McGovern, with a strong ideological position on issues (the Vietnam war, advocacy of school busing, relaxation of regulations on the use of marijuana, and clearly suggested approval of abortion) and favored with an efficient organization can outpace a centrist candidate such as Edmund Muskie, whose doughty occupancy of the middle ground caused him to appear bland on issues.

The primary interlude is excessively long, three and a half months in 1972, or twice the length of the postnomination campaign. Primaries are also expensive, soaring to an expenditure of more than $13 million in 1972,[8] with shortages of funds a curse that overtook all major Democratic candidates and ultimately caused Muskie, Jackson, and Fred Harris to drop out.

The National Nominating Convention

The national nominating convention itself, the final arbiter, is as uniquely American as the hot dog and salt-water taffy. Everyone knows its spirit of carnival, the marching, shouting delegates, the frothy oratory, the grating brass bands. Like most citizens, H. L. Mencken, sage and cynic, viewed the nominating convention with mixed sentiments. "One sits through long sessions wishing heartily that all the delegates and alternates were in hell," he wrote, "—and then suddenly there comes a show so gaudy and hilarious, so melodramatic and obscene, so unimaginably exhilarating and preposterous that one lives a gorgeous year in an hour." [9]

CONVENTION REFORM, 1972 Traditionally, the major parties choose delegates to their national convention by elaborate formulas that recognize the state and local organizations as the basic units of the party and that reward the performance of these organizations in past elections. In 1972, in the spirit of democracy, the national conventions, particularly the Democratic, applied "reforms" to delegate selection processes designed to make each delegation more representative of the diversity of a state's population. The Democratic party's reforms focused on improving the representation of several "left-out" population categories—blacks, women, and youth—and a remarkable upsurge occurred in their presence in the party's 1972 national convention.

Representation of "Left-Out" Groups at the 1972
National Democratic Convention

	Percentage of delegates, 1968	Percentage of delegates, 1972	Percentage of population
Blacks	6	14	11
Women	14	36	51
Youth (30 years or under)	2	23	30

Source: Denis G. Sullivan et al., *The Politics of Representation* (New York, 1974), p. 23.

By singling out certain population groupings for studied treatment, the Democratic reforms necessarily slighted others. Among the heaviest losers at the hands of the reformers were white urban ethnics—Catholics most of all, but also Protestants and Jews. Organized labor, although favorably represented in numbers of delegates, exerted only a shadow of its usual influence upon convention business. Accustomed to applying a decisive hand in selecting the Presidential nominee, labor leaders had to swallow a candidate—George McGovern—to whom they were, and remained, largely hostile. [10] Prominent among the underrepresented were state and local party leaders, public officials, and big contributors. For all of the pretense of openness and fairness, the reform delegations in effect slighted the establishment figures who had for so long underrepresented them.

McGovern's overwhelming defeat tarnished the allure of delegate selection reform, and in the Democratic party a protracted struggle commenced over how much the 1976 convention would modify the 1972 changes. In actuality, the struggle over delegate selection is a struggle for dominance between "regulars" and "reformers"—between labor, party regulars, centrists, and old lib-

erals, on the one hand, and insurgents, new liberals, leftists, and newer groups
such as blacks, on the other.

THE CONVENTION AT WORK   The convention poses for the top contender
and his managers two vitally important tasks, failure in either one of which
might spell the difference between victory and defeat. The first is to keep the
bloc of pledged or promised delegates "nailed fast" to prevent their straying
"off the reservation" to another candidate. The second is to control the convention machinery to permit its manipulation for, rather than against, the candidate. In a contested convention these undertakings are a high-tension ordeal.
Jim Farley wrote of the 1932 Democratic convention,

> The nervous strain during this period of suspense was very close to the limit of
> physical endurance. . . . I was working eighteen or nineteen hours a day, con-
> versing with hundreds of people, constantly consulting with other leaders, receiv-
> ing reports from every delegation, and meeting at least twice daily with several
> hundred newspapermen. I . . . slept a few hours just before dawn if the opportu-
> nity offered. . . . Hundreds of other men were caught in the same dizzy whirl
> and were trying to keep up the same maddening pace.[11]

In facing their convention tasks, the managers of the modern candidate resort
to specialization, as they do in the preconvention phase. In 1932 Farley
operated the main Roosevelt reception center at Chicago, where he greeted the
Roosevelt delegates and tried mightily to win others over from the opposition.
One of Farley's props was a huge map of the United States on which the
Roosevelt states were blocked out in red. So vividly and convincingly did the
map demonstrate that Roosevelt was the choice of a big majority that the wor-
ried opposition took pains to deride it as "Field Marshal Farley's Map." In negotiations with delegates in his hotel suite, Ed Flynn, the suave and astute
Bronx boss, supplemented Farley's efforts to build Roosevelt's strength. Louis
Howe, too, wooed the delegates, and he had installed in his suite a microphone
attached to a direct wire from Albany. Roosevelt's exhilarating voice would
come booming into the room full of visitors, "My friends from Iowa," and
launch into a personal message. Roosevelt would expound his views, answer
questions, and delight and impress the delegates. Thanks to the direct wire,
Roosevelt, remaining at home, could electioneer and share in nearly every important decision at Chicago. The Roosevelt floor manager was Arthur Mullen
of Nebraska, an old hand at conventions and one well-liked by all factions.[12]

The managers of a serious modern candidate coordinate their far-flung effort
through an internal communications network at the convention itself. One of
the most elaborate of these was Kennedy's in 1960. From the Kennedy liaison
post, a cottage outside the Los Angeles Sports Arena, ran a net of direct communication lines to special telephone posts fixed on the chairs of friendly delegations. Eight of Kennedy's forty "state shepherds" who roved the convention
floor carried walkie-talkie sets that were linked to a communications control at
the cottage. From there the floor managers, Governor Abraham Ribicoff and
Robert Kennedy, directed the whole body of shepherds. Another set of lines

ran to Room 8315 at the Biltmore Hotel, the strategic center of the candidate's top command. Other lines were connected with Kennedy's private hideaway in Hollywood and his public Presidential suite.[13]

To control the convention machinery, the candidate and his managers must concentrate upon several key parts. Much of their effort occurs before the convention begins and centers upon the national committee and the national chairman who decide when and where the convention is to be held and make the local arrangements. The national committee selects the temporary chairman of the convention, who delivers the keynote address. Since the tone and tendency of this oration shape the convention's initial and sometimes decisive mood, the selection of the temporary chairman may touch off a fierce struggle. His further power to hand down parliamentary rulings helpful to the candidate he favors adds zest to the combat.

In 1932 the Roosevelt camp had to maneuver forcefully to prevent Jouett Shouse from becoming temporary chairman. Shouse, who fiercely opposed the Roosevelt candidacy, had powerful support. The Roosevelt emissaries were able to install their own nominee, Alben Barkley, for temporary chairman when the New York governor agreed that the arrangements subcommittee of the national committee might "commend" (Roosevelt's word) rather than "recommend" Shouse for a second major convention post, the permanent chairmanship.

Well before the convention, however, the Roosevelt forces decided to oppose Shouse for permanent chairman as well and advance their own candidate, Senator Thomas J. Walsh of Montana. Following Roosevelt's agreement to commend him, Shouse had campaigned ardently against the New York governor in Massachusetts and Pennsylvania and had convinced Roosevelt's managers that a loyal permanent chairman was imperative. Cries of "unfair" greeted disclosure of the Rooseveltians' decision. The fight grew so furious and the outcome so unpredictable that Charles Michelson, the party's stellar ghost writer, carried in one pocket an acceptance speech for Shouse and, in another, one for Walsh. Roosevelt's candidate, Walsh, was elected 626 to 528, the convention high-water mark for the opposition. The Roosevelt forces rounded out their control of convention machinery by installing Cordell Hull as chairman of the committee on resolutions and Bruce Kremer of Montana as chairman of the rules committee. Roosevelt chose no nominees for two other committee chairmanships to leave Farley free to dangle them before wavering delegations.[14]

In contrast to Roosevelt's struggle is the assured control that can be wielded over a convention by an incumbent President seeking reelection. Nixon's direction of the 1972 Republican convention illuminates the phenomenon to the point that his White House aides induced conservative Republican delegates to swallow the bitter pill of omitting an antilabor plank. Nixon, courting the labor vote, could not bear a discordant sound on the subject, and there was none.[15]

A race's outcome is often determined by "deals" arranged by the candidates' convention representatives. Franklin Roosevelt was eventually put across in 1932 by a bargain for the Vice-Presidency, which not a few times in the nation's history has determined the choice of the Presidential nominee. Farley suggested to Garner's representative, Sam Rayburn, that if Texas threw its support to Roosevelt, Garner could have the Vice-Presidency. Rayburn answered crustily that he and his co-workers had come to Chicago to nominate Garner for President, although they did not want a stalemate. Eventually Garner made the decision. Fearful that an ugly convention deadlock might damage public confidence and cost the Democrats the election, Garner released his delegates and reluctantly exchanged his proud Speakership for the quietude of the Vice-Presidency. Texas and California went over to Roosevelt and the nomination was clinched.[16]

The Convention Decides

The convention can also be viewed as a series of decisions, climbing, by phases, to the climax of the Presidential nomination. The proceedings of the convention committees—credentials, rules, permanent organization, and platform or resolutions—are often the harbinger of things to come. The committees' reports to the whole convention often provide an early test of strength of the rival candidates. The credentials committee, for instance, acts as a kind of court to decide which one of two or more contesting delegations from a given state is entitled to be seated. At the Republican national convention of 1952 nearly a hundred delegates were involved in seating contests. Supporters of Robert A. Taft controlled the credentials committee and reported favorably on delegations pledged to his candidacy from Louisiana, Georgia, and Texas. The Eisenhower camp carried the fight to the convention floor, waved the banner of "fair play," won the uncommitted delegations over to their side, seated their own delegations from the contested states, and opened the way for a first-ballot nomination.

The convention's balloting may simply be a routine ratification of the candidate's success constructed in the previous months of careful effort. The first-ballot nominations of Nixon and McGovern in 1972 were no surprise. A succession of ballotings, which is not uncommon, reflects the continuing struggle for delegates and requires adroit maneuvers. It may seem that the prize of the nomination goes to the man with the best organization and the most compelling political personality. But actually nominees are weeded out in advance to some extent; not all able individuals are eligible in practice. One of America's favorite candidates has been the military hero. Of the thirty-six men who have been elected President, thirteen have been military veterans. Both parties have thrice nominated former military men in the same year. The Republicans tapped no less than four Civil War generals; Theodore Roosevelt was the glamorous Rough Rider of the Spanish-American War; and Dwight Eisenhower achieved international military renown in World War II. John Kennedy's valor in that war was not forgotten, either. In this century governors have been the leading source of Presidential candidates, sixteen of them having been nominated after 1900. The United States Senate, once a liability, is fast becoming a factory of Presidential candidates. The chief Democratic contenders in 1972—McGovern, Muskie, Jackson, and Humphrey—were all Senators, and the Republican standard-bearer—Richard Nixon—was a former Senator. The Senator's importance has been enhanced in recent years by television and the dominance of foreign affairs, a subject that traditionally receives heavy attention in the Senate.

The Mountain States did not provide a candidate until Barry Goldwater in 1964, nor did the South for more than a century until Lyndon Johnson's nomination in 1964. Of the sixty-one men nominated by the two parties since 1856, forty-one have come from either New York State or the Middle West. Religion, race, and sex have also been selective factors for the nomination. Kennedy's breakthrough in 1960 as the first Catholic to become President may, before many more elections come to pass, throw the gates open to all. Before this only a white Anglo-Saxon Protestant male was considered eligible.

As to a black for President, a succession of Gallup polls, taken between 1958 and 1972, disclosed a marked rise in the view that race would not matter to the voter. In 1958, 38 percent said they would vote for a black for President and in 1972 the figure rose to 70 percent. But, paradoxically, a 1972 poll revealed that most voters thought that a black Vice Presidential candidate would handicap a national ticket that year.[17] The increasing incidence of women candidates for offices at all levels of government enhances the likelihood of a woman being nominated for President or Vice President.

After the Presidential nomination comes the usually anticlimactic selection of the Vice President. This decision is ordinarily governed by the tradition of "balancing the ticket" geographically. (Among the exceptions is the Truman-Barkley, Missouri-Kentucky, border state ticket of 1948.) After Wilson's nomination in 1912, his manager, A. S. Burleson, telephoned to say that the convention was leaning toward Thomas R. Marshall of Indiana. "But, Burleson," Wilson remonstrated, "he is a very small caliber man." Burleson did not argue the point but noted that Marshall was from the Middle West and a doubtful state. His candidacy would ideally supplement Wilson's. "All right, go ahead," Wilson said, not too agreeably.[18] Wilson notwithstanding, the opinion of the Presidential nominee is also weighty in choosing the Vice President. The degree to which the choice is specific varies.

THE CAMPAIGN   Radio and television, wider press coverage, and a burgeoning transportation technology have made campaigning strenuous for the modern candidate and have driven him to enlarge his staff. His increased exposure reduced the utility of that ancient standby, the set speech. The candidate must make many and varied speeches respectably adorned with an array of ideas. For this phase of his needs, Franklin Roosevelt's innovation, copied and adapted by his successors, was the brain trust, a body of professors and researchers who dealt with policies and issues for the candidate's speeches and other statements. A second distinct group, comprising Farley, Flynn, and others who had marshaled delegates for the convention, redirected their talents to gathering popular votes in the campaign.

Kennedy's postconvention campaign organization in 1960 enlarged upon the
Roosevelt pattern. There were new brain-trusters, professors recruited largely
from Harvard through Archibald Cox of the university's law school. Ideas and
speech drafts spewed from the group that followed Cox to Washington. In
addition, Kennedy's idea-generators included his personal brain trust, Sorensen
and Richard Goodwin, who dealt with high affairs and pronouncements.

For the political management phases, each member of Kennedy's prenomina-
tion entourage adapted his special skill to the new environment of the postconvention campaign. O'Donnell handled campaign scheduling, a difficult art concerned with allocating every minute of the candidate's time, with due regard for
transportation and speech schedules, the necessities and feuds of local leaders,
and the shepherding of newsmen following hard on the candidate's heels.
O'Brien became Director of Organization for the National Committee and
Byron (Whizzer) White, Director of the Kennedy-Johnson Volunteers Organization. Robert Kennedy presided over the entire enterprise—idea men and political managers—aided and abetted by Richard Donahue, Ralph Dungan, and
other personal Kennedy lieutenants and a half-dozen members of the Kennedy
family. The vast realm of the communications media was handled by Salinger,
polltaker Harris, and a speech coach brought in to pare away the candidate's
regional accent.[19]

The postconvention campaign, like other phases of the route to the Presidency, requires a series of major strategic decisions. Strategy on one level is
the selection of an array of voter entities, which when pieced together will provide an electoral majority. Kennedy's 1960 strategy focused upon nine large
states (New York, Pennsylvania, California, Michigan, Texas, Illinois, Ohio,
New Jersey, and Massachusetts) comprising 237 of the 269 electoral votes
required to elect a President. These plus sixty more electoral votes added by
Lyndon Johnson in the deep South or by several New England and Middle
Western states would make victory certain. Indispensable to Nixon's narrow
1968 victory was a "Southern strategy" that produced a sufficient number of
Southern electoral votes to bring success. Formulated in partnership with Senator Strom Thurmond of South Carolina, the strategy called for moderation on
civil rights and a running mate unobjectionable to the South, an ideal that
resulted in the selection of Governor Spiro Agnew of Maryland.[20] But as Vice
President, Agnew proved to represent other values more strongly.

A further phase of strategy is the welding of groups—national, racial, ideological, and economic—into a winning coalition. In both his 1968 and 1972
campaigns, Richard Nixon pursued a strategic vision of "a new American majority." In one of his most extended discourses on this subject, Nixon perceived a "new alignment" of political forces that "is already a new majority"
that would endure "for generations to come." Strange bedfellows comprised
the alignment—long-time Republicans committed to freedom and enterprise
and wary of "centralized and domineering" government; the "new South,"
emancipated from "racist appeal" and one-party voting habits and moving rapidly in industrial development; the "black militant" who preferred black pri-

vate enterprise to "handouts or welfare"; and the "new liberal" who valued participatory democracy with "more personal freedom and less government domination." [21] In 1972, Nixon further defined this "new American majority" to include at its core blue collar workers and Catholics, who, Nixon said, lived "in the rings around the cities, they're a new middle class." [22] He sounded themes alluring to workers and ethnics outside the central city, stressing the high note of patriotism and the work ethic. Nixon also pitched his appeal to many older Jews who had fled the cities for the suburbs and who were moving to the right of their usually liberal position on busing, scatter-site housing, and law and order.*

The candidate must also make several basic organizational choices. He can choose between relying heavily upon the regular party machinery or supplementing it with "independent" citizens' committees. In 1952 the independent Citizens for Eisenhower organization figured importantly in the Republican victory, particularly in drawing dissatisfied Democrats over to support the Eisenhower candidacy. For his 1972 campaign, Nixon too worked outside the party organization, utilizing the Committee for the Reelection of the President, headed by the President's campaign manager, John Mitchell, and his successor, former Minnesota Congressman Clark McGregor. Their top aides were drawn from the White House staff and such key Presidential assistants as H. R. Haldeman, John Ehrlichman, and Charles W. Colson. Generally, the committee was disdainful of the regular party organization; nearly all the members were amateurs in politics and young men on-the-make, and the President's campaign resembled the style of California politics where candidates offer themselves as public figures rather than as party men, with their roles defined by such non-party types as public relations experts and tactical strategists.[23] The reelection committee recruited some three dozen "surrogates"—chiefly senators and governors—as stand-ins for the President, who did little campaigning himself. A finance committee raised untold quantities of money that would have left Mark Hanna aghast, using high pressure means that often strayed into extortion. "The November Group," a cadre of accomplished public relations and advertising specialists, handled media operations and coordinated all national and local media advertising. Within the Committee were divisions for courted voting blocs: the young, ethnics, the Spanish-speaking, Jews, farmers, women, teachers, businessmen, and the elderly. All were targets of a computerized direct mail operation focusing on their particular interests and the Administration's related accomplishments.[24] Be it also noted that the reelection committee, closely meshed with the White House staff, perpetrated the break-in at the national Democratic headquarters and acts of political espionage and sabotage. For democracy's sake, it is essential to recognize that these transgressions could be committed more easily in a personal campaign organization of the President than if the campaign had been conducted by the regular party organization with its more salutary participation of many centers of power—the state

---

* For an evaluation of "the new American majority," see pp. 144–46.

and local organizations, Congressional and interest group leaders, constellations of autonomies that would have been less pliant to Presidential bidding and the manipulations of his law-breaking associates. Soon after becoming President, Gerald Ford made plain that he would not create a separate organization to conduct his electoral campaign in 1976.

Another strategic problem concerns the candidate's personal involvement in the campaign. How much of the campaign emphasis should be on issues and how much on personality? Eisenhower, national hero and international personage in 1952, was under less pressure to emphasize issues than the lesser known Kennedy in 1960, whose campaign stressed issues. In his 1972 reelection campaign, Nixon made a minimum of campaign appearances. "He doesn't have to campaign," said his chief of staff, H. R. Haldeman. "He doesn't have to establish his identity. He's been exposed for twenty-five years. Because of TV and his trip to China and the man on the moon, he's probably the best-known human being in the history of the world. For him to campaign would be counter-productive, superfluous." [25] To the extent that Nixon campaigned, he did so in discharging the duties and exploiting the resources of the Presidency. Chiefly, he dominated the news media by attention-getting foreign policy moves, set the tone of the campaign, and kept the initiative securely in his own hands.[26]

Should the candidate concentrate on mass appeal via radio, television, and big rallies? Or should he do the whistle-stop routine, as Harry Truman did in 1948, with folksy talks to hundreds of small audiences across the nation? For all of the magic of radio and television, candidates still heavily invest their time and treasure in going out to the voters. Although in 1960 the four television debates supplied the candidates with an audience of unsurpassed size, both Kennedy and Nixon traveled by rail and air to give brief talks in hundreds of communities and to shake thousands of hands. A powerful inducement for whistle-stopping is Truman's extraordinary success at it in 1948 in achieving a victory unpredicted by the public opinion polls or by any reputable politician save Truman himself.

Truman made his whistle-stop speeches from the back of a reconstructed Pullman car, the *Ferdinand Magellan,* purchased in 1942 for one dollar from the Association of American Railroads. According to the 1948 routine, the local high school band blared out "Hail to the Chief" upon Truman's arrival. Then came a gift for the President, his expression of thanks, his welcome to local Democratic leaders, and compliments to the citizenry for their new highway or factory. Hereupon Truman ripped into the Republicans and the Eightieth Congress with wild ridicule. His Republican listeners heard their party brethren referred to as "gluttons of privilege" and "bloodsuckers with offices in Wall Street." ("Ridicule is a wonderful weapon," Truman told his aides.) After his political talk, Truman asked the crowd, "Howja like to meet my family?" and he proceeded to introduce Mrs. Truman as "the boss" and his daughter Margaret as "my baby" and "the boss's boss." The family bit delighted the crowds.[27]

In 1960 Presidential campaigning took a new turn when the traditional political debate of Congressional and local elections was adapted to the Presidential canvass and the idiosyncracies of television. The resulting Kennedy-Nixon TV debates had enormous impact upon the electoral outcome. An audience of 120 million viewed one or more of the Kennedy-Nixon encounters. When the debates began, Nixon appeared the likely electoral winner, with Kennedy rather well behind; when they ended, the contestants' positions were reversed. The result will hardly prompt future candidates who are leading at the outset of a campaign to take on TV debates gladly. Nonetheless, debates helpfully provide the voters with a close-up of the candidates without their props of speechwriters and idea men. The candidates can be seen thinking and speaking under stress, a situation that casts a great shaft of light upon character. In 1960 the debates undeniably quickened voter interest in the campaign.

But the debate system is not without flaws. The Presidency has a limited need of forensic talent; the office is far more than a great debate. No President, fortunately, is expected to formulate in a matter of seconds answers to great questions of foreign policy. The 1960 debates, while they revealed the candidates' personalities in sharp topographical relief, added little to public understanding of issues. Indeed a built-in drawback of TV debates may be overattention to personality and superficial examination of the issues.

THE NEW TECHNOLOGY   The selection of the contemporary President is assisted by a cluster of gadgetry contributed by science and technology. The computer has become a mighty sword of the Presidential campaign, and in 1972 its employ attained new degrees of sophistication. Beginning in the New Hampshire primary, computers played a major part throughout Nixon's quest for reelection. In New Hampshire, the name of every registered Republican and every registered independent was fed into a computer by the Nixon organization. Everyone on the list was telephoned by a volunteer and was sent a letter typed and addressed by computer. The letter asked the voter if he supported Nixon, and, if he answered that he did, a second computer letter asked if he would work in the President's behalf. Those who acquiesced received a further letter specifying how they could help, and just before primary day all those who answered "yes" to the first letter but did not volunteer to work received another letter reminding them to vote.[28]

In the postconvention campaign, computers carved census tracts into patterns; selected counties whose waverings in the past proved critical to their state's electoral vote; and had the names of their citizens sorted into categories labeled "independents," "gettable Democrats," and "don't knows," the information for which was obtained by massive telephone inquiries. The names, thus sorted, were stored in computers. Near the end of the campaign, in the nine largest states, eight million exhortative mailgrams were prepared and coded according to many variables (for example, county, age, income, Spanish-speaking, black, ethnic origin), while nine million letters were addressed to registered Republicans. Eventually seventeen million mailings ensued, the mightiest direct mail effusion in American political history.

Is not the computer a boon to the ideal of an effective democratic Presidency? In facilitating the dissemination of campaign material, in discovering the voter—independent or undecided—who might benefit from that material, the computer serves the higher vision. Clearly the quality of the material itself that the computer assists is crucial—well and good if it is reasoned and informed, but a disservice and even a danger if it falsifies and divides. As yet, computer services are unregulated by campaign laws, whether used for the compiling of mailing lists or for the identification of voters.

During the 1950s and 1960s, outlays for television time rose at a galloping pace that finally slowed in 1972. Television expenditure for the Presidential election of that year increased relatively little from 1968. The 1972 total for all broadcast and cablecast advertising was $59.6 million, an increase of $700,000 over 1968. Several factors contributed to slowing the pace, a welcome development for democracy, whose interest is not served by spiraling costs that make candidates more dependent on self-seeking benefactors and that penalize candidates who cannot command such support. In 1972 a new law forced broadcasters, for the first time, to charge their lowest rates for political advertising. The lack of primary contests for the Republican Presidential nomination also reduced spending, and, even more important, campaign strategists were impressed with research revealing that TV advertisements ranked low (twenty-fourth) among factors influencing undecided voters. Television news ranked first; spot ads proved highly effective only in introducing voters to candidates. Consequently, TV commercials became less entertaining in 1972 and somewhat more imitative of news broadcasts, more issue and problem oriented.[29] But as the campaign wore on, the TV effort became more intense, and one of the most commonly displayed commercials symbolized McGovern's proposed cuts in defense spending by showing a hand sweeping away toy soldiers and miniature ships and planes, leaving only a small portion of the toys untouched. After explanatory commentary, the spot shifted to President Nixon aboard a Navy ship and visiting troops in Vietnam. To the strains of "Hail to the Chief" in the background, the announcer identified the President with "a strong America." [30]

At best, television is proving a mixed blessing in linking Presidential selection processes to acceptable democratic standards. On the positive side, television can enable candidates who are little known to gain rapid recognition, as Kennedy did in 1960, or to bring into the national political arena a serious latent issue, as Eugene McCarthy presented the Vietnam war in 1968. Since the Presidency is a highly personal office, television, in its better moments, can be incredibly efficient in providing a national close-up of the candidate and his manner, which may be a key to his character and his thinking processes. But television also bears consequences inhospitable to democracy. Its enormous costs favor the candidate with access to wealth over his more deprived opponent; it may overstress the candidate's appearance and style at the expense of personal substance and depth on issues. It injects new breeds of functionaries into Presidential politics—advertising and marketing specialists and opinion manipulators—whose comprehension of, and commitment to, democratic ways may be frail.

A major component of the modern Presidential campaign is the public opin-ion poll conducted in the candidate's behalf, often by specialists in market research. From polls, the candidate learns how to reach voters better through television, radio, and the press, what issues to stress, what portions of his projected image to refurbish. Polls reveal candidate effectiveness in regard to issues and geographic areas and illuminate the impact of major campaign themes. Early polls of a campaign can pinpoint weaknesses and imply appropri-ate remedial action. And polls can have a psychological dimension; if favor-able, they buoy the confidence of workers, potential contributors, and voters. If starkly unfavorable, they fall like a palsied hand on the candidate's effort.[31]

THE MONEY PROBLEM   The costs of Presidential campaigning are rising faster than costs for other elective offices, with an estimated outlay of $100 million in 1968, a figure higher than that for 1972 when the Republican nomi-nation was uncontested. In the Presidential elections of the 1960s and 1970s, the abilities of the two parties to foot the prodigious expenditures have con-trasted markedly. Invariably the Democrats emerge with a forbidding deficit, while the Republican habit, even in the overwhelming defeat of 1964, is to sus-tain a robust surplus. In 1972, the treasure available to reelect Richard Nixon was the most bountiful ever amassed in American politics, with a reported net balance for the Finance Committee to Reelect the President of $3.5 million. In contrast, the Democrats emerged with a forbidding deficit, and, even more serious, they entered the 1972 election year with a debt of $9.3 million.[32] Clearly, democracy is not served if the financial capabilities of the major par-ties are excessively disparate. In recent elections the contrast has been widen-ing, but, fortunately, it has not yet stretched to a peril point.

Where does the money come from to feed the voracious appetite of the cam-paign? The most responsive givers number among the best-heeled Americans, big business executives and investors, and their contributions in the Presidential elections of 1968 and 1972 flowed far more insistently to the Republicans than to the Democrats. In 1968, members of the Business Council, an elite group who own, finance, or manage the country's largest enterprises, contributed by better than three to one to the Republicans. In a study of the contributions in 1968, in amounts of $500 or more, by the officers and directors of the twenty-five largest industrial corporations, the Citizens' Research Foundation likewise discovered an overwhelming Republican sentiment. Not even heavy depen-dence on government contracts affected these business executives' preferences. A lopsided proportion of contractors with the Pentagon, NASA, and the Atomic Energy Commission gave to the Republicans—and this during an eight-year Democratic reign in the White House.

Since the 1950s, both parties have toiled to increase the number of small donors, a democracy-serving tactic, which, if successful, would reduce the dependence of candidates on the big givers. Until 1972, Republicans had well surpassed the Democrats in mobilizing small givers. In 1964, for example, even with the Democrats controlling the Presidency, large contributors ($500 or more) provided about 69 percent of the dollar value of individual contributions, compared with the Republican figure of 28 percent. But in 1972, the picture was reversed. Thanks to McGovern's strong local organizations and a potent direct-mail effort, small contributors outnumbered by about 5 to 1 those who gave more than $100 each. Reports of Nixon's cornucopian financing revealed three large contributors for every two small contributors.[33]

As the postconvention campaign moved into high gear, the President's campaign treasurers took in an unprecedented $100,000 a day. At the forefront of the donors were two open-handed benefactors of the 1968 campaign, the Pew family of Philadelphia, heirs to the Sun Oil Company fortune, and the W. Clement Stones, a wealthy Chicago insurance family, who reported a contribution of $500,000 to Nixon in 1968. Close behind came donors identified with leading major industries, such as the Tropicana citrus drink company; Montgomery Ward stores; Warner-Lambert Pharmaceuticals; McCormick & Co., the spice, tea, and flavoring house; the Chase Manhattan Bank; Dow Chemical; Nabisco; Westinghouse; Douglas Aircraft Corporation; the Borden Company; and the like, a roll call of major industry.[34] The fund raiser without parallel who compiled the prodigious sums that poured into Nixon quarters was Maurice H. Stans, former Secretary of Commerce and chairman of the Finance Committee to Reelect the President. Hundred dollar bills—the standard remittance—inundated him to the point that he sometimes had as much as $350,000 to $700,000 in cash sconced in his safe at one time. Suspected of extortion and other illegality, the hard-pressing Stans was eventually indicted.

Notwithstanding the rampant malfeasances of 1972, the early 1970s were a rare interval in American political history, when several reforms of campaign financing were instituted. The Federal Election Campaign Act of 1971, which became operative in April 1972, seeks to regulate the problem through publicity and disclosure. All political committees that anticipate receiving or spending more than $1,000 in any year for any federal candidate must register and submit periodic reports. The Act requires reporting of every expenditure and every contribution of $100 or more. Comprehensive disclosure is based on the assumption that in democracy voters have a right to know the sources of candidates' funds and that if questionable sources are publicly exposed, they will either cease or offend the voters to the candidate's detriment. The 1971 Act also limits the amount that federal candidates may spend on campaign advertising via radio, television, newspapers, magazines, and other means, to ten cents per voting age person in the area covered by the election. Past limitations on spending have eluded enforcement, but architects of the 1971 law assume that the expenditures it regulates are the most visible and difficult to disguise, and therefore are easiest to enforce. At most, the 1971 law applies a particular, although narrow, theory to reform—publicity as an inducement toward good practice, a theory that was quickly battered and shorn by the malfeasances of the 1972 campaign. The law does not touch two prime problems of electoral reform—imbalances in the distribution of resources between candidates, and the potency of big contributors. But a second reform responds to the latter problem, the Revenue Act of 1971, designed to increase the number of small contributors. The Act provides that campaign contributors may claim a tax credit against a portion of their federal income tax, or a tax deduction for the full amount of contributions, up to specified limits. The 1971 law also allows the taxpayer to designate $1 of his tax obligation to go to a fund to subsidize Presidential campaigns. Slated for initial application to the Presidential election of 1976, the provision has a tumultous history and an uncertain future.

POLITICAL SABOTAGE   The employment of falsehoods and smears, malicious tricks and calculated sabotage are, unfortunately, not uncommon in Presidential campaigns. But since the 1960s, these assaults upon democratic norms have sharply worsened; while Presidential candidates vie on the high road, some of their henchmen claw in the dirt. The lowest tactics in Presidential campaigning transpired in the 1972 elections and were illuminated in the Watergate investigations. According to the Fair Campaign Practices Committee, a private citizens' organization that has monitored campaigns for twenty years, the tactics employed in the Nixon reelection effort exceeded in malfeasance any other campaign and amounted to "a conscious conspiracy to violate laws, to manipulate voters, and to make a mockery of the democratic system of self-government." [35]

A sample listing of acts of sabotage launched under the auspices of the Committee to Reelect the President and the White House staff affirms this severe indictment. To foster the nomination of George McGovern, viewed as the weakest potential nominee to oppose the President, the saboteurs fomented tricks to hobble the efforts of other Democratic contenders: a fabricated slur on French-Canadians was attributed to the most feared potential opponent, Edmund Muskie, in the New Hampshire primary; in Florida, signs were stapled to trees and telephone polls, reading, "Help Muskie Support Busing Our Children." Through a planted volunteer worker in Muskie headquarters, information seeped out concerning the Senator's scheduling problems, dissension in his organization, and the texts of impending speeches. Stories were sprung on Jackson, Muskie, and McGovern of sexual misconduct; the national Democratic headquarters were broken into and bugged in a quest for material that would discredit the Democratic chairman, Lawrence O'Brien, and the Democratic party.

Is there cause for concern, in light of these and other nefarious acts? Yes, in the sense that they attest to a spreading activity, the concommitant of a new manipulative "image" politics, which Bruce Felknor, former Fair Campaign Practices Committee chairman, has described as the handiwork of "a new wave of amoral political technicians who are clever, indefatigable, poisonous and brilliant." [36] In purpose, this breed is unabashedly antidemocratic, intent upon destroying rival candidates and discrediting the opposition party. Fortunately, the impact of these often sophomoric misdeeds in 1972 was minor. It would be too much to claim that they were instrumental either in McGovern's triumph in the primaries or in his overwhelming defeat in the elections. A range of other factors was far more decisive. Meanwhile, democracy's chief bulwarks against the devastations of campaign sabotage are the alertness of opposing candidates and parties, publicized exposure of wrongdoing, arousal of voter sentiment against the candidate in whose behalf the malfeasances are perpetrated, and the application of criminal penalties against the wrongdoer. The best of all defenses is an informed and sophisticated electorate, fallow ground for the appeals to prejudice and ignorance that are the saboteur's stock-in-trade. Fortunately, dirty tricks are by no means standard, but they have been increasing since the 1960s when the Democrats' Dick Tuck sprang innovative pranks.

The Electoral College

The final stage of selecting the President—his actual election—was a very knotty, much debated issue at the Constitutional Convention. Eventually the electoral college method of choosing the President emerged as a compromise. In actuality, there are fifty electoral colleges, one in each state. The number of electors in a given state equals the number of its Senators and Representatives in Congress.

Each elector has one vote, and a majority of the whole number of electors appointed is required to choose the President. If no Presidential candidate receives a majority, the Constitution directs the House of Representatives to complete the election of the President. The House is limited in choice to the three candidates receiving the greatest number of the electors' votes.

The Constitution authorizes each state to appoint its electors "in such manner as the legislature thereof may direct." In the first three Presidential elections the electors were chosen chiefly by the state legislatures. Thereafter, popular choice gradually took hold. By 1824 electors were chosen by popular vote in all but six states, and in 1832 in all states but South Carolina, which clung to legislative election until 1864. Popular choice has been registered through two main systems—election of electors by districts and election of electors on a "general ticket." Each system spawned numerous variations. In the former method, the people would vote in districts relatively equal in population, each district choosing one elector. Districts often coincided with Congressional districts. The district system was widely employed in the early days of the Constitution; indeed, according to Madison, most of the Founding Fathers strongly preferred it. In practice, electors were pledged to particular candidates. Whichever candidate's elector then carried a district was the official elector of that district. Since, in a given state, the elector of one candidate might triumph in one district, and the elector of a different candidate might win in another district, the total electoral vote of a state might be divided among several candidates. The division tended to follow the pattern of the Congressional elections in the House districts.

In time a political party, having gained control of a state, would sniff an opportunity to avoid the division of its electoral strength by introducing the general ticket system, which applies an ancient principle of gamesmanship— "winner take all." The party carrying the state, by however small a popular plurality, wins all the state's electors and the minority party or parties get none. Since 1836 all states have used the general ticket system, except for a brief relapse in Michigan to the district system following the 1892 election.

Although the states determine the method of choosing their electors, the timetable of a Presidential election is set by national law. On the first Tuesday after the first Monday in November, every fourth year, the qualified popular voters of the several states choose the Presidential electors. On the first Monday after the second Wednesday in December the electors meet in their respective states to cast their votes for President. On January 6 the electoral votes are counted in the presence of the two houses of Congress and the results are announced by the presiding officer—the Vice President.

The Founding Fathers' expectation that the electors would exercise an element of free judgment in choosing the President was quickly crushed by the appearance of political parties, the Federalists and the Anti-Federalists, the latter soon becoming the Republican-Democratic party. George Washington's two Presidential candidacies were untouched by electoral vote politics. Following his departure from the Presidential scene, the electors took to party-line voting in choosing John Adams as President in 1796 over his chief rival, Thomas Jefferson. Thereafter, with rare individual exceptions, the electors have functioned as the automatons of their parties. Only rarely has an elector violated his pledge to vote for a particular Presidential candidate. In 1820 William Plumer voted for John Quincy Adams instead of Monroe. In 1956 a Democratic elector in Alabama, though pledged to vote for whomever the Democratic national convention nominated, voted for a leading segregationist judge. In 1960 Senator Harry F. Byrd of Virginia, who was not a candidate on any ticket, received six of Alabama's eleven Democratic electoral votes, all eight of Mississippi's votes, one vote in Oklahoma, or a total of fifteen electoral votes. But none of these lapses affected the outcomes.

Custom, which dictates the electors' voting conduct, has been reinforced by legislation and court opinion. State statutes range from those calling for a party nomination of electors, which itself is a presumption of pledged electors, to the laws of two states prescribing that electors vote for the party nominees, regardless of personal preference. In *Ray* v. *Blair* (343 U.S. 214, 1952) the Supreme Court gave its blessing to these arrangements, upholding a state law empowering party organizations to fix the qualifications of candidates for nomination as electors. The state law, the Court said, simply converted custom into legal obligation. Anticipating the 1964 elections, Mississippi and Georgia in 1961 passed laws permitting the election of unpledged electors. In Alabama, electors, although identified with a major party, are not required to vote for its Presidential nominee. In 1963 Governor Wallace of Alabama disclosed that his 1964 efforts would be devoted to spreading the unpledged elector movement in lieu of launching a third party. Unpledged elector slates were entered in Alabama and Mississippi in the 1964 election, but they were foiled when the popular vote in both states chose electors committed to the Republican candidate, Senator Barry Goldwater.

The selection of electors has also been altered by revisions of the Presidential

ballot that confronts the popular voter in the polling booth. One is the requirement, first adopted in Nebraska in 1917, that electors be listed and voted for as
a party group rather than individually. Another change brought the names of
the Presidential nominees on the ballot with those of the electors. The latest
evolutionary step is the Presidential short ballot, on which only the names of
the Presidential and Vice-Presidential nominees appear, an innovation speeded
by the use of voting machines, which impose severer limitations of space than
the paper ballot does. Each popular vote cast by the Presidential short ballot
counts for the elector whose name, although unknown to the voters, is on file
with the state secretary of state.

Originally, under the Constitution, each elector cast two votes for President,
one of which had to be for a candidate who was not an inhabitant of the elector's state. This provision, coupled with the necessity of an electoral vote majority for victory, barred even the largest state from choosing by itself a President from among its own inhabitants. The double-vote feature virtually
compelled the selection of a candidate of national reputation. The candidate
receiving the second highest number of electoral votes became Vice President,
a method that brought into the number-two post men of Presidential caliber like
John Adams and Thomas Jefferson. The double-voting system, for all of its
seeming merit, was abandoned in 1804 with the adoption of the Twelfth
Amendment. The double vote had crashed on the rocks in the election of 1800,
when a deadlock developed between the Republican candidates, Jefferson and
Aaron Burr. The election passed into the House of Representatives, where the
rival Federalist party, which controlled the outcome, favored Burr but was
pressured by Alexander Hamilton, its national chieftain, into backing Jefferson.
Snatched from a disaster they wished never to encounter again, the Republicans
championed the Twelfth Amendment, establishing separate electoral votes for
the President and the Vice President.[37]

Defects of the Electoral College

The existing electoral vote arrangements have long been the object of heavy
criticism and dire warnings. The critics hold that the electoral system violates
basic tenets of democracy and that its many mechanical flaws invite breakdown
and the eruption of a Presidential election into a nightmare of civil strife.[38]

The electoral college system has been employed in forty-seven elections and
has failed three times to elect a President: in 1800, 1824, and 1876. Three elections are also often indicted for flaunting the voice of the people, for electing
Presidents who received fewer popular votes than their opponents. The suspected elections are John Quincy Adams' triumph over Jackson in 1824, Rutherford B. Hayes's over Samuel J. Tilden in 1876, and Benjamin Harrison's
over Cleveland in 1888. Jackson's showing in 1824 is clouded by the fact that
no popular votes were cast in six of the twenty-four states. In 1876 Tilden

received some two hundred thousand more popular votes than Hayes. Since fraud and violence marked the popular voting in the South, North, and West, Tilden's popular margin is not unblemished. Harrison's victory by a popular minority over Cleveland cannot be gainsaid.

Of all the features of electoral college practice the general ticket system has raised the severest criticism. The general ticket, as Lucius Wilmerding demonstrates, puts the Presidency on a federative rather than a national basis. It has taken "the choice of the President from the people of the nation at large and given it, in effect, to the people of the large states." [39] The principle of winner take all serves to disenfranchise a substantial minority of popular votes or even more outrageously transfers them to the use of the candidate against whom they were cast. Charles Evans Hughes in 1916, for instance, carried Minnesota by a popular plurality of only 359 but received all twelve of that state's electoral votes. A large part of those electoral votes were made possible by thousands of Minnesotans who voted against Hughes. On a national scale, John W. Davis received six million popular votes in 1924 that earned him no electoral votes at all—or in reality were transferred to the use of his rival, Calvin Coolidge—while two million others brought him 136 electoral votes.

The general ticket system's rough handling of minority popular votes extravagantly favors the large states. The pluralities of the twelve largest states control 281 electoral votes. If these states should vote for a single candidate, he would be elected regardless of the strength of his opposition in those states and in the remaining thirty-eight states. The general ticket system, this is to say, enables the popular voter in the large states to participate in the choice of a larger number of electors than the voter of a small state. In 1964 a popular voter in New York shared in the choice of forty-three electors, and in Nevada only three. The candidate of the popular majority of the nation is far from certain to prevail in an electoral college where the representation of each state is not that of its people but of its plurality. The likelihood of minority Presidents will surely increase in our present era of close Presidential elections.

The general ticket system, with its winner-take-all principle that rewards the victor more lavishly than any other system, wreaks other distortions. It prods parties into seeking out their candidates in big states such as New York and Ohio, while ignoring the small states, whose sons may be equally talented. The general ticket system also encouraged the historic one-party solid South. The Republican party, faced with a hopeless minority position, for years maintained no serious organization in Southern states. The general ticket system also causes party campaigning to be concentrated in doubtful states and in large states. New York, Ohio, and Illinois are regularly showered with relatively more campaign dollars and rhetorical fervor than states such as Maine, Nevada, or Georgia, which are safe or small. In 1960 Kennedy was hailed for his political wisdom in concentrating on the large industrial states, and McGovern pursued a similar strategy in 1972.

The general ticket system is also attacked for grossly inflating the bargaining power of pressure groups and minority parties in large doubtful states. A well-organized national, racial, religious, or economic group whose votes are concentrated upon a Presidential candidate can more powerfully exact his commitment if the group is situated in a large state.

Defenders of the existing electoral system argue that its distortions serve the cause of social justice, that the system enables smaller masses of people to strike bargains that unshackle their oppressions. A more perfect system, presumably, would afford fewer liberating opportunities. Yet a standard that judges the quality of the electoral system in terms of whether the bargains struck are good or bad is of dubious merit. Wilmerding argues in *The Electoral College,*

> If the President is to be the man of the people, if all the people are to stand on the same footing, equal masses of people must be given equal votes, equal bargaining power. Their weight in the electoral count must be proportional to their numbers and not to the rightness or wrongness of their causes.[40]

The pretensions of distinguishing good groups from bad and of assigning greater electoral weight to the former than to the latter cannot be justified in democratic theory, nor can it long be asserted satisfactorily in practice.

Alternatives to the Electoral College

Hardly a session of Congress passes when legislators, distressed by the flaws of the electoral college system, do not introduce proposals, embodied in drafts of constitutional amendments, to reform it. Although differing in detail, the proposals that perennially appear can be grouped into several broad categories:

A NATIONAL POPULAR VOTE According to this proposal, the President would be chosen by the majority of the national popular vote. Electors and electoral votes would be tossed upon the political scrap heap.

The plan of national popular election offers powerful attractions. It is the only plan extant that assures against the election of a President receiving fewer popular votes than his opponent. Every voter, be he a New Yorker or a Nevadan, would have one vote of equal weight. Majoritarian democracy would be cleanly applied, in which 51 per cent and above would rule. The several evils of the general ticket system would be banished at one fell swoop. The principle of Presidential selection would be national rather than federative; minority votes of states would at least be counted; large states would be barred from consolidating their votes to the disadvantage of the small. The power of pressure groups and minor parties would be more nearly proportionate to their numbers. Political activity in safe states would rise and be meaningful.

The national popular vote carries several formidable defects. It would jeopardize our two-party system by encouraging minor parties, giving them a weight in the national popular vote that they lack in the electoral college system. It violates the federal principle by redistributing political power among the states:

The proposal would shift power from the smaller states to the larger states; from states that are politically passive to states that are politically active.

Individual plans for popular elections introduced in Congress over the years have offered different provisions for the eventuality wherein no candidate wins a majority. Some would permit a plurality to elect; others would hold a run-off election limited to the two or three candidates polling the highest initial vote. Still others would throw the election into the House of Representatives, with each member having one vote.

PROPORTIONAL VOTING   Under this plan, which has many variations, each candidate who polled a fraction of a state's popular votes would win the same fraction of its electoral votes. The candidate's national electoral vote would be the sum of his electoral votes in all fifty states. The President would continue to be chosen by electoral, not popular, votes. If no candidate received 40 per cent of the entire electoral vote, the contest would be decided between the two highest candidates by the House and Senate jointly, with each member having one vote. The state legislatures would lose their present freedom to decide the methods of choosing electors and of voting.

The minority popular vote in each state would be accurately reflected in the electoral vote. The plan would abolish the evil of the one-party state and diminish the disproportionate influence of local pressure groups and the dread possibility that a candidate with a minority of the popular vote will win a majority of the electoral vote. The plan harmonizes with the federal structure by preserving the interests of the small states.

But proportional voting has heavy disadvantages. It would encourage the development of minor parties and would in time weaken or destroy the two-party system. The Presidential constituency would cease to be primarily geographical and would become, instead, primarily mathematical or ideological. Groups rather than areas would be the focus of appeal. The geographical constituency encourages the candidate to be moderate in view and balanced in appeal to its diverse groups. To win an ideological constituency, the candidate must tend to extremes and subordinate himself to its special purposes. Proportional voting would increase rather than reduce the danger of electing minority Presidents. If, for example, proportional voting rather than the present electoral system had operated in the elections of 1880 and 1896, their outcomes would have been reversed. In 1880 James A. Garfield received more popular votes than Winfield Scott Hancock, and in 1896 McKinley more than Bryan. Proportional voting, however, would have converted Hancock and Bryan from losers into victors because of the way their popular votes were distributed among the states.

THE SINGLE-MEMBER DISTRICT SYSTEM   Each state would be divided by the state legislature into districts equal to the number of Representatives the state is entitled to in Congress. Ideally, the districts would comprise contiguous and compact territory and, as nearly as possible, equal numbers of inhabitants. (Ideally, also, the electoral college districts would correspond with the districts of the House of Representatives.) Each district's voters would choose one elector. In addition, two electors would be chosen from the state at large. The candidate winning a majority of the electoral votes (some proposals require only 40 percent) would be deemed elected. If no candidate qualified, the House and Senate would jointly choose the President.

Like other proposals, the district system would take the method of electing the President out of the hands of the state legislatures and more nearly make the President the man of the people. It would end the power of large states, or their dominant party, to override the dominant party in the country at large. It would hamper minor parties and pressure groups in doubtful states from defeating, for their own ends, the will of the nation. Finally, it would force the parties to lift their eyes beyond the big states and into the country at large in their quest for candidates.

The district system has several forbidding weaknesses. It is vulnerable to the gerrymander. Its champions face the gerrymander evil by incorporating into their proposed constitutional amendment precise standards concerning population and territory by which districts would be made up. These the courts presumably would enforce. The districts still would not be equal in each state; large states would have districts with more populous constituencies than small states. Worst of all, the district plan would probably convert the present system, by which the American people engage in a national act focused upon national problems, into a series of petty campaigns in local districts. The district system, would encourage minor parties by giving them a stronger opportunity to choose an elector in a district than the traditional system permits in a state. In a close election, a minor party might hold the balance in the national tally of electors.

KEEPING THE ELECTORAL VOTE BUT DROPPING THE ELECTORS   In 1801 Jefferson wrote to Albert Gallatin of an "amendment which I know will be proposed, to wit, to have no electors, but let the people vote directly, and the ticket which has a plurality of the votes of any state to be considered as receiving the whole vote of the state." Presidents Johnson and Nixon both urged the step. The accompanying argument is undeniable. If the elector is faithful to the popular vote, he is useless; if he is not, he is dangerous.

ALTERING THE PROCEDURES OF THE HOUSE OF REPRESENTATIVES   The Twelfth Amendment specifies that if no candidate receives a majority of the electoral votes, the House of Representatives, voting by states, shall immediately choose the President by ballot "from the persons having the highest numbers not exceeding three on the list of those voted for as President." A majority of all the states is necessary for election. The present system of a single vote for each state is unjust in making one Representative from Nevada equal to forty-one Representatives from New York.

Most proposals would have the Representatives vote by heads rather than by states, patently a fairer procedure. Still others would have the Senate and House sit jointly and vote by heads. Including the Senate would be a sop to the small states, who would lose strength if the House shifted from voting by the states as units to voting by heads. This method also preserves the advantage of the populous states in the electoral college and carries it into a possible multicandidate Presidential election in which no one candidate received a majority. The advantage, of course, would not have the solid impact of the general ticket system. Most state delegations in Congress would divide on party lines, although New York with forty-three members would still wield more power than Mississippi with seven. A deadlock could be precluded by limiting the Congressional voting to the two leading candidates.

The Future Presidency

In the interest of strengthening and democratizing the Presidency, several innovations might advantageously be made in its selection procedures.

1. We ought, at the very least, to abolish the electoral college, which is a standing invitation to trouble. Even if we abolished the college, we could retain the electoral vote, which should automatically reflect the plurality of the popular vote.

2. We ought to review periodically the question of whether we might advantageously abandon both the electoral college and the electoral vote and substitute a plan for selecting the President on the basis of a national popular vote. A national popular vote is most in accord with democratic principle, and it would apply a standard of absolute fairness of "one American, one vote," which is badly violated by the present system. It would avoid the dread possibility, under the present electoral vote system, that the candidate winning a national popular majority will not prevail because he does not command a majority of the electoral votes. A serious drawback of the national popular vote plan is the possible necessity of a run-off election. But this is better in the bargain than the present danger that the popular vote winner will lose in the electoral college. There is, however, a formidable difficulty that to this writer makes prohibitive the adoption of the national vote system now. The system would encourage minor parties by affording them a recognition in the national popular vote that they do not have in the present electoral vote. The fact that their votes would count under the national popular vote plan would induce them to extend themselves nationally. Such a development would further weaken our already much too weak major parties.

3. When the House of Representatives is called upon to choose a President, it should vote by heads rather than by states. A vote by heads clearly would better approximate the popular vote than the existing system. Best of all would be a combined Senate-House vote by heads, since Senators are chosen by the states at large and therefore reflect state-wide opinion.

4. The assassination of President Kennedy should teach us for all time that the only valid criterion for choosing a Vice-Presidential candidate is his suit-

ability for the Presidency. The folly of the traditional formula of "balancing the ticket"—the North-South tandem of the Democrats and East-West one of the Republicans—is exposed by the stark statistic that four out of eleven Presidents in the twentieth century were brought into the highest office from the Vice-Presidency by the death of the President.

5. Let government subsidize the entire electoral system, and let us be done, therefore, with private financing, which enables insurance executives and milk lobbies, among others, to contribute fat sums to Presidential campaigns and reap manifold profits, thanks to the accommodation of subsequent public policies. This scenario of influence and plunder makes a mockery of democracy and feeds citizen moods of cynicism and withdrawal. Reform legislation adopted in 1974 providing for public financing of Presidential elections, primaries, and conventions is a major improvement. In primaries, to qualify for public funds, the candidate must raise $100,000, with $5,000 each from 20 states in contributions of $250 or less. Similar contributions will be matched up to $5 million, with the total expenditure limited to $10 million. The eventual major party nominees can obtain $20 million of public funds for the general election, or can use private contributions only, up to $20 million. Individual contributors are confined to $25,000 in a single year, and to no more than $3,000 to a particular candidate. The 1974 law can be manipulated to discriminate against candidates and minor parties. Clearly the law depends on vigorous enforcement, a fatal flaw of earlier campaign legislation.[41]

6. Although television debates between the Presidential candidates are not without flaw, in an era of public relations slickness that is spreading rapidly in the political arena, they are a strong antidote, and they afford the nation a better view of the real candidate than it would get in any other way. But with television taking such a great chunk of campaign costs, is it not time to ask this medium to donate a goodly quantity of hours to the task of choosing a President? Conceivably, providing free time for candidates could be a condition for holding a broadcasting license. The proposal becomes all the more important when an incumbent President is a candidate. Thanks to his office, he enjoys opportunities for publicity, financial advantages, and broadcasting facilities readily available at minimal cost, but not to his opponents. As a step toward equalizing the struggle, for the sake of democracy, facilities should become more accessible to his challengers at lower cost.

7. Finally, acts of political sabotage have clearly become overstretched, beyond all reasonable tolerance in a democratic system. Dependence on exposure by rival parties and citizens' committees and the presumed constraining effect of embarrassment to candidacies in whose behalf sabotage has been done, have plainly been inadequate to check the spreading malfeasance. Senator Walter F. Mondale (D-Minn.) has wisely proposed the establishment of an office of federal elections to act as a "permanent independent prosecutor" for all election-related federal crimes and to cooperate with the states when their laws are applicable.[42]

4

TENURE

Tenure is power. Whether the Presidency is a center of energy and direction or of weakness and futility depends in no small way upon the length and security of the Chief Executive's term of office, his eligibility for reelection, and the adequacy of arrangements available to bolster the office if his health—physical or mental—should falter. Tenure, therefore, depends partly upon the structuring of the office and partly upon the President's ability to escape the afflictions of biological frailty. If he does succumb to serious illness, the office, to function adequately, requires provision beforehand for a substitute President to take over with adequate preparation and authority.

But fixity of tenure can collide with the democratic imperatives of Presidential power. With a term of defined duration that can be broken only with extreme difficulty, the President can embark on acts offensive to democratic norms and destroy public confidence but persist in office. Such was the case when Richard Nixon remained in office after Watergate and a host of other offenses that in a parliamentary system, where tenure is more readily interrupted, would have promptly resulted in his overthrow. In contrast to Nixon's tenacity through every storm and stress, West German Chancellor Willy Brandt felt behooved to resign when an East German spy was discovered among his personal staff—a minor lapse by the Nixon Presidency's standards. Tenure poses formidable dilemmas for the strong Presidency and its necessary balance with democratic needs.

The Founding Fathers, aware of the importance of tenure to the strong, but responsible, Executive, debated the President's term and his reeligibility long and anxiously. The Fathers' anxiety about the President's term of office was reflected in their consideration at successive junctures of a term first of seven, then of six, and finally of four years. If Congress chose the President, as many favored, a long term without eligibility for reelection seemed best because a President otherwise might become a Congressional yes-man in courting reelection. But once the electoral college system had been adopted, a shorter term with unlimited eligibility was agreed upon.

The Founding Fathers expected that George Washington would become the first President and would willingly serve the rest of his days. Their acceptance of the principle of indefinite eligibility ran counter to another American political principle deeply ingrained since Revolutionary times—that rotation in executive office is essential to liberty. The principle of unlimited eligibility for reelection was irreparably undermined by the man in whose behalf it had been established, George Washington himself. Washington announced upon completing his second Presidential term that it was his personal wish not to serve another. By the Civil War, Presidential observance had established the two-term principle in the core of American political doctrine.

Despite its formal observance, with only a single exception throughout Presidential history, the two-term practice has occasionally been under siege. Although Franklin D. Roosevelt alone exceeded the two-term limitation, he was far from the first to try. In the decades between Lincoln and Franklin D. Roosevelt there was seldom a period when the third-term fever did not seize the Chief Executive. So menacing in fact did the third term boom of Ulysses S. Grant become in 1875 that the House of Representatives felt duty-driven to resolve, by a vote of 234 to 18, that departure from the two-term tradition would be "unwise, unpatriotic and fraught with peril to our free institutions." [1]

Theodore Roosevelt, like Grant before him and Calvin Coolidge later, took the pragmatic view that the two-term limitation applied only to a third consecutive term. He had sworn fealty to the two-term custom in the exuberance of his electoral victory of 1904, a pledge his foes gleefully recalled when he entered the Presidential race of 1912. But Roosevelt was a supreme rationalizer and saw no contradiction between his words in 1904 and his actions in 1912. If he were to decline "a third cup of coffee," he explained, no one would suppose he meant never to take another cup. By his 1904 pledge, he said, "I meant, of course, a third consecutive term." [2]

Franklin D. Roosevelt's distinction in achieving reelection to a third and a fourth term was prevented from becoming more than a personal triumph by the Twenty-second Amendment. The amendment inscribes in the nation's fundamental law the prohibition, "No person shall be elected to the office of the President more than twice." For anyone like Ulysses S. Grant, who after two terms and an interlude of retirement strains to possess the office a third time, the amendment would provide a clear and unequivocal negative. For Presidents such as Theodore Roosevelt, Calvin Coolidge, and Lyndon Johnson, whose incumbencies stretched across a partial and a full term, the amendment continues in a fashion too clear to be misinterpreted: ". . . and no person who has held the office of President, or acted as President, for more than two years of a term to which some other person was elected President shall be elected to the office of the President more than once." Admirers of former President Eisenhower, the first casualty of the amendment, concluded after reading its text that he could well be restored as Chief Executive by electing him Vice President and then having the President elected with him step down in his favor. The Twenty-second Amendment is a mixture of political motivations, both partisan and personal. It was a posthumous revenge against Franklin Roosevelt for breaking the two-term tradition. It was also a desperate attempt to push back the rushing flood of Executive authority. And to the career politician it was an assurance that the foremost prize of American politics would be available at regular intervals.

The amendment also instills certain weaknesses into the office of the Presidency, however. It can gravely weaken the President's influence during the entire span of his second, and final, term. In 1957, the first year of Eisenhower's second term, the President was hampered by a noticeable weakening of his grip on Republican legislators and a softening of his hitherto staunch support from the press and business. Yet Eisenhower had been returned to power only a year earlier with a fresh and overwhelming mandate. Even worse is the amendment's potential mischief in a foreign affairs crisis. The nation could conceivably be deep in war, or on the brink of it, when the tenure of its Chief Executive was suddenly cut off. The amendment would require the nation to violate that wise old adage warning against changing horses in mid-stream. The electorate would be wrenched into choosing new leadership at a time when national unity was imperative; it would be deprived of a Chief Executive whose experience and knowledge of the ongoing crisis could not be duplicated. The crisis of war kept Franklin Roosevelt in office because the electorate concluded that the continuity of leadership and policy could not be safely shattered midway without peril. Had the Twenty-second Amendment then been in force, Roosevelt would automatically have been disbarred and new leadership imposed contrary to the electorate's judgment. The Twenty-second Amendment, whatever may be said in its favor, is antidemocratic in spirit, a frustration of the will of the people out of fear that the people might choose unwisely.[3]

Resignation

The Presidential tenure can be interrupted not only by restriction on reelection but by other means—resignation, for example, a means for which the Constitution provides. Only Richard Nixon has ever resigned, but Woodrow Wilson came close to committing that final act of voluntary separation. An admiring student of British governmental practice, which turns upon the Prime Minister's periodic resignation to seek a vote of public confidence for his party, Wilson twice as President contemplated resigning. If his rival in the 1916 Presidential race, Charles Evans Hughes, had won, he proposed to resign to avoid a lame-duck Presidency in the midst of world crisis. His plan was first to ask his Secretary of State, Robert Lansing, to resign so he could appoint President-elect Hughes as his successor. Thereupon President Wilson and Vice President Marshall would both resign, permitting Hughes's ascent to the Presidency under the existing succession law.[4] Wilson's electoral victory rendered the novel plan unnecessary. In a later crisis, the fight for the Versailles peace treaty in 1919, Wilson briefly weighed the tactic of resigning and then immediately running again in a special Presidential election permitted by the Succession Act of 1886 then in force. His election presumably would have expressed a national desire for membership in the League and sustained confidence in him. Wilson dropped this plan. The approaching elections of 1920 seemed to him to promise to be "a great and solemn" referendum on the treaty.[5]

In 1974, less than two years after his overwhelming reelection, Richard Nixon became the first President to resign from the office, a decision reached in the face of his probable impeachment by the House and Senate. Resignation was a way of avoiding the disgrace implicit in a successful impeachment, and it preserved the pension rights and other perquisites of a former President that would have been lost in a completed impeachment. Further, resignation avoided an authoritative finding concerning Nixon's conduct by the constitutionally designated tribunal, the Senate. Resignation enabled Nixon to define his situation and judge his Presidential incumbency himself, which he did in terms calculated to imply minimum culpability: He was resigning, he said, because "I no longer have a strong enough political base in Congress," and he acknowledged only that "if some of my judgments were wrong—and some were wrong—they were made in what I believed at the time to be in the best interests of the nation."

For Nixon, resignation was a painful and reluctant decision. "I have never been a quitter," he said, "and to leave is abhorrent, . . ." but he took the step after Barry Goldwater (R-Arizona) disclosed that no more than fifteen votes against impeachment existed in the Senate, well short of the thirty-four necessary to escape conviction, and on the strong recommendations of his staff—including his chief of staff, General Alexander M. Haig, Jr.—and of Secretary of State Henry Kissinger that he step down in the national interest.[6]

Impeachment

According to Article II of the Constitution, the President can be "fired" via an impeachment process, for "treason, bribery, or other high crimes and misdemeanors." [7] Imitating existing state constitutions, the Founding Fathers empowered the House of Representatives to impeach the President, and the Senate, sitting as a law court with the Chief Justice of the United States presiding, to conduct the trial. A two-thirds vote of the Senators present is necessary for conviction. The penalties that the Constitution brings down upon the convicted President are removal from office, disqualification for "any office of honor, trust, or profit under the United States," and liability to "indictment, trial, judgment, and punishment, according to law." Although the introduction of impeachment resolutions is a favorite indulgence of members of Congress embittered by particular Presidents, Andrew Johnson enjoys distinction as the only President who has walked the impeachment gangplank to the point of a Senate vote. Far more importantly, he, and the Presidency with him, came out of it alive. By a single vote Johnson missed conviction and the Presidency was spared. The Johnson case demonstrates the capacity of legislators to convert a solemn judicial function into what Gideon Welles, Johnson's Secretary of the Navy, termed "a deed of extreme partisanship." [8] The impeachment was built upon the creaky foundation of the Tenure of Office Act of 1867, which denied the President the right to remove civil officials, including members of his cabinet, without Senatorial consent. Presidents had been removing cabinet Secretaries since the days of Washington. By the act of 1867 Congress was contravening precedent, stripping Johnson of control of his administration, and unconstitutionally violating his power to remove a member of the cabinet. Convinced that the Tenure Act was unconstitutional, Johnson requested and then ordered Secretary of War Edwin M. Stanton to resign and appointed General Lorenzo Thomas his successor. When Thomas appeared at the War Department, Stanton barricaded himself behind his office door.

Johnson himself was not without fault. Though principled and reverential toward the Constitution, he was barren of political skill. Incapable of seeing any merit in the opposition's position, he was disinclined to solve his problems by bargaining and compromise. Even when his most respected counsellors urged that he refrain from removing Stanton, for the sake of retaining a modicum of his party's support, Johnson was adamant. Nor was he deterred by events, by reports of whites committing atrocities against blacks in the South, reports that moved even moderate Republicans to concede the necessity of some military rule. Worst of all, Johnson himself was floundering in a state of acute political weakness: rejected at the polls, condemned by most of the Northern press, and loathed as an apostate by the Republicans, who controlled both Congressional houses. [9]

On February 28, 1868, the House voted to impeach the President for "high crimes and misdemeanors." Eleven articles of impeachment were drawn, ten centering upon Stanton's removal. The remaining article, contrived from garbled newspaper accounts of the President's speeches, charged, among other things, that he used unseemly language and spoke in a loud voice. Johnson meanwhile expected to knock the props from under the impeachment proceedings by obtaining a ruling from the Supreme Court endorsing his views on the Tenure of Office law. But the Court, in a mood of "judicial restraint," declined to act.

The ensuing impeachment enterprise reeked with self-serving politics. If Johnson were convicted and deposed, the new President of the United States, owing to the Vice-Presidential vacancy and the line of succession in the applicable law of 1792, would be Ben Wade of Ohio, the vituperative President pro tempore of the Senate. When Wade's participation in the trial was objected to because of his not inconsiderable personal stake, the Senator replied with simple finality that he saw nothing wrong with serving as a judge. He would do impartial justice, he said, and was sworn. Chief Justice Salmon P. Chase, who presided, also wanted to be President, having for the office a craving that Lincoln once likened to insanity. By day Chase conducted the trial; by night he wrote letters building his claim to the next Democratic Presidential nomination. That the trial would ooze with low politics was instantly apparent when after the President's counsel requested forty days to prepare their case, with its numerous intricacies of law and fact, they were permitted ten. The Chief Justice, empowered within narrowly defined limits to rule on points of law, heroically put political ambition aside and rose to the full height of his responsibilities. According to the Senate rules specially adopted for the trial, if one Senator objected to the Chief Justice's holding, the matter was voted by the entire body. The Chief Justice was overruled seventeen times, in most instances for the purpose of suppressing evidence favorable to the President.

President Johnson, for all of his reputation for wild epithet and the big blunder, was a model of decorum. His chief act of self-assertion lay in putting his case before the people in interviews with several friendly reporters. Said the President,

Suppose Congress should pass a bill abolishing the veto power. . . . Suppose it should pass a dozen bills of this character—would the President be constitutionally bound to execute them as laws? Would it not be his duty, as in the present instance, to seek immediately judgment in the Supreme Court? [10]

The Radicals were desperate. The vote on Article XI, the first impeachment article to be disposed of, fell short of the two-thirds majority necessary for conviction. To revive their wilting plot, the Radicals maneuvered the Senate into an adjournment of ten days for the known but carefully unacknowledged purpose of lining up votes for Johnson's conviction. The adjournment occurred only after the Chief Justice's ruling against it was overridden. But the massive machinery of pressures and intrigue, unloosed upon Senators who were still on the fence or who conceivably might be lured or bullied into abandoning Johnson, failed. Johnson and the Presidency were saved by a single vote. Senator Lyman Trumbull, who sided with the President, captured the significance of the lamentable episode in explaining his vote:

Once set, the example of impeaching a President for what, when the excitement of the hour shall have subsided, will be regarded as insufficient cause, and no future President will be safe who happens to differ with the majority of the House and two-thirds of the Senate on any measure deemed by them important, particularly if of a political character. [11]

IMPEACHING RICHARD NIXON   Richard Nixon is the only other President to be seriously threatened by impeachment. Like Johnson, Nixon faced a Congress dominated by the opposing party and many legislators long resented his treatment of them, but unlike Johnson, whose trial and its outcome centered on constitutional questions, the potential case against Nixon embraced his possible criminal conduct plus that of his subordinates who in steady numbers were prosecuted, convicted, and jailed. Also at issue were a range of noncriminal acts, which suggested that the President had failed to carry out his constitutional duty to "take care" that the laws are faithfully executed.

Under prevailing political realities, the possible impeachment of Nixon derived primarily from what he himself did rather than from his subordinates' malfeasances. Although, normally, a chief executive in the private sector is, and should be, held responsible for his subordinates' conduct, and would be promptly ejected into the outer darkness for failings comparable to those of the Nixon men, the practical politics of impeachment made clear that removal of the President must derive its force from his own specific acts. Not otherwise, it appeared, could a majority vote of the House be mustered, nor the more formidable two-thirds vote of the Senate. In its preparatory studies, the staff of the House Judiciary Committee focused on five major areas of Presidential conduct.[12]

1. The President, within days of the Watergate burglary, instructed his aides to order the CIA to block an FBI inquiry, instructions that resulted in a two-week delay of the investigation. Moreover, the President approved his aides' efforts to conceal facts about the burglary for six months; he knew of the Watergate break-in at least within six days after it occurred, was aware of the payment of "hush money" to Watergate defendants, and discussed executive clemency for them with his aides.

Repeatedly, the President sought to hobble investigations by the Special Prosecutor. This office was created when the Senate delayed approval of the President's nominee for Attorney General, Elliott Richardson, until the administration accepted the establishment of the post of Special Prosecutor, endowed with extraordinary independence to investigate Watergate and related scandals. In clear violation of the new post's authority and autonomy, Nixon refused to hand over tapes to the initial Prosecutor, Archibald Cox, and, after the Court of Appeals ruled against the President, he fired Cox, who declined to accept what the President termed a "compromise." A federal district court found the firing illegal. Nixon likewise withheld tapes of White House conversations and evidence on a wide range of matters from Cox's successor, Leon Jaworski, and made similar withholdings from the impeachment inquiry of the House Judiciary Committee. Frequently, when requested to turn over tapes to the special prosecutor, the President supplied only "transcripts," which were of questionable accuracy. When Nixon did hand over the tapes, some were found to have blank spots. One crucial tape bore an 18½ minute deletion that technical experts concluded had been accomplished by manual erasure. Since the tapes were in the President's custody, he was responsible for the destruction of evidence.

2. The President misused government agencies and accepted illegal campaign contributions. He ordered the compilation of a list of political opponents preparatory to their harassment by the Internal Revenue Service following the 1972 elections, though little evidence of actual I.R.S. activity materialized. Further, the President granted favors to milk producers in return for campaign contributions by imposing import quotas on dairy products and by having the Agriculture Department reverse a decision against raising milk price supports soon after milk producers met with him. (Nixon was not alone in accepting contributions from dairymen. Sixteen members of the House Judiciary Committee accepted donations from dairy cooperatives, including chairman Peter Rodino, whose Congressional district produces not milk but beer.) [13]

The President also ordered a favorable settlement of an antitrust suit against the International Telephone and Telegraph Company (ITT) in exchange for a campaign donation. This accusation was weakened by tapes rebutting charges that Nixon perceived any linkage between the two actions. However, the matter was not conclusively dispelled because the President withheld a score of other tapes on ITT affairs.

From a representative of Howard Hughes, the multi-millionaire, the President's close friend Bebe Robozo accepted $100,000 in hundred dollar bills, which he returned three years later. Investigatory concern centered on a possible connection between the donation and an Administration decision permitting the Hughes interests to buy a Las Vegas casino.[14]

3. The President established a secret police force for domestic surveillance, the "Plumbers," a special White House unit to plug leaks of information to the press. This unit burglarized the office of Daniel Ellsberg's psychiatrist. The President at first withheld from law enforcement authorities information about the burglary but then permitted its submission to the court where Ellsberg was on trial. The President attempted to bribe the judge in that trial when the White House staff, with his knowledge, inquired if the judge would be interested in an appointment as FBI director. In addition, the President approved, and later rescinded, a plan for widespread domestic surveillance that included burglary, wiretapping, and mail inspection.

Early in his administration, Nixon approved the wiretapping of more than a dozen aides and journalists, presumably to detect sources of leaks of government information. But Nixon contended that the taps were legal at the time, since the Supreme Court did not, until 1972, declare such wiretapping without court warrants unconstitutional.

4. President Nixon, while in office, paid only nominal federal income taxes based on an enormous deduction for the donation of his Vice Presidential papers to the National Archives and on unreported capital gains on the sale of property in California and New York. His lawyers conceded that the deed on the papers transaction was backdated to show that the gift transpired before the law was changed to bar deductions for such donations. Though the President subsequently paid nearly a half million dollars to overcome tax liabilities, the House Judiciary Committee investigated for possible fraud.

5. The President misused the powers of his office in foreign affairs in initiating, without Congressional authorization and without disclosing it publicly, a bombing campaign in Cambodia and ground operations in Laos, the latter in violation of specific Congressional prohibitions. Domestically, the President impounded $40 billion, most of it appropriations for social programs. Repeatedly, the courts ruled that the actions were unconstitutional.

Against this formidable bill of particulars, Nixon provided defenses and explanations in speeches, news conferences, and court actions. Likewise, he constructed an extended web of strategies to withstand impeachment and maintain his hold on the Presidency. In public addresses and comment he depicted himself as the defender of the Presidential office, pledging to "do nothing that will weaken this office.'' He invoked his ''constitutional responsibility'' to employ his official powers to thwart an impeachment inquiry concerning whether he had abused those very powers. To justify his refusal to supply evidence requested by the House Judiciary Committee, the President made the dubious claim that he was defending the ''separation of powers'' doctrine against impeachment. Impeachment, as the nation's ultimate inquest, has no such subordination. Neither the Presidency nor separation of powers was in danger, only Nixon's own survival. Nixon's counsel, James D. St.Clair, pursued the classic defense lawyer's course—get your client off by any means you can; stretch the law to its farthest imaginable limit; yield nothing to the opposition and seize every advantage by exposing flaws in the opposition's legal reasoning, by discrediting its witnesses, and by challenging its right to proceed.[15] Both the President and his counsel strove to limit sharply the charges that might be brought in impeachment proceedings by contending that the Chief Executive is impeachable only for criminal acts of ''a very serious nature,'' committed in one's ''governmental capacity.'' This contention blithely overlooked the Johnson precedent, in which charges were noncriminal, and the preponderance of other impeachment proceedings against judges and department heads based on allegations of noncriminal offenses.

To the embattled Nixon, time was a priceless jewel; though protesting that ''one year of Watergate is enough'' and demanding speedy resolution of the impeachment question, he played a game of delay. Thus he fought subpoenas in court, sparking litigation that required months to complete. Nixon pursued a strategy of confusion, exploiting the silences and ambiguities of the terse Constitutional language covering impeachment. Although the Constitution clearly established the Senate as the trial court for impeachment, with the House confined to bringing charges, the President nudged the latter body toward a trial posture by requesting that his counsel have the right to interrogate witnesses in hearings of the House Judiciary Committee. The Constitution provides no guidance on the matter of how the President's testimony, if any, is to be received. At another juncture, Nixon offered testimony to the House Judiciary Committee, though only on terms favorable to himself. He agreed to submit to written questions from the Committee and to interviews with the Committee chairman and ranking minority member, if unattended by counsel—''a very forthcoming offer,'' the President contended.[16]

Since impeachment is a political as well as a legal process, Nixon's experience, not surprisingly, unfolded beneath a full panoply of politics. Nixon's politics focused on the retention of support from one-third of the Senators, the minimum number necessary to his survival. The targeted Senators were conservative, largely Southern Democrats and western Republicans, and Nixon steadily linked his decisions of program and policy to their preferences. A land use bill that he once hailed as a high priority environmental measure was defeated on Capitol Hill with his acquiescence. The President's change of heart set in when conservative western Republicans remonstrated that the measure would hamper private enterprise. Likewise, the President delighted Senate conservatives when he terminated administration efforts to promote a bill providing federal aid to secondary education. Candidly, Secretary of Agriculture Earl Butz acknowledged that he found himself "playing pretty closely," in dispensing his department's favors, with those legislators who supported the President against impeachment.[17] In arranging his speaking schedule, Nixon concentrated his appearances in states with conservative Senators.

One of the more vulnerable spots of Nixon's antiimpeachment politics was the expected devastation the Watergate scandals would wreak on Republican candidates in the 1974 Congressional elections, and the dread conclusion his party might reach that its chances could improve if it rid itself of its Presidential albatross via the impeachment process. To stem this possibility, Nixon risked much in campaigning personally in a special Congressional election in Michigan. Although the Republican candidate, James M. Sparling, Jr., was defeated, his position in the polls improved subsequent to Nixon's appearances.[18] But with dreary regularity other special Congressional elections went against the Republicans. Between the President and his party relations were tense and gingerly, with the Administration contending that because Nixon's roles as President and party leader were "indistinguishable," the party and the President had to sink or swim together. In contrast, Republican leaders doggedly proclaimed that Watergate had nothing to do with their party, that the scandals were the progeny of a miscreant, disavowed entity, the Committee for the Reelection of the President, whose existence and depredations transpired wholly outside the party structure.

For Nixon, foreign policy was a mighty sword against the impeachment dragon. He labored to demonstrate that foreign policy needs and his accomplishments made his continuation in office imperative, a theme illuminated by his elaborate tour of the Middle East after Secretary of State Henry Kissinger's extraordinary success in stilling the Arab-Israeli war in 1974. Foreign leaders generously reinforced Nixon's theme. President Sadat of Egypt proclaimed Nixon's indispensability; King Faisal of Saudi Arabia feared that continued efforts for peace in the Middle East might falter if Nixon were impeached. Similar sentiments were not heard from another party of interest, Israel. Soviet leaders were openly concerned about Nixon's future, with the offical press agency, Tass, lamenting that his Watergate troubles were "being fanned by the President's political adversaries." [19] Soviet leaders readily cooperated in arranging the 1974 Moscow summit conference that bolstered Nixon's image of indispensability. Conspicuously less demonstrative were the Western European and Japanese allies, who had suffered repeated slights in Nixon's foreign policy.

But the President's antiimpeachment politics eventually proved inadequate to halt the process's sure momentum. The House Judiciary Committee adopted three articles of impeachment, delineating many specific charges. Article I contended that Nixon engaged in a plan to obstruct investigations of the Watergate burglary and to cover up the facts of that undertaking. A second article accused Nixon of violating his oath to execute the laws and of broadly abusing Presidential power in misusing the Internal Revenue Service, imposing illegal wiretaps, in creating a "secret investigative unit" in the White House, and the like.

A third article charged the President with conduct "subversive of constitutional government" in his refusal to comply with the Judiciary Committee's subpoenas for 147 tapes of his conversations and related documents.[20]

Almost simultaneously, the Supreme Court, in an 8-0 decision, rejected the President's contention that he had absolute power to withhold from the courts tapes of his conversations with assistants and ruled that he must provide quantities of tapes required in the criminal trials of his former subordinates.[21] The unanimity and breadth of the decision spurred the impeachment drive in Congress.

Among the tapes the President was required to turn over to trial court Judge John Sirica were those of three discussions Nixon held on June 23, 1972, with his chief of staff, H. R. Haldeman, that disclosed, beyond doubt, that Nixon had attempted, but failed, to use the CIA to deflect an FBI investigation of the Watergate scandal. For more than two years Nixon claimed to be innocent of involvement in any cover-up, and the disparity between his previous statements and the newly revealed evidence swiftly eroded his remaining Congressional and public support, and made his impeachment inevitable. Its course was halted by his resignation.

An unused process for more than a century, impeachment worked in 1974. A contemporary President, possessing power well beyond the design and imaginings of the Founding Fathers, had been forced from office. The Nixon experience is a reminder to future Presidents that, despite the heady temptations of their office to think otherwise, they are subject to the Constitution, as befits democracy. This includes their prescribed duty to see that the laws are faithfully executed. That duty is not faithfully executed when the President manipulates laws to favor friends, to violate the constitutional rights of private individuals, and to punish his political opponents. From their skillful curbings of a Presidential aberration, Congress and the courts gained new and needed prestige and a sense of accomplishment. Congress, and more particularly the House Judiciary Committee, functioned with a caution and deliberation that drained any possible validity from the contention of President Nixon's staunchest advocates that he had been "hounded from office."

But another perspective on the Nixon events and the impeachment process, with its adjunct, a virtually unbreakable four-year term, results in a less charitable appraisal of the Presidential system. In a parliamentary system, Nixon, after only a few of his infractions, would have been swiftly ousted from office. But the cumbersome impeachment machinery and a fixed term of office enabled Nixon to dodge and parry for more than two years while the nation suffered and drifted.

The President and Legal Processes

With the Constitution's language so sparse and experience limited, important unanswered questions remain about impeachment and related legal processes.

Some of these surfaced in the Nixon proceedings and were responded to by the courts, Congress, or the executive, while others were avoided and therefore left to another day.

1. Although the Constitution acknowledges that the President is liable to criminal indictment after his removal by impeachment, can a grand jury indict him without, or prior to, impeachment? Following the cover-up of the Watergate burglary, the federal grand jury investigating Watergate named President Nixon as an unindicted coconspirator. Watergate Special Prosecutor Leon Jaworski dissuaded the jury from directly indicting the President, contending that the House Judiciary Committee was the proper forum for considering "matters of evidence relating to" a President.[22] Ultimately, the grand jury report and accompanying materials were turned over to the House Committee. In *Nixon* v. *United States,* the Supreme Court let the grand jury's action stand.[23]

2. Yes, the President can be subpoenaed, but can anyone subpoena him in any court, in any state, in any trial? A California superior court judge subpoenaed Nixon to appear as a witness at the trial of his former aide, John Ehrlichman. But Nixon rejected the subpoena, citing the contention of Thomas Jefferson that if the President were obliged to honor every subpoena, the courts could overwhelm the separation of powers principle and "keep him constantly trudging from North to South and East to West, and withdraw him entirely from his constitutional duties." That a state court was requesting his appearance enabled Nixon to cite traditional intergovernmental immunity.[24]

3. Must the President testify before the Watergate grand jury? When Special Prosecutor Jaworski requested that he do so, Nixon declined on grounds that it would be constitutionally improper, and Jaworski did not press the matter, nor did he accept the President's offer of written, or indirect, testimony.[25] Nixon drew on precedents set by Jefferson and Monroe. In the treason trial of Aaron Burr, President Jefferson was subpoenaed, and he responded by making evidence available to the federal trial court but did not testify personally. In 1818, Monroe was subpoenaed as a witness in a court martial but satisfied the request with written responses. Be it noted that unlike Nixon, Jefferson and Monroe were not objects of criminal inquiry.

4. Must the President honor subpoenas calling for White House papers and tapes? For Nixon, the question arose in various contexts and partook of different outcomes:

☐A U.S. Circuit Court of Appeals ruled that Nixon had to turn over to a federal district court White House tape recordings that possibly bore on Watergate crimes. The court could then give the Watergate grand jury any relevant material unless it felt some public interest must be served by withholding particular information. Faced with Presidential claims of executive privilege for the tapes, the Appeals court decided the case on narrow grounds. It acknowledged that "wholesale public access to executive deliberations and documents would cripple the executive as a coequal branch" but concluded that observance of executive privilege depends on "a weighing of public interests that would be served by disclosure in a particular case.'' The court was impressed that the President did not assert that the tapes involved contained military or state secrets.[26]

□Special Prosecutor Jaworski requested sixty-four tapes needed as evidence for a pending Watergate cover-up trial, but the President refused to surrender them. Federal district judge Sirica ordered the President to turn over the tapes, rejecting his claim of executive privilege and his contention that since Jaworski was a subordinate in the executive branch he had no standing to sue his superior, the President, and that therefore the district court had no jurisdiction to enforce Jaworski's subpoena. The Supreme Court ruled unanimously that the President must provide potential evidence for the criminal trial of his former subordinates and rejected his contention that he had absolute authority to withhold the material.[27]

□Nixon rejected the dictum of James K. Polk that in a House impeachment proceeding "all the archives and papers of the executive departments, public or private, would be subject to the inspection and control of a committee [of the House] . . ." After partly complying with requests by the House Judiciary Committee for tapes and documents as it considered impeachment, Nixon informed the Committee that he would not comply with two existing subpoenas nor with any future requests. Contending that he had already provided the committee with "a voluminous body of materials" that give "the full story of Watergate," the President declared there would be "no end" to the requests "unless a line were drawn somewhere by someone. Since it is clear that the committee will not draw such a line, I have done so." Nixon cited "the principle of the separation of powers and of the executive as a coequal branch." Committee chairman Peter Rodino, Jr., warned that the President's action was "a very grave matter," implying that it could ultimately provide grounds for impeachment. Rodino wondered aloud whether the Watergate cover-up was not continuing at full-sail even at the House stage of impeachment.[28]

5. After the President resigns or is successfully impeached, can his successor pardon him before he has been subject to possible indictment, trial, and judgment, to which Article I, Section 3 of the Constitution makes him liable? Yes, according to President Ford, who pardoned former President Nixon for all federal crimes that he "committed or may have committed or taken part in" while in office.[29] Ford's position is supported by long-standing English cases and by *ex parte Garland* (4 Wall. 333, 1867) in which the U.S. Supreme Court held that a pardon could be issued before conviction in a case involving a Confederate officer who was pardoned and reinstated as a member of the bar. The Nixon pardon, however, was a stark contradiction of the democratic ideal of equal justice. Other Watergate defendants underwent trial and punishment while the man who gave their orders remained free in comfortable enjoyment of a generous pension and other bountiful allowances accorded a former President. Ford's ultra-secrecy in preparing the pardon, and his failure to follow customary procedure and consult the Justice Department, inspired accusations that a "deal" existed with Nixon. In the blanket protection it accorded Nixon from federal indictment, the pardon was a cover-up of the ex-President's cover-up of Watergate.

Disability

The President, as the Constitution anticipates and history demonstrates, may fall victim to crushing illness or to death. Eight Presidents (almost one out of five) have died in office, four by assassination. A sick President may be unable to discharge the duties of his office. According to Richard Hansen's computations, the cumulative periods of actual Presidential disability add up to a full year in which the country was "without a President." Such periods unfortunately occurred during difficult times, when large issues demanded the Chief Executive's full vigor and skill. Until the Twenty-fifth Amendment was adopted in 1967, the problem of disability was treated by provisions in Article II, whose language was a quagmire of ambiguity.[30] Article II reads,

> In case of [the President's] inability to discharge the powers and duties of the said office, the same shall devolve on the Vice President, and the Congress may by law provide for the case of . . . inability, both of the President and Vice President, declaring what officer shall then act as President, and such officer shall act accordingly, until the disability be removed or a President shall be elected.

Neither here nor elsewhere in the Constitution were the following questions answered: Who is authorized to say whether a President is unable to discharge the powers and duties of his office? If he is unable, does the office become vacant? To what does the Vice President succeed when the President is disabled—to the "powers and duties of the said office" or to the office itself? What is the election referred to—the next regular Presidential election or a special election called by Congress?

Twice in American experience Presidents have been incapacitated for extended periods. President Garfield lay stricken after July 2, 1881, when an assassin's bullet struck a vertebra of his spinal column and became deeply embedded in the muscles of his back. The White House was converted into a hospital, and fans in the President's sickroom blew cool breezes over ice cubes to provide relief from the capital's broiling summer.[31] The President, a large, rugged man who faced his ordeal with unflagging heroism, rallied through most of July. In August he passed through cycles of decline and improvement. On September 6 he was transported by rail with maximum precautions to Elberon on the New Jersey coast, where it was hoped the sea air would by some miracle rally him. But his strength only dwindled, and in a few days he died.

During his entire illness, President Garfield committed only one official act. He signed an extradition paper, prepared in the State Department, after a physician read it aloud. He saw only Mrs. Garfield and his doctors and had no visitors except one day at Elberon, when members of his cabinet filed in for brief interviews. The Star Route frauds,* inherited from the previous Hayes administration, still bedeviled the Post Office Department, and the gush of illicit

---

* These frauds occurred in the carriage of mails over roads marked by asterisks in the official records and popularly known as "star routes." The Post Office scandalously overpaid certain persons operating such lines, including the chairman of the Republican National Committee.

dollars from the United States Treasury into corrupt hands continued. The President's isolation brought to a standstill Secretary of State James G. Blaine's effort to modify the existing Clayton-Bulwer Treaty in the interest of the proposed Nicaraguan canal. (Blaine's ultimate purpose in this complex maneuver was to establish an isthmian canal under United States control.) A conference of American republics that the President had called was postponed.[32]

As the neglected problems accumulated, demands spiraled in the press, in Congress, and among the cabinet that Vice President Chester Arthur take over the duties of the incapacitated President. The cabinet, which was most distressed by the ravages of neglect, earnestly discussed the Vice President's possible assumption of Presidential authority, a prospect that repelled them. Agitated meetings in the Secretaries' offices and homes quickly revealed disagreement on a thorny issue of constitutional interpretation. Four of the seven Secretaries believed that Arthur's exercise of Presidential power would make him President for the remainder of the existing term and would immediately and permanently oust Garfield from the office. Legalistic interpretation was not the only bond joining those in the cabinet in opposition to the Vice President's assumption of Presidential duties. Arthur, in their view, belonged to a low order of politicians—the "Stalwart" Republicans—who had wished Grant to be nominated for a third term and had fought Garfield with waspish oratory and savage deed ever since the onset of his Presidency.

Chester Arthur, for his part, was facing the question of his assumption of the Presidency with characteristic prudence. He stayed out of public view, dodged the press, and remained in New York as much as possible. The most painful element in Arthur's situation was the cold suspicion with which the President's friends beheld him. Arthur felt the full bite of the frosty atmosphere when he called one night at the White House, shortly after the attack, as a courteous demonstration of concern for the stricken President. The Vice President was ushered to an office where the full cabinet sat gathered in vigil. He paused uncertainly in the doorway, waiting for an invitation to enter. None came; no one moved to greet him. The cabinet stared with unanimous hostility. Arthur was about to withdraw in painful confusion when another visitor who came along greeted him cordially and drew him into the room. Several cabinet Secretaries then extended the Vice President the minimum amenities.[33]

For all their revulsion toward Arthur, the cabinet in the later days of Garfield's illness again considered the question of the Vice President's succession. To the harried Secretaries the mounting pile of neglected problems left no choice. Postmaster General Thomas L. James was dispatched to New York to ascertain Arthur's views. The Vice President's answer was swift and categorical. Under no circumstances would he assume the responsibilities of the Presidency while Garfield was alive. The Vice President held to his point and public problems drifted. Not until his own formal investiture in the Presidency after Garfield's death did Arthur touch the power of the office.[34]

The other occasion of extended Presidential incapacity occurred during the second administration of Woodrow Wilson, at a time immeasurably more serious than Garfield's. During the ailing Wilson's taxing Western trip in September 1919 intended to rally the people behind the League of Nations, the President collapsed and was rushed back by train to Washington. Conflicting versions persist of the onset of the President's illness. One, by Mrs. Wilson and Rear Admiral Cary T. Grayson, the President's physician, contends that Wilson "collapsed" in the West, returned to Washington, and three days later suffered a stroke described by Mrs. Wilson as "paralyzing the left side of his body. An arm and one leg were useless." [35] A contrasting version by Joe Tumulty, the President's trusted secretary, holds that the stroke occurred in Colorado, during the Western journey. At 4 A.M. September 26 in Pueblo, where the Presidential train had stopped, Tumulty was aroused by a knock on the door of his sleeping compartment. It was Dr. Grayson with word that the President was seriously ill. Tumulty rushed to the train's drawing room where the President, fully dressed, was seated in a chair. Tumulty stood transfixed by the spectacle. "His face was pale and wan," the secretary later described it. "One side of it had fallen, and his condition was indeed pitiful to behold. . . . His left arm and leg refused to function. I then realized that the President's whole left side was paralyzed." [36]

The White House was again transformed into a hospital. The President, who was not expected to live long, somehow clung to the edge of existence. Although his body was broken, his mind was clear. "Physically he was very weak," observed Grayson, "but mentally very alert." [37] Meanwhile, the nation was caught up in the cumbrous transition from warmaking to peacemaking. The peace treaty, with its controversial League of Nations provision, was before the Senate at midcourse, where it faced the hostility of the President's arch rival, Henry Cabot Lodge. On the autumn agenda were scheduled visits of European dignitaries with the President. Domestically, the economy was demobilizing to peacetime footing. In the din and lash of public business, the President lay crippled, his true condition known only to his wife, his physician, and the little ring of medical specialists who surrounded him and desperately administered their skills. The President, in their general opinion, was hopelessly beyond recovery. A year and a half of his term stretched ahead. What was to be done?

Dr. Francis X. Dercum, the eminent nerve authority, told Mrs. Wilson, "Madam, it is a grave situation, but I think you can solve it. Have everything come to you; weigh the importance of each matter, and see if it is possible by consultations with the respective heads of the Departments to solve them without the guidance of your husband. In this way you can save him a great deal. But always keep in mind that every time you take him a new anxiety or problem to excite him, you are turning a knife in an open wound. His nerves are crying out for rest, and any excitement is torture to him."

"Then," replied Mrs. Wilson, "had he better not resign, let Mr. Marshall [the Vice President] succeed to the Presidency and he himself get that complete rest that is so vital to his life?"

"No, not if you feel equal to what I suggested," Dr. Dercum said. "For Mr. Wilson to resign would have a bad effect on the country, and a serious effect on our patient." [38]

The *modus operandi* suggested by Dr. Dercum was quickly instituted for the remainder of Wilson's term. Officials coming to the White House took up with Mrs. Wilson business that hitherto they had discussed with the President. The brave First Lady applied herself conscientiously to understanding the intricacies that poured upon her and to reporting them in as precise a language as possible to her husband. Mrs. Wilson said in describing her stewardship,

> I studied every paper, sent from the different Secretaries or Senators, and tried to digest and present in tabloid form the things that, despite my vigilance, had to go to the President. I, myself, never made a single decision regarding the disposition of public affairs. The only decision that was mine was what was important and what was not, and the *very* important decision of when to present matters to my husband.[39]

In deciding what was important, Mrs. Wilson, of course, was making a vital kind of policy decision.

Even the trusted Tumulty, who had been accustomed to seeing the President whenever he chose, bent to the new procedure. Only Mrs. Wilson and Dr. Grayson saw the President. Somehow the public business limped forward. The hurdle of the State of the Union message, an annual and unalterable constitutional requirement, was managed when cabinet Secretaries, acting in accordance with the traditional procedure, submitted paragraphs reflecting their departmental concerns to the White House. There Tumulty received them and wove them together into a single document of reasonable coherence. It was read to Wilson and, with a few changes, the President approved it. On his better days, the President read state papers or listened as Mrs. Wilson read. He signed documents and in bursts of strength dictated notes for Senator Gilbert Hitchcock's guidance in the treaty fight.

But the President's dedicated helpers and his own valiant effort could not tame the mounting suspicion and unrest in the world outside. Secretary of State Robert Lansing believed that the President was not really writing the papers purporting to come from him. The Senate, collectively overcome by curiosity, appointed Hitchcock and Albert B. Fall, soon destined for exposure in the muck of Teapot Dome, as a committee to inquire into the condition of the President. After a visit with Wilson, they reported publicly that his mind was clear and that he was recovering. The baseless and misleading character of the latter finding appalled Mrs. Wilson. Nor did the Senators' reassurances deter several sensational newspapers from contending that the President was tightly secluded because he was insane, or that he was dead and his death was being kept secret.

The cabinet Secretary most concerned over the leaderless state of affairs was the head of the senior executive department, Secretary of State Robert Lansing. A responsible man of granitic integrity, he decided it was time to act. He arranged a private meeting with Presidential secretary Tumulty in the cabinet room. As diplomatically as possible, Lansing said he wished to suggest that in view of Wilson's incapacity the Vice President be called in to act in lieu of the President. To reinforce his suggestion, he cited the disability provisions of the Constitution. Tumulty was outraged at this seeming invitation to mutiny, and candidly vented his displeasure. Who, he asked, could authoritatively determine the fact of the President's disability? Those having the best information of it, answered Lansing—Dr. Grayson and Tumulty himself. Dr. Grayson, when he learned of the proposal, helped Tumulty to kill it quickly. If "anyone outside the White House," Tumulty warned Lansing, attempted to certify that the President was unable to carry on his duties, the President's physician and secretary would jointly repudiate the notion.[40]

Tumulty's rebuff did not quiet Lansing's conscience, agonized by the drift of affairs. The Secretary of State tried another tactic. The cabinet, the President's chief body of counselors, had not met since the commencement of Wilson's illness. If the cabinet were to meet occasionally on its own initiative, Lansing reasoned, the country's confidence would be buoyed. He placed this new inspiration before his fellow Secretaries. Their response was favorable, and Lansing as senior Secretary began calling and holding meetings of his fellow department heads in his office. That Lansing took the venture seriously is attested by the fact that in the first four months of Wilson's illness twenty-one cabinet meetings were called. When Wilson ultimately learned of them, he promptly wrote to Lansing pointing out that under established Constitutional procedure only the President could convene the department heads into conference and no one but he and Congress were entitled to request their views, collectively or individually, on public questions. Wilson's letter blazed with implications that Lansing's resignation would not be unwelcome. It was quickly forthcoming.[41]

The several illnesses of Dwight D. Eisenhower, although fortunately less severe than those of his predecessors, stirred national and world concern. In 1955 President Eisenhower sustained a coronary thrombosis, in 1956 an ileitis attack and operation, and in 1957 a mild stroke. In his first and most serious illness the President was totally removed from governmental affairs for only four days, after which he initialed papers. Sixteen weeks passed, however, before the President resumed his normal workload. Scarcely had he returned to full duty when the second illness crashed upon him. The combination of both illnesses left the President partially disabled for twenty-two weeks.

Eisenhower's first illness raised a question that was settled then and for his subsequent lesser illnesses. During the President's disability, full or partial, who should discharge his duties? Although the Constitution pointed to the Vice President, Richard M. Nixon, the smooth-working team of White House staff and department heads posed an alternative. So freely had Eisenhower delegated duties and authority to his aides since the outset of his administration that they could function almost autonomously in his absence forced by illness. The "team's" director was Sherman Adams, "the assistant to the President," widely viewed as the President's chief of staff. Another member of large importance was James Hagerty, the administration's chief public relations officer, the press secretary, who stood high in the President's esteem.

Two days after the President's heart seizure, Hagerty touched off the issue of who acts for an incapacitated President by disclosing that he had asked the Acting Attorney General, William P. Rogers, "for an opinion on any action that might be necessary at any time for delegation of powers." The next day Vice

President Nixon told the press, "It is quite clear, of course, that the Attorney General must give an interpretation as to how some technical details can be handled during the time the President is away. There are many legal problems involved." The Nixon and Hagerty statements were interpreted as faintly auguring a Vice-Presidential takeover. Thereupon Sherman Adams arrived in Washington from a European sojourn and quickly dominated and recomposed the situation. He conferred with Nixon and Rogers. The discussion's outcome and Adams' mastery are disclosed in Rogers' statement to the press afterward that "it may not be necessary to make a formal delegation of powers." Thereafter Hagerty in press statements referred to Adams repeatedly as the President's "deputy" rather than the President's "assistant." [42] "The announcements served to emphasize," noted the *New York Times*, "that the powers of the President still rested with General Eisenhower and no one else [and] that in the exercise of these powers, Mr. Adams, and not the Vice President, was the chief assistant to the President."

Under the emerging formula Adams and the department heads handled the regular operations of the executive branch. Nixon took on certain established, more or less ceremonial capacities. He made public addresses and appearances and presided at meetings of the cabinet and the National Security Council, as he had done during past Presidential absences. Press conferences with Hagerty were supplemented by occasional Nixon press conferences where a top official's comment was indispensable. Eisenhower's administrative machinery displayed an impressive capacity for self-direction, and thanks largely to Vice President Nixon's exemplary restraint there were no struggles for power.

Eisenhower's only incapacity of any duration, the heart attack, struck during a governmental lull. Congress was in recess, no international meetings or moves were afoot, public urgencies were few. In contrast, the third illness—the stroke—occurred during a critical period. The Russians had put their first Sputnik into orbit only a month before, and the prestige of America's military and technological might had become murkily suspect at home and abroad. A NATO meeting of heads of state was three weeks off, and the early signs of the acute 1958 economic recession were visible. But the gathering crisis was confined by the President's quick recovery.

Handling Disability:
The Twenty-fifth Amendment

The nation's several encounters with Presidential illness and its attendant constitutional and administrative problems stirred wide and thoughtful concern, which finally led to the passage of the Twenty-fifth Amendment in 1967. The amendment, often known as the Bayh amendment, after its chief Congressional manager, Senator Birch Bayh of Indiana, was carried by an irresistible momentum following President Kennedy's assassination. Senator Kenneth Keating reflected the mood of Congress when he declared that "as distasteful as it is to entertain the thought, a matter of inches spelled the difference between the painless death of John F. Kennedy and the possibility of his permanent incapacity to exercise the duties of the highest office of the land." [43] An awareness swept through Congress that careful action could no longer be postponed to protect the nation from the peril of a headless government in the nuclear age. However, discussion and action were complicated by the multitude of proposals advanced and by the dispersal of attention over several key questions.

1. What is disability? The Founding Fathers did not answer the question in the Constitution, nor does the Twenty-fifth Amendment undertake to define it. Disability encompasses literally dozens of conditions that defy exhaustive cataloguing. Ruth Silva, the leading authority on the subject, concludes that the Constitution contemplates "any *de facto* inability, whatever the cause or the duration, if it occurs at a time when the urgency of public business requires executive action." [44]

Disability is clearly not limited to physical illness but extends to mental illness as well and covers periods when the President is missing or captured in military operations. In an era of intercontinental missiles, when decisions on which national survival may turn must be taken in minutes, any definition of inability must be made carefully to include all contingencies. "The everpresent possibility of an attack on the United States was always hanging over us," Richard Nixon wrote of the brief period of Eisenhower's unavailability following his heart attack. "Would the President be well enough to make a decision? If not, who had the authority to push the button?" Or again, Eisenhower's ileitis seizure necessitated an operation at Walter Reed Hospital, where the President was under anesthesia for two hours. "The country," Eisenhower commented afterward to Nixon, "was without a Chief Executive, the armed forces without a Commander-in-Chief." [45]

2. Who determines disability? The Twenty-fifth Amendment provides that the President determine his own disability but requires that he communicate his finding in writing to the President pro tempore to the Senate and the Speaker of the House.

But what if the President refuses to proclaim his disability or because of his physical and mental circumstances cannot? The amendment stipulates that the Vice President, acting in concert with a majority of the cabinet, or of such "other body" as Congress may by law provide, could advise the President pro tempore of the Senate and the Speaker that the President was disabled. The "other body" was described in Congressional debate as a commission of private citizens, doctors, or psychiatrists, who might be summoned to pass judgment upon the President's competence.

Most discussions of the disability problem agreed that the Vice President should not have to bear sole responsibility for finding the President disabled but that he should have help, preferably from the cabinet. The cabinet, the argument goes, thanks to its daily contacts with the President, would be best informed of his plight. The department Secretaries' deepest inclination would be to act loyally and fairly to the President, since their job security depends upon him.

The cabinet's critics hold that it would be too blinded by self-interested loyalty ever to certify the President's disability. The possibility of retaliation by the President, when he recovered sufficiently, would encourage cabinet inaction. Wilson dismissed Lansing, and Harry S. Truman once declared in post-Presidential utterances that if his cabinet had ever declared him disabled while he was confined on the flat of his back, his first act upon rising would be to fire every culprit who had supported the finding.

The cabinet's limitations suggest the wisdom of the "other body," the alternative contained in the Twenty-fifth Amendment, whose members might include distinguished citizens and leading physicians and psychiatrists. Disability is most likely to be largely a medical question, for which authentic answers are best provided by qualified professionals. Disability is never only a medical question, however. It poses a tandem political question: Does the public interest at the time require the exercise of Presidential power? Doctors have no inherent superiority over other citizens in assessing "public interest." Even in medical questions genuine professional differences hold sway in diagnostic judgment.

3. If the President is disabled, to what does the Vice President succeed—to the "powers and duties" of the office, or to the office itself? Does he become Acting President, serving temporarily until the disabled President has recovered, or does he take over permanently for the remainder of the term? Vice Presidents Arthur and Marshall were deterred from taking over from their infirm Presidents by the wide opinion of their fellow public officials that a disabled President once pushed aside could never return. The Constitution, they reasoned, did not allow for two Presidents to exist simultaneously, one acting and the other ailing. The Twenty-fifth Amendment should settle the whole problem once and for all. It declares that when the President is disabled the Vice President shall assume "the powers and duties of the office as Acting President."

4. Who determines when the President's disability ends? The amendment provides that the President shall decide. But what if the President wants to get back to work too soon, before he is sufficiently recovered from his disability? The amendment specifies that if the Vice President and a majority of the cabinet or of the "other body" did not agree that the President had recovered, then Congress would resolve the issue. It could, by two-thirds vote of each house, decide that the President was still unable to discharge his duties, whereupon the Vice President would continue as Acting President.

While under Congressional debate, the features of the Twenty-fifth Amendment permitting the Vice President and the "other body" to find the President disabled, as an alternative to a finding by the Vice President endorsed by the cabinet, were criticized. It was charged that such provisions would enable the Vice President to "shop around" for support of his view that the President was disabled. Senator Albert Gore warned that "this nation could undergo the potentially disastrous spectacle of competing claims to the power of the Presidency.'' [46] Senator Bayh contended that such a power scramble was unlikely, and the bulk of the testimony before his subcommittee stressed that the amendment's disability provisions would be invoked only in the most extreme circumstances and that in the attending atmosphere of crisis executive officials and Congress could be expected to act responsibly. Witnesses paid no heed to the ghost of Andrew Johnson weeping at their folly. They were more impressed that in the nuclear age ambiguity was no longer tolerable and that it must be displaced with clearly defined rules and procedures. Committee witnesses, representatives of the legal profession, and citizen groups sounded a loud ''amen'' to Walter Lippmann's observation that the Twenty-fifth Amendment is ''a great deal better than an endless search . . . for the absolutely perfect solution . . . which will never be found, and . . . is not necessary.'' [47]

Succession

The Founding Fathers, who were geniuses at spotting thorny problems and passing them on to hapless posterity to wrestle with, applied their sure touch to Presidential succession. The all-seeing Fathers anticipated the calamitous day when a double vacancy might befall the nation—when both President and Vice President might be unavailable because of death, resignation, impeachment, or disability. The Fathers, accordingly, posed no solution, but simply empowered Congress to enact a law ''declaring what officer shall then act as President.'' Congress has thrice passed such laws, the last in 1947, and each time its labors have provoked criticism and sent citizens scurrying for better remedies.

In its three laws, Congress vacillated between drawing upon its own leaders and the members of the cabinet in laying the lines of succession. Considerations of pure political science have seldom motivated Congress's actions. The first law of 1792 was not a solution rooted in Olympian wisdom but a narrow partisan act. The law's object was to prevent the succession of Secretary of State Thomas Jefferson. The conservative leaders of Congress, who abhorred Jefferson, simply by-passed him and voted one of themselves into the succession. If the Presidency and the Vice-Presidency were vacant, the President pro tempore of the Senate, and after him the Speaker, would succeed. Neither officer was to become President upon the takeover, but only Acting President. If the double vacancy happened within the first two years and seven months of the Presidential term, Congress was required to call a special election ''forthwith.''

In 1886 Congress passed a new law, the pendulum now swinging to the cabinet. In a future double vacancy the succession would run from the Secretary of State to the Secretary of the Interior in the order in which the departments were established. No Secretary could be wafted by fate and the act into the Presidential chair if he could not satisfy the regular constitutional qualifications for the Presidency. The 1792 act's special election feature was dropped.

During Harry Truman's first weeks in the Presidency, into which he had been catapulted by Franklin Roosevelt's death, he perceived grievous limitations in the 1886 act. He incorporated his concern and recommendations for a new succession law in a special message to Congress on June 19, 1945. The 1886 act, placing the Secretary of State, an appointed and not an elected officer, next in line for the Presidency in effect permitted Truman to name his own successor. "I do not believe that in a democracy," the President declared, "this power should rest with the Chief Executive." In the new legislation he proposed, Truman contended that after the President and Vice President in the succession line should come the Speaker of the House of Representatives, because he "is elected in his own district" and "is also elected to be the presiding officer of the House by a vote of all the representatives of all the people of the country." After the Speaker, in the Truman plan, would come the President pro tempore who is elected first by the people of his state and then by the whole Senate. Following the President pro tempore would be "the members of the Cabinet as provided now by law." [48]

Since Edward Stettinius, Jr., a career businessman, was Secretary of State at the time and Sam Rayburn, a career politician, the Speaker, the House of Representatives passed a bill reflecting Truman's views with vast cheers for Rayburn and a proud sense of doing something nice for one's own. When the bill reached the upper chamber, however, James F. Byrnes, a distinguished and popular former Senator and Congressman, had replaced Stettinius as Secretary of State. Congressional enthusiasm for the succession bill shriveled. It was nearly dead when the Republican triumph in the 1946 Congressional elections suddenly revived it. The bill passed in 1947, and Truman dutifully signed it, thereby establishing not a Democratic but a Republican Speaker, Joe Martin, as his successor. After the Speaker, under the 1947 act, come the President pro tempore of the Senate, the Secretaries of State, the Treasury, and Defense, the Attorney General, the Postmaster General, and the Secretaries of the Interior, Agriculture, Commerce, and Labor. The Secretaries of Health, Education and Welfare, Housing and Urban Development, and Transportation now also figure in the succession.

Like bygone succession laws, the 1947 act stirred more reproach than praise. It trampled upon the separation of powers principle by bringing two legislative officers into the Presidential line. Truman's estimable image of the Speakership as a popular "democratic" office is open to challenge. The Speaker's electorate is local rather than national, his district a patch of a few square miles on the face of a continental nation. His elevation to the Speakership reflects not simply the "popularity" Truman valued, but seniority, parliamentary skill, party fidelity, and finesse in personal politics. Even worse, Speakers as a lot compare unfavorably with Secretaries of State, the Treasury, or Defense as Presidential timber. As executive officers the Secretaries would afford better continuity in succeeding to the Presidency than an "outsider" like the Speaker. Ironically, the 1947 act revived the Ben Wade–Andrew Johnson "temptation" by creating for the Speaker and the President pro tempore a vested interest in the President's impeachment.

The 1947 act also stumbled upon the imperatives of the nuclear age. The act did not face up to the possibility that in a future nuclear war one tolerably aimed bomb could destroy Washington and with it the whole company of Presidential successors. Earlier succession laws would have done no better.

The Twenty-fifth Amendment seeks to minimize the possibilities of a double vacancy occurring in the Presidency and Vice-Presidency. The amendment requires the President in the event that the office of Vice President is vacant to nominate a Vice President who will take office upon confirmation by a majority vote of both houses of Congress. This feature of the Twenty-fifth Amendment attracted the greatest unanimity in the Bayh subcommittee hearings.

But history can be prankish with surprises, and the Vice Presidential provision of the amendment was invoked under grotesque, totally unanticipated circumstances. In 1973, Vice President Agnew suddenly resigned under an agreement with the Justice Department by which he admitted evasion of federal income taxes and bartered away his office to avoid imprisonment. The stage was therefore set for President Nixon, who had himself already moved under the shadow of impeachment, to fulfill the requirements of the Twenty-fifth Amendment and nominate a new Vice President. Initially, Nixon veered toward John B. Connally, an erstwhile Democrat who had become a Republican, but Democratic Congressional leaders announced that they would oppose him, a fortunate judgment in light of Connally's subsequent indictment, stemming from his dealings with the potent milk lobby in the 1972 campaign. Nixon's ultimate selection, House Republican leader Gerald R. Ford, a popular figure on Capitol Hill, was instantly acclaimed.[49] Nevertheless, the episode itself is abhorrent to democratic standards. At a point when he was badly discredited and was soon to be driven from office, Nixon chose his own successor, thanks to the Twenty-fifth amendment. The public had little, if any, voice in the selection of the new President. Even more, Ford chose his potential successor, Nelson Rockefeller, to fill the Vice Presidency, vacated by his own succession to the Presidency. Again, the people's impact was minimal.

Presidential Transitions

The environment of the modern Presidency makes imperative not only a rational method of succession but a smooth transition between the outgoing and the incoming Chief Executives. In an age when several foreign affairs crises can flame simultaneously around the globe, when weapons systems consume an average of seven years in passing from drawing board to operation, when the economy grows ever more intricate and sensitive, a snarl or lapse in public policy invites disaster. Foreign leaders calculate their moves with an eye on the United States Presidential calendar. Several weeks after President Hoover's electoral defeat in 1932, Britain requested "adjustment" of her World War I debt and suspension of her payment due December 15. Other debtor European nations quickly made similar demands. The Europeans caught the United States during an interlude of governmental paralysis, with a President discredited by defeat, a Congress controlled by the opposition party, and the President-elect, Franklin Roosevelt, visibly and understandably reluctant to plunge onto a terrain full of economic and political booby traps, without the protection of official responsibility.

Succession presents a variety of problems: The President and the President-elect may be of the same party or of different parties; or the transition may be from Vice President to President, a reminder of the Vice President's function as the President's understudy. Of modern Presidents, Hoover was the first to seek consultations and joint policy-making with the President-elect. Both Franklin Roosevelt and Truman, when running for reelection, permitted aides to supply the opposing candidates with vital information on foreign affairs. President Truman, mindful of his own sudden and unbriefed trajectory into the Presidency, smoothed the transfer to the incoming Eisenhower administration, thus becoming the first outgoing Chief Executive to accept the responsibility squarely for orderly transition. President Eisenhower reciprocated by easing the Kennedy administration's advent in 1961.[50]

The Johnson-Nixon transfer of 1968–69 advanced the developing institutionalization of transition. Following his announcement on March 31, 1968, that he would not be a candidate for reelection, Johnson offered briefings by the CIA and the State and Defense Departments to all major candidates, and, following their nominations, Johnson summoned Nixon and George Wallace to the White House for consultations. Nixon designated Franklin B. Lincoln, Jr., a former Defense Department official and a partner in Nixon's law firm, as his representative. Throughout the campaign, Johnson briefed the candidates on his policies, including the bombing halt in Vietnam, and they in turn abstained from directly criticizing the war or in any way undercutting the President and negotiations for peace—a remarkable exercise of restraint, given the potential of the war issue for political gain.

In the 1972 elections, Nixon offered to brief his opponent, George McGovern, on the Vietnam War through his national security assistant, Henry A. Kissinger, which the Senator discounted, asserting that "I've frankly learned more about the realities of Vietnam from following the dispatches of good newspapermen than I have from official briefings in the White House." Nevertheless, McGovern deputed Paul C. Warnke, a former Assistant Secretary of Defense, to receive information "that the White House thinks would be useful." Throughout the campaign, McGovern maintained a distant and wary stance toward the Nixon administration. His approach to ending the conflict in Vietnam was poles apart from the administration's, and he did not mean to blur the difference by consorting with the White House.[51]

Generally, transitions are easier if the incumbent President is not a candidate for reelection. Transition is also facilitated if party turnover occurs at short intervals, since a party returning to power after a hiatus of only two Presidential terms is still mindful of the complexities of policy problems and enjoys acquaintanceship among the higher echelons of the career service. And, as recent transitions suggest, a war or foreign policy crisis is a salve for partisan differences.

In 1974, the apparatus for transitions underwent novel strains when Nixon's political strength was ebbing fast, to the point of his certain impeachment, while his successor, Vice President Ford, felt behooved to preserve his loyalty to, and even to defend, his beleaguered friend and benefactor. Clearly, it was inconsistent with these purposes, and unseemly for Ford, to engage personally in preparations for his assumption of the Presidency. It was equally awkward for the Nixon staff to consort with Ford's Vice Presidential staff to arrange for a possible sudden transition.

Nevertheless, at least three months before Nixon's resignation, Philip Buchen of the Vice President's staff commenced conversations with Clay T. Whitehead, director of the Office of Telecommunications Policy in the Nixon White House and a participant in the Johnson-Nixon transfer. Others of Nixon's and Ford's staff and friends were brought into the conversations, and meanwhile, Ford, laboring doggedly to preserve a fitting decorum, declared that if any of his staff were working on transition plans, "they are doing it without my knowledge and without my consent."

In meetings in Georgetown houses, the Ford and Nixon representatives proceeded through a checklist of items that included the "principles, themes, and objectives" Ford might espouse in his early Presidential pronouncements, the kind of staff required in the transition, the precise timetable of Nixon's withdrawal from and Ford's accession to the Presidency.[52] Despite the inevitably sudden nature of Nixon's resignation, Ford assumed the Presidency well briefed, and the hold-over Nixon staff were tolerably cooperative. But in time frictions prickled between the Ford and Nixon staffs, just as they had between the Kennedy-Johnson staffs in the early Johnson Presidency.

In the final days of the Nixon Presidency, Secretary of Defense James R. Schlesinger and the Joint Chiefs of Staff asserted exceptionally close control over the lines of command to insure that no unauthorized orders were given to military units by the White House or by service officers to impede the "constitutional process" (impeachment). Fortunately, no signs of any such moves materialized. As well, the Defense Department leaders were watchful for a genuine international emergency in which military units might have to be placed on alert or go into action. Schlesinger wanted to insure that he could justify the step publicly, mindful of the widespread skepticism when American forces were placed on alert in October 1973 as the Soviet Union appeared to contemplate dispatching forces to the Middle East.[53]

For all the surface appearance of cooperation and harmony, transitions are beset with the tensions and cross-purposes of the outgoing and incoming Presidents. The outgoing President, as Laurin Henry demonstrates in *Presidential Transitions*, prizes continuity and order, the preservation of his policies, and the maturing of his half-begun projects in the next administration. The President-elect is cautious and aloof, watchful of involving his freedom and the mandate and prestige of his electoral victory in policies of the incumbent administration over which he has no control. When in its closing days the Eisenhower administration decided to break diplomatic relations with Cuba, the incoming Kennedy administration was invited to associate itself with the move. The Kennedy camp, not surprisingly, declined. "In the absence of complete information on all the relevant factors," a Kennedy spokesman declared, the new administration could not participate.[54] The new President's personal philosophy may be radically at odds with the incumbent President's, as Eisenhower's laissez-faire preferences were miles removed from the welfare-state commitment of Truman. The new and old Presidents may differ in their view of Presidential method: Harding's Whiggery was a long way from Wilson's dynamism. But the most pressing difficulties of Presidential transitions are constitutional rather than administrative. Although the Twentieth Amendment helpfully moved the Presidential inauguration from March to January, a yawning hiatus still stretches between the end of the old administration and the beginning of the new one. A lapse of eleven or twelve weeks between popular election and inauguration is absurd, given the gallop of today's affairs. The dates of the two events need to be juxtaposed within not more than four weeks of each other. Likewise, the interval between the national party conventions and the election, scheduled originally in horse-and-buggy days, has become thoroughly antiquated and ill serves the nation's interests. Following the conventions in July or August is a lull of four or five weeks of inactivity before the campaigns begin in earnest after Labor Day. Then come eight or more weeks of campaigning as compared with two weeks or less in Great Britain and Canada. The increasing efficiency of American campaign media could easily support a shorter campaign period. Our historical political calendar has plainly become outmoded. Wise compression could eliminate two months or more between the dwindling reign of a lame duck President and his successor's arrival at the seat of power.

The Future Presidency

Thoughtful concern and discussion regarding disability, succession, and transition is apt to wax well into the future. Viewing the President, as we do, under the cruel pressures of the nuclear age, what seems best on each of these scores for keeping the Presidency continuously strong and responsive to democratic standards?

1. Although the Twenty-fifth Amendment is not flawless, it would probably be best to leave the subject of disability at rest and to anticipate, confidently and prayerfully, that its provisions could be applied in workable manner by responsible officials should the need arise.

2. There are several possible, although remote, contingencies of Presidential tenure that never troubled us in quieter, bygone times. In the nuclear era,

however, with its infinite perils and ever shrinking timetables, we should put our minds to them although the cloud they make on our political horizon is no larger than a person's fist.

(a) Suppose the Presidential or Vice-Presidential candidate should die or become disabled prior to the popular election in November. The situation is not covered by law. Both major parties have empowered their national committees to fill the vacancy, and the Republican committee has the further option of summoning a new convention. We would be on firmer legal ground if the procedure were incorporated into law.

(b) Suppose the Presidential or Vice-Presidential candidate should die after the November popular election but before the electors met in their respective state capitals in December to cast their votes. Under present law the electors could vote for anyone they pleased. Both major parties, however, have authorized their national committees to fill the vacancy, and the likelihood is that the electors would vote for the new nominee. If the Presidential nominee should die, the country would likely expect the Vice-Presidential nominee to fill the vacancy, and his place, in turn, to be filled by a new nominee. All this is a darkling plain, barren of precedent.

(c) Suppose that after the electors vote in their respective states and before January 6, when the electoral votes are opened, announced, and counted in Congress, the Presidential candidate should die. The possibilities are grisly. The candidate's death would raise the question whether votes for a dead man could be counted. If they could and if he were the winner, the election would be thrown into the House of Representatives. Some authorities argue that Congress could reconvene the electoral college to permit the electors to change their votes. Still others hold that Congress could make the Vice-Presidential winner the President-elect. Probably the easiest way out would be to declare the dead candidate, if he was the winner, the President-elect, and, under the Twentieth Amendment, the Vice President–elect would become President on Inauguration Day, January 20.

(d) Suppose no Presidential candidate receives a majority of the electoral votes, and the election is thrown into the House of Representatives, but before the House acts, one of the candidates eligible to be voted upon dies. No procedure exists for filling the vacancy. The Twentieth Amendment, however, empowers Congress to resolve the situation. Conceivably, Congress could permit the national committee of the party affected by the death to propose a replacement.

Fortunately, the law of probabilities runs strongly against the occurrence of these several nightmares. But on the theory that the governmental structure must never falter in our troubled day, these are fit subjects for study by Congress and interested citizens.

3. For reasons we have explored, the 1947 Succession Act is a mistake, and it ought to be repealed. To replace it, the act of 1886 might be restored with the line of succession proceeding through the cabinet, beginning with the Secretary of State. In addition, the line of succession might well be extended. Those now in the line pass most of their time in Washington, a circumstance that makes possible the extinction of the entire body of successors in a nuclear attack on the capital. Congress might well add to the succession persons distributed around the country. One possibility might be to include the governors ranked according to the population of their states in the last census.

4. In the interest of easing the transition between Presidencies, we might well cast a critical eye on our present scheduling of the national nominating convention, the duration of the postconvention electoral campaign, and the date of the inauguration. Each could be revised to shorten the transition. A three- or four-week electoral campaign should be altogether efficient and desirable. We could use a shortened campaign as a springboard for revising other parts of the Presidential calendar. We might redress the awkwardness of the Budget and Accounting Act of 1921, which requires a new President, days after his inauguration in January, to submit a budget that has been prepared largely by his predecessor. A rearranged Presidential calendar would give the new President more time to prepare a budget of his own for presentation in January or to amend the one inherited from his predecessor. On the basis of these necessities, one could project the following calendar, with approximately a four-week interval between most steps: August—the nominating conventions; September—the postconvention electoral campaign; October—the election; November—the inauguration; December—recruiting administration members and preparing initial policies; January—presentation of the new President's State of the Union and budget messages and the economic report.

5. Let every good friend of the strong Presidency and the democratic ideal of free electoral choice pledge himself or herself to work unstintingly for the repeal of the Twenty-second Amendment. Even more, let us do a better job in choosing Presidents who are democratically fit, as an easier alternative than the belated discovery of their defect after they are in office, with the anguish of impeachment or forced resignation as the only remedies.

5

PUBLICS

Τhe hours when the American Presidency has enjoyed its most brilliant effectiveness, when democracy and the strong executive seem in finest congruence, are those when the Chief Executive rallies public sentiment behind policies addressed to the common good. Theodore Roosevelt moving against the abuses of giant railroads, Woodrow Wilson advancing his New Freedom program of social justice, Franklin Roosevelt combating the Great Depression and reforming the economy were achievements of leadership that stirred the understanding and support of the generality of the people.[1]

The President and Public Opinion

Given the realities of the political system in which he works, it is well that the President enjoys impressive resources for reaching the public and rallying public opinion. Because the national parties are weak organizations, they are unreliable and often pusillanimous as sources of help for Presidential programs. The built-in conflict between the President and Congress assured by checks and balances, the ease with which Congress can rebuff him, leaves the President dependent upon his ability to summon broad public support as his most substantial means of bringing Congress around to an accommodation productive of policy and action.

THE PRESIDENCY AND SOCIALIZATION   Ordinarily, the adult public takes a favorable view of a President's performance, as the following data from Gallup polls suggest. Before the Watergate disaster engulfed him, Nixon attained a high of 68 percent, but as the scandal unfolded he plummeted to 23 percent, a low known only by Truman among contemporary Presidents.

During periods of crisis, especially in foreign affairs, public opinion tends to

Popular Approval of Presidential Performance		
	Highest %	**Lowest %**
Roosevelt	84	50
Eisenhower	79	49
Kennedy	69	57

rally around the President. Even after the disastrous Bay of Pigs invasion, Kennedy's popularity did not fall, as logic might suggest, but rose 10 points, and Truman's in the onset of the Korean War increased 9 points. If the strong Presidency is perceived as an organ for achieving policy and program, the concept is not assisted by the public's tendency to evaluate Presidents merely as persons beset by critical events, rather than in terms of policy accomplishment or demonstrated political skills.[2] Fortunately, there are also periods during which the public is more prone to question the President when its critical faculties are more aroused. Typically, after the President has handled a crisis successfully, his support in the polls tends to fall off. Some Presidential acts evoke marked public disapproval—President Ford's precipitant pardon of former President Nixon, for example, following which Ford dropped twenty-one points in a public opinion poll, the steepest decline in so short a time in thirty-five years of poll surveys of Presidents.[3]

A sizeable part of the President's ready popularity is attributable to processes of socialization. The President richly benefits from attitudes the public entertains about his office and its incumbents. Studies disclose that children know about the President at a very early age and that their knowledge is idealized. Already highly visible to the young child, the President is seen as benign, honest, exceptionally competent, better than most individuals, hard-working, and devoted to protecting all Americans. The young child's picture of the President is not democratic—a failing that may infiltrate adult perceptions—for the President is beheld as a boss who does more than anyone to make the laws, with Congress and others functioning as helpers. Generally, in early school grades, textbooks are uncritical of Presidents, identifying them with accomplishment and pride in the country's history and showing them as remote figures, untainted by flawed performance. As the child grows older, admiration for the President diminishes somewhat, but not until the seventh or eighth grades do children venture to make negative judgments about the Presidency.[4]

In the adult world, the results of early socialization by family and school are reinforced by the regularly recurrent events of Presidential elections and successions, and the tolerable effectiveness of the incumbents. A disruptive event such as the assassination of President Kennedy evoked many similar emotional reactions among primary and secondary school children and adults—sadness and mourning, shame and anger. Many college students displayed profound feelings of reassurance that the Presidency's institutional feature of automatic succession by the Vice President had functioned effectively, and their impressions of Lyndon Johnson immediately became more favorable because of his assumption of the Presidential role.[5]

Not surprisingly, the benevolent leader image burns brightest among the comfortably situated and weakest among those who fare less well in the distribution of society's benefits, such as blacks and the poor. In the Nixon era, public opinion analyst Louis Harris found that no more than 3 percent of all blacks expected significant assistance from the President; instead, according to the prevailing view among blacks, they must extract their own progress from a grudging white society.[6]

For both children and adults, the Watergate scandals were jarring and disruptive of the Presidency's normal connections with socialization. Parents feared a loss of their own credibility in the socialization process. According to one parent, "The chief problem in raising children is our desire as parents to teach them the ethical approach to people in life situations. That's a difficult enough lesson without Watergate, and now they're seeing a total lack of conscience at the highest level. Our message doesn't relate to what they're seeing now." Interviews with children disclosed that they perceived the morality of Watergate in simple terms, with the President appearing to have been bad, according to their criteria, and answerable to harsher standards than they applied to themselves. "He's the President," said a ten-year-old, "and is supposed to be protecting the people against crime, not making crime. He should be punished more." [7]

PRESIDENTIAL POPULARITY AND THE VIETNAM WAR Despite the normally sturdy underpinnings of socialization, as American combat involvement in the Vietnam War escalated and the struggle dragged on inconclusively, leading journalists wrote condemning it as "the most unpopular" American war "of this century" or "in American history." A study group of the National Commission on the Causes and Prevention of Violence declared that it "commands less popular support than any previous American international war." [8]

These assessments are disputed by empirical studies, which found, for example, that opposition to the Vietnam War was not more substantial than opposition to the Korean War. Doubtless what overimpressed the journalists, commentators, and possibly Lyndon Johnson, was that the Vietnam opposition was more vocal, a condition attributable, at least partly, to the intellectual nonunion left, sometimes called the journalistic-academic complex, and their contrasting perceptions of the Korean and Vietnam wars. The Korean conflict was tolerable as an episode in the cold war against Stalinist Russia, but by the mid-1960s, with a spreading Vietnam War and Stalin no longer alive, the Russian threat seemed abated.[9]

The new left of the late 1960s was the old left of the earlier civil rights movement, experienced at vocalizing through demonstrations, and drawing heavily on young people, with their stamina, freedom from occupational and familial responsibilities, and a proclivity for thinking in absolute moral terms. Though vocal, the intellectual left chiefly influenced elite groups; it never became a mass movement. In fact, the Vietnam protesters acquired a highly negative public image, even among doves, a circumstance that may actually have hurt the peace movement by linking it to an unpopular reference group.[10]

According to a 1966 survey, the war was a salient problem for the public, which possessed relatively high levels of information concerning it. The President enjoyed strong support (61 percent) for his conduct of the war, though many respondents to opinion polls were influenced by their general support of the President rather than by approval of his war policies. The public majority was receptive to moves to end the war but was not in favor of sudden withdrawal from Vietnam and abandonment of commitments.

Public Approval of Alternatives for Ending the Vietnam War	
Alternative	**Percentage of public approval**
Negotiating with the Vietcong	88
Free elections, even though Vietcong might win	54
Coalition government with the Vietcong	52

Source: Sidney Verba et al., "Public Opinion and the War in Vietnam," *American Political Science Review* 61 (June 1967), 318–21.

The majority, however, was also opposed to further drastic escalation. In all, the majority was relatively permissive, moderate and responsible and desirous of a negotiated settlement, thereby granting Johnson and Nixon generous latitude for conducting and concluding the war.[11]

Indeed, Louis Harris has demonstrated that the electorate was consistently ahead of its leaders in the Presidential elections of 1964 through 1972 in yearning for peace in Vietnam. In Nixon's landslide victory in 1972, the chief force contributing to his success was his ability to convince the public that he had moved the world closer to peace. His rhetorical promise of a "generation of peace" gained credibility with the voters thanks to North Vietnam's announced agreement to tentative peace terms on October 8, 1972, and Henry Kissinger's assurances in late October that "peace was at hand." Less influential were McGovern's occasional ineptitudes in handling the Vietnam issue.[12]

Constituencies

In addition to the general public, the President deals with many lesser publics or constituencies whose demeanor toward him embraces a wide range of positive and negative behavior, from furious disdain to imperishable approval, dispositions that can shape his policies, their success and failure, his political future, and even his place in history. Constituencies express their feelings toward the President in diverse ways—with supportive and obstructive acts and sheer passivity, by giving and withholding benefits and penalties that are theirs to confer. The following are major constituencies that populate the President's world.

POLITICAL CONSTITUENCIES   This category includes the President's most vital public, his bread-and-butter constituency, the national electorate, upon whose favor his reelection or his party's continued control of the Presidency depends. Because of this incomparable power, the electorate is exceeded by no other constituency in its importance to the President. Elsewhere, the landscape is dotted with political publics: members of Congress, governors, mayors, the Chief Executive's prospective opponents in the next Presidential race, the leaders, subleaders, and workers of his own and the rival parties.

If the President slips or falters, as he did when the Vietnam War dragged on inconclusively, he becomes prey to Congressional critics and opponents, to derision and attack, and to competing policy initiatives, claimed to be superior to his own, from out-party leaders and even from his own party. From her gallery seat, as she witnessed her husband's rendering of a State of the Union Message to Congress, Mrs. Lyndon Johnson noted two of his more formidable constituents among the applauding Democrats: "Senator Fulbright sat silent, above it all, the whole evening. Bobby Kennedy was stony-faced. He applauded once, two or three light claps." [13] Severer penalties were to follow.

Outside the United States, the President has countless political constituencies, including foreign leaders and subleaders of countries friendly, hostile, or on-the-fence. These further publics range from the general population to specialized groupings just as the President's domestic publics do.

ADMINISTRATIVE CONSTITUENCIES   Traditionally identified most closely with the Presidential administration, the department heads are valuable for the prestige they bring, their political and administrative skills, their own constituencies or publics that they are linked to or can appeal to. But they can also hamper the President with administrative lapses, jar him with public criticism, or enlarge the rift in the Presidential team by resigning. In 1967, Robert McNamara's resignation as Secretary of Defense meant the departure of a prestigious hold-over of the Kennedy administration and a symbol of the essential continuity between the two administrations that had stilled the incipient criticism of many a Kennedy Democrat. McNamara's withdrawal "hung a pall" over the Johnson administration and, amid the instantaneous furor of political speculation, Johnson confided to his family, "Except for one, this is the hardest day I have spent in this job." [14]

A huge, varied constituency is the bureaucracy, both civilian and military. Winning its benign regard is no easy task for any President, and eeked-out gains can be quickly dissipated.

ECONOMIC CONSTITUENCIES   Business can raise prices, invest abroad, and cut back production with deleterious consequences to the President and his goals of restraining inflation, improving the balance of payments, and reducing unemployment. Labor too can exacerbate these problems by heightening its demands for wages and benefits and by invoking strikes. Acknowledging the formidable power of business and labor, contemporary Presidents bestow upon them alert attention and solicitude.

Something of the deference Richard Nixon accorded the great corporations is evidenced in his stance toward "Big Oil" early in his administration. The major oil companies had contributed generously to his 1968 campaign, and when an administration task force moved toward recommending in 1969 a drastic scaling down in governmental protection of the industry, replacing existing import quotas with a tariff that would sharply reduce costs to the consumer, the large oil firms, consternated and battle-ready, made clear to Presidential campaign manager and Attorney General John Mitchell that if the plan moved ahead, they might look elsewhere in throwing support to Presidential candidates in the 1972 election. In a visitation to the task force, Mitchell laconically urged caution: "Don't put the President in a box," he said, and the task force quickly trimmed back its recommendations, thereby killing long months of research supportive of its original position and casting on the consumer the future ordeals of shortages and higher prices.[15]

SOCIAL CONSTITUENCIES   In the operating realities of the Presidency, Americans are perceived in terms of social criteria, in racial and ethnic identifications, in sex and age differentiations, as occupants of rungs in the class structure. In launching his poverty program, Johnson responded to several social constituencies. His new program was a major weapon for quieting black discontent and a shiny lure for low-income votes, regardless of race. To those constituencies and even others more comfortably situated and liberal-minded, the program would enhance the image he was assiduously cultivating of a "compassionate" President.[16]

For Johnson, one of the most elusive of constituencies was the young, or, more precisely, a particular subcategory of that diverse constituency, the college student activists of the 1960s. For a time, early in his administration, Johnson and the activists joined in harmony. In their initial enterprises, the activists concentrated on winning rights for blacks in the South, with sit-ins, Freedom Rides, and voter registration drives. The foundation of their efforts consisted of laws that Johnson had promoted and that guaranteed the rights for which the students demonstrated. The students were also sensitive to the maltreatment of the poor, and Johnson again fostered harmony by inducing Congress to pour millions in appropriations into his remedial poverty programs.

But whatever bridges were built between Johnson and the activist youth constituency proved fragile in the Vietnam War and soon collapsed, even though the opponent in that war was a totalitarian power, a trampler of the very rights the activists cherished. Suddenly Johnson became a caricature to the activists, an object of repugnance and scorn. Certainly, the horrors of war did much to provoke and widen the chasm between the President and his critics, but, as sociologist Seymour Martin Lipset has suggested, the split was also the product of a generation gap in which the young identify with an "ethic of absolute ends" and thus judge society in light of its professed ideals and blemished realities and invariably find it wanting. Neither Johnson nor his more exalted Presidential predecessors could satisfy such lofty standards. Older people, including Johnson and Presidents generally, identify with an "ethic of responsibility," or a willingness to compromise in order to make progress and shoulder, not always gladly, its accompaniments of "deals," manipulations, and dissemblings, accompaniments which offended the activists who prized candor and autonomy.[17]

CRITIC CONSTITUENCIES   In a democratic society observant of civil liberties, the performance of all components of the political system, including the Presidency, is subject to critical review. Several major constituencies provide continuity and expertise in political criticism. For them, criticism is inherent in their function. At the forefront of the critical constituencies are the news media, the clergy, and the intellectual community. From ample experience, the media conclude that their reading and viewing publics are more interested in bad news than good news, a tilt that draws the media into revealing shortcomings and conveying criticisms of officials, including Presidents, and thereby contributing indispensably to democratic purposes. Sometimes the clergy are prominent critics, spurring the President to greater effort, notably in behalf of the abolition of slavery, the realization of modern black civil rights, and other social measures. By the nature of their function, the clergy are disposed to perceive and elucidate the inadequacies of temporary society and to measure them against more demanding spiritual standards. As well, intellectuals—thinkers, writers, artists, scientists, academics—are sensitive to the shortcomings of the existing order, can perceive them more accurately and express them more eloquently than other citizens, and are more keenly and expertly attuned to amelioration.

Of contemporary Presidents, Kennedy fared best with the news media and with intellectuals. He installed several intellectuals and journalists in significant positions in his administration, and he was aided by the fact that the Vietnam War did not assume, in his term, the proportions that later offended sensitive observers.

The President-Constituency Influence Process

The President and his constituencies are mutually dependent; each can do things that will help or hamper the other, and frequently their dealings have the appearance of a quid pro quo. Often their relationships are channeled by common processes, in which the following are major elements:

TARGETS   The President and his constituencies serve as targets to each other, a focus of positive or negative behavior—of petition, influence and support, on the one hand, or attack, rejection, obstruction, on the other. The President is not a solitary target; his White House aides, department secretaries, and the executive bureaucracy are subsidiary targets that constituencies can aim at, to reach the President indirectly. Early in the 1974 "energy crisis," truckers and truck drivers, distressed by lowered speed limits and soaring gasoline prices, blockaded highways and articulated grievances to the Secretary of Transportation as steps toward influencing the President, who could not be reached or pressured directly but whose approval of major revisions of policy was necessary and eventually materialized.

Presidents choose targets from among their constituencies, as Nixon did in advancing his 1974 education proposals. He singled out several targets, soliciting support from some (affirmative targets), and attacking others (negative targets). His message to Congress was tailored to win approval from suburbanites with its high commendation of neighborhood schools where "parents know that the education of their children can most effectively be carried out." Among the targets the President attacked were inner city people, eager for genuine school integration, when he expressed support for antibusing legislation and disparaged "bureaucrats in Washington" who "cannot educate your children" and who must never be placed "in the role of master social planners." [18]

In choosing his affirmative targets, or those whose support he seeks, the President calculates their readiness of response, the compatibility of their needs and aspirations with his own interests, and the likely costs and gains. The greater the costs of influencing the target, the less the President is apt to select it, and his choice is shaped by memories of past constituency performance, or the record of responsiveness to his attentions, and the kinds and amounts of political expenditure required.

CONSTRUCTION OF SOCIAL REALITY   Each of the President's constituencies possesses its own construction of social reality—the beliefs, values, attitudes it holds that provide a frame of reference, a cognitive map for interpreting reality—that guides the exchange of information and influence. [19] Some constituencies depend upon the President, in whole or in part, for information and even for interpretation of reality. The degree of dependence differs sharply among subject matters—typically much less for domestic affairs that constituencies can observe readily and directly, and much more for foreign affairs that are more remote, whose surrounding secrecy curtails constituency scrutiny and therefore enlarges dependence on the President. What passes for "social reality" consists of great chunks of unreality, with the President selecting what he wants to tell and shaping his interpretations according to his interests, while the constituencies, for their part, are disposed to hear what they want to hear, a disposition that itself is a mighty censor of the President's selective interpretations.

But, as befits a democratic political system, the President is subject to constraints even in realms where he enjoys a nearly monopolistic sway over his constituencies' information. Hence, even in the Cuban missile crisis, a situation of acute constituency dependence on the President, Kennedy, as a source of information and interpretation, faced competition from Senators who had their own sources and enjoyed credibility with constituencies. The worst calamity the President can suffer in his role as reporter and interpreter of social reality is the onset of a "credibility gap," his constituencies' loss of confidence in his truthfulness and candor.

The President interprets reality in terms of a constituency's needs and entitlements, and articulates what redress social realities will tolerate and the commitment of his leadership might produce. The President can create demand, arousing among his constituencies a desire for products of his leadership. Toward the black community, for example, Kennedy and Johnson were creators of expectations, formulating goals of betterment and launching programs to obliterate injustices and long-suffered deprivations. In practicing the politics of expectations, Kennedy and Johnson, in addresses and statements, spoke glowingly of the power of their office, its possibilities in the pursuit of heroic goals, its shining historic accomplishments, all of which augured a ready actualization of black people's needs and their leaders' demands.

But, as sometimes happens in the Presidency, Kennedy and Johnson, although providers of sizeable gains, raised expectations that exceeded the political system's capacity to deliver and that spurred black dwellers in the ghettos to overestimate the likely responses to their plight. To a degree, the consequent frustration and despair contributed to the rioting that was costly to themselves and their neighborhoods and which aroused the hostilities of whites.

INFLUENCE MODES   In their dealings and exchanges, the President and his constituencies employ several major modes of influence. His possible choices, for instance, include both *open* and *clandestine* modes. Open modes embrace threats and impositions of punishment and reward as well as the persuasive and dissuasive use of warnings. President Ford, in his initial package of proposals for Congress and the public to adopt to fight inflation and conserve energy, added the admonition, "Now if all of these steps fail to meet our current energy-saving goal I will not hesitate to ask for tougher measures." [20]

Clandestine modes utilize manipulation and concealed assertion for gaining compliant behavior from the target, sometimes without the target's awareness of the source and motive of control. The President employs cues to evoke predictable and what to him are desirable responses. Nixon could cry that the likely grounds offered for his impeachment would constitute a threat to the Presidential office, a contention that could ignite support among many publics for a narrowing of the charges against him, quite apart from the merits of his case. The President can filter information to block the perception of possible alternative actions and to manipulate outcomes that are less than expected constituency gains. Initially, in offering his welfare reform proposals, Nixon projected gains for both the public and the welfare recipient. Later he altered his proposals, stressed "workfare" and took other steps that wrote off the welfare constituency, and appealed to such opposing constituencies as blue collar workers and white suburbanites, whose support Nixon valued as the 1970 elections approached.

In their evaluations of relevant constituency behavior, Presidents as a lot exhibit no clear preference for open or clandestine modes. Kennedy, for one, was suspicious and disparaging of "howlers," particularly in the domain of civil rights, where he felt that some of that genre exploited the issue for self-gain among minority and urban voters in lieu of undertaking the hard work of constructive action.[21]

In their mutual dealings, Presidents and their constituencies also employ *hard* and *soft* modes of influence. Beleaguered by incessant revelations by the news media of Watergate wrongdoings, Nixon exclaimed, in a tense news conference, "I have never heard or seen such outrageous, vicious, distorted reporting in twenty-seven years of public life." Almost invariably, when he dealt with the media, Nixon resorted to the hard modes.

Fortunately, most Presidents are less combative than Nixon, and, ordinarily, constituencies shower a fiercer opprobrium on Presidents than Presidents do on them. Washington, Lincoln, and Jackson were mercilessly vilified, but the all-time record set by a target of sustained punishment is held by Lyndon Johnson, who was repeatedly termed a "murderer" and a full load of synonyms of that condemnation tumbled on him, unloosed even by members of his own party on the floor of the Senate, where, presumably, more than ordinary restraint prevailed. Even his announcement that he would not seek the Presidency again did not diminish the attacks.

At least in their public conduct, Presidents are prone to employ soft modes of influence. Johnson assiduously courted dissidents of the Vietnam War, calling critical reporters into the Oval Office for long talks about the conflict, sugared with hints that his listener might soon be favored with an important exclusive. He sent forth aides for "good talk" with influential groups behind closed doors. He systematically presented his case to selected Congressmen at mealtimes and in a chain of White House receptions.[22] Playing over a broad range of soft modes, Johnson employed ample doses of cajolery, flattery, humor, and favors.

The President and his constituencies employ *offensive* and *defensive* modes of influence toward one another. The first is exemplified by Lyndon Johnson's resolve to liberate the black constituency from enduring racial discrimination and to make the American black a first-class citizen. The resolve launched Johnson on a positive (offensive) civil rights program of legislation and administrative action, unmatched either before or since his Presidency.

In resorting to defensive modes of influence, the Chief Executive enjoys a well-stocked armory of weapons and battle options. A favorite is the flanking movement and strategic retreat, in which Nixon was well-practiced. Rather than engage in frontal combat with hostile constituencies, especially when he was vulnerable, Nixon chose to retreat to more tenable ground, while simultaneously proclaiming his action to be a spectacular advance. Pressed, for example, by critics of the Vietnam War and heavy U.S. defense spending, he began pulling troops out of Vietnam, pared the defense budget and the antiballistic missile program, and reduced American commitments abroad by proclaiming "the Nixon Doctrine." By these modest moves, he kept both doves and hawks tolerably quiet, and, at least for a season, accrued to himself credit for generosity and astute compromise. During the high moment of these maneuvers he appeared virtually as one who had originated the idea of peace in Vietnam and more harmonious relations with the Soviet Union.[23]

Roles

In providing leadership and in otherwise dealing with his constituencies, whether the general public, the electorate, or more specialized components, the President acts through roles, or, in actuality, through a complex of roles that comprise his office. His roles, or patterns of behavior, derive from his major continuing tasks in party affairs, legislation, administration, and diplomacy, among others, which will be examined in subsequent chapters. Since roles tell the individual what he ought to do, the nature of role is crucial for the objective of achieving a strong Presidency that is also compatible with a democratic political system. Roles can be structured in ways consistent with both purposes. Once established, roles must be preserved against destructive activity, whether emanating from Presidential incumbents or their constituencies. Consequently, a Presidential role can be defined as embracing the activity the incumbent would engage in were he to act solely in accord with the essential requirements of a strong, but democratic, Presidency. *Role* is distinguished from *role performance,* or the actual conduct of a President, whose particular behavior will harmonize with, fall below, or sometimes exceed his roles' norms.[24]

A role, including Presidential roles, possesses certain properties. It incorporates rights and obligations, and role performance embraces their assertion and defense, including their expansion, modification, and surrender. Hence, early in the Watergate investigation, President Nixon cited executive privilege, in the broadest imaginable terms, as an inherent right of his office and forbade his White House aides and former aides from testifying before the Senate's Watergate investigating committee. The committee chairman, Sam J. Ervin, Jr. (D-N.C.), and others contended that the President had no power to withhold information and testimony relevant to a committed crime, such as the break-in at the national headquarters of the Democratic party, but an obligation to cooperate in the quest for wrongdoers and lawbreakers. Eventually, Nixon retreated somewhat from his absolute position.

Presidential roles have boundaries, or a range of behavior that conforms with the norms of constitutional democracy. But boundaries are also vague and are therefore subject to manipulation, a condition that strong Presidents are prone to exploit. Fortunately for democracy, and often, too, for the strong Presidency, the Chief Executive is surrounded by boundary-watchers capable of restraining incumbent Presidents within limits of acceptable activity. The Courts provide surveillance of the President's conduct of his office and its accordance with the Constitution and statutes and can checkmate his transgressions. Congress pushes the President to and fro in its quest for acceptable boundaries, resorting to varied tactics that include investigations, overriding his veto, reviewing his appointments and treaties, and even impeachment. Boundaries are political as well as legal. Congress underfunded Johnson's many-faceted social programs, with the implicit rebuke that he was going too far too fast, after which it showered Nixon with more appropriations than he wanted, a remonstrance that he was falling well short of doing enough for the country's serious social problems.

Finally, role is a means of socialization, a regulator of an incumbent President's behavior. Thus the structuring of roles is a principal means of satisfying the requisites of democracy by prescribing specific behavior patterns for which the President is accountable. In roles, his tasks are allocated and defined, and they can be revised, if necessary, to bring the conduct they prescribe more into harmony with democratic ideals. And the constituencies are available to demand and enforce the President's observance of role norms that are also democratic. A constituency such as the courts can press for his deference to the civil liberties protections of the Constitution. Various constituencies can prevent or punish his overindulgence in deception and other acts of that genre that impair both democracy and the strong Presidency. That largest of constituencies, the public at large, can inflict a most devastating penalty by withdrawing its confidence and trust. In ways obvious and subtle, in amounts large and small, the President can suffer the drain of real political power. In effect these are penalties, coupled with democratic socialization, that can befall him for behavior that violates role norms.

The Mass Media

Formulations of ideal democracy accord the communications media an heroic role as purveyors of information to citizens concerning public issues and events and the performance of those who govern. The media are also critics of officials and their work, and this function is indispensable in a democracy, since it serves to actualize a body of informed citizens and fosters the organization and expression of opposing opinions.

How well do the media perform these vital tasks in the context of the Presidency? A study directed by Newton Minow, a former Federal Communications Commission chairman in the Kennedy administration, concluded that one component of the media, television, and the President's towering command of it, have altered the balance of political forces. Most people, it is clear, acquire their information about public affairs not from the press but from television, and deem it the most objective and believable of all the media.[25] Far more than any other national political figure, including leaders of Congress, the President dominates the television airways, and for him the medium is a working tool of fabulous potential. When Lyndon Johnson renounced his candidacy for reelection in 1968, his television audience exceeded seventy-five million. Television enables the President to reach the people, not indirectly through a journalist, but through his own presence and statement.

How do Presidents themselves view the media as organs of power? Near the close of his administration, Johnson told a reporter, "Our most tragic error may have been our inability to establish a rapport and a confidence with the press and television. . . . I don't think the press has understood me." [26] Johnson attributed his failure partly to geography, "to where Mother was living when I was born"—to biases of Eastern reporters toward a Texan in the Presidency, especially since the assassination of his predecessor had taken place in Texas.

But others attributed Johnson's difficulties to the decaying Vietnam War, which increased his vulnerability and his lapses into high-pressure sales pitches to reporters who became resentful of such tactics. Unlike Kennedy and Eisenhower, Johnson was less a chief of state than a chief of government, and the latter role injected him into the manipulation of machinery, into bargaining and propagandizing, and into other soiling activities that were repugnant to reporters. Cherishing secrecy and the element of surprise, he fended off inquiries concerning alternatives he was considering preparatory to decision and discredited stories that would antagonize others or raise expectations that might preclude his own last-minute change of mind. In the phrase of the day, Johnson liked to keep his options open. Above all, he preferred freedom from pressure, to operate the Presidential and governmental machinery according to his own lights, preferences that clashed with democratic openness and the necessities of newsmen. Once Johnson, who was impressed that a wide gap existed between the general success of government and a specific or isolated failure that a newsman might spotlight, complained of the chasm to Henry Luce, publisher of *Time*. "But Mr. President," replied Luce, "good news is no news. Bad news is news." [27]

Communications Experts

Although the President is normally his own best publicity agent, he is assisted by a large and growing staff of communications experts. Presidents got along with a press secretary and a speech-writer or two earlier in this century, but it is possible for a present-day Chief Executive to become an enclave surrounded by communications specialists. Nixon's White House staff included more experts from the worlds of broadcasting, advertising, and public relations than any previous Presidency.

The President's key helper for dealing with the news media is his press secretary, provider of advance texts and reports, daily briefings, and announcements of new policies and aspirations. In confronting reporters, he dodges questions, pleads ignorance, erupts in righteous anger, and stresses positive themes. He helps prepare the President for his news conferences and arranges Presidential meetings with individual reporters and writers. Ideally, he points out lapses to the President, goads him into better effort, and somehow maintains both the President's and the reporters' confidence.

President Johnson was known to employ the same secrecy in dealing with his own press secretaries as he did with reporters. He employed a series of press secretaries—Pierre Salinger, George Reedy, Bill Moyers, and George Christian—which in itself suggests that the function was handled uneasily. Because of his desire to preserve his options, to act only when, politically, he was ready to act, he was largely his own press secretary. The post of press secretary suffered something of a decline, owing to Johnson's working methods. Pierre Salinger, who stayed on with Johnson after service with Kennedy, discovered that he no longer enjoyed the privilege of walking into the President's office at any time to be filled in on matters for the press. His successor, George Reedy, also suffered the uncomfortable experience of working for a chief who did not supply him with the information necessary for his job. It was not until Bill Moyers, Johnson's former chief assistant, took on the added duty of press secretary that the post was finally upgraded. Moyers struggled manfully to set aright Johnson's badly deteriorated press relations. For a time, a new atmosphere of reason and trust prevailed, but it collapsed when reporters perceived that it was the work of Moyers rather than of Johnson. Moyers' successor, George Christian, gained the respect of both warring sides, the President and the press, but unlike Moyers he did not vent to Johnson his disagreements with the President's policies and practice.[28]

Richard Nixon, whose relations with the press plunged to a nadir well below Johnson's, further demoted the press secretary in White House ranking. Ronald Ziegler, who endured in that post, sometimes miraculously, was subordinated to the White House general manager, initially H. R. Haldeman, and later General Alexander Haig. But Ziegler was also a part of Nixon's small inner circle and, after the Watergate scandal erupted, was one of a few who saw the President regularly. Nixon too was secretive toward his press secretary, and Ziegler often had to face the press handicapped by incomplete information.

After serving only a month as press secretary to Gerald Ford, J. F. terHorst resigned, his credibility with reporters having been damaged by the President and the White House staff. Days before Ford granted a full pardon to Richard Nixon, terHorst confidently informed the press that reports that the step was imminent were unfounded. The press secretary's assurances grew from consultations with key White House staff members, who, as events proved, misled him. Earlier terHorst and Ford had pledged a "completely open" White House, a commitment that was mocked by the secrecy of the pardon decision that left the press secretary compromised and dangling. Ruefully, terHorst recalled that he had hoped to persuade his White House staff colleagues that "by being frank with me, I could do a better job of talking with the press." [29]

The News Conference

To reach their publics, most contemporary Presidents rely upon the news conference, an institution that harks back only to the administration of Woodrow Wilson. Soon after his inauguration, reporters gathered by general invitation in his office for a question-and-answer exchange on the administration's business. The reporters assembled with lofty expectations encouraged by Wilson's solemn invocation of "pitiless publicity" for public business in his pre-Presidential writing on political science. The new practice of the press conference replaced the old arrangement by which Presidents had granted interviews only to selected reporters, a tactic permitting favoritism and penalization. In the news conference, reporters enjoy equal footing.

Unfortunately, the sessions under Wilson and his early successors fell far short of the initial optimism. Wilson's glacial reserve inhibited interchange. He was often irritated by the reporters' habit of speculating about the news and of persisting with questions before he was prepared to release information. He considered the reporters' cross-examining a reflection upon his honesty.

The advent of Franklin Roosevelt finally brought the little-tried institution into its own. Roosevelt set up two news conferences a week, canceled his predecessor's requirement of written questions, and with his facile charm turned the sessions into lively occasions on which he provided the public with a running account of what he was doing and what he proposed to do and why.[30] Eisenhower permitted the innovation of televising his news conferences and presenting them, with minor editing, to the public. With John Kennedy there was no editing; the televised presentation was made exactly as his encounters with the reporters occurred. Kennedy's news conferences were highly effective, his responses to questions revealing an almost photographic memory for detail and a gift for keeping abreast of policy development from incubation to implementation. His brisk assurance and his opening statements charged with newsworthy content lent zest and excitement to his administration.

Kennedy's news conferences took place in the vast State Department auditorium, with about three hundred newsmen on hand. Millions of citizens later took in the half-hour's proceedings on television and radio. Although superficially the news conference appeared informal and off-the-cuff, Kennedy, like his predecessors, did considerable preparing beforehand. He and his aides engaged in intensive pondering to anticipate the questions. His wide reading of newspapers and magazines and his listening to broadcasts apprised him of the mental stirrings of the journalists and therefore of what they were apt to ask. On the afternoon before the conference, the President's press secretary, Pierre Salinger, summoned the information chiefs of the executive departments to his White House office to share their experiences of the past week with press inquiries. On the day of the news conference Salinger, with his sundry notes, breakfasted with the President. Also partaking of the meal were Secretary of State Dean Rusk; Walter Heller, chairman of the Council of Economic Advisers; Theodore Sorensen, the President's counsel; McGeorge Bundy, assistant for national security affairs; and Myer Feldman, deputy counsel. The breakfast group canvassed the news questions that occurred to them and supplied Kennedy with data for answers.[31]

President Johnson, who excelled more in conversation and in encounters with small groups than in large, formal presentations, was always seeking for the most suitable forum for his news conferences. He tried such places as the vast, windowless, international conference room of the State Department; the New York World's Fair; a two-mile walk; his own office; the office of the White House press secretary; the cabinet room; the LBJ ranch; and the East Room, the White House's largest and most formal room, where reporters sat on gilt chairs in a semicircle around the President, who stood in front of a golden drapery flanked by huge portraits of George and Martha Washington. A talker rather than a performer, Johnson fared best in a setting where he was most natural.

For Nixon, the new conference was both a useful arrangement and an object of neglect. Despite a pre-Presidential background of pugnacious press relations, Nixon in his early months as President conducted highly effective news conferences. Employing a stand-up format, with only a microphone between himself and reporters instead of the usual podium or desk, Nixon was deft at analyzing ideas and issues and persuasive in presenting his program.[32] But he soon allowed the news conference to languish into disuse, a pattern that deepened as his tenure wore on. Thus, in 1971, he permitted ad hoc questioning by the White House press on only nine occasions, compared with an annual average of twenty-four to thirty-six by Presidents over the past quarter century. During the Watergate crisis his news conferences became even less frequent.

Nixon's original withdrawal from news conferences coincided with the advent of the first major controversies of his administration: Clement Haynsworth's nomination for the Supreme Court, school desegregation, and the war in Vietnam. Even more than Johnson, Nixon was rankled by criticism, but his rationale for constraining it was different. Nixon regarded reporters as personal adversaries who were threatening, prosecuting in intent, and conspiratorial in method. As Chief Executive, he likened himself to a corporation president who dealt with the press only through public relations assistants.

For both democracy and the Nixon Presidency, his disuse of news conferences had serious costs: important issues and events came and went without public comment from the President—the India-Pakistan War, the release of Jimmy Hoffa from prison, increasing budget deficits, and the rising crime rate. Reticence deprived Nixon of a weapon that compels the bureaucracy to supply the President with reports and explanations of its lapses in policy making and implementation.[33]

In contrast, Gerald Ford, aspiring to an "open Presidency," a reversal of Nixon's seclusiveness, reverted to more frequent conferences, sometimes before a symbolic open door in the background, and selected his questioners from a balanced mix of men, women, blacks, young and old, old hands and new among White House reporters. He called those with journalistic specialties in for smaller conferences and held impromptu meetings. Instead of Nixon's bitterness toward the press, Ford radiated friendliness.[34]

For all its slow start and erratic progress, the Presidential news conference occupies a vital place in American political life. It is the only regular occasion on which the nation can view the Chief Executive in an active interchange with people outside his administration and without the props of speech writers and idea men. The sessions are also invaluable opportunities for the President to present his opinions and raise trial balloons. He can be sure that what he wants to say gets said by having it arranged beforehand for a reporter to ask a convenient question—a planted question—an old, productive device. The President can easily dodge and parry questions; no mere reporter can nail an incumbent of the awesome office to the wall. But despite its faults, the news conference merits jealous vigilance to assure its perpetuation.

The Art of News Management

In the estimation of political analyst Arthur Krock, the Kennedy administration practiced the art of news management "boldly," "cynically," and "with the utmost subtlety and imagination." The reward of this effort, Krock contended, was a portrayal of the administration in the press with a radiant aura of approval that neither its achievement nor the country's circumstances warranted. In the Kennedy era, as in other eras, many critics voiced concern for the continued integrity of Thomas Jefferson's dictum that the people have a right to "full information of their affairs thro' the channel of the public papers." [35]

News management, which is a craft of many tricks, can cultivate the image of the President as infallible even in the face of flagrant error. If things go wrong, blame is placed upon others, usually his subordinates. A major tool of news management is the use of selective personal patronage, whereby those reporters who "behave," or write favorably of the administration, are granted privileges unavailable to their fellows. Thus Stewart Alsop and Charles Bartlett, coauthors of a widely noticed magazine article on the Cuban crisis, which could not have been undertaken without the unparalleled privilege of access to National Security Council proceedings, were candidly referred to by the President in a news conference as "old friends." Another plum was a 1962 year-end informal televised interview of the President by three cooperative reporters covering an extraordinary range of subjects and witnessed by a vast audience. A contrasting and less selective Kennedy tactic was the use of "social flattery," by which a succession of groups of editors and publishers were feted at the White House. Over several months, for example, the President had to luncheon eight editors from Florida, a throng of New Jersey publishers, and twenty-four publishers and news executives from the state of Washington. Kennedy reached reporters and editors on a large scale in occasional intimate, far-ranging background briefings. The press participants emerged, Krock observed, "in a state of protracted enchantment evoked by the President's charm and the awesome aura of his office." The mood carried over into the news columns and editorials.[36]

News management was not a creation of the Kennedy administration, however. It is an ancient and common practice of the Presidency. Management assumes a variety of forms, from the complex to the simple little expedient Chester A. Arthur employed to present to his critics the appearance of being busy. Having a large reputation for indolence, Arthur maintained a "property basket" filled with official-looking documents that a secretary would carry into the President's office when he was with visitors to create the impression of industry.[37]

MANAGEMENT BY THREAT   In the Nixon era, news management evolved into new forms, clearly directed toward Presidential domination of the media. The fact that Nixon appeared on prime time television more than any other President, and during some intervals more than Eisenhower, Kennedy, and Johnson combined, did not allay his displeasure with the networks.[38] Through a variety of means, the Nixon administration moved to become the first in Presidential experience to impose prior restraint on news reporting, an objective that violates the First Amendment and the civil libertarian base of American democracy.

In its several moves, the Nixon administration used the subpoena power to force reporters to turn over their raw notes. The administration opposed a shield bill before Congress that had been advanced by press and television representatives to protect the confidentiality of news sources. The director of the White House Office of Telecommunications Policy, Clay T. Whitehead, drafted and ardently promoted a broadcast license-renewal bill that would hold local television stations accountable for the balance and taste of all network news and entertainment programs they broadcast. In effect, local stations were to censor network programing. "Who else but [station] management," Whitehead asked, "can or should correct so-called professionals . . . who dispense elitist gossip in the guise of news analysis?"

The administration's influence and pressures took on many shadings. Herbert G. Klein, Director of Communications, acknowledged that the White House occasionally telephoned television stations to ask what their editorial treatment of a Presidential action or policy would be. Klein once stressed that "All of the news media needs to reexamine itself in the format it has and its approach to problems of news to meet the current issues of the day. . . . if you look at the problems you have today and you fail to continue to examine them, you do invite the Government to come in. I would not like to see that happen."[39] Another White House communications specialist, Patrick Buchanan, proposed antitrust action against the networks in order to overcome what he beheld as widely prevalent antiadministration tendencies.[40]

Himself a close monitor of the media and their "biases," President Nixon was a fertile source of counterstrokes. He requested a White House aide to generate letters to *Newsweek* magazine detailing his "tremendous reception" in a visit to Mississippi and at a professional football game in Miami. Another time he directed his aide, Herbert G. Klein, to "have the *Chicago Tribune* hit Senator [Charles H.] Percy hard on his ties with the peace group." A log of the President's requests for the month between mid-September and mid-October

1969 reveals that he spurred complaints about coverage that were lodged with all three commercial television networks as well as with *Time, Newsweek, Life,* and with columnist Jack Anderson. Although nearly "double or triple" the total of the President's requests were made by others in the White House, an aide, in a comprehensive memorandum reviewing the media problem, concluded that this "shotgunning" was not really effective, that the administration could better "get the media" if it used harrassment by the Internal Revenue Service and the Antitrust Division of the Justice Department.[41] But the President's principal avenging angel was Vice President Spiro Agnew, who regularly blasted network commentators.

THE PEOPLE'S RIGHT TO KNOW   The sorties of various Presidents into the fine, and sometimes dark, art of news management raise difficult but basic questions involving democratic values and practices. In deciding what to tell the nation, the President must strike a balance between the people's right to know what their government is doing and planning, the nation's safety and welfare (which may not always be served by disclosure), and his own political interests. Disclosures to the public might embarrass our relations with a friendly nation. But secrecy also may do nothing more than enable him to make gross errors in solitude. The opinion has been expressed, and Kennedy agreed with it, that less official secrecy and more publicity before the invasion of Cuba at the Bay of Pigs might have saved the nation from that debacle.[42] Clearly beyond the pale of tolerance in a democratic system is governmental intimidation of the news media and the imposition of censorship, including the media's self-censorship spurred by governmental pressure.

No neat formula for resolving the dilemma of secrecy versus disclosure can be constructed that would be meaningful or useful. The choices must be worked out in specific instances, with careful sensitivity for democratic necessities. Fortunately, the President has no monopoly of power or influence on this difficult terrain and can be buffeted toward a different course by those who raise their voices in criticism: legislators, group interest leaders, prestigious private individuals, and the press. In confronting the ways and wiles of the Chief Executive in managing the news, the press is not without defenses; it mustered sufficient strength to withstand the most concentrated onslaught yet launched, that of the Nixon Presidency. Against lesser, more usual pressures, if the press is alert and professionally responsible it should be able to cope with the President's slickest manipulations. The media can, with ingenuity and enterprise, do their share of "managing" as well. They can, if they choose, put before the public an impression of the Chief Executive that is utterly contrary to reality. The newspapers converted the dour, colorless, futile Calvin Coolidge into a forceful, red-blooded, two-fisted, strong and silent "sage of Vermont," a man who never was. They can oppose and harass the President and overlook every shred of merit his administration possesses. Many of the most powerful press organs of Lincoln's day, for example, fought his administration without letup. "Mr. Lincoln deemed it more important to secure the [New York] *Herald*'s support than to obtain a victory in the field," explained Thurlow Weed, the administration's principal intermediary with the newspaper.[43]

The President as Consensus Leader

The President, in his cumulative roles of chieftain of party, Congress, administration, and public opinion, tends to conform to two general patterns of leadership: leadership by consensus and majoritarian leadership. A given President may first veer toward one pattern and then toward the other.

The most common form of Presidential leadership is rooted in the politics of consensus. According to Lyndon Johnson, one of its most thoroughgoing practitioners, there is for every national problem a national answer that reasonable men can construct through discussion and accommodation. The national answer is not simply what the majority wants. Majorities are transitory and ought not to dominate the minority whose thought and action too might contribute valuably to consensus.

To produce consensus and action rather than disagreement and inaction, the President is at the center of the effort, possessing political means capable of invoking a fundamental unity of interest, purpose, and belief in all the nation. As a consensus leader, the President formulates goals having the broadest possible appeal and charts the route to them by offering the specifics of immediate action. The President tends to undertake what Johnson liked to call the "doable"—or that for which there are enough votes or support, a consensus. The President extends the scope of consensus by discovering and developing common denominators of agreement. Prior to the Education Act of 1965, bills providing general aid to education were steadily wrecked on the issue of public aid to church-supported schools. Through discussions with the National Education Association and the National Catholic Welfare Council, the Johnson administration developed a formula acceptable to both groups: to aid not schools as such but their children, whether in public or private schools, and especially in poor areas. With the two major education lobbies brought into a consensus, the administration incorporated the new-found formula into its education bill with an eye to securing maximum votes in Congress. The bill passed without major amendment and a political deadlock that had endured for decades was finally overcome.

The President who is a consensus leader uses his powers with restraint and prefers bipartisan support to partisan strife. For the legislative achievements of his Presidency, including its remarkable record in the Eighty-ninth Congress, Johnson was careful to give credit to the minority Republican party and to praise Congress. The consensus President also seeks to broaden the base of his party by making it a party "which serves all our people." [44]

But the consensus approach, even in the hands of its most devoted Presidential practitioners, carries certain weaknesses. When the hard business of constructing policy reaches the phase of choosing between competing interests, men divide, partisanship rises, and agreement is lost to conflict. Johnson was bedeviled by breakdowns or the sheer unavailability of consensus in the perversity of Ho Chi Minh in the Vietnam war, in the rioting in American cities, and in the unwillingness of Congress to flesh out his Great Society programs with substantial appropriations.

The Majoritarian President

Instead of pursuing the consensus method, a President may act as a majoritarian leader who is prepared to take up, if necessary, the politics of combat. He puts himself at the head of a program behind which he rallies majority support and moves toward his goal by persuasion, manipulation, and conflict. His program is more definite and stable than the offerings of the consensus President, and his administration has more of an ideological coloring or emphasis. Andrew Jackson constructed a majority following and, among other things, engaged in a full struggle with the Second Bank of the United States, an agency of largely private economic power and regional rule.

The President who chooses the majoritarian path and the politics of combat uses different methods and resources than the consensus President and applies different values. The program or purpose of the majoritarian President takes precedence over the claims of his individual supporters. If a particular supporting group rejects portions of his program, he will hold to it and try to push it through, hoping that his remaining supporters still add up to a majority. He will take up causes in the full anticipation that in doing so the wrath of powerful groups will tumble down upon his head. Harry Truman pursued a strong response to the Soviet Union in the general deterioration of U.S.-U.S.S.R. relations following the Second World War, even though it meant the alienation of Henry A. Wallace and other influential New Dealers and the loss of a substantial heritage of political support left by his predecessor, Franklin Roosevelt. Truman offered a national health program even though he knew he would earn the unflagging opposition of the American Medical Association.

The majoritarian President who takes up the politics of combat tends to use certain resources of his office more than others. He is apt to "go to the people" to "educate" them on the issues, and, he hopes, to rally them to his side in the strife. He uses the veto power more, not simply to resist and reject, but as a dramatic weapon that serves well to identify him with his cause. His discourse carries a strong vocabulary and he is prone to be mercilessly specific in identifying his enemies. Harry Truman startled his whistle-stop audiences in the 1948 campaign by attacking the "bloodsuckers of Wall Street." An even more useful "enemy" in that election was the Republican Eightieth Congress, labeled the "Do-Nothing Congress."

The majoritarian President is willing to lose battles in order eventually to win wars, even those where, in the final moment of victory, he may no longer be in office and another may bask in the success that rose from his efforts. He takes a broad view of success and is willing to sustain defeat as the price for changing, or setting into motion the forces that may change, the country's prevailing opinion. He appeals to emotion as much as to rationality and is apt to view Presidential politics as not simply a continuing dialogue, seeking adjustments and accommodations, but as an enterprise analogous to a military campaign, with strategies and maneuvers, and fierce clashes of those with opposing interests.

The Future Presidency

The strong President has the gift of rallying public opinion, of bringing it to perceive the nation's problems and interest and the rightness of his measures. But public opinion, speaking through public and private leaders, through the communications media, and through the electorate, can also reach the President. Democracy requires this two-way flow of information and ideas, which makes the following questions crucial: How are the channels of communication and exchange to be kept in optimum working order? How, on the one hand, is the future President to be strong in his high task of educating and rallying the public? And how, on the other hand, is he to be subject, as befits democracy, to the competition of other political leaders, particularly on television, and to ideas and policy alternatives emanating from sources other than his own?

1. Toward such ends, the television roles of Congress and the opposition party might be expanded. The Congressional houses should permit televised coverage, scheduled several or more times a year, in prime-time evening sessions, during which important issues would be discussed and voted on. Both here-and-now problems and likely longer-term questions could appear on the agenda.

The national committee of the opposition party should be given, by law, the right of response to any Presidential radio and television address. Upon request, the networks would be obliged to provide equal broadcast opportunities and free time, if the President's time was free. Incidental Presidential appearances in documentaries and newscasts would be exempted from this right. The national committee would choose one or more spokesmen, would possess the same control over format as the President, and would not be limited to issues raised by the President.[45]

2. The slender interest of the viewing public in televised political programs might be enhanced by use of the debate format, on the order of the 1960 Kennedy-Nixon "Great Debates" that drew huge audiences. The debate could deal with both present and future issues, with the participants chosen by the na-

tional party committees, whose interest would be to provide arresting personalities and accomplished debaters. The proposal would encourage the parties to develop positions on serious issues and to become more responsive to changes in public sentiment. If, as often happens, the President's party is divided on an issue, it could conceivably oppose his policies in these ''national debates.'' Something of the imbalance between the President's domination of television relative to the opposition party could thus be redressed.

3. If the President wants to communicate effectively, he will need speech writers and other aids of whom at least some are not public relations professionals. The professional's attachment to the status quo and his tendency to subordinate policy to image mean that the President will need a representation of communications people of altogether different backgrounds—men like Samuel Rosenman, a lawyer of wide public experience who was a draftsman for Franklin Roosevelt; Malcolm Moos of the academic community, who served Eisenhower; or Theodore Sorensen, Kennedy's draftsman, whose background combined law and politics.

4. To promote the purposes of this chapter a variety of legal changes to ease the flow of information to the public are necessary. The Chief Justice Earl Warren Conference on Advocacy urged the establishment of a national journalists' privilege to exempt reporters from compulsion to reveal the sources of information gained in confidence, abolition of all governmental power to regulate program content on television and radio, creation of an independent agency to review national security documents to determine if the classification system is being abused, a requirement that the government pay costs for successful information suits, and that government be forced to justify the withholding of any portion of a document. The urgency of these proposals is spurred by the darkening clouds of uncertainty over freedom of information created by the Watergate cover-up and the 1972 Supreme Court ruling that journalists possess no right under the First Amendment to withhold confidential information from grand juries.[46]

6

PARTY CHIEF

If there is an aspect of the Presidency that is hobbled by uncertainty and frailty it is the office's uncertain specifications for the role of party leader. The President is largely deprived of the advantage of strong party organization that the heads of other governments enjoy; the American national party organizations are strikingly weak. Parties are the best political invention yet struck by the mind of man to stabilize political influence and to transpose promises into policy. Yet little of the invention and less of its fruits are made available to the President, and even to the extent that they are, he may be disinclined to use them. Richard Nixon conducted his 1972 reelection campaign through a personal organization and almost wholly ignored the Republican party. The result was his overwhelming victory and, simultaneously, the near undoing of his subsequent administration. For so corrupt and criminal was his personal organization, committing misdeeds that could hardly have transpired in a national party structure, that Nixon himself was overtaken by the threatening shadow of impeachment. In 1972, what might be termed the Presidential party superseded the national party, which eased the way for Watergate, since the Presidential party does not possess the potent internal checks provided by the national party—the largely autonomous Congressional, state, and local organizations and leaders that could have questioned and limited the Watergate malfeasances more readily than the controlled and acquiescent Presidential party.

The President and His Party

Under more normal circumstances, the major American party does well as a vehicle of power and badly as a vehicle of policy. The contemporary President who abides by democratic norms needs both these means of political success in steady quantity. But while the party can serve the President well as a campaign organ to bring himself and his party brethren into office and as a forum for broadcasting his platform to the people, it serves him ill in transposing his campaign promises into law. American parties, unlike those of any other major nation, fail to stabilize the Chief Executive's impact on policy making. His party

115

capacity endows him with only a fraction of the strength that the British Prime Minister has to transform campaign promises into established policy.

The lack of an effective national party institution forces the President into a heavy dependency upon his personal skills as party leader and makes the use of a personal organization tempting. His ability as a manipulator of party resources, such as funds and organization, and his exploitation of passing advantages produced by political events and circumstance are keys to his success as party leader. A few Presidents, notably endowed with party skills or favored by exceptional circumstances, have reaped impressive political harvests as party leaders. They have dominated the governmental machinery and scored glittering legislative victories. But because success in party leadership depends so heavily upon personal skill, the role has never stabilized. One President who excels as party leader has never been followed by another who even approximates his predecessor's accomplishment.

The party role was plastered onto the Presidential office after the main structure was built. The Founding Fathers made no provision for parties in the Constitution, and their later emergence was attended with awkwardness. Although parties appeared in Washington's time, he abstained from functioning as party leader, deeming it incompatible with the nature of his office. For his successor, John Adams, the party was not an adjunct of the Presidential office but an instrument that his political enemies employed against him. Under Jefferson, Jackson, and a sprinkling of their successors, party leadership flourished, but it has flourished even more in the states and localities, in the hands of governors, mayors, and local politicians.

The President's uneasy party role is aggravated by the continual tension between his responsibilities to his office and the claims of his party. His office, and therefore its duties and problems, presumably exceed any obligation the party can impose upon him. He is a politician who must also be a statesman. Yet the party often insistently violates this assumption. Senate Republicans, blithely heedless of President Eisenhower's struggle with great and manifold problems of state, required him to work in harness with their chosen leader, William F. Knowland, who opposed most of his foreign and much of his domestic policy. President Kennedy was expected, at the first electoral opportunity, to stump against Senator Everett Dirksen, Republican leader, who had provided indispensable support for the test ban treaty and a string of other important measures.

The tension between office and party is heightened by the party's and the President's almost frivolous disregard of their obligations to each other. He may by splendid electoral triumph plant the party standard in the White House and carry many a legislative party colleague on his coattails across the victory line only to see his proposals spurned, sometimes seriatim, by a Congress whose two houses his party controls. President Truman, despite his stunning electoral victory in 1948, which restored the Democrats to power in both Congressional houses, was able to obtain in the ensuing session the enactment of only several of a score of Fair Deal measures. President Kennedy, who summoned his fellow Democrats on Capitol Hill to rally behind an ambitious and popular program, did little better. He could well paraphrase for his own party role the memorable instruction of his inaugural address, "Ask not what your party can do for you; ask what you can do for your party."

President Eisenhower, just before his spectacular reelection victory in 1956, was questioned pointedly concerning the affinity of several old guard Republican Senators to his own Modern Republicanism. His perceptive response suggested several limits the President suffers as party chief. Eisenhower said,

> Now, let's remember there are no national parties in the United States. There are forty-eight state parties, then they are the ones that determine the people that belong to those parties. There is nothing I can do to say that [anyone] is not a Republican. The most I can say is that in many things they do not agree with me. . . . We have got to remember that these are state organizations, and there is nothing I can do to say so-and-so is a Republican and so-and-so is not a Republican.[1]

The President is an uncertain monarch of a loose and far-flung party empire of several satrapies and dependencies and a host of self-governing commonwealths. His sway is full over a few parts; over most it is little or nonexistent. He is a chief among chiefs. The local and state party organizations are beyond his control and are subject, at most, to his influence. The major parties function as viable national organizations only quadrennially, when their state and local parts more or less unite to win the Presidency and its stakes of power. Thereafter the parts conduct themselves with jealously preserved autonomy. The state and local organizations command a solid corps of workers and followers, assert their own discipline, control the selection of Senatorial and Congressional candidates, and possess financial resources of their own. The Senate and House of Representatives maintain a quantity of party organizations: caucuses, steering committees, campaign committees, and policy committees. Senators and Congressmen render their principal allegiance not to the Chief Executive but to the state and local organizations to which they owe their nomination and election. Legislators of the President's party both help and hobble his program of legislation. The fact that an Eastland and a Church march under the Democratic banner and a Tower and a Javits under the Republican demonstrates how undependable the party label is as a guide to how legislators debate and vote. Nowhere in the vast party structure is there a constant and effective source of power that the President can confidently turn to for support. The national committee, where his strength is greatest and where the state and local organizations converge, is chiefly concerned with the choice and election of the Presidential candidate.

The unreliability of his party, the likelihood that numbers of its Congressional members may oppose him, must lead any President to ponder privately just what good his party really is to him. Indeed, if he reads the texts of Presidential history, he will discover that Presidents achieve many, if not most, of their important policies and programs, whether in domestic or foreign affairs, only with bipartisan support. The loyalty of his own party is never so dependable that it can assure a succession of program victories. This undependability makes it necessary for the President studiously to cultivate support in the opposition party. His own party's ambiguity of support promotes the President's necessary ambiguity as party leader. For his program's sake, he must not be so fiercely and devotedly the leader of his own party as to preclude his gaining support from the opposition.

The case for the President to treat his party role pragmatically and to conduct himself in a fashion that will pick up support beyond his party can be made in another way. The President, is brought into office by a popular vote that is greater than his party vote. His electoral majority is a patchwork of voters from his own party, from the opposition party, and from the steadily growing body of "independents." He may have large support from big groups such as organized labor and national and racial groups. His own party may have chosen him as its standard-bearer principally because of his presumed ability to attract broad support. Ironically, the Republican party denied Robert A. Taft its nomination because he was too much a Republican ("Mr. Republican," in fact), and therefore thought unable to lure Democratic and independent voters into his column. Without substantial outside support, he could not possibly have become a winner.

The President and Vice President are the only officers chosen by a national popular majority. In seeking to convert his promises to that majority into policy, the President is frustrated by the skillful arrangement of the governmental structure that permits what at most can be only limited majority rule. The system of checks and balances enables Congress, which is a series of disparate local majorities, to reject what the President, the voice of a national majority, purposes. The weakness of the parties assures that the principle of checks and balances, and therefore limited majority rule, will enjoy the full play the Founding Fathers intended. Congress's local constituencies, in contrast to the President's national constituency and Congress's internal organization (its powerful committees with chairmen chosen by seniority), tend to produce a legislature and an executive of dissimilar policy outlooks, even when the same party controls both branches. Contemporary Democratic Presidents have been more progressive than Democratic Congresses, and the single Republican President, Eisenhower, who, for a time, had a Republican Congress, was more "moderate," or "progressive," than his party's legislators.

The President is forced by checks and balances and party weakness to scramble for support by a variety of expedients. He must court approval in both Congressional parties. He may endeavor as best he can to dominate portions of his own party by building alliances with state and local leaders and by discreetly influencing the choice of legislative candidates. He may rely heavily on his own personal organization—if he has one—to make his way in party affairs. He can move to change the popular base of his party by extending it to groups to whose interests his program is akin. Desperation is nowhere else so much the mother of invention as it is in the Chief Executive's party plight.

The Presidential Nominee

Even in its most serviceable roles—selecting the Presidential nominee and conducting the electoral campaign—the party's relation with its chosen candidate is uneasy and imperfect. The party provides no assurance that the platform he runs on accords with his wishes. His ability to make his preferences prevail depends upon a complex of factors—the power of his rivals, the nature of the issues, his own general political health. Franklin Roosevelt could confidently expect that the Democratic convention of 1936 would approve the platform prepared under his supervision. "I would like to have as short a platform as possible this year," he instructed his draftsmen, "and . . . I would like to have it based on the sentence of the Declaration of Independence, 'We hold these truths to be self-evident.' " [2] The convention approved the several parts of the Roosevelt-made platform with waves of ovations.

Grover Cleveland in 1888 had more difficulty. The tariff was the prickly issue of the day between progressives and conservatives, and the President's general political situation was not without weakness. Cleveland himself drafted the platform, carefully stating in moderate language the tariff question. For the sake of his own political necessities, Cleveland wished to provide the Republicans no opportunity to charge the Democratic party with free-trade principles. At the St. Louis convention, unfortunately for Cleveland, the low tariff men unshackled their bonds. They and Cleveland's emissaries of moderation were about evenly divided on the platform subcommittee on the tariff. The subcommittee met at dusk in a steaming room of the Southern Hotel and fought over the issue all night. The free-trade men, led by Henry Watterson, the Kentucky editor, ultimately prevailed.[3] In the ensuing election, tariff reform became the leading issue, and, although the election did not turn on the issue, Benjamin Harrison, staunch defender of the tariff, defeated Cleveland.

Many a Presidential nominee views the available party organization as an enterprise of limited dependability and feels it the better part of wisdom to build a personal organization to conduct much of the postconvention campaign. John Kennedy relied upon an elaborate personal organization, consisting of his brothers, his brothers-in-law, a cadre of aides from his earliest political campaigns, and several members of the Harvard faculty, among others. In 1972, Richard Nixon conducted his campaign through a personal organization so complete and so pervasive that for him the Republican party almost need not have existed.

The Presidential nominee may be driven to build up a personal organization by the fickleness of state and local party organizations in providing support. Instead of devoting their resources in a substantial way to his race, they may concentrate upon local campaigns, especially in years when the Presidential nominee is deemed a likely loser. Adlai Stevenson, who campaigned under such circumstances, resorted to a trifurcated organization in 1956. In addition to the regular national party organization, a Stevenson-Kefauver Committee appeared in Washington, headed by James A. Finnegan, Stevenson's campaign director, and housed across the street from Democratic headquarters. A third organization was Volunteers for Stevenson, whose province was the independent voter. The poverty of support that the regular party organization gave Stevenson made his decision in behalf of a personal organization eminently wise. The duplication of the Stevenson experience in other similar episodes raises a strong suspicion that a Presidential nominee cannot securely depend upon the regular organization unless his victory appears clear and imminent. In such a happy eventuality, when Senatorial and Congressional candidates eagerly press to ride his coattails, the Presidential nominee might be able to bar access to that privileged place to those whose known positions on policy promise to make them future saboteurs of his program. If the Presidential nominee distributed his support selectively at this juncture, he might gain more than by applying gentle pressures at the midterm elections when there are no Presidential coattails and his power is consequently very much reduced. Nowadays the legislative campaign committees of the President's party insist that he hit the campaign trail in Congressional elections. His cabinet Secretaries are expected to take their full turn too.

But the President works with something less than total ease and comfort with the Congressional and Senatorial campaign committees of his party. The midterm election is often a season for exposing divergences in the policy views of the President and legislators of his party. The lengths to which the malaise may go was suggested in a remarkable statement by Republican Congressional campaign committee chairman Richard M. Simpson of Pennsylvania, in 1958. Republican candidates, Simpson counseled, should forget about Eisenhower's favor in the 1958 elections and "make known" to voters any "disagreement with the President's policies." Simpson, a conservative Republican, often opposed the President's Modern Republicanism.[4]

Despite the varying cordiality of the invitations he receives, the President has for many years now led the party in Congressional elections. The results, like the invitations, are mixed. Woodrow Wilson began the practice by appealing for a Democratic Congress in 1918, with a disheartening result. His party lost control of both houses. Franklin Roosevelt launched his purge in 1938, for which the electorate slapped him hard. Not only did the purge fail, but the Democrats lost the incredible total of seventy seats in the House and seven in the Senate. In the 1966 Congressional elections Lyndon Johnson apparently concluded that he could help the Democratic cause most by staying away from the campaign trail and attending to his official duties. Many of his party's candidates for state and national office concurred in his judgment. The President and his policies at the time were sagging in popularity. In the South Johnson was a symbol of desegregation, which many local politicians in both major parties were profitably exploiting. His coming as a campaigner would only spur their attacks upon desegregation as a local political issue. Elsewhere he symbolized an unwanted war, mounting prices, and the bane of neglected farmers. Many a Congressional race seemed to turn on local issues and personality contests in which the President's influence was irrelevant.

Richard Nixon, in the 1970 Congressional elections, presented an opposite picture of hyper-involvement, stumping in twenty-two states and following up Vice President Spiro Agnew, who bombarded the Democrats with heavy rhetorical cannonade. In hard campaigning, Nixon toiled to secure an "ideological majority" in Congress to reflect a presumed conservative majority in the country, and he worked heartily for conservative Republicans like Senators Winston Prouty of Vermont and George Murphy of California and against such liberal Democratic Senators as Albert Gore of Tennessee and Vance Hartke of Indiana. The President endeavored to bring into the Senate conservative candidates like Cramer of Florida, Brock of Tennessee, Roudebush of Indiana, and Wold of Wyoming, while undercutting a liberal Republican like Charles Goodell of New York and supporting the Conservative party nominee, James Buckley. In the 1974 Congressional elections, Gerald Ford toiled overtime for Republican candidates and warned of the dangers of a "veto-proof" Democratic Congress.

On occasion the President undertakes a further function in Congressional elections. His encouragement may be vital to inducing able citizens to become their party's nominees for legislative office. The national Republican chairman, Leonard Hall, concluded in 1956 that John Sherman Cooper, then ambassador to India, was urgently needed to run for the Senate in Kentucky. Cooper had triumphed in the Senate race in 1952, but in 1956 he was unwilling to sacrifice contentment in India for the travail of a Senate race. Eisenhower, who thought it inappropriate for the President to persuade anyone to run for office, was pressed to take on Cooper by both Hall and Presidential Assistant Sherman Adams, who had tried and failed. Cooper was brought to Eisenhower's office, and the President, who never did ask him to run, spoke eloquently of the opportunity for service in the Senate. Cooper capitulated, ran, and won.[5]

Winning Renomination

The most important of a President's personal political objectives, needless to say, is securing renomination, and normally, the party almost automatically grants this Presidential wish. Even the likelihood of defeat may not bar his renomination, as it did not for Hoover in 1932. Yet a few Presidents, such as Pierce, Buchanan, and Arthur, were denied renomination, and Benjamin Harrison achieved it only after a hard struggle.

Chester Arthur, who became President upon Garfield's assassination, failed to be renominated, although he approached the Chicago convention of 1884 with imposing credentials. Old-line political leaders, independents, and liberals all endorsed him. George William Curtis, distinguished reformer and old-time foe, wrote enthusiastically, "I say that a President whose accession by means of a most tragical event was generally regarded as a serious misfortune, if not calamity, has not only allayed all apprehension, but his pacific and temperate Administration has gained the general approval of the country." Henry Ward

Beecher declared, "I can hardly imagine how he could have done better." And Mark Twain proclaimed, "It would be hard to better President Arthur's Administration." [6]

Arthur's defeat for renomination was the product of his alienation of key factions and bosses, his consequent weakness in key states, and poor convention strategy. A Stalwart, he acted moderately toward the Half-Breeds, the faction of James A. Garfield, his predecessor. Arthur's conciliation was resented by his own Stalwarts as ingratitude and weakness. Garfield men in Ohio, for all of Arthur's consideration, remained cool. Former governor Charles Foster bludgeoned the Arthur movement by declaring that Arthur would be "a very weak candidate in Ohio." In New York, Arthur's own state, Whitelaw Reid and Thomas C. Platt, ancient foes, united for a common cause against Arthur. Platt, having had small success with the Arthur administration in its dispensations of patronage, now believed that Arthur's rival, James G. Blaine's, "turn had come." The upshot was a badly divided New York delegation. Blaine went into the convention with a plurality, but not a majority, of the delegates. Arthur's convention campaign, which with modest skill might have weaved together a victory, was badly managed. The nominating speeches in his behalf were downright inferior. His managers were dull and laggard in fashioning deals with rival factions. "The management of Mr. Arthur's canvass here was a botch from beginning to end," an aide wrote. [7]

Both more difficult and more successful than Arthur's ordeal was Truman's quest for renomination in 1948, which he achieved in a steep uphill fight by a combination of pluck and luck. Before the convention, Truman's political stock was at rock bottom. The Republican Congressional victory in 1946 foreshadowed a Republican Presidential victory in 1948. Scandals had crashed upon the administration in waves. Henry A. Wallace had broken off from the Democratic party and announced his Presidential candidacy. Labor and New Deal liberals were restive, and Southern Democrats stood at the brink of revolt. Truman's popularity in the opinion polls had fallen dismally. To hold back the avalanche, Truman, in January of 1948, used his State of the Union message to project a platform for his party. The message recapitulated a quantity of Fair Deal proposals with a request for an improbable tax cut thrown in. Truman's choice of theme sought to hold together the crumbling Roosevelt Democratic coalition and to forestall liberals and independents from drifting to Wallace. In June, Truman made a fiery whistle-stop tour through the Middle and Far West to show local Democratic leaders his strength with the crowds before the convention began.

But Truman's ability to be renominated depended not upon his own power and enterprise but upon the outcome of a caucus that gathered in Philadelphia, shortly before the convention, to arrange his overthrow. The caucus was called by Jacob M. Arvey, Chicago Democratic leader, James and Elliott Roosevelt, the late President's sons, and sixteen other party leaders. The active coalition against Truman was a cross section of the Democratic party and the old Roosevelt coalition. It included Mayor Hubert Humphrey of Minneapolis, Chester Bowles of Connecticut, Mayor William O'Dwyer of New York, and the Americans for Democratic Action. These Northern Democrats were joined by Southern Democrats such as Senator Lister Hill of Alabama, Governor Strom Thurmond of South Carolina, Governor Ben T. Lancy of Arkansas, Governor William M. Tuck of Virginia, and Senator Claude Pepper of Florida. Harold Ickes and James F. Byrnes, Secretary of the Interior and War Mobilization Director, respectively, in the Roosevelt administration, both opposed Truman.

The Philadelphia caucus saw inevitable electoral defeat unless a substitute candidate for Truman could be found. Their acquisitive gaze fell upon General Dwight D. Eisenhower, then on the crest of his popularity from his European military triumphs. But Eisenhower dashed the hopes of his would-be benefactors by issuing a statement a week before the convention, saying, "I will not at this time identify myself with any political party and could not accept nomination for any political office." Leon Henderson, the ADA chairman, futilely urged the Democrats to ignore the Eisenhower statement and to go ahead with the general's nomination as "the best man the country can provide." The ADA next brought forward the name of Supreme Court Justice William O. Douglas, but many Democratic leaders balked, and Douglas issued a declining statement.

Truman was eventually renominated by default of the old coalition's failure to unite on an alternate candidate. The vote was not unanimous as befits a President seeking reelection but 947½ for Truman, 263 for Richard B. Russell of Georgia, and ½ for Paul V. McNutt of Indiana. The New York *Post* reflected the convention's mood when it wrote, "The Party might as well immediately concede the election to Dewey and save the wear and tear of campaigning." As everyone knows, Truman went on to win in one of the most dramatic election upsets in the country's history.[8]

But Truman in 1952 and Johnson in 1968, confronted with formidable competitors for the nomination and an unhappy trend in the primaries, withdrew early in the struggle.

The Congressional Party

But once nominated and elected, or reelected, a President is concerned with getting his program through Congress, a venture in which the party leadership and rank and file are as likely to fail him as to help him. Few Congressmen view their loyalties to their own careers, constituents, and party as related to their loyalty to their party's national standard-bearer and his program. Eisenhower's Senate leaders were successively Senator Taft, his chief rival for the Presidential nomination, and Senator Knowland, who opposed him on a wide range of policy. President Eisenhower steadily received more support from Democratic legislators than from Republicans. In Kennedy's time the House Democratic floor leader, and later Speaker, was John W. McCormack of Massachusetts, whose nephew contested with the President's brother Edward for the 1962 Democratic Massachusetts Senatorial nomination. Mike Mansfield,

Senate Democratic leader and long-time ally of President Johnson, broke with the administration on the wisdom of the Vietnam War policy and registered his dissent publicly, pointedly, and repeatedly. In no other governmental system in the world are such oddities of party life to be found.

Creative and well-intended efforts to improve President-Congress relations in the party realm have gone awry. The Congressional reorganization legislation of 1946 founded what might fairly be called a noble experiment to build up Congressional party unity by establishing a policy committee for each party in the Senate. The House later also instituted such committees. The committees were conceived by their creators, Senators Robert La Follette, Jr., and Mike Monroney, as councils that would meet periodically with the President to improve interbranch understanding on questions of national policy. Like many other noble experiments, the policy committees have achieved only small success. President Truman met with the Democratic Senate Policy Committee of his day only once. In the Eisenhower administration's first days, the Senate Republican Policy Committee more or less accepted the President's program, although it quickly turned out that the legislative party for which it appeared to speak did not. There is no record of any Eisenhower meeting with the entire Senate Policy Committee. The committees have developed not as institutional organs, as their creators hoped, but largely as instruments by which Senate chieftains exerted their personal leadership. Lyndon Johnson and Robert Taft used the committees as vehicles for building up their personal influence. But most important of all, the committees have become effective not for policy-making but for service and research and legislative scheduling.[9] In the House's 1974 reforms, the power to fill Democratic vacancies on committees was shifted from the Ways and Means Committee to the Democratic Steering and Policy Committee.

The President's party equips him with remarkably few pressures he can apply to Congress, and these are highly imperfect at best. His most ancient pressure is, of course, patronage. Earlier Presidents were wholesale dispensers of offices, a part of their job that they dislike. In Lincoln's day job-seekers crammed the White House rooms, stairs, hallways, and even closets, prompting that noble spirit to cry out, "It is not the rebellion that is killing me, but the Pepperton post office."[10] The Civil Service Act of 1883, and its later extensions, protecting the tenure of designated employees, has gradually but sweepingly reduced the relative numbers of federal jobs tagged for patronage. A contemporary President's patronage appointments number a mere few thousand.

Patronage enables the President to strike at the legislator in his home district, to attract or alienate local groups on whose support he depends. For the favor of his juicy patronage plums, the Chief Executive can exact a quid pro quo. Many a President, before handing out jobs, first checks the voting record of the interested Congressman on the administration's legislative program. The search may bring down the heavens upon the errant. When Samuel J. Randall, Democratic high tariff advocate, fought Grover Cleveland's grand enterprise to lower the tariff, retribution was swift and severe. Word went forth from Washington that no Randall man need expect any patronage. At Randall's political base in

Pennsylvania, reaction was quick. Two key Randall organizations, the Randall Club of Pittsburgh and the Eleventh Ward Democratic Association of Philadelphia, hastened to repudiate their leader and endorse Cleveland's tariff position. When the state Democratic committe met to elect a chairman and adopt resolutions, Randall's candidate lost to a low tariff man and the committee voted a hearty endorsement of Cleveland's tariff stand.[11] Yet, as Presidents well know, many legislators whom they might strike at by withholding patronage are by no means defenseless. "It was a smart practice in government," Roosevelt's party chairman, Jim Farley, once said, "to avoid antagonizing the men who vote the appropriations." [12] He could add, too, legislators of large influence on other key Congressional committees and those enjoying full sway over local party organizations.

The patronage weapon is not without flaw. Its worth rests upon the assumption that human gratitude is enduring, an assumption that sometimes falters in practice, especially in politics. Further, an appointment that recognizes a local political faction may antagonize competing factions. William Howard Taft, after a wealth of experience, concluded that every time he made a job appointment he created "nine enemies and one ingrate." Virtually anything the President does in the patronage field stirs bleats of disgruntlement.

In contemporary Presidencies, far more important than the patronage of jobs is the patronage of expenditure and the untold variety of executive decisions that can waft windfalls of largess into the laps of deliberately selected beneficiaries. A key ingredient of Nixon's Southern strategy was succor for textiles, a major industry of the region. Nixon pressed negotiations with European nations and Japan for treaties helpful to American textiles, and although the treaties failed to materialize, awareness of textiles' preeminence in White House concerns spurred flows of investment capital into the industry. In distributing funds for the Model Cities program, Lyndon Johnson allocated not on the basis of need but according to political criteria intended to reward the home towns of key Congressional committee chairmen. Of the initial list of sixty-three cities, Cleveland and Los Angeles, scenes of severe racial outbreaks, received no grants, while Smithville, Tennessee (population 2,300)—a community represented by Congressman Joe L. Evans, a Democrat and chairman of the House Housing and Urban Development Subcommittee on Independent Offices Appropriations—was favored. Ordinarily subtle, Johnson sometimes coupled his dispensations with naked threat. When Senator Frank Church (D-Idaho) tendered an article by Walter Lippmann to explain his opposition to the Vietnam War, an annoyed Johnson replied, "All right, the next time you need a dam for Idaho, you go ask Walter Lippmann." [13]

THE OPPOSITION PARTY The party, when it does not control the Presidency, may be expected, according to general political practice, to take on the democracy-serving function of responsible opposition. Difficulties afflict this expectation due to the low capacity of the Congressional party organization to achieve party coherence. Soon after the 1956 election of Eisenhower, Senator Hubert Humphrey proposed that Congressional Democrats adopt their own legislative program, consisting of sixteen points, including civil rights, as a responsible opposition alternative to the President's program. "If you have a platform," Democratic Mayor David Lawrence of Pittsburgh commented to reporters, "you ought to follow it up with a legislative program, not just throw it out after you are defeated in an election." Senate Democratic floor leader Lyndon Johnson and Speaker Sam Rayburn declared their opposition to Humphrey's step and suggested that Congress wait and act upon the Eisenhower legislative program. When later Rayburn and Johnson proved fairly congenial to the Eisenhower program, Truman, Stevenson, Humphrey, and other Democratic leaders moved to form a Democratic Advisory Committee (or Council, as it came to be called) to keep alive the spirit of creative opposition. But the Speaker and majority leader agreed only to "consult" the committee, holding that they must retain their independence of action for their Congressional responsibilities. In such a tangled situation it is difficult if not impossible to find meaningful national party leadership. Stevenson was discredited because of his two defeats for the Presidency, and Johnson's own party-mindedness, in light of his course, was a trifle obscure.[14]

Any incumbent President looks for support in the opposition's Congressional party, an aspiration that constrains his stance toward that group. For his defense and foreign aid programs, Eisenhower appealed for help to Democratic Congressional chieftains Rayburn and Johnson; at critical junctures in quests for civil rights legislation, Presidents Kennedy and Johnson sought much-needed aid from Senate Republican leader Everett Dirksen. Nixon's strongest Congressional support came not from Republicans but from Southern Democrats.

Like other Presidents, Nixon's demeanor in Congressional elections toward opposition party members who helped him was conspicuously more benign than toward resolute foes. Consider the tender concern lavished on the reelection in 1972 of Senator James O. Eastland of Mississippi. As Senate Judiciary Committee chairman, Eastland had staunchly supported the Administration's embattled Supreme Court nominees, Clement Haynsworth, Jr., and G. Harrold Carswell, and in the disputed and politically dangerous International Telephone and Telegraph Corporation case. When Vice President Agnew alighted in Mississippi, he announced that he could not associate himself with Eastland's Republican opponent, Gil Carmichael, and that the administration could do nothing to "help defeat someone who has been so helpful to us in the past." In a speech at the state capital, Agnew elaborately endorsed Mississippi's three Republican nominees for the House of Representatives but never mentioned Carmichael, who was conspicuously absent from the platform.[15]

The Jeffersonian Success Model

The President's success in party affairs is a mixture of many things: his own personality, his public popularity, his skill at maneuvering, his intuitive sense.

It is a game played not with rules but with a master's instinct for the shifting sources of power. Some Presidents revel in their role as party commander. Jefferson, Franklin, Roosevelt, and Kennedy, for example, enjoyed the game and usually played it with skill and finesse. John Quincy Adams and John Tyler, at the other extreme, were failures. And a President like Eisenhower accepted his party leadership reluctantly, holding that the White House should be above the party. It was as party leader that Lyndon Johnson accumulated considerably less success than he enjoyed in other branches of Presidential endeavor. Eminent among Presidents as a legislative leader, as party leader he secured for himself a quantity of black marks in the books of political professionals. The experience of each of these men is, in different ways, instructive.

Of all the Presidents, Thomas Jefferson is unsurpassed in the authority he asserted as party leader and in the fealty he commanded from state and local party organizations. He held sway by means of a thoroughly formulated theory of party principles and functions and a sure grasp of the means of party action. For Jefferson, the party was preeminently the instrument of majority rule. The party joined the executive and Congress into a majoritarian unit. The President and his department Secretaries provided the legislative agenda; the party members in Congress transmuted it into law.

The Presidential program was the party program, and fidelity to it in debate and vote was a principle to be jealously guarded and enforced. Jefferson wrote critically of his Congressional party brethren,

> Our friends have not yet learned to draw well together, and there has been some danger of a small section of them, aided by the feds [the Federalist party], carrying a question against the larger section. They have seen however that this practice would end in enabling the feds to carry every thing as they please, by joining whichever section of Republicans they chose; and they will avoid this rock.[16]

Jefferson could not abide Republican legislators who acted independently of their party. He called them "wayward freaks, which now and then disturb the operations." [17]

Jefferson worked through and dominated the Congressional party machinery. Caucuses of Congressional Republicans were summoned at his direction, and sometimes reportedly he presided. Secretary of the Treasury Albert Gallatin devoted no little time and skill to laying before the caucus the President's messages and requests. Jefferson, Gallatin, and other cabinet Secretaries watched over the progress of administration measures in Congress at all stages until their enactment. Jefferson and his aides invented the "floor leader," a legislator in each house who efficiently shepherded the administration's fondest projects over the craggy terrain of votes, committee hearings and reports, and parliamentary maneuver.

At the outset of a legislative session John Randolph, House floor leader and Ways and Means Committee chairman until he fell from Presidential grace, would dine with Jefferson to go over the administration's agenda. As the session proceeded, the Congressman was in almost daily touch with executive officials. Gallatin spoke of his "free communication of facts and opinions" to

Randolph. Most of Gallatin's proposals were steered through the Ways and Means Committee and onto the House floor in the manner his fastidious tastes desired. Appropriations to purchase Florida, to establish a Mediterranean Fund, and to retire the debt moved steadily under Randolph's sure hand. As floor leader, he managed such major Presidential projects as the repeal of the Judiciary Act, the reduction of civil expenditures, and the bringing of charges of impeachment against Supreme Court Justice Samuel Chase, a loud, violent Federalist who denounced Republicanism from the bench as a mash of anarchy, atheism, and the devil.

Jefferson viewed Congressional elections as a grand opportunity to eliminate obstructors and import supporters. Although James A. Bayard, Federalist Congressman of Delaware, had by his vote finally ensured Jefferson's triumph over Aaron Burr in their struggle for the Presidency, Bayard's subsequent leadership of the Congressional opposition alienated the Chief Executive. The President, as he was wont to do, searched for a candidate to beat Bayard at the polls. "For God's sake, run for Congress against him," he implored Caesar A. Rodney of Delaware. Bayard's "long speeches and wicked workings at this session have added at least 30 days to its length, cost us 30,000 D. and filled the union with falsehoods and misrepresentations." Rodney ran and was elected. The President's occasional manipulations had their costs. Major lieutenants like Joseph Nicholson and Nathaniel Macon were sometimes bedeviled with rumors that he was maneuvering to throw them over. To such men he wrote what became known as his "tares" letters: "Some enemy, whom we know not, is sowing tares among us. Between you and myself nothing but opportunities of explanation can be necessary to defeat these endeavors. . . . I must therefore ask a conversation with you." [18]

Jefferson employed patronage to induce legislators to cooperate and to assure executive loyalty to his policies. When things went awry in the party organization, he was quick with redress. Randolph was dropped from his two high posts soon after he erred. He had managed and botched the prosecution of Justice Chase and had demurred at the President's seeming tenderness to the culprits of the Yazoo land fraud and at the President's request for a secret appropriation of two million dollars to purchase Florida if circumstances warranted. Randolph announced his dissents with merciless invective on the House floor. The affronted Jefferson dropped word to Senator William Plumer that "Mr. Randolph's late conduct is very astonishing and has given me much uneasiness." Jefferson and his followers moved to depose Randolph as floor leader and to substitute Barnabas Bidwell of Massachusetts. This plan was foiled when Bidwell was defeated for reelection. Administration business that normally went to the Ways and Means Committee was routed elsewhere as long as Randolph remained chairman. In a speech on the House floor Congressman Thomas Mann Randolph, Jefferson's son-in-law, savagely attacked John Randolph as a betrayer of secrets and an inciter of clamor. From his constituency in southern Virginia, the embattled Randolph complained that "every engine has been set to work to undo me in the estimation of my constituents, and not without effect." The local press maintained a steady, hostile chant, and two prestigious

Virginia politicians, William B. Giles and Wilson Cary Nicholas, campaigned mightily against him. Another Jefferson son-in-law, John W. Eppes, took up residence in Randolph's district, contested his House seat, and eventually won it in 1813, when Jefferson was long retired.[19]

Those Who Failed

If Jefferson achieved crowning success as party leader, John Quincy Adams and John Tyler floundered in the uttermost depths of failure. Adams won the disputed Presidential election of 1824 in the House of Representatives and then only, his enemies said, by a corrupt bargain with Henry Clay. In return for Clay-controlled House votes to assure Adams' election, Adams promised the Kentuckian the post of Secretary of State. Andrew Jackson, one of the vanquished candidates, termed Clay "the Judas of the West."

Adams was endowed neither by personality nor by circumstance to be a party leader. Austere and principled, he faced a wretched political situation. His cabinet contained no one who had openly supported him for President. Although his party controlled the House, the opposition ruled the Senate. Key Senate committees like the Foreign Relations Committee constantly opposed him. Adams' perilous situation in the upper chamber came into sharp relief when he requested authority to dispatch a mission to the Panama Congress of Latin-American states. The Foreign Relations Committee rejected his plan with a warning against entangling alliances, but somehow he managed to squeak through the Senate by a vote of twenty-four to twenty despite a punishing debate.

Randolph, who had returned to Congress in 1815, had a field day with the Panama Congress proposal. Charging that Clay had forged the invitations to the Congress, he resumed the attack upon the political partnership of the President and the Secretary of State. They were, he cried, "the coalition of Blifil and Black George . . . of the Puritan with the black leg." * For Adams, the worst aspect of this rowdy day in the Senate was not Randolph's crudity but the fact that the President's own party permitted it. Not a single Republican Senator called Randolph to order, and Vice President John Calhoun, in the chair, permitted the breach of privilege. Adams, furious at Calhoun's laxity, made a slashing attack upon the Vice President, writing under the name "Patrick Henry," in the press. Calhoun, who used "Onslow" as his pen name, reciprocated fully. The two party giants, the President and Vice President, demonstrated their rich talents for controversy in several exchanges.[20]

Adams' personal encounters were never softened by the favors at his command as party chieftain. He conceivably could heal wounds by applying the slave of patronage. But his principles stood in the way, taking precedence over

---

* A reference to two conspiratorial characters in Fielding's *Tom Jones*.

the claims of party, as General James Tallmadge, lieutenant governor of New York and Tammany chieftain, sadly learned. Tallmadge had backed Adams unstintingly in his narrow victory. In a savage fight the lieutenant governor had stopped a move by Martin Van Buren's New York machine to break up a joint session of the state legislature before the electors could be chosen. If Van Buren had succeeded, New York's electoral votes would have been wasted and Adams defeated. Van Buren and his ally, Governor De Witt Clinton, had their avenging knives poised. Tallmadge clearly needed to escape New York for a distant foreign mission if his political life was to be saved. Thurlow Weed, Tallmadge's emissary, laid the situation before the President. In a meeting that was "embarrassing and constrained," Adams quickly demonstrated his capacity to ignore political obligations. He could not appoint Tallmadge to any diplomatic post, he said, because another New Yorker, Rufus King, had just been named minister to Britain, and New York could not claim more than one overseas appointment. Weed sickened when he reflected that King had opposed Adams' election and Tallmadge had risked, perhaps given, his political life to assure it.[21]

John Tyler, like Adams, is at the bottom of the league of party chieftains, although for different reasons. A sure-footed politician, he was the victim of the relentless ambition of the leader of the Whig party in Congress, again Henry Clay. The New York *Herald* wrote of Clay,

> He predominates over the Whig party with despotic sway. Old Hickory himself never lorded it over his followers with an authority more undisputed, or more supreme. With the exception of some two or three in the Senate and fifteen or twenty in the House, Mr. Clay's wish is the paramount law to the whole party.[22]

Clay coupled with his great power a fierce drive to become President. A towering obstacle was the incumbent President Tyler and his likely desire to be reelected.

Not without reason, Clay scornfully spoke of Tyler as "a President without a party." Tyler's Whig following in Congress was so small that it was called, half-derisively, "the Corporal's Guard." In the Senate, only William C. Rives supported Tyler in the heavy fighting. The President's party weakness extended to his cabinet, which he had inherited from his late predecessor, William Henry Harrison. All the cabinet Secretaries except Secretary of State Daniel Webster and Postmaster General Francis Granger were allied with Clay. Even of Webster and Granger, Tyler could not be certain. The President's chief sustenance in his political weakness was his personality—"approachable, courteous, always willing to do a kindly action"—and his unlimited courage.[23]

Without a party Tyler could not well put his chief measures through Congress; with a party Clay had Congress in his hand and the President largely at his mercy. Time and again Congress rebuffed the President and the President vetoed Congress. Clay, pursuing his American system, a series of measures to promote the nation's economic development, put through a bill creating a new bank of the United States. Tyler, whose state rights disposition was offended, vetoed it, earning plaudits from Andrew Jackson. The Clay men drenched the President with invective. "The vocabulary of the language," a witness wrote, "seems to have been ransacked for words to express their angry denunciation." [24] A second bank bill passed, and Tyler vetoed it. At Clay's command, all his men in the cabinet resigned.

Tyler, bereft of party aid, saw many a favorite measure hacked to death in Congress. His proposed treaty with the German *Zollverein* was tabled in the Senate. His nominations to office habitually encountered rough handling in the same body. His fond project to annex Texas by treaty was lost, with every Whig but one voting against it. Eventually, almost miraculously, Tyler brought Texas into the Union by joint resolution.

Tyler's troubles lay not only in Congress. He was treated roughly in the organs of political communication, in the party press, and in the talk of the political professionals. Henry Clay was known to say that if it could have been foreseen at the Harrisburg convention, which created the Harrison-Tyler ticket, that Harrison would die after a month as President and that Tyler would veto the Whig's bank bill, either the convention would have ignored Tyler or he would not have received a single electoral vote in the subsequent election. The Clay press reechoed its leader's hostility. The Richmond *Whig* called Tyler "the accident of the accident," "a vast nightmare over the Republic." And when a dread influenza epidemic overtook the country, the Whig press was quick to name it "the Tyler Grippe." [25]

Franklin Roosevelt as Party Leader

Franklin Roosevelt, the most powerful of modern Presidents, was also the most assertive as party leader. Commanding unprecedented popular support, attested by his four-time election to the Presidency, he dared to attempt drastic renovations of his party: to expand its voting base by extending its commitment to programs and to displace the Democratic Congressional foes of the New Deal with those who promised to be its friends. Bold ventures almost inevitably involve a mixture of success and failure, and they did for Roosevelt. [26]

A rare President may intervene not only in the elections themselves but also in his party's primaries for Congressional seats, seeking the nomination of candidates pledged to his support. Because of the grave hazards such an enterprise involves, most Chief Executives know all too well that the local voters resent the intrusions of outsiders. Franklin Roosevelt, however, mounted the heaviest Presidential assault yet upon the inviolability of the local primary in his attempted 1938 purge of a handful of Democratic Senators and Congressmen. If it had succeeded, it would have brought about a major revision of the Congressional Democratic party and the party's historic heterogeneity would have been displaced by loyalty to the New Deal program. The purge was sparked by the defeat of Roosevelt's Court-packing plan of 1937.* That defeat, the first major rebuff in five years of glittering victories, had rankled the President. Not a few Democrats who opposed the Court plan, he noted, had steadily voted against his New Deal measures. Roosevelt turned a receptive ear to his aides, Harold Ickes, Thomas G. Corcoran, and Harry Hopkins, who for months had talked of the desirability of a purge. On a hot June night he fired the opening salvo of the purge venture in a fireside chat. He declared,

> As the head of the Democratic party . . . charged with the responsibility of the definitely liberal declaration of principles set forth in the 1936 Democratic platform, I feel that I have every right to speak in those few instances where there may be a clear issue between candidates for a Democratic nomination involving these principles, or involving a clear misuse of my own name.[27]

The purge took on more definite form in Roosevelt's zigzag trip across the nation. He proceeded to distinguish between those who were with and those who were against him. In Texas he beamed on liberal Congressmen Lyndon Johnson and Maury Maverick and punished Senator Tom Connally, a Court bill foe, by announcing from the back platform of his train the appointment to a federal judgeship of a Texan whom Connally had not recommended. In Kentucky Roosevelt worked hard for Alben Barkley, his faithful Senate leader, embattled in a close race for his Senate seat with Governor Albert "Happy" Chandler, a strong campaigner with a potent machine. Roosevelt, upon reaching Kentucky, invited both Barkley and Chandler into his car for a drive to a huge political crowd at the Latonia racetrack. Roosevelt and Barkley were nettled when Chandler kept bowing to the right and left, acknowledging the great applause that presumably was directed chiefly to Roosevelt, and the President came roaring back with a speech heaping praise upon Barkley and dismissing Chandler as a young man who required many years to match Barkley's knowledge and experience. In a later statement Roosevelt hinted that Chandler had approached the White House with a deal in judicial appointments in an effort to clinch his Senate seat.[28]

The President was spurred on by the primary victory of Barkley and of another favorite, Senator Elmer Thomas of Oklahoma. He now concentrated his fire anew on several selected purge targets. High on the list was Senator Walter F. George of Georgia. George's defeat, Roosevelt reasoned, would provide a lasting lesson to Southerners in Congress who had been opposing his social legislation. Other marked men in the Senate were Democrats Guy M. Gillette of Iowa, Bennett C. Clark of Missouri, Pat McCarran of Nevada, "Cotton Ed" Smith of South Carolina, Millard Tydings of Maryland, Frederick Van Nuys of Indiana, Alva Adams of Colorado, and Augustine Lonergan of Connecticut. In the House the men slated for defeat by the President were Howard W. Smith of Virginia, John J. O'Connor of New York, and E. E. Cox of Georgia, all determined foes of his New Deal program.

---

* Faced with a Supreme Court that repeatedly declared his New Deal legislation unconstitutional, Roosevelt sought to "pack" the Court with new members who presumably would be more favorable to his purposes. He proposed to add one new justice, up to a maximum of six, for every justice of the Court who, having passed the age of seventy and serving for ten years, failed to retire.

Roosevelt personally carried the fight against his principal purgees. En route for a vacation at Warm Springs, he stopped at Gainesville, Georgia, to dedicate a public square named in his honor. Senator George introduced the President, who proceeded to ignore the Senator and beam approval upon Governor E. D. Rivers, who he hoped would run against George. When Rivers declined, Roosevelt recruited Lawrence S. Camp, United States District Attorney at Atlanta. In another Georgia visit, this time at Barnesville, and with Camp and George on the platform, Roosevelt referred to the Senator as "my old friend" and proceeded to demonstrate his inadequacy by New Deal standards. The President described his test:

> First, has the record of the candidate shown, while differing perhaps in details, a constant active fighting attitude in favor of the broad objectives of the party and of the Government as they are constituted today; and secondly, does the candidate really, in his heart, deep down in his heart, believe in these objectives? [29]

The President proceeded to the excommunication. "I regret," he said, "that in the case of my friend, Senator George, I cannot answer either of these questions in the affirmative." Mixed boos and cheers rose from the crowd. Roosevelt shook hands with George who said, "Mr. President, I want you to know that I accept the challenge." "Let's always be friends," Roosevelt answered.

For all of Roosevelt's effort, the purge ended a wretched failure. Although certain of his favorites triumphed, every Senator and Congressman he marked for defeat won except Congressman O'Connor of New York, and O'Connor's loss was attributed by New York Democratic professionals not to the President's intervention, but to O'Connor's own shortcomings—a poor campaign and a fat roster of enemies who joined together to take electoral revenge. In Georgia Roosevelt's candidate, Camp, ran a poor third; in Colorado Alva B. Adams was nominated without opposition; in Connecticut Augustine Lonergan prevailed in the Democratic state convention. "It's a bust," Jim Farley observed, as Roosevelt's political stock plummeted. In the face of Franklin Roosevelt's grisly and unforgettable failure, no President has ventured onto the purge trail since his day.

Yet despite Roosevelt's failure to transfer his own power and personal magnetism into victory against Congressmen who were entrenched in their local regions, he did shake his party at its roots and transform it through his own great political talent. The traditional Democratic party, on which he performed his drastic surgery, was a classical alliance of Northern city bosses and Southern and Western agrarians, held together by states' rights beliefs and federal patronage, and enlivened with intermittent bursts of progressivism. He replaced this old party order with a new Democratic coalition enduringly committed to positive government acting for national and group welfare. He had found the Democratic party a minority party. His graftings upon it of new group allegiances left it the instrument of the majority.

Roosevelt's vision of the new party was of one free from business domination and its debilitating effect upon political morality and public policy. He attracted into the party fold labor, farmers, racial and national groups, intellectuals, and women, all disadvantaged in the business culture. He brought in as well those businessmen who were restive under Wall Street and Eastern ascendance. Roosevelt established the new coalition by a lengthy, circuitous route. In staffing his administration after his 1932 victory, he drew talent not from the traditional Democratic organization but from the coalition. He brought Hugh Johnson, an independent, and Donald Richberg, a progressive, into NRA; Henry A. Wallace, a progressive, into agriculture; another progressive, Ickes, into public works; Hopkins, an independent, into relief administration; John Winant, a progressive, into social security; and Joseph P. Kennedy, a new entrepreneur, and James Landis, an independent, into securities regulation.

In Roosevelt's hands lawmaking was also an instrument of party reorganization. Major laws of his administration—the Social Security Act, the National Labor Relations Act, and the like—furnished the base of a new Democratic party, Northern and urban in orientation, attractive to city-centered groups, labor, Negroes, the new immigrants, women, and intellectuals. Policy and the unifying force of Roosevelt's personality, rather than pork barrel and patronage, cemented the new party. The breadth of his success was apparent as early as the 1934 Congressional elections. The Democratic returns showed an upsurge of labor and Negro votes, and of Northern Democrats in Congress with an ebbing of the relative strength of the South. Of 69 Democrats in the Senate, only 24 were Southern; of 322 Representatives, the South had 108.

The next major stroke in the Democratic party's transformation was the infiltration of New Dealers, or coalitionists, into the party's councils and operations. New Deal emissaries Edward Roddan, Stanley High, and Leon Henderson took up stations in the national committee. In electoral contests the party's chief campaigners were the New Deal coalitionists: Roosevelt himself, of course, and Ickes, Wallace, and Hugh Johnson. Administration policy was readily manipulated to feed the political necessities of the coalition. Roosevelt, mindful of the approaching 1936 elections, told Agriculture Secretary Wallace in February, "Henry, through July, August, September, October, and up to the fifth of November, I want cotton to sell at 12 cents. I do not care how you do it. That is your problem." When a WPA cutback in relief funds threatened the dismissal of many workers on October 1, Roosevelt instructed Secretary of the Treasury Henry Morgenthau, Jr., "You tell Corrington Gill that I don't give a god-dam where he gets the money from but not one person is to be laid off on the first of October." [30]

The courted urban groups provided not only votes but money, organizing energy, and publicity. In 1936 organized labor created Labor's Nonpartisan League, whose wealth and manpower were consecrated to Roosevelt's candidacy. Spurred and indefatigably aided by Eleanor Roosevelt, he won the enduring loyalty of blacks to the New Deal. J. E. Spingarn, president of the National Association for the Advancement of Colored People, said of Roosevelt, "he has done more for the Negro than any Republican President since Lincoln." [31]

Roosevelt's experience showed that a powerful President can change the national image—and the reality behind the image—of his party. He succeeded by shrewd political finesse and also by promulgating a program with which many alienated groups could identify. And it was in defense of his new alliance, held together by a program—as well as in annoyance at the opposition—that he undertook the 1938 purge. The test of a party's success, he felt, was achievement of its program, and if a few entrenched party leaders had to go to achieve it, then this was a reasonable sacrifice. But he miscalculated local loyalties to long-time leaders and the refusal of local groups to think of the good of the party as a whole.

Eisenhower as a Bipartisan

Most Presidents climb to their office by superior political skill and, upon arriving, eagerly take up their duties as party chief. But to a few Chief Executives, especially to hero-Presidents like Washington and Eisenhower, party activity is unwelcome, if not distasteful. Washington gladly delegated the partisan function to Alexander Hamilton, his Secretary of the Treasury, preferring to remain above the heat and dust of party battle himself. The new country, launched in perilous circumstances, required bipartisan unity in Washington's day. There was rather less compulsion for it in Eisenhower's. Nevertheless, during his two terms, Eisenhower resolutely, but not always successfully, shied away from partisan political duty. He immensely preferred nonpartisan and bipartisan politics to partisan. He could have been nominated for the Presidency by either party, and, indeed, a concerted effort for his Presidential services had been made by both parties. His most forceful lapses into partisanship occurred on the campaign trail, most notably his attacks upon the Truman administration in the 1952 electoral struggle. His foreign policy, which he largely entrusted to Secretary of State John Foster Dulles, was also hardly bipartisan.

Eisenhower's penchant for nonpartisan or bipartisan politics was a matter partly of temperament and partly of necessity. The strongest elements of his political faith were negative: return federal activities as far as possible to the states and to private responsibility, and balance the budget. His Modern Republicanism appeared to call for federal social measures, but these he chose not to push very hard. He eschewed partisan conflict, therefore, as something neither necessary nor relevant to his program, and avoided it if possible as activity that was troublesome and petty.

Eisenhower as President faced a Congress that had been dominated by the opposition party for a longer time and in greater numbers than any President since Zachary Taylor. Even in his first two years, when the Republicans controlled Congress, hard political reality necessitated cooperation with the Democrats. The Republicans' majority in the House was eleven, and in the Senate a mere one. Even more important was the inexperience of Republican legislators in cooperating with the Chief Executive. Not since 1931, nearly a quarter century before, had Republicans controlled the Presidency and both houses of

Congress simultaneously. Not a single Republican Senator of the Eighty-third Congress, which began on January 3, 1953, had ever served with a President of his own party. Of the 221 House Republicans, only 15 had ever experienced a Republican President. The Republican habit of opposition did not cease with Eisenhower's advent. Indeed, it is not impossible to argue that Republicans gave Eisenhower a harder time than they ever gave Kennedy and Johnson. In the Senate Joseph McCarthy, William Jenner, Henry Dworshak, Herman Welker, Hugh Butler, and George Malone were relentless foes of the President's program in maneuver, speech, and vote. McCarthy, who was largely a gathering storm during the Truman administration, reached maximum fury during Eisenhower's first term. Most Presidents would have agreed with Eisenhower, who decided, as he faced the Congressional session of 1953, that the coming effort of the administration and of legislative Republicans should be devoted to redeeming the 1952 party platform and his own campaign pledges. Eisenhower's State of the Union message of February 2, 1953, diligently mirrored these party pronouncements. But in the early Eisenhower Presidency, the Senate Republican leader was William F. Knowland of California, of whom Sherman Adams wrote, "It would have been difficult to find anybody more disposed to do battle with much of the President's program in Congress." [32] Franklin Roosevelt, in contrast, worked steadily—particularly in his first years—through a legislative party leadership that ran up a high batting average of support for his measures.

On April 30, 1953, a historic explosion occurred when Eisenhower, meeting with Congressional leaders, broke the news that despite severe cutting he could not balance the new budget as Robert A. Taft and others who were present had hoped. The President and Defense Department officials explained that part of the difficulty was that certain revisions were necessary in the nation's defense program. Suddenly Taft erupted, losing control of himself, pounding his fist on the cabinet table, and shouting at the stunned President seated opposite him. "With a program like this, we'll never elect a Republican Congress in 1954," Taft cried. "You're taking us down the same road Truman traveled. It's a repudiation of everything we promised in the campaign!" Taft went on excitedly, and when he stopped, tension gripped the room. Fortunately, several of those present commenced an aimless conversation until Eisenhower, flushed and upset, recovered himself to state in measured tones the necessities of global strategy.[33]

Republican legislators were the most relentless foes of Eisenhower's mutual security program. Some Republicans wanted to reduce taxes at once regardless of the costs of the ongoing Korean War. Others wanted to scuttle the Reciprocal Trade Agreements Act and restore the high tariff Smoot-Hawley Act of the Hoover era. In jest and in no little truth, Harry S. Truman declared as the 1954 Congressional elections neared, "It seems to me that President Eisenhower should be secretly wishing for a Democratic Congress . . . and hope that we can save him from the misdeeds of his own party." Not surprisingly, Eisenhower sometimes speculated privately with his aides whether he really belonged "in this kind of Republican party." [34] He mused over the desirability of forming a new political party, internationalist, welfare-oriented, but conservative in spending and economic regulation.

Out of such experience, Eisenhower, understandably, never wore his hat as party chieftain gladly. To the Republican faithful, he denied even that he was a politician. "Everybody knew I wasn't a politician—and I'm not yet," he told a group of Republican workers. He clung to his chosen nonpartisan demeanor, declaring at a news conference,

> I don't believe in bitter partisanship. I never believe that all wisdom is confined to one of the great parties, and I certainly have never in general terms criticized the other party, that is, to include its great membership. I believe there are good Americans in both parties, and I believe that the great mass of both parties is fundamentally and naturally sound.[35]

As the 1954 Congressional elections neared, he cautioned his cabinet against an overly partisan approach, adding that he must take care himself to remain nonpartisan in using the national radio and television networks except on programs paid for by the party. When Republicans everywhere, with the eagerness of those whose bread and butter was at stake, pressed Eisenhower to stump the country for the party tickets, he refused, acknowledging at a press conference, "I am deeply interested in what happens to the complexion of the Senate and the House of Representatives, but I do not intend to make of the Presidency an agency to use in partisan elections." And yet, as the 1954 elections came closer and the party pressures mounted, Eisenhower finally yielded and took off for ten thousand miles of travel and forty speeches. His spreading involvement never overcame his distaste for campaigning. "By golly, sometimes you sure get tired of all this clackety-clack," he remarked to Jim Hagerty, his press secretary, on election eve.[36]

Soon after the Democrats captured Congress in 1954, Eisenhower informed his cabinet he did not see how there could be any question of the need for the White House to work with the Democratic leadership. He held bipartisan meetings with the legislative leaders and, when major happenings were afoot, diligently kept both sets of party leaders informed. Upon returning from his 1956 Bermuda meeting with Prime Minister Harold Macmillan, for instance, he invited spokesmen from both parties on the Hill to the White House for a report on the conference. In public pronouncement, as well as in private act, Eisenhower maintained a moderate demeanor toward the Democrats. "Whenever he thought any one of us became too harsh," Sherman Adams wrote, "he would remind us that we were not going to get anywhere in Congress without Democratic votes."[37]

Each President, as party leader, is expected to assist the campaigns of Congressional candidates indiscriminately, including the campaigns of those whose election would injure his program more than their opponents' victories would. Roosevelt's attempt to flaunt this tradition had ended in failure. In the 1954 Congressional elections President Eisenhower permitted himself to be photographed with a hundred or more Republican candidates, an imposing advantage in a local campaign. He also promised to make speeches delineating his program if he happened to be in the vicinity of a candidate who supported it and invited him to speak. Asked how he chose from among the Congressmen for bestowal of his photographic and rhetorical favors, he acknowledged that there was ''a little bit of a check'' on the legislators' voting record. In actuality, he was not known to withhold support in 1954 from any of the more recalcitrant legislators in his party who asked for it. For the President, loyalty to party generally transcended loyalty to program during campaigns.

Roosevelt and Kennedy took the position that support for their program *was* loyalty to the party. Perhaps a strong President inevitably assumes that he and his program and the party are synonymous. The party professional, however, makes no such assumption, except for pragmatic reasons in Presidential election years.

So Eisenhower, whose temperament was bipartisan, or perhaps more accurately apolitical, was forced by circumstances into assuming a highly partisan role in election years and a bipartisan role in between in his relations with a Democratic Congress. He was a man of uncomplicated loyalties and ideological simplicity, a man for whom conflict over program or over people was uncongenial. His election-year loyalty to his party, therefore, proved nearly absolute. Is it a political paradox that those Presidents who are less party-minded can be counted on to support the party most (but with least effect) and that those who are genuinely partisan—and strong—will defy the party when a few block the fulfillment of the party's promised program?

Kennedy and the Urban Era

President Kennedy had paid considerable heed to the lessons of both Roosevelt and Eisenhower. He was deeply concerned over the fact that a party's national program supported by its Presidential candidate may falter or fail at the hands of the party's own leaders in Congress. Was the answer not to wait for the election year to initiate a purge but to move upon the source of power ahead of time—in the state and local party organizations, where the seeds of trouble germinate?

The state party organizations are allegedly self-governing principalities, but Kennedy, who pursued his duties of party chief with zest, remorseless diligence, and ingenuity, moved upon them with aggressive enterprise. He acted principally through his personal organization—Lawrence F. O'Brien and Kenneth O'Donnell, his brother Robert and his brother-in-law Stephen E. Smith, and other associates, all of whom enjoyed close personal ties with state and local Democratic power centers in the big Northern industrial states on which Kennedy concentrated. His own organization in these states was in some ways more powerful than the regular Democratic organization. He maintained close ties with state leaders such as Jesse M. Unruh of California, city leaders such as Ray Miller of Cleveland, and local potentates such as Charles A. Buckley of the Bronx, dealing them considerable preferment. After the 1962 elections Smith, a man of quiet competence, served the Democratic National Committee as a trouble shooter in the key states of New York, Pennsylvania, Ohio, and Michigan, all of which had chosen Republican governors. Smith's chief responsibility in his uneasy capacity was to prevent fractious Democrats from feuding with one another. His early assignments included the laying of olive branches on such adversaries as "reform" Senator Joseph Clark of Pennsylvania and Philadelphia "machine" leader Congressman William Green, Jr. In Michigan Smith toiled to heal the rift between the United Auto Workers and Democratic regulars, and in New York to quell the party's long-standing strife and chaos.[38]

Kennedy did much "coordinating" himself. Soon after taking office, he worked mightily to revise the New York State Democratic leadership. He gave the cold shoulder to two top Democratic chieftains, Carmine De Sapio, New York County leader, and Michael Prendergast, state chairman. The more luscious patronage appointments credited to New York were awarded to members of a reform Democratic group dedicated to Prendergast's and De Sapio's ouster. Kennedy's cold treatment of the latter had a social dimension. During his inauguration ceremonies, Kennedy had pointedly distinguished between New York Democrats in good and bad standing. Congressman Charles A. Buckley, the long-time Bronx Democratic leader, Joseph T. Sharkey, the Brooklyn leader, and Peter J. Crotty, the Erie County chairman, all enjoyed places in the Presidential box at the Inaugural Ball. Prendergast and De Sapio were among the fifteen thousand dancers who milled about on the floor. In a visit to New York City several weeks later, Kennedy rode with James A. Farley through the city streets, visited Lehman at his apartment, interviewed Sharkey, and talked with Buckley on the telephone. De Sapio was totally ignored and Prendergast heard only from a member of the Presidential staff.[39] By these and other means Kennedy implied he would never deal with Prendergast and De Sapio, and encouraged lesser New York Democrats to challenge their leadership.

Kennedy resorted to several expedients to advance the candidacies of legislative Democrats whom he viewed favorably. To further the cause of Wilkes T. Thrasher, Jr., an all-out New Frontiersman running in the Third Congressional District of Tennessee in 1962, he picked the candidate to represent him as a special ambassador at independence ceremonies in Trinidad. The scarcity of such plums underscored the importance of the President's action. As the 1962 elections neared, Kennedy seemed to take a giant step toward Roosevelt's method when he announced that he was "going to help elect Democrats" who supported his legislative program. The incumbent Representative Leonard Farbstein of Manhattan, who was running for reelection, faced a primary contest with Assemblyman Bentley Kassal, the reform Democratic candidate. In a letter to Farbstein, Kennedy praised his "clear judgment, wisdom, dedication and energy" and expressed "my personal appreciation for your sustained support of our legislative program." Farbstein made the letter public, terming it an endorsement.[40] His opponent, Kassal, contended that it was not, that he had been assured indeed that Kennedy would not take sides in the primary. The President said no more, and Farbstein swept on to victory. Reform groups are common casualties of Presidential party decisions, especially where the rival individual or group represents power the President cherishes or respects. Farbstein, as a member of the House Foreign Affairs Committee, had been an ardent advocate of bills favorable to Israel. In turn, the administration's attitude toward Israel was considered important by large numbers of Jewish voters in New York.

In his attentions to the states, Kennedy generally slighted reformers—if support for the regulars strengthened his own position. At a Democratic fund-raising dinner in New York City, he sent Charles A. Buckley a lavish verbal bouquet, described by a Kennedy staff member as "the most personal message I've ever known in all my twelve years' association with the President." The message, which was read at the dinner, was signed, significantly, by "Joe, Jack, Bobby and Teddy Kennedy." This fulsome tribute to one of the most encrusted and anachronistic of bosses brought the New York *Times* to protest the President's knowing recognition of a figure who needed to be "decried and deplored" rather than "promoted and protected." [41] Not the least importance of Buckley was that as chairman of the House Public Works Committee he was admirably situated to help the administration by influencing other House Democrats to vote for the President's bills.

Publicity is another weapon a President can employ to promote his legislative party friends, and in one publicity gambit Kennedy moved to wrest from the Republican party one of its proudest possessions, the observance of Abraham Lincoln's birthday. He celebrated that event in 1963, the centenary of the Emancipation Proclamation, with a White House reception for black and civil rights leaders and a host of Democrats, chiefly legislators who supported the Kennedy program. More than a thousand celebrants were on hand, including blacks distinguished in endeavors ranging from law to jazz. The day was ripe with suggestion of the solid harmony between Lincoln's ideals and contemporary Democratic action. Prior to a buffet, Kennedy received at a ceremony in his office a report on civil rights progress in the hundred years since Lincoln's Emancipation Proclamation. The report noted that "as the century following emancipation draws to a close, more forces are working for the realization of civil rights for all Americans than ever before in history. Government is active in every branch and at every level, if not in every region." But it added, with a solid air of commitment, "The final chapter in the struggle for equality has yet to be written." [42]

Kennedy's death cut short the experiment that was to have been tested in the 1964 Presidential election and probably in the 1966 Congressional election. He died in the line of duty as party leader. The purpose of his visit to Texas, which ended in his assassination, was to reduce the widening cleavage between Texan Democratic factions identified with Senator Ralph W. Yarborough and the then Vice President Johnson. It is left for future Presidents to see whether the stalemate between the party's Presidential leadership and its Congressional leadership can ever be resolved in favor of the President and the majority of the nation who support him. The Kennedy formula looked for the eventual dominance of urban politics over Congressional politics. His legislative program was heavily directed toward the urban vote, and his personal political organization concentrated upon winning and holding the allegiance of the great Democratic organizations in the Northern urban states. The combination of a program geared to urban groups and a personal political organization that mobilized local party organization could conceivably have added up to a force that Democratic legislators would have found difficult to resist after 1964.

Johnson the Consensus Leader

Lyndon Johnson came into the Presidency with only a modest background in partisan leadership. The bulk of his political career was passed in a one-party setting in his home state of Texas, in an interval when only the Democratic organization could win at the polls. A one-party state, by definition, precludes indulgence in the arts of partisanship. As Senate Democratic leader he spent most of his tenure working in bipartisan cooperation with a Republican President. Neither did his initial years as President produce emphasis on partisan leadership. The 1964 Presidential race was conducted under circumstances that made an "unpartisan" campaign Johnson's most logical choice. The identification of his opponent with an ultraconservative political philosophy that repelled the great body of the electorate inevitably prompted Johnson to soft-pedal Democratic partisanship and appeal to the broadest possible group of Republican and independent voters.

More important than the several circumstances of his career was Johnson's own philosophy of politics. As Senator and President his fundamental working principle was "consensus," a method that employs discussion, reason, compromise, and accommodation; that seeks to create the largest common denominator of agreement among the broadest combination of group and sectional interests. By its nature, consensus tends to eschew partisanship and takes the road of nonpartisan and bipartisan politics.

Against such a background of experience and philosophy, it is not surprising that Johnson as party leader did not compile a glittering record and sometimes even appeared to falter. A totaling up of errors and an articulating of grievances followed the 1966 elections that dealt the Democatic party substantial defeats across the nation. Among other things, the Republicans gained forty-seven seats in the national House of Representatives and eight governorships. In the aftermath, Johnson assembled many Democratic governors at the LBJ ranch to hear their complaints and to formulate plans for 1968. Elsewhere other Democrats made known their unsolicited views. Criticism centered upon Johnson's chief resource as national party leader, the Great Society program, with its substantial expenditures for education, health, housing, poverty, and other political staples that bring advantage to vast reaches of the electorate. The dispensing of these program benefits presumably would be a great boon to the Democratic party, an expectation that the 1966 electoral results dashed.

The governors who assembled at the LBJ ranch complained that the administration of the Great Society programs was politically deleterious.[43] They were little consulted, or even informed, concerning the policies administered in their states. Governor Hulett C. Smith of West Virginia, a state that has a big stake in federal aid because of its severe poverty as a part of Appalachia, complained of local dissatisfaction with penalties—such as reductions of grants-in-aid—that the federal government imposes for failure to meet its standards. The governors also contended that they were, in effect, called upon to campaign in 1966 in support of the national administration without having been consulted on national policy.

A second species of complaint sprang from the evident steep decline of the Democratic National Committee following the 1964 election. The committee, by tradition, is a Presidential adjunct, and the Chief Executive decides its policies and chooses its top personnel. Johnson ordered a cutback in services performed by the committee in an effort to retire the debt inherited from previous campaigns and increased in 1964. By dint of Johnson's economy measures, the committee liquidated its debts and even accumulated a reserve for the 1968 struggle. But the financial achievement was politically expensive. The committee was so weakened that it could not even mount a national registration drive in the 1966 campaign. There was also a curbing of the committee's influence. The White House regularly by-passed it on patronage. And, according to Governor John B. Connally, Jr., of Texas, the President's long-standing political friend, neither were the state Democratic leaders consulted.[44]

From other quarters came complaints that President Johnson's policies of financing had a weakening effect on state and local organizations. His principal fund-raising device, the President's Club, drained money out of the states and into the national party coffers. Democratic leaders in New York State, for instance, found it difficult to attract contributions for state party programs from many members of the President's Club. In 1966 almost seven hundred New Yorkers belonged to the club, a privilege that required a contribution of at least one thousand dollars a year. The President thus siphoned off from New York a sum more than twice as large as the expenditure of the 1966 Democratic gubernatorial candidate, Frank O'Connor, whose Republican opponent, Nelson Rockefeller, ran a multimillion-dollar campaign. The outflow of funds also saps party strength at the grass roots and hinders the normal development of young potential candidates and party leaders. Having limited resources, young aspirants encounter difficulty in attracting financial help from those already contributing substantially to the national party.

The feature of Johnson's conduct as party leader that rankled Democratic professionals most was his seeming aloofness from the 1966 elections. The campaign of that year was for him a noncampaign. Seldom did Democratic candidates receive less help from the White House. As the campaign moved

into its climactic weeks, Johnson resorted not to the speaking stump but journeyed to the Far East for consultations on international affairs. A decision to
undergo surgery prompted the President to cancel a plan to venture onto the
campaign trail after his return from the Pacific. Following his operation and
convalescence, the President, in a news conference shortly before the election,
failed to make a ringing endorsement of such embattled Democratic candidates
as Pat Brown in California, Paul Douglas in Illinois, and Robert Duncan in
Oregon. For that matter, although offered the opportunity by questions posed in
his news conference, the President made no endorsement of any Democratic
candidate. One disillusioned Democratic leader in California growled, "When
it comes to working for Johnson in '68 he may find a loyalty gap here."

With a full backlog of resentments, and the 1968 elections on the horizon,
Johnson in 1967 launched an intensive drive to improve his relations with Democratic governors and local party organizations. To smooth out administrative
snags in federal programs, the President dispatched Farris Bryant, former Governor of Florida and Director of the Office of Emergency Planning, with a
squad of experts from the federal departments to visit forty state capitals. In a
further move, the President installed a plan by which each member of the cabinet is assigned four or five states as his personal responsibility, with instructions to facilitate personal contact between the governors and the White House.
Late in 1967 and early in 1968 each of the fifty states was scheduled for a
"day" in Washington, when a planeload of its key officials was to be flown in
for conferences with departmental officials, capped by a meeting of each governor with the President. In Washington, state officials would sit across the conference table from their federal counterparts, and any important unresolved
questions would be left to the governors to take up in their visit to the White
House.[45]

In President Johnson's defense, it is clear that the protestation against his
Great Society programs came chiefly from governors of the South and Southwest, whose states insisted upon more local autonomy and were habituated to
standards of social and economic policy substantially lower than federal standards. The President was caught in a vise between his duty to upgrade the quality of the nation's life through federal programs and the pressures upon the state
leaders of his party to maintain local autonomy, which resulted in lower standards. Johnson's noncampaigning in 1966 was encouraged by counselors impressed by the dominance of local issues and the President's dipping popularity
at that moment in the public opinion polls. By disposition and philosophy,
Johnson was a centralist, or one who tended to gather power into his own
hands, and to distrust institutions whose autonomy and inclination might produce resistance to his purpose. His centralism was also encouraged by the
strength of a competitor, Robert Kennedy, in state and local party organizations. With Kennedy men well stationed around the country, it was only natural
for Johnson to use his most available resources of party leadership, the resources of centralism—federal programs, the national party structure, the Presidential office.

Nixon and the New American Majority

Richard Nixon is one of a small handful of Presidents who strove to restructure his party by enlisting sufficient numbers of new adherents to transform it from a minority party into the majority party of future decades. As he advanced in his term of office, Nixon defined ever more clearly the constituencies to be melded into the new majority.

At its core were blue-collar workers, denizens of suburbia, a new middle class. Nixon perceived this constituency to cherish law and order, patriotism, and the work ethic. In the domestic furor over the Vietnam War, the members of this constituency were an absolute rock of support; Nixon's campaigning celebrated their values, and he entertained their leaders in the White House. With policy decisions, governmental favors, and concessions, Nixon courted union leaders and workers. The administration released former teamsters' union president James R. Hoffa from prison and dropped plans for antistrike legislation in the transportation field. The teamsters' union promptly endorsed Nixon's re-election. The construction unions benefited when their industry was favored with a separate wage control board, and construction wage increases ran ahead of increases in the rest of the economy. The administration's relaxation of the Philadelphia Plan, originally designed to increase the numbers of minority workers in the building trades, also pleased the construction unions.[46]

Nixon's perception of the new majority possessed a religio-ethnic dimension. His aides spoke of a Catholic strategy; in major industrial states, Catholics were heavily represented among blue collar workers and in the expanding suburban population, and their preferences on issues were strongly asserted in Nixon's discourse, which left his rival, George McGovern, securely identified with the "wrong" side. Accordingly, in traditionalist rhetoric, Nixon was perceived as rejecting abortion, marijuana, and amnesty for Vietnam deserters and draft dodgers.

The new majority also had definable geographic contours. Its favorite habitat was the burgeoning suburbs. The 1970 census indicated the gross population shifts in progress—declines in the cities and sharp increases in the suburban belts around the cities, resulting in two sharply contrasting worlds. Millions of white people were leaving the cities and moving to the suburbs, while black people and Spanish-speaking people replaced them. To suburbanites generally, Nixon's policy appeals to workers and ethnics seemed apt and welcome.

The new majority was also geographically delineated in Nixon's long-standing "Southern strategy," the essence of which incorporated his other appeals; here too were "white ethnics," living in scarred metropolitan areas and embittered by crime and busing. The South and Southwest were loci of the greatest population growth, according to the 1970 census, and their plethora of retirement homes and military and technological centers reinforced a conservative outlook on issues.[47]

To promote his Southern strategy, Nixon freely employed the resources of the Presidency. He proposed that the original Voting Rights Act be revised to

eliminate its "regional" provisions. His administration shifted school desegregation enforcement from HEW to the courts and with it any attendant voter
resentments. His initial Supreme Court nominees, Haynsworth and Carswell,
were Southerners, and their nominations were received warmly in the South.
Nixon took on Harry S. Dent as a chief political aide. Dent had been chairman
of South Carolina's Republican party and a former assistant to Senator Strom
Thurmond (R-S.C.).[48]

It was not a "Republican" majority but an "American" majority, necessitating a Presidential stance that would appeal to detachable non-Republicans. The
campaign organization therefore became Nixonian rather than Republican. Not
the National Committee, but a specially created Committee for the Reelection
of the President, administered by key Presidential aides, ran the campaign. The
Republican party played virtually no national role in the 1972 Presidential elections. The President's handpicked national Republican chairman, an aggressive
Kansas Senator, Robert Dole, was enchained in futility. An admirer of Nixon,
Dole, despite repeated effort, was not even allowed by the White House staff to
see the President. One day, after months of seeking an appointment, Dole
received a telephone call from "an assistant President," as he characterized
several staff members. "Hey, Bob, do you still want to see the President?" a
youthful voice asked crisply. "When?" said Dole. "Tune in on Channel 9,
he's coming on the tube in ten minutes." [49]

For the other Republican races of 1972, the Committee for the Reelection of
the President did almost nothing; it released precious little of its huge money
hoard to other party candidates. Nixon himself campaigned minimally, less
than any modern President since Franklin Roosevelt's fourth term candidacy
during the Second World War. Presumably, Nixon could better win the new
majority of detachable Democrats and independents plus Republicans by keeping busy as President than by involvement as a Republican candidate. As thus
conceptualized, the new majority served to rationalize Nixon's belief that his
own campaign would flourish most if he soft-pedaled his Republican affiliation. Meanwhile, professional Republicans were distressed by the President's
newly conceived role as party leader, which he had redefined virtually to the
point of its disappearance. One Republican Senator, frustrated by the President's seeming indifference to the fate of Republican candidates, exclaimed
that 1972 was "the most selfish campaign in history," [50] to which extra sting
was added when Nixon's prodigious landslide victory was coupled with Republican losses in Congress and the states.

The new American majority—if there really is one—remains up for grabs. If
Nixon claimed that he embodied it, by dint of his 1972 victory, so did the
Democratic Congress created by the same election. And whatever grip Nixon
had on it was weakened by the Watergate scandals, inflation, and the oil crisis,
all of which contributed to his drop of forty-one points in popularity in the
Gallup poll after one year of his new term. Whatever else it is, the new majority, or more accurately the electoral center, is, according to history, a phenomenon ephemeral in its perceptions and beliefs, as the following comparison
suggests.

What a Majority Considered Most Dangerous
or Harmful to the Country
1967
(The year before Nixon's initial successful Presidential candidacy)

People who don't believe in God

Black militants

Student demonstrators

Prostitutes

Homosexuals

1973
(after a year's exposure of the Watergate scandals)

Political spies

Generals who conduct secret bombing raids

Politicians who engage in secret wiretapping

Businessmen who make illegal political contributions

Politicians who try to use the CIA, FBI, or Secret Service for political purposes

Politicians who try to restrict freedom

Sources: Interview with Louis Harris, *New York Times,* January 21, 1974; Louis Harris, *The Anguish of Change* (New York, 1973).

In every Presidential election, the successful candidate must discover afresh "the new majority," or political center, in its most recently evolved, evanescent form and respond seriously to it.[51] As Louis Harris has suggested, the American people are pragmatic, and therefore shifting in the priorities they accord to issues, rather than ideological. Nixon's perception of "the new American majority" is founded on the opposite assumption. In fact, Harris's opinion analyses reveal, the foremost preoccupations of this majority in 1972 were not those that Nixon ascribed, but ending the war and establishing peace in Vietnam. Also, the stress on a new ideological majority has roots in the tendency of leaders who lack charismatic appeal, such as Nixon and Johnson, to read into their mandates, provided by massive outpourings of voters, deeper messages than are actually there.[52]

The Future Presidency

At most, the President can be only a quasi–party leader. A variety of forces and pressures compel him to temper and contain his partisanship. He must at times give higher priority to his calling as leader of the nation, facing needs and goals greater than those of his party. He may face a Congress one or both of whose houses is dominated by the opposition party. The body of independent voters has increased to such a degree that it exceeds those identifying as Republicans and is rapidly overtaking the majority Democratic party. The ability to appeal to independents both during his quest for the Presidency and after gaining it is an ever more crucial test of the Chief Executive. Thanks to weak party discipline, a President knows the difference between a "paper," or party, majority in Congress and a "working" majority. In many of his waking hours he is forced to be bipartisan or nonpartisan if he is to pick up needed legislative votes from the other party. Bipartisan leadership is exerted at a price. It rests upon consultation and compromise and necessarily reduces the forcefulness of policy and the President's program image.

Viewed another way, although the party system has enabled a national popular majority to choose a President, when he attempts to translate his electoral promises into policy he finds himself in a government that permits only limited majority rule because of separation of powers and checks and balances, among other things. Only a rare President, such as Jefferson or Franklin Roosevelt, succeeds in building enough strength as party leader to enable him to extend substantially the principle of majority rule. Despite the limiting realities of the party and the governmental structure, what can be done to help the strong President also be a strong party leader?

The President's party role is also highly relevant to a second proposition of this book; that is, that the strong Chief Executive should be confined within the boundaries of democratic practice. Parties are unsurpassed as the means by which the people, or organized masses of voters, can hold government—including Presidents—accountable to their will. Voters, acting through the party victorious at the polls, can throw out the Presidential incumbent or bar the successor proferred by his party. At its best, the opposition party supplies the alternative candidate and therefore offers a choice for the voter, provides a different perspective on issues, and induces masses of people to vote. A crucial question emerges. If recent Presidents measure up poorly as conformers to democratic standards, can parties be improved as regulators to produce candidates whose behavior, according to democratic norms, is more acceptable?

1. Within the past two decades, disparate forces have been effecting alterations of the parties to the point that, compared with their historic appearance, they have become scarcely recognizable. Television, primaries, campaigning by jet aircraft, the increasingly augmented ranks of the independent voter, ticket-splitting, and such potent social forces as affluence, more widespread education, and enhanced population mobility have swiftly outmoded the traditional parties. Parties of yore consisted of baronies ensconced in state capitals, county courthouses, the cities, and, sometimes, in Congressional incumbencies. Supported by interest groups, the barons' approval—or at least the avoidance of their veto—was requisite for winning the Presidential nomination. After their designee took office, these groups enjoyed access to the President and dealt with him directly—not merely with his staff—to press demands and communicate dissatisfactions. All this was done from a vantage point of independent power and limited attachment to the President.

But now the older party fiefdoms are diminished and the power of the barons has been reduced. The barons have been replaced by candidate politics, campaign management firms, television, financing by fat cats, and direct-mail drives, and the tasks of getting out the vote are handled by bands of dedicated volunteers. The supreme examples of the rout of the barons were provided by the 1972 Democratic convention, from which they were largely excluded, and by Nixon's personalized campaign.

What can be done to restore the parties to their former place as constraints—for the sake of democracy—on the President? Can these traditional institutions of mass democracy undergo revival and renewal? Conceivably, governors of the major states may become the future barons, raising money in the contemporary fashion and utilizing the latest managerial expertise and campaign technology. Mail drives, telephone campaigns, and zealous volunteers can flourish for the Governor as they do for the President. With these accouterments, the governors can again become arbiters and bargainers in the business of Presidential selection, and the eventual Chief Executive will feel obligated to negotiate with these potentates for his own reelection or his party's continued retention of the office, for the progress of his programs in Congress, and for concordats on such matters of mutual concern as revenue sharing and natural resources regulation. Interaction will be direct and personal and not, as was characteristic in the Nixon era, discharged through staff.[53]

Or, the parties may revive and serve as a constraint on the Chief Executive by better representing the disparate forces of society. The reforms preceding the 1972 Democratic convention were a significant, if clumsy, effort toward that end. Although the reforms were modified after the disastrous electoral defeat, the pressures of contemporary political forces, one can confidently predict, will compel parties in the future to better represent the less powerful—blacks and the Spanish-speaking, women and youth, people on welfare, consumers, the elderly, and others. As each left-out group becomes better organized, develops national leadership, and formulates specific programs and policies, it should become a force to be reckoned with at national conventions for both Presidential nominations and platform making. Given their continuing power and role, the future President would feel that interchange with these groups was advisable after assuming office.

2. Both for the sake of a strong Presidency enhanced by a more competent national party and for a Chief Executive who is subject to democratic safeguards through the party system, attention might be directed at improving the parties as forums for the discussion of issues and the review of policy. The Democratic party adopted a proposal for more frequent national conventions, including a "national issues convention" midway in the Presidential term. The first "mini-convention" was held in Kansas City in 1974.

In spirit and method, an issues convention might profitably imitate the annual conference or convention of British parties. A step in this direction was the Democrats' 1974 mini-convention which adopted a national party charter and a sweeping resolution detailing specific measures necessary for the nation's troubled economy. In future years, the convention might more closely approximate the British model. Accordingly, participants would include delegates representing state and local party organizations, members of Congress, and the President and his department heads. Since the purpose of such a convention would not be to nominate candidates, which is the primary task of the regular quadrennial convention, attention could center on serious issues and vigorous debate. Ideally, the delegates could introduce resolutions embodying stands on issues, although their confinement to reasonable numbers might require regulation. The President and other party leaders would expound their policies, and, as in the annual conference of the British Labor party, an effort would be made to air every important issue. In effect, the President and other party leaders would be called on to explain and defend their policies to the general party membership.

Even if his administration won the likely approval of the convention, expressed through supportive resolutions, the President doubtless would be influenced by any vigorous criticism or dissent. At its best, the issues convention could expose weaknesses in Presidential policies and exert moral and psychological pressure for reform. But near unanimity of support for Presidential policies could enormously strengthen the President in future quests for Congressional support of his program. At its worst, the issues convention can be unattended and ignored by the President, or it can be furiously and inconclusively split over important issues.

In any event, it would be superior to that quadrenium of quietude following a national election, during which the President meets with no party assembly, which enables him and his White House staff all the more easily to ignore or hold at arm's length other party leaders and representatives.

3. Although television has weakened traditional party roles, it can also serve as a potent source for party renewal. A Twentieth Century Fund study has wisely proposed that the major parties be allotted greater shares of television time as a counterbalance to the inordinate amounts of time accorded the President.

First, the national committee of the opposition party should be empowered by law to claim time to respond to any Presidential address broadcast during the ten months preceding a Presidential election or within ninety days preceding a Congressional election in non-Presidential years. In addition, "national debates," held four times a year (but only twice in federal election years), should take place between spokespersons for the major parties. The debates should be scheduled in prime time and broadcast simultaneously by the networks.[54] This further spur to the parties' development as expositors of issues could rally both broader public and party support for Presidential programs and policies and thereby promote the strong Presidency. It could also diminish the undesirable withdrawal of the Chief Executive behind walls guarded by janissaries of the White House staff. As conduits of issues, the parties could force the President to explain and defend his policies before the court of public opinion. Thus, an invaluable link could be forged between the strong Presidency and democratic processes.

7

LEGISLATIVE LEADER

In the tradition of great legislatures, Congress can be a potent instrument for keeping the strong President within democratic bounds. Congress can impose its positive will on the President and require him to do what he does not want to do. President Ford, for instance, reluctantly acquiesced to Congress's insistence that he cut off aid to Turkey, in certain contingencies, in the Cyprus war, despite two vetoes and his protest against the wisdom of the restriction.[1] Congress is master of the Grand Inquest, the legislative investigation into executive malfunction. To the grosser misdeeds of the President and executive officers, Congress can, if it chooses, apply the most drastic of remedies, impeachment and removal. Seldom can the President act for long without appropriations, which only Congress can provide and it can, within constitutional limits, set such conditions as it wishes. Presidents are often recruited from the houses of Congress, and some (though unfortunately not all) may bring to the executive branch democratic habits inculcated in the legislature: awareness of the legitimacy of the opposition and tolerance of its expression, habituation to the sharing of power, to compromise and accommodation, and regard for lesser power units.

The function on which Congress concentrates most of its energy and skill is legislation, which, by specific constitutional arrangement, is shared with the President. To some scholars, the combined elements of the President's role appear so magnitudinous that they speak of him as ''Chief Legislator,'' but the reality is less impressive than this grandiose title suggests.

No function of the President is more beset with uncertainty, is more vulnerable to breakdowns, and is more readily the victim of the will and whim of individuals whose outlooks and responsibilities tend to be different from his own than his duty to lead in legislation. Nowhere else in the Presidential enterprise is there found a greater gap between what the Chief Executive wants to do, what he promises to the electorate in his contest for the office, and what he can do in bringing Congress to enact the laws that alone can give effect to the party program of the previous campaign. In no other major nation is the program of a head of government more susceptible to rebuff in the legislature, to delay and crippling amendment, and to absolute, uncompromising rejection. The President runs an obstacle course on Capitol Hill that other heads of government would find strange and even incredible.

Even a President like Dwight Eisenhower, who generally viewed Congress with good will, was sometimes seized with sensations of futility.[2] In delineating his program at the outset of his term, he took pains to remind his cabinet and legislative leaders that the Republican platform of 1952 comprised "the minimum limits of achievement below which we must not fall." Eisenhower's dedication to the platform was received with open amusement by the legislative leaders. "To my astonishment," Eisenhower wrote, "I discovered that some of the men in the room could not seem to understand the seriousness with which I regarded our platform's provisions. . . . More than once I was to hear this view derided by 'practical politicians' who laughed off platforms as traps to catch voters." [3]

In his 1960 campaign John Kennedy spelled out a program by which alert and assertive leadership might move the country forward again. He put forth several hundred specific proposals, including parity for the farmer through a supply program, medical care for the aged under social security, full employment, equal rights for women, price stability, freer foreign trade, urban renewal, a new civil rights law, and the like. Most of Kennedy's campaign pledges required legislative fulfillment and therefore provided a ready foundation for his legislative program as President. But what came forth was a shrunken image of the earlier promises. Kennedy dropped permanent improvements in unemployment compensation and repeal of right-to-work laws, among other things; he trod softly on aid to education, oil depletion allowances, and medical care for the aged; and he postponed civil rights. There were no radical new ideas, no great transformations of policy like those implied in the rhetoric of the 1960 campaign. In the main his items were familiar holdovers from the Eisenhower era, items that might have been passed if Eisenhower had chosen to push them. Kennedy, in a sound appraisal of Congressional realities, chose to set his sights low.

Richard Nixon, the first conservative President of contemporary Chief Executives, often found the torpor of Congress harmonious with his personal philosophy. In a Presidency dedicated to holding the start of new social programs to a minimum, Nixon's purpose was seldom impaired by Congress. The Democratic Congresses of his two Presidential terms yielded a meager harvest, chiefly mild environmental and consumer laws and revenue sharing. Welfare reform, which Nixon promoted in 1969 but soon lost his zeal for and half-heartedly reverted to in 1974, never evoked sufficient Congressional enthusiasm to produce a new law. Nixon's most positive interlude, in 1971, when he advertised his legislative program as "a new American revolution," eventuated in barren results for two of its principal components, health insurance and welfare reform, and much of what he proposed never came to a vote that year.[4] Generally, Gerald Ford's conservative tilt was well served by the ineffectuality of Congress.

The Good Legislative Years

Congress, the historical record discloses, consistently follows the Presidential lead only in three types of situations. One is crisis, when the survival of the nation or its social system may be at stake. In the gravity of the peril, national opinion demands action and the population looks to the President for initiative and brooks no denial. The crises of the two world wars and of the Great Depression created popular opinion that demanded nothing less than Congress's full support of Presidential leadership.

The second situation in which Presidential leadership is assured is found in national security and foreign affairs since the Second World War. In these, the President has enjoyed a high batting average of success. A Marshall Plan, a Truman Doctrine, a NATO, and wars in Korea and Vietnam (at least until its final months) were well supported, although the cement of union was provided not by Presidential skill or legislative charity, but by the doings of the Russians, the Red Chinese, the North Koreans, and the North Vietnamese.

The third situation of outstanding Presidential success is produced by rare occurrences of political abnormality under circumstances highly favorable to the Chief Executive. Theodore Roosevelt in intervals during his two terms, Woodrow Wilson in 1913 and again in 1916, and Lyndon Johnson in 1965 and to a lesser degree in 1966, enjoyed this special status. All three were uncommonly skilled at manipulation in legislative encounters and basked in the sunlight of exceptionally favorable political circumstances. Roosevelt and Wilson thrived upon the nation's expanding progressive sentiment. Johnson reigned at an interval when the explosive urgency of urban problems no longer permitted Congress to sleep upon the President's program.

Both Wilson and Johnson were favored with towering working majorities in the houses of Congress. In the Senate, Wilson and his social program enjoyed the presence of progressives whose numbers comprised a majority in both parties. His Democratic majority in the House was large, and he was doubly blessed by the fact that 114 of 290 House Democrats had been elected for the first time. Eager to please, their future careers depending heavily upon executive patronage and the administration's general success, they were amenable to Presidential direction.

In 1965, Johnson, too, reaped rich legislative harvests with the aid of a substantial corps of freshmen Democratic Congressmen. Coming into office in an era when Presidents enjoyed strong success in the Senate only to meet steady rebuff in the House, Johnson derived from the 1964 elections a crop of seventy-one freshmen Democratic Congressmen. Sixty-seven of these voted for the top items on his agenda—the education bill and Medicare—and the entire body of them supported the President more than 80 per cent of the time on roll call votes. For most of 1965, House Democrats enjoyed a lopsided 152-vote margin over Republicans, which included a net gain of thirty-five seats from the 1964 elections. In certain instances, the President and his program twice profited when some conservative Democratic seats in the South were lost and some liberal Democratic votes in the North were added. A precious by-product of the top-heavy Democratic supremacy was the corresponding increase of Democratic party ratios on House committees. The Ways and Means Committee, a graveyard of key measures in the Kennedy years, was changed from a Democratic-Republican ratio of fifteen to ten to a ratio of seventeen to eight. The three Democratic vacancies on the committee were filled by staunch supporters of the President, and the committee proceeded to function in close harmony with the administration.[5]

With such imposing political resources at his command and with shrewd strategy and relentless drive, Johnson in 1965 presided over more legislative innovations on the home front than any other President in any other single session of Congress in the twentieth century. In scope as well as in number, the measures passed were impressive. These included medical care for the aged under social security, which had been on the Democratic agenda for twenty years; the first comprehensive aid to education legislation; a voting rights bill; immigration reform; a broad housing program that included rent subsidies to low income families; programs for highway beautification; programs for combatting heart disease and cancer and strokes and water and air pollution; and income guarantees for wheat farmers. With ample reason, Johnson could call the Congress of 1965 the greatest Congress ever and "my Congress." Following the 1966 elections and the upsurge in Republican strength, Johnson's fortunes on Capitol Hill veered toward the more usual pattern of inaction and rebuff for key items on the Presidential agenda.

Congress and the President: An Imbalance?

The Founding Fathers, in providing for a strong President and a strong Congress, intended that a balance should persist between the branches, that neither would become unduly ascendant at the other's expense. As history unrolled, one branch, at some intervals, amassed superior power and impact at the expense of the other, followed by intervals when the pendulum of power swung back in favor of the other branch. The fluctuations of events foster the shift; public opinion soon wearies of whichever branch is dominant, and the diminished branch soon develops a mood of reassertion.

In important respects, the balance has moved sharply in the President's favor since the Second World War, pushed both by events and Presidential methods. A potent factor feeding the trend was the long-running Indochina war, a Presidential war, conducted without exercise of the Congressional power to declare war. In the period 1969–70, Nixon initiated a secret air war in Cambodia, dispatched ground forces into Laos in contravention of an express Congressional prohibition, and made the lion's share of decisions in winding down and terminating direct American military involvement in the Indochina war. For the better part of two Presidential terms, Congress and Nixon struggled over priorities, and most of the victories fell to the President. Nixon was the first President to become entrapped in a collision between the steadily rising costs of government programs and the objective of controlling inflation. The President aimed to hold government spending within a preestablished budget ceiling to forestall a rise in taxes. The Democratic Congress shared that goal, but differed with Nixon over which programs to cut. The President applied the budget cleaver to domestic, and particularly to social, programs, while Congress preferred to decrease military expenditure.

The flow of undue power to the President was also induced by Nixon's methods. He moved his office away from its traditional accountability to Congress to a posture of autonomy and secrecy. In effect, Nixon asserted that the President alone determines what programs to cut and by how much, a contention made with the assurance derived from a landslide reelection victory, which he viewed as an overwhelming popular ratification of his definition of priorities. Nixon's posture toward Congress was the reverse of that of most contemporary Presidents, which also magnified his apparent power. Whereas his predecessors struggled to get laws passed, and suffered many a Congressional rebuff, his stance was negative: he aimed to scale down programs, phase them out, and, most of all, prevent them from starting—objectives that spurred him toward autonomy and negation.

In the magnification of his power, Nixon employed several major weapons:

THE VETO   On a scale unmatched by any previous President, Nixon applied the veto * to a broad range of social programs. None seemed beyond his disapprobation—he vetoed appropriations for hospital construction, for aid to the handicapped, for education, health and antipoverty measures, pollution control, and the sums expunged were not merely millions, but billions of dollars. Nixon did not apply even the least shadow of a comparable scrutiny to military and space programs. Toward those programs he was the soul of liberality.

IMPOUNDMENT   When his veto failed, Nixon's further recourse was impoundment, a historic process by which Presidents have withheld from programs funds Congress has appropriated. Prior to Nixon, Jefferson refused to purchase gunboats, Truman impounded appropriations for the Air Force, and other impoundments were applied to antimissile systems, flood control projects, and highways. Congress sometimes explicitly empowers the President to withhold funds, and, in impounding, Presidents frequently cite deficiencies in program design or operations and the need to make savings, justifications that normally delight Congress. Typically, past Presidents impounded funds only for a time, after which they became a matter of negotiation with Congress, and eventually most funds were released. But Nixon's procedure was quite different. He made perfectly clear that he would not release any impounded funds unless the courts forced him to do so.

To the impoundment process Nixon added radical new dimensions. While other Presidents impounded because of statutory directives or to enhance efficiency, particularly in military weaponry, Nixon concentrated on domestic, and especially on social, programs incompatible with his professed philosophy

---

* According to the Constitution, the President can "veto" ("I forbid") legislation that Congress enacts. By a two-thirds vote of each house, Congress can override the veto, whereupon the legislation becomes law without the President's approval.

of self-reliance—for most people, that is. Other Presidents withheld millions of dollars; with Nixon it was billions. Often the programs cut most severely were those addressed to the poor. In 1972, for example, the Nixon administration turned over to the Treasury some $400 million from the food stamp program, an act that one critic termed "pickpocketing the poor."

What could those who were harmed or outraged by the Nixon's impoundments do—the needy, the old, the poor, the cities, and Congress, which expressed its will by providing the appropriations in the first place? Some Nixon impoundments were pried loose by political pressure and protest. In 1971, the administration moved to impound Model Cities funds to help finance its revenue sharing plan. Letters explaining the procedure were drafted for dispatch to many mayors, but they got wind of the moves, shrieked angrily in unison, and the letters were never sent out. But even at best, political pressure is far from a satisfactory check on manipulative Presidential power. Sizeable exertions are required to bring sufficient pressure to bear, and the sheer number of Nixon impoundments precluded the constant effort necessary to create such pressure.

Another recourse is the courts, which in 1973 alone ruled against Presidential impoundments a dozen times. But court holdings too suffer limitations; they were narrowly drawn, addressed only to the specific impoundment involved, a circumstance that can be overcome only if the Supreme Court chooses to tackle the broad constitutional questions involved in the type of impoundment practiced by Nixon. Since the Court is loath to decide major constitutional questions if it can avoid them, the likelihood of an encompassing decision is poor.

Judicial reticence puts pressure on Congress to enact a thoroughgoing law dealing with the excesses of impoundment. In 1973, both houses passed muscular bills on the subject but failed to agree on a common measure. The tougher Senate version required that impounded funds be freed within sixty days unless both houses of Congress, acting jointly, approved the President's declination to spend.[6]

EXECUTIVE PRIVILEGE   Nixon also applied his style of expansive interpretation to the old doctrine of executive privilege. Again he stretched the elastic vagueness of the concept to an almost infinite dimension. The resistance he evoked moved toward precise definition of a practice that, as history suggests, is better left flexible and adaptive. Executive privilege was invoked by President Washington, who refused to supply the House with working papers developed in negotiations for the Jay Treaty. Succeeding Presidents applied the doctrine to preserve the confidentiality of information in foreign affairs and contended that the power to keep executive secrets was implied in the executive power clause. In support of executive privilege, Presidents have also cited the necessity of maintaining the confidentiality of advice from their staff and the loyalty of executive subordinates.

Later Presidents enlarged the doctrine of executive privilege, particularly Eisenhower, for whom the doctrine was a bulwark against Senator Joseph McCarthy's assaults on the executive branch, and Richard Nixon contributed to the pattern of expansion with gusto, particularly as the Watergate crisis began building. At one juncture, he contended that not only members of the White House staff, but former members as well, are covered by the privilege, and acknowledged no time limit for their immunity. Attorney General Richard Kleindienst asserted that every employee and communication was covered, but, fortunately, the administration retreated from this interpretation that threatened to turn the executive branch into a walled city.

Inasmuch as it has been used to cover up waste and corruption and the unsavory Watergate and allied scandals, executive privilege has acquired a bad name. Thus Air Force Secretary Robert C. Seamans, Jr., declined to disclose his conversations with White House aides concerning the dismissal of A. Ernest Fitzgerald, who exposed huge cost overruns on the C-5A transport plane. Nearly as important as the formal assertions of executive privilege were the many occasions when the Nixon administration simply withheld information without expressly invoking the doctrine or responded only partially to Congressional queries.[7]

In view of the galloping expansions of executive privilege and their evident inconsistency with the ideal of Presidential accountability, what can be done to keep the doctrine within salutary democratic bounds? For one thing, the play of political pressures has a regulatory effect. Typically, Nixon, after making sweeping claims of executive privilege, retreated in the face of Congressional and public outcry. His claim of privilege for former White House aides dissolved when they testified before the Senate Watergate investigating committee or succumbed to criminal indictment. In the ITT affair, when trouble boiled over, Nixon came around to permitting White House aides to appear and answer questions before a Senate committee, although in a fashion as restricted as the political pressures of the situation allowed. Various judicial rulings compelled Nixon to supply the federal district court of the District of Columbia with tapes of conversations held in his office and in which he participated that might bear on Watergate crimes.[8] The court holding was narrow and restrained and therefore left the executive privilege doctrine with its historic flexibility much intact. In more typical Presidencies, executive privilege, like impoundment, is used sparingly, and it remains a necessary Presidential defense against overreaching Congressional committees like the McCarthy investigation of the 1950s. There are less dramatic needs stemming from national security and legitimate needs for secrecy in decision processes. The border between these and the equally legitimate claims of democracy for openness cannot be precisely delineated and is best regulated by the comity that normally prevails between the executive and legislative branches.

Gerald Ford took something of a step toward comity when he chose to appear before a Congressional subcommittee to answer questions about his pardon of Richard Nixon. Although a notable retreat from his predecessor's claims of absolute privilege, Ford's presentation provided more symbolic value that substantive disclosure.[9]

APPOINTMENTS   Presidential appointments that required the Senate's advice and consent were a major battleground in the interbranch struggle of the Nixon era. To dent Nixon's reluctance to provide information on the administration's dealings with ITT, the Senate dragged out its hearings on the nomination of Richard G. Kleindienst as Attorney General. In all, the hearings, which concentrated on ITT, consumed twenty-four days. One Senator referred to the hearings as "the longest in history." [10] Likewise, the Senate used the subsequent nomination of Elliott Richardson as Attorney General to extract from the President agreement for the appointment of a special Watergate prosecutor with highly autonomous powers. In effect, Nixon bargained away the President's customary control of the prosecutorial function.

The most tumultuous conflict over appointments stemmed from Nixon's initial nominations to the Supreme Court. For the first time since 1894 a President suffered the rejection of two Court nominations by the Senate. In rebuffing Nixon's nominees, Clement Haynsworth, Jr., and G. Harrold Carswell, the Senate viewed itself as a defender of the Court and a variety of interests that felt aggrieved by the nominations. Nixon was perceived as using the nominations to serve his Southern strategy, and labor and civil rights groups protested that Judge Haynsworth had blemishes on his ethical record, that his labor and civil rights rulings as a federal judge disclosed hostility to those interests. The Nixon camp stressed the President's right to appoint a Southerner and a conservative to the Court. After a free-swinging struggle, the Senate rejected the nomination. Nixon retaliated by nominating a less qualified candidate, another Southerner and conservative, G. Harrold Carswell. Again controversy erupted. A 1948 speech by Carswell was discovered that supported white supremacy, and civil rights advocates charged that Carswell was still a segregationist and that his record as a judge revealed no significant change in his views or philosophy. Organized labor, through George Meany, president of the AFL-CIO, termed the nomination "a slap in the face to the nation's Negro citizens." [11] Distinguished judges and law school deans and professors joined a full chorus of opposition, even though a committee of the American Bar Association found both nominees qualified. All three Republican Senate leaders voted against Haynsworth and only one supported Carswell. Their combined opposition signified the extreme lengths to which Nixon had resorted in order to "rectify" the Court and its decisions, such as those on school desegregation, that he perceived as troubling his key constituencies, the South and the suburbs. [12]

The Carswell nomination and Nixon's active consideration of other possible nominees whose records were highly undistinguished suggested that the President held the Court in low esteem and, through the appointing power, was bent upon despoiling its quality. Earlier he had questioned the Court's capacity to act as arbiter on such issues as school desegregation, and he openly challenged the Court when he urged Congress to nullify its ruling on school busing. Nixon's combined tactics suggest that his overriding objective was to establish his own construction of the Constitution, at whatever cost to the Court, but the Senate intervened and he was forced to provide more professionally respectable nominations—Harry Blackmun, William Rehnquist, and Lewis Powell, whose competence was uncontested, and who shared some of the President's conservative preferences. [13]

Congress and the President: Basic Differences

Congress repeatedly checks and balances the President—whether to challenge his abuses of power or his proposals of constructive legislation—largely because it represents altogether contrasting constituencies. The President, chosen by the nation, is the natural instrument of majoritarian rule—is, as Max Lerner has written, "the greatest majority-weapon our democracy has thus far shaped." [14] It is, to be sure, a contrived majority, one normally more difficult to maintain than to create, an association of purposeful pressure groups and the great mass of little-organized citizenry, distributed across the several sections of the country, each with its distinctive social and cultural tradition and economic organization. Congress, in contrast, is the product of local constituencies: the Senate emerging from the substantial land mass of the states and the House, except for its members at large, from the smaller Congressional districts. The validity of both the national and the local viewpoints found in the executive and legislative constituencies is affirmed by the federal principle of government incorporated in the Constitution.

Congress's relationship to the "national majority" differs in other respects from the President's. The totality of the two-house Congress is never the product of any conceivable national majority, since only one-third of the Senate is chosen in any given election. The President's national majority and the Senate's and House's local majorities have varying periods of legitimacy expressed in the terms of office allotted to the candidates they elect: the Senators six years, the President four, the Congressmen two. The Senator or Congressman is identified with several kinds of majority: with the majority of his constituency, with the party majority in his house, and with the voting majority in his house. In carrying on the legislative process, the houses of Congress contain no continuing majority. A majority accumulates or emerges for limited purposes but never hardens into a durable entity. The legislative majority that passes a particular bill develops from a series of processes by which members are elected, the internal authority of the House and Senate are allocated, an agenda is selected, and procedures of debate and vote are followed. But once the bill is passed and others arise, new and almost invariably different majorities must be constructed. Congress is also the haven for the minority: the minority party, the maverick legislator. Congress speaks with many voices. The Chief Executive, with his concentration of authority and use of hierarchical organization, aims to speak with one. Congress represents the rich diversity of American life, the President its necessary unity.

Despite their imposing differences, no one branch, executive or legislative, can claim inherent superiority in articulating the national or public interest. A Washington and a Wilson are shining beacons of public interest, but who can say that in the quest for the common good President Harding was superior to Senator George Norris, or President Coolidge to Senator Robert La Follette? During certain eras legislators sometimes speak with more initiative, force, and freedom on national issues than Presidents do. Webster and Clay are better remembered than most of their Presidential contemporaries. In the 1960s, Senator William Fulbright could undertake a candid and comprehensive review of the prevailing foreign policy in terms unthinkable, at least in public utterance, for the Chief Executive and his principal subordinates. Many of the nation's foremost economic and social policies were first championed by legislators well before Presidents were prepared to exert their influence. Thus the Federal Reserve System was preceded by the legislative spadework of Senator Carter Glass, the Tennessee Valley Authority by years of advocacy by Senator Norris, and key New Deal policies by the pioneering effort of Senator Robert F. Wagner. In 1965, when Johnson reigned so fully over legislative-executive relations, Congress passed a voting rights bill broader than the one he proposed, and the House Ways and Means Committee produced a major expansion of his Medicare bill. It would be folly, in light of the historical record, to view the executive branch as the seat of national omniscience and Congress as merely negative and local. For Theodore Roosevelt a strong Presidency was premised upon a strong Congress.

But distinguished legislators are more common than strong Congresses. In brutal truth, Congress is far more often weak in accomplishment than strong. However memorable a La Follette or a Norris may be, the houses of Congress are more than assemblages of individuals; they are also corporate bodies with a hearty preference for inaction and cautious leadership. Both the House and the Senate work with a body of procedures that have an awesome capacity either for preventing Congress from acting at all or for ensuring that it will act only after unconscionable delay.

Inside Congress

Congress's internal organization and processes constitute a vast terrain of booby traps for the Presidential program. The standing committees and their chairmen, the negative power of the House Rules Committee, and the Senatorial filibuster are all potential occasions of disaster for the President. The regular center of the President's concerns is the standing Congressional committee, where party discipline is least potent.

Committees provide the money and authority indispensable to executive action. The committee chairman is a potentate presiding over a great satrapy, calling meetings when he chooses, setting the agenda, allocating time for testimony, and personally reporting the committee's measures to the floor. The sole principle by which he is chosen is seniority. He rises to his eminence not by proven excellence or loyalty to President or party but simply by being present year in and year out. Since seniority is most easily built by legislators from "safe districts," chairmen emerge most steadily from the Old South and Northern rural districts, and with such backgrounds they prove beyond doubt that a safe seat cultivates independence both from the national party and from the

President. The geographic distortion of Senate committee chairmanships is evidenced by the fact that in 1968, the final year of the most recent progressive Presidency, nine of sixteen of these posts were occupied by Southerners. These included such crucial committees as Finance, Judiciary, Foreign Relations, Labor and Public Welfare, Government Operations, and Banking and Currency, where most of the legislation that was of major concern to the Johnson administration reposed.

Accordingly, any modern progressive President who advocates positive measures addressed to serious social and economic problems faces an array of chairmen instinctively and philosophically hostile to his programs. In 1968, for example, major civil rights legislation was long delayed in the House Rules Committee, chaired by William M. Colmer, an antiadministration conservative Democrat from Mississippi. From 1967 onward, President Johnson was bedeviled by the opposition of Wilbur D. Mills, chairman of the House Ways and Means Committee, which enjoys jurisdiction over such vital subjects as taxes, social security, and tariffs. Mills kept bottled up Johnson's request for a tax increase and demanded deep cuts in federal expenditures before taking it up in his committee. In the Senate the chairman of the Judiciary Committee, a key committee where civil rights legislation is traditionally considered, was Democrat James O. Eastland, who on occasion has withheld his support of his party's Presidential ticket and platform.

But what for progressive Presidents was often a nightmare was for the conservative Nixon a sweet political dream. To Nixon, Senator Eastland was a political paragon, an unstinting collaborator for the Haynsworth, Carswell, and other Court nominations. Other Southern Democratic chairmen rallied around planks of Nixon's Southern strategy: his proposals for a weakened voting rights bill; aid for predominantly black schools to deter integration; and parsimony for social programs. Ford's conservatism was equally bolstered by these sources.

The dominance of the seniority principle—which is a custom, since it is not incorporated in any rule—is a standard but not an inexorable procedure. In 1913, for instance, it was overthrown when Senate progressives of all parties united into a majority to displace senior committee chairmen with young men, some of whom had not served in the Senate for more than two years. This enterprise speeded enactment of Wilson's New Freedom program. In 1975 Wilbur Mills, ill and criticized for his personal life, was overthrown as Ways and Means Committee chairman. "Reforms" that modified procedures of the House Democratic caucus made challenge of other chairmen easier, though practical politics largely precluded it. Seniority remained undisturbed in the Senate.

The President also may be a reforming force in the committee power structure. President Kennedy set as his first order of legislative business an assault on the most powerful of committees, the House Rules Committee, which schedules or refuses to schedule the time and conditions under which important bills come before the House. Thanks to the exertions of Speaker Sam Rayburn, the Rules Committee was enlarged by three members, a change designed to provide a safe voting margin for administration measures.[15] But thanks also to the behind-the-scenes bargaining over the new memberships, the administration emerged with only a precarious eight-to-seven vote advantage on liberal-conservative issues. The injection of religious, racial, or special economic factors, as events soon proved, was enough to capsize the administration's narrow majority. Later the Rules Committee was permanently enlarged, an action Kennedy encouraged by declaring that if the committee were not continued in its expanded state, his program would be "emasculated." [16] In 1975 the capacity of Rules Committee conservatives to obstruct was further diluted when the Democratic caucus empowered the Speaker and the Majority Leader to appoint members to the committee.

There is no better proof that Congress is often more the instrument of minority than of majority than the Senate filibuster. It is an ancient and favorite weapon of legislative minorities. President Johnson's severest task in 1964 was to steer a meaningful civil rights bill past the shoals of a Southern filibuster. He prevailed, thanks to a rare imposition of cloture, which brought debate to an end, with indispensable Republican support. But this sudden political bliss was short-lived. A 1966 filibuster killed two key Johnson measures, the civil rights bill and the bill to amend the Taft-Hartley Act.

Congressional Majorities

Congress and the President, for all their built-in antagonisms, must somehow work together to secure enactment of beneficial legislation. "I am part of the legislative process," Eisenhower rightfully said in 1955.[17] Article II, section 3, of the Constitution is the launching ground for Presidential leadership in legislation. The President is called upon to "give to the Congress information of the state of the Union, and recommend to their consideration such measures as he shall judge necessary and expedient." But what the President proposes Congress disposes, by approval, defeat, delay, or amendment. Congress, too, can initiate and the President dispose, by approval, or by veto that Congress, needing to muster a two-thirds vote of both its houses, can seldom override.

Although in the face of an overwhelming emergency Congress may cooperate with the President, it enhances its self-image when it rejects the President or compels him to compromise. Congress can be irresponsible in its dealings with the President because with two houses, hundreds of members, powerful committees, and dispersed leadership blame cannot be readily allocated. The Senator or Representative acquires and keeps his seat not by supporting the President but by maintaining the approval of groups and interests in his local constituency. A labor union, a Chamber of Commerce, or a citizens' group normally has greater impact upon a Senator's or Representative's future than all the will and might of the President of the United States.

The President may have a paper majority of his party in Congress but no working majority. Dwight Eisenhower, brought into the Presidency by the largest popular vote that had ever been cast and with his Republican party in control of both houses of Congress, quickly discovered the harsh realities of his new existence. A succession of hostile maneuvers were launched by his Republican colleagues on Capitol Hill, and all were directed at the White House. Not a few of the President's antagonists had been swept into office on his coattails, but neither sentiment nor gratitude dulled their purpose. Senator John Bricker of Ohio, a former Republican Vice Presidential candidate, sponsored an amendment that would have emasculated the President's power to make executive agreements and convert the treaty power, already difficult in the constitutional arrangement, into the most cumbersome in the world. Senator Joseph McCarthy was in open war with the executive branch. Daniel A. Reed, the octogenarian chairman of the House Ways and Means Committee, fought for an income tax cut that threatened to throw the budget into gross imbalance and wreck the President's program set out in his State of the Union message. The President's nomination of Charles Bohlen as ambassador to Russia was severely and protractedly challenged by Senator McCarthy and other formidable Republicans. Congressman John Taber, the economy-minded House Appropriations Committee chairman, slashed nearly one billion dollars from the President's mutual security request. The President was steadily harassed by riders to bills contrived by Republican legislators. Small wonder that Eisenhower after six months of office was driven almost to despair of being able to succeed in the Presidency.[18]

The President's problem of getting voting majorities is twice compounded by the bicameral system, which provides for two legislative houses chosen by different constituencies for different terms. The Senate, the traditional "rich man's club" of the late nineteenth century, was the nemesis of Theodore Roosevelt and his Square Deal program; Franklin Roosevelt fared conspicuously better in the House than in the Senate. Eisenhower and Kennedy, in contrast, enjoyed strikingly greater success in the Senate than in the House. Measures approved by Kennedy and the Senate were rejected in the House or rewritten to its specifications. Johnson's program, too, proceeded with less assurance in the House.

Why did the Senate, historic slaughterhouse of Presidential designs, give John Kennedy and Lyndon Johnson almost everything they asked for, while the House dealt out struggle and defeat? A possible explanation may lie in the great population shifts to the cities since the 1940s. The Senator, answerable to a state-wide constituency, had become heavily dependent upon the great mass of urban voters for election. Kennedy's and Johnson's electoral campaigns and subsequent legislative programs were directed chiefly to the urban industrial United States. A basic and growing convergence of interest existed between Senate and President, extending across party lines. Representatives, in contrast, are answerable to a smaller, less complex constituency.

Nixon, however, fared better in the House than in the Senate. Since the 1972 elections, because of population shifts and fairer districting, more Congressmen come from the suburbs than from either cities or rural districts, and Nixon's legislative program was targeted at the suburban voter, described as white, middle-class, middle-aged, and middle-educated.[19] Typically, Nixon's program included appeals for "welfare reform," which stressed "workfare," or putting welfare people to work in exchange for their benefits, and revenue-sharing, which permitted the states and localities—where the suburbs are even stronger than in federal politics—wide discretion to determine what federal funds shall be used for. Nixon's other suburban items included crime control, economy in government, and protection for the consumer and the environment.

The vagaries of Congressional party loyalty compel the President, estimating his legislative prospects, to acknowledge two coalitions in which members of each major party are joined. One is a "conservative" coalition of Republicans and Southern Democrats who, voting together in Kennedy's first two years, comprised a majority in both chambers. This stark, imposing fact illuminated the necessity for the Kennedy administration to concentrate upon weaning away Republicans and Southerners from opposition to its bills. Notwithstanding the administration's acumen and zeal, the conservative coalition did heavy damage. In the Senate it defeated the proposals for an urban affairs department and medical care for the aged. In the House it likewise killed the urban affairs cabinet post and the college aid bill. When the conservative coalition lost, as it often did, it was because the administration won over sufficient numbers of Republicans or Southern Democrats to support the rival "liberal" coalition. This coalition consists of a majority of voting Northern Democrats and minorities of Republicans and Southern Democrats, mostly from urban and suburban constituencies. Many of Kennedy's victories were owed to liberal and moderate Republican support. In the House, Republicans provided the margin of victory in the fight to enlarge the Rules Committee and the passage of the emergency feed grains, depressed areas, and minimum wage bills. Similar victories were won in the Senate. A *de facto* liberal coalition of Northern and Western Democrats and "liberal Republicans" provided the Kennedy administration with most of its successes.

Johnson's extraordinary legislative successes in 1965 were built over the collapsed foundations of the old Southern Democrat–conservative Republican coalition. The 1964 elections decimated the coalition's rank and reduced it to a shadow of its former power. In 1961, a Kennedy year, for example, the coalition won 74 percent of the roll calls for which it was present. In 1965, the big year for Johnson's Great Society program, the coalition's successes fell to a low of 33 percent. But in the 1966 elections the coalition rose again and promptly took charge of the House of Representatives.[20]

In the Nixon era, the conservative coalition of Republicans and Southern Democrats thrived even more, and in 1971 it compiled the highest percentage of victories on votes taken in the House and Senate in more than a decade—83 percent against a previous high of 73 percent in 1968. But, while for earlier Presidents this coalition was a bane, for Nixon it was a boon. Time and again, the coalition in both houses took positions agreeing with the President's. In the House, the coalition formed twenty-nine times in 1971, for example, and won twenty-four of the votes on which it agreed with Nixon; in the Senate, the coalition-Nixon position appeared twenty-one times and won seventeen votes.[21] In his other Presidential years, Nixon's success was more modest. In 1973, for example, the victories of the conservative coalition fell to 61 percent. In the Senate, the President and the coalition disagreed only once in 40 major votes, and in the House, he and the coalition coincided on 36 out of 43 votes. The Nixon-conservative coalition success rate in each house also underwent a comparable decline.[22] Conversely, Nixon was most embattled in his dealings with the liberal coalition.

The President conducts many of his legislative enterprises through the floor leaders of each house. Floor leaders, with their split role as party leader and the President's legislative leader, vary widely in interpreting their total responsibility. Robert Taft and William F. Knowland in the Eisenhower administration cherished their independence and the long mile between the White House and the Hill. Taft, of course, was Eisenhower's chief competitor for the 1952 Republican Presidential nomination, and Knowland, when invited to switch California to Eisenhower to provide the general with a big victory, answered coldly, "We don't want any credit or any responsibility for *that* nomination." [23] In true Congressional paradox, Eisenhower's best leader was Lyndon Johnson, the Democratic floor leader, whose entire distinguished service was spent under the Republican Eisenhower. Johnson consistently refused to turn Senate Democrats loose on Eisenhower at will but worked with the President with dispassionate professionalism, supporting or opposing as he believed he should. "We prod him," said Johnson of Eisenhower, "into doing everything we can get him to do, and when he does something good we give him a 21-gun salute." [24] In Johnson's own Presidency, Everett Dirksen, the Senate Republican leader since 1959, helped push administration measures through with such success that some of his party colleagues were dismayed, particularly as the 1968 elections approached.

Nixon's relations with his legislative leaders were burdened by Watergate and fears of consequent voter hostility to future Republican candidacies, and by the fact that the leaders had to nudge the President toward terminating his incumbency by resignation. Ford's dealings with the leaders were denoted by comraderie but in his early Presidency seldom yielded positive results.

Open and Closed Politics

The President advances his program in Congress by means which C. P. Snow, the British novelist and scientist, terms "open politics" and "closed politics," one visible and the other covert. In open politics the President sets forth his proposals for legislation, sends appointments and treaties to the Senate, brings Congress into extra session and puts an agenda before it, and makes public statements explaining and defending his legislative actions. His chief weapon in open politics is his messages—his State of the Union message rendered each January, followed since Woodrow Wilson's day by special messages that focus on single issues. These messages provide the record and delineate the scope of the administration's program.

Congress, too, invites messages, and therefore leadership, from the President. The Budget and Accounting Act of 1921 bids the President to submit an executive budget each January. This ponderous tome, equal in bulk to several metropolitan telephone directories, with its accompanying message is a detailed statement of policy objectives with means of achieving them for Congress's guidance. The Employment Act of 1946 calls for an Economic Report from the President that permits him to lay out policies fostering free competitive enterprise and maintaining employment, production, and purchasing power at maximum levels.

Theodore Roosevelt began the practice of supplementing his messages with actual drafts of bills. Although Roosevelt, mindful of the niceties of separation of powers, was a trifle sheepish and clandestine about it all, Wilson did it openly. Since then all Presidents, even Calvin Coolidge, despite his strict constitutionalism and tired blood, have drafted bills.

The Constitution endows the President with the veto, a most powerful weapon in the game of open politics. The veto's grave defect is that it is total and not partial. The President must accept or reject a bill as a whole; he cannot veto particular items and approve the rest. This permits Congress to engage with merry impunity in pork barrel legislation in appropriation bills and to attach riders like the one Senator Pat McCarran attached to the general appropriations bill for 1951, "That of this appropriation $100 million shall be used only for assistance to Spain." Nothing at the time was more alien to President Truman's foreign policy than to provide aid to Franco, the Spanish dictator. Early Presidents seldom used the veto and then chiefly to object on constitutional grounds. Andrew Jackson first employed the veto as a weapon of policy and of popular appeal in his war on the Second Bank of the United States. Franklin Roosevelt, who brandished the veto more than any other President, was known to say to his aides "Give me a bill that I can veto" to remind legislators that they had the President to reckon with. Harry Truman, taking his cue from Jackson, vetoed a string of measures of the Republican Eightieth Congress, peppering his sentences with vivid expletives like "dangerous," "clumsy," "arbitrary," "impossible," and "drastic," not so much for the legislators as for the public. Truman's vetoes were no small factor in his 1948 victory.[25] One of the busiest of vetoers, Nixon was also rejecting social programs. After a short-lived "honeymoon" with Congress, Ford too resorted frequently to the veto.

The President's enormous power to command the nation's attention endows him with a capacity no legislator enjoys. By skillfully leading the public, Presidents have brought Congress around to actions from which, left to its own instinct, it would refrain. Theodore Roosevelt was the first of the modern Presidents to rely heavily upon appeals to the public. Gifted and joyous in public combat, Roosevelt, blocked in Congress, went to the people. Woodrow Wilson perfected what Theodore Roosevelt had begun. "He is the spokesman of the Nation in everything," Wilson said, describing the President's special capacity. A spellbinder in times when oratory was admired, Wilson's lean, gripping prose and romantic moralism stirred his audience's better senses.[26]

Wilson and other successful practitioners of the popular appeal follow several rules. Wilson went to the public sparingly and only when the need was strong. The issue chosen must be important to the people and one about which their feelings can be instantly rallied. There must be careful preparation; when issues are sprung, they fare badly. As Wilson well knew, the venture carries the high risk that the people will respond only fleetingly or not at all. The appealing President is laying both his own political reputation and the prestige of his great office on the line. Worst of all, the secluded executive session of a legislative committee and the artful parliamentary maneuver, where the controlling decisions on the President's program may be made, are not directly accessible to the legions of public opinion.[27]

The President in his relations with Congress also engages in the processes of closed politics. Relatively unpublicized, unseen, and unofficial, closed politics employs the personal contact, the patronage lever, the choice viands of the pork barrel, and sundry other exertions of power and influence. The negotiation in the White House office or Congressional cloakroom, the Presidential phone call to the legislator deciding how to vote, the accommodations and compromises necessary to patch together a legislative majority for an administration bill, are the warp and woof of closed politics. The resort to closed politics is a constant reminder of the weakness of open politics. Because the Founding Fathers made so little provision for Presidential leadership in legislation, the Chief Executive is driven to rely heavily upon the extraconstitutional resources of closed politics.

The President personally is, or should be, at the center of closed politics. There is no substitute for the force of his word and gesture. He therefore must explain and exhort to win backing for his program. His dealings and exertions cover the entire range from soft to hard sell. Kennedy, endowed with personal charm and a zest for closed politics sharpened in his legislative years, labored hard and sometimes fruitfully in this vineyard. He met weekly with the legislative leaders of his party and breakfasted or lunched with the Speaker of the House and the majority and assistant leader of the Senate. He also conferred systematically and individually with the chairman of each of the standing committees of both houses, and sometimes with the entire committee when it was mulling over an item of the administration's program.

Kennedy was often found in the thick of battles on Capitol Hill. When a crucial vote approached, he not uncommonly put in long hours on the telephone, carrying his case to legislators who had not yet made up their minds or seeking to detach others from the opposition camp. Kennedy's attentions embraced Republicans as well as Democrats. Everett Dirksen was the object of various blandishments, including privileged rides in the President's helicopter. When the Democratic leader, Senator Mike Mansfield, hailed Dirksen as a "tower of strength" on foreign policy, Dirksen found it necessary to deny good-naturedly, for the partisan record, that he had "gone soft on Kennedyism."

Lyndon Johnson brought to the Presidency a high reputation and rich experience in the art of closed legislative politics, with service in both houses of Congress and a record as one of the most illustrious floor leaders in Senate history. He was master of two indispensable competences in closed politics. He was ingenious at discovering politically feasible compromises, and he commanded a relentless, overpowering persuasiveness at bringing those he confronted around to supporting them. His former occupancy of high Senate station provided him with an access to the centers of legislative power that Kennedy, whose Senate influence was considerably less, did not enjoy. Johnson as President seemed to range further and more insistently over legislative affairs than Kennedy ever did. "Kennedy came too late to many of his problems in Congress," said an official of both these Presidential administrations, learned in the fauna of Capitol Hill. "He would hold back, let things develop, come in at the top of the crisis. Johnson likes to stay ahead and anticipate what will happen and how to meet it." [28]

In dealing and bargaining with legislators, the President operates from an array of vantage points. He can dole out various degrees of help in the next Congressional elections. He manipulates the several executive beneficences like pork barrel and defense contracts. The Kennedy administration, laboring mightily to induce Southern Democrats to vote for its measures, generated good feeling by increasing price supports for Southern cotton and awarding Southern plants big defense contracts, such as the million-dollar order allotted Lockheed Aircraft of Georgia. The depressed areas bill forged ahead when its rural aid outlays were doubled. A map demonstrating how nicely the gravy would flow to Dixie under the amended bill circulated on the floor.

Not the least of the President's loaves and fishes is federal patronage, the art of bestowing offices upon legislators' protégés—with votes, it is hoped, the *quid pro quo*. Wilson sometimes disciplined legislators who persistently failed to support his policies by cutting off their patronage. "We not only ought to pay no attention to Senator Vardaman's recommendations for office," he wrote his Attorney General, "but we ought studiously to avoid nominating men whom he picks out." [29] Truman, exasperated in his futile efforts to force the repeal of the Taft-Hartley Act in the Eighty-first Congress, thundered that how Democrats voted on that matter would be weighed in handing out patronage. But patronage by Truman's day, thanks to the spreading coverage of the civil service merit laws, had been reduced to a light weapon. For all of Truman's ferocity, Taft-Hartley was intact when he left the Presidency.

Despite the weakness of his individual weapons, if the President chooses to direct his available means of both closed and open politics upon a selected objective, he can gather an imposing arsenal. An impression of the administration's diverse weaponry is provided by Congressman Otto E. Passman, chairman of the House Appropriations Subcommittee, charged with responsibility for foreign aid. A skillful, doughty foe of foreign aid, Passman offered this picture of the Kennedy administration's legislative technique in its first foreign aid fight. The administration, Passman noted, relied heavily upon the testimony of Treasury Secretary Douglas Dillon, a Republican, "with his usual smile and personality." Passman continued,

Then Democratic National Chairman Bailey sends wires to Democratic officials all over the country, trying to get them to put the pressure on Congress. . . .

Then there were letters from Dillon and Rusk. . . . The program was talked up at a State Department briefing for editors. . . . There was the Ayub [President of Pakistan] pep-talk [urging foreign aid]. . . . The Citizens Committee for International Development was organized to exert more pressure. . . . McCormack [then House Democratic leader] sent letters to 2400 mayors across the United States including some in my own district. . . . Shriver [then Director of the Peace Corps and the President's brother-in-law] made a personal visit to every office on Capitol Hill. Although he came for the Peace Corps, foreign aid was mixed in. . . . The White House kept contacting business groups all over the country. . . . I jotted down some figures to show my thinking [i.e., of possible cuts in foreign aid spending]. A Republican subcommittee member leaked the figures to the President a few hours before the subcommittee was to act. . . . While I was presenting the subcommittee report in the full committee meeting, administration agents continued to place phone calls to committee members in the room. In the same meeting, letters from an Assistant Secretary of State to members of the committee, all calling for more funds, were actually slipped under the door.[30]

Yet for all the unstinting commitment of the President and his cohorts, Congressman Passman cut the foreign aid appropriation by 21 percent, or $896 million. After the deed was done, Passman observed simply, "This is a great day for the taxpayers." President Kennedy and his aides were reported "stunned and angry."

Approaches to Legislative Leadership

A Chief Executive can choose between several possible approaches in setting the tone, pace, and pressure level of his legislative leadership. No President, to be sure, limits himself to any one approach. Like baseball pitchers, he prefers to mix his delivery, and the choice of an approach, like a pitch, depends upon how the game stands at the moment. The sheer number and variety of approaches are themselves witness to Presidential weakness in legislative leadership. The following are some of the possibilities from which the President may choose.

"FOX" VERSUS "LION"   All Presidents engage in periods of the foxlike, or diplomatic, approach. The Constitution's endowment of Congress with vital powers of legislation and the President's consequent necessity of inducing its cooperation force him to be diplomatic in method. The President's personality and political ideology may bring him to prefer it. So also may special circumstances.

Gerald Ford, attaining the Presidency after nearly nine years of executive-legislative estrangement commencing in the later years of Lyndon Johnson's tenure and culminating in the storm of Nixon's threatened impeachment, immediately accorded the highest priority to constructive relations with Congress. He had ample reasons to do so. The ever-deepening conflicts of his predecessors had been barren and unresponsive to domestic problems. Ford's prior tenure as House minority leader had schooled him in the give and take that could actualize his desire as President for "partnership" with Congress. Shortly before becoming President, Ford, recalling his legislative past, spoke confidently of working with a Democratic Congress—with all Democrats, "from Jo Waggonner," an ultra-conservative, "to Mo Udall," a liberal. In his initial address to Congress, Ford chose the diplomatic approach when he declared that his motto toward Congress would be "communication, conciliation, compromise and cooperation." Among the strengths that Ford commanded to further his motto were a staff he brought with him from Capitol Hill that was sensitive to Congressional realities, a personal preference for "testing the waters" before proposing legislation, for negotiating with legislators rather than vetoing, and resolute faith that individuals of good will can sit together and solve difficult problems.[31]

In the foxlike approach the President fraternizes with legislators and plies them with blandishments. Franklin D. Roosevelt excelled at the art of Congressional gratification, at giving out the easy first name, the warm handshake, the contagious smile, the intimate joke, the air of concern, the quasiconfidential interview, the picture snapped at the White House desk, the headline in the hometown newspaper.

One Saturday afternoon in blossom time in 1961, when Senator Harry F. Byrd's friends and neighbors gathered in his Virginia apple orchard to commemorate his birthday and eat fried chicken, there suddenly burst from the azure skies President Kennedy's whirring helicopter. The President had taken time from his heavy duties to come personally to honor the Senator. The attention did not deter Senator Byrd, one year later, and in the same apple orchard, from publicly criticizing Kennedy for requiring an excessive number of airplanes, yachts, and limousines to move about, and from proposing that he "set an example by getting along with a little less."[32]

The President who resorts to the direct, or lionlike, approach brandishes the veto power freely, turns on the pressures of patronage, pork barrel, and the ministrations of alert aides. He churns up public sentiment for his program to spur the legislators into support. The supreme example of the strong approach was Franklin Roosevelt in his first one hundred days, when in the depths of economic crisis Congress time and again put aside established procedures in the rush to do the President's bidding.

The President is apt to be lionlike in seasons when his political prestige is riding high. Truman, after his spectacular surprise reelection in 1948, was soon giving the pressure valves a full twist. He jarred the gaiety of a Jackson-Jefferson Day dinner of 1948 by threatening, in his address to the celebrating Democrats, to tour the country to force Congressional enactment of the party's platform pledges. Later he termed the vote on the Taft-Hartley Act's repeal a good test of party loyalty and uttered several strictures on the seniority principle and the inattention of Democratic legislators to their party's national platform.[33]

In fashioning his remarkable legislative successes in 1965, Lyndon Johnson, in many an interlude, moved about in his Congressional dealings as a menacing lion. Favored by extraordinary legislative majorities as a result of the 1964 elections, he acted quickly to reap a maximum yield on his wealth of political resources. He insisted that Congress begin work at once on two measures that had long eluded legislative action—education and medical care for the aged geared to the social security system. After impressive success with these, he pushed an avalanche of proposals upon Congress. In 1965 alone, in sixty-three separate documents, he requested a staggering variety of legislation and maintained a close personal watchfulness over its progress.

SYSTEMATIC VERSUS "BUCKSHOT"   President Eisenhower applied to legislative affairs the high degree of system apparent in other phases of his Presidency. His legislative program was elaborately coordinated, setting forth the President's choices and priorities in every major area of federal action. The cycle began at midyear when the Bureau of the Budget called upon the executive agencies to submit by September 15 a statement including "*all* items of legislation (other than appropriations) which the agency contemplates proposing during the ensuing twelve months." A month after the Bureau's call in 1953, Eisenhower, looking toward the coming State of the Union message, asked each cabinet Secretary for substantive ideas based upon a "thorough rethinking of the mission of your department and the . . . means to achieve it." The response was a vast outpouring of measures, many long advocated by the career service. Sherman Adams, the President's chief assistant, and several aides spent two weeks with Bureau of the Budget help studying and sifting the proposals and checking with the President. Many complex and controversial measures of high policy and partisan significance—social security, taxation, agricultural assistance, and foreign aid—were tagged for presentation to the cabinet by the sponsoring department head. The White House staff previewed the presentations and gave advice. In November and December seven were presented to the full cabinet, with Eisenhower himself a leading participant, his questions and views sparking most of the changes made. In mid-December the President unveiled his program to Republican Congressional leaders in a series of carefully staged eight-hour sessions at the White House. The Vice President, the Speaker, the majority leaders, whips, most of the cabinet, and several White House aides were also present. Congressional committee chairmen participated when their subjects were discussed. When legislative leaders expressed concern over some item, the President was apt to modify it. The principal purpose of the sessions, however, was to inform the legislators, not to secure their approval or commitment.[34]

In the three weeks between the leaders' meetings and the presentation of the President's messages in January, the several messages—the State of the Union address (put together by the White House largely from agency submissions), the Budget Report (written largely by the Bureau of the Budget), and the Economic Report (largely the work of the chairman of the Council of Economic Advisers)—were coordinated for consistency and coverage by the White House staff. Meanwhile, the departments concentrated on drafting special messages and detailed bills to follow promptly each proposal advanced in thm more general messages. The State of the Union message of January 7, 1954, stated the President's program in general terms. Specifics were advanced in a series of seven special messages, delivered from January through March, on individual subjects such as social security, agriculture, Taft-Hartley, and foreign aid. An administration bill quickly followed each special message.

Eisenhower's successors have continued his emphasis on system, each with his own variation. President Johnson, in setting his goals for each session, made intensive searches for new legislative programs. He used study groups of private citizens, sent emissaries to university campuses to corral new ideas, and pressed an earnest search among departmental planners and thinkers for responses to national needs. In one ground-laying memorandum, he asked department heads to "insist that your staffs consider the issues objectively, free from what they think may be overriding political obstacles to constructive change. I want to pass judgment personally on such alleged political obstacles." [35] To weigh and choose from the ideas that flowed in, Johnson employed a study group pulled together from the Executive Office, which included his special assistant for legislation, and top personnel from the Bureau of the Budget, the Council of Economic Advisers, and the Office of Science and Technology. Johnson was also a busy and skilled employer of the special message and meetings with legislative leaders.

President Truman was addicted to the buckshot method of presenting a legislative program. His message of September 6, 1945, "one of the most important of my administration," projecting the nation's conversion from warmaking to peacemaking, contained nothing less than twenty-one points of domestic legislation, ranging from agriculture to Congressional salaries. Sixteen thousand words in all, the message was the longest since Theodore Roosevelt's marathon twenty thousand words in 1901.[36] Nor was this all. In subsequent weeks Truman sent up special messages with additional proposals. In his legislative presentation of 1962, President Kennedy followed a similar tactic by deluging Congress with requests for civil rights, special Presidential authority to cut taxes and start public works to avert a recession, medical care for the aged, higher education, foreign aid, urban affairs, an international communications satellite, permanent unemployment compensation, and other things. Judged by its fruits, the buckshot approach is unimpressive. Only a few of Truman's and Kennedy's requests ever became law. Both sets of defeats were easily predictable beforehand.

Why, then, do Presidents resort to buckshot? In both the Truman and Kennedy instances, the Presidents were faced with approaching elections—the national elections of 1948 and the Congressional elections of 1962. Both Presidents, firing a barrage of requests at Congress that were foredoomed to failure, aimed to exploit the Republican tendency to ride the brakes, to build a record for labeling it the "do-nothing" party in the electoral campaign. The buckshot approach is usually asserted in a cantankerous style. Truman blasphemed Congress, and Kennedy, who regularly employed a sober approach puffing Congressional dignity, picked a fight on selected issues, particularly the creation of a department of urban affairs, which cast him in the hero's mold with masses of metropolitan voters. In the buckshot approach, the President invests noticeably less effort in working out compromises and patching together majorities.

INVOLVED VERSUS ALOOF   Far more than most Presidents, Woodrow Wilson was deeply involved personally in the legislative struggle. As a political scientist and an admirer of British public affairs, he had long been convinced that the President must be a kind of "prime minister, as much concerned with the guidance of legislation as with the just and orderly execution of law." Wilson oversaw the development of a body of legislation promoting economic and social justice, the "New Freedom." He believed that only the President could assure an integrated legislative program. Wilson, therefore, regularly planned it, shared in the toil and sweat of drafting bills, and oversaw their progress through Congress.

Preceding each Congressional session, Wilson drew up lists of measures to be pushed, discussed them with the cabinet, and then conferred personally with House and Senate leaders or sent his "political ambassador," Postmaster General Albert S. Burleson, in his stead. Carter Glass, chief legislative sponsor of the Federal Reserve Act, has written that Wilson "dominated" the act's preparation. Congressman E. Y. Webb maintained that Wilson personally drafted the Clayton Act's famous clause that says "the labor of human beings is not a commodity or article of commerce," that he pressed legislative committees to report his bills out, watched the Congressional calendars, and scrutinized amendments to forestall damaging changes. He also managed to keep in touch with conference committee deliberations, a traditional graveyard of progressive legislation.[37]

Wilson used his legislative influence selectively, pushing one measure at a time, but the key to his legislative approach was collaboration. The President, he said, in coming personally before Congress to promote his tariff legislation, should not be viewed as "a mere department of the Government hailing Congress from some isolated island of jealous power . . . he is a human being trying to cooperate with other human beings in a common service." Wilson put in a heavy schedule of hours on Capitol Hill. "Did you ever hear of a President occupying a room in the Capitol called 'the President's Room'? What would be thought of it," he asked the politically sophisticated Josephus Daniels, "if instead of asking Senators with whom I wished to consult to call at the White House, I should occupy that room for such conferences?" Daniels answered candidly that Senators would resent it. Wilson went ahead anyhow. When important bills were in the Congressional crucible, Wilson would see a score of legislators in his Capitol Room. At the White House he saw even more and installed a special telephone to reach Senators quickly from his office. If Congress balked, he went to the people.[38]

Presidential involvement in the contemporary era also includes a readiness to fight on issues that count, even where they concern Congress's internal organization. The big breakthrough, Lawrence F. O'Brien believes, came in the 1961 fight to enlarge the Rules Committee, which the Kennedy administration won by five votes.[39] Under Johnson, the White House involvement deepened. He reminded his cabinet members that "no persons in their respective departments could be more important than the heads of their Congressional relations activity." [40] The departments did not conduct their affairs on Capitol Hill independently but under the watchful eye of the White House. Each department or agency would give a weekly report to the office of the assistant for legislative affairs at the White House, covering its activity on Capitol Hill for the previous week and its forecast for the coming week. The White House assistant then reviewed the reports and prepared an analysis for the President plus an agenda for his weekly breakfast meeting with the Congressional leaders.

Johnson's interest in legislative relations covered the whole waterfront of executive concerns, large and small. "The President we have in the White House now," Representative Peter H. B. Frelinghuysen of New Jersey said, "follows with intense interest everything that affects his legislation. He apparently objects to any modification. He doesn't like a comma changed in anything he's proposed." [41]

In contrast to Wilson and Johnson, who were intensely involved, some Presidents have scrupulously held themselves aloof from the heat and dust of legislative combat. The progenitor of this approach was President Washington. The aloof style custom-fits the hero-President by removing him from the rough and tumble that might scratch the gilt of his flawless prestige. The aloof President addresses Congress in stately, general discourse and with a degree of deference. He avoids the specifics of issues, leaving them for Congress to determine, untutored by the Chief Executive. Washington's first annual message, eagerly awaited as a guide to major policy, was chiefly a general and thankful exposition of "the present favorable prospects of our public affairs." His recommendations were rendered up in broad, innocuous proposals such as "protecting the frontiers," "extension of the postal system," and "promotion of science and literature." The last proposal was delivered in a perfect straddle: "Whether this desirable object will be best promoted by affording aids to seminaries of learning already established, by the institution of a national university, or by any other expedients will be well worthy of a place in the deliberations of the Legislature." At every turn where controversy reared its ugly head Washington nimbly sidestepped.

A century and a half later another hero-President, Dwight D. Eisenhower, visualized his Presidential service as a kind of unifying and moderating influence above the struggle. He was the good man above politics who eschewed conflict, reconciled differences, and healed divisions. He avoided involvement in political controversy and expressed frank distaste for partisan politics. "In the general derogatory sense," he declared in a press conference, "you can say that, of course, I do not like politics." [42] In legislative affairs Eisenhower took on the pleasant missions and left to his colleagues, principally Vice President Nixon and chief Presidential assistant Sherman Adams, the tasks of conveying the harsh word and springing the fierce maneuver. Deeply respectful of the tripartite character of the government, Eisenhower was reluctant to assume executive leadership over a vast area that he viewed as legislative business.

BIPARTISAN VERSUS PARTISAN   A modern President chooses between a partisan and a bipartisan approach to legislation. In certain areas of affairs, bipartisanship is preferable, even imperative. In crisis, in much of foreign policy, and in major social legislation political realities require the modern President to employ bipartisanship to build his legislative majorities. In the depths of economic crisis Franklin Roosevelt conducted a nonpartisan administration, drawing large support from both parties. After 1936, with the crisis subsiding and with huge Democratic legislative majorities created by the elections, his administration took on a more partisan attitude.

President Eisenhower depended heavily upon bipartisan support throughout his two terms. His dependence was not less in his first two years, when the Republicans possessed a legislative majority, than in the following six years, when the Democrats controlled both houses. Eisenhower, writing to the House majority leader, Charles Halleck, early in 1954, said,

> Because of the thin Republican margins in both Houses, both you and Knowland obviously require Democratic support in almost every tough vote. This being so, we must by all means quickly show our readiness to cooperate in every decent way, and particularly in those areas where bipartisan action is vital to the national interest.[43]

Eisenhower's conciliatory pitch was well rewarded. From Democratic leaders Johnson and Rayburn he received, according to Adams, "more sympathy" than from the Republican Senate leader, William F. Knowland, who plagued the President with his one-track mind on the menace of Red China, and Joe Martin, the House leader, whose support of the administration was spoken of in White House circles as "uninspired and lackadaisical."[44] Cooperation with the Democrats paid off at voting time. "Fifty-eight times," according to the *Congressional Quarterly Almanac* for 1953, the administration's worst legislative year, "Democrats saved the President . . . their votes providing the margin of victory when Republican defections or absences imperiled the happy glow." But Eisenhower paid a price for his collaboration. "This added more strain on his relationship with the right wing of his own party," Adams has written.[45] Though Gerald Ford shot flaming arrows of vituperation at the Democrats in the 1974 Congressional elections, he sedulously maintained a bipartisan stance in Washington. He had to; the Democrats possessed overwhelming majorities in both Congressional houses.

Bipartisanship is attractive to the President whose party lacks or barely enjoys a majority in Congress. It may appeal to a President such as Johnson, whose party, thanks to the 1964 elections, gained overwhelming majorities in both houses. In putting through his record-breaking program of legislation in the Eighty-ninth Congress, he steadily courted Republican support and abstained from partisan conduct likely to offend Republicans. He consulted with the Republican opposition constantly before settling on his budget or announcing his domestic legislative program. He relied on Senator Dirksen almost as if the Republican leader were the Democratic leader in the Senate. In assessing the output of the Eighty-ninth Congress he was always careful to recognize the

Republican contribution. "I think the Congress has done a good job," he said on one occasion. "I am not just talking about Democrats. I am talking about Congress generally." [46] Or again, "Most of the key measures have received some support from progressive and moderate Republicans, and all Republicans in some instances." [47]

Some Presidents have traffic with bipartisanship only from sheer political necessity. Otherwise, by instinct and preference they take the partisan road. Left to his own devices, Kennedy preferred a partisan approach to legislation. "Legislative leadership," he said, "is not possible without party leadership." Wilson's Presidency was a telling application of this principle. In forwarding his New Freedom program, he acted true to his conceptions of the President as prime minister, party leader, and champion of a legislative program. Wilson advanced his legislative purposes through party means. He worked through Democratic legislative leaders and committee chairmen, cracked the patronage whip, and employed House and Senate caucuses in the English style. His tariff bill, for example, was taken up in the Democratic caucuses of each house at his insistence. The Senate occasion was termed "the first caucus of Democratic Senators that anyone can remember." Wilson triumphed in both forums. The House and Senate caucuses voted to support the tariff as a party measure. When the federal reserve bill was advancing, Wilson again resorted to caucus with happy result. The act was passed without any Democratic Senators opposing it; in the House only three Democrats dissented.

Wilson as legislative party leader traveled a rough road, given the divisiveness of parties and the localism of Congress. He had to cut through thickets of factional differences and convert the high-tariff Senator F. M. Simmons, the Finance Committee chairman, to espouse the administration's tariff reductions. The House Democratic caucus on the tariff teetered upon collapse when seven Ohio Congressmen threatened to revolt against free wool and the Louisiana delegation fought to break the sugar schedule. But the skillful majority leader, Oscar Underwood, held his ranks, and only thirteen Democrats refused, because of pledges to their constituencies, to abide by the caucus's decision endorsing the tariff reform bill.[48]

INDEPENDENT President-Congress relations may deteriorate into such a state of futility that one or both branches may seek its purposes not through the usual channels of cooperation, but by independent action. The President, for his part, despairing at legislative obstruction, resorts to his prerogative. Franklin Roosevelt, administering price controls in the Second World War, concluded that his efforts to hold the lid on inflation were imperiled by several farm support provisions of the existing Emergency Price Control Act. In a message of September 7, 1942, he asked Congress to repeal the objectionable provisions by October 1. "In the event that the Congress shall fail to act, and act adequately," Roosevelt added, "I shall accept the responsibility, and I will act." How could the President legally carry out this threatened self-assertion? "The President has the powers, under the Constitution and under Congressional acts," said Roosevelt rather generally, "to take measures necessary to avert a disaster which would interfere with the winning of the war.'' Here in slightly different guise was the ''stewardship theory'' of Cousin Theodore.[49]

It is Abraham Lincoln who provides the most sweeping illustration of executive independence. At the outset of the Civil War he delayed calling Congress into session, judging presumably and altogether justifiably, in light of history, that the legislators might delay and obstruct while rebellion spread. Lincoln the Commander-in-Chief became for twelve crucial weeks the nation's lawmaker. The normal joint legislative-executive processes were suspended, and America had its first taste of dictatorship, fortunately a benevolent one.

Executive-legislative relations can also collapse into general debacle at Congress's instigation. In two of the worst crises the nation has known, Congress discarded every vestige of cooperation with the Chief Executive and pursued a bitter course of general sabotage. James Buchanan, who toiled hard and prayerfully to prevent the Civil War, and Andrew Johnson in the Reconstruction era were the victims of rampant Congressional hostility. In Buchanan's case Congress denied the President nothing less than the essentials of governance. As the South continued to mobilize in spite of his entreaties, Buchanan requested more military funds. Congress responded by cutting his estimates to a fraction of their original amount and restricting the service of any additional volunteers who might be raised to the Utah territory. Buchanan justifiably asserted that the last Congress he had the misfortune to experience had ''throughout the entire session, refused to adopt any measures of compromise to prevent civil war, or to retain first the cotton or afterwards the border States within the Union.'' Congress was derelict in other vital duties. It failed to provide for any judicial process in South Carolina following the resignation of every federal court officer. Congress declined to provide the President with authority to call out the militia or volunteers to suppress the insurrection flaming in Charleston. Even after Buchanan's message of January 8, 1861, declaring the existence of revolution and reminding Congress that it alone could muster troops, three weeks passed before a bill was introduced, only to be immediately withdrawn. Not until two months after South Carolina seceded and ten days after the Confederacy was formed was another, more modest, militia bill proposed. The House killed it with a resolution to postpone.[50]

The Future Presidency

''There is nothing more important for the future of popular government in America,'' Charles A. Beard once wrote, ''than an overhauling of congressional methods and the establishment of better relations with the Executive.'' The problems to which Beard pointed have over the decades stirred thought in political and academic circles and have evoked a quantity of proposals for reform. The more extreme of these have urged that separation of powers and checks and balances be rigorously altered and that some variant of the British parliamentary system be adopted. The seeds of this alternative have always

fallen on barren soil since it is alien to the entire American tradition. A historically assertive Congress would never bear the subordination of the legislature to
the degree implied in the British system. Any changes, if they are to occur,
must be in accord with the spirit of an autonomous Congress endowed with
considerable power.

We need a strong President and a strong Congress. The two are not incompatible but mutually reinforcing through their representation of valid constituencies—the President the nation, and the Congressional houses the locality,
state, and region. Both the national and local sectors of political society must
be rallied behind major policy. Accordingly, neither Congress nor the President
can have a monopoly of wisdom and an exclusive claim to the exercise of leadership. What we seek is effective cooperation between the two branches, with
each a positive, constructive participant. We need to avoid both Lincoln's tendency toward exclusive leadership and the executive-legislative deadlocks of
the past four decades.

A second essential contribution of Congress is to help keep the Presidency on
the path of constitutional decorum. Congress is a principal instrument, potentially the best of all governmental instruments, for holding the President accountable, for assuring that he functions as a responsible executive, within the
law, and with sufficient conformity to the democratic ethos—its values and
processes. As a lot, Chief Executives need to be coached and pushed by other
political institutions to stay within constitutional parameters, and Congress is
well qualified for the task, with members who are powerful and self-assertive
and with resources and decision, to extend or withhold, on which the President
depends. Criticisms of the contemporary Presidency as an institution that is
abusive of power imply that Congress has been performing less than adequately
its vital task of holding the Chief Executive to the standards of constitutional
democracy. Explanations that are offered of Congress's insufficiency of accomplishment appraise the national legislature as lethargic, timid, and married
to outmoded methods.

1. The President, the Senate, and the House should be simultaneously
elected for a common term of four years. Historic data establishes that we
could rightfully expect that an election so administered would produce a President and two houses of Congress better attuned in party and political outlook
than their present staggered elections permits. It is a rare Congressman who
will repudiate his party's platform in a Presidential year. Under existing practice, the Senate, with its six-year term, is never wholly elected during a President's four-year term, and it is not until he is at his own midterm that even a
majority—two-thirds—of the Senators who will serve during the President's
tenure has been chosen. Also, the House's two-year term, and consequent election at the President's midterm, subjects his administration to a severe test of its
popularity at an interval that is unfair, coming when his administration has
barely started. Defeat in the election can be damaging to the President's prestige in both foreign and domestic politics. All too often, either his party loses
control of the House or Senate, or its majority is reduced.

2. Control of the purse strings is the hallmark of the democratic legislature. Those who perceive a dangerous enlargement of Presidential power rightly point to the frail and tattered state of the Congressional purse strings. Control has been slipping freely to the President, thanks to the conferral of a sweeping budgetary power on him and Nixon's little inhibited impoundment of funds.

In a potentially important counterstroke, Congress enacted new budgetary legislation in 1974, expanding the legislative role.[51] Henceforth Congress, after submission of the Presidential budget and before acting on appropriations and spending legislation, must adopt a budget resolution, setting target figures for total appropriations and spending and defining related tax and debt levels. Congress will also set subtargets for particular functions—health, defense, agriculture, and the like. In each house, new committees are established to analyze budget options and prepare budget resolutions, and a new timetable of deadlines has been set for various steps in the Congressional finance process, adding three months to legislative review of the Presidential budget. A Congressional budget office is also established, equipped with experts and computers, to analyze the President's budget. Most important, the new law enables Congress to force the President to spend impounded funds. To work effectively, the 1974 law will require serious and continuous commitment from Congress, for embedded in its language are provisos for its undoing: at any time, Congress can waive its procedures and postpone its deadlines.

3. The internal organization of the houses of Congress can be viewed as a maze of contrivances to assure inaction or minority rule. The majority is prevented from voting upon measures that by every indication it would approve, or it is able to act only after unconscionable delay. Often the thwarted majority opinion equals or approximates the President's positive view of social programs—Kennedy's and Johnson's domestic programs in general, and Nixon's initial proposals for welfare reform and revenue sharing. Consequently, a liberation of the legislative majority would frequently produce Congressional approval of key items in the President's program. The devices of minority rule are well known: the seniority principle in selecting committee chairmen, the method of assigning legislators to committees, the vast power of the House Rules Committee, and the Senate filibuster, to mention several of the most powerful. Symptomatic of the gravity of the problem is the fact that not only was Nixon's welfare reform not enacted during two Presidential terms, but Congress substituted no plan of its own.

The seniority principle of choosing committee chairmen, which assures that the preponderance of these eminences will oppose much of the President's positive social program, urgently needs to be modified. Legislators and thoughtful citizens have often advanced proposals to this end. In hearings held in 1965, the Monroney-Madden Committee on the reorganization of Congress heard testimony containing various proposals for substitutes for the seniority principle: election of the chairman by majority vote of the committee, rotation among senior members, election by the party caucus, removal of the chairman by majority vote of the committee after he has served a single term and reached age seventy, and the setting of meeting dates, agenda, and other procedures by majority vote in lieu of the chairman's decision. In urging the seventy-year age limit, former Senator Joseph S. Clark has noted that it is the same limit that Congress itself has placed upon federal judges to induce their retirement. Under the Clark proposal, the overage chairman could still continue as a member of the committee.

Study and discussion have led to positive action. In 1971, House Republicans adopted procedures by which they selected by secret ballot the party member to serve as highest ranking Republican member on each House committee. If Republicans gain control of the House in the future, they could elect committee chairmen. This would provide the opportunity to challenge the workings of the seniority principle. The Republican innovation placed pressure on House Democrats to modify their seniority system, which they did in reforms adopted in 1974.

The House Democratic caucus likewise modified its procedures to make it easier to challenge the workings of seniority in the selection of committee chairmen as well as Appropriations subcommittee chairmanships. The sole early casualty of the new procedures was Wilbur Mills, who was overthrown as Ways and Means Committee chairman. The 1974 reforms did not prevent the committee and subcommittee chairmanships to continue to go to senior members who generally were more conservative than the House Democratic caucus as a whole. Another 1974 reform directed at House seniors barred committee chairmen from serving as chairmen of another standing committee or of a joint House-Senate committee, a step that sheared authority from octogenarian Congressman Wright Patman of Texas, who was chairman of both the House Banking and Currency Committee and the Congressional Joint Economic Committee. However, since joint committees lack authority to send legislation to the floor for passage, they possess little power. In contrast, the Senate remained untouched by reform and the traditional seniority principle continued intact.

To assure that legislation receives fair and prompt attention, several further adjustments might well be made in the standing committees. Because of their present size and memberships, many committees do not accurately reflect the majority opinion in each house, nor the strength of the apparent disposition of the houses' majorities. Accordingly, its items encounter delay, crippling amendment, or death in committee. In 1974, the House through its reforms, but not the Senate, responded to the problem. The House Ways and Means Committee, historic mutilator of tax reform and other progressive legislation, had its membership increased from 25 to 37, with most new appointees liberal in outlook, a perspective long underrepresented on the committee. Key House subcommittees were made more available to junior members. Other 1974 reforms pulled power away from mighty committee chairmen and their fiefdoms to leaderships more sympathetic to progressive social and economic legislation. The power to fill vacancies on committees was shifted from the conservative Ways and Means Committee to the Democratic Steering and Policy Committee, an arm of the rather more progressive House leadership, Speaker Carl Albert and Majority Leader Thomas P. O'Neill, Jr. For the first time in years, an aggressive liberal, Representative Phillip Burton of California, was elected chairman of the Democratic caucus.

Caution is necessary to avoid exaggerating the consequences of these changes for policy and program. Albert and O'Neill are oriented more to politics than to program, and leadership of the party caucus has not been a stepping stone to policy accomplishment.[52]

Still other reforms of the 1970s virtually abolished was the old practice by which members could avoid having their votes recorded on floor amendments, enabling them to vote counter to their announced general positions on issues. All committees were required to function according to written rules, rather than according to the whims of the chairman, as in the past.[53]

A variety of other Congressional reforms can be advanced to improve the ability of the legislative majority to act and the President's program to receive its just consideration: the conference committee, which often mutilates bills with arbitrary abandon, ought to include in the majority of its members from each house only those whose votes demonstrate their support of a bill that their house has passed and with which the other house disagrees. In addition, committees with an overburdening volume of business, such as House Ways and Means and Senate Finance, might have their excess redistributed to other committees, a step that might speed their work.

To ask how, after decades of waiting, the reforms of the 1970s finally transpired is to evoke an answer that suggests a likely route to further reforms. Fortunately, the House's leadership in the 1970s, Speaker Carl Albert and majority leader Thomas J. O'Neill, proved more responsive to the reform tide than previous leaderships. Reform also benefited from public interest group lobbying, most notably by Common Cause. For years, the Democratic Study Group, a small band of liberal House Democrats, hammered away at reform and constructed an understanding and ultimately an accepting climate for the reform agenda. Evidently, House members were moved by polls showing that public confidence in Congress had sunk to virtually a record low, indeed to a point lower than that for the harried President Nixon. The way to reform was also eased by the inroads of the 1970 primaries and elections into the ranks of senior legislators, resulting in the retirement of many aging and powerful members and their replacement by younger activists in both parties. Finally, President Nixon himself was an unwitting catalyst of reform. His frontal attacks on Congressional prerogatives, expansions of executive privilege, united Democrats in the House and moderates and liberals of both parties as no other recent force has and rekindled among the members a certain pride in Congress as an institution.[54] Reform became a prime defense against executive encroachment. But the question of how much can be gained in program initiatives and coherence awaits further testing.

8

ADMINISTRATIVE CHIEF

It is good for democracy but bad for the strong Presidency—though by no means always for either—that the Chief Executive possesses a highly imperfect capacity to induce the vast officialdom of the executive branch to abide by his purposes and follow his directives. If there were any saving moments in the Watergate scandals, they occurred when two bureaus, the Internal Revenue Service and the FBI, beat back demands from White House associates of President Nixon that they approve or share in acts of malfeasance. Nixon and the country might have been spared the agony of Watergate and the strength of his Presidency saved rather than dissipated by that scandal if other bureaus—the Justice Department, for example—had been a force for probity rather than mischief, and had resisted the wrongdoing emanating from the White House.

But democracy is also enhanced when government through administrative program enables the private individual and group to utilize their freedoms more effectively, by overcoming illiteracy, for example, by raising levels of health care, by opening employment to racial minorities. More often than not the Presidency is a force for good, and its capacity for positive accomplishment in forwarding programs responsive to society's problems is hobbled by administrative limitations. Unlike the typical business chief, the President finds no designation in his fundamental charter, the Constitution, as administrative chief, and neither do its collective provisions confer any equivalent authority. The Constitution does grant him the "executive power," language the Supreme Court has sometimes interpreted to include certain powers normally associated with an administrative chief. He is charged to see that the laws are "faithfully executed," which suggests a general administrative responsibility, but duty is not power. He also enjoys express powers such as the power to make appointments. Still other authority is conferred by act of Congress and by weight of custom. As well, he functions vis-à-vis the departments and agencies with a highly imperfect communications system. Although avalanches of papers and reports constantly threaten to engulf him, the President lacks the most rudimentary administrative information. He has only a sparse and disjointed impression of the quality of performance by the departments and to what degree they are fulfilling his policies and purposes. Worst of all, he lacks any dependable system that will forewarn him of incipient malfunctions in the departments.

Although the President has a mighty array of counselors in the White House staff and the Executive Office of the President, his office is relatively weak in policy analysis. His limited band of associates live in constant danger of being out-thought and out-flanked by the vaster armies of the departmental bureaus and their interest group clienteles. At best, the President and his helpers can tinker and adjust, but the preponderance of the world of policy and action belongs to the departments.[1]

With this gift of imperfect power, the President engages in varied administrative activities. He shapes and determines policy, from "grand policy" to clerical minutiae, from the Monroe Doctrine to a common spectacle in Eisenhower's day, when scores of commissions for notaries public were spread out on his office floor waiting for the ink of his signature to dry.

The President prepares for decisions by absorbing oral briefings and reading and pondering memoranda. Many a President would vouch for Truman's complaint that the reading is hard on the eyes and on the attention, for "nearly every memorandum had a catch in it." [2] The President supervises his executive subordinates with an attitude ranging from the tolerance of Harding, who approved everything his Secretary of State, Charles Evans Hughes, did, to the definitiveness of Polk, who required his Secretaries, seated before his desk, to read their reports aloud before forwarding them to Congress. The President has only limited power to recruit, train, and promote the personnel of the executive branch. Most of his key appointments require the advice and consent of the Senate, and even more are subject to vagaries of Senatorial courtesy. Since the first days of the republic he has shared general personnel powers with Congress, and since 1883, when the Civil Service Act (the Pendleton Act) became law, with a civil service commission.

His power to make removals, a subject on which the Constitution is silent, is likewise circumscribed by the civil service laws and by the courts. In *Myers* v. *United States* (272 U.S. 52, 1926) on President Wilson's removal of a postmaster, the Court seemed to find the President's removal authority unlimited. This sweeping ruling was trimmed back in *Humphrey's Executor* v. *United States* (295 U.S. 602, 1935). Humphrey, a Federal Trade Commissioner appointed by President Hoover, was removed by President Franklin Roosevelt not for causes cited in statute but, as Roosevelt candidly disclosed, because of policy differences between Humphrey and himself. The Court, finding for Humphrey, held that Congress can protect officials such as a Federal Trade Commissioner, who wield legislative or judicial power, against Presidential removal. An "executive officer," however, or one "restricted to the performance of executive functions," the Court took pains to declare, could not be similarly protected. The distinction between an "executive officer" and one exercising "legislative or judicial power" remains blurred, although in *A. E. Morgan* v. *TVA* (115 Fed. [2d] 990, 1940) the Circuit Court of Appeals viewed a member of TVA's board of directors as an "executive officer."

The President delegates functions and authority, and by grace of the Budget and Accounting Act of 1921, develops an executive budget—his budget—covering federal income and outgo. He coordinates the several agencies of the executive branch or, as Harry Truman put it, he makes a "mesh" of things.[3]

Almost continuously since the Reorganization Act of 1939, a consequence of the famous Brownlow Committee, he has had a limited power to reorganize executive agencies by redistributing functions and overhauling structures.

Congress as Administrator

The executive branch has not one but two managers—the President and his rival, Congress. Nearly everything the President does Congress can do, sometimes with greater effect. The mission and structure of the departments are determined by act of Congress. Congress can give authority to subordinate officials to act independently of their department heads, prescribe specific and detailed administrative procedures, petrify the internal organization of an agency by statute, and require Senate confirmation for bureau chief appointments. Congress can establish independent regulatory commissions, like the Interstate Commerce Commission and the Federal Reserve Board, well removed from the President's direction and control. All executive agencies require annual appropriations that Congress provides as it chooses. The programs they administer Congress authorizes and amends. Congress can investigate departmental work in close detail, and its habit is not merely to query the leadership but to reach far down into the hierarchy. A dominant fact of life for the department Secretary is that he must respond not merely to his official superior, the President, but to the standing committees and subcommittees of the House and Senate watching over his department, aided and abetted by the pressure groups whose needs it serves. But as the Watergate hearings of the Ervin Committee (Senate Select Committee on Presidential Campaign Activities) reveal, the legislative investigation is a mighty force for exposing executive misdeeds that threaten democracy's well-being.

By tradition, Congress is closely involved in personnel administration. In detailed laws, Congress sets down the elements of a classification structure, rates of pay, service ratings, retirement, and the like. Although Congress gives the President the power to develop an executive budget, legislative action on its parts may be so extensive that much of the document's original validity may be lost.

Some Presidents, accepting the realities, give the Congressional power centers a substantial part in the development of administrative decisions affecting program, budget, and personnel before consummating them and dispatching them to Capitol Hill. Lyndon Johnson was of this school. His appointment of a public commission, for example, to reconsider the entire foreign aid program served to diminish the rising outcry of Congressional economizers. In the Nixon era, characterized by running conflict between the President and Congress over domestic programs, the legislators, typically, championed the bureaus against the President's budget cuts and impoundments of funds, and the depredations of department secretaries, who, reflecting Nixon, interpreted program intent restrictively and even contrary to legislative mandates that often were drafted by the bureaus in the first place. But Congress's supreme accomplishment was blowing the whistle on Watergate.

The Bureaucracy

Even more resistant to the President's quest for dominion over the executive branch is the giant bureaucracy itself, with its layers of specialists, its massive paper work and lumbering pace, its addiction to routine, its suspicion as a permanent power center committed to program and policy of a transitory, potentially disruptive Presidential administration. The single most powerful figure in the great pyramid is the bureau chief, who in many subtle ways can frustrate the President's purposes when they diverge from his own. He cultivates ties with the pressure groups whose interests his organization serves and the Congressional committees that provide him with money and authority. Congressional committees and subcommittees welcome his attentions. The subcommittee on veterans' affairs does not wish to permit any facet of veterans' services to fall into other hands. The bureau chief may enjoy impregnable prestige with the public. John Kennedy as President-elect yielded to that reality when he announced at the time of his first appointments the retention of J. Edgar Hoover, a public hero, as Director of the FBI. Richard Nixon made a similar judgment when he abandoned a plan to fire Hoover. However, in light of consequences in the longer run, the decisions of both Presidents seem questionable. Between the President and the massive departments are natural antagonisms of interest. The President wants to keep control, to receive early warning of items for his agenda before his options are foreclosed, to pick his issues and lift them out of normal channels, to obtain the bureaucracy's full support for his initiatives. The great departments represent a wholly different bundle of purposes and needs. They cling to orderly routines, mountainous paper work, and time-consuming clearance procedures. They tend toward caution, and to the departments the President may represent a temporary intruder who threatens established policy.

At times, Kennedy and his aides despaired more over their travail in winning cooperation from the departmental bureaucracy than over their deadlocks with Congress. After one heavy interval of bureaucratic obstruction, the Kennedy administration in its private comment seemed to adopt the notion that the President must contend not merely with Congress but with a further branch, a fourth branch, the bureaucracy. There were distressing signs of the force of the bureaucracy's hostile impact. Kennedy despaired of the State Department's ability to manage foreign policy effectively. The military services teamed up with the Congressional committees against the President's military policies, and the Bay of Pigs disaster taught Kennedy, according to his own avowal, the folly of relying completely on subordinates down the line.

But the bureaucrat can also be an heroic figure asserting democracy's interests against malpractices and the towering hostility of the Presidency. In the Nixon years, for example, Gordon W. Rule, director of the Procurement Control and Clearance Section of the Navy Materiel Command, testified to a Congressional committee that government was rescuing giant concerns of the military-industrial complex while smaller companies were allowed to fail. Furthermore, according to Rule, military contracting was becoming a "quasi-welfare industry," and the appointment of a former official, Roy L. Ash, of one of the more dependent of these enterprises, Litton Industries, as the President's chief budget director was "a mistake." Retribution fell swiftly upon this civil servant, who was valuable to democracy for his courage and candor. Rule was reassigned to other duties where he would find less occasion for critical utterance.[4]

The Presidential Staff

To assert his influence over the executive branch, the President resorts to his White House staff, the cabinet, and the cluster of agencies composing the Executive Office of the President. The White House staff consists of approximately a score of senior assistants who bear such diverse titles as press secretary, special counsel to the President, appointments secretary, and special assistant for national security, science and technology, or a miscellany of other affairs. There are many other staff members—the precise number in recent administrations is unknown. Some may be unlisted and unannounced publicly, and many are "loaned"—paid for by the departments, in which, technically, they continue to be employed, while toiling full-time in the White House. In the federal budget for 1974, 480 persons were listed under the White House Office, with a budget of $9,100,000. Of this sizeable number, probably fewer than a dozen occupied positions of important policy influence. The staff is the President's "lengthened shadow." Staff members help prepare his messages, speeches, and correspondence; arrange his appointments; oversee the inflow and outflow of his communications; analyze and refine the problems confronting him; advance his purposes with legislators, departments, private groups, and party officialdom. Although White House aides cherish their anonymity, they cannot escape importance. Few cabinet Secretaries can rival leading White House staff members in influence and authority. Collectively, the staff tends to be more powerful than all other groups in the executive branch, including the cabinet and the National Security Council.

The cabinet, founded by Washington early in his Presidency, has seldom been a source of advice upon which the President continuously relies. It exists by custom and functions by Presidential initiative and is therefore largely what the Chief Executive chooses to make of it. "It lives," Richard F. Fenno has written, "in a state of institutional dependency to promote the effective exercise of the President's authority and to help implement his ultimate responsibilities." [5] Wilson, Franklin Roosevelt, and John Kennedy used it little. Quick and hard-driving, they chafed under extended group discussion. Truman and Eisenhower resorted to it more but with uneven result. Johnson was more inclined than Kennedy to employ it, although often his purpose was not to secure counsel but to develop understanding and support in the cabinet "team" for a pending administration decision. In no Presidential administration of the past four decades has the cabinet emerged in the forefront of influence in Presidential policy making.

Unlike the British Prime Minister, who, typically, brings into office a team of ministers or department heads who have long been associated in common legislative and party enterprises with houses of Parliament, many of the President's department Secretaries arrive with no acquaintance with each other and indeed little with the President himself. The two principal appointees of the Kennedy administration, Secretary of State Dean Rusk and Secretary of Defense Robert McNamara, were both strangers to the President until the moment he interviewed them for their respective jobs. Historically, all sorts of considerations have governed the selection of department heads, including geography, to a degree: The Interior Secretary is ordinarily a Westerner, and the Secretary of Agriculture is hardly apt to hail from an Eastern metropolis but more likely from corn, wheat, or hog country. The Secretaries of Commerce and the Treasury will probably emerge from the business and financial worlds. The Secretary of Labor may be picked from the organized labor movement, as was the case with Martin Durkin in the Eisenhower administration and Peter Brennan in the Nixon and Ford administration. Ordinarily, the major party factions must be represented. Eisenhower dealt out recognition to protégés of Robert A. Taft, his rival for the Presidential nomination, by appointing George Humphrey and Ezra Taft Benson Secretary of the Treasury and Secretary of Agriculture. For Johnson, the retention of cabinet Secretaries inherited from the Kennedy administration was useful as a bridge to the "Kennedy wing" of the Democratic party. A cabinet that includes strong political figures and personalities—a Charles Evans Hughes or a William Jennings Bryan—can be one of the most effective counterbalances to the strong President, with status and experience enabling them to question and resist Presidential actions that they consider unmeritorious. The strong Secretary is a potent safeguard against Presidential abuse.

In addition to the White House Office and other units, the Executive Office of the President includes the National Security Council, patterned after the British Committee of Imperial Defence and created by the National Security Act of 1947. It advises the President on national security objectives and commitments and the integration of national security policy. The NSC's top-level membership comprises the President, the Vice President, the Secretary of State, the Secretary of Defense, and the statutory advisers—the chairman of the Joint Chiefs of Staff and the director of the Central Intelligence Agency. The President can invite such other officials as he chooses to attend NSC sessions. In the Truman and Eisenhower administrations the NSC included a substructure of several working levels that was dropped in the Kennedy administration. Nixon, however, added to the NSC's committee structure in ways that expanded the influence of the assistant for national security affairs, Henry Kissinger.[6] The Office of Management and Budget (OMB), whose director may be involved in a wide range of Presidential concerns, was created by the Budget and Accounting Act of 1921. In the President's behalf the OMB prepares a single executive budget or consolidated financial program, although Congress has not committed itself to pass a consolidated appropriation bill. The OMB also clears and coordinates legislation for the President and promotes management improvement in the executive branch. The Council of Economic Advisers, a child of the Employment Act of 1946, thinks, plans, and reports on the maintenance of economic prosperity. The Council on Environmental Quality advises the President on how pollution can be controlled and diminished. Nixon established a Domestic Council, patterned after the NSC, with a staff, department heads, and an executive director who was also a principal member of the White House staff. The council generated ideas from the bureaucracy for coping with domestic problems, prepared and promoted legislation, and was a focal point for relations with the states and cities. Less professional than the NSC and more political, the council enjoyed Nixon's and Ford's confidence and, therefore, a steadily expanding influence.[7]

The Vice Presidency, whose first incumbent, John Adams, termed it "the most insignificant office that ever the invention of man contrived or his imagination conceived," [8] has, after dormancy through most of the nineteenth century, acquired occasional usefulness in the twentieth. A President prefers to work closely with associates whom he can discard easily, which he cannot do with the Vice President, whom he cannot fire. The Constitution also makes the Vice President the presiding officer of the Senate, a duty which, although light, makes difficult his assumption of large and fixed executive responsibilities. Vice Presidents of the past three decades have participated increasingly, although unevenly, in the President's administrative enterprises. Henry A. Wallace, as Vice President in the Franklin Roosevelt administration, took on important administrative duties during the Second World War. Alben Barkley in the Truman administration became a statutory member of the National Security Council. Richard Nixon in the Eisenhower administration presided over the cabinet and the National Security Council in the Chief Executive's absence, was chairman of the interdepartmental government contract committee, and undertook good-will missions abroad. He did not, however, discharge any important executive responsibilities. Vice President Johnson in the Kennedy administration continued in the Nixon pattern, with assignments overseas and chairmanships of several interdepartmental committees concerning space programs and government contracts important for civil rights policy. That Johnson also held a substantial place as a counselor in the Kennedy administration is suggested by his membership in the "Ex Com" of the National Security Council, an *ad hoc* group of a dozen top administration officials who aided the President in working out his responses to the 1962 Cuban crisis.

In the Johnson administration, Hubert Humphrey's most consequential toil was promoting the progress of Great Society legislation on Capitol Hill. Like his recent predecessors, he ventured abroad to serve as a prestigious official symbol of American concern for the countries visited. Humphrey was also charged to keep in touch with farm and urban affairs programs and was made White House liaison with the nation's mayors, governors, and major interest groups, such as the Leadership Conference on Civil Rights. Humphrey was also a link to the liberal community, seeking to diminish its outcry against the Vietnam War. As Nixon's Vice President, Spiro Agnew was a stellar electoral campaigner, the darling of the conservative Republican banquet circuit, whose speeches depicted America as a place of deteriorating values, induced by, among others, violent demonstrators ("those tomentose exhibitionists"); and Vietnam peace marchers ("an effete corps of impudent snobs"). In the daily operations of the Presidency, Agnew was an excluded figure. He rarely saw Nixon, and the recognitions conferred upon him proved no springboard to influence—member of the cabinet, the National Security Council, the Domestic Council, and the national councils on Indian Opportunity and aeronautics and space. Almost invariably, if Agnew was to preside, a White House staff member would appear and run the meeting. For a time, Agnew headed the Office of Intergovernmental Relations and was a principal liaison between the federal government and the states and cities, but the function was subsequently taken over by the White House staff.[9] After exposure of his criminal behavior, Agnew resigned. His successor, Gerald Ford, also became an electoral campaigner and a defender of a Nixon imperiled by Watergate and impeachment.

A transition study group recommended to Ford that Vice President Nelson Rockefeller be closely enmeshed in White House operations. Rockefeller became vice chairman of the Domestic Council, where conceivably he could assume a major role in the country's grave economic problems, and as vice chairman of the National Security Council, he could become active in foreign and national security policy. Ford stressed that the Vice President would engage in "explaining" administration policy "throughout the country." [10] Rockefeller's fulfillment of these duties would make his impact greater than that of other Vice Presidents. But, like his predecessors, he faced obstacles: maintaining the President's confidence and relating effectively to the President's personal assistants.

The acute question facing the President is how to best harness the administrative resources of the executive branch to his democratically legitimate purposes—how can he transmute goal and plan into program and policy? How can he best awaken a sense of urgency in the bureaucracy and bestir its creativity? Presumably his best ally in these causes is the Presidential staff, which after small and slow beginnings has, since the New Deal era—and especially since the Second World War and in the Nixon years—burgeoned into a substantial bureaucracy itself, with more than four thousand employees occupying several buildings plus the east and west wings of the White House. Will the Presidential bureaucracy succumb to supreme irony and itself assume the very qualities of the greater bureaucracy it is designed to combat?

On the other hand, the President himself is a bundle of frailties and inadequacies—of limited knowledge and imperfect information, of biases and blind spots, and, sometimes, unfortunately, of stunted ethical sensitivities, for which a well-functioning staff could be a corrective force. The President-staff relationship is therefore a problem of balance, of sufficient Presidential dominion to advance his program and fulfill his electoral mandate, while simultaneously the staff retains a capacity to question the Chief Executive's thinking and worthiness of purpose, to put forward alternatives, to warn of pitfalls. But the staff too can bear the same human and policy weaknesses as the President, and as the sad events of Watergate remind us, the White House staff can be a fabricator of criminal acts that subvert democracy. Moreover, the staff's incessant accumulation of power, well removed from Congressional and public scrutiny, is incompatible with democracy. Can Presidents manage their staffs in ways that advance the legitimate needs of the strong Presidency while simultaneously holding them within democratic norms?

Roosevelt as Administrator

Franklin D. Roosevelt reigned as chief administrator by a highly unconventional system that gave the utmost play to his influence and enabled him to retain great power in his own hands. In pursuit of this supreme good he resorted to means that time and again violated the most sacred canons of efficient administration as taught with unflagging zeal in schools of business and public administration. For Roosevelt, organization blueprints were often scraps of paper, and the rules by which good executives, according to the texts, delegate authority were honored by their breach.

The textbooks warn that duplication must above all else be avoided in administration. Roosevelt went out of his way to indulge in it. He instituted the New Deal and its revolutionary changes, notwithstanding the bureaucracy he inherited from the previous Republican era. Roosevelt triumphed over the established bureaucracy with its elephantine pace and resistance to change partly by ignoring it. He established his own bureaucracy to adminster much of the New Deal. The job of regulating stock exchanges was given not to the Treasury or Commerce Departments but to the newborn Securities and Exchange Commission. The Wagner Act, enhancing labor's opportunity to organize and engage in collective bargaining, was consigned not to the Labor Department but the National Labor Relations Board. The bold new Tennessee River Valley project fell not to the Interior Department but to a special Tennessee Valley Authority. Before the normal pathologies of bureaucracy could mature, the New Deal was a going operation.

Roosevelt as administrator drew freely from a large bag of tricks to get what he wanted done. He had little regard for the administrative niceties that are observed in most organizations. He was given, for example, to end-running his department heads and dealing directly with their subordinates. He applied a competitive theory of administration, which kept his administrators unsure, off balance, confused, and even exasperated. With ambition pitted against ambition, the power of decision remained more securely in his own hands. In Roosevelt's Presidency, competition was also democracy-serving. Those of Roosevelt's staff who opposed the trend of policy or an incipient decision had every inducement to illuminate weaknesses—ethical flaws, transgressions of democratic values and electoral mandates, faulty assumptions, and misperceptions of events and situations. But, as the stormy intervals of Lincoln's cabinet often demonstrated, competition can be excessive and disruptive, as it sometimes was with Roosevelt. Roosevelt at times deliberately kept the lines of authority blurred and jurisdictions overlapping. The administration of work relief thus was divided vaguely between Harry Hopkins, successively the Federal Emergency Relief Administrator and Works Progress Administrator, and Harold Ickes, the Public Works Administrator. Secretary of the Treasury Henry Morgenthau, Jr., was given, with Presidential approval, such large powers of interference in the expenditures of WPA that Hopkins nearly resigned. "There is something to be said," Roosevelt observed in behalf of his method of planned disorder, ". . . for having a little conflict between agencies. A little rivalry is stimulating, you know. It keeps everybody going to prove that he is a better fellow than the next man. It keeps them honest too." [11]

Roosevelt's devotion to the competitive principle and checks and balances led him often to prefer boards, commissions, and other variants of the plural executive to the single administrator. One of his more bizarre creations in the Second World War was the Office of Production Management, charged with administering much of the economy's mobilization. For this intricate and massive task, he resorted not to the leadership of a single administrator but to a biheaded authority consisting of William Knudsen of General Motors as Director General and Sidney Hillman of the CIO as Associate Director General. Although Knudsen's and Hillman's titles differed slightly, their authority, Roosevelt disclosed at a press conference, would be equal. But suppose, an incredulous reporter queried, Knudsen and Hillman disagreed, an altogether likely prospect given the conflicting premises of their respective worlds of management and labor. Might not the war effort be imperiled by dissension and impasse in OPM's biheadship? There would be no trouble whatever, Roosevelt answered confidently. If Knudsen and Hillman disagreed, he would simply lock them up in a room and not let them out until they could agree. [12]

In maintaining competition, Roosevelt was adept at cutting down or building up his aides as situations might require. He disciplined them by withholding honors and distinctions, by assigning new authority and programs to someone else. He rewarded administrators with his intimacies. Harold Ickes, a jealous and cantankerous administrator, suffered his most distressful period when a year elapsed in which he never saw his chief alone. In Roosevelt's hand the simple, small White House luncheon became a mighty sword of reward and fear. If Ickes or Wallace lunched with the President, every other member of the official family instantly knew of the event and speculated anxiously about what had been discussed and its consequences for their interests. [13]

Roosevelt sometimes had to knock an administrator down, but he was quick to help him up. If Ickes had been shorn of a coveted jurisdiction and Hull had lost an interdepartmental dispute, Roosevelt would favor the losers with attentions days later. The building-up might take the form of an elaborate compliment in cabinet for the way the vanquished Secretary had handled what was described as a difficult and sensitive matter. Another restorative was "hand-holding," as Roosevelt called it, a process of consolation at which his talent, in the discerning judgment of William Phillips, was "rare" and which took up, according to Grace Tully, the President's secretary, "hours and days" of his time.

Roosevelt, in the interest of competition, filled his administration with human opposites. His original Secretary of the Treasury, Will Woodin, was a conservative, respectable, trustworthy financier, and his first Director of the Budget, the economy-minded Lewis Douglas, viewed New Deal spending as "the end of Western civilization." Yet Roosevelt could also import a free-spender like Hopkins and legions of young lawyers schooled in the progressivism of Louis Brandeis and Felix Frankfurter. The philosophical pluralism of his administration enabled Roosevelt to play off not merely men against men but dogma against dogma. It was a kind of double insurance of Roosevelt's own retention of the power of decision.

The jewels in the crown of the formal organization, the department Secretaries, were individuals of initiative and drive, deep in their commitment to program. Roosevelt permitted them great scope. Their collective organization, the cabinet, however, he restricted to a modest role. He did not value the cabinet as a source of collective wisdom, and its meetings were apt to be hollow affairs. The President began typically by engaging in a monologue of pleasantries, recounting stories and joshing selected Secretaries. He would then throw out a problem, usually one that he had been considering just prior to the meeting. Discussion rambled and was inconclusive. Roosevelt's next move was to turn to the Secretary of State and say, "Well, Cordell, what's on your mind today?" The same query continued around the table in order of the Secretaries' precedence. They responded usually with items of minor importance, preferring to take up larger matters privately with the President just before or after the meeting. Large matters, the Secretaries feared, might be excessively mauled or leaked to the Hill or to the gossip columnists.[14]

Roosevelt steadily employed a free-roving assistant who shepherded the President's fondest projects over the assorted hurdles in the executive branch and outside. The assistant, acting for the President ("This is the White House calling"), made short shrift of departmental hierarchy and red tape in expediting action. He was a major tool by which the President might prevail against the vast, sluggish executive branch. Among these general assistants were Raymond Moley, Rexford Tugwell, Thomas Corcoran, and Harry Hopkins. Corcoran in his day was a stellar administration lobbyist on Capitol Hill; a Presidential speech writer; a channel to Roosevelt for those with ideas; a trouble-shooter who would rush to New York City and rescue the PWA housing program bogged down in an internecine brawl; a hirer and firer of personnel, and doyen of a vast body of young lawyers catacombed in the departments—his "chicks," he called them—a government within a government whose hallmark was action. In the Second World War Harry Hopkins was Roosevelt's number-one trouble-shooter. Known as "Generalissimo of the Needle Brigade," he prodded industry to speed war production, harassed laggard military administrators, and oversaw the distribution of supplies to the fighting fronts. Hopkins was Roosevelt's personal liaison with the war overseas. In conferences with Churchill and Stalin and military chieftains he did the legwork on which Roosevelt's central decisions were founded.

The Roosevelt method is the surest yet invented for maximizing the President's personal influence and for asserting his sway over the executive branch. It spurred the flow of information and ideas into his possession and magnified his impact on policy. It released the energies of men from confining bureaucratic routine. In the main, Roosevelt's competitive administration operated within the bounds of the New Deal's purposes, which were humane (democratic), and they saved many administrators, though not all, from becoming merely self-seeking in their striving. For the 1970s and beyond, however, the Roosevelt method has limited relevance. The new costliness of error in foreign affairs makes the Rooseveltian system of haphazard consultation, by which some departments may be left out, unthinkable. The internecine strife which marked the system is also barred by the necessity that the national executive appear before the world with the face of unity. Roosevelt enjoyed a luxury his successors are doomed never to know. He could create much of his own bureaucracy, first in the New Deal and then in the war. His successors must work with an inherited bureaucracy.

Eisenhower's Staff System

At a far opposite extreme from Franklin Roosevelt's highly personal managerial method was Dwight D. Eisenhower's preference for institutionalizing Presidential relationships in the executive branch. The Eisenhower method was a product of his military experience and several long-entertained convictions concerning White House practice. "For years I had been in frequent contact in the executive office of the White House," Eisenhower has written, "and I had certain ideas about the system, or lack of system, under which it operated. With my training in problems involving organization it was inconceivable to me that the work of the White House could not be better systemized than had been the case in the years I observed it." [15]

Eisenhower's key tactic was to delegate duties, tasks, and initiatives to subordinates. After their study and formulation of decision, he, as Chief Executive, might ultimately accept or reject. "The marks of a good executive," he advised his department heads, "are courage in delegating work to subordinates and his own skill in coordinating and directing their effort." Eisenhower's subsequent illnesses speeded his inclination to delegate. [16]

The vehicle of his delegations was the staff system. At its apex was the assistant to the President, Sherman Adams, a former Congressman, governor of New Hampshire, and early organizer of Eisenhower's Presidential candidacy. Eisenhower, Adams has written, "simply expected me to manage a staff that would boil down, simplify and expedite the urgent business that had to be brought to his personal attention and to keep as much work of secondary importance as possible off his desk." Any issue, no matter how complex, Eisenhower believed, could be reduced to some bare essence. "If a proposition can't be stated in one page," he declared, "it isn't worth saying." Impatient with the torrential paper work of the Presidency and not one who took to reading gladly, Eisenhower insisted that his subordinates digest lengthy, involved documents into one-page summaries, "which," said Adams, "was sometimes next to impossible to do." [17]

Except in the singular case of Secretary of State John Foster Dulles, cabinet Secretaries approached the President through Adams. Policy proposals were made in writing, the fruit of staff study and recommendation. Adams' task was to see that every expert in the executive branch who could contribute to a proposal had his opportunity to do so. Many final decisions were made not by the President but by Adams. Eisenhower was brought in only if the matter was very important or if the executive experts disagreed. The President was not bothered very often, according to Adams, who has explained, "I always tried to resolve specific differences on a variety of problems before the issue had to be submitted to the President." He adds, "Sometimes several meetings were necessary before an agreement was reached. But with a few exceptions I was successful." [18]

Eisenhower kept the system on its toes by his own close knowledge of governmental detail mastered in a long military career and a capacity to put sharp, piercing questions that could reduce premises and argument to a shambles. He could not bear flawed performance, a sentiment conveyed at times by fierce outbursts of the Presidential temper. Both Eisenhower's queries and Adams' zealously pursued mission to see that no relevant opinion, fact, or option eluded the President were democracy-serving. Both fostered competition among the departments and representation of their functional viewpoints; both permitted questions to be raised concerning the values, morality, and practicality of pending decisions. Eisenhower, his questions often revealed, was acutely aware of the nature of democratic administration, of sensitivity to and regard for the opposition, and the need for policy to extend beyond responsiveness merely to a narrow, privileged economic class. But there was also danger: that the emphasis on order and system, on paperwork and routine, could create busyness without accomplishment and dampen zeal for innovation and risk, qualities that sometimes produce policies and programs leading to major democratic gains.

Adams was an ubiquitous influence. When a caller or official sprang a new proposal, Eisenhower was prone to say, "Take it up with Sherman." If a paper came to the President, he would run his eye over it for the familiar notation, "O.K., S. A." If it was missing, Eisenhower was sure to ask, "Has Governor Adams approved this?" Although each cabinet Secretary had an ivory telephone connecting directly with the President's line, the connection—except for that of Secretary Dulles, who consulted Eisenhower constantly on foreign policy—was seldom used. Cabinet Secretaries found it wise to call Adams instead. For the several specialists constituting the White House staff—the press secretary, the appointments secretary, the staff secretary, and the cabinet secretary— Adams was a coordinator. Though all these colleagues enjoyed direct access to the President, only Adams by dint of the breadth of his responsibilities could speak with the President on broad, general affairs. Adams dealt with policy in sweep, his colleagues in chunks. The major staff positions interlocked smoothly with Adams' undertakings; his controls extended over the communications system running to and from the President. The appointments secretary, for instance, in setting up the President's daily list of visitors, routinely checked with Adams, enabling him to veto prospective callers or fit others in. Adams also could arrange his own schedule in order to be on hand, if necessary, when Eisenhower met with visitors. The staff secretary, who presided over a system installed under Eisenhower's supervision, was a great boon to Adams. He kept records on hundreds of papers, many of high import and secrecy, dealing with national security and domestic affairs. Within minutes, Adams, thanks to the staff secretariat, could track down the location and status of reports, memoranda, and letters that had come into the White House or gone out for clearances in the far reaches of the executive branch. He could tell who had prepared a given document, the concurrences received and objections encountered, who was dragging his feet, and other essential facts of paper-work life. Although the Eisenhower staff system stressed hierarchy and order, its highly formal structure also assured that multiple participants and opposing views and values—all potentially contributory to the variety necessary for democratic administration—would flow into a developing decision. Adams was no mere merchant of dry-as-dust routine. He uplifted some of the administration's finest achievements in their wobbliest beginnings—the Atoms for Peace plan, the civil rights program, and the Refugee Relief Act.

The ancient institution of the cabinet also felt Eisenhower's reforming hand. Shocked that the department Secretaries, the government's principal executives, should gather without any preconception of the business to be considered, Eisenhower created the post of cabinet secretary. This new official arranged an agenda for cabinet meetings, circulated it beforehand among the members, oversaw the preparation of "cabinet papers" presenting proposals for the President's action, and recorded the results of cabinet discussion. Keenly aware of the gap between Presidential decision and departmental reliability in carrying it out, Eisenhower had his cabinet secretary meet after a session of the cabinet with "cabinet assistants," a group of assistant secretaries and departmental executive assistants with responsibilities for implementation. Every several months a cabinet meeting was converted into "Judgment Day" on the "Action Status Report," in which each department head revealed how much (or little) he had honored his obligations to take actions called for by the President's decisions in cabinet.

In adapting the military staff system to the Presidency, Eisenhower viewed his cabinet Secretaries essentially as theater commanders. Like field generals, the Secretaries were invested with broad initiative and responsibility for their allotted sectors of operation. For their assertions, the President, most of the time, provided political defense. When a score of Middle Western Republican Congressmen, with elections in prospect, grew restive over Agriculture Secretary Benson's hard line on farm price supports and suggested it would help politically if he would resign, Eisenhower, controlling his fury, answered at a press conference that "for any group of congressmen, either informally or formally, to raise a question concerning my appointment to the Cabinet would not seem to be in order." [19] If dispersal of executive power, to a degree, befits democracy, Eisenhower's concept of the initiating, responsible department head warrants imitation by future Presidents.

One of the more complex and important elements of of Eisenhower's institutionalized Presidency was the National Security Council. Eisenhower, who utilized the NSC heavily, often met with it two or more times a month, with an agenda of intelligence reports, policies to be innovated or revised, and reports on progress in fulfilling established policies. Backstopping the council proper in the Eisenhower administration was the Planning Board, considered the most influential part of the NSC system and consisting of representatives and observers from member agencies, usually at the assistant secretary level. The Planning Board provided an unremitting flood of documents with each drop painstakingly considered. "The Planning Board normally does not send a paper forward without meeting three or four times on it," said Gordon Gray, Eisenhower's National Security Affairs assistant. Planning Board members, according to report, debated not merely high policy but the subtleties of idiom and terminology. Hours of anxious effort were invested in clearance procedures, with intensive review and interdepartmental negotiation of words and phrases. Critics hold that papers worked out in such proceedings were highly watered down, lowest-common-denominator-of-agreement affairs, and there were snide remarks about this being "the century of the comma man." Defenders of the stress on paper work hold that such exercises foster exactitude in an area of utmost sensitivity and complexity.

Another NSC offshoot was the Operations Coordinating Board, created by the Eisenhower administration, which was made up of deputy-level officials who tackled the job of getting things done, of devising ways to put into operation, at home and overseas, NSC policies ranging from psychological and economic warfare to international cooperation in science. Like the Planning Board, the OCB reveled in paper work and meticulously negotiated detail.

The attraction of the Eisenhower system is the assurance it promises that the President will have the benefit of coordinated counsel in an age when major problems require the expertise of several or more departments. Adams' operation strove systematically to include every relevant department. The omission of skill and information, given the world's dangers, could be severely costly. At its best, it maintained a kind of competition and system of administrative checks and balances that provided parameters for Eisenhower's administrators and staff that were conducive to ethical and democratic behavior. At its worst, it could, engrossed in its managerial procedures, ignore or downgrade rising social problems like civil rights, health, and education, and postpone serious responses to another day and another Presidency. Meanwhile the problems worsened at public expense.

The Eisenhower system also can be viewed as purporting to provide a security that is unattainable, given the vastness of the executive branch, the interminable Niagara of executive transactions, and the severely limited timetable imposed by events. The Eisenhower experience indeed bears instances of human and organizational failure in spite of all the elaborate safeguards. As the Dixon-Yates contract episode,* a major political disaster, was building, Republican Senator John Sherman Cooper of Kentucky, whom Eisenhower highly esteemed, called at the White House to lay before the President his several objections to carrying the project forward. Adams refused to grant the Senator an appointment. When the Bureau of the Budget and the Atomic Energy Commission prepared chronologies of the principal facts of Dixon-Yates for the President's use and for distribution to the press, an essential detail was omitted: that Adolphe Wenzell, a Bureau of the Budget consultant for the contract, was simultaneously an official of the First Boston Corporation, which was financing the Dixon-Yates group. Eisenhower's staff left him helpless and exposed while the administration's foes leaped with full cry upon the error.[20]

In some respects, the Eisenhower system appears to afford the President both too little initiative and too little total impact upon policy. He depends overmuch upon others to discover and assess the magnitude of problems. He enters into policy-making only in the final stage of decision, when his area of choice is small and his dependence upon his staff great.

Kennedy's Personal Management

John F. Kennedy's administrative method veered decidedly toward Roosevelt's. Like Roosevelt, Kennedy aimed to carve out a maximum personal role in the conduct of the Presidency but without some of the more jagged methods and much of the turmoil of the Rooseveltian model.

Unlike Eisenhower, who stressed institutional structure, Kennedy placed great store in personal relationships. The person—his talent, perception, and reliability—counted more than his organization. Kennedy's person-centered approach reflected his pre-Presidential career, passed chiefly in legislative politics and in political campaigning, in both of which working relationships are highly personal. Accordingly, in dealing with department Secretaries and White House staff members Kennedy insisted upon direct relationships, unhampered by organ-

---

* The Atomic Energy Commission's increasing demands upon the TVA for power, coupled with Eisenhower's reluctance to expand TVA, resulted in the so-called Dixon-Yates contract with a combination of private utilities that were to supply the necessary power to TVA. Disclosures of irregularities in the negotiation of the contract led the Eisenhower administration to cancel it.

ization and hierarchy. He, for his part, remained highly accessible to a large circle of colleagues.

At Kennedy's hands, democracy was enhanced by a President who picked good associates, maintained surveillance over their performance, and devoted his administration to a broad range of interests. But those who are "the best and the brightest" do not necessarily perform as persons of wisdom and judgment on every Presidential working day. Those whose gifts Kennedy esteemed most contributed to his worst troubles, as initiators and encouragers of those banes of democracy, violence and warfare. The miscalculations of Kennedy's talented associates stepped up American involvement in Vietnam and entrapped the President in the fiasco of the Bay of Pigs invasion.

Kennedy, dealing with the departments, did not stop with the department head, but reached down the hierarchy to lesser levels. A loud, clear hint of this practice was sounded in the preinaugural period in the manner of the President-elect's selection of his foreign policy aides. He designated an Assistant Secretary and an Undersecretary of State and the ambassador to the United Nations before selecting his Secretary of State. In a television interview he was asked, "Is it true that during your first year, sir, you would get on the phone personally to the State Department and try to get a response to some inquiry that had been made?" "Yes," Kennedy replied, "I still do that when I can, because I think there is a great tendency in government to have papers stay on desks too long. . . . After all, the President can't administer a department, but at least he can be a stimulant." [21]

Kennedy injected himself at any point along the decision-making spectrum from problem selection to final judgment. He wanted to know a problem's facets and alternative answers, keeping decision for himself in consultation or "dialogue," as the administration called it, with advisers. Kennedy's keen nose for detail took him far into the interior of problems. Although interested in general principles, he was essentially a pragmatist and had, as a colleague said, "a highly operational mind." Policy separated from operations, in his view, was meaningless. His desk, not surprisingly, was piled high with reports and memoranda that he read closely. Conferring with an official, he would reach into the pile, pull out a memorandum, and resort instantaneously to a paragraph to make a point or raise a question. "President Kennedy," a colleague said, "is a desk officer at the highest level." [22]

Kennedy entertained well-defined views of the proper role of the individual department. His tactic was to devolve upon individual department heads and on identified subordinates the responsibility for recommending policy initiatives and overseeing the execution of decisions. He took a stern view of a luxuriant bureaucratic phenomenon, the interdepartmental committee, beholding it as an intruder upon departmental responsibility and therefore something inherently bad, to be extirpated if at all possible. In lieu of committees the Kennedy administration resorted to "task forces," a name appropriately suggestive of vigor and purpose. Task forces, which consisted of departmental representatives and usually one or more White House staffers, were not merely committees by another name. "They operate with a consciousness of having a mandate, often from the President himself," a participant explained. Task forces carried a sense of the importance of getting things done, which often stirred bureaucracy to faster, more constructive effort. The attendant White House staff member was a powerful reminder of the Chief Executive's need and interest, a bearer of his influence upon decision, not merely in the moment of final choice but along much of the journey of its formation. Departmental participants in the task forces were not altogether enthusiastic about the contribution of their White House colleagues. "When the President's man says something, you don't know whether he is speaking for himself or for his boss," a department man exclaimed. "The effect can be, and often is, to cut off discussion too soon." [23]

Kennedy's White House staff, unlike Eisenhower's, was not organized by hierarchy or pyramid, but like a wheel whose hub was the President and whose spokes connected him with individual aides. Five aides occupied major functional posts. The staff assistant to the President, Kenneth O'Donnell, handled appointments and Presidential travels and was an omnibus "chief White House official for party politics," in touch with the Democratic National Committee and local party figures. The special counsel, Theodore C. Sorensen of Nebraska, whose association harked back to Kennedy's Senate days in 1953, had responsibilities running across the board. His office, comprising two assistants, focused Presidential objectives, planned programs, broke impasses, and passed judgment on timing. Sorensen drafted Presidential messages and speeches with high artistry and a capacity that Richard Nixon once hailed as "the rare gift of being an intellectual who can completely sublimate his style to another intellectual." [24] Sorensen sat with department Secretaries formulating their budget and legislative programs and attended the President's meetings with legislative leaders and pre–press conference briefings. Sorensen had an acquisitive, cosmopolitan intelligence, which, as a colleague put it, "can understand anything from sugar subsidies to bomb shelters." [25]

McGeorge Bundy, a former Harvard graduate dean, was special assistant for national security affairs. Bundy, aided by a small band of assistants ("the Bundy group"), kept watch for weakness and trouble in defense and foreign policy administration and saw to remedies and repairs. In the President's behalf he occupied a central place in the stream of intelligence. He received copies of virtually all the incoming cables to the Secretaries of State and Defense and the Director of the CIA. He sorted these out and put the most important before the President. Other key aides were the assistant for Congressional relations, Lawrence F. O'Brien, and the press secretary, Pierre Salinger.

Kennedy deployed his White House staff as critics of departmental performance and as emergency repair crews when departmental undertakings went awry. He restored direct work-flows between departments and himself and made his staff responsible for "monitoring," but not "obstructing," departmental access to him personally. A key function of the White House staff was to spot political and policy weaknesses in departmental proposals. Staff members played a decisive part in heading off a tax increase that may have made sense economically but not politically during the Berlin crisis of July

1961; they delighted liberals by implanting several public-ownership features into the communications satellite bill; they knocked down a State Department proposal that action on the trade bill be postponed for more than a year, until 1963. There was wide agreement that a large advantage of the Sorensen-Bundy service was penetrating analysis. "When Sorensen gets into something," a Bureau of the Budget career man said, "it gets a thorough scrubbing." It was also the lack of such a scrubbing that plunged the staff to the far depths of its worst failure, the abortive Cuban invasion in the young administration's fourth month. The staff was admittedly timid about raising questions that should have been asked. "At that point," a White House aide confessed, "we just didn't have the confidence to tell the veterans of the bureaucracy, 'Look, you're crazy.' " [26]

In another blow at the institutionalized Presidency, Kennedy performed drastic surgery on the most advanced expression of that phenomenon, the National Security Council. He abolished the NSC's nerve- and work-center, the Planning Board, and its organ for implementing decision, the Operations Coordinating Board. Most important of all, he shunned the NSC by seldom bringing it into session. He sought counsel for major crises like Berlin of 1961 and Cuba of 1962 by bringing together an ad hoc group of advisers in whom he had special confidence. In lieu of the Planning Board and the OCB was the Bundy office, which greatly scaled down the former mountains of paper work.

Kennedy also largely dispensed with cabinet meetings, holding that the entire body of Secretaries should be assembled only for matters of full breadth and significance. He saw no reason for the entire cabinet to ponder matters affecting only three or four departments. The cabinet, consequently, met infrequently. In the summer of 1962 various department heads, then occupied with the political campaign, happened to converge upon Chicago. There they laughingly acknowledged that what had not transpired in Washington for some months was at last happening in the Middle West, a cabinet "meeting"!

The Kennedy technique clearly maximized the President's involvement and imprint upon policy, breathed vitality into sluggish bureaucracy, and extended the reach of a highly knowledgeable President and his staff into the departments. Yet there were also disadvantages. There was feeling that Kennedy was too accessible to operating personnel, too much "in the thick of things," overimmersed in minor policy and small detail, with too little time for major business. Or again, that Kennedy's emphasis on swiftness—terse statement, quick strides from one problem to the next—resulted at times in inadequate consideration of alternatives. Much public business, like reducing the arms race or overhauling the tax system, does not permit quick, concise expression. "The system now," a frequent participant said, "favors people who know exactly what they want to do. It is tough on people who have dim misgivings—even if those misgivings happen to be very important." [27]

One strength of the Kennedy system may also have been a weakness. His method rested upon the realistic view that the executive branch, lacking the apparatus of collective responsibility found in Great Britain, depended heavily, for action and decision, upon the President's judgment. Yet what ordinarily was plausibly realistic may have caused at times an overdependence upon the time, energy, and talent of the President. The great risk of the Kennedy method is that no single mind, even a Presidential mind, can absorb the information or muster the wisdom necessary for sound judgment of many intricate issues pouring upon the President.

The problems with which American statesmanship must deal have acquired a complexity that renders them no longer fit for individual insight and judgment, no matter how perceptive. To be dealt with adequately, they must at some stage be subjected to collective study involving diverse technical skills, specialized knowledge, and organizational viewpoints. Decision without collective study is apt to be founded on inadequate information and to lack roundness of judgment.

Johnson's Consensus Method

President Lyndon Johnson's method blended elements of the Franklin Roosevelt-Kennedy, President-centered style, on the one hand, and the Eisenhower tendency to system and institutionalization on the other. Like Roosevelt he tried to maximize his personal influence in the executive branch, and he deployed and used his staff with similar unorthodox managerial methods. Like Roosevelt he often sought counsel outside the government. He frequently consulted Dean Acheson, once Secretary of State in the Truman administration, and old New Dealers Benjamin Cohen, Thomas Corcoran, and James Rowe. Abe Fortas numbered in this group until his appointment to the Supreme Court somewhat curtailed his availability, and Clark Clifford until he took over as Secretary of Defense.

Johnson also had a sturdy streak of administrative orthodoxy. He placed greater reliance upon the departments than Kennedy or Roosevelt did. Promptly after coming into office, Johnson accorded new recognition to the departmental Secretaries. Secretary of Defense McNamara quickly achieved an influence surpassing his considerable status under President Kennedy. When Dean Rusk faced heavy criticism over Vietnam on Capitol Hill and from public quarters, Johnson expressed openly his admiration for his Secretary of State. Johnson also made greater use than Kennedy did of the cabinet and the National Security Council. For the cabinet, Johnson adopted the Eisenhower practice of a formal agenda and assignment of a special assistant to act as cabinet secretary.

The way Johnson used his staff was shaped essentially by his own political goals, prior career, and work habits. His chosen, often proclaimed purpose was to bring the executive branch to work with a consensus that the President discovers or constructs. His working method resembled the Congressional leader's, a role he occupied for much of his own career. As a broker in political consensus, he would withhold his own commitment until the commitments of other men were reconciled, or, in effect, until a majority was built.

From his White House staff Johnson expected help in defining issues, in articulating his views, and in protecting his freedom of movement. In calculating and constructing his position, Johnson preferred to be in touch himself with labor, business, local leaders, Congressmen, the press, and chieftains of the executive bureaucracy. Sometimes he acted as his own press secretary, Congressional liaison officer, and speech-writer. His staff constantly experienced the phenomenon of their leader both delegating power to them and taking it away. Johnson needed a staff that could move rapidly without getting in his way and without attracting attention or committing his position prematurely. No one on Johnson's staff approached the influence of Harry Hopkins or Samuel Rosenman under Roosevelt, Clark Clifford under Truman, or Theodore Sorensen under Kennedy. Bill D. Moyers, a young, bright, articulate fellow Texan enjoyed impressive influence before departing for private employment. As assistant to the President, he oversaw departmental preparations of the vast legislative program of 1965, supervised the drafting of Presidential messages, was in constant touch with Johnson, and reviewed the whole Great Society program with the President just before its launching in the State of the Union message. Unlike the top aides of past Presidents, Moyers shared his duties with other White House staff men, including Douglas Cater, a former editor. Democracy and governmental ethics stand to gain if the President has on his staff individuals with sufficient status and capacity to say "no" to the boss, to point out his errors and wrongheadedness. Fortunately, several of Johnson's associates, notably Moyers and Cater, served that function. Why? Because their futures did not depend on Johnson, they could determine their own time to depart from the administration, a strength that enabled them to tell the President sometimes what he did not want to hear.

The fluidity of the Johnson staff was reinforced by the background and personality of its members. Heavily represented in its ranks were writers and others with public relations experience, a breed of men of high adaptability. They were not especially identified with any policy area, and if they shared a personality characteristic, it was that they were self-effacing. Thus they were able to adjust to the President's moods and demands and to refrain from attracting attention to themselves in the press and from building ties with special interest groups—tendencies that might have impaired their ability to move on to other assignments. But the adaptability and acquiescence of the staff to Johnson's demands were also the limits of its usefulness. Verging on the sycophantic, it could not deter him from decisions, particularly in foreign affairs, that were costly to his administration. By constraining and minimizing the roles of individual staff members through his consensus method, Johnson maximized his own impact, including the full weight of his faults. These faults included his overconfidence in power and his underestimation of the average citizen's capacity to comprehend foreign affairs, which constituted a giant stride toward the eventually fatal credibility gap.

Johnson also leaned heavily upon two new institutions that emerged within the White House staff in the Kennedy era. Where once Colonel Edward M. House and Harry Hopkins were personal advisers to Presidents Wilson and

Franklin Roosevelt on national security matters, McGeorge Bundy in the Kennedy and Johnson years handled the duty more systematically. He and his successor, Walt W. Rostow, made the White House staff a regular and substantial participant in foreign policy. Bundy installed and Rostow continued to use a handful of assistants specializing in Africa, Europe, Latin America, Southeast Asia, international economics, and science and defense. Rostow, like Bundy, participated regularly in the President's meetings with his Secretaries of State and Defense. Similarly, the President's dealings with Congress were institutionalized during the Kennedy-Johnson era by Lawrence O'Brien. He, too, expanded his office, developed a staff and secretariat, and was a regular participant in the President's meetings with Congressional leaders.[28] But Johnson's staff, whether personal or institutional, could not save him from the decisions that escalated American involvement in the Vietnam War, incurring political costs that eventually drove him from the Presidency. Ironically, the consensus-building for which Johnson often so skillfully utilized his staff in domestic politics was a neglected art in his foreign policy. Consensus seemed to stop at the water's edge, as Johnson, in privacy, surrounded by acquiescent aides, made costly foreign policy decisions with little heed for enhancing public understanding and support.

Nixonian Centralism

Determined to be an "activist President," oriented toward intervention in the departments, Nixon was confirmed in his resolve by his perception of the bureaus as hostile, comprised largely of Democrats recruited by previous Presidents of that party. The bureaus were proponents of "the welfare state" that he was resolved to prune back and reform, and therefore a source of potential obstruction.[29] Important in shaping his White House staff's structure and processes were Nixon's lack of physical stamina for the hurly-burly of administrative work and policy formation, his abhorrence of conflict inherent in administration, and his aversion to delivering criticism personally. Nixon was a loner who found little surcease in mingling with his fellow humanity. In deploying his staff, Nixon, like other Presidents, gave vent to his needs and preferences. Essentially, the staff helped assure his privacy, his removal from the unwelcome demands of administration, and his transaction of business with a tiny circle of associates with whom he felt at ease.

Nixon adapted and embellished on the formal staff systems he had observed as Vice President in the Eisenhower years. His Sherman Adams, or chief of staff, was Harry Robbins (Bob) Haldeman, who, before becoming encoiled in the Watergate scandal, was called, like Adams, "the second most powerful man in Washington." An executive of the J. Walter Thompson advertising agency where he promoted Seven-Up and Black Flag insecticide, with periodic leaves for service in Nixon's earlier campaigns, Haldeman was injected by the

1968 electoral victory into his post as "Special Assistant to the President," to which he brought little familiarity with democratic practice and the power centers of national politics.

A Janus-like guardian of Nixon's door, Haldeman determined whom the President saw, as well as what he read. With the air of a Marine Corps drill sergeant and a manner that bespoke his conviction that "every President needs his s.o.b., and I'm Nixon's," Haldeman fortified Nixon's isolation by running a grim, efficient operation that facilitated the President's desire to reach decisions through staff papers rather than oral argument and to have ample "opportunity to react, partly to initiate on his terms rather than someone else's." So adept was Haldeman at keeping unwanted visitors from the President that his protective network became known as "the Berlin wall." Without ceremony or ado, Senators and cabinet Secretaries were steadily rebuffed.[30]

A second top position on the Nixon staff was the assistant for domestic affairs, initially John Ehrlichman, who too was a veteran of Nixon's early campaigns, including service as an "espionage agent." A former land-use lawyer in Seattle, Ehrlichman as a presidential assistant became known for hard-nosed efficiency and cool enforcement of the Presidential will—"He leaves no more blood on the floor than he has to," noted a colleague.[31] Through a half dozen youthful deputies, Ehrlichman watched over transitory "project groups recruited from the departments and agencies and the White House staff to develop proposals on matters like welfare reform, manpower training, and pollution control. Ehrlichman's office also helped draft the necessary legislation and scrutinized the expected costs of programs against their benefits. When Presidential decision was required, he prepared a concise summary of the issues and options, which Nixon studied in seclusion. After the President disclosed his basic decision, Ehrlichman developed details and besought cooperation from the relevant agencies. Ehrlichman's power was enlarged by his role as chief executive officer of the Domestic Council and by his working relationship with the President. As well, Ehrlichman profited from the opportunity to pick and choose among the ideas that reached his desk for presentation to the President, and from his control over follow-up. In his heyday, Ehrlichman commanded more influence over domestic policy than any cabinet Secretary.[32]

For foreign policy and national security affairs, the instrument of Nixonian centralism was the assistant for national security, Henry Kissinger. Although such predecessors as McGeorge Bundy and Walt W. Rostow wielded great power, Kissinger, in the hospitable clime of centralism, exceeded them and institutionalized his office to unprecedented degree. As Nixon's chief adviser on foreign policy, Kissinger, more than Ehrlichman or Haldeman, became the formulator, negotiator, and implementer of Presidential decision. No special bonds united Kissinger with the Haldeman-Ehrlichman tandem. The latter, with their contrasting backgrounds and interests, were content to let Kissinger work freely in his bailiwick while they toiled in theirs.

For the rest, the White House staff was studded with young men, in their twenties and thirties, some of whom gained notoriety in the Watergate scandals. Typically, they emerged from comfortable, even wealthy, families and from business—especially advertising—backgrounds. In impeccable Brooks Brothers attire, with an enamelled flag in their lapels, articulate and socially poised, they were orthodox in their view of the world, ambitious, intelligent but not thoughtful, and bereft of any controlling ethic except to do what their bosses wanted. Typically, they were unhampered by democratic socialization— by awareness of democratic values and processes or of American history and philosophy, which nourish such appreciation. The youth, modest talents, and outlook of these juniors facilitated Nixonian centralism by assuring the presence of a cadre of eager, compliant subordinates, none of whom could challenge the older established top command of Haldeman and Ehrlichman.[33]

In addition to the "advertising crowd," Nixon's staff contained several "tough political handymen," including, at various times, Murray Chotiner, Harry S. Dent, and Charles W. Colson. Seasoned and aggressive, they reported to Haldeman, who gave them wide latitude but kept track of their activities and transmitted special assignments in the President's behalf. These no-holds-barred political sophisticates were expected to overcome the lack of political savoir faire of the advertising men, and, as one staff man said, to "do the dirty work when it is necessary."[34]

The Nixon staff functioned in an atmosphere akin to a state of siege; its centralism was intensified by fear of violent upheaval in the country at large. The roots of this mood reached back to the campus disorders and demonstrations erupting from the Cambodian invasion and the killings of students at Kent State and Jackson State, after which some 400 colleges were disrupted or shut down. Simultaneously, violence flared between militant blacks and police in communities across the country. Growing antiwar demonstrations kindled staff fears that just as the protests had unhinged Lyndon Johnson from the Presidency, they might break Richard Nixon. An "us versus them" psychology developed, with gravely deleterious consequences for staff functioning. Colson's office developed an "Opponents List, Political Enemies Project," that eventually included several hundred persons, among them university presidents, business executives, reporters, news commentators, theater personalities, and athletes. Undercover operatives were added to the White House staff and a staff assistant oversaw the development of an expanded domestic security and intelligence gathering plan, which, among other things, called for "surreptitious entry." After approving the plan, Nixon, faced with objections from FBI director J. Edgar Hoover, withdrew his decision. Nevertheless, following the publication of the Pentagon Papers and other leaks, the President authorized the establishment within the White House of a Special Investigations Unit, whose task, he said, was to "stop security leaks and to investigate other sensitive security matters."[35] "The Plumbers," as they became known, burglarized the office of the psychiatrist of Dr. Daniel Ellsberg, disseminator of the Pentagon papers. In the 1972 Presidential campaign, another squad of White House assistants, including the President's appointments secretary, launched "dirty tricks" against the campaigns of Edmund Muskie, George Wallace, and other candidates. White House personnel were also apprehended in the break-in of Democratic headquarters in the 1972 Presidential campaign, for which they were subsequently indicted and convicted. The disclosures of burglaries, of contributions to the 1972 campaign extorted from business, of spying on dissident citizens, and of the sabotaging of feared electoral rivals number among the first known multifaceted attack by the Presidency upon basic democratic processes.

Nixon's participation in the criminal acts of his administration were facilitated by centralism, since it permitted his conduct to be more private and furtive. His lamentable courses of action were beyond reach of fresh opinion capable of offering ethical perspectives. Through centralism, Nixon imprisoned himself in the company of a small band of compliant, like-minded men whose values and instincts duplicated his own. Likewise, Haldeman and Ehrlichman erred more easily because they had no competitors or coequals among the staff to regulate them. In centralism, the principle of hierarchy was carried to excessive extremes. Traditionally powerful White House staff posts, sources of potential competition, were reduced to middling status, to the point that John Dean, the President's counsel, whose predecessors numbered such luminaries as Rosenman, Clifford, and Sorensen, lacked direct access to the President. Even in the developing malfeasances of the Watergate scandal, Dean hesitated to request so much as an interview. The staff was recruited from too narrow a base; too few knew little more about politics than releasing balloons at rallies at the right moment. Worst of all, the staff was remote from those organs of the political system that might have stopped incipient malfeasance: from Congress, against which the barrier of executive privilege was raised; from the Republican party, which was held at arm's length; and from the press, which was vilified.

Nixonian centralism also ran aground on the shoals of "the closed door boss," which the President was, in contrast to "the open door boss" that other Presidents have been. Like other contemporary major executives, Nixon faced the problems of ever-expanding floods of data and of awaiting visitors who sought his decisions while devouring his time. Nixon became the executive type who turned inward and used his staff for insulation, feeling that he must be protected from extraneous intervenors and data in order that he might set priorities and concentrate on projects that were most productive.[36] The open door boss, typified by Lyndon Johnson, is an indefatigable accumulator of information. No detail of operations or morsel of political gossip was unworthy of his attention. He used his staff to maintain a wide range of contacts and he encouraged at least a limited competition of ideas among his counselors. Although Johnson cherished secrecy, he confined it to a tactical level. The danger facing the closed door executive is that secrecy may degenerate into stealth and consume the mutual trust that should suffuse the staff's work. Outsiders are beheld as adversaries, loyalty is perceived in negative terms, and the staff becomes engrossed in protecting the boss and each other. A team-player mystique luxuriates, and dissent and discord become untolerated. Conflicting ideas and initiatives that might jar the internal equilibrium are withheld, and a disposition develops to make any established game plan succeed by means fair or foul. When performance falters, unwanted information is rejected and deception becomes tempting. Hence the often heard Watergate testimony, "I don't know and you don't want to know." "Don't tell me the details." Principles fade away fast in such an atmosphere. But all need not be lost for the inward boss and his staff. In the Nixon years, their secluded efforts worked well in opening relations with China and in expanding relations with East Europe, situations where concentration appeared useful to the point of reducing information on other problems, and, at least to a degree, tactical secrecy seemed productive. But the inward-turning Chief Executive, to function well, requires top staff aides with a wide-ranging curiosity about policy and operations (like Kissinger), a voracious appetite for detail, and the courage to be candid with the President.

To a degree that no President had attempted before, Nixon aimed to control, even dominate, the departments and agencies. Dissenting department heads and bureau chiefs like Interior Secretary Walter J. Hickel and Education Commissioner James E. Allen, Jr., were banished summarily into the outer darkness. Following his smashing 1972 electoral victory, Nixon moved to tame the department that most inherently contradicted his Horatio Alger precepts of individual self-reliance, the Department of Health, Education and Welfare (HEW). In 1973, he appointed as the new Secretary Caspar W. Weinberger, who in earlier service as Director of the Office of Management and Budget demonstrated such flair at program reduction that he became known among the disgruntled as "Cap the Knife." In HEW, Weinberger quickly demonstrated the potency of the President's appointment of a hostile Secretary by drastically cutting HEW's budget and by employing the discretionary rule-making power of his office as a blunderbuss against social programs.[37] In HEW, as in other departments, Nixonian lieutenants were installed at secondary and tertiary levels, where they maintained surveillance on the top command and intervened down the line to stamp out incipient heresies.

Nixon regulated the bureaucracy by threat of reorganization—no other President has unloosed a heavier barrage of departmental reorganizations. Through them, Nixon moved to reduce or abolish agencies that were ill-suited to his administration's philosophy. The poverty program and its agency, the Office of Economic Opportunity (OEO), were favorite objects of attack. Functions and administrative units were detached and assigned elsewhere or lost in consolidation. Entire programs and even OEO itself were headed for liquidation, catastrophes that were slowed as clientele groups appealed successfully to the courts. The loose-strung HEW underwent a consolidation of grants and the delegation of functions and authority to state and local governments.[38]

In the Executive Office of the President, Nixon effected reorganizations that extended his reach into the departments. He transformed the Bureau of the Budget into the Office of Management and Budget, thereby increasing that agency's supervisory and management powers, and thereby, indirectly, the White House's power over the departments. He established a Domestic Council in the Executive Office, directed it to devise new programs, and endowed it with supervisory powers designed to foster greater conformity in the agencies to his policies and wishes. For a time, Nixon designated as counselors to the President four of his cabinet Secretaries and charged them with overseeing broad domains—the economy, community development, and human and natural resources—while retaining their Secretary functions. The effect was to centralize power further in the Presidency, with the counselors reporting directly to the Chief Executive and supervising clusters of activity in several or more departments and agencies. By executive fiat, Nixon had embarked on a potentially far-reaching reorganization, but, facing outcries following the Watergate disclosures, which contended that the Presidency had fallen into deep trouble because it had become excessively centralized, Nixon dropped the counselor structure.

Convinced that personnel changes, to be really effective, must reach below the most senior level, Nixon called for relaxation of civil service rules that protected tenure and seniority. Potentially, this would be a mighty scythe in Presidential hands with which to mow down recalcitrant civil servants, whose most humane fate might be reassignment to other duties. Most audacious of all was Nixon's proposed transformation of seven cabinet departments—HEW, Labor, HUD, Agriculture, Interior, and Transportation—into four departments for natural resources, community development, human resources, and economic affairs. The plan would have left the remaining departments intact. These and other proposals that Congress rejected were weakened by the President's own political enfeeblement following the Watergate disclosures.[39] Nonetheless, the plan contained the promise of developing more coherent domestic policies usually precluded by the present diffused departmental structures and their consequently fragmented programs. It was also alluring because it seemed to promise cost reduction and more efficient operation.[40] Smaller agencies that had functioned as independent fiefdoms, would, under the Nixon plan, have passed under a larger command powerful enough to evoke allegiance to broad departmental goals. But on the other side of the coin lurks a formidable danger: in large organizations, such as Nixon contemplated, top leadership can more easily starve and suppress particular programs that fall into disfavor.

Many of Nixon's efforts at centralism by reorganization are of a piece with what students of political science and public administration have long been urging. Others are the climax of trends that commenced under Eisenhower and persisted with Kennedy and Johnson. In theory, democracy, to be fulfilled, requires the election of political officers, such as the President, who run on platforms containing program pledges and who are faithfully supported by the tenured bureaucracy. At least to some degree, the President must be able to direct and control the bureaucracy if he is to accomplish the goals promised in his election campaign and on which the voters expressed approval. Historically, the Presidency is replete with incumbents' complaints of the bureaucracy's ability to resist and frustrate the Chief Executive. A succession of Presidents have endeavored to make the bureaucracy more responsive, and Nixon's performance illuminates the dangers lurking in that objective.

Against the centralized Presidency that Nixon and other Presidents have dreamed of and striven for, several objections must be raised. His plans would consolidate power not merely in the President's hands but in the grasp of an elitist corps, the White House staff and the Executive Office of the President, the members of which are appointed with little public scrutiny and who function in a veiled domain removed from review by Congress and beyond the normal vision of the press. Hardly a picture of robust democracy. Moreover, the men in the White House and Executive Office, as Nixon's centralism illuminates, may possess extraordinary similarity of social background, previous employment, and outlook—a concentration of attributes that hardly accords with the variety of American society. In contrast, the untidy departments, with their breadth of functions and wide recruitment of personnel, offer diversity, valuable, if not indispensable, for democracy. Department leaders are subject to scrutiny by Congress and the news media, and the lesser departmental echelons include a polyglot of program advocates and professionals, skilled politicians, transplanted academicians, pressure group axe-grinders, and innovators—a mélange surely not found in the White House, but which articulates, better than the narrowly based White House staff, the interests and aspirations of much of society.

Ford: Centralism Diminished

That Gerald Ford was impressed that Nixon's staff system was a root of his fatal trouble was evidenced when the incoming President appointed a committee of "transition advisers" to study the functioning of the White House Office. Soon forthcoming were recommendations for paring back some of the more potent elements of Nixonian centralism. In a reconstituted White House Office, there would be no chief of staff in the Haldeman image, but one of significantly reduced power. The chief of staff prescribed for Ford would no longer be the single channel through which all the President's business, except foreign and national security affairs, flowed; instead, the chief of staff would be principally an administrative facilitator and coordinator, with diminished functions and influence, who would share power more with other members of the staff. Concerning the latter, the transition advisers contemplated some five or six assistants and advisers, each covering a particular function of government, such as national security, the budget, domestic policy, the economy, personnel, and legal counsel. The chief of staff would "coordinate" but not "control" these colleagues. In effect, Ford was advised to adopt a kind of hybrid of the Roosevelt-Eisenhower models.[41]

Early in his administration, Ford heeded these recommendations. Robert T. Hartmann, a former newspaperman and Congressional aide of the President, functioned as a deft political factotum, coordinating, but not controlling, other key White House staff members, whose ties with Ford were, like his own, personal, strong, and long-standing. These included former Congressman John O. Marsh, Jr., whose domain is legislative relations; Philip W. Buchen, as Presidential counsel in charge of all legal matters; Ford's former law partner, L. William Seidman, also of Michigan, who dealt with economic policy; and Donald Rumsfeld, a former Congressman, ambassador to NATO, and a transition adviser. Rumsfeld too was beheld as a coordinator of White House operations and procedures, a scaled down model of a chief of staff. But was not Hartmann a likely rival? Predictions sprouted of an impending power struggle between Rumsfeld and Hartmann. A staff member observed that "Rumsfeld will tend to look upon Hartmann as a staff person, whereas Hartmann will tend to look at Rumsfeld as the chief paper pusher." Hartmann enjoyed the advantages of having the only door with private access to the Oval Office and a will for combat, conveyed by his abrasive personality, which a colleague characterized as a case of "terminal ego." [42]

Whether, over time, a pattern of more or less evenly distributed power among the nine senior White House assistants privileged by a reorganization to communicate directly with the President will develop and endure depends heavily on Ford's willingness and capacity to commit sufficient time and energy to deal daily with a number of key aides in lieu of the less demanding regimen of relations with a single chief of staff. As for the staff, its susceptibility to the system recommended to Ford depends on the personalities involved, their compatibility and sharing of public policy values, and the distribution of roughly equal talent and will in the personal power politics of the White House staff that would keep influence relatively well distributed rather than allowing it to become excessively concentrated in a single staff member whose avidity for power and skill in amassing it could disrupt a balanced dispersal.

Centralism has been diminished by Ford's generous accessibility to department and agency heads. A clear early signal sounded when he met with Russell E. Train, administrator of the Environmental Protection Agency, to review a number of long-building environmental issues. A hold-over Nixon appointee who had served in the post for more than a year, Train had never met with Nixon.[43] Like other Presidents, Ford diminished centralization by moving outside the White House and the executive branch for advice and policy initiatives. Unprecedented in kind and scale were his summit conferences on inflation with industry and labor representatives and economists of widely differing persuasions, who discoursed on their favorite remedies, with the President taking notes.

For his greater accessibility, Ford paid several prices. Conflicts between agency administrators became more frequent, intense, and open, and spilled into the President's lap. His 1974 speech to the United Nations on food and energy was a compromise of sharp differences within his administration, with Secretary of State Kissinger and his department eager to double the food aid program, while the Office of Management and Budget and its director Roy Ash and the Council of Economic Advisers opposed any increase. In public statements, Secretary of Agriculture Earl Butz sided with the OMB, while privately he supported Kissinger. Ford's speech was a compromise, with something for everybody.[44]

As President, Ford followed a regimen typical of his tenure as House minority leader and subsequently as Vice President—long days and nights of seemingly endless conferences and talks with a wide variety of people on diverse subjects, major and minor, in Washington and out. He appeared to violate the recommendation of his knowing transition advisers that he set aside some time to be alone, to think, and plan. Critics who had scarcely finished lamenting that Richard Nixon was excessively secluded and out of touch with Congress, administrators, and the public, now beseeched Ford not to spend so much time with people. But the President confidently defended his style, declaring, "I have enough time to decide what's right and what's wrong." [45]

The Future Presidency

The activist President, bent upon extracting as much mileage as possible from his resources as general manager, must plainly commit great quantities of his own personal energy and talent fully to the task. The Presidency is no place for semiretirement. The President does best with a small cadre of assistants, with flexible assignments and responsibilities of both action-forcing and program-building nature. Yet he must be watchful that his immediate staff does not, intentionally or no, exercise its enlarging authority for its own purposes rather than his, and, even worse, for antidemocratic activity of the Watergate genre. The competitive principle of advice and action has been successfully used by activist Presidents since the days of Washington. It is the surest means yet devised for extending their influence and control and for inducing behavior consonant with democracy.

But no contemporary President can live by personal assistants alone. He must make large use of the Presidency's institutions such as the Office of Management and Budget, the NSC, the CEA. Given the enormity of his problems and the dangers of the times, he can no longer reign with the informal splendor of a Franklin Roosevelt of the 1930s. The institutionalized Presidency is the best available guarantee that the multiple specializations a major problem requires will be addressed to that problem. With an independent power base and more security of tenure than the personal staff, the institutions are better able to warn the President of impending decisions that are not well honed to democratic and ethical criteria.

In the 1970s, the personal staff, the White House office, has come under increasing attack on grounds of efficiency and democracy. The staff is excessively powerful, removed from even the minimum accountability required by democratic standards. Secretive, aloof from Congressional inquiry, distant from the electoral process, the staff functions with an autonomy that flaunts the pretensions of democratic government. And, as experience discloses, the staff can lapse into corruption, criminality, and gross errors of policy. It can misinform and mislead the President and, as Watergate reveals, can seriously—if not irreparably—cripple his administration. For the sake of democracy and efficiency, what safeguards are in order to ward off the disaster of a misguided, overweening White House staff?

1. The President must strike a balance between the "open door" and "closed door" stances toward his staff. If he employs a chief of staff, an Adams or a Haldeman, he should restrict such types to facilitative administration—to monitoring, but not unduly diminishing, the flow of visitors and paperwork, while simultaneously according direct access to other staff who represent diverse approaches to policy issues. Above all, the President must not become overcommitted to the chief-of-staff concept. If he does, he will see too few people and hear an insufficient variety of interests and viewpoints. He should remain directly accessible to department heads, key bureau chiefs, the heads of his institutional staffs, and such central figures of his personal staff as his special counsel, appointments secretary, and policy aides, as well as a diversity of legislators, party figures, and interest group representatives.

2. The President can function with better regard for democracy and efficiency if he builds links with a wide gamut of interest and opinion in American life. He must be in touch with not only the corporations and labor unions but with the professions, the city and state governments, minorities, youth and the elderly, with those on welfare, and with other disadvantaged groups. In a word, Presidential decision-making should reflect the pluralism of society in order to foster the representative and participating phases of democracy and rational efficiency.

In many ways, President Johnson sought to advance this concept by perceiving Presidential administration as a consensus process and by setting priorities and fashioning key policies through consultation with multiple sectors of opinion. In Johnson's view, legitimate sources of counsel were not limited to the White House staff or government in general, but extended to the business executive, the labor leader, the universities, to spokesmen for minority groups.

The President-group relationship can also be structured and regularized by extending processes flourishing in recent Presidencies. The task force device lends itself well to pluralism in Presidential counsel. It can be used to study and report on a full range of Presidential subjects, and its membership can constitute a representative cross-section of concerned interests. Consultation could occur at more or less regularized intervals, in the sense that recent Presidents, or their representatives, have met with the Business Council, a body of corporation leaders, or the annual civil rights conference that flourished in the Kennedy-Johnson era, the conferences on nutrition of the early Nixon years, and Ford's summit meetings on the economy. Admittedly, such meetings can become manipulated and desultory, but whatever their faults, they will expose the President and the Presidency to a variety of opinion, as befits democracy, and spare the office from intolerable insulation and overresponsiveness to narrow, usually well-heeled interests.

3. Key White House staff members such as a chief of staff and top assistants for national security and domestic affairs ought, if they engage in operations, to be subject to at least a minimum of democratic control external to the Presidency itself. Since they exercise enormous power over national policy, their ap-

pointments warrant Senate confirmation. The Senate's review of their qualifications might stress several ingredients highly germane to democracy and efficiency. Above all, the quality of democratic socialization of the prospective appointee should be probed: how well they comprehend democratic values and processes as evidenced by their past behavior. A distressing aspect of the Watergate investigations was the obtuseness of a lengthy parade of Presidential assistants to the nature and imperatives of democratic deportment. If conspicuous gaps appear in the democratic socialization of any nominees, they should be rejected, since their inadequacy is then self-evident. Likewise, the known malfeasances of Ehrlichman and Haldeman in Nixon's pre-Presidential political campaigns should have been assessed in a Senate review, and should have disqualified them for White House service.

Senate confirmation would constitute a pressure on the Chief Executive to nominate individuals with a more rounded sophistication in politics than merely that derived from service in campaigns as advance men. Broader political experience is apt to produce a better understanding of democratic processes than a life history lacking that exposure.

4. To avoid possible future lapses of the Presidential staff into the antidemocratic excesses of Watergate, it might be salutary to establish a permanent commission on democratic government. The commission has several analogues, including the commission on civil rights, created by the first modern civil rights legislation in 1957, charged with pointing out flaws in civil rights administration and ways to improvement, and the British Royal Commission of Inquiry, composed of distinguished persons, who study major issues and draft authoritative reports that lead to legislation and administrative action.

A commission on democratic government would constitute a permanent inquiry into trends and developments affecting the health and prospects of democracy. The Presidency and the White House staff would be included in its ambit. The commission would be empowered to conduct studies, take testimony, and make public reports that would stress both positive and negative features of current developments.

Ideally, the commission, in the manner of its British prototype, should be composed of citizens who have gained eminence in a profession or calling, including previous public service, and who are not currently engaged in nor envision a further political career. Father Theodore Hesburgh, president of Notre Dame, former chairman of the civil rights commission, typifies a suitable member. One third of the proposed commission might be appointed by the President, one-third by the Speaker of the House, and one-third by the president pro tempore of the Senate, as the two Hoover Commissions were, with a substantial tenure of at least six years. The prestige of the members and the importance of their business would command attention from the news media, and the desire to avoid its criticism would induce the President and his staff to shun even a shred of the transgressions against democracy committed in the Watergate era.

9

CHIEF DIPLOMAT

"I make American foreign policy," said Harry S Truman, discoursing on his office one day to a visiting body of Jewish War Veterans.[1] Truman's candid dictum finds support in the pronouncement of another Chief Executive, Thomas Jefferson, who once termed the conduct of foreign affairs "executive altogether."[2] But from no less venerable authority than James Madison comes an opposite view, that Congress determines foreign policy, by dint of its power to declare war, with the President limited to instrumental powers and circumscribed discretion.[3]

The trend of power has long run in the President's favor.[4] Since the Second World War, the Presidential contribution has attained flood-tide proportions, moving responsible critics to complain of the erosion of legislative authority while executive power crests at dangerous heights. Time and again, Presidents exercised power with fewer constraints and readier self-indulgence than Soviet leaders Khrushchev and Brezhnev. A formidable dilemma taunts the American political system: How can the President be entrusted with the amplitude of powers necessary to defend the nation and its interests in times of nuclear danger and assertive Communist states while sharing power meaningfully with Congress and remaining accountable to the people?

The Two Presidencies

Both the essence of the dilemma and its possible solution are mirrored in the circumstance that there are, and for some time have been, two Presidencies in foreign affairs. Both have been constructed and shaped by the Founding Fathers, by the adaptation of the office to changes in the world with which it deals, and by its own peculiar suitability for the management of foreign affairs.

The two Presidencies have parallel powers and functions, and yet they are radically opposite in nature. One possesses a maximum autonomy, in which the President in relative privacy can make decisions that choose between war and peace, that commit treasure and lives, and that may determine the nation's foremost priorities for years to come. The President may take these decisions in secrecy and freedom, beyond the reach and even the knowledge of Congress and the people. Or, if Congress or the people are related to the decision, they can act only marginally. They have no real choice but to ratify what the President has done or will do. It is this Presidency that has grown by leaps and bounds in the nuclear age. It is this Presidency in which the largest decisions in foreign affairs repose and that invites one to coin the maxim that the larger the issue the more freedom the President has to act upon it. This is the Presidency that allowed Truman to order the use of the atomic bomb against Japan and to make his choice risking only the private criticism of a limited circle of counselors. This is the Presidency that can act on an instant's notice, that could respond to the outbreak in Korea in 1950, that could launch an indirect invasion of Cuba in 1961, and that could send an ever-increasing force to Vietnam.

The two major wars the United States has fought since 1945 have been "Presidential wars," or conflicts in which Congress did not exercise its constitutional power to declare war. If anything (unfortunately for democracy), this Presidency has tended increasingly toward omnipotence and self-containment. In confronting North Korea's invasion of South Korea, Truman secured a mandate from the United Nations; in the Cuban missile crisis, Kennedy derived a measure of empowerment from the Organization of American States. In neither instance did the President seriously approach Congress. Their successors have been even less assiduous in seeking authority outside their office.[5]

Without doubt the worst defilement of democratic norms were the secret B-52 bomber raids in Cambodia, commencing in 1969, which were not disclosed publicly until 1973 when a Congressional investigation uncovered them. While more than three thousand raids were flown in 1969 and 1970, White House and State Department spokesmen declared repeatedly that American policy respected Cambodian neutrality.[6] To preserve the secrecy of the raids, the Defense Department sent falsified reports to the Senate Armed Services Committee.[7] Even more, when the press disclosed in 1969 that the raids were occurring, at least seventeen wiretaps were imposed, many directly authorized by President Nixon and concurred in by his national security assistant, Henry Kissinger. These acts were, at least in part, but the culmination of long-building trends of secrecy and deviousness of the Presidencies of the 1960s.

The other Presidency in foreign affairs is marked by its dependence upon Congress and upon public opinion. Instead of operating with autonomy, its method and emphasis are cooperation and accommodation. It fits the democratic image of the powerful, responsible executive whose decisions are open to external view and debate. In a bygone day, this Presidency embraced the largest questions of foreign policy: McKinley and Congress reaching a consensus on whether to go to war with Spain; Wilson trying and failing to secure the Senate's approval for the nation's entry into the League of Nations. But in the era since the Second World War, the activity of this Presidency falls to a secondary level of importance.

To a remarkable degree, each Presidency can, action for action, discover constitutional powers and institutional resources that are counterparts of the other's. The independent Presidency employs the executive agreement to commit the United States in its relations with others, freely uses special agents or personnel to carry forward the President's missions and purposes, and utilizes the Commander-in-Chief power to conduct the enterprise that might well be called Presidential warmaking. The "dependent," or cooperative, Presidency has legal powers and institutional resources that include the treaty power, which involves Senate participation, and the executive agreement when money or other Congressional support is required for its effectiveness; the appointment of ambassadors, ministers, and other officers of foreign affairs with the advice and consent of the Senate; and the concrete provision of the Constitution by which war is declared by Congress. To understand the nature of the two Presidencies in foreign affairs, we need to look more closely at their several kinds of resources.

Constitutional Limitations

The Constitution, in Article II, section 2, provides that the President "shall have power, by and with the advice and consent of the Senate, to make treaties, provided two-thirds of the Senators present concur." Significantly, this language associates the President with the Senate throughout the course of treaty-making. President Washington, interpreting the Constitution literally, understandably felt obligated to secure the advice of the Senate on certain questions arising in the course of treaty negotiations with the Southern Indian tribes. But the Senate chose to respond churlishly, resolving to consider the questions privately, without the Chief Executive present. Washington, incensed by this treatment, withdrew, according to Senator William Maclay, "with sullen dignity." [8] This little set-to finished Washington, and for that matter all future Presidents, on consultations with the full Senate. Not, however, with individual Senators. Although the Executive negotiates treaties, he has deemed it wise on occasion to involve key Senators in the enterprise. Senators Tom Connally and Arthur Vandenberg were members of the United States delegation to San Francisco to construct the United Nations Charter. Negotiations of the 1963 test ban treaty were conducted in the presence of a panel of Senators. Some historians blame Wilson's League of Nations defeat on his failure to include Senators in the United States delegation to the Paris peace conference.

In practice, the Senate can approve or reject a treaty outright or impose conditions or reservations that may or may not be acceptable to the President. When the test ban treaty was in the Senate's hands, President Kennedy, at the urging of Senator Everett Dirksen, the Republican minority leader and a supporter of the treaty, sent a letter to the Senate carrying "unqualified and unequivocal assurances" that the treaty would not deter him from maintaining a vigorous weapons program. Kennedy gave other explicit assurances, including one that the treaty would never be amended by Executive action but only by treaty procedure. [9] The President's action headed off possible Senatorial reservations. The constitutional requirement that two-thirds of the Senate give its advice and consent establishes for the President the unavoidable and sometimes difficult test of winning support from the opposition party. Wilson's failure to attract sufficient Republican backing wrecked United States membership in the League of Nations. Franklin Roosevelt, anxious to avoid the Wilsonian disaster in his quest for a United Nations organization, took elaborate precautions to win both Republican and Democratic cooperation.

The President may choose to disregard the treaty procedure and resort to "executive agreements." These entail no Senatorial review, and may stem from several types of independent Presidential authority—the executive power clause or his power as Commander-in-Chief—and from statute or treaty. Executive agreements are not mentioned specifically in the Constitution. The exchange of United States destroyers for British bases in the Second World War was founded upon the Commander-in-Chief power and executive power clauses and a statute permitting the transfer of "obsolescent" military materiel. Presidents have used executive agreements for nearly every conceivable diplomatic subject: fishing rights, boundary disputes, the annexation of territory, and so on. In *United States* v. *Curtiss-Wright Corp.* (299 U.S. 304, 1936) the Supreme Court seemed to contemplate an almost limitless variety of matters for executive agreements. Yet what the President can do in law he may be unable to do in politics. Most executive agreements depend for their effectiveness upon support from Congress, which can assert itself, if it chooses. Hence, when the United States and the Soviet Union reached agreement in 1972 on a sweeping trade package, an impressive by-product of détente, the diplomatic enterprise depended upon Congressional approval for granting credits and tariff concessions. Immediately, no less than seventy-six Senators served notice that they would block passage of the accords if the U.S.S.R. did not lift its oppressive exit fees on Jews and others seeking to emigrate.[10]

The President, the Constitution says, "shall nominate, and by and with the advice and consent of the Senate, shall appoint ambassadors, other public ministers and consuls. . . ." Ordinarily, the Senate raises no objections to the President's nominees for diplomatic posts, but trouble is by no means unknown, and President Eisenhower drew a full draught of it early in his term when he nominated Charles E. Bohlen as ambassador to the U.S.S.R. A leading expert on the Soviet Union, Bohlen numbered among his experiences service as Franklin Roosevelt's Russian language interpreter and adviser on Russian affairs at the Yalta conference. Bohlen's presence there made him a renegade in the eyes of many Republican Senators. His prospects did not improve when he testified to the Senate Foreign Relations Committee that he saw nothing wrong with the Yalta agreements. Senators Joseph McCarthy and Pat McCarran questioned Bohlen's loyalty, compelling Eisenhower to come out strongly for Bohlen in a press conference. Senator Robert A. Taft, the Republican leader, backed up the President and the Bohlen nomination finally prevailed. Mopping his brow, Taft got word to Eisenhower that he did not want to carry any more Bohlens through the Senate.[11]

The Constitution empowers the President to receive the diplomatic representatives of other nations. The power to receive or exchange ambassadors enables the President to recognize new governments without consulting Congress. Congress, however, can pass resolutions expressing its wishes and intent, as well as providing or withholding appropriations. As Nixon's dealings with Communist China reveal, the President can engage in a range of actions, short of formal recognition and the exchange of diplomatic representatives. Following his visit to Communist China, Nixon appointed David E. K. Bruce as a "contact point" in Peking, and subsequently President Ford named George Bush, former Republican national chairman, to succeed Bruce. Though not regularly accredited envoys and not formally members of the diplomatic community in Peking, Bruce and Bush were active agents who expanded constructive relations between the countries, and Congress supported their efforts with appropriations and bipartisan approval. Since Bush ranked high among those Ford considered for the Vice Presidency, his appointment signaled to China that he was one who had the President's ear.[12]

Presidential War

Although the Constitution vests in Congress the power to declare war, the United States has declared war in only five of its eleven major conflicts with other countries. In each of the five instances, Congress declared war only in response to the President's acts or recommendations.[13] The five declared wars were the War of 1812, the Mexican War, the Spanish-American War, and the two world wars. A declaration of war was neither made by Congress nor requested by the President in the naval war with France (1798–1800), the first Barbary War (1801–05), the second Barbary War (1815), the Mexican-American clashes (1914–17), and the Korean and Vietnam conflicts. Presidents, evidently, have tended to apply to the fullest limits the view of Alexander Hamilton that the Constitution intends "that it is the peculiar and exclusive province of Congress, when the nation is at peace, to change that state into a state of war;" but "when a foreign nation declares or openly and avowedly makes war upon the United States, they are then by the very fact already at war and any declaration on the part of Congress is nugatory; it is at least unnecessary."[14]

The President claims authority for involvement in violence or potential violence as Commander-in-Chief, as custodian of the executive power, and, on certain occasions since the Second World War, under Article XLIII of the United Nations Charter. Sometimes Congress prods the President to exercise his initiative. Within a period of two weeks in 1962, for instance, the House of Representatives adopted resolutions expressing determination to use all means, including force, to defend United States rights in Berlin, about which a crisis was stirring, although the wall went up some months before, and a similar resolution was adopted for the Cuban missile crisis.

President Eisenhower introduced a novel variation to Presidential war-making when in 1955 he initiated and Congress approved a resolution authorizing the President "to employ the Armed Forces of the United States as he deems necessary for the specific purpose of securing and protecting Formosa and the Pescadores against armed attack." Communist China had been engaging in some menacing activity directed at those off-shore areas. In his request, Eisenhower was careful to say that "the authority for some of the actions which might be required would be inherent in the authority of the Commander-in-Chief." [15] He believed that by associating Congress with his effort, his declaration of his readiness to fight for Formosa would have greater impact on Peking. Furthermore, Eisenhower did not want to repeat what he considered Truman's mistake in sending forces into Korea without consulting Congress. When, eventually, the Korean conflict became politically unpopular, President Truman took the brunt. Eisenhower invited Congress to share any similar liability in a drawn-out Formosan struggle. The technique of the Formosa resolution was renewed in the 1956 Middle Eastern crisis. Eisenhower again brought Congress to authorize the President to resist "overt armed aggression" by "any nation controlled by international Communism" in the "general area" of the Middle East.[16]

THE INDOCHINA WAR   A similar resolution, which subsequently became the subject of bitter controversy, was adopted in 1964 following a reported attack on two United States destroyers by North Vietnamese PT boats in the Gulf of Tonkin. The resolution, which Congress passed with only two dissenting votes, was couched in sweeping language. It authorized the President to take "all necessary measures" to "repel any armed attack" against United States forces and "to prevent further aggression." As the Vietnam War escalated, critics, including members of the Senate Foreign Relations Committee, contended that the President had exceeded the intent of the resolution, that he used the resolution to dispatch ground forces to Vietnam and to order bombing attacks upon North Vietnam, including territory close to the border of Communist China—actions that were uncontemplated when the resolution was passed. The response to a minor incident was used to undergird a major war. Nor was friction diminished when many legislators subsequently became convinced that the incident in the Tonkin Gulf had not been fully reported by the President and the Executive Branch, that American and South Vietnamese provocations had instigated the Communist attack.[17] Eventually, as division over the protracted war mounted, Congress repealed the resolution.

The phenomenon of independent Presidential war-making continued to blossom as the Indochina war waxed on. Beginning in 1969, secret American air raids were conducted over Cambodia. In 1970, Nixon dispatched American forces into neutral Cambodia to destroy supply centers and staging areas for North Vietnam's operations in South Vietnam. In 1972, the President ordered, again on his own, the mining of North Vietnamese ports to forestall the flow of arms to South Vietnam, a decision that risked incidents involving Russian and Chinese supply vessels in the harbors and confrontations with those powers.[18]

When, in 1973, North Vietnam dallied in concluding a truce, the President ordered carpet-bombing of Hanoi and Haiphong, again without consulting Congress. But eventually North Vietnam returned to the negotiating table and a truce was concluded. The truce and its terms were wholly the enterprise of the President and his aides, without significant consultation of Congress. The 1973 Paris accord established a "cease-fire" to end all fighting in North and South Vietnam, with the United States withdrawing its troops from Vietnam and dismantling its military bases in Indochina, while Vietnamese Communist and all other foreign troops were to be withdrawn from Laos and Cambodia. All American prisoners and captives on both sides were to be released. Both the United States and North Vietnam recognized "the South Vietnamese people's right to self-determination," and the South Vietnamese government agreed to a national election organized by that government, the Communists, and neutralists. President Nixon hailed the truce as bringing "peace with honor," [19] while Senator George Aiken (R-Vt.) declared that the President had finally accomplished what the Senator had urged six years earlier: "We said we had won and got out." [20] Best of all, American forces were extricated from combat in Vietnam, and American prisoners, after agonizing delays, returned. But for South Vietnam and neighboring Cambodia there was no "peace." Despite the "cease-fire," North Vietnam allowed no let-up in the fighting, and the great powers—the Soviet Union, Communist China, and the United States—continued to pour in armaments unrelentingly to their respective allies.

The claimed authority for these actions was the President's power as Commander-in-Chief, his investiture with the executive power and, as is therefore implied, with the military power ordinarily possessed by heads of government. Historic practice is also cited—Jefferson sending naval frigates to fight the Tripolitan pirates, McKinley dispatching troops to China to subdue the Boxer Rebellion, Roosevelt ordering the Navy to fire "on sight" at Axis naval craft, Kennedy throwing a naval blockade around Cuba.

But as a practical matter, so lengthy and costly a war as the Indochina conflict could not have been waged by the President alone, no matter how expansive were his claims to independent power. Over its long years, the war could not be sustained without positive acts of Congressional cooperation, and, throughout the war, these were amply forthcoming. The Senate approved the SEATO treaty, providing commitment and structure for American military support of the Southeast Asian region. Congress overwhelmingly approved the Tonkin resolution, a step for which, despite any possible executive legerdemain, it must shoulder responsibility. Most important of all, the engines of war required vast and repeated infusions of money, which only Congress could and did supply. Over the drawn-out course of the war, and until its final stages, Congress provided funding unstintingly and without reservation. In a war whose duration traversed five Presidencies, Congress attached no serious qualification to its own cooperation until the late date of 1973, when it specified that its appropriations were not to support American ground combat in Laos. Thanks to its appropriations power, Congress could review annually its commitment to the Indochina war, and its decision was almost invariably a reaffirmation.

THE WAR POWERS ACT OF 1973 Congress's most significant challenge to Presidential authority is the War Powers Act, passed in 1973 during Nixon's political enfeeblement from Watergate. As its sponsor, Senator Jacob K. Javits (R-N.Y.), pointed out, the act is a towering reminder of Congressional rejection of the little-inhibited exercise of Presidential power represented by the Indochina war.[21] Under the Act, the President can undertake emergency military action in the absence of a declaration of war, but within forty-eight hours after committing the armed forces to combat abroad he must report the event to Congress in writing. The combat action must end in sixty days, unless Congress authorizes the commitment. But this deadline could be extended for thirty days if the President certified the extension's necessity for the forces' safe withdrawal. Most important, at any time within the sixty-day or ninety-day period, Congress could order an immediate removal of the forces by adopting a concurrent resolution, which is not subject to Presidential veto.

Is this law to be hailed as a useful containment of Presidential power? Certainly it well reminds the Chief Executive of the Congressional presence as a sharer in decisions of war, and it is a constructive effort to adapt Congress's war-declaring power, fashioned in the eighteenth century, to the swift tempo of today's affairs. For delicate international security emergencies of the future, however, it provides cumbersome procedures that could become snarled in Congressional delays and deadlock between the houses. Decision-making will become less assured and American intentions less clear. Since foreign affairs crises often arise from obscure communications and misreadings of intent, the new law could add immeasurably to these maladies.

The War Powers Act bears seeds of future constitutional crisis. Passed in an hour when an incumbent President was drained of political effectuality, the law is unlikely to be accepted with equanimity in future, more normal Presidencies.

The act's constitutionality is dubious, and it is unclear that the courts could effectively intervene to decide the controversies it might engender, which would then be left to wrangling between the branches, most likely in time of crisis. Precisely how Congress, as a practical matter, could reverse Presidential commitment of the armed forces strains one's imagination. Worst of all, despite the appearance of limiting the President, the law may actually enlarge the Executive's war-making capacity to extremes that even the most bellicose Presidents would never dream of. For the War Powers Act can be read as a blank-check empowerment of the Chief Executive to fight anywhere, for whatever cause, subject only to a sixty- to ninety-day time-limit, indefinitely renewable. With ample cause, after making this reflection, Senator Thomas F. Eagleton (D-Mo.) exclaimed to his Senate colleagues, "How short can memories be? My God, we just got out of a nightmare." [22]

Cooperation with Congress

When the President needs money or new authority—and for an abundance of his policies he needs one or the other—he must forsake the independent Presidency and enter into the cooperative phase of his office.

President Johnson, aiming in 1967 to launch a major foreign policy initiative by promoting "peaceful engagement" with the communist bloc, had no choice but to travel to Capitol Hill to seek approval of five pieces of legislation: a treaty with the Soviet Union barring nuclear weapons in outer space; a consular convention, also with the Soviet Union; an East-West trade bill authorizing the President to extend "most favored nation" tariff treatment to the Soviets and communist countries in eastern Europe; removal of restrictions to the Food-for-Freedom program; and a ban of food shipments to any nation trading with North Vietnam or Cuba. Congress of course can, if it chooses, amend or thwart the President's proposals.

By his own acts the President may stiffen the opposition to what he wants to do. Johnson, to the extent that he created indispensable public and Congressional support for his prosecution of the Vietnam War, had also created a body of opinion unfriendly to his policy of "building bridges" to the communist world. His staunchest Congressional supporters for the war became the most resolute opponents of his bridge-building. Since legislation in foreign affairs is less apt to enjoy the group interest support prevalent in domestic legislation, the President's foreign projects were more susceptible to the several species of mishap lurking in legislative processes. Parliamentary delays, crippling amendments, and headline-capturing investigations can erupt from many places.

The Foreign Aid Program

Congress's potency for restricting the President is amply conveyed by its annual review of his foreign aid proposals. Power is widely scattered among autonomous legislative committees run by chairmen with little, if any, political attachment to the President, and they can act with minimum detection and maximum effect. The foreign aid program of military and economic assistance, a keystone of United States foreign policy involving billions of dollars of annual expenditure, demonstrates the lengths and hazards of Congressional policy-making. The program runs the gauntlet of six committees: the foreign affairs, armed services, and appropriations committees of each house. It presents an annual suspense drama in which the President's proposals are subject to drastic cuts, partial restorations, and great delays, and the eventual result is usually well below his original request. The first foreign aid bill of Gerald Ford's Presidency was slashed by the Senate Foreign Relations Committee by nearly $1 billion, to $2.5 billion, and was crammed with limitations on the President's freedom to employ aid for South Vietnam, Cambodia, and South Korea.[23] After Turkey invaded Cyprus, Ford twice vetoed Congressional measures designed to cut off military aid to that NATO ally, and eventually, after determined effort, extracted a stop-gap money bill that enabled him to continue aid to Turkey for less than two months, subject to close restrictions.[24]

Foreign aid's worst troubles have been suffered at the hands of hostile Congressmen such as Otto E. Passman, Democrat of Louisiana, chairman of the Subcommittee on Foreign Aid Operations of the House Appropriations Committee. Passman, who delights in referring to himself as a "country boy," though he is modestly wealthy and indulges a fondness for snow-white silk suits, applies his "countryman's axe" to the President's foreign aid requests. Although there is some redress elsewhere in the legislative review, the net damage is severe. Once, after deleting nearly $1 billion, or about one-fourth, of the President's request, Passman justifiably exulted, "We cut the gizzards and some of the liver out of the bill." The fund-cutting bestirs chilling concern in some of the President's foreign constituencies. In 1972 a State Department official on a tour of Asian and Pacific countries discovered more worriment concerning Congress's growing opposition to foreign aid than about any possibly disruptive effects of President Nixon's trip to China.[25]

To counter his legislative hazards, the President resorts to two major strategies. He resists chiefly by mobilizing bipartisan support for the aid program. He goes along by deferring to Congress, indulging in expedients that silence or win over the legislative critics. In his bipartisan campaign for his 1961 foreign aid request, President Kennedy was backed by the nation's two leading Republicans, Eisenhower and Nixon. When Passman, in a single flourish of his axe, severed 21 percent of the administration's request, Eisenhower cried out from his Gettysburg farm that "these slashes are incomprehensible to me, especially in light of present world tensions."

The President is also given to a drastic reshuffling of foreign aid administration, a hopeful by-product of which is a resurgence of Congressional confidence and support. Choosing foreign aid administrators is a busy task for contemporary Presidents. Since Paul G. Hoffman took over direction of the Marshall Plan in 1948, eleven different administrators, with an average tenure of about two years, have guided the aid program. Eisenhower had four aid administrators, Kennedy three. Each new administrator is accompanied by a busy reshuffling of functions, promises of saner working principles, and sometimes a change in the agency's name. While these deeds are committed to build Congressional confidence, they also have certain costs: a slowdown of effectiveness as the program adjusts to the new structure, an erosion of employee morale, and an impairment of public, if not Congressional, confidence in the validity of foreign aid.

The Secretary of State

Given the high moment of foreign policy to their administrations' success, many Presidents have become, as the cliché goes, "their own Secretaries of State." The Roosevelts, Woodrow Wilson, and John Kennedy are rightly remembered as such. A President who is his own Secretary of State closely involves himself in major problems, sets high policy, intrudes upon routine, and engages heavily in diplomatic negotiation. He is both general commander and front-line soldier. But an activist President by no means requires a passive Secretary of State. The dynamic Theodore Roosevelt successively retained two eminent Secretaries, John Hay and Elihu Root, whose distinction increased with their tenure.

At another extreme are the Presidents who delegate freely to their Secretaries of State, as Harding did to Charles E. Hughes and Eisenhower to John Foster Dulles. But this pattern presents difficulties for both the ideals of the strong President and democratic norms. Dulles enjoyed an unparalleled authority as policy formulator, negotiator, and chief spokesman in foreign affairs. Indeed Dulles' sweeping power brought Senator J. W. Fulbright to protest that "Secretary Dulles seemed at times to be exercising those 'delicate, plenary, and exclusive powers' which are supposed to be vested in the President." [26] Eisenhower himself contended that Dulles never made a major decision without Presidential knowledge and approval. In the judgment of Sherman Adams, "Far from relieving Eisenhower of the burden of foreign problems, this unique partnership required him to spend more time in consultation with Dulles than he did with other department heads." [27] As Nixon's Secretary of State, Henry Kissinger roamed the world with an equally sweeping gift of authority from the President, matched the prodigious travels of Dulles, and brilliantly patched together an accord that halted the Middle East war of 1973, its provisions evidently harmonizing with the wishes of Nixon, who was distracted by pressures for his impeachment. Early in the Ford Presidency, Kissinger continued his peripatetic global ways, with key missions to the Middle East, India, and the Soviet Union.

The tension between the strong President and democratic needs can be most intense when the Secretary of State is a major political figure. The least promising appointee is one who believes the higher office should have been his. Lincoln's Secretary of State, William H. Seward, had expected to win the 1860 Republican nomination and regarded the victorious Lincoln as an upstart. Ability was now serving mediocrity. Seward in his rationalizations began thinking of the President as monarch and the Secretary of State as Prime Minister, and the train of these quaint ideas led to a memorandum entitled "Thoughts for the President's Consideration," probably the most extraordinary document ever presented to a Chief Executive by a subordinate. "We are at the end of a month's administration," it read, "and yet without a policy, domestic or foreign." Further delay will "bring scandal on the administration and danger upon the country." Seward generously offered to take on the great task of policy-building himself. Lincoln's reply, fortunately, was an unsparing squelch. "If this must be done," he said, "I must do it." [28]

Later Presidents who have brought in erstwhile political rivals as Secretaries of State have fared no better. Wilson chose for his Secretary the perennial Democratic Presidential nominee, William Jennings Bryan. His stubborn pacifism and neutrality eventually collided with Wilson's drift toward involvement and its risk of war, and the nation was rocked by the Secretary's resignation.[29] Harry S. Truman appointed as his Secretary of State James F. Byrnes, his rival for the 1944 Vice-Presidential nomination, the route to the Presidency upon Roosevelt's death. Truman indeed had nominated Byrnes for the Vice Presidency. After the convention made its choice, Truman wrote that "Byrnes, undoubtedly, was deeply disappointed and hurt. I thought that my calling on him at this time might help balance things up." [30] Again, the relationship did not work.

The President's Staff

Power for the President reflects, among other things, the quality and usefulness of his staff. Upon them he depends for the funneling of information and problems to himself and the communication and interpretation of his directives to those sectors of the huge, sprawling executive branch that administer the diplomatic, economic, military, scientific, intelligence, and psychological phases of foreign policy. Whether the executive agencies are alert and effective, whether they can perceive his own interests and necessities, instead of representing merely their own preferences, may have much to do with how well or ill the President fares in foreign policy.

THE WHITE HOUSE STAFF AND THE NATIONAL SECURITY COUNCIL   John Kennedy regularly used the White House staff to maximize his own involvement in foreign affairs. He relied heavily upon his national security assistant, McGeorge Bundy, and a small band of aides to monitor foreign policy and national security problems and the progress of decisions throughout the executive branch. President Johnson continued to employ Bundy as national security assistant at a level of influence equal to that under President Kennedy. In the Washington community, Bundy, in both Presidential administrations, was widely regarded as the virtual equal of Secretary of State Dean Rusk and Secretary of Defense Robert McNamara. However, unlike the Secretaries, who were subject to the constant scrutiny of legislative committees, Bundy conducted his duties in well-protected privacy. His status as Presidential assistant made him privileged against Congressional inquiry while allowing him to function as a leading adviser on policy. After Bundy's departure for a private career, his title and most of his functions passed to his former deputy, Walt W. Rostow. A leading influence in foreign policy-making, Rostow nevertheless was a step removed from the pinnacle of influence enjoyed by Bundy.

With Henry Kissinger's incumbency in the Nixon administration, the post of national security assistant came into fullest flower. Like his predecessors, Kissinger helped to create policy, but unlike them, he conducted crucial international negotiations to carry it out.[31] On policy, Kissinger and Nixon seemed in fullest accord. Prior to the administration, both had published articles on the Vietnam War and other international questions, and their views were extraordinarily similar. In the subsequent administration, the general harmony persisted,

with the more informed Kissinger improving on Nixon's instincts and judgments.[32] Kissinger was assisted by a large staff, some fifty-four "substantive
officers," compared with Rostow's twelve. In addition, Kissinger was chairman of a half dozen interagency committees covering the entire range of
foreign policy, and manager of "working groups" that prepared staff studies
for top-level policy-making.[33] Eventually the power that accrued to Kissinger
enabled him to assert an impact on foreign policy that plainly exceeded that of
the Secretary of State, and a leading member of the Senate Foreign Relations
Committee, Senator Stuart Symington (D-Mo.), was moved to exclaim that the
national security assistant had become "Secretary of State in everything but
title." [34]

Symington's assessment was symptomatic of the lack of congruence of Kissinger's position with democratic norms. In a Presidential administration notable for its undervaluing of democracy, Kissinger was a consistent part of the
pattern. The heroes of his academic studies were not American democratic politicians, but Castlereagh, Metternich, and Bismarck, autonomous master diplomats, intellectually and politically superior, who ran the worlds of their day
with maneuver, threat, secrecy, and surprise. They played their diplomatic
power game remote from public scrutiny, legislative interrogation, and even
from their heads of state. Kissinger's own deportment reflected his admired
prototypes. Sometimes he operated free of Nixon's oversight, and pitilessly
excluded the State Department from serious participation in his policy-making
ventures. The few State Department officials who were recruited to Kissinger's
staff were abjured not to disclose their activities to the department. In their
meetings with Chou En-lai and Brezhnev, Kissinger and Nixon used Chinese
and Russian interpreters rather than a State Department interpreter who might
inform the Secretary of State of matters in progress.[35] Kissinger was also distant from Congress, declining to testify publicly and limiting himself to private
appearances on Capitol Hill. Doubtless Kissinger's sharpest departure from
democratic deportment was his acquiescence to wiretaps imposed on members
of his staff who were regarded as possible sources of information leaks.

While the claims of the strong Presidency to confidentiality for the national
security assistant are necessary and tolerable, Kissinger's extension of his post
into operations—negotiating an armistice, reviewing the military budget—
makes the claim challengeable, at least for operations. Clearly too much
foreign policy is removed from public discussion if these operations are included, a contention encouraged by the clear evidence of recent American experience that no one has a monopoly of wisdom in foreign affairs. The plain
lesson of the Vietnam War is that it is salutary and necessary to challenge assumptions and question policy. For all of its successes, which easily place him
in the front rank of American diplomats, Kissinger's performance was not
without blemishes—the slights to Japan in the lack of forewarning of the coming American rapprochement with Communist China, the flagging attention to
Western Europe, the stumblings of international economic policies, the dubious
"tilt" that favored Pakistan in its futile 1971 war with India.

Later, when he became Secretary of State in the Nixon and Ford administrations, Kissinger, though continuing as Assistant for National Security Affairs, became more accessible to Congress, the press, and other sectors of the political system, and more prey to their pressures and criticisms.

Other institutions that the President may turn to include the Central Intelligence Agency, the cabinet, the National Security Council, and the Joint Chiefs of Staff. The cabinet originated in the diplomatic crisis of 1793, when it charted United States neutrality in the Franco-British war. The cabinet's role has been erratic. It reached the height of its influence in fashioning the Monroe Doctrine; in the two world wars its activity was slight. The fortunes of the National Security Council, which has largely displaced the cabinet in foreign affairs, have also wavered. Truman and Eisenhower regularly resorted to the NSC, but Kennedy used it infrequently, preferring instead meetings with administrators individually, and in small groups. Johnson and Nixon turned more to the NSC, particularly during critical decisions concerning Vietnam and the Middle East. Ford, faced with Turkey's invasion of Cyprus, instability in the Middle East, and other international perils and opportunities in his early Presidency, frequently resorted to the NSC. Potentially, the NSC is democracy-serving, since several agencies with diverse functions and perspectives participate jointly, permitting different views to be advanced and debated in the Chief Executive's presence.[36] But in the Nixon-reorganized NSC, consequences ensued that were inimical to democracy. Power gravitated excessively to the assistant for national security affairs, Kissinger. The committee structure, which Kissinger headed, facilitated his access to the various departmental power centers, and his own elite staff, expanded by recruits from the State Department, helped push the Secretary of State, William Rogers, to the outer perimeters of the NSC system, while Kissinger occupied its center, and progressively cut off the Secretary from access even to his own departmental staff.[37] The cumulative changes of the NSC, according to one critic, tilted the decision machinery in favor of the military and were responsible "for some of the most serious misjudgments" of recent Presidencies.[38]

The ideal of democratic policy-making based upon the interaction of administrators, with perspectives drawn from differentiated bureaucratic functions, is also advanced by the common practice of modern Presidents who throw together *ad hoc* groups to provide counsel in diplomatic crises. To weigh the American response when Israel invaded Egypt in 1956, Eisenhower summoned to the White House Secretary of State Dulles, chairman of the Joint Chiefs of Staff Admiral Arthur Radford, Secretary of Defense Wilson, CIA Director Allen Dulles, and Sherman Adams.[39] Eleven years later, when Israel scored its lightning military success against Arab arms, President Johnson sought to prepare policies for the "new peace." For this purpose he drew together a group that included McGeorge Bundy, on leave from the presidency of the Ford Foundation, to serve as executive secretary; Secretary of State Rusk as chairman; Secretary of the Treasury Henry Fowler; General Earle G. Wheeler, chairman of the Joint Chiefs of Staff; Richard Helms, director of the Central Intelligence Agency; Clark Clifford, then a part-time chairman of the Foreign Intelligence Advisory Board and subsequently Johnson's Secretary of Defense; and Walt W. Rostow.

THE CENTRAL INTELLIGENCE AGENCY   Created by the National Security Act of 1947, with Truman's firm approval, the CIA has had a mercurial career. Housed in architecturally sterile headquarters, above whose entrance are chiseled the words, "The Truth Shall Make You Free," the CIA enjoyed its strongest influence, in playing its advisory role to the President and the NSC, in the Truman and Eisenhower eras of the 1950s and early 1960s. In pursuing its standard duties of gathering raw intelligence, interpreting its meanings, and in estimating the likely consequences of policy moves by the United States or other nations, the CIA churned into top policy-making circles a steady flow of intelligence analyses and projections on a wide range of subjects. Under Kennedy, who preferred to deal with selected individuals rather than institutions, and even more so under Johnson, the CIA suffered a declining influence. Strikingly, Johnson, who was preoccupied with Vietnam and who refers extensively in his memoirs [40] to memoranda and reports that influenced his thinking, makes no allusion to any CIA study. In the Nixon era, the NSC system, expanded under Kissinger's impress, produced no marked enhancement of the CIA's role. Ironically, the Pentagon Papers released by Daniel Ellsberg make the CIA "look good" in its studies and forecasts on Vietnam. Alas, they commanded little readership in top policy circles.[41]

In the Ford Presidency, the CIA stirred national attention and criticism when its long-standing clandestine and disruptive activities against adversaries burst into prominence with revelations of its role during the Nixon years in the overthrow of the Allende government in Chile. In an $8 million campaign (from 1970 to 1973) against the Marxist leader, the CIA, among other things, helped finance strikes and demonstrations to "destabilize" Allende's government. Eventually, the government fell and Allende was murdered—how much the government's collapse was due to the CIA and how much to its own errors remains problematical. A considerable body of informed opinion holds that the Allende regime would have toppled by itself and that the CIA's intervention was superfluous and foolish.[42]

For the CIA to engage in subversion of foreign governments seems a blatant contradiction of the democratic pretentions of the American political system. How, in ethics and conscience, can such a system practice abroad what it professes to abhor at home? President Ford justified the CIA's activity in the name of that ready cover-all, "national security," a concept whose easy abuse had been demonstrated in the Watergate malfeasances by the Nixon Presidency. Furthermore, Ford contended, "I am reliably informed that Communist nations spend vastly more money than we do for the same kind of purposes." [43]

At the very least, ought not the CIA be subject to more rigorous political oversight, including that of the President? Actually, it has been under Presidential rein to a degree, and the projects in question require approval at the Presidential level. Kennedy, Johnson, and Nixon all knowingly employed the CIA for political action in counter-insurgency programs. The 40 Committee, consisting of top-level executive officials who oversee the CIA's clandestine activities, approved its undertakings in Chile. Despairing of the adequacy of executive surveillance, J. W. Fulbright and other Senators urged the establishment of a joint Congressional committee to oversee the entire intelligence community.

A more modest, and perhaps more politically attainable proposal calls for selected members of Congress to sit with the NSC when it considers secret action projects for the CIA.[44] But the CIA has many friends in Congress, the more influential of whom doubtless would find their way to the NSC's table.

THE STATE DEPARTMENT   For counsel and action the President turns also to the Department of State, home of a vast assemblage of specialists, and to the United States Foreign Service, a distinguished career organization. Many activist Presidents have become disenchanted with the State Department and the Foreign Service, however. Woodrow Wilson and Franklin Roosevelt, for example, held them in low esteem. Forewarned by Adlai Stevenson that he would find the State Department a "tremendous institutional inertial force," John Kennedy soon spoke of the department as "a bowl of jelly" and complained bitterly, "They never have any ideas over there: never come up with anything new." [45] Presidents and their aides regard the State Department's staff work as lacking in quality, as unduly devoted to established policy at the expense of alternatives, as bereft of thorough and broad analysis and prone to reflect pained reluctance in carrying out Presidential decisions. To department officials, the President is a temporary intruder whose idiosyncratic interests and work habits are both resented and somehow coped with. When asked by John Kennedy what was wrong with "that goddamned department of yours," career ambassador Charles Bohlen replied, "You are." [46]

SPECIAL AGENTS   Presidents enjoy almost limitless freedom to employ special agents on high missions abroad if for any reason they prefer not to use the regular ambassadors. Unlike ambassadors and ministers, special agents are appointed solely by the President, without referral to the Senate; they are not mentioned specifically in the Constitution, although their employ is implied by the treaty power and the all-purpose "executive power" clause. George Washington dispatched John Jay to England to negotiate the treaty bearing his name; Thomas Jefferson sent James Monroe to the court of Napoleon to help Robert Livingston arrange the Louisiana Purchase; and Lyndon Johnson had Attorney General Robert F. Kennedy go to Indonesia to induce Indonesian President Sukarno not to fulfill his threat to crush the new country of Malaysia.

Special agents command the President's confidence and trust, which is not always the case with ambassadors. Special agents know better than anyone else the latest intentions and objectives of their Chief Executives. They radiate prestige because they come directly from the White House, and at their approach the gates of foreign ministries open wide. But special agents are at best a mixed blessing. They often lack relevant diplomatic training or experience—Harry Hopkins, who was Franklin Roosevelt's chief liaison with foreign affairs and the Second World War overseas, was a former social worker and administrator of domestic New Deal programs. Special agents undercut the resident ambassador, whether intentionally or not. During the blooming of American-Soviet détente, Kissinger conducted close-to-the-vest diplomacy in Moscow in which the American ambassador, Jacob D. Beam, did not participate. Pictures in the

Soviet press showed Leonid Brezhnev, the Communist party leader, Andrei Gromyko, the Foreign Minister, and Anatoly Dobrynin, the Soviet ambassador to Washington, together with Kissinger accompanied by two White House aides. Ambassador Beam was conspicuously absent. At the time, American and other diplomats commented that Soviet officials would surely note the omission and that it would hurt the embassy's prospects for gaining regular and easy access to Soviet leaders once the special agent departed. "When Kissinger is here, we're left out in the cold," said a middle-level American diplomat, "and when he's gone, we're still out in the cold." [47]

Foreign Leaders

For the President, power in foreign affairs lies in the ability to persuade foreign leaders, whether friend or foe or neutral, to back or accept his policies. His chief policy objectives—stepping up or winding down the Vietnam War, building constructive relations with the Soviet Union and China, recasting the alliances with Western Europe and Japan in recognition of their new strength and autonomy—have usually led him to pursue these contacts diligently with meetings and correspondence.

The Johnson era witnessed a steady trek by heads of other governments to the White House. To the President these occasions are valuable not so much for the specific agreements they produce, which are few, but for several intangibles. The meetings may clear away suspicions, cement personal relations, and lead to broad understanding of positions.

The many personal letters that Kennedy dispatched to a wide circle of foreign leaders were no mere puffs of good will, but dealt with major problems. At the height of the 1962 Cuban crisis, the Kennedy-Khrushchev exchanges opened up an understanding that averted general war. An essential feature of the arrangement was the secrecy both countries maintained about the exchange. Personal communication permitted greater privacy and was less susceptible to leaks than regular channels, and, unlike formal diplomatic notes, custom does not require its publication. The Soviet news media did not mention the exchange at all. The White House kept secret the number of letters involved, the content of most of them, and the channels used. Top-level communication was also nicely attuned to Khrushchev's preference for personal diplomacy and to that of his Foreign Minister, Andrei Gromyko, who functioned as a technician rather than a policy-maker. Nevertheless, the Kennedy-Khrushchev notes were not a substitute for normal diplomatic endeavor, but a supplement, resorted to when the diplomats were unable to agree or when the problem exceeded the bounds of the forum in which they were negotiating.

A President's relationship with world leaders may be buffeted by the vagaries of American domestic politics. With American domestic opinion clamorous against the Vietnam War, Israeli leaders grew accustomed to Johnson's and Nixon's habit of linking that war, in expositions of its rationale and validity, to the cause of Israel in Middle East crises. The comparison presumably would discomfort some critics of the Vietnam War who nevertheless favored strong support for Israel. For Nixon's speech, opposing "precipitate withdrawal" of American troops from Vietnam as a possible trigger of violence in the Middle East, Israeli Premier Golda Meir offered praise, since it "encourages and strengthens freedom-loving small nations the world over." [48]

The domestic politics of foreign countries too may be a jarring influence. At times the President has to shore up other chief executives whose perpetuation in office suits his purposes. When the 1953 West German elections left Adenauer's Christian Democratic Union party badly weakened in the Bundestag and dependent upon votes of several smaller parties, cries went up for the Chancellor to step down as Foreign Minister, the first presumably in a series of steps to curb his large powers. Faced with this serious political crisis, Adenauer badly needed a success in foreign affairs to bolster his imperiled fortunes. President Eisenhower, who viewed the Chancellor with great favor, moved to provide it by personally superintending the admission of Germany into the NATO alliance. Adenauer's long campaign for a rearmed German Federal Republic was now realized, and his political stock for a time resurged.

But the President can also become a terribly disruptive force to the political fortunes of foreign leaders, as Nixon was to Premier Eisaku Sato of Japan. While Japanese exports were pouring into the United States, the American economy, in the early 1970s, was lurching along with heavy unemployment and no foreseeable recovery. Nixon pressed Sato to curb textile exports and believed he had the Premier's promise to do so. Japanese businessmen resisted, and only after concerted American pressure were exports slowed, with Nixon meanwhile feeling that Sato had broken his word. [49] Then came Nixon's surprise announcement that he would visit Peking, a step taken without any advance consultation with Japan, a key American ally. Sato (who learned of the venture from television) and his government felt slighted, if not humiliated, and assessed Nixon's conduct as revenge for the textile embroglio. America's sudden new China policy sent shock waves through Japan, and opposition leaders and even key figures in Sato's own party assailed him for ineptitude. Soon Sato was departing as premier, a development that could be attributed, as much as anything, to his jagged relations with Nixon. [50]

In pursuing a major foreign policy, the President faces an array of nations, each with its purposes and needs, and its leaders with their domestic political necessities and career ambitions, all of which he must venture to put together as a kind of grand jigsaw puzzle of nations and leaders, whose many pieces must somehow fall into place if he is to succeed. Consider, for example, the full scene that confronted President Nixon and Secretary of State Henry Kissinger in the 1973 Arab-Israeli War. Nixon's overriding purposes were to assure the survival of Israel, to avoid the swelling of the crisis into a U.S.-U.S.S.R. confrontation, and to utilize the Middle East conflict as an opportunity for a long-term settlement.

For the Soviet Union, a cluster of needs, interests, and oportunities were at stake. It had to avoid the humiliation of having the Arab forces it supported routed by the Israelis. In the atmosphere of emerging détente with the United States, the Soviet desired most-favored-nation status in trade, which only Congress could provide. Already balky because of Soviet restrictions on Jewish emigration, Congress, now faced with the Middle East war, would doubtless reject the legislation. Aware of the certain damage that would then befall détente, administration representatives rushed to Capitol Hill to induce Congress to postpone action.[51]

As for the Middle East combatants, Nixon and Kissinger recognized Egypt's desire to transform its military successes in crossing the Suez Canal into a lasting settlement that would restore its territories occupied by Israel since the 1967 war. To Nixon and Kissinger, the Egyptian aspiration was an opportunity to engage in serious dialogue with the Arab world, which they furthered by quickly establishing formal diplomatic relations with Egypt.

Israel wanted Egypt punished for starting the 1973 war, and a central task of Kissinger's frenetic negotiations was to persuade the Israelis that their long-term security interests would gain more by a political settlement than by continued retention of Sinai and other Arab land.[52] Premier Golda Meir had potent political resources for resisting the Nixon-Kissinger formula—broad support both in her own country and in the United States. Yet there were implicit pressures to accede to assure the Nixon administration's continued good will and the flow of American arms supplies that Israel needed to survive. And in the background hovered the domestic political opposition to Mrs. Meir, which was critical of her management of the war.

Among the other parties of interest were America's Western European allies whose acute dependence on Arab oil brought them to assume a circumspect posture toward the crisis. West Germany proclaimed her strict neutrality and asked the United States to stop transferring arms cached within her borders, "from and over" her territory, to Israel. Equally cautious, France and Britain failed to support American opposition to the inclusion of U.S.-U.S.S.R. membership in a United Nations peace-keeping force dispatched to the Middle East.[53]

Summit Conferences

The President as chief diplomat often engages in diplomatic ventures himself, notably the summit conference. From Franklin D. Roosevelt onward, the summit, a rare experience prior to the Second World War, has become standard Presidential fare: Roosevelt at Yalta, Truman at Potsdam, Eisenhower at Paris, Kennedy at Vienna, Johnson at Glassboro, Nixon at Moscow and Peking, and Ford at Vladivostok.

Most Presidents have displayed no great enthusiasm for summitry. Truman did not go to Potsdam gladly, holding that the State, War, and Navy Departments should negotiate with their foreign counterparts instead. Kennedy early in his administration pointedly expressed appreciation for the quiet, normal diplomatic channels. Johnson, soon after taking office, proclaimed his readiness to meet with any world leader, including Premier Nikita Khrushchev, should such a meeting contribute to his loftiest goal, achieving "peace and prosperity." But in actuality, Johnson, with the exception of the one with Kosygin at Glassboro, did not indulge in meetings of the kind implied by his statement.

Pressures for summit meetings beat most insistently upon the President in time of great crisis. Indeed, an almost invariable Soviet tactic in such moments, especially during the peak of the Cold War, was to propose a chief executives' meeting. Khrushchev did so in the 1962 Cuban crisis and at several junctures when Berlin issues were at their crest. For the Soviets, the move was a fruitful propaganda stroke and a brake on the momentum of the President's moves. Most Presidents have found that summits work best when dealing with questions well prepared at lower diplomatic levels. Sometimes they unfreeze disagreements that regular diplomacy cannot resolve. Kennedy, meeting Khrushchev in Vienna, was eager to size up the Soviet leader. Even more, Kennedy said afterwards, "The direct give and take was of immeasurable value in making clear and precise what we consider vital." But the sizing up of Khrushchev was also a grim experience, as Kennedy made clear in reporting to the nation. The U.S.-U.S.S.R. quarrel over Laos, then at high flame, was "not materially reduced," and his hopes for a nuclear test ban agreement had received "a serious blow." With the thawing of the Cold War, the stiffness of summitry diminished and the possibilities of constructive results became enhanced. Johnson's meeting with Kosygin at Glassboro was valuable in underscoring the interest of both powers in avoiding situations threatening nuclear war, in permitting first-hand exchanges of views, and in establishing a potentially useful personal acquaintance.

Yet, for all of the cordiality at Glassboro, the Johnson-Kosygin meetings yielded no substantive agreements and provided no clue concerning a key question of the moment: Did the Soviet Union propose to continue arms shipments to the Arab nations of the Middle East, and, in actuality, did the Soviet Union intend to make that region a place of future East-West confrontation?

For Nixon, the summit conference was the forum for the most acclaimed achievements of his Presidency. The visit to Communist China, after a quarter-century void of suspended official relations between the countries, was in essence an Event, a televised extravaganza, commanding an audience of the magnitude that witnessed the first landing on the moon. Peking's Great Hall and north China's Great Wall were stages for the Presidential television drama in which the long-dedicated anti-Communist, Nixon, was undertaking what no Presidential predecessor dared to do, making "the long march" to China as a prelude to expanded future relations. For Nixon, the Peking summit also commanded rewards at home—heightened validity to his claimed role as the great peacemaker despite the then little-abated Vietnam War, and the exhilaration of widespread public approval.[54]

Of equal profit to Nixon was his 1972 summit meeting in Moscow, hard on the heels of his visit to Peking. A new element of competition had been introduced—where once the U.S.S.R. was the only major Communist power conducting relations with the United States, now China did too, and the Russians seemed resolved that their summit was not to be overshadowed by the Chinese. Long before the conference, a series of agreements were completed and in readiness for signature by the leaders, thus guaranteeing the conference's success. Nixon and Brezhnev agreed to a treaty limiting antiballistic missile (ABM) defensive systems to 200 missiles at two sites in the United States and the U.S.S.R. In addition, Nixon entered into an executive agreement restricting the number of intercontinental ballistic missiles (ICBMs) and submarine missiles.[55] The agreements did not limit the number or power of the warheads accompanying the missiles, and both nations remained free to make existing systems even deadlier. The even more formidable issues, concerning the Vietnam War and the Middle East, remained unsolved, and even the accords reached were at the mercy of future events and the unknowable intentions of leaders on both sides, present and future.

A year later, two Brezhnev-Nixon conferences were a welcome surcease for Nixon, who was beset by the fires of Watergate. But the American objective of a comprehensive permanent agreement on limiting offensive nuclear arms failed.[56] However, in late 1974 at Vladivostok, Ford and Brezhnev reached a tentative agreement limiting each side to 2,400 offensive strategic nuclear weapons, including up to 1,320 land-based and submarine-launched missiles with multiple warheads (MIRVs). Valid until 1985, unless superseded by a permanent agreement, the Vladivostok accord was criticized as excessively generous to the U.S.S.R., which, for example, had few MIRVs and could now produce them in great numbers.[57]

Alliances

Alliances can trigger Presidential war. The conflicts in Korea and Vietnam evoked United States involvement in response to alliances and understandings, and, as the war in Indochina stumbled on, a web of agreements evolved that was fashioned by Presidential deputies functioning with high autonomy and secrecy. In 1972 the Senate Foreign Relations Committee spotlighted a hitherto secret American commitment to provide up to $100 million a year to support a Thai "irregular army" of 10,000 men in Laos, using American equipment and ammunition and flying American helicopter gunships. Indignant legislators cited the 1971 Defense Procurement Act, which prohibited the use of defense funds for forces of a third country, such as Thailand, fighting in support of Laos or Cambodia. By dint of some tortuous semantical hair-splitting, the executive branch contended that the act was inapplicable to the Thai volunteers, thus rounding out a common scenario of the Indochina war, that of Congressional prohibition and executive circumvention.[58]

Keeping an alliance intact may sometimes become a major Presidential preoccupation. Gerald Ford had scarcely assumed the Presidency when war erupted in Cyprus and two long-standing allies of the United States entered a passage of tense relations as Turkey invaded the island and Greece mobilized its forces. Greece, to express displeasure with an initial American preference for Turkey, withdrew from NATO. Ford and his aides had the arduous task of restraining Turkey's spreading military dominion over Cyprus, of dispelling Greece's ill-feeling toward the United States, and of curbing Congressional opinion that Turkey be punished for its aggression.

Today's intricate network of alliances reaches back to the Second World War. Alliances or understandings exist with individual countries and with regional groupings around the globe: Europe (NATO), Southeast Asia (SEATO), Australia and New Zealand (ANZUS), the Middle East (CENTO), Latin America (OAS), and Central America (OACS). When NATO was forming, Truman promised "the support which the situation requires," backed the bipartisan Vandenberg resolution endorsing the United States' association with NATO, featured the treaty in his 1949 inaugural address, urged upon Congress a vast program of military aid to the NATO countries, and assured its passage by announcing the first atomic explosion in the Soviet Union. Presidents have led in NATO's sharper turns of direction, too. Truman pushed West Germany's rearmament and inclusion in the western European defense system. Eisenhower promoted the European Defense Community treaty to merge the armed forces of six western European nations into a "hard and dependable core" for NATO. Kennedy advocated a NATO missile fleet of surface ships manned by crews of mixed nationality. Johnson led in the adjustment of NATO following De Gaulle's assault upon its military structure in requiring the removal from France of all military units or bases not under complete French control.

The Nixon Presidency departed in important particulars from alliance commitments maintained by Presidents since the Second World War. The magic weapon of the Nixon-Kissinger effort was ambiguity. The Nixon Doctrine, a masterwork of obfuscating generalities, looked toward sizeable reductions of American forces overseas and enlarged responsibility of local peoples for their own defense. The withdrawal of American forces from Vietnam left the South Vietnam ally reeling in uncertainty over just what American guarantees would persist after troop withdrawals were completed. In a general statement reaffirming treaty commitments, Nixon left unsettled whether he intended to continue protection to protocol states, such as Cambodia and Laos, provided for in the SEATO treaty. Ambiguity enables the President to support or ignore the Indochina states in future crisis, and it left those states uncertain of American intentions, more driven to self-reliance. In American domestic politics, the Nixon Doctrine helped diminish antiwar opinion while reinforcing the lack of clarity in American political thinking generally concerning the nation's long-term interest in the balance of power in Asia.[59] And domestically, the American public had to restrain its expectations from being lifted to unrealistic heights by the sometimes extravagant claims of Nixon and Kissinger concerning their foreign policy accomplishments—their proclaiming that "peace is at hand" in Vietnam, followed by acts that intensified the war.

A second Nixonian departure from the inherited Presidential alliance system was the solidification of relations with the Soviet Union, to the point of at least a quasi-alliance. A consequent malaise developed in the ranks of the NATO allies, not so much because of the substance of the agreements made with the Russians as the methods of the Nixon Presidency in concluding them. NATO leaders bemoaned the "deceptions" involved and the callous disregard, if not contempt, for the allies. When a Western European diplomat asked American officials, including the Secretary of State, "Will you talk about things (in Moscow) that concern all of us," the response was negative. NATO representatives knew nothing of a U.S.-U.S.S.R. statement of principles until it was released in Moscow during the 1972 summit. Even worse, the statement contained provisions that contradicted portions of a NATO draft, in which the United States had joined, of a comparable declaration by the alliance. The latter, for example, called for freer movement between East and West, a resolve that was dropped in the Soviet-American text. "You abandoned in Moscow what you were urging us here to support," said a NATO official to a Presidential representative.[60]

Alliances in which the United States as a superpower associates with powers of far lesser strength pose temptations for behavior that is flagrantly undemocratic, and sometimes, for Presidents, the opportunities prove irresistible. With the war going badly in South Vietnam, and therefore constituting a threat to his own domestic political welfare, President Kennedy sought to force the removal of Ngo Dinh Nhu, whose influence over his brother, President Ngo Dinh Diem, was apparently great and the cause of several unfortunate turns of policy. In a televised interview President Kennedy criticized the Vietnamese regime for losing touch with the people whose support against the communists was essential in the local war. The President attributed much of the declining popularity to repressions against the Buddhists, which culminated in attacks by secret police on their pagodas. Popular support, Kennedy suggested pointedly, could be regained only by "changes in policy and perhaps with personnel." [61] As Kennedy spoke, a Vietnamese newspaper accused the United States Central Intelligence Agency of planning a coup d'état against against President Diem's government. The United States ambassador Henry Cabot Lodge, Jr., was soon advising President Diem that the United States regarded the removal of Ngo Dinh Nhu as vital and that unless the regime could solve its problems, mounting Congressional pressure might force the Kennedy administration to cut economic and military aid to South Vietnam. The Vietnamese regime continued intact, and Mme. Ngo Dinh Nhu, President Diem's sister-in-law, journeyed to the United States in a highly publicized transcontinental tour, launching counterblasts against the Kennedy policy. Midway in her campaign, President Diem's regime was overthrown, he and his brother were murdered, and the "changes" of "personnel" proceeded.

The United Nations

In setting his foreign policy, the modern President must reckon, of course, with the United Nations. Kennedy, striving to alter the tone of U.S.-U.S.S.R.

relations, found the UN General Assembly a useful forum in which to urge that in the future the two nations compete in "leadership and responsibility" instead of competing in a search for better methods of destruction.[62] In Kennedy's 1962 confrontation with the U.S.S.R. over Cuba, the UN served its classic functions as a forum in which the American complaint could be ventilated and world opinion courted, and where machinery could be found for negotiation and conciliation. But for the President the UN may also be a hazard. Kennedy, in the agony of a Berlin crisis, was urged by certain of his counselors to lay the problem before the UN General Assembly. Charge Khrushchev, they said, with threatening the peace over Berlin and call for economic sanctions if he fails to accept the UN verdict. Kennedy quickly spurned this advice, pointing out that a UN verdict might favor Khrushchev and that the neutralist nations might be persuaded to accept his suggestions for a free city.

For the President faced with situations where military forces must be utilized, the United Nations will often provide a better alternative than the direct engagement of American power. Bringing to bear the UN's international policing apparatus has entailed less expense, misunderstanding, and abuse than the direct involvements that Presidents have chosen to make in Korea and Vietnam. UN policing in the Congo and Cyprus, and the insertion of a UN buffer force between Israeli and Egyptian troops in 1973 plainly displayed the attractions of international action. UN procedures are also valuable as a face-saving or cooling-off device, as the *Pueblo* crisis of 1968 demonstrates. The President, faced with a grave affront to the United States, was able, by resorting to the UN, to provide a semblance of action rather than undertake a more direct and dangerous response.

Faced with a burgeoning international food crisis in 1974, the Ford Presidency, in proposing remedial measures, urged the utilization of the UN and its related organizations. For example, as a means of improving nutrition through food of higher quality Ford recommended the establishment of a "global nutrition surveillance system" by the World Health Organization, the Food and Agriculture Organization, and the United Nations Children's Fund.[63]

But except for an occasional speech by the President or the Secretary of State at the United Nations, which provides a useful forum, the world body has largely been neglected and shunned by contemporary Presidents, who look askance at the frequently hostile vetoes of the Security Council and the unfavorable votes emanating from the General Assembly.

The Future Presidency

The Presidency's most serious problem is the autonomous model, an aggrandizing machine that never stops, whose ever-building potency is inimical to democracy, as are its indulgences in secrecy and deceit, and the Chief Executive's susceptibility to impetuousness and overreaction. Democracy, the nation, and the world suffer, and the political costs can become unbearable to the President himself.

Can the autonomous Presidency be effectively constrained? Can it become more responsive to democratic norms, more open to public discussion and to more meaningful sharing of power with other members of the political system?

1. Attention turns to Congress as the alternative political branch, constitutionally endowed with sizeable power, and a participant whose historic role has been significant, though sporadic. Can Congress do more and be more continuously effective?

Congress's mightiest weapon for halting overreaching Presidential policy is the appropriation power. It was applied belatedly in the Indochina war, but when it finally was used in 1973 to cut off support for the engagement of American forces in Cambodia, it was decisive. The possibilities of executive subterfuge were limited and the enormous powers of the autonomous Presidency were unavailing. The appropriations process permits an annual Congressional review and its application is free of constitutional ambiguity and crisis.

Senators J. W. Fulbright (D-Ark.) and Clifford Case (R-N.J.) have promoted proposals requiring the President to submit new international undertakings that are not incorporated in treaties to Senate review. Fulbright championed a national commitment resolution, by which the President would consult with the Senate and obtain expressions of its views before entering any new international commitments. The Case proposal provided that international agreements other than treaties must be transmitted to the Senate and House within sixty days of their execution. Case hoped for broadened consultation before the President entered into commitments, and the procedure would cover both oral and written agreements and any expression "intended to induce a reliance by another government upon the United States." [64] Doubtless these and similar plans could precipitate a Presidential challenge of their constitutionality, spurred by long historical practice in which the President has enjoyed wide independence in making executive agreements. For the President, however, the plans could sometimes be politically attractive. By consulting with Congress in the formative stages of decision, the President could better secure its support for necessary appropriations later.

2. Both for the sake of democracy and the strong Presidency, the major decisions of the Chief Executive in foreign policy ought to be based on advice that is broadly representative of the functional perspectives of relevant agencies of the executive branch, especially those devoted to the peaceful arts of diplomacy and trade such as the State, Treasury, and Commerce departments, as well as the military. Advice should also be competitive, with the advocates of one perspective presenting their case in a forum where it can be challenged by executive colleagues speaking from a different functional perspective. In recent Presidencies, the ideal of competitive advice-giving has been diminished by the marked flow of control to a single Presidential helper in the White House office, the Assistant for National Security Affairs. Since the Assistant can invoke

the doctrine of executive privilege more easily than department Secretaries and their aides, the expansion of power of the national security assistant is attractive to the President, since it helps shut out the unwanted intrusions of Congress.

The practices of Truman and Eisenhower pose an alternative that is salutary for both democracy and the strong Presidency. In those administrations, the national security assistants were Sidney Souers and Robert Cutler. Unlike later appointees—Bundy, Rostow, and Kissinger—neither was particularly versed in national security affairs, and the modest relevance of their backgrounds is cause for celebration, for it helped limit their activities to a narrow compass. Essentially facilitators who assisted the operation of the decision process, they made certain that every pertinent departmental source contributed to the development of alternatives the President might weigh in making decisions. Meanwhile, they scrupulously abstained from influencing policy or the selection of alternatives. Presidential decisions developed in accord with the Souers-Cutler model are apt to be more broadly based, more complete in corralling the diversity of relevant perspectives than the prevailing hierarchical model provided by more recent national security assistants. Presidential decisions under the earlier version of the national security assistant's office are apt to be more prudent, as indeed they were time and again.[65] But a caveat must be entered. An amateur background is not in itself an automatic guarantee of constrained decorum. The Chief Executive's preferences and the staff member's own character and definition of role are the basic factors. Witness Nixon's staff of amateurs who ruthlessly dominated and perverted domestic policy to their own selected ends.

3. Interest groups too might help in the quest for better structuring of Presidential decision-making. Unfortunately, interest groups are closely oriented to domestic affairs and much less so to foreign affairs. Normally, they stand to lose or gain most in their bread-and-butter concerns in the domestic arena. Presidential decision might be more representative of the forces and interests of American life, and more prudent, if the domestic-oriented interest groups, particularly those preoccupied with urban problems and social policy, contributed their views and advice to Presidential foreign policy-making. Their exclusion, disinterest, or reticence, as the Vietnam War demonstrated, can be costly to themselves. Social policy expenditure suffered a reduced priority while outlays for the battlefield became profligate.

Accordingly, Martin Luther King acted harmoniously with this proposal in urging the civil rights movement to address itself to the task of bringing the Vietnam War to a close. Likewise, the National Welfare Rights Organization astutely examined the war and concluded that it was a barrier to genuine welfare reform. Clearly, domestic interest groups, especially those concerned with social problems, need to increase their organizational effectiveness and concentrate more on foreign affairs. Thereby they may enhance their impact on the President and his counselors and provide a perspective in decisions that choose between war and peace that has been singularly lacking.

10

COMMANDER-IN-CHIEF

A democracy, like any other state, must be capable of defending itself and assuring its survival. If a democracy is powerful, like the United States, it is also expected to defend other less powerful states, some of them democracies and others embarrassingly not. Equally paradoxical, the chief agency of defense, the military, is in structure and organization antithetical to democracy, stressing obedience to authority, hierarchy and command. Its central enterprise—war—with its concommitants, death and destruction, is the negation of democracy, whose actualization requires life and peace.

As the constitutionally designated Commander-in-Chief, the President is the focus of the unresolved dilemmas of democracy and force as the maker of decisions that can be costly, hazardous, and, in the nuclear age, horrendous. Since the Second World War, military matters have been a top priority item for all Presidents. The most formidable criticisms of the Presidency have centered upon its military power, viewed as expansive and encroaching, to the point that those accouterments of democracy, legislative oversight and electoral review by informed public opinion, are evaded and frustrated. Not only are Presidents perceived as abusing power; their active role as Commander-in-Chief has entrapped them in prolonged wars that, for all of America's military power, they have been unable to win, and, worse, little able to extricate themselves from. Caught and flailing in military quicksands, Presidents have paid a high political price. Truman, bogged down in the Korean War, abstained in 1952 from running for reelection, wisely declining to test a war-weary electorate. The chief Presidential casualty of the protracted Vietnam War was Lyndon Johnson, who refrained from seeking reelection, in the face of tumultuous country-wide protest and dissent, much of which stemmed from his continued waging of the Vietnam War.

Limitations on Presidential Power

As active Commanders-in-Chief, contemporary Presidents have given off contradictory images of themselves and their office. Time and again, they appear to wield arbitrary power—commencing an invasion of Cuba, enlarging the war in Vietnam, conducting a secret war in Cambodia, without even a gesture of consultation with Congress, which the Constitution empowers to declare war. But a glance at history and the participants in national security policy-making reveals that there are also limitations upon the President's military power, and its exercise can be affected by potent regulators. Despite his designation as Commander-in-Chief, the President enjoys no monopoly of direction over American military power but shares it with others who may withhold what he needs, challenge or even veto what he does, or commit acts that leave him no choice but to respond within channels that they, rather than he, establish. Congress has a substantial military power. It can provide or withhold appropriations, reduce the numbers of American forces abroad, and bar specified kinds of military action. The professional military, some steps removed from an image of absolute obedience, may resist, delay, and amend. The courts may upset what the President does in their duty to protect the rights and liberties guaranteed by the Constitution. And in wartime the electorate may weigh the quality of his military stewardship and decide whether to keep him in office or fire him. Power that is shared and balanced, as the Framers wisely perceived, is more apt to be used prudently than if it is concentrated or monopolized.

The Defense Department

The President's main reliance and help in his duty as Commander-in-Chief is the Defense Department, which shelters most of the military endeavor. In the Kennedy-Johnson era, power was centralized in the department, as never before or since, during Robert McNamara's assertive tenure as Secretary. A systems analysis staff attached to his office utilized techniques of cost effectiveness and strategic analysis in reviewing the military's proposals. Often what eventually emerged from the thoroughgoing top-level review were decisions so different from the original proposals that they materialized into a series of independent weapons programs and strategic studies geared to both conventional and nuclear war.[1]

Clothed in trappings of quantification, McNamara could speak on complex national security matters with confidence and authority, and his Presidents, impressed and grateful, showered encomiums upon him. Unfortunately, the Vietnam War exposed latent weaknesses of the Secretary's approach. During his visits to Saigon, those who viewed the war as a hopeless quagmire were troubled by McNamara's imperturbable certitude and facilely summoned statistics.[2] McNamara's system stumbled when it was addressed to the less measurable aspects of national security policy. It underestimated the tenacity of North Vietnam and the psychological drain of corruption and dependence on the United States upon South Vietnam's will to fight. Assumptions underlying McNamara's tidy analyses endured too long without serious questioning, and guerrilla warfare in the Asian jungle possessed nuances that escaped the tabulators and chart-makers in remote Washington.

Every President revises to some degree his predecessor's structuring of Defense Department operations. Variation imparts a sense of fresh policy-making and identity to his administration, and it may be forced by new realities and by the trend of his own work habits. In the Nixon era, the initial Secretary of Defense, Melvin R. Laird, launched changes, perpetuated by his successors, embodying clear departures from the McNamara system. Roles were now reversed. The Joint Chiefs of Staff and the service departments were restored to something of their pre-McNamara influence. Laird and Nixon preferred to seek out military counsel in decision-making and allotted to the Joint Chiefs full opportunities for advocacy in both the Defense Department and the National Security Council. Nixon's reorganization of the latter facilitated the Joint Chiefs' access.[3]

Practical politics also undergirded the Laird-Nixon pattern. The hazardous task of extricating the United States from the Vietnam War, through graduated troop reductions, required at least the acquiescence of the Joint Chiefs; their dissent would have enormously complicated, even jeopardized, that difficult maneuver. But Nixon's restructuring of the NSC also promoted the principle of civilian direction. The reorganized National Security Council in effect substituted rigorous civilian institutional procedures at the President's level for McNamara's Defense Department-centered civilian systems analysis.

With the Joint Chiefs of Staff, his principal military advisers, the President's relations are frequently attended by tension and conflict. Truman, reluctant to depend on the military as primary policy advisers, was forced, with the outbreak of the Korean War, to adopt a stance of closer dependence. As an impeccable military hero, Eisenhower could indulge his preference to hold the military at arm's length, and his wish to avoid the likely charge of his political opponents that because of his background, he would allow the military excessive influence. But as his administration proceeded, he was faced with a series of international crises in Indochina over the Chinese offshore islands and the Suez, and in Hungary and Berlin, which, in their cumulative effect, brought the JCS chairman, Admiral Arthur W. Radford, into a position of uppermost influence in foreign policy councils second only to Secretary of State John Foster Dulles. Kennedy, who felt that Eisenhower was sometimes too severe with his generals, especially on budgetary questions, initially accorded the JCS freer access to his policy councils. Unfortunately, the new relationship fell flat on its face in the Bay of Pigs disaster.

The Joint Chiefs' chairman, General Lyman Lemnitzer, was shifted to Europe as commander of United States forces and was replaced by General Maxwell Taylor, whose return from retirement into private life reflected badly upon the military. Trouble again fell upon the Joint Chiefs when certain of the incoming Taylor's views proved sharply at odds with those of Admiral George W. Anderson, Chief of Naval Operations, and General Curtis E. Le May, Air Force Chief of Staff. Not the least of these differences were Taylor's proposals for an expanded Army and the abolition of the Joint Chiefs and their replacement by a single chief.[4] In less than a year the forces of conflict were resolved, thanks to resourceful Presidential intervention. President Kennedy failed to reappoint Admiral Anderson as Chief of Naval Operations and hence to the Joint Chiefs. General Le May was not reappointed for the standard two-year term but only for one year.

The President's fluctuating dealings with the military reflect a malaise that springs at least partly from several kinds of acute dependence. First, it is difficult for the Chief Executive to find alternative sources of military advice. He can summon retired military, as Kennedy did General Maxwell Taylor, but their access to operational information is limited. The President's chief civilian deputy, the Secretary of Defense, depends upon data and evaluations supplied by the military. And military chieftains gain leverage in the executive branch from the influence they enjoy with Congressional leaders. Legislation empowers the military to inform Congressional committees of their reservations and differences respecting Presidential policy, if asked, and Presidential proposals to reorganize military structures and programs stand little chance of moving through Congress without military assent. If he fears right-wing attack, the President will act all the more guardedly toward the military, aware of their strength in that constituency. Above all, the President is acutely dependent on the military to implement his decisions. The military's penchant for standard procedures may cause his orders to be distorted through simplification, and the JCS is apt to defer to field commanders and not oversee closely their compliance with Presidential direction.[5]

But the President, fortunately, can fight back against these threatened limitations on his power to gain information and advice he needs and support for implementing his decisions. He can launch reorganizations to secure cordinated advice rather than separate advice from the services, and he can enlarge the NSC system to augment the variety of views on military problems. He can install an independent military counselor in the White House, as Kennedy did General Maxwell Taylor and as Nixon did General Andrew Goodpaster. The assistant for national security affairs is a civilian adviser in the White House, aided by an expert staff, and is a source of additional information, advice, and options. As a free-roving Presidential assistant, he can press for compliance with the Chief Executive's decisions. Other officers and bureaus of the Executive Branch provide the President alternative information and advice—scientists who counsel on weapons systems; the Office of Management and Budget, which provides professional scrutiny of the military budget; and ad hoc groups, commissions, and individuals, who can report on military questions. Nixon, for example, accepted advice from British guerrilla war expert Brigadier General Sir Robert G. K. Thompson, who was sent to Vietnam to assess the conduct of the war, and from the Fitzhugh Commission, which recommended a large-scale reorganization of the Pentagon.[6]

The President and the Generals

As Commander-in-Chief the President appoints and removes his field generals. In wartime the responsibility is especially important because of the consequences of the President's choice for the nation's survival and his own political future. Lyndon Johnson's grip on the Presidency was loosened by the inability of his generals to win a decisive victory in Vietnam, despite prodigious escalations of American military commitment. For Richard Nixon, a most perilous shoal to be circumnavigated was the withdrawal of American troops without sustaining defeat or serious loss, disasters that might inflame domestic opinion, but from which he was spared by the skill of his generals.

Several Presidents have faced major crises either in bringing their field generals to engage in battle or in keeping them within bounds, not simply on the battlefield but within the framework of constitutional government. General George B. McClellan, the most lagging of field generals, was a great trial to Abraham Lincoln. Bold in his strategic conceptions, McClellan nevertheless dreaded execution. His standard tactic was to demand more reinforcements after overestimating the enemy's strength and deprecating his own. He was a wonderfully imaginative procrastinator. If he had Lee at a disadvantage, he almost invariably failed to exploit it. He must wait, McClellan would report to his impatient superiors at Washington, until the Potomac rose to be sure that Lee would not recross it; he must finish drilling new recruits, reorganize his forces, and procure more shoes, uniforms, blankets, and camp equipment. McClellan also passed some of his battle-idle time pouring his innate arrogance into a letter of July 7, 1862, to Lincoln, pointing out that it was high time the government established a civil and military policy to cover the full canvass of the nation's troubles. The general generously offered to inform the President of what it should be.

The McClellan question became critical with his failure to exploit his victory at Antietam by pursuing Lee's fleeing army. Lincoln worked mightily, as his secretary John Nicolay put it, at "poking sharp sticks into Little Mac's ribs." When the general included among his ingenious excuses one that an epidemic had afflicted his army's horses with sore mouths and weary backs, Lincoln was goaded into a sharp reply. "I have just read your dispatch about sore tongues and fatigued horses," he telegraphed. "Will you pardon me for asking what the horses of your army have done since the battle of Antietam that fatigues anything?" [7]

Lincoln and his administration were now at a critical juncture. Winter was approaching and would assure that except for Antietam the long record of Eastern defeat and stalemate would remain intact. Congress, restive with this state of affairs, was soon to convene. Governors were nervous, the cabinet was divided, and the extreme-war men and advocates of immediate peace were thundering against the President. Replace McClellan? The available generals were a sorrowfully undistinguished lot, many already well-scarred with failure, and others abysmally inexperienced.

After heavy deliberation, Lincoln cast aside the adverse factors and on November 5, 1862, relieved McClellan and appointed General Ambrose E. Burnside in his place. Upon reading the President's order, McClellan exclaimed, "Alas for my poor country!" [8] Certain of his officers urged him to disobey. He later wrote that he might have marched his troops into Washington and taken possession of the government. Instead, he handed over his command of

120,000 men in an elaborate ceremony. But this was by no means the last en-
counter between McClellan and Lincoln. In 1864, two years after his removal,
McClellan met Lincoln on a new terrain—as the Democratic nominee for the
Presidency.

In another day, President Truman experienced a confrontation with a field
general prone to do too much rather than too little. General Douglas Mac-
Arthur, commander of the United Nations forces in Korea, possessed a military
career of rare distinction: peerless hero of the Pacific theater in the Second
World War, successful viceroy of postwar Japan, and a widely mentioned potential Republican Presidential nominee. His handsome, erect presence and ma-
jestic eloquence were marks of an imperious figure.

Truman's difficulties began when the general, midway in the Korean War,
visited Chiang Kai-shek at Formosa. After their meeting, Chiang declared,
"The foundation for Sino-American military cooperation has been laid." [9]
Since these words were both obscure and potentially expansive and the administration was anxious to keep Formosa neutralized, Truman dispatched
Averell Harriman to review with MacArthur the entire Far Eastern political situation. Harriman's apparent success was shattered when MacArthur released a
statement to the commander of the Veterans of Foreign Wars urging a more dynamic United States–Formosa partnership. The President himself now went
forth to see MacArthur in a hastily cleared-out Quonset hut on Wake Island.
According to information released to a subsequent Senatorial investigation, the
whole Eastern policy was broadly and congenially discussed. The part of Truman's visit that the public saw seemed entirely happy. The President pinned the
Distinguished Service Medal on the general and presented a five-pound box of
candied plums to Mrs. MacArthur. The general reciprocated by declaring,
through the President's press secretary, "No commander in the history of war
has had more complete and admirable support from the agencies in Washington
than I have during the Korean operation." [10]

MacArthur pressed the war forward, routed the North Koreans, and received
approval from the United Nations General Assembly to pursue the fleeing foe
across the thirty-eighth parallel, the division between the two Koreas. Hereupon Communist China entered the war. The struggle proceeded to seesaw between MacArthur's forces and the enlarged enemy. On March 17, 1951, in a
public statement issued from his United Nations headquarters, MacArthur lamented the "abnormal military inhibitions" upon his command and pointed to
the necessity for "vital decisions—yet to be made." These presumably were to
incorporate his proposals to the Joint Chiefs for broadened military action
against Red China, including a blockade, air bombardment, and ultimately invasion. MacArthur's public statement was issued simultaneously with efforts of
the President and the State Department to end the Korean conflict by reopening
diplomatic negotiations. [11]

MacArthur made other public statements, not the least of which was a reply
to Joseph W. Martin, the House minority leader, who had asked the general for
his views on the use of Chinese Nationalist troops. MacArthur indeed believed
they should be employed, and added, in words implying that it was necessary

to vastly expand the Korean conflict, ''Here we fight Europe's war with arms while the diplomats there still fight it with words. . . . if we lose the war to Communism in Asia the fall of Europe is inevitable.'' Congressman Martin read MacArthur's letter on the House floor.[12]

Anxiety flowed like wine in foreign capitals. President Truman now concluded that decisive action was unavoidable if Presidential authority, civil supremacy, and established policy were to be preserved. He wrote to a friend, ''I reached a decision yesterday morning after much consideration and consultation on the Commanding General in the Pacific. It will undoubtedly create a great furor but under the circumstances I could do nothing else and still be President of the United States.'' On April 11 the President announced MacArthur's removal from his command.[13]

Truman explained his decision in an address to the nation. MacArthur, returning to the United States, addressed Congress and advanced his policy tenets with superb oratorical skill. Several legislators moved to impeach Truman, and the Senate Armed Services and Foreign Relations Committees commenced a joint investigation. The top military unqualifiedly supported the President.

Presidential power was eventually vindicated by Truman, as it had been earlier by Lincoln. In both episodes, civil supremacy had been maintained over the professional military, a cardinal arrangement of the democratic state. Both Presidents in their self-assertion faced grave political risks: the possibility that the successors of the deposed generals would compile a less favorable military record, that public opinion would feel affronted, and that legislators would exploit the situation for personal political gain. But both Presidents clung to duty and brushed aside political expediency and the temptation not to act. The military rallied around them, the public understood, and ultimately the Chief Executive, as Commander-in-Chief, was reaffirmed, but he trod no unperiled, primrose path.

Sources of Authority

The President, functioning as he does in a democratic state, requires legal authority to pursue his military purposes. The quest sends him to the Constitution to contemplate how much authority its lean language really provides, or to enactments like the War Powers Act of 1973.* And in what he does he must reckon with the courts, guardians of the fundamental law and private right against governmental, and therefore Presidential, encroachment.

Presidents in the nation's major wars have invoked two contrasting patterns of legal justification for their acts. One, the Lincolnian, asserts an expansive view of the President's independent authority based on the Commander-in-Chief clause in Article II, section 2, of the Constitution and on the duty ''to

---

* The President's constitutional and statutory authority is discussed in Chapter 9, pp. 215–17.

take care that the laws be faithfully executed" expressed in section 3. In the twelve weeks between the outbreak at Fort Sumter and the convening of Congress in special session on July 4, 1861, Lincoln employed these two clauses to sanction measures whose magnitude suggests dictatorship.

In the twelve-week interval, Lincoln added 23,000 men to the Regular Army and 18,000 to the Navy, called 40,000 volunteers for three years' service; summoned the state militias into a ninety-day volunteer force; paid $2 million from the Treasury's unappropriated funds for purposes unauthorized by Congress; closed the Post Office to "treasonable correspondence"; imposed a blockade on Southern ports; suspended the writ of habeas corpus, which protects the citizen against arbitrary arrest, in certain parts of the country; and caused the arrest and military detention of persons "who were represented to him" as engaging in or contemplating "treasonable practices." He later instituted a militia draft when voluntary recruiting broke down and extended the suspension of the habeas corpus privilege to a nation-wide basis for persons "guilty of any disloyal practice." His first Emancipation Proclamation freed the slaves in states in rebellion against the United States and pledged "the Executive Government of the United States, including the military and naval authority thereof," to protect the freedom conferred. Lincoln invited Congress to "ratify" his enlargement of the armed forces, which it did, and it sanctioned his handling of the writ of habeas corpus. Altogether, Lincoln's actions, as Edward S. Corwin has written, "assert for the President, for the first time in our history, an initiative of indefinite scope and legislative in effect in meeting the domestic aspects of a war emergency." [14]

In 1973 the pretensions of Presidential power were stretched to hitherto unimagined extents when former leading Nixon aides, testifying before the Senate Watergate investigating committee, stated that in behalf of "national security" Presidential deputies could commit crimes, including burglary. Such crimes had indeed occurred when Presidential agents broke into the office of the psychiatrist of Dr. Daniel Ellsberg, who had leaked the "Pentagon Papers." President Nixon never renounced these astounding claims; if anything, he seemed to support them. In effect, what the Nixon men asserted for the Presidency was the power to commit any act, including criminality, not in order to prosecute a war, but simply to maintain "national security" at any and all times, regardless of the level of peril.[15] The claim was tantamount to abrogating democracy and laying a justifying base for permanent dictatorship. Unlike Nixon, most Presidents have displayed due sensitivity to legality and perceived how indispensable it is to democracy.

The world war Presidencies of Woodrow Wilson and Franklin Roosevelt afford a contrasting pattern. The spreading character of war, its encroachment upon the economy, the involvement of growing numbers of people, and the resort to propaganda necessitated Presidential approaches to Congress both for legal authority and political support, and the process fostered an executive-legislative partnership in war leadership. In both world wars statutes were passed delegating broad powers to the Chief Executive. Selective service laws in both wars enabled the President to administer a vast manpower draft. The

Lever Act of 1917 empowered the Executive to license the mining, importation, manufacture, storage, and distribution of necessities; it authorized the seizure of factories, pipelines, mines, and the like; and it fixed the prices of wheat, coal, and other basic commodities. In the Second World War the Lend Lease Act permitted the President and his deputies to transfer "defense articles," meaning anything from bacon to battleships, to the "government of any country whose defense the President judged vital to the defense of the United States," on any terms he "deems satisfactory."

By gift of legislation, Roosevelt managed much of the domestic economy in the Second World War. Through deputies, he allocated "materials," fixed prices, controlled rents, settled labor disputes, and seized strikebound plants. Like Wilson, Roosevelt as Commander-in-Chief created "executive agencies," such as the Office of Price Administration and the National War Labor Board, to administer delegated legislative power.

The President needs not only laws from Congress but a variety of other cooperative deeds to assure effective military policy and administration. By grace of the Constitution, with its mechanisms of checks and balances, the Chief Executive shares a wide range of military powers with Congress. Congress raises the armed forces, provides for their regulation, and investigates the military enterprise; the Senate gives its advice and consent to military nominations; Congress passes laws governing military organization, appropriates vast funds for equipment and materiel, and declares war. Its powers, Presidents would gladly testify, enable it to act forcefully in military affairs. The results are not always positive and cooperative. Checks and balances, bolstered by rivalries between the armed services, sometimes bring the President and Congress into incipient or actual conflict.

In 1962 President Kennedy faced a gathering crisis that threatened to become a head-on clash not simply over the merits of a military artifact, but between Congress's and the President's respective military powers. The subject of controversy was the RS-70 bomber, then in its final stages of development. Air Force leaders strongly backed the RS-70, stressing the necessity of a manned bomber program to avoid excessive reliance upon missiles. Substantial Soviet bomber advances were cited. Army and Navy leaders, and President Kennedy, like President Eisenhower earlier, opposed the RS-70, holding that great numbers of long-range missiles would be available before the new bomber could be produced in sufficient quantity. When the Kennedy administration requested $180 million in 1962 to continue the RS-70 development program, the House Armed Services Committee lavishly authorized $491 million. The committee's bill "directed" that the funds it authorized be spent. The choice of this particular word signified the beginning of a possible massive constitutional confrontation between Congress and the President for dominion over military policy. The House committee based its wording "direct" upon Article I, section 8, of the Constitution, which vests in Congress the responsibility for raising and maintaining the military forces.

President Kennedy refrained from picking up the gauntlet of the constitutional issue thrown down by the House Committee and its chairman, the powerful Congressman Carl Vinson of Georgia. Instead he took the "Swamp Fox of Georgia," as Vinson was otherwise known, for a stroll one sunny March afternoon in the White House rose garden. The President and the Congressman fortunately arranged an honorable, peacemaking compromise by which the administration agreed to spend more than was originally budgeted for the RS-70 if a new review and technological developments warranted an increase.[16]

Presidents must also reckon with a favorite preoccupation of Congress in the military realm—investigation. Truman's Senate Committee to Investigate the Defense Program was a model of searching, but constructive, criticism that produced fruitful change in the administration of the Second World War. Success as a wartime investigator established Truman's chief claim upon his subsequent Vice Presidential nomination. A contrasting view of the investigatory power is provided by a great cross Lincoln had to bear in the Civil War, the Joint Committee on the Conduct of the War, which, in a typically unflattering estimate of the administration, wrote, "Folly, folly, folly reigns supreme. The President is a weak man." Lincoln reciprocated in his judgment of the committee. He said,

> I have never faltered in my faith of being ultimately able to suppress this rebellion and of reuniting this divided country; but this improvised vigilant committee . . . is a marplot, and its greatest purpose seems to be to hamper my action and obstruct the military operations.[17]

The Courts

As Commander-in-Chief the President also faces tensions with the remaining governmental branch concerned with military affairs—the federal courts—with its high duty in a democratic state to protect the Constitution and the laws against encroachment. The most perplexing and consequential issues between the Executive and the courts may arise during actual war, when the President feels driven to curtail, or even to suppress, key liberties sanctioned in the Bill of Rights. To further the progress of war, to safeguard what he cites as the nation's imperiled safety, the President has set aside political and economic liberties that in peacetime are inviolable.

The Civil War, fought within the nation's borders and jeopardizing its capital, was resented and resisted in many sectors of the North sympathetic to the Confederacy, to the point that President Lincoln promulgated several orders and proclamations restricting individual liberty. The most important of these was his suspension of the constitutional privilege of the writ of habeas corpus. Lincoln's first habeas corpus proclamation, issued in the war's early weeks, was triggered by events in Maryland. Underground resistance and open defiance were rampant in that state. Federal troops were attacked by mobs in Baltimore, communications to the capital were severed, and the mayor and police chief were unabashedly pro-Confederate and anti-Lincoln. Bridges were destroyed to hamper the passage of Union troops, and newspapers hostile to the administration fanned disunion sentiment. The state legislature was soon to convene, and a formidable bloc of its members aimed to have the state secede from the Union.

Union generals moved to nip the growing conspiracy by arresting the mayor of Baltimore, the chief of police, and several police commissioners. Even more sensational was the arrest of members of the Maryland legislature. To forestall the passage of an act of secession, Union General Nathaniel P. Banks barred the legislature from meeting and arrested nine of its members and the chief clerk of the senate. Still other Marylanders were arrested, including one John Merryman "charged with various acts of treason." Merryman was languishing in Fort McHenry when the Chief Justice of the United States, Roger B. Taney, on circuit duty, ordered "the body of John Merryman [produced] and . . . the day and cause of [his] capture and detention" made known. A head-on clash between the President and the Court, between the war and the Constitution, was in the making. Taney, to the administration's great relief, confined himself to declaring that the power to suspend the writ, which should be exercised only with "extreme caution," belonged to Congress, and not to the President (17 Fed. Cas. 144). Taney's opinion, nevertheless, put the administration under the cloud of the likelihood of a hostile Supreme Court decision, an event the Attorney General, Edward Bates, said would "do more to paralyze the Executive . . . than the worst defeat our armies have yet sustained." [18]

The administration's position was strengthened when Congress, after much struggle, passed the Habeas Corpus Act of 1863, affirming the President's power to suspend the writ. Despite several procedural devices incorporated to placate the courts, the act left to the Executive the setting of policy concerning arrests and imprisonments. Prisoners were tried, as before, by military tribunal and punished or released under authority of the War Department. Arrests continued apace. Clement L. Vallandigham, fiery Copperhead, after his arrest, trial, and sentencing by a military commission, appealed to the United States Supreme Court to lift his case into civil court. But the Supreme Court ruled that it had no jurisdiction, since a military commission was not a "court," to which the federal judiciary was limited under existing law (*Ex parte Vallandigham*, 68 U.S. 243, 1864).

Although Vallandigham never lived to see it, his legal position was ultimately vindicated in the celebrated case of *Ex parte Milligan* (4 Wallace 2, 1866). Milligan too was a Copperhead, tried by a military commission for "treasonable" speeches. Condemned to hang, he invoked the habeas corpus writ. But the war was now over, and the Court was prepared to act boldly. It ruled that Indiana, where Milligan resided and spoke, was not part of the "theater of war" and that the civil courts there were "open" and therefore available to conduct his trial. Under such a combination of circumstances, the writ could not be constitutionally suspended. The *Milligan* case, needless to say, has become the source of permanent consternation to the friends of Presidential power and of hope to the friends of civil liberties. In *Milligan,* the interests of the latter clearly were paramount.

Despite the potential restrictiveness of the *Milligan* doctrine, the Court proved tolerant of Presidential power in the two world wars. In *Ex parte Quirin* (317 U.S. 1, 1942) the Court broadly construed the Commander-in-Chief's capacity as executor of the Articles of War, enacted by Congress to further the United States' obligations under the laws of war, a branch of international law. The Articles of War provide for their enforcement through courts-martial and military commissions. *Ex parte Quirin* concerned eight saboteurs, seven Germans and one American, who were trained in a Berlin espionage school and deposited on Long Island and the Florida coast by German submarines in 1942. They doffed their German military uniforms for civilian attire, and with their tools of sabotage set out for New York City, Jacksonville, and other points to practice their art on American war industries. Arrested by the FBI before they could get down to work, they were turned over to the provost marshal of the District of Columbia. As Commander-in-Chief, President Franklin D. Roosevelt appointed a military commission to try the would-be saboteurs for violating the laws of war by not wearing fixed emblems revealing their combatant status. Midway in the trial the defendants petitioned the United States Supreme Court and the District Court for the District of Columbia for leave to bring habeas corpus proceedings.

The defendants argued that the offense charged against them was not known to the laws of the United States and was not one "arising in the land and naval forces," as described by the Fifth Amendment of the Constitution. Nor was the military tribunal that was trying them, they said, constituted in keeping with the Articles of War. The Court struck down the latter contention by declining to distinguish between the powers of the President as Commander-in-Chief and of Congress to create a military commission. The Court rejected the other arguments, holding that cases involving enemy personnel had never been deemed to fall under the constitutional guarantees of the Fifth and Sixth Amendments. The Court also cited the long-standing practice represented by an act of 1806 that imposed the death penalty on alien spies "according to the law and usage of nations, by sentence of general court martial." The saboteurs, accordingly, were tried and sentenced by military commission.

The most extreme application of the Commander-in-Chief's power to designate the theater of military operations was President Roosevelt's executive order of February 19, 1942, directed at the presumed danger of Japanese sabotage on the West Coast. In the high excitement over the Japanese bombing of Pearl Harbor, Roosevelt was pressed by the military, Congress, West Coast groups, and the newspapers to remove persons of Japanese ancestry from that area farther into the mainland. By Executive Order No. 9066 Roosevelt empowered the Secretary of War to establish "military areas" from which "any or all persons" might be excluded to prevent espionage and sabotage, and he designated military commanders to police these areas. The Secretary of War was directed to provide food, shelter, and transportation for persons evacuated. Soon the three westernmost states and a part of Arizona were declared "military areas 1 and 2" by Lieutenant General J. L. DeWitt. In a brief resolution of March 21, 1942, Congress endorsed the Presidential action by making it a misdemeanor "to knowingly enter, remain in, or leave prescribed military areas" of the Secretary of War or of the commanding officer. A War Relocation Authority was established to care for persons cleared out of the military areas. In all, some 112,000 persons were removed from the West Coast, of whom the vast majority—70,000—were United States citizens. Both the transplanted United States citizens and the aliens were eventually placed in ten "relocation centers" in California, Arizona, Idaho, Utah, Colorado, Wyoming, and Arkansas.

The relocation enterprise was challenged several times, but never effectively. In *Hirabayashi* v. *United States* (320 U.S. 81, 1943) the Court, by the drastic surgery of legal technicalities, reduced the issue to the right of the West Coast commander to subject citizens of Japanese ancestry to a special curfew order. The Court stressed the nation's plight and the state of the war in reaching its decision. Japan was achieving striking victories in 1943, the West Coast lay exposed, defense plants were heavily concentrated there, and, in the eyes of the Court, the ethnic affiliation of Japanese-Americans with the enemy posed a danger unknown from those of other ancestry. The Court deemed relocation within the powers of the President and Congress "acting in cooperation." In *Korematsu* v. *United States* (323 U.S. 214, 1944) a United States citizen, a Japanese-American, was convicted in district court for remaining in his California home. The Supreme Court again severely narrowed its decision and reasserted the reasoning of earlier relocation cases, though Japan was now in full retreat throughout the Pacific.

The most general abrogation of civil liberties in the Second World War occurred in the territory of Hawaii. Soon after the Japanese bombed Pearl Harbor, Governor J. B. Poindexter of Hawaii invoked section 67 of the Hawaiian Organic Act of April 30, 1900, proclaimed martial law throughout the territory, and turned over to the commanding general of the Hawaiian Department the exercise of all normal gubernatorial powers "during the present emergency and until the danger of invasion is removed." President Roosevelt approved Poindexter's decision, and a regime of martial law commenced that remained in force until October 24, 1944, when a Presidential proclamation terminated it. Habeas corpus was suspended and the civil courts were supplanted by military tribunals in which civilians were tried for crimes by summary procedures.

The Hawaiian arrangement was challenged in 1943, when District Judge Delbert E. Metzger issued a writ of habeas corpus in behalf of two naturalized Germans interned by the Army. The Hawaiian commander, Lieutenant General Robert C. Richardson, countered by forbidding writs of habeas corpus, including those of Judge Metzger. The issue was soon settled administratively.

Eventually, the Court, in *Duncan* v. *Kahanamoku, Sheriff* (327 U.S. 304, 1946) cited section 5 of the Hawaiian Organic Act, which declares that the Constitution of the United States has "the same effect within said Territory as elsewhere in the United States." The war was now well past, and the Court declared that the suspension of normal judicial processes had been unlawful. The Organic Act of 1900, it found, did not authorize the supplanting of civil courts by military tribunals.

In addition to seizing persons, the President as Commander-in-Chief has also seized property. Six months before Pearl Harbor, while the nation was still officially at peace, President Roosevelt, citing his earlier proclamation of an "unlimited national emergency," seized the strikebound North American Aviation plant at Inglewood, California. Roosevelt's claim of authority was sweeping and somewhat imprecise—"the duty constitutionally and inherently resting upon the President to exert his civil and military as well as his moral authority to keep the defense efforts of the United States a going concern," and "to obtain supplies for which Congress has appropriated money, and which it has directed the President to obtain." Both before and after the United States became a belligerent, Roosevelt seized other aircraft plants, shipyards, and a railroad.

In the Korean conflict President Truman brought the Supreme Court down upon his head when he ordered the seizure of most of the nation's steel mills in the face of a threatened strike, citing "the authority vested in me by the Constitution and laws of the United States." The President ignored the Taft-Hartley Act, which established special procedures for national labor emergencies but did not give him the power of seizure. The Supreme Court, in *Youngstown Sheet and Tube Co.* v. *Sawyer* (343 U.S. 579, 1952), ordered the President and his executive colleagues to stay out of the steel mills, holding that in seizing them he had seized legislative power. Only Congress could have ordered the mills seized; the President lacked power to seize them without its authorization. Like the *Milligan* case, this hastily improvised opinion throws a lasting shadow of doubt over the President's independent seizure power.

Labor too has felt the pressure of the Commander-in-Chief's power. In the Second World War the President by executive order created a War Manpower Commission to manage the mobilization of manpower for employment in the war production industries. Later Roosevelt added to the commission's province the administration of the Selective Service System. The WMC was not long in issuing a "work or fight" order reqiring all workers designated as "nondeferable," or those engaged in "nonessential" enterprise, to choose between induction into the armed services and transfer to war production jobs. Draft requirements were simultaneously lowered, and the nation's workers faced a categorical choice: work in a war plant or be drafted into the armed forces.

Conceivably, the courts might declare that the hostilities in which the President has engaged the armed forces are unconstitutional. In the concluding weeks of American air bombing of Cambodia, a federal district judge ruled that the bombing must stop because it was "unauthorized and unlawful." But the ruling was overturned by the Court of Appeals, and the Supreme Court declined to review the case. In effect, the high court acquiesced to the appellate court's view that the legality of the Cambodian action was a political question not reviewable by the courts.[19]

Communist War-making

What the President does as Commander-in-Chief, how he uses his power, is not the simple choice of a self-willed Chief Executive. Not the least of the novelties the President has had to cope with are the several species of warfare that the communist powers choose to wage and with which the United States had little, if any, experience. These are the techniques of guerrilla warfare, infiltration, and takeover waged by communist operatives. Contemporary Presidents have faced large-scale "police action," or undeclared war, in Korea, civil war in Greece, guerrilla war in Indochina, insurrection in the Canal Zone, a communist revolution in Cuba, and communist infiltration and threatened takeover in other lands.

A favorite Soviet tactic is war by proxy, by which it supplies arms and encouragement to other peoples and nations, such as North Vietnam and sundry Arab states, who bear the burden of fighting. According to a 1972 report by the Stockholm International Peace Research Institute, the Soviet Union, apart from its contributions to the Vietnam War, had become the largest supplier of weapons to third world peoples.[20] The recipients of Soviet assistance, particularly if they are communist states or forces, often prove their deserts by unstinting dedication to the battlefield. The unflagging North Vietnamese outdo even the Prussians in warlike tenacity. Since 1945, they have fought to impose their will on the people of South Vietnam and neighboring Laos and Cambodia as well. In addition to arms, the Soviet Union supplies justificatory doctrines to help spark wars that are to its advantage and to forestall those that are not. Consequently, in Europe it insists on the finality of territorial changes that transpired in the wake of the Second World War and upon the inviolability of all frontiers of that continent as indispensable for European security. But in the Middle East, the Soviet Union has denied these very same principles and has promoted the inflammation of tensions that ultimately exploded in the 1973 war.

Presidents have committed American forces to combat, as in Korea and Indochina, and to watch over a change of government in the Dominican Republic. The President oversees vast programs of military and economic aid to nations around the globe, particularly on the communist periphery. He engages in a range of other acts of fluctuating subtlety and success through the CIA. And he can launch bold indirect counterthrusts at the U.S.S.R.'s promotions of war by proxy. Thus Nixon, in 1972, eager to complete the American withdrawal from Vietnam and with a summit meeting in Moscow impending, was dismayed when the North Vietnamese opened an offensive, which, thanks to sudden infusions of heavier and more sophisticated Soviet weapons, would have devastated the South Vietnamese army had not a panoply of American airpower protected it. Hereupon Nixon embarked upon a response that Johnson had considered but never risked taking—he ordered the mining of Haiphong and other North Vietnam harbors to block further inflow of Soviet and Chinese armaments.[21] The gamble worked; the offensive slowed, the United States continued its withdrawal, and the Moscow summit proceeded.

Something of the strains upon Presidential method caused by communist assertion is conveyed by President Eisenhower's moves to foil a takeover in Guatemala in 1954. In that brief drama's early stage, a ship from the Skoda arms factory in Czechoslovakia bearing two thousand tons of small arms, ammunition, and light artillery pieces, a quantity far beyond Guatemala's normal military requirements, was bound for that country. Nicaragua, alarmed at communist infiltration from neighboring Guatemala, broke off relations. Guatemala's procommunist government suspended constitutional rights, made mass arrests, and executed the leaders of the political opposition. To offset the incoming Czech weaponry, the Eisenhower administration flew arms into Honduras and Nicaragua, threw up a naval quarantine around the beleaguered countries, and detained in the port of Hamburg, Germany, still another shipment of arms destined for Guatemala. Anticommunist forces led by Carlos Castillo Armas, a former Guatemalan colonel, crossed from Honduras into his country and made good progress until they lost two of their three bombers. President Eisenhower, mindful of Latin-American sensitivities and taking anxious counsel, decided to replace the planes. The existing procommunist government was soon deposed, and a new anticommunist ruling junta was established under the watchful eyes of United States Ambassador John Peurifoy, with Colonel Armas at its head.[22]

Alliances

In another major response to the division between the western and communist worlds, the contemporary President is heavily engaged as a builder and custodian of alliances, a responsibility his forebears never had to face. He and his deputies have constructed bilateral alliances with nations around the world, committing money, technicians, armaments, and even American soldiers. He has played a leading role in the founding of such multilateral alliances as NATO, SEATO, CENTO, and OAS. He buoys up the alliances when their inspiration lags in seasons of communist quiet and enheartens them when disaster threatens. He is apt to view alliances at times as a step toward a world community, a vehicle for advancing objectives urgent for all mankind. He and his fellow chief executives are restrained and goaded in the common task by the pressures of their inescapable domestic political necessities. The promise and frustration alliances hold for American Chief Executives are illustrated by several encounters John Kennedy experienced with allies.

Kennedy included among his objectives the adoption by the United States and its allies of efficient and economical American-built weapons systems. He also worked mightily to forestall individual European nations from building their own nuclear weapons, but proposed that their development and use be integrated into the NATO alliance. Kennedy, whose keen sense of political realism extended to the international plane, took up his task conscious that "you can't possibly carry out any policy without causing major frictions."

Kennedy and his principles were severely tested in his confrontation with British Prime Minister Macmillan at their meeting in the Bahamas in December 1962. The subject of discussion was Skybolt, a nuclear-tipped missile with a thousand-mile range launched from high-speed bombers. In a conference with President Eisenhower at Camp David in 1959, Macmillan had arranged for the purchase of one hundred Skybolts at a relatively low price for delivery in 1964. The United States Air Force's candidate for the top weapons vehicle of the next generation, Skybolt was being developed in competition with Polaris and Minuteman. Relying upon Skybolt, the British abandoned their own Blue Streak, a land-based missile, in 1960. The Kennedy administration, faced with climbing weapons costs, decided to abandon Skybolt and concentrate upon other weapons systems. The land-based Minuteman, tests proved, could reach any Skybolt target from underground launching silos in the United States. The administration felt that Minuteman plus Polaris, a submarine-launched missile, would satisfy both American and allied needs for long-range weapons. Abandoning Skybolt would slow the big weapons drain on the United States budget, and, if the British could be induced to accept Polaris, Kennedy could advance another valued objective—the vesting of nuclear weapons not in individual nations but in the trust of alliances to which the United States belonged.

At Nassau, Kennedy gave Macmillan the tidings that Skybolt would be no more and proposed instead that Britain adopt Polaris within a framework of NATO control. Macmillan apparently had little forewarning of the proposal, the President and his aides having just emerged from the engrossing Cuban missile crisis. The Skybolt cancellation was a hard blow to the Royal Air Force and its manned bomber. It was bad budget news for Macmillan because Skybolt, coupled with existing British bombers, was the cheapest possible way of maintaining an independent British deterrent. The cancellation also had implications for British domestic politics. Several days before venturing to Nassau, Macmillan had been a supplicant at the court of Charles de Gaulle, seeking entry to the European Common Market. The Prime Minister suffered the political ignominy of rebuff. At Nassau, with Kennedy's sudden confrontation, he was threatened with a second major political defeat. His party's fortunes were already badly in eclipse at home and an election was impending. Looming political disaster brought Macmillan to drop his accustomed Edwardian gentility and roar back at his Presidential antagonist. But Kennedy held fast and offered Polaris to the British at the lowest possible price, with the proviso that although the missiles would operate under NATO, they would pass under British command in "supreme national" emergency. Macmillan ultimately acquiesced, enabling Kennedy to improve his budgetary position and advance his purpose of internationalizing nuclear weapons.[23]

Major events and shifts in American objectives can jolt even the sturdiest alliances. For both Asian and European allies, Nixon's initiations of rapprochement with the Soviet Union and Communist China evoked nightmares of uncertainty concerning future American resolve to live up to the traditional military commitments of its alliances. The distress was exacerbated by the minimum forewarning given to allies and the modesty of subsequent assurances.

In both East and West, allies reacted with defiance and distress. In South Korea, President Park Chung Hee declared that his country would not accept any big-power decision on the fate of Korea made without the consent and participation of his government.[24] In western Europe, improved U.S.-U.S.S.R. relations were beheld as a prelude to the withdrawal of some American forces from the continent while the heavy build-up of Soviet strength continued, steps that could lead to an overwhelming preponderance of Soviet power at the threshold of Central Europe.[25]

Nixon's blossoming rapport with the giants of the communist world, Russia and China, also had implications of an unusual sort for the concept of alliance. With Russia, he established what might be termed a nonallied alliance. In effect, the U.S. and U.S.S.R. were both enemies and allies, who, since the 1962 missile crisis, became accustomed to reading each other's signals and respecting each other's external obligations and internal necessities. Actually, Nixon forced Moscow to formalize in the 1972 summit meeting various prevailing implicit agreements. His forcing agent was his resumption of relations with China, an event that rushed to the forefront of Soviet calculations. Russia's relations with China were tense and had led to the concentration of huge forces on their mutual border. The entrance of China into the U.S.-U.S.S.R. equation afforded Nixon more room to maneuver in dealings with the Soviet, including the blockading of North Vietnam ports to the jeopardy of Russian ships. Notwithstanding that affront, the U.S.S.R. moved ahead with summit agreements in preparation with the United States. As for China, its interest in the tri-part relation was to retain and enhance its American option as a depressing force on the Soviet military machine sitting at its borders.[26]

Nuclear Weaponry

The President bears the awesome responsibility to our allies, to his own people, indeed to all mankind, of deciding when, if ever, to use the vast arsenal of American nuclear weaponry. Under law only he, the Commander-in-Chief, can give the order. He has done so on but one occasion—near the end of the Second World War, when Truman ordered atomic bombs to be dropped on Hiroshima and Nagasaki in 1945. Later Presidents have threatened to use nuclear weapons. In 1953 President Eisenhower threatened Communist China with nuclear attack unless it supported a truce in Korea.[27] In his 1962 confrontation with the Soviets over their emplacement of offensive missiles in Cuba, President Kennedy put the Strategic Air Command and Air Force missile crews on maximum alert. In the 1973 Middle East War, with signs that Soviet forces might intervene to rescue entrapped Egyptian army units, Secretary of Defense James R. Schlesinger instructed the chairman of the Joint Chiefs of Staff, Admiral Thomas H. Moorer, to put U.S. armed forces on general stand-by alert, including the Strategic Air Command and the North American Air Defense

Command, custodians of nuclear arms. Although Schlesinger acted without talking directly with the President, the Secretary asserted that Nixon was "in complete command at all times" and later approved "a whole series of decisions" adopted by the National Security Council.[28] This example of a remote President who merely ratifies the deliberations of subordinates is dangerous and distressing. Without the President in active command, communications can more easily become confusing in the leaderless negotiations of coequal department Secretaries, and the dreaded risks of accidental war increase. And subordinates, unconstrained by the responsibility that is vested in the President alone, are more prey to temptations to overreach themselves. More typically and rightly, Presidents are active participants as major decisions develop that can potentially affect the use of nuclear weapons.

In facing their responsibilities for nuclear weapons, Chief Executives, typically, have been absorbed in two concerns. One is keeping the ultimate decision in their own hands. "I don't want some young Colonel to decide when to drop an atomic bomb," President Truman was known to say. The other is the avoidance of the dread possibility of an "accidental" nuclear war. Both problems thrust the President well into a complex of mechanisms and procedures regulating the release of nuclear weapons.[29]

The complex begins at the Ballistic Missile Early Warning System (BMEWS) in Thule, Greenland, where radar screens are poised to pick up Soviet missiles, if they are ever launched against the United States. BMEWS intelligence is simultaneously flashed to the North American Air Defense Command (NORAD) in Colorado Springs, Colorado, for interpretation; to the Strategic Air Command (SAC) control post near Omaha, Nebraska; to the Joint War Room of the Joint Chiefs of Staff in the Pentagon; and to the President. Several kinds of radio systems, telephones, teletypes, and television link these points. Multiple routings, frequencies, and circuits; alternate locations; verifications by senders and recipients that the messages actually come from their presumed source; procedures to challenge and counterchallenge the verifications; hundreds of men to pass the word to the button-pushers, who also number in the hundreds, all contribute to the vast effort to find safety.

The policy-makers, generals, psychologists, sociologists, and physicists charged with tightening the safety factor must deal with several types of possible human failure. Elaborate testing and "redundancy" procedures help thwart the kind of situation that arose in 1958 when a berserk sergeant threatened to fire a pistol at a nuclear bomb but was fortunately talked out of it by a supervisor. Suppose the President of the United States "goes ape," as the military say? Or suppose he singlehandedly decides to reverse national policy and launch a preventive war? The President too is subject to checks. Even he cannot simply pick up his telephone and order "go," nor does he know the one signal for a nuclear strike—the "go code." In an emergency he would receive intelligence via the "gold phone circuit" that connects him with the offices, action stations, and homes of the Secretary of Defense, the Joint Chiefs of Staff, the SAC commander, and others, all of whom could assist in his decision. An agenda with key questions concerning the probable emergency has been prepared, which could be administered quickly and in code. Time is a slight safety factor. In the existing state of weapons systems, the President has a possible thirty minutes after the report of launched enemy ICBM's to consult and await further information before unleashing a full, irrevocable "go" order.

Chief Executives have been concerned with several types of safety and control. Kennedy arranged the "hot line" to Moscow to deal with breakdowns and miscalculations of the kind featured in the novel *Fail-Safe*.[30] The Kennedy administration also instituted a new lock system for the nation's huge and far-flung nuclear weapons arsenal. Kennedy consummated the 1963 test ban treaty with the Soviet Union and Johnson promoted the treaty prohibiting states from placing nuclear arms or other weapons of mass destruction in orbit around the earth or installing those weapons on the moon or on other celestial bodies.[31] In 1968 Johnson could hail the adoption of a treaty to prevent the spread of nuclear weapons by barring the five nuclear powers from transferring nuclear weapons to nations that do not have them.

The 1972 Nixon-Brezhnev arms accords limited each side's defensive missile systems, with a commitment not to build nationwide antimissile defenses. In addition, an interim five-year agreement concerning offensive systems froze land-based and submarine-based intercontinental missiles at existing levels. Although a solid advance, the accords were nevertheless flawed by gaping loopholes that were quickly exploited. A further Nixon-Brezhnev agreement, reached during their Washington 1973 summit, called for immediate and "urgent consultations" if relations between their countries, or between one of them and another country, "appear to involve the risk of nuclear conflict." Thereupon the two superpowers shall "make every effort to avert this risk."[32] In 1974 at Vladivostok, Ford and Brezhnev reached a tentative agreement to limit the number of all offensive strategic nuclear weapons and delivery vehicles through 1985. The agreement left wide latitude for quantitative and technological expansions.

Neither the 1972 or later agreements contained provision for on-site inspection to check violations, but American officials were confident that other means of verification would suffice. According to an "open sky" provision of the 1972 agreements, neither side would "use deliberate concealment measures which impede verification" of compliance through the employment by both the U.S. and the U.S.S.R. of reconnaissance satellites.[33] But by 1974, Defense Department officials suspected that the Soviet was camouflaging some weapons programs and concealing its deployment of strategic missiles. Pentagon officials cited the placement of canvas covers over construction ways at a shipyard near Murmansk where nuclear-powered missile-carrying submarines are constructed. As well, the Soviet Union, according to these officials, was employing countermeasures to thwart American electronic methods.[34] Electronic intelligence surveillance is important for monitoring Soviet missile programs during their development phases, while photographic intelligence through reconnaissance satellites keeps watch of missiles once they are deployed.

Nixon also sought to impart to the Presidency a greater flexibility in responding to different kinds of nuclear attack or its threat. He initiated the development of weapons improvements, some designed to make specific retaliatory strikes more precise, particularly against "hard" Soviet military targets. With more flexibility, the President would not be limited to "soft" targets, such as cities, war plants, shipyards, and petroleum refineries, but could concentrate on military targets, on missile sites, bomber bases, radar installations, command control centers, and submarine pens.[35]

The Scientific Community

A major by-product of the President's preoccupation with nuclear weapons is the deepening of his relationships with the scientific community. The capability of his military establishment depends increasingly upon the efficiency of scientific research; in hard decisions he looks for scientists' counsel. Scientists were consulted when Truman weighed how he would use the newly developed atomic bomb. Then, as they often have been in facing momentous Presidential issues, the scientists were divided. Some advocated a purely technical demonstration, others a military application best designed to induce Japanese surrender.

Scientists, like the Presidents they serve, have lived in the coils of a continuing predicament. Some spend their lives improving the United States' weapon capability, but they feel conscience-bound to reduce the possibilities that the terrible weapons will ever be used. Scientists counseled the President when he took his first steps toward committing the United States to the international control of atomic weapons. The result was the Truman-Atlee-King declaration of November 15, 1945, which called upon the United Nations to establish a commission to develop proposals to promote peaceful uses of atomic energy, eliminate nuclear weapons, and foster an open world.

The Soviet Union's development of an atomic bomb in 1949 hurtled the scientists and the President into a formidable new issue. Should the United States, in the face of the Soviet achievement, forge ahead in the race by developing a hydrogen bomb? The President again received divided scientific counsel. One sector of scientific opinion deemed the bomb both feasible and necessary to the nation's security. Another sector urged the President "to tell the American public and the world that we think [it] wrong on fundamental ethical principles to initiate the development of such a weapon." America's abstention, these scientists also argued, would set an example that might limit the extent of war and raise the hope of mankind. President Truman ultimately ordered the development of the hydrogen bomb.

The Russians' atomic achievements also thrust the President into a difficult and at times agonizing new relationship with scientists. He had to determine, for example, whether particular scientists were "security risks" and therefore should be barred from access to classified government information. After 1949 the suspicions of legislators and administrators of the loyalty of scientists rose markedly. Late in 1953 William L. Borden, a former executive staff director of the Congressional Joint Committee on Atomic Energy, wrote to FBI Director J. Edgar Hoover that it was his "own exhaustively considered opinion, based upon years of study, of the available classified evidence, that more probably than not J. Robert Oppenheimer is an agent of the Soviet Union." An FBI report on Oppenheimer was prepared and ultimately forwarded to President Eisenhower. "This report," he has written, "jolted me." [36] The President, after consultations, directed that sensitive agencies were to erect at once a "blank wall" between Oppenheimer and classified information. With the President's approval, a three-man board headed by Gordon Gray, president of the University of North Carolina, was appointed to conduct a hearing. The hearing drew upon forty witnesses and produced three thousand pages of testimony. By a vote of two to one the Gray board found Oppenheimer a security risk, although a loyal citizen. The Atomic Energy Commission (AEC), Oppenheimer's employer, approved the Gray board's finding by a vote of four to one. President Eisenhower concurred in the finding and Oppenheimer's clearance was not reinstated.

But the President not only taketh away, he also giveth. Shortly before his death President Kennedy concluded plans for a White House ceremony for the presentation of the Enrico Fermi award to Oppenheimer for his "outstanding contributions to theoretical physics and his scientific and administrative leadership." When Kennedy's assassination intervened, President Johnson made the presentation in an early act of office-holding, to the satisfaction of many in the scientific community, who had long been seeking a symbolic clearance of Oppenheimer's name. [37]

Before the Soviet Union's launching of Sputnik, in October 1957, the President, for all of the importance of science in national life, had no regular, full-time scientific staff in his White House organization. In the wake of Sputnik the post of special assistant to the President for science and technology was created, with James Killian, president of the Massachusetts Institute of Technology, as the first incumbent. The existing Science Advisory Committee was brought to the White House level. President Eisenhower was soon turning to his scientific associates for alternative advice to the views of the Pentagon and Atomic Energy Commission. In Eisenhower's closing Presidential years, his scientific counselors debated intensively the scientific feasibility and the political desirability of a nuclear test ban. Ultimately Eisenhower, spurred by certain scientific advisers and Secretary of State Dulles, embarked upon negotiations for a nuclear test ban agreement, a major reversal in American nuclear policy that was finally consummated in the test ban treaty of President Kennedy.

In the test ban venture scientists served Presidents Eisenhower and Kennedy as both negotiators and counselors. [38] Eisenhower dispatched a scientific delegation to Geneva in mid-1958 to meet with their British and Russian counterparts and consider methods for policing a nuclear test ban. Out of their work emerged Eisenhower's proposal on August 22, 1958, that the three nuclear powers negotiate a treaty for the permanent suspension of nuclear weapon testing. To provide himself with continual advice on test ban problems, Eisenhower appointed a Committee of Principals—outside the National Security Council, interestingly—whose membership included the special assistant for science and technology plus the heads of the State and Defense Departments, the CIA, and the AEC.

Although the Eisenhower disarmament effort ended in an impasse, President Kennedy, upon entering office, resolved to try again and convened a panel of scientists to evaluate the American position and recommend modifications. As the negotiations advanced, Kennedy, like Eisenhower, was faced with absolute cleavage within the scientific community on the technical feasibility of a control system to monitor a nuclear test ban. Ultimately, Kennedy drove himself to choose between the conflicting schools. Contemporary Presidents, mindful of the experiences of the 1950s and 1960s, would readily concur with C. P. Snow that the task of decision-making in the modern scientific world is "one of the most intractable that organized society has thrown up." [39] Although scientists did not provide neat, reassuring guideposts in Presidential policy-making in the field of nuclear weapons, they achieved full partnership with political administrators and the military.

But in the 1970s the influence of the Science Adviser and his office sharply declined, as evidenced by his diminished access to the President. Potent contributing factors were the widespread opposition of scientists to Presidential policies in the Vietnam War and science's growing involvement in domestic social and environmental issues. In 1973, the post of the adviser and his office were abolished and their functions transferred to a government agency, the National Science Foundation. With the importance of science in the nation's life, in its national security and technology, science, like economics, ought to be represented at the Presidential level to facilitate communication between the Chief Executive and the scientific community. [40]

The Future Presidency

The Commander-in-Chief must be both strong and restrained, qualities that are vital to the well-being of democracy and Presidential power. Like any other form of government, democracy must maintain and reconcile to its processes a military establishment. A major means to that end is civilian control over the military, and the effective assertion of that principle depends centrally upon the President, who as Commander-in-Chief is a civilian officer to whom the military are subordinate. In an era of huge military budgets and devastating weapons, the Presidency's effectiveness as the vehicle of civilian control becomes crucial. How can the President, in the best sense, function both as a strong and a democratic Commander-in-Chief?

1. The most costly decisions that escalated the American commitment to the Vietnam War were made in an interlude when power in the Pentagon was concentrated in the Secretary of Defense and military advice from the Joint Chiefs

of Staff was "unified" in the hands of the Chairman. The quality of the advice rising to the President suffered from the tendency to compromise among the services to produce a common position, or to engage in log-rolling in which recommendations of all the services are endorsed.

Better military advice might be forthcoming if the Chairman of the Joint Chiefs of Staff is separated from the service chiefs (Army, Navy, Air). Thereupon the President and the Secretary of Defense would invite the separate views of each service chief and the JCS Chairman, and even, when useful, the views of field commanders, such as those for Europe and Asia and the head of the Strategic Air Command. Under this structure of multiple sources of advice, the President and the Secretary of Defense would be apprised of different viewpoints rather than simply a negotiated compromise. Instead of being engrossed in developing the compromise, the JCS Chairman could formulate a military judgment separate from the perspective of the services—with a military overview supplied by the Chairman and the opinions of the operators provided by the service chiefs. In making his decisions as Commander-in-Chief, the President, under this arrangement, is more apt to obtain proposals that are imaginative and innovative and is more likely to be aware of the diversity of military opinions rather than to become lulled by the misbelief that the views of his advisers are unified.[41] Also, the President would be freed of the awkwardness of having to develop a new position that in effect overrules all the military. Clearly, a further vital ingredient is the President himself. Unless he is receptive to structural diversity, a system such as that sketched will not work. Nixon was not attuned to multiple advocacy, nor was Johnson through most of his encounter with the Vietnam War, but Truman and Eisenhower were, and likewise Johnson in domestic affairs.

2. In addition, the Secretary of Defense should be allotted a role reduced from its grand scale of the 1960s. Decision-making concerning the military budget and the invocation of military force ought to flow, after initial preparation, to points outside the Defense Department, into broader arenas where participants are drawn from other departments and agencies as well as from the White House office. Nixon moved in that direction in his restructuring of the National Security Council. Consequently, one NSC group became a forum in which military, diplomatic, and intelligence evaluations of possible use of force could be brought together systematically. Another NSC committee reviewed the Defense budget, its size and major programs, and the participants included Defense, State, the Arms Control and Disarmament Agency, the Council of Economic Advisers, and the Office of Management and Budget.[42] In the Nixon years, these and other NSC committees were chaired by the powerful assistant for national security affairs, Henry Kissinger, which suggests that the net change was minimal, that centralized power had moved from the Defense Secretary to a new locus, the national security assistant. Such unwanted concentration could easily be dissipated by future Presidents simply by designating a different official as chairman of each of the NSC committees and thereby enhancing the possibility of varied advice emerging from the NSC structure.

3. The general imbalance of power over military affairs, running against Congress and heavily in the President's favor, might be significantly improved upon through innovative utilization of that most powerful of Congressional weapons, the power of the purse. Congress might establish a joint Congressional committee to examine the relationship of military to other spending and to establish national priorities between all kinds of major outlays. Domestic social needs would be compared with military and foreign policy needs, and, from the vantage point of a general overview, informed deliberations could allot limited governmental resources to the competing claimant fields. The effort could lead to a comprehensive study and careful formulation of national goals and priorities, resulting in guidelines for expenditure policy.[43]

The process might be assisted if a practice of the Defense Department were extended to other agencies, a practice by which the Secretary of Defense provides the Congressional Armed Services Committees with an annual statement on the military posture of the United States, with due protection of classified information. A similar statement might also be prepared by the Secretary of State, still another on domestic social posture by HEW, and another on the economy by the Council of Economic Advisers, a need already partially fulfilled by the President's annual Economic Report. Nixon's innovative annual State of the World Report approximated the proposed foreign policy posture statement. What is proposed here would be tailored to the historic Congressional function of assessing the President's budget and converting it into appropriations.[44]

4. The limitation of the arms race through international agreement will remain a large preoccupation of the President. Only a strong Chief Executive can press the case upon Congress and the people that an upward spiraling arms race is a threat to the nation's security. The individual services and the Congressional committees to which they are allied can be expected to provide resistance that only the Chief Executive can overcome. He is best situated to keep alive useful proposals that at first are rejected and to assure that new possibilities are considered. The Commander-in-Chief does not simply conduct war or stay prepared for the threat of it. He has a further mission upon which the nation's and the world's future depends—the Commander-in-Chief also keeps the peace.

11

THE ECONOMY

In his economic duties the Chief Executive is caught in a power gap. He functions in the one major nation of the world whose economic order and tradition are founded on private enterprise. He presides over a pluralistic economy in which private enterprise makes the key decisions of what and how much to produce, when and at what price, and how profits shall be used. The extent of private decision is evidenced by the gap that may exist between what the President tries to do and what he accomplishes. The President can toil, plan, and hope for prosperity, but there may be only depression. He can thunder against the trusts, but big enterprise may grow apace. He can come into office pledged to get the country "moving again," but for all his exertion the economy may only lag. He can place a WIN button on his lapel in defiance of inflation, but prices continue their upward rush.

The several administrative and policy-formulating agencies of the executive branch dealing with the economy differ widely in their responsiveness to the President. The Office of Management and Budget and the Council of Economic Advisers are *his* agencies and behave accordingly. The great operating departments—Treasury, Commerce, Labor, and Agriculture—are part of his cabinet family and partners to large and intimate decisions of his administration. An array of independent regulatory commissions—the Federal Reserve Board, the Securities and Exchange Commission, the Interstate Commerce Commission, and the like—make basic decisions in vital economic areas such as banking and credit, the sale of securities, the conduct of the stock exchanges, transportation, and communications. The independent commissions are carefully removed from the President's line of command. He has influence but lacks authority over them.

The limitations of his economic powers enthrone the President on the jagged prongs of a predicament. His authority over the economy does not equal his responsibility for its condition. Legally and administratively, he has important but severely limited means to influence its health and growth. As Martin Van Buren and Herbert Hoover would gladly have testified on the election nights of 1840 and 1932, the voters hold the Chief Executives responsible for the plight of their jobs and their pocketbooks above all else. Virtually from the moment he ascended to the Presidency, this appeared to be the acid test of Gerald Ford's incumbency and of his entitlement to continue in the office after 1976.

Yet for all the limitations he suffers in his authority, the President has more

264

impact upon the economy than any single source or possible combination of private power. The substantial authority and influence he possesses make him the head of the economic administration of the country. He applies quantities of laws promoting, regulating, and planning economic affairs. The Employment Act of 1946, a grand codification of his responsibilities, broadly charges him to lay before Congress each January an economic report on levels and trends of production, employment, and purchasing power, and to recommend ways to stimulate them. He is empowered to administer controls of prices, wages, and rents, which in the Nixon years were applied with widely varying and suddenly altering degrees of intensity, with each shift determined solely by the President. He collects taxes to provide roads, airports, research, and other services vital to industry. Thanks to its military needs, the executive branch, which the President manages, is the nation's largest purchaser. The aircraft and shipping industries would indeed be in a perilous state and railroads that were once great would vanish altogether if the United States government were not their best customer or guarantor. Through loans and guarantees administered by executive agencies, the President reduces or erases the risk to private enterprise.

In effectuating the confinement of the strong President within the norms of democratic accountability, the economy plays a vital part. It embraces the most powerful of the domestic constituencies, to which, to attract their valued approval and support, he must justify programs and policies and plead for cooperative private economic decisions, on which his own policies critically depend. Labor and business leaders play fluctuating roles in Presidential nominations and provide wherewithal for political campaigns, a basis for future demands on the President for concessions on program and policy. Pluralist democracy requires the flourishing of a variety of private economic enterprises and labor organizations and depends upon the existence of multiple power centers that assert initiatives and checks toward other centers, including the Presidency. In turn, the Chief Executive can weaken or strengthen economic pluralism by formulating policies that assist the concentration of private economic power or that resist it and foster increases of power units.

The President as Friend of Business

Living as they do in an economic world where decisions of private industry have much to do with economic health, Presidents as a lot assume that harmony and confidence between government and business are profitable to both. This benign assumption burns weakest in economic depression and brightest in war, when the nation's survival depends upon coordinated public and private economic effort. Presidents, for all their good intentions, differ widely in their individual dispositions toward business. Calvin Coolidge's worshipful dictum "The business of America is business" bespeaks his administration's total dedication to helping business. Richard Nixon was the first contemporary President to align himself squarely on the side of business and property and to view sternly those of his fellow citizens who falter in the economic race. As President he preferred the company of self-made millionaires and cherished the comforts of their luxurious estates. In his lengthy Congressional career, Gerald Ford developed his closest friendships with several of Washington's most powerful corporate lobbyists, including those for the Ford Motor Company, Procter and Gamble, and U.S. Steel. The day before Nixon resigned a Presidential transition meeting between representatives of the outgoing and incoming Presidents took place at the Georgetown home of William G. White, vice president and top Washington representative of U.S. Steel, and Ford's old and trusted friend.[1] No President can be said to be antibusiness. Franklin D. Roosevelt, who waged fierce struggles to reform the worst business malpractices and said harsh things about "economic royalists" and "unscrupulous money-changers," accepted the basic structure and premises of the business community. "I am certain," his Secretary of Labor, Frances Perkins, well observed, "that he had no dream of great changes in the economic or political patterns of our life." [2] Roosevelt limited his rejection of private enterprise to TVA and several sister projects in the belief that popular and business power needs could not be adequately supplied by private means. He apparently never wished government to take over the railroads, the coal mines, or any other basic industry. He considered government ownership both clumsy and unnecessary.

Republican Presidents view business fondly, and their modern Democratic brethren tend to be critical, although Lyndon Johnson's position was somewhere in between. He treated business as a most favored constituency against a background of pulsating prosperity and record profits, conditions of well-being that he never tired reminding his business audiences of. Johnson won business support for his 1964 program of tax cuts by promising to hold down government spending and by blotting out tax reforms that Kennedy had asked for earlier. As well, Johnson let it be known that business was not to be harassed, a sentiment that quickly prompted federal regulatory agencies to curb any aggressive tendencies that might have been budding. Johnson put through a relaxation of tax rules on depreciation, affording hundreds of millions of dollars in bonuses to corporations. He promised to sell off government enterprises competing with private business and pushed through a big reduction in excise taxes long clamored for by manufacturers. Although he nurtured liberal social programs, he held them to moderate size by feeding them modest budgets and developed an image of fiscal respectability that delighted the business community. On the several occasions when he went to the mat with giants of the business world, Johnson avoided head-on conflicts and preserved a framework of ever-renewable relations. He acted as though consensus politics is the key to economic prosperity. The economy does best when confidence unites business and government, and consensus politics is the wand that weaves the magic spell.

The President's relations with the components of the business community may differ widely at any one time. The community is not a monolith but a sprawling, continental—indeed intercontinental—pluralism whose members' interests differ markedly by region (Wall Street and the East versus the West), by size (big, intermediate, and small business), and by function (manufacture, wholesale, and retail). A single industry may contain both "liberal" enterprises that are public-minded and public-relations conscious and "conservative" enterprises whose self-interest blinds them to national necessity and who habitually fight governmental regulation in Congress and the courts. Presidents are wily enough to exploit business differences. The easiest and most commonly employed tactic is to pursue policies toward the business community that appeal to the many and offend the few. In launching his famous antitrust suit against the Northern Securities Company, a giant consolidation of the James J. Hill, J. P. Morgan, and E. H. Harriman railways, which embraced nothing less than the Northern Pacific, the Great Northern, and the Chicago, Burlington, and Quincy systems, Theodore Roosevelt scored a ten-strike in the esteem of the majority of the business world. They hailed Roosevelt's crusade joyfully because the Northern Securities Company was the outcome of a massive struggle between Morgan and Harriman on which most businessmen blamed the panic of 1901.

By word and deed the business community bestows its approval or disfavor upon the Presidents. The United States Steel Corporation abstained from raising its prices in the eight Presidential years of Dwight Eisenhower but boosted them twice during the three years of John Kennedy. The New Deal's cleansing and chastising of business created a lasting embitterment. No President has been more widely hated in the upper economic stratum than Franklin Roosevelt was. Visitors to J. P. Morgan in New Deal days were forewarned against mentioning the Roosevelt name lest it launch the mighty financier into apoplectic rage.[3]

Winning Business Confidence

If democracy is denoted by communication exchange and mutual confidence, Presidents respond to those norms by their attentions to the sometimes hard task of securing business approval, aware that their own powers can be used more effectively if business's resistance is minimized. At the very least, Presidents desire to rouse business confidence in their administrations, for which they apply a variety of old and proven nostrums. A standard remedy is the appointment of businessmen to responsible administration posts. Even Presidents like the Roosevelts, with large reputations for ferocity toward business, carefully provided "balance" in their administrations by including prestigious businessmen in them. Franklin Roosevelt counted heavily upon Jesse H. Jones, chairman of the Reconstruction Finance Corporation, to maintain an image of respectability in the eyes of the business community. A wealthy, monumental Texan who had built a fortune in the grand manner in banking, real estate, and newspapers, Jones was a paragon of success by business standards. The price of his services came high, but Roosevelt cheerfully paid it. "Whenever we did anything of importance, that was on the borderline of our authority," Jones said once in explaining the ground rules at RFC, "I would try at first opportunity to tell the President about it, but after the fact. He was always interested, and he never criticized." Roosevelt, in turn, never failed to appreciate the usefulness of Jones's gilt-edged prestige with business and Congress. "Your conservatism is a good thing for us in this Administration," the President would reassure the great Texan.[4] In the Kennedy and Johnson, as well as in the Nixon, years, the Treasury and Commerce posts were reserved for appointees who stood high in the confidence and regard of the business community.

In cultivating business confidence, Presidents work hard at tilling an image of fiscal responsibility. When national circumstances force the budget into imbalance, Presidents, with the aid of wizard-technicians of the fiscal arts, resort to elaborate hocus-pocus to maintain at least the window-dressing of fiscal respectability. For example, in his early Presidential years Franklin Roosevelt could face the nation with a balanced budget by the simple expedient of putting his costly recovery programs into a separate account. Invariably he included among his counselors those whose lives represented an unbroken consecration to conventional fiscal policy. Lewis Douglas, Director of the Budget, chanted the virtues of the balanced budget and a Hoover-like program of subsistence relief, with wages, hours, and prices shaped by natural economic forces. When Douglas eventually departed, Henry Morgenthau, Jr., as Secretary of the Treasury, made temperate public spending his special cause.

A President may keep business confidence at high flame by fraternizing with leading businessmen conspicuously more than with any other species of citizenry. The guests most frequently invited to President Eisenhower's stag dinners, social functions with incidental discussions of the administration's purposes, were businessmen. In his hours on the golf course Eisenhower's favorite companions were George E. Allen, a puckish corporation director; William E. Robinson, president of Coca-Cola; and Clifford G. Roberts, a New York banker. A President and his aides may seek to rally the business community behind their cause by wooing it with speeches. During his first year in office Kennedy waged a campaign of proportions unequaled in Presidential history to induce industry's cooperation in his efforts to maintain stable prices, without which he could not hope to secure labor's vital support in paring down its wage and fringe demands. Business could swallow the bitter price medicine more easily if it were sweetened with evidences of the administration's general concern for its interests. Administration officials plied business with sympathetic speeches and promised a balanced budget, better depreciation allowances, and other policies that business cherished.

A President may cultivate business by consulting it on problems and policies of mutual concern. In 1962, following his head-on collision with the United States Steel Corporation over its rising prices, which had resulted in part at least from a failure in business-government communications, Kennedy moved to avoid any similar lapses in the future by establishing the Business Council. The President took up with the council, composed of the presidents and chairmen of large corporations, such knotty problems as the balance of payments and the outflow of gold. One year after the steel price encounter, at the council's meetings at Hot Springs, West Virginia, Kennedy could listen with high satisfaction to the testimony of corporate executives that they were less nervous about business-government relations than they had been at any time since his inauguration.

Much of the President's economic policy may advance both the President's and business's purposes. The income tax, established by constitutional amendment in 1913, is not merely an enormous producer of revenue but a reflector of an administration's underlying economic philosophy and a means of slowing or quickening general economic activity. Presidents Harding, Coolidge, and Hoover were more or less the spokesmen for the view of their Secretary of the Treasury, Andrew Mellon, that "the prosperity of the middle and lower classes depended upon the good fortunes and light taxes of the rich." Taxes that were too high, Mellon believed, would prevent the rich from saving and would make them reluctant to invest. If they failed to save and invest, the economy would ultimately falter.

The most pervasive of all taxes—the tariff—can also advance or obstruct a broad sweep of the President's economic policies. Harding and Coolidge, employing discretionary authority under the Fordney-McCumber Act, raised rates and fostered the concentration of domestic economic power.

But discretionary Presidential authority to adjust rates may also promote trade, as demonstrated by the Trade Expansion Act of 1962, which authorizes the President to cut tariffs in general as much as 50 percent and to eliminate tariffs on certain goods. But mounting trade deficits and grave weakening of the dollar abroad moved Nixon to devalue the dollar and request from Congress new authority to raise, as well as lower, trade barriers to gain a "fairer shake" for American products in world trade.

Appropriate to his premier orientation to business's interests and approval, Nixon is the first contemporary President to have a top-ranking, wide-ranging White House assistant—Peter M. Flanigan—to nurture those objectives. An investment banker, Flanigan became a pro-business surrogate of the consumer affairs program, promoted the administration's oil policy, supervised the White House's relations with the regulatory agencies, and drew plans to revitalize the nation's near-moribund merchant marine.

Flanigan's skill at achieving results pleasing to business in the torpid federal bureaucracy was acclaimed from every side. "He's the guy who people in our industry turn to," said a steel executive. "And we wouldn't turn to him unless he came through." A Commerce Department official observed that at top echelons "the business community pays no attention to this department; if you have a policy problem, you go see Peter Flanigan—and he is available." But to critics, he was a fixer. A Democratic Congressman noted that "Flanigan is a manipulator of the first order. He's a master of the compromise that works out best for vested interests." A bureaucratic critic added, "It's very subtle, very discreet. You create an atmosphere, a relationship, a sense of debts, a series of understandings. There are political pay-offs all the time. But nothing is written down. Things don't have to be said. Most things are left unsaid and there are just 'understandings.' Anyone who looks for specific deals is just naive." [5] The incipient conflict between these assessments and the ethical standards of democratic government came to a head in the International Telephone and Telegraph (ITT) affair, in which a developing antitrust action against the company was settled on a basis highly favorable to ITT. In reluctant testimony to a Congressional investigation, Flanigan declined to discuss his contacts with that huge conglomerate. Flanigan's reticence was a negation of democratic norms and his functions aligned the Presidency with dominant economic power at the expense of small and weaker economic units, the consumer, the worker. To function by democratic criteria, the President must be responsive to all of the economy, not merely to the dominant segment.

Frictions

The President's dialogue with business takes on a tougher weave when, more in keeping with democracy, he endeavors to persuade the business community to come around to some action that, although vital to national welfare, does not altogether square with business's self-interest. One of the more emphatic passages of Presidential discord with private enterprise occurred in 1916, when a major railroad strike confronted the nation. President Wilson summoned the railroad owners to the White House and eloquently appealed to them to accept a compromise he had devised to resolve the dispute. Wilson's formula called for an eight-hour day, no raises, and time and a half for overtime. For all Wilson's exhortation that his plan was fair and that the national interest required its acceptance, the railroad owners were negative and adamant. The President was butting his head against the rock of Gibraltar. Upon reaching this conclusion, Wilson, not a man of any great patience, rose from the conference table. His face twisted with anger, he exclaimed, "I pray to God to forgive you; I never can," and left the room. [6]

A President may also negotiate with individual titans of industry with great consequence to the economy. The most fabulous of these negotiations took place in 1905 between Theodore Roosevelt and the unsurpassed presence, J. Pierpont Morgan. Morgan was building his empire with no-holds-barred fury; the administration had mounted its trust-busting policy. A head-on collision was a matter of time. Morgan decided to talk to Roosevelt. In the lengthy interview Theodore Roosevelt was bemused by the mighty Morgan's notions of the character and status of the United States Presidency. "Mr. Morgan," Roosevelt noted afterward, "could not help regarding me as a big rival operator, who either intended to ruin all his interests, or else could be induced to come to an agreement to ruin none."

The Morgan way of dealing with the United States Presidency came into full play on a January day in 1905 when an official of the Bureau of Corporations of the Department of Commerce and Labor appeared in the offices of Elbert Gary, board chairman of the United States Steel Corporation, a Morgan enterprise, to discuss the bureau's impending investigation of the company. With Morgan's encouragement, the astute Gary, a suave erstwhile judge, arranged a meeting at the White House with Secretary of Commerce and Labor Victor H. Metcalf, Commissioner of Corporations James R. Garfield, and Theodore Roosevelt. Gary opened the session by amiably declaring that he would not challenge the constitutionality of the Commerce and Labor Department's request that U.S. Steel open its books and records. In return for this benevolence, Gary tactfully invited the administration to pledge that any information gleaned from U.S. Steel's files would be used not by subordinate government officials but "by the President alone for his guidance in making such suggestions to Congress concerning legislation as might be proper, expedient, and for the actual benefit of the general public." If questions should arise over the use of material that Gary deemed confidential, he, Garfield, and Metcalf would seek agreement, and that failing, the President would decide. A memorandum of the conference was prepared to Theodore Roosevelt's satisfaction.

The Gary-Roosevelt concordat was put to a test one year later when the administration brought International Harvester, another Morgan company, under scrutiny. Would International Harvester be satisfied with whatever the Commerce and Labor Department's findings were, Theodore Roosevelt teasingly asked George W. Perkins, the Morgan representative. Perkins responded uninhibitedly. The company expected, he said, "the Department frankly [to] come to us and point out any mistakes or technical violations of any law; then give us a chance to correct them, if we could or would, and . . . if we did, then we would expect the Attorney General not to bring proceedings." [7] Although Roosevelt, in ensuing brass-tacks discussions, was somewhat more demanding than Perkins anticipated, International Harvester pretty well passed muster at the White House.

In making secret deals with Morgan and his men, Roosevelt risked raising the hackles of progressives who surely would interpret his behavior as a betrayal of the people. But Roosevelt was not merely doling out approval to the Morgan interests. The President was playing a game, too. In arranging secret pacts, Roosevelt was achieving a cherished peace with Wall Street at a juncture when its aid was critical to the advance through Congress of the top-most item of his economic program, the Hepburn railroad bill. Roosevelt also aimed to achieve in the Morgan consultations new and mutually more rewarding government-business dealings than the barren negativism of the Sherman Act had thus far permitted.

How Presidents Fight Business

When business fails to cooperate or openly fights the President, he may resort to an armory of diverse and potent weapons. Here Presidents may burst beyond democratic bounds and resort to actions that sometimes violate due process and civil liberties.

The President may choose to regulate business by drawing upon his "prerogative," or power directly granted him by the Constitution. The most enriching provisions for the prerogative-minded President are the opening clause of Article II ("The Executive power shall be vested in a President of the United States of America") and his designation as "Commander-in-Chief." Prerogative is usually exerted in crisis, in war or economic decline, and it is often buttressed by statutes delegating broad powers to the President. From the First World War on, industry's growing involvement in war-making has made it the frequent object of Presidential prerogative. Before the Pearl Harbor attack, for example, Franklin Roosevelt, citing his earlier proclamation of "unlimited national emergency," seized an aviation plant and pointed to the "duty constitutionally and inherently resting upon the President to exert his civil and military as well as his moral authority to keep the defensive efforts of the United States a going concern" and "to obtain supplies for which Congress has appropriated money, and which it has directed the President to obtain." [8]

The employ of Presidential prerogative in labor-management disputes was set back firmly in the Supreme Court's review of President Truman's seizure of the steel industry midway in the Korean "police action." In *Youngstown Sheet and Tube Co.* v. *Sawyer* (343 U.S. 579, 1952) the Court struck down the President's action as unconstitutional. The President, in moving upon the steel strike, had relied upon prerogative and ignored the Taft-Hartley Act passed by a Republican-controlled Congress in 1947, subjecting Presidential intervention in labor-management disputes to a specified procedure. Truman had vetoed the bill, holding partly that his prerogative was sufficient for labor-management crises. Congress, in turn, overrode his veto and Truman solemnly avowed he would observe the new law. When a steel strike loomed in April 1952, however, the President ignored the Taft-Hartley Act and its eighty-day no-strike provision and, brandishing his prerogative, seized the steel mills. Pointing to the mountainous military requirements of the nation and its allies, he invoked "the authority vested in me by the Constitution and laws of the United States," language so general that it said almost nothing. The Supreme Court intervened and struck a blow for democracy and against arbitrary, unlimited Presidential power by ruling that since Congress could have ordered seizure of the steel mills, the President lacked the power of seizure without specific legislative authorization.

In addition to statutes and prerogative, the President can summon a variety of "pressures" to encourage industry's "cooperation." These too can easily stray into excessive power, trampling upon constitutional rights and liberties. Glimpses into the character of these pressures are provided by John Kennedy's sharp encounter with U.S. Steel in 1962.[9] Eager to hold the steel price line against inflation, the Kennedy administration, by energetic persuasion, had brought the steel union to curb its wage and fringe demands and agree to a two-year compact with the United States Steel Corporation. The administration emerged with the blissful expectation that the steel industry in reciprocal sensitivity to the nation's welfare would make no price increases. Suddenly U.S. Steel raised its prices, and other big steel companies quickly followed its lead.

Kennedy and his aides, deeming the steel companies' action nothing less than a double-cross, unloosed a barrage of pressures. Kennedy hoped that the few steel companies that had not raised their prices could be induced to refrain from doing so. Several administration aides even dared to surmise that if only a few companies held out, market forces would induce the giants to drop their price increases. The administration gave the pressure faucets a quick full turn. In a nationally televised news conference, the President questioned the patriotism of the "tiny handful of steel executives—whose pursuit of power and profit exceeds their sense of public responsibility." The President asked Senator Estes Kefauver, Democrat of Tennessee and chairman of the Senate Antitrust subcommittee, to express publicly his "dismay" over the price rise and to consider an investigation. These the Senator gladly did. The Justice Department and the Federal Trade Commission announced that the price action would be closely scrutinized for possible violations of the antitrust laws. The President, Secretary of Defense McNamara, and leading officials of the Treasury and Commerce Departments and the Council of Economic Advisers put in friendly low-key telephone calls to contacts in the steel companies that had not raised prices, gently suggesting the wisdom of continued abstinence.

At Democratic national headquarters calls were made to Democratic governors across the nation inviting them to make public statements supporting the President and encouraging local steelmakers to hold the price line. When it appeared that the proceedings of a stockholders' meeting of Bethlehem Steel Corporation, held shortly before the price rise, might be relevant in possible antitrust prosecutions, the Justice Department moved to secure the potential evidence. In the middle of the night overzealous FBI agents routed out for questioning three newspaper reporters who had covered the Bethlehem meetings. In testimony on Capitol Hill administration officials unloosed alarming analyses of the impact of the steel price rise upon military and economic foreign aid and the nation's relationship to the Common Market. In the Defense Department, Secretary McNamara ordered military agencies to shift their buying to the few steel companies that had not raised their prices. The Kennedy administration's "divide-and-conquer" strategy ultimately paid off when the several hold-out companies announced they would not raise prices. Fearful of a disastrous loss of sales, U.S. Steel and all other companies that had followed its lead quickly canceled their rises. But U.S. Steel and other companies bounced back, nearly a year later, by raising prices, this time without administration opposition.

One of Johnson's favorite economic weapons was the manipulation of government stockpiles of critical and strategic materials. The United States government has stockpiles of about one hundred strategic materials, from asbestos to zirconium, in more than two hundred storage sites throughout the country. Congress established the stockpiling program under legislation that specifically provided that stockpiled commodities might be sold publicly in a manner that would not disturb the commercial market. The use of stockpiles for price regulation in the civil economy is patently beyond the statutory intent of Congress, but Johnson was not deterred from manipulating the stockpiles to advance his war against inflation. For example, he induced the Aluminum Company of America (Alcoa), the nation's largest aluminum producer, to roll back a schedule of price increases. Secretary of Defense Robert McNamara announced that 200,000 tons of aluminum would be released from the federal stockpile. Both the quantity and the price of the stockpile releases was expected to "relieve price pressures." Unlike Kennedy in his encounter with steel, Johnson remained personally silent and made no demand that Alcoa rescind its price increase, and administration officials took pains to stress that the stockpile move was unconnected with the price problem. Of such stuff are credibility gaps made, the bane of Presidential effectiveness and democratic candor. Within days, Alcoa and other aluminum companies that had followed its action announced that the price increases were rescinded, and McNamara, speaking for Johnson, hailed Alcoa's decision as "an act of industrial statesmanship." [10]

Johnson, who viewed both Presidential and democratic politics as consensus politics, endeavored to minimize the damage of conflicts such as those with business by refraining from hostile public utterance and by quickly repairing breaches in the relation. There was no crisis of confidence such as had followed Kennedy's assault on U.S. Steel, which was manifest in a drastic decline in the stock market. And Nixon, who too had moments of conflict with business, took leaves from the Kennedy-Johnson book. When the Bethlehem Steel Corporation threatened the President's 1971 drive against inflation by raising prices, Nixon, through his press secretary, expressed concern over the "enormous" steel rises and threatened to relax existing policy limits on steel imports from Japan and Europe. Nixon also fought back at soaring industrial prices by moving to sell from strategic stockpiles in order to drive prices down. His success was as modest and tentative as that of his predecessors. Gerald Ford, who enjoyed wholehearted acceptance in the business community, publicly reprimanded General Motors for raising automobile prices. The President deplored the inflationary consequences of the higher prices, and the company responded with a modest price reduction. [11] A similar protest budged U.S. Steel even less.

The "New Economics"

The Kennedy-Johnson era marked the advent of the "New Economics," by which government is becoming a manager of prosperity, in addition to its long-standing role of savior in the depths of a depression or recession. Presidents are coming into their new prosperity role not by legislative mandate, judicial decision, group consultation, or public discussion, but largely by autonomous executive decision, goaded by the importance of the economy to their own and the country's well-being. One example of the President's new role, in the Kennedy-Johnson years, is his use of "guidelines," which he can apply to labor-management wage negotiations and to industry's price policies. The guidelines provide a formula for testing whether particular wage or price increases are inflationary; that is, whether they exceed the nation's average annual gain in productivity, or output per man-hour, over the last five years. The generally prevailing gain in the Kennedy and Johnson years was 3.2 percent. If, in a given industry, the productivity gain equals the national average, the wage increases can be absorbed by the gain without necessitating a price increase. The Council of Economic Advisers provided the guidelines, with the aim not of preventing all price or wage changes but of preserving overall economic stability.

A difficulty that constantly bedeviled the guidelines was that they were enforced more effectively against prices than wages. Industry leaders show more sensitivity to Presidential pressures than labor leaders. Although industry disliked the guidelines, it disliked even more the publicity and other costs of embroilment with government. Union leaders, in contrast, were apt to feel that to accept a governmental decision that determined labor's slice of the economic cake was to abdicate their responsibilities. In many important industries, bargaining is local and remote from Presidential influence. Paradoxically, although industry was held more closely to account for its prices, its profit levels have well outdistanced wage gains. From 1960 to 1965, profits after taxes rose 67 percent, while the weekly take-home pay of factory workers climbed 21 percent.[12] Guidelines were applied only to so-called basic industries and not to hundreds of other industries affecting the cost of living, such as food, clothing, and housing. Under labor's pressure to regain lost ground in the economic race, President Johnson decreed in 1966 that the guidelines should be more "flexible," that their limits should be breakable to enable labor to catch up with rising living costs.

A second bastion of the President's New Economics is his manipulation of tax policy to restrain a business boom or to stop the plunge toward a recession. In 1966, for example, Johnson recommended to Congress the temporary repeal of incentives for business investment. Earlier that year, he asked Congress to restore previously reduced excise taxes on automobiles and telephone service to help avoid an overheated economy. Likewise, the President's 1967 proposal of a special surcharge on the income tax was intended not only to raise needed revenue but to check the economy's fast tempo.

In its initial sorties the Nixon Presidency transformed the New Economics into what often became "no economics," with less governmental manipulation of the economy, more reliance on monetary policy (money and credit), and less on fiscal policy (taxing and spending) to bolster prosperity and slow inflation. Nixon's economists perceived the economy as inclined toward relatively steady growth, thus occasioning no need for shifting public budget and monetary policy to offset economic swings. Likewise, the Nixon team rejected their predecessors' tactic of manipulating the federal budget through changes in taxation and spending to hold the economy to a track of noninflationary growth, when, ideally, tax revenues should cover expenditure. But the dynamics of economic forces unsettled this scheme. Unemployment rose above expected levels, inflation soared, and Nixon, who like other Presidents gladly left economic policy to the experts, developed understanding of that occult subject through the political microscope. He was spurred to this sudden comprehension by the 1970 elections, when the voters, who perceive economics in stark bread-and-butter terms, reacted negatively to Republican Congressional candidates whose economic preferences were similar to Nixon's. With his own electoral test of 1972 approaching, the President suddenly shifted economic gears. Whereas earlier he had denounced his Democratic predecessors for accumulating a long string of deficits, his new budget, for fiscal 1972 projected a huge deficit. Ruefully, Nixon announced, "I am now a Keynesian." Soon the President was moving to easier money and credit, and to what Kennedy and Johnson, in their most embracing formulations of the New Economics, never dared invoke—wage and price controls.[13]

But just as the economic direction of Presidential policy can shift, so can the political. After his overwhelming 1972 reelection, Nixon's political world was again transformed, thanks, in part, to the Twenty-second Amendment, which ruled out his further Presidential candidacy. With the removal of that deterrent, he quickly redefined the New Economics along lines that better reflected his personal economic values, which emphasized self-reliance and constrained government activity. Price controls were greatly reduced. Yet, ironically, Nixon's further budgets, for all his proclaimed austerity, showed ever larger deficits, thanks to increased military expenditures, inflation, and the profusion of program items so solidly built into the budget that no President can disturb them. And, even in his second term, whenever recession loomed it was fought with stepped-up public expenditure.

For Gerald Ford, inflation was "public enemy number one," an enemy whose depredations were compounded by a sluggish economy, rising unemployment, record high interest rates, and a severely depressed stock market. In his initial assault on inflation, Ford resorted to the Old Economics rather than the New, and to astute political tactics. With a fervor that would have delighted Herbert Hoover, he focused on a reduction of the federal budget and allowed only a meager concession to the New Economics in encouraging the Federal Reserve Board to permit a modest easing of interest rates. He emphatically ruled out price and wage controls. Simultaneously, he embarked upon a passage of political entrepreneurship by moving to make his economic policy bipartisan, much in the fashion that foreign policy traditionally has been. He convened a series of "summit" conferences on inflation whose participants included Congressional Democratic leaders, labor chieftains, who are mostly Democrats, and a wide range of economists and experts. Ford meant to spread the blame if his policies failed to stabilize the economy, and his moves put Democratic leaders and Presidential aspirants on the defensive. After the Democrats' landslide success in the 1974 Congressional elections, Ford persisted in his invitation to bipartisan endeavor by calling for a shared Congressional-Presidential attack on inflation.

His own initial package of proposals for dealing with the number one enemy was slender. He asked for expanded agricultural production through removal of acreage limitations, legislation to increase antitrust violation penalties, tax incentives to business to stimulate industrial expansion, enhanced benefits to the unemployed, encouragement of home construction, relaxation of environmental standards, a one-year tax surcharge of 5 percent on corporate and individual incomes, with families having a gross income of under $15,000 excluded, and cuts and deferrals of federal spending with an expenditure target of $300 billion for the fiscal year 1975.[14]

Altogether, Ford's was a pallid response to problems of crisis magnitude. Prices continued to soar. In choosing an essentially do-nothing approach, Ford eschewed what to many seemed the only promising weapon against inflation, price and wage controls, imposed, if not across the board, at least selectively on such major industries as oil, steel, automobiles, copper, and chemicals. Prices in these industries are administered by giant corporations rather than determined by competition, and the potent economic power of such corporations can be checked only by government intervention. Nonetheless, Ford, in public statements, repeatedly disparaged price controls: "From past experience controls show us that they never really stopped inflation . . . not even during and immediately after World War II. . . ."[15]

Late in 1974 rising unemployment induced Ford to acknowledge that a recession had hit the country and required the same top priority he had previously accorded to inflation. His insistence on budget-cutting and a surtax as steps to fight inflation softened in favor of governmental liberality to fight the recession, including public jobs for the unemployed.[16] But how far down this new road Ford, whose economics were conservative, would go remained problematic. His 1975 State of the Union Message urged a tax cut to jog the faltering economy and moves to diminish American dependence on foreign petroleum sources, chiefly by driving up gasoline and petroleum prices to encourage a declining of consumption and expansion of American production.

Business's Weapons

Business, too, has an abundance of muscle that it can flex in encounters with the Presidency. Not the least element in business's potency is money, which takes on an added allure when elections are approaching. The iron baron and political boss Mark Hanna dexterously intertwined the national Republican organization and a coterie of top-level businessmen into a working alliance. By assessing the magnates shrewdly, Hanna assured a perpetually well-stocked campaign fund and, to gladden his generous donors, a respectably conservative program. Hanna's crowning success came when he handpicked William McKinley for the Presidency and installed him in the office.

Theodore Roosevelt's campaign manager, George B. Cortelyou, gave the Hanna technique an added twist by employing methods approaching blackmail in enlisting contributions from the large industrial trusts. When Alton Parker, the Democratic Presidential nominee, began charging that the trusts were underwriting the Republican campaign, Roosevelt was put upon to denounce the accusations as "unqualifiedly and atrociously false." [17]

But the champion money raiser is Maurice H. Stans, who amassed, as chairman of the 1972 Finance Committee to Reelect the President, "the largest amount of money ever spent in a political campaign." An investment banker, Stans excelled at extracting huge sums from businessmen, and a major factor in his unmatched success was his insistence on raising the big money by chasing after the fat purses himself. According to a colleague, "Stans presses very hard. He would tell them what it was worth for them to assure that George McGovern not spend four years in the White House. One man made a commitment of $10,000 to me, but Stans got him up to $50,000. The next day the guy called me back and said, 'I've been thinking about what Maury told me. I'm going to make it $100,000.' " Stans scored highest among businesses facing trouble with government or seeking a government decision or favor whose potential worth was incomparably more valuable than a generous campaign donation. [18] From the major oil companies, he extracted far more than a million dollars in campaign contributions, a generosity that was prodigiously rewarded in the lavish profits the companies enjoyed in the "energy crisis," extracted from consumers, without any significant restraint by the Nixon administration.

Businessmen or their proven servants may fill strategic elective and appointive offices of government whence they can exert a channeling influence upon the President. For example, Theodore Roosevelt, bent upon a progressive program, was faced by the "Big Four" Republican leaders in the Senate: Nelson W. Aldrich of Rhode Island, John C. Spooner of Wisconsin, Orville H. Platt of Connecticut, and William B. Allison of Iowa. Time and again Theodore Roosevelt, in inescapable reckonings with these hard-line conservative leaders, had to trim his progressive measures. In the executive branch, businessmen may dominate the cabinet Secretaryships, lesser departmental posts, and the independent regulatory commissions. President Eisenhower's original cabinet, for example, was described, not without exaggeration, as a "millionaires' corporation." So captive were the millionaires to their traditional economic doctrines that Eisenhower had the steady chore of lecturing to his cabinet on the importance of avoiding actions lending credence to critics' epithets that his was a "business administration." The administration, Eisenhower would say, must never fail to demonstrate its concern for the little man. [19]

Business's political attention is constantly focused on the independent regulatory commission: the Federal Trade Commission, the Securities and Exchange Commission, the Federal Reserve Board, and the like. These are the principal regulators of the economy, and their policies can do much to curb the practices and profits of business. The best insurance against inconvenient regulation, business has found, is to fill the commissions' positions with its own men. Undoubtedly, the most complete take-over of the commissions was engineered by the Harding-Coolidge appointments to those bodies. But Richard Nixon at least rivals these predecessors in making the regulatory commissions the preserve of business and industry. Nixon used the appointing power to produce commission memberships with less diversity than in the past by appointing fewer academics, liberals, and consumer activists.

Presidents who champion progressive social programs are both sensitive and vulnerable to economic pressures from the business community. Theodore Roosevelt was visited with two economic "panics," as they were known, each a large threat to his political fortunes. In the late spring of 1903, when his nomination and election appeared certain, economic panic suddenly struck. The stock market fell into deep decline, wiping out $2 billion in security values; credit tightened and business failures soared. The high priests of finance, in their analytic incantations, attributed the disaster to a single and simple cause— Roosevelt's harassment of business. Only a few business spokesmen mentioned the contributing factors of an inflexible monetary structure and the overcapitalization of trusts like U.S. Steel. Roosevelt's own analysis of the ominous events, confided to his Secretary of State, Elihu Root, was that "certain of the big men" in Wall Street were not reluctant to see the panic get worse to discredit the administration and "to force the Republican party back into the path of conservatism." Mark Hanna, waiting in the wings, was a tailor-made conservative candidate, in fact. Root, for his part, brought the President corroborative intelligence that a pro-Hanna, anti-Roosevelt campaign among "the substantial men" of New York was blooming in the Union League Club, of which Root was president. When the further bludgeon of the 1907 panic smote his fortunes, Theodore Roosevelt made no bones about articulating his suspicions in a public statement charging that "certain malefactors of great wealth" had combined to intensify the panic "in order to discredit the policy of the government." [20]

Labor Leaders and the President

The second member of the great economic tandem, labor, like other groups, attracted significant attention from the President of the United States only after it attained major political strength. Samuel Gompers, president of the American Federation of Labor, was not given the privilege of visits with Presidents until the late nineteenth century, and even then the occasions were few and brief. Gompers first extracted sustained Presidential interest from Theodore Roosevelt. Roosevelt invited the labor leader to the White House socially, consulted him on a wide range of subjects, and meted out honorific recognitions. Upon receiving the Nobel prize, for example, the President set up an industrial peace foundation and named Gompers to its board of directors.

Of all Presidents, Franklin Roosevelt maintained the most extensive relations with labor leaders. With labor he employed the same technique he applied to other private organizations. Viewing the nation's politics as essentially group politics, Franklin Roosevelt was wont to approach groups whose support he cherished through their leaders. Roosevelt's dealings with labor leaders ran the gamut from intimacy to mortal enmity. Dan Tobin of the Teamsters' Union was such an exalted favorite that Roosevelt made his "labor speech" of the 1944 campaign at a Teamsters' dinner, after rejecting entreaties of a dozen other unions for his presence.

Roosevelt's most intimate and profitable rapport was with Sidney Hillman, president of the Amalgamated Clothing Workers and vice president of the CIO. Hillman's sensitivity and appreciation of social workers, intellectuals, and others outside the labor movement set him apart from rougher-hewn colleagues. He served in responsible government posts in the New Deal and the Second World War, on NRA's Labor Advisory Board, on the National Defense Advisory Council, and as Associate Director of the Office of Production Management. To Roosevelt, Hillman was one of "the longest-headed individuals I have ever met." A constant visitor at the White House, Hillman enjoyed the rare privilege of a right-of-way by telephone to the Chief Executive. By the mid-1930s, a CIO official could plausibly assert that "a whisper from Sidney Hillman of the Amalgamated is louder than the loudest shout of almost anyone in the national Cabinet." And CIO president John L. Lewis, even when he was beholding the CIO vice president with a critical eye, declared, "Sidney Hillman was after all the driving force behind many of the measures attributed to the New Deal. If it had not been for him there would probably have been no Fair Labor Standards Act." [21] Probably Hillman's thorniest assignment in the mid-1930s was smoothing the troubled waters that kept churning up between his superior, John L. Lewis, and Franklin D. Roosevelt. Hillman's busy diplomacy was made doubly difficult by Lewis' resentment of his aide's privileged closeness to Roosevelt. The ordeal ended when Lewis finally broke with Roosevelt in 1940.

The Hillman-Roosevelt nexus, although resting upon a sturdy underpinning of personal regard, was mutually advantageous. For Hillman, an unrivaled access to the White House meant speedy advancement in his labor career. For Roosevelt, Hillman was a constant friend in the court of labor who could cushion the blows of unwelcome policy decisions such as the administration's proposed labor draft in the Second World War. In the New Deal and the early war years, Hillman was a kind of auxiliary Secretary of Labor at the White House's beck and call on myriad problems. Indeed, Roosevelt seems to have seriously considered making Hillman his Labor Secretary at several junctures, but was dissuaded by Mrs. Roosevelt, who did not like having her old friend, Secretary Frances Perkins, the only woman in the cabinet, superseded.[22]

With John L. Lewis, the leonine, bushy-browed master of ornate rhetoric, Franklin Roosevelt's relations were unceasingly tempestuous. Lewis, like Roosevelt, loved power and position; when they met, giants clashed. A stickler for the amenities for himself and his office, Roosevelt was offended by Lewis' spiny arrogance. The President, who had a large talent for noncommittal generalities, would be brought up short when Lewis would stop him in mid-sentence to ask, "Well, will it be yes or no?" Roosevelt was also distressed by Lewis' occasional crudity in exploiting his White House access. Soon after Section 7a of the National Industrial Recovery Act (a provision designed to encourage union organization) went into effect, for example, Lewis' United Mine Workers organizers raced through the coal fields shouting, "The President wants you to join the Union." This unseemly and wholly unauthorized use of the Presidential office put Roosevelt squarely on the spot. Politically, he could not disavow the organizers' activity but could only writhe in private anguish. By 1936 Lewis was referring to Roosevelt as "my man." Roosevelt conveyed his own estimate of the labor leader in an interview with Max Lerner. "You know, Max," said the President, "this is really a great country. The framework of democracy is so strong and so elastic that it can get along and absorb both a Huey Long and a John L. Lewis." Lewis, when he heard the remark, growled, "The statement is incomplete. It should also include 'and Franklin Delano Roosevelt.' " [23]

In 1940 the fragile Roosevelt-Lewis connection was snapped by the coming of the war and Roosevelt's third-term candidacy. During a White House visit in January 1940, according to Frances Perkins (whose report of the interview was corroborated by Philip Murray, a later CIO president, and denied by Lewis), the United Mine Workers chief made a startling proposal. He suggested to the President that he, Lewis, should run for Vice President of the United States on the third-term ticket. A strong labor man, Lewis argued, would ensure full labor support plus the support of all the liberals who, he added pointedly, would be a little troubled by the constitutional irregularity of a third term. [24]

The rebuff of Lewis' Vice-Presidential aspirations launched a train of bizarre events that widened the chasm between himself and the President from miles to oceans. After weeks of intensive wooing by the camp of Wendell Willkie, the Republican Presidential candidate, Lewis abandoned Roosevelt. "He is not an aristocrat," Lewis said, endorsing Willkie in a labor-oriented statement, "He has the common touch. He was born to the friar and not to the purple. He has worked with his hands, and has known the pangs of hunger." In a radio address Lewis urged the workers of America to vote against Roosevelt. In a flourish that left his fellow labor leaders gasping with disbelief, Lewis declared he would consider Roosevelt's reelection a vote of no confidence in himself and would thereupon resign from his CIO presidency. The labor rank and file, forced to choose between Roosevelt, beloved as their President, and Lewis, their adulated leader, chose Roosevelt at the polls. Honoring his threat, Lewis resigned from the CIO leadership. [25]

Differences cropping up between John Kennedy and the unions were handled with scrupulously quiet decorum. Kennedy in his 1960 race and Johnson in 1964 received invaluable help from labor. In the great Northern industrial states, where Johnson's party ties were weakest, union officials pitched in to get out the electorate, both for registration and for the election. Later in the din of criticism of his policies in the Vietnam War, Johnson enjoyed the comfort of publicly spoken approval by George Meany, president of the AFL-CIO, and by David Dubinsky, who declared that the President "deserves the support of the American people and of liberty-loving people everywhere for his vision, determination and vigor in such a crucial period." [26] On occasion, Johnson called upon labor to support the administration's key projects on Capitol Hill, such as his 1967 effort for increases in social security benefits. The President's plea was conveyed in a filmed message to thousands attending social security rallies sponsored by the AFL-CIO in major cities.

Although George Meany labored mightily to keep Richard Nixon out of the White House, the AFL-CIO leader, a doughty pragmatist beneath his gruff exterior, scrupulously preserved his White House connection, developed in the previous Democratic administrations. Access to the White House had long been a dynamic element in Meany's own power in the labor movement. And he gratifyingly found in Nixon a sharer of valued sentiments. As long-standing anti-Communists, both were united on the Vietnam War, and both were antipathetic to long-haired war protesters. Meany was further propelled into Nixon's embrace by the necessity of softening the President for future ample wage settlements that would have adverse inflationary effects and by his growing view that the Democratic party was disintegrating, with "extremists" taking over, ejecting good labor men from their accustomed places of influence, and causing union workers to look outside the party for acceptable candidates.[27]

Nixon was responsive, at least in symbolic ways. He quickly let it be known that Meany, and Meany alone, was the only true voice of labor. Even more, Nixon accorded what Democratic Presidents had never granted, a celebration of Labor Day 1970 at the White House for labor leaders and their wives, and a fiesta on the White House lawn for scores of lesser lights among the guests. Thereafter, the Nixon-Meany relation went down hill. Many of the President's emerging policies sparked Meany's opposition. He and the AFL-CIO lobbied the Senate against the Supreme Court nominations of Clement Haynsworth and G. Harrold Carswell, grumbling that the President went shopping for his Court choices on a dark night with Senator Strom Thurmond of South Carolina as his guide. For Meany, Nixon's price and wage controls were "Robin Hood in reverse," robbing the "poor to give to the rich." [28]

Even in this atmosphere of growing recrimination, Nixon and Meany were useful to each other. The 1972 campaign was approaching, and throughout his lengthy career as a campaigner Nixon thrived most when he had a foe to excoriate. Meany, thanks to these recent fracases, suddenly qualified as a new Nixon villain, a target for blame if the prevailing wage-price control schemes failed. But Meany also profited from his altercations with the President. He had chosen an issue—Presidential discrimination against the working man—on which the badly divided ranks of labor could unite, on which the huge unions that had left the AFL-CIO—the Teamsters and United Auto Workers—could join hands and, what counted most for Meany, line up behind him as chief gladiator for all of labor on this vital issue. A construction union official voiced the welcome sentiment: "Nobody but George Meany has had the guts to stand up to Nixon." [29]

Consistent with the recent Presidential pattern, Gerald Ford's relations with organized labor began on a high note, even though in his quarter century in Congress Ford's average of "right" votes on the AFL-CIO scorecard was a wretched .148. Meany was an early White House visitor, who counseled the President on how best to combat inflation and unemployment, and organized labor played a premier part in Ford's 1974 summit conference on the economy. Meany and other union leaders welcomed Ford's early announced aversion to wage and price controls and endeavored to nudge the President a step or two away from his selection of inflation as the nation's top economic problem. Union leaders stressed the need to check growing unemployment by stimulating economic activity. They were critical of the President's antiinflation policies—such as monetary restraints, high interest rates, and federal budget cutting of social programs beneficial to labor. The leaders contended that Ford's policies would worsen the developing recession and expand the intolerably high jobless rate. Ford responded by promising to make more funds available for public service employment.[30]

The affability reigning between Ford and Meany was reinforced by the President's selection of Nelson Rockefeller for the Vice Presidency; Rockefeller was also Meany's number-one choice. As Governor of New York, Rockefeller had exceeded the pharaohs of Egypt in his lavish public building programs, and among the prime beneficiaries were the construction unions, including the plumbers from whose ranks Meany had sprung to leadership of the AFL-CIO.

How Presidents Are Useful to Labor

Twentieth-century Presidents, particularly those of Democratic vintage, perform various functions to further labor's interests. Since 1933 all Presidents, Republican and Democratic alike, have promoted new legislation beneficial to labor. The removal of obstacles to the effective exertion of labor's economic power, the increase of labor's legal rights, and the enlargement of the government's welfare services are areas of legislation that vitally interest labor. Since labor legislation ordinarily is not passed without a long and impassioned struggle, a President proposing it sets the agenda not merely of his own administration, but often of future administrations. In 1905 Theodore Roosevelt proposed that Congress "regulate" the "procedure" for granting labor injunctions. Not until twenty-seven years after his initiative, in the Norris–La Guardia Act of 1932, did Congress finally do it.

Although most of the laws promoting labor's fundamental interests were enacted in Franklin Roosevelt's administration, and he of all Presidents is the most revered in the labor community, the truth of the matter is that Roosevelt was not an eager champion of labor's causes, but a reluctant hero. In the enactment of each of the three basic labor laws of his administration—Section 7a of the National Industrial Recovery Act, the Wagner Act of 1935, and the Fair Labor Standards Act of 1938—his participation was cautious and halfhearted. Section 7a was included in the National Industrial Recovery Act not because Roosevelt rushed to put it in, but because John L. Lewis insisted on it. Roosevelt's principal involvement in the NIRA's preparation was to order the industrialists and labor leaders who drafted individual bills to "get into a room and weave it all together.'' In the ensuing Congressional phase of the NIRA, Lewis was fearful that 7a, blessed with little Presidential support, might be dropped, so he entered into an intrigue with a labor-minded White House assistant. Lewis would write to the President, and the compliant assistant, who drafted Franklin Roosevelt's reply, would slip in a dash of exhortation for 7a. The tampering, according to Lewis, passed unnoticed. With the letter in hand, the labor leader spread the word among fence-sitting legislators that Roosevelt really wanted 7a.[31]

Roosevelt's commitment to the Wagner, or national labor relations, bill, which enhanced labor's right to organize and obliged employers to engage in collective bargaining, was also mild. In 1934, indeed, a Presidential decision had sidetracked the Wagner bill. Senator Robert Wagner was encouraged to reintroduce his measure the following year, not by the President, but by the labor movement. Franklin Roosevelt, to Wagner's dismay, despite expressions of mild approval the year before, now took a hands-off attitude. Even in the bill's late stages, Secretary of Commerce Daniel Roper was predicting a Presidential veto. After the bill had passed the House, and just before the Senate's final action, Roosevelt convened a White House conference where Senator Wagner and Donald R. Richberg, the administration's labor adviser who opposed the bill, debated its merits at the President's invitation. Midway in the discussion, Roosevelt, whose position still was unknown, finally made clear that he wanted the bill. On the fair labor standards bill of 1938, Roosevelt likewise engaged in belated, feet-dragging decision. It was not the President or his administration, but Sidney Hillman, the CIO vice president, who rallied the labor bloc of legislators and worked out the minimum wage of twenty-five cents an hour in a hard-wrought compromise with the Southern Democrats. Roosevelt, ever skeptical of the bill's chances, gave help only when its success was assured and political prudence required that he quickly identify himself with it.[32]

Why was Roosevelt so chronically reserved and reluctant? For one thing, born into comfortable gentility, he had no firsthand understanding of labor problems. Instinctively and intellectually he sympathized with labor's objectives, but he had little grasp of its needs and feelings. On setting the priorities of his administration, he gave labor's objectives a secondary place. In the depression years of 1934 and 1935 and in the recession of 1938 his primary interest was economic recovery. Time and again he seems to have been impressed by the argument that production might climb faster in the depression-bound economy if labor decisions could be postponed until business was on its feet again. Labor's most drastic weapon, the strike, sometimes annoyed him, especially when it obstructed his own political and economic purposes. In the main, he envisioned himself not as labor's champion but as a balancer and adjuster between labor and management in which he approached both sides with a good measure of judicious detachment.

In the post–Franklin D. Roosevelt era the fate and substance of labor legislation have varied strikingly between the Republican Eisenhower and Nixon Presidencies and the Democratic Presidencies of Harry Truman, John Kennedy, and Lyndon Johnson. Eisenhower's personal preference for state rather than federal action and his apparent lack of philosophical sympathy with labor's aims wrought results considerably below labor's aspirations. Kennedy, in contrast, stressed national action in labor matters, pushed through legislation for depressed areas, which Eisenhower had vetoed, and the $1.25 minimum wage, which Eisenhower had resisted. Kennedy also won liberalizing amendments to the Social Security Act that increased minimum benefits and lowered the eligibility age. He won legislation extending unemployment compensation for up to thirteen additional weeks and giving special benefits to the children of the unemployed.

Despite the frequent acrimony of their relations and labor's revulsion at Nixon's wage-price policies, Nixon and the AFL-CIO were united on various legislative enterprises that produced greater employment and fatter paychecks. Labor was an unfaltering friend of the full-blown national security budget. In the President's determined, but unavailing fight for the SST, the unions, which had much at stake, led the intensive lobbying on Capitol Hill. Their efforts were equally unstinting for another bread-and-butter program, the Rail Passenger Service Act of 1970, which created a semipublic corporation to operate a nationwide railway passenger system.[33] Nixon's social policies synchronized with the fears and predilections of the blue-collar worker. The President's deploring pronouncements on crime, on welfare recipients and the work ethic, on long-haired youth and antiwar demonstrations, articulated the workers' deeper resentments. With perfect ideological ease, Nixon could indulge in the gesture of entertaining hardhats in the White House and donning a hard hat himself to affirm the bonds between them.

But while Nixon played artfully on the harp of labor's fears, he pursued economic policies that devastated the workingman's bread-and-butter interests. Following his 1972 reelection, he abruptly terminated price controls, a move that unleashed record-breaking inflation, while wages increased only modestly. His tight credit and monetary policies fostered steadily climbing unemployment and sharply curtailed new housing construction and the tempo of other industries vital to labor. While Nixon fraternized with hardhats, he simultaneously cut their jobs from under them.

Since the days of Franklin D. Roosevelt, labor has expected Presidents, particularly Democratic Presidents, to resist legislation hostile to its interests. The noisiest and most politically profitable instance of Presidential jousting in labor's behalf was Harry S. Truman's veto of the Taft-Hartley bill of 1947. An omnibus measure that was passed in the wake of a large upsurge in strikes, Taft-Hartley aimed to equalize employer-employee responsibilities by regulating union organization and practices. After polling the Democratic National Committee and the state Democratic chairmen and vice chairmen for advice, Truman delivered a fiery veto that was overridden by the Republican-controlled Congress. For Truman, the defeat was merely the beginning of a long, implacable, politically rewarding crusade. In the 1948 Presidential campaign and after, he lost no opportunity to identify the legislation with Republican conservatism, though a majority of the Democrats in both houses had voted for it.

From Truman's day on, Democratic Presidents have been expected to put their shoulder to the wheel to bring about the repeal of the most objectionable features of the Taft-Hartley Act. Faithful to this political custom, Lyndon Johnson, following the 1964 election, urged Congress to repeal Section 14b of the act, which allows states to pass laws banning the union shop. Johnson was able to compress his enthusiasm to the point that his recommendation required merely a single sentence in a lengthy message touching on many subjects. In taking this step, Johnson paid his principal political debt to organized labor for its considerable help in his 1964 campaign. Johnson's recommendation, however, proved fruitless; repeal of Section 14b was killed by a Senate filibuster in 1965, a year when the President was fashioning brilliant successes on Capitol Hill. The contrast between the President's general success and his failure to bring off labor's most cherished purpose prompted some union leaders to grumble that repeal could have been obtained if the President and Senate Democratic leaders had worked a little harder.[34]

The President may bring labor into his official family by appointing as his Secretary of Labor a figure from the organized labor movement. Woodrow Wilson inaugurated the practice when he made William B. Wilson of the United Mine Workers his Secretary of Labor in 1913. The precedent was renewed not by his Democratic successors Roosevelt and Truman but by the Republican Eisenhower, who named Martin Durkin, president of the plumbers' union, Secretary of Labor. Likewise, Nixon appointed Peter J. Brennan, president of the Building and Construction Trades Council of Greater New York, as Secretary of Labor. Kennedy's first Secretary of Labor, Arthur Goldberg, general counsel to the United Steel Workers' Union, did not, like Durkin and Brennan, hail from the workers' ranks, but from labor's growing professional wing. In appointing a nonlabor man as Labor Secretary, a contemporary President will make a selection that is inoffensive to the labor movement.

Since the 1930s the great bulk of leaders of organized labor have made a clear and absolute choice in Presidential politics by casting their lot with Democratic candidates and opposing the Republicans. The single aberration was the Presidential election of 1972, in which Meany and most labor chieftains tacitly supported the Republican nominee, Richard Nixon. After that election, the AFL-CIO acted to assure that its voice would be heeded in the Democratic Presidential nomination of 1976. A successful initial move was launched that terminated Jean Westwood as Democratic national chairwoman, and her replacement, Robert S. Strauss, was installed by an intraparty coalition, of which the AFL-CIO was a leading member.[35]

When a Republican occupies the White House, labor constitutes a major opposition force second only to the Democratic party. If the Democratic party is divided and dominated by moderates and conservatives, as it was in Eisenhower's first term, organized labor "plays a role of *the* major loyal opposition within American politics," as James Tracy Crown has put it.[36] In the Nixon era, on the supreme bread-and-butter issue of wage and price policies, George Meany and the AFL-CIO ranked foremost among the administration's critics. No one attacked the President with more barbed vehemence than Meany. "This fight between Meany and the President," an AFL-CIO official observed, "should stiffen the back of Congress. Now the Democrats on the Hill will have to take sides." [37] Nonetheless, the strongest institutional supporter in American society of the Vietnam War was the AFL-CIO. When Nixon launched his controversial 1970 incursion into Cambodia, one of the earliest voices raised in his support, above the cacophony of criticism, was George Meany's.

From Franklin D. Roosevelt onward until George McGovern's nomination in 1972, labor has played a central part in selecting Democratic candidates for the Presidency. Indeed, no Democratic candidate during that time was named without its approval. There was truth in Kennedy's jest when he acknowledged in a speech to the 1961 AFL-CIO convention that he was "one whose work and continuity of employment has depended in part upon the union movement."

Labor has displayed an almost equal interest in the selection of Democratic Vice Presidential candidates. In the fateful selection of Harry S. Truman for the Vice Presidency in 1944, labor had at least as great a part as the incumbent President, Franklin Roosevelt. The latter's frail health, a fact well known to the labor leaders, lent urgency to their task. Roosevelt himself contributed only confusion by recommending no less than four candidates for the Vice Presidency. Robert E. Hannegan, Franklin Roosevelt's representative embarking for the Chicago convention, beseeched his chief for instructions on the Vice Presidential question. Before making a final selection, Roosevelt was heard to say Hannegan and his aides must first "clear it with Sidney" (Sidney Hillman), the CIO vice president. The union leaders, after rejecting James M. Byrnes and expressing indifference toward Henry Wallace, the incumbent Vice President, settled upon Truman. "Clear it with Sidney" quickly took its place in the national lexicon and raised a drumfire of conservative indignation. Cried Westbrook Pegler, "How came this nontoiling sedentary conspirator who never held American office or worked in the Democratic organization to give orders to the Democrats of the United States!" [38]

Also since Franklin Roosevelt's day, Democratic Presidential campaigns have counted heavily upon labor's contributions of funds and legwork. "The election of John F. Kennedy is Labor's number one job," proclaimed George Meany in 1960.[39] Union halls across the nation were turned into Kennedy campaign centers, and union registration drives in the cities were indispensable to his success. Franklin D. Roosevelt cemented labor and the Democratic Presidency into close bond in the embittered election of 1936, when he courted the aid of AFL and CIO leaders. They responded lavishly in the conviction that for labor's fortunes and future everything turned on Roosevelt's reelection.

Sidney Hillman made it plain that labor expected something of a *quid pro quo* in a telegram to Franklin Roosevelt after his union pledged its financial backing. "Labor anticipates your support," Hillman wired bluntly, "for decent labor legislation . . . the guarantee of the right to organize and the enactment of minimum labor standards." Roosevelt in a letter to "Dear Sidney" expressed gratitude and blithely ignored the suggestion of a bargain, saying merely that Amalgamated's action had given him "new strength and courage." Following the electoral victory, when Lewis began growling that Roosevelt had better start reciprocating, the labor leader expressed impatience with those who were shocked by his temerity in demanding a dividend on labor's investment. "Is anyone fool enough to believe, for one instant," asked Lewis, "that we gave this money to Roosevelt because we were spellbound by his voice?" [40]

The Lewis-Hillman technique of direct financial contributions was banned by law in 1943 and again by the Taft-Hartley Act in 1947, which also prohibits direct union expenditures for candidates for public office. Similar restrictions apply to business corporations. Both unions and corporations freely circumvent the laws, however, sometimes with Presidential acquiescence, if not encouragement.

Labor-Management Disputes

Twentieth-century Presidents have regularly become entangled in labor-management disputes over union recognition, collective bargaining, and bread-and-butter issues of wages, hours, and general working conditions. The President's participation ranges from leadership in labor-management negotiations—personally or through deputies—to the seizure of struck properties and the use of the military to maintain law and order. In his earliest interventions in labor-management disputes, the President used military force under acts of Congress of 1792, 1795, and 1807 to enforce national laws in local disorders and to guard the states against domestic violence as guaranteed in Article IV, section 4, of the Constitution. In the 1877 railroad strike that affected ten states, Rutherford B. Hayes furnished state authorities with arms from national arsenals and, as Commander-in-Chief, transferred troops from remote posts to the scenes of trouble. In the Pullman strike of 1894, President Cleveland, against Governor Altgeld's strenuous protests, dispatched troops to Chicago to protect United States property and "to remove obstructions to the United States mails." The Supreme Court upheld Cleveland in *In re Debs* (158 U.S. 564).

Theodore Roosevelt reversed the Presidency's promanagement tendencies in resolving the anthracite coal strike in 1902, the largest work stoppage up to that time. The severity of approaching winter, the popularity of the miners' cause, and the anthracite industry's membership in a close-knit trust drew Roosevelt actively into the crisis. He ordered his commissioner of labor to investigate the strike and make recommendations, which furnished the basis of a compromise solution that Roosevelt proposed to the operators and miners. When the operators rejected it, Secretary of War Elihu Root rushed to New York to confer with J. P. Morgan, and together they drafted an agreement to submit the dispute to an arbitration commission. The imperious Morgan pressed the agreement upon George Baer, president of the Reading Railroad Company and the operators' chief negotiator. Morgan's achievement approaches the awesome, for Baer had sprouted a bad case of self-righteous intransigence. "The rights and interests of the laboring man," he maintained, "will be protected and cared for not by the labor agitators, but by the Christian men to whom God in his infinite wisdom has given the control of the property interests of the country, and upon the successful management of which so much depends." [41]

Acting on the Root-Morgan agreement, Roosevelt appointed an arbitration commission. To assure that the award would not go too decidedly against the miners, Roosevelt took pains to include a cleric and a union official, the latter filling the place designated for an "eminent sociologist." The commission's findings were made and accepted by both sides, and the strike ended. It remains a landmark of Presidential innovation in labor policy. For the first time in a labor dispute, representatives of both capital and labor were called to the White House, where Presidential influence induced a negotiated settlement. For the first time, both sides promised to accept the decision of a Presidentially appointed arbitration board. If the board had failed, Roosevelt, in an equally innovative step, was prepared to "put in" the army to "dispossess the operators and run the mines as a receiver."

Franklin D. Roosevelt clung to his preference for keeping out of specific labor-management disputes even in the most ruinous confrontation of his time, the sit-down strikes of 1936. Both the sprawling General Motors organization, the focus of the strikes, and the CIO pressured Roosevelt to intervene. His personal political interest was to end the conflict quickly without becoming involved in the specifics of its settlement—a purpose calling for fine maneuver. At one juncture Roosevelt called the CIO leaders to the White House and asked them bluntly to "get the men out of the G.M. plants." John L. Lewis would only promise that the men would leave "when the company begins to bargain with them or even with me, in good faith." To balance the scales, Franklin Roosevelt publicly spanked Alfred Sloan, the General Motors president, for breaking off negotiations. In a characteristic tactic, Roosevelt forced negotiations to proceed at lesser levels of authority—between the disputants themselves and through the good offices of the Conciliation Service and Governor Frank Murphy of Michigan, where the strikes were heaviest. Roosevelt viewed the Presidency as a supreme arbiter, to be held jealously in reserve and used only as a last resort. Ultimately, Roosevelt brought General Motors to begin what it had never done before—negotiation with union representatives and the CIO to end the strikes. [42]

In the Second World War strikes were few, thanks largely to Roosevelt's and Truman's insistence that labor-management disputes must not hamper war production. When strikes erupted in vital war industries, both Presidents seized and operated the struck industries. In the Truman era of postwar reconversion, with labor meaning to hold its wartime gains, strikes soared. A corporation-wide General Motors strike, national steel and railroad stoppages, the CIO Electrical Workers strikes against General Electric, General Motors, and Westinghouse, and several coal strikes hobbled the economy and blanketed the nation's cities with "dim-outs" and "brown-outs." The embattled Truman resorted to fact-finding boards, and his principal assistant, John R. Steelman, was not for nothing plucked from the directorship of the U.S. Conciliation Service. Much of Steelman's time was devoted to White House conferences with the disputants in key labor-management impasses.

Dwight Eisenhower and John Kennedy both avoided Truman's personal involvement in labor-management disputes. Truman's successors have benefited from increasing labor-management stability and by labor's marked shift in tactical emphasis from the strike to the bargaining table. In contrast to Truman, Eisenhower and Kennedy had no Steelmans, but kept labor-management issues largely locked up in the Labor Department.

Under pressure of the Vietnam War, President Johnson moved strongly to avert strikes in vital industries. He invoked the emergency provisions of the Taft-Hartley Act, which establish an eighty-day "cooling off" period for strikes affecting the national interest. He brought Congress to pass special legislation to prevent a national railroad strike and masterminded and participated in the negotiation of contracts between management and labor in vital industries. In 1965 Johnson, with the scrupulous attention he would give to a foreign policy crisis, watched over contract negotiations between the steel industry and the steelworkers' union. After special mediators failed to resolve the parties' differences, the President summoned the negotiators to Washington and in the cabinet room quietly exhorted them on the necessity of avoiding a strike for the sake of the national interest; he pointed out that a strike would harm troop morale in Vietnam and comfort the nation's enemies, asked that negotiations continue in the Executive Office building next door, and kept in close touch with their progress. After several days of futile meetings, he stepped up the pressure—"this is not a ladies' game you're playing over here and I think the time has come to do more." Acknowledging that each negotiator had a constituency to keep faith with, the President added, "Mine, I think, is a little larger—190 million people." He asked both the industry negotiator and the union negotiator "to go 51 percent of the way" to "wrap this up." As days passed without agreement, Johnson told his aides that the late Sam Rayburn had once told him that the most important thing in politics, as in poker, was knowing when to "put the stack in." Convinced that such a time was at hand, Johnson instructed his aides to give the negotiators specific suggestions for resolving the remaining issues. The aides feared that both sides might be hostile, but Johnson's instinct proved sound, and an agreement soon emerged. As a negotiator, Johnson correctly assumed that administration suggestions that split the labor-management differences nearly down the middle would be acceptable because they enabled both sides to back off gracefully from firm bargaining positions.

Despite Johnson's sparkling success, the President's personal intervention in labor-management disputes has certain drawbacks. The knowledge that the President is available through ultimate appeal may prompt the parties, particularly labor, to treat less seriously the earlier stages of negotiations. The President, in intervening, also takes substantial risks. If the parties do not agree, after his best efforts, his prestige and influence suffer damage, which can wilt his effectiveness in other interventions. He cannot intervene too much, or his efforts shrink in value. He can intervene successfully only if he can exert sufficient pressures, and these in turn depend upon the presence of a genuine national danger if a work stoppage occurs in the industry involved.

Like his predecessors, Nixon, too, personally intervened in critical labor disputes. His other major sortie into the labor-management arena consisted of recommendations for stronger legislative machinery to forestall transportation strikes. Nixon proposed that both sides in a transportation dispute agree to a final settlement before a strike begins. A special panel would choose the last, best offer of either management or labor and require both sides to abide by the decision. Nixon's proposals, if enacted, would have constituted the only major changes in the nearly half-century-old Railway Labor Act and the more than quarter-century-old Taft-Hartley Act. The long-standing record of legislative passivity was a monument to labor's political prowess, which did not fail in this new threat. Any passion Nixon may have generated for labor-management reform was exceeded by his political passion to entice and keep the vote of the workingman in the Republican fold. Not long after making the proposal, the President withdrew his support.[43]

In the Nixon-Ford era, the principal regulator of labor-management disputes was the high-inflation, high-unemployment economy, which undermined labor's capacity to bargain and strike. "What's the point of striking," asked a union leader early in the Ford Presidency, "if you lose a month's pay to get more money that isn't worth anything when you get it?" [44]

The Future Presidency

Both democracy and the objective of a strong but safe Presidency are advanced if business and labor serve as constraints on the Chief Executive, as constituencies whose understanding and support must be solicited and whose veto can block Presidential excesses. But he in turn merits, and needs, strong powers over them to assert public interest against their narrower, selfish interests and to protect those of weaker economic power—the poor, the unorganized worker, the consumer, the local community.

1. The ideal of a Presidency functioning in an environment of politico-economic pluralism and asserting the general interest is threatened when the Presidency and business become allied for nondemocratic ends. The lavish contributions of the petroleum industry to Nixon's 1972 campaign, although to a degree extorted by the Presidential staff, brought the richest payoffs to the industry in the form of soaring prices and profits that commenced in the 1974 "energy crisis" and went unchecked by significant public regulation. In what was anything but a democratic scenario, these boons to the oil interests were aided by a Presidential veto of legislation confining the industry's profits.

2. The ability of the strong Presidency to function simultaneously as a democracy-serving Presidency has depended, historically, upon the Chief Executive's capacity to use his powers to improve the distribution of economic bene-

fits by assisting the less powerful groups in the economy in their struggle for more power. Thus Franklin Roosevelt used and enhanced Presidential powers over the economy by speeding the growth of the organized labor movement, with a consequent improvement in the distribution of income.

For later Presidents, unions do not offer similar democracy-serving opportunities. Structural changes in the economy, the shift in the national job pattern toward more white-collar workers, and the absence of the organizing spirit of the 1930s and 1940s all contribute to making union memberships static or declining. Unions have become an elitist component of the economy, with less than a fourth of the work force unionized. Their doors are opened only a crack to racial minorities, and the incomes and hourly wages of union workers are far above those of nonunion workers.[45] The impaired utility of organized labor to the President as an avenue to the economic betterment of the general body of citizens may require the President to rely more heavily upon racial and national groups and to direct his appeal more pointedly to consumer interest.

3. As long as the vital processes of collective bargaining are adequately safeguarded, the President might be given increased, although carefully limited, authority to intervene in disputes that might create a national emergency. The President might be provided more possibilities of action than he now enjoys under the Taft-Hartley and Railway Labor Acts. If the President's alternatives are increased, both labor and management will be uncertain that he will intervene at all, and if he does, what he will do. Presidential intervention will be taken less for granted than it is now. If Presidential authority were used sparingly, it would hold to a minimum strikes that are deemed emergency-creating, and genuine collective bargaining would be best preserved.

4. The President will gain strength and will function in accord with democratic means if he regards his economic policies as enterprises in consensus building. He and his aides can use the conference method more widely to spread information and to help form opinion as, for example, among industry and union leaders and consumer representatives on issues of price and wage stability. Power can be more safely entrusted to the President if the full diversion of interested groups are consulted and participate in policy development. Since business and organized labor have ample records of placing self-interest above the public good, the President needs to forge communication ties with groups that can provide critical assessments of axe-grindings by the economic giants. The likely articulators of concepts approximating the public good include Common Cause, the Ralph Nader organization, and various environmental and consumer groups. Since, generally, these groups express middle-class perspectives and values, the President ought to extend his consultations to the lower classes and to others inadequately represented by established groups—to the poor and the unorganized worker. The future President must devise means to make their voices heard in the framing of national economic policies, which have so much effect, often for the worse, upon their lives.

12

SOCIAL JUSTICE

Presidents face a struggle that they can neither direct nor control—a struggle that goes on in our society, as in any other society, between those who have wealth and power and are loath to share them and those who do not have wealth and power and seek to get them. The advantaged want to hold to their privileged position and the disadvantaged to improve their condition. A dynamic democracy makes no lasting arbitration between the contestants, and their conflict is an enduring feature of politics. The President, as the principal elective officer of American democratic society, has made no enduring and unqualified commitment to either the advantaged or the disadvantaged. Particular Chief Executives have been heavily committed to one of the sides; others have remained largely indifferent or have been distracted by other problems of their administration. Nineteenth-century Presidents were uneven and chiefly negative in their attention to social justice; in the twentieth century unevenness still prevails, but positive actions have become far more numerous and more forceful. Yet if one thing is clear, it is that the President can effect no lasting accommodation that will bring the struggle for wealth and power to a close. Its endurance and the likelihood that it will move on to new phases and intensities provide some of the more formidable facts of the President's political life.

Social justice and its policies are addressed to sensitive problems whose complexity is aggravated by a political system of dispersed power. So dependent is the President upon sources in society and the political system, each highly autonomous and self-assertive, that what he loftily promises in electoral campaigns, he cannot accomplish through the resources of the Presidency. Nor can social problems be resolved merely by sweeping legislation. A President dared declare war on poverty, with Congressional sanction and support, but poverty remains little diminished as a national blight.

Many factors contribute to Presidential frustration. Because the individual human being comprises almost infinitely varied combinations of needs, talents, perceptions, and lacks even the most elementary self-sufficiency, because he is vulnerable to disease, accident, and age, to prejudice and embitterment, to the free-wheeling self-interest of exploiters, the task of responding to the problems that the individual creates or is a victim of poses great risk of error and inadequacy and eludes neat, systematically calculated solutions. In dealing with social problems and social justice, the President is one among many participants. Most of the time he shares power with Congressmen mindful of the imminent test of reelection, bureaucrats with iron-clad tenure, and delivery systems with a high probability of faulty performance. Contemporary Presidents are well aware that lapses in social policy and implementation are distinctly less well tolerated than inadequacies of military equipment and space gadgetry. Any contemporary President suffers the added pressure of responding to social problems with reduced reaction times and decision time-frames. In the age of television and a better educated citizenry, the President conducts social policy under the blare and glare of relentless criticism by interest-group leaders and militants who can skillfully generate and escalate dissatisfactions and force the President's priorities, timing, and decision.[1]

Social justice has a dimension beyond social rights and social welfare. It includes the civil liberties of the individual and their protection against encroachments by government. In this sense government is conceived of not simply as the promoter of social justice but as the perpetrator of social or individual injustice. Government and the individual are linked in a basic tension that Lincoln expressed in his message to Congress about the newborn Civil War on July 4, 1861: "Must a government of necessity be too *strong* for the liberties of its own people, or too *weak* to maintain its own existence?" In the deepest sense, Lincoln was expressing a fundamental problem of democratic society—finding the proper balance between the individual's liberty to live his life as he will and government's authority to protect and enhance the welfare of its people.

A Historical View

Except for an occasional landmark development, like Andrew Jackson's emergence as a rallying point for the rights and welfare of the common man and Lincoln's Emancipation Proclamation, which commenced a lengthy, erratic reversal of injustices suffered by a massive class, the nineteenth century was not an era of notable advance for social justice. As the century wore on, the country was engrossed in its own development, wealth dominated commonwealth, the ethics of business was the ethics of politics, and the President, most of the time, was little more than a titular leader.

If the history of social justice possesses turning points, one indeed is the ascent of Theodore Roosevelt to the Presidency. The talents and instincts of that extraordinary man and the climactic momentum of forces that had gathered great speed in the final decades of the nineteenth century combined to produce an epoch of Presidential social achievement. The forces were many and diverse. The two great groups most injured by big industrialism—agriculture and labor—were well astir. The first President to wage large-scale war upon economic abuse, Roosevelt viewed his office as a "bully pulpit." Endowed with moral fervor and oratorical gifts, he awakened Congress and the people to the urgency of reform. The curbing of railroad rate discriminations, the pure food and meat inspection laws, the brassy warfare upon the trusts, and the federal employers' liability act typify his trail-blazing achievements. Certain of his proposals were so far-reaching that they were not adopted until the distant day of the New Deal.

Theodore Roosevelt was spurred by his own large capacity for social initiative and moral fervor and the play of forces about him. Progressive sentiment was at a crest. If social reform tends to come when economic power becomes too concentrated too fast, when disparities between wealth and poverty become too glaring, the times indeed were right. Huge corporate profits and the lack of graduated income or inheritance taxes had created at the economy's apex a set of fabulously wealthy people.

Woodrow Wilson could hardly have gained his New Freedom's social and economic reforms without the thunderous schooling of the Democratic party in progressivism by William Jennings Bryan in his three races for the Presidency. Wilson also prospered from the progressive's infiltration of Middle Western Republicanism. A majority of both Democratic and Republican opinion demanded tariff, tax, and currency reforms; increased federal aid to farmers, workers, and other disadvantaged groups; and national controls over banking and industry. Wilson did not have to create a progressive public outlook in 1913; it was already there. He came to power at a time when social reform was in its ascendancy and the elections of 1912, with their overwhelming progressive sentiment, produced a President's dream of opportunity. With good working majorities in both houses of Congress, Wilson swept through a bulging social program. But the closer the United States drew to involvement in the First World War, the more strenuously Wilson campaigned to ease tensions between government and business. He cut back his antitrust prosecutions as a first step and petted the business community with soothing deeds and honeyed words of confidence. War or threat of it smothers the ardor for reform.

Franklin Roosevelt, more than any other Democratic President, identified his party with social and economic reform and with the desires of major disadvantaged groups, such as labor and blacks, to better their position. The New Deal, like the "deals" of other reforming Presidents, implied that in the game of life a beneficent superintending government can deal out a better playing hand to the great mass than can the unregulated market place of society. In the breadth and number of its innovations, the New Deal stands at the head of the list. Relief for the jobless, insurance against unemployment, pensions for the aged, help for labor to organize, aid to the farmer, protection for blacks against discrimination in employment, regulation of securities and the stock exchanges, the Tennessee Valley Authority—the list is lengthy. The depths of the Great Depression provided Roosevelt with a magnificent opportunity to act. Social justice, paradoxically, advances most in times of misery.

Like other reform Presidents before him, Roosevelt had his most productive period in the first half of his first term, marked by the election of a new President and Congress, both Democratic. With the coming of the Second World War his revelation that old "Dr. New Deal" was henceforth superseded by new "Dr. Win-the-War" signaled the primacy of military victory and a shut-down on social legislation for the duration. Restraints upon civil liberties again took over, although on the whole the Justice Department functioned with commendable moderation. The wartime administration's worst offense to civil liberty was the relocation of the persons of Japanese descent residing in West Coast areas at the war's outset.

The post-Roosevelt administrations have undertaken, in varying degree, extensions and adaptations of the New Deal. Truman's Fair Deal ventured further into civil rights, championed a vast program of national health measures, and gave social justice an international dimension through his Point Four program by making "the benefits of our . . . industrial progress" available to "underdeveloped areas." The Eisenhower administration brought off the largest extension of social security coverage since the law was first established. Eisenhower trod cautiously on civil rights, preferring to leave responsibility to the states and the private citizen. Yet his administration also witnessed the passage of the first civil rights laws since the post–Civil War era.

John Kennedy's New Frontier program in the 1960 campaign was a large-scale program of social services and reforms pointedly addressed to the great urban groups. Kennedy's narrow popular victory, however, and his lack of a "working majority" in Congress led him to lower his sights. Lyndon Johnson's Great Society program would have made William Jennings Bryan, the Roosevelts, and other stalwarts of social justice beam with pride as he succeeded in putting on the statute books measures long struggled for in American political life and as he took on new goals that earlier Presidents would never have dared to entertain. The Great Society program aimed to erase poverty and the inequities that afflict the underprivileged. Johnson sought to make blacks equal partners with whites in American society. In its further dimensions, the Great Society program offered something to everybody, privileged and underprivileged, by waging intensive drives against disease, crime, and ugliness. The beautification of the nation through the development of national park areas, the elimination of billboards and junkyards from highways, the reduction of pollution in air and water, and the encouragement of the arts and humanities promised a better life for all and testified to a basic working principle of the Great Society that maintained that social justice is indeed for everyone. In the same vein, Johnson took up causes beneficial to the consumer—and everyone is a consumer—by promoting higher safety standards in automobile production, the control of pesticides, truth in lending, and the like. A host of evils that Americans have endured beyond memory were marked for extinction in the Great Society. But the drain of the Vietnam War and modest appropriations relegated the Great Society program more to the realm of promise than to here-and-now fulfillment.

In contrast to the full plate of social policy initiatives of the Johnson era, Nixon offered consolidation and digestion of his predecessor's fare, and prescriptions for reform of faltering administrative machinery: a revamped welfare system to provide a guaranteed income to poor families, an overhauled poverty program, a revenue-sharing plan devolving many social programs to the states, cost-of-living adjustments in Social Security, elimination of the military draft, and a quantity of lesser reorganizations and reforms. To hold down social expenditures, Nixon freely vetoed appropriations and impounded funds. But when elections neared, whether Presidential or Congressional, Nixon invariably displayed more tolerance of social measures. With his own election test awaiting in 1972, and with unemployment at unacceptable levels, Nixon proclaimed a "new American Revolution," whose components included his newly proposed national health program, environmental and antipollution measures, enhanced consumer protection, and more vigorous advocacy of his welfare reform and revenue-sharing. Typically, after an election, Nixon's ardor for social policy evaporated, and he reverted to his tactics of curtailment. The chief exception, subsequent to his massive 1972 victory, was his national health insurance program, which, despite some national governmental participation, depended chiefly upon private financing and management. Significantly, Nixon did not advance his program until Senator Edward Kennedy (D-Mass.) offered a more ambitious plan.

Nixon's sudden departure from the Presidency left something of an unfinished agenda of social policy for his successor, Gerald Ford. Welfare reform, which Nixon began advocating in 1969, was passed by the House but rejected by the Senate in 1972. In his 1974 State of the Union message, Nixon again urged welfare reform through direct cash assistance for those with low incomes.

In the early Ford Presidency, HEW Secretary Caspar W. Weinberger developed a welfare reform plan more comprehensive than Nixon's, but like the former President's, it was patterned after the "negative income tax," or "guaranteed annual income." Weinberger's proposal would terminate food stamps and such programs as Aid to Families with Dependent Children, in lieu of which a jobless family of four would receive $3,600 a year. To provide a "work incentive," the plan would permit the family to earn money, with half the earnings deducted from the basic benefit. Critics of the HEW plan contended that the level of support was too low and that needy families stood to gain more from the mélange of established programs.[2]

Despite a conservative voting record in Congress, Ford as President proved receptive to social policies. He supported the Housing Act of 1974, the first omnibus housing and community development legislation to be enacted since 1968.[3] Ford also backed long-term mass transit legislation, but it became stuck in the House Rules Committee in 1974, and the President's efforts to pry it loose were less than strenuous.[4] After opposing, in his later Congressional days, the Equal Rights Amendment, which proposed to ban sex discrimination based on governmental action, Ford as President rallied behind the amendment and approved legislation prohibiting corporations from denying credit to women on the basis of sex.[5] Ford also urged the passage of a national health insurance plan, as Congressional committees and leaders vied over rival proposals.[6] In these and other gestures in behalf of social betterment, Ford acted without the manipulative bravado of the Roosevelts or the moral fervor of Wilson. His contribution was uniformly low-key.

The Ford Presidency was the first to bear the heavy brunt of the energy crisis, with its plain message that the supply of petroleum and other nonrenewable resources, once believed to be almost infinite, was diminishing rapidly. An economy accustomed to full and free opportunities for growth was rapidly approaching confrontation with the necessity to adjust to an increasingly energy-short and commodity-short world. To whom and in what proportions should the burdens of adjustment be distributed? Should not the President be an arbiter of such questions, the dispenser of equity and justice in the distribution of burdens and sacrifices?

According to history, the Presidency faces a choice between two roads. It can tend toward democratic pluralism, toward concern and responsiveness to a broad variety of Americans—to the consumer as well as the corporation, to the powerless as well as the powerful. The other road is elitist, or high Presidential acquiescence to the interests of the great aggregations of economic power—to the gigantic petroleum companies, the automobile industry, and other huge energy producers and users—while treating indifferently the consumer, the poor, the small enterprise, the local community.

In its early responses to the energy crisis, the Ford Presidency displayed disquieting signs of an elitist rather than a pluralist preference. For example, John C. Sawhill was forced by the President to resign as Federal Energy Administrator. Though a defender of oil company profits as necessary to finance investment and future energy supplies, Sawhill was an ardent champion of energy conservation as a means of diminishing American dependence on imported oil and of lessening the pressure for environmentally costly development of shale oil and exploitation of the outer continental shelf. His resignation evoked expressions of regret from the Consumer Federation of America and Friends of the Earth, an environmental organization.[7] President Ford veered toward the elitist tendency when he initially nominated as Sawhill's successor Andrew E. Gibson, an oil executive, whose name was withdrawn after disclosures of a million-dollar severance agreement with his company, and the eventual appointee, Frank G. Zarb, a Wall Street management specialist.[8]

Growing commodity shortages, as the 1974 World Food Conference in Rome revealed, inject the President into a new set of dilemmas concerning social justice. If, for example, many elderly Americans are living on dog and cat food while in Bangladesh starvation is rampant, to which constituency should the President give priority in regulating the distribution of limited agricultural supplies? Should national security policy, in which food is a factor, be subordinated to international humanitarian purposes? At the Rome conference, officials of other nations and Democratic Senators who were members of the American delegation urged President Ford to declare that American humanitarian food aid would be doubled in the approaching year. But the President declined, and explanations of his decision cited tight supplies, budget constraints, and an adverse impact on American consumer prices, which were already badly inflated.[9]

The President as Social Critic

Social reform depends upon more than a set of special circumstances; it also requires the vital ingredient of the man—the President. Without his talent and involvement, circumstances, however favorable, will be wasted. If circumstances are not advantageous, we may well wonder whether a President endowed with conviction and creative gifts can bring off major achievement in the face of limited opportunity. Those Presidents who have wrought the greatest social achievements—the two Roosevelts and Woodrow Wilson—were all endowed with certain personal qualities. However much they differed otherwise, each possessed a strong sense of right, a confident faith in man's capacity for progress, and an aristocratic heritage of *noblesse oblige*. Wilson, the Calvinist, *knew* what was right and faced public questions with bristling faith in his predestined ability to find righteous solutions with God's help. "Talking to Wilson," Clemenceau once remarked, "is like talking to Jesus Christ." [10] Theodore Roosevelt, morally, was rather different. He had a strict sense of personal morality that he followed impeccably in private life and held others to in public life. In pursuing public or political ends, however, Theodore Roosevelt often forgot his moral code in choosing means. Gifford Pinchot once told Roosevelt that he had to be either a great politician or a great moral teacher; he couldn't be both. But as historian John M. Blum has pointed out, Theodore Roosevelt had to be, and he was, both. [11]

The Roosevelts and Wilson were all, in their way, aristocrats—Wilson by dint of his Calvinistic faith; the Roosevelts by birth and fortune. They were men apart from the usual run of aristocrats who evidence no particular sense of responsibility for others. The Roosevelts each bore a hard vein of benevolent paternalism; Theodore Roosevelt often articulated his conviction that superior station meant superior responsibilities to the less fortunate and to the state. Wilson was inspired by the ideal of service as man's highest endeavor. By grace of their aristocratic condition, all three Presidents enjoyed detachment from the existing economic order. Neither their material sustenance nor their moral tenets depended upon it. They were free to be its critics. Franklin Roosevelt's limited experience in business—he dabbled briefly in law and insurance—his lack of understanding of the importance of making a profit, Frances Perkins, his Secretary of Labor, deemed all to the good. "It gave him freedom to think," she was convinced, "in fields in which common people need their leaders to think." [12]

All three Presidents were cosmopolitan, endowed with a sturdy intelligence and curiosity to seek out new and provocative ideas. They were not rigid and inflexible in their sympathies and associations, as aristocrats tend to be, but were eager to know the world about them and excelled as assimilators of ideas. They represented, in a word, the aristocratic tradition at its best. No modern President has brought to the office a more enterprising or cosmopolitan intelligence than did Theodore Roosevelt. At the age of forty-three, when he assumed the Presidency, his far-ranging interests had established him as a naturalist, a discoverer of rivers, and a prolific author. Scientists, labor leaders, corporation executives, and religious chieftains numbered among his friends, and for them, as indeed for anyone of distinction, the welcome mat was always out. The White House calling lists in Theodore Roosevelt's day read like an occupational encyclopedia.

Woodrow Wilson began his gubernatorial candidacy as a spokesman of Democratic conservatism, which was the viewpoint of his sponsor, boss James Smith, Jr. Quickly learning the issues that were agitating the people, Wilson displayed his capacity for assimilation by cutting loose from the Smith machine and supporting the reforms that progressives of both parties had been pressing for a decade.

Franklin D. Roosevelt was also a great assimilator. "He was easy of access to many types of mind," Frances Perkins noted. The roots of his social philosophy, nourished by many sources, reached far back into his life. "One who is trying to discover the economic origins of New Deal," Rexford G. Tugwell has written, "cannot ignore the Harvard class of 1903." [13] There Franklin Roosevelt took in W. Z. Ripley's strictures on corporate finance and the lectures of O. M. W. Sprague, a future New Deal adviser, on the merits of central banking and credit control as devices for economic stability. Certainly one of his foremost teachers in the elements of social justice was Eleanor Roosevelt. Observant and reportorial, especially after his illness, Mrs. Roosevelt excelled at bringing to her husband persons expert and stimulating in social subjects. Among Mrs. Roosevelt's importations were Rose Schneiderman and Maude Schwartz of the Women's Trade Union League, who subtly tutored Roosevelt in the mission of trade unionism. He habitually preferred to assimilate background from conversations rather than from books. "I doubt," acknowledged Frances Perkins, "that he had ever read any of the standard works on trade unionism." It was during his Albany days that Roosevelt, with the encouragement and guidance of his counsel, Samuel I. Rosenman, founded his brain trust of Raymond Moley, Tugwell, Adolf Berle, and other Columbia professors. In gubernatorial seminars with his university friends, Roosevelt, as Tugwell put it, was brought "to grapple with the complex realities of industrial life, and to move beyond his oversimple reactions which were insufficient as guides to policy." [14]

Wilson and the Roosevelts all had a faith in man's capacity for progress and in government's ability to help achieve it. All had a vision of Presidential leadership that was positive and assertive. They discovered what the people wanted or needed and rallied them with great gifts of oratory. Social justice requires in large degree the passage of legislation, and all three possessed a dynamic philosophy of the Presidential role as legislative leader and a sturdy knack of success. Indeed, they exploited the full legal and political potentialities of the Presidential keyboard. "I believe in a strong executive," Theodore Roosevelt exclaimed, "I believe in power." [15] To this Wilson and Franklin Roosevelt would add a firm amen.

Richard Nixon too was a social critic, though of a different stripe and working in a different historical milieu. Like his predecessors, he addressed his campaign appeals and social policies to a massive constituency, which he defined as wronged and aggrieved by the prevailing dispensations of politics. Both Roosevelt and Nixon, this is to say, perceived social justice in terms of "the forgotten man" or "the forgotten people." Roosevelt's "forgotten man" of the 1930s was unemployed, incapable of providing his family with the basics of food and shelter, a wretchedness that afflicted the permanent poor and the far more numerous members of the middle class whose generally satisfying life had been crushed by the cataclysm of unemployment. Roosevelt and his Democratic successors diligently fashioned policies to erase the deprivations of these "forgotten people."

From his 1968 campaign onward, Nixon also appealed to "forgotten people," and paradoxically, many who responded to his call had earlier harkened to Roosevelt's summons and had faithfully voted for Democratic standard-bearers for decades. In the 1970s, many of Roosevelt's forgotten people became Nixon's forgotten people. By the 1970s their fortunes had changed, seemingly for the better. They were employed at comfortable wage scales, they had acquired property, assisted by the welfare state and a planned economy, and had moved from the decaying, tumultuous cities to the suburbs. But they did not, in their new world, find total happiness. As homeowners, they abhorred rising taxes and viewed distastefully the militant blacks and poor whites left behind in the cities. The new middle class, beneficiaries of earlier social programs, resented the racial unrest and rising crime rates, the result, they were convinced, of permissive social programs that their hard-earned tax dollars were paying for.[16] Just as Roosevelt, a generation earlier, defined "the forgotten people" to embrace a majority of the electorate, so Nixon confidently delineated his constituency as a majority. His two election victories and research on trends in electorate opinion confirmed his perceptions. Those who are deprived, according to the several economic and social criteria of poverty and unemployment, are no longer a majority as they were in Roosevelt's day. Instead, "the new American majority," as Nixon termed it, was composed of "unpoor and unblack," "middle-aged, middle-class, middle-minded." [17]

The Limitations of Politics

The President's political necessities take priority over ventures in social justice. No matter how lofty the cause or how intense the Chief Executive's dedication, he obeys a higher law of political survival. He must win the next election and carry on his coattails his fellow party candidates on national and local tickets. One day Franklin Roosevelt, pressed by the impatient idealism of several youthful aides, discoursed on the realities of the political world in which he and they worked. Roosevelt began,

> You know, the first thing a President has to do in order to put through good legislation? He has to get elected! If I were now back on the porch at Hyde Park as a

private citizen, there is very little I could do about any of the things that I have worked on. So don't throw away votes by rushing the gun—unless there is some good sound reason. You have to get the votes first—then you can do the good work.[18]

The subordination of ideology to politics means that even those Presidents whose achievements of social justice are monumental often make their way by a course that is bafflingly erratic. Their social undertakings evolve according to no master plan but piecemeal, with quick, and not too costly, visible results preferred. The President's course is full of half-steps, forward and backward, covered with smoke clouds of obfuscation.

Like any other political leader, the President can at most push his ideas only a little beyond the tolerance of his constituents. As Tugwell has written, he must balance "the risk of alienating support against his conviction about what must be done and his desire to put it into practice." [19] Franklin Roosevelt thus had to find a broad base of support and gain the specific consent of powerful groups he had to work with: labor, national and racial groups, and the like. He had to impress upon them that no matter what happened, he cherished their interests at heart. Yet he also had to carry a Congressional majority. He could not alienate articulate groups such as business, the press, the lobbyists, or vote-rich groups like the several immigrant bodies and the Catholic Church. Or, more precisely, he could not alienate enough of them at once to bring real trouble.

No President of the United States has been or is ever likely to be a social zealot. The political system which selects him for the great office precludes it. To win election, he must cast the net of his promises wide; the more he can offer to more people of diverse economic interests, geographic sections, and national and racial groups, the more likely he is to triumph. The balancing effect of promise upon promise keeps the President from extremes. Indeed, the political system sifts so finely that it has invariably produced Presidents who are "safe" not merely in public utterance but in personal conviction. Franklin Roosevelt was altogether accurate in speaking of himself as "a little left of center," despite his opponents' fierce characterizations of him as a "socialist" and a "Bolshevik." Theodore Roosevelt likewise was a safe man. He is well described by George E. Mowry as an orthodox heretic, a respectable agitator, an intellectual Philistine, and a conservative revolutionist.[20] "At times I feel an almost Greek horror of extremes," Theodore Roosevelt once said. He abhorred "the dull, purblind folly of the very rich men, their greed and arrogance." At the other extreme, he possessed an almost morbid fear of socialists and social violence. To Theodore Roosevelt, the Populist William Jennings Bryan and the Socialist Eugene Debs were the monstrous American replicas of Marat and Robespierre.[21] His own high and solemn function, as Roosevelt saw it, was to bring balance between the greedy rich and the violent poor.

Likewise, social justice politics imposes constraints on Presidents whose preferences carry them to the opposite side of the ideological street from the Roosevelts. Richard Nixon, despite his hearty subscription to his ideal that all Americans should work hard like Horatio Alger heroes and make their way in an economic market place asserted to be as pristine and free as in the days of Adam Smith, the President was constrained from indulging his preferences by a variety of regulators. For considerable time he was inhibited by his likely opponents in the 1972 elections. They and their public policy preferences determined his stand on social issues as much, if not more, than his convictions. Two potential Democratic rivals, Senators Edmund Muskie and Henry Jackson, became proponents of successful environmental legislation. To forestall their taking over this rising social issue, Nixon moved to identify himself with it. When Muskie proposed a single independent agency to administer environmental policies, Nixon countered by recommending a close variant, and when Muskie proposed to enhance the federal role in checking water pollution, Nixon men worked to enlarge the role of the states.[22]

Against another potential rival, Senator Edward Kennedy, who championed national health insurance, Nixon countered with a competing plan. His eventual 1972 opponent, Senator George McGovern, stressed the problem of hunger, and Nixon depicted his welfare reform proposals as its eradicator. Similarly, what Gerald Ford and future Presidents do for social justice will depend partly upon the assertions of their political competitors.

Among other regulators of Nixon's parsimonious ideals was the budget. Despite the President's fervid prayers for reduced outlays, the budget contained many items that, as inexorably as the tides, required steadily increasing expenditures—already legislated increases in Social Security benefits, caseload and unit cost increases under Medicare and Medicaid, and expanded outlays for pollution control and housing. Although Nixon sometimes sounded like Scrooge, he often followed the path of political practicality suggested by Daniel P. Moynihan, to "talk conservative and act liberal." Thus for fiscal 1974, Nixon's budget called for federal outlays of more than $21.7 billion for health purposes, the largest amount ever expended, nearly twice as much as the expenditure for fiscal 1969, when Nixon assumed office. His call for more state, local, and private action did not reduce national outlays; they were increased.

Congress too was a regulator. While Nixon tirelessly recommended curtailment of social policies, Congress increased his budgets substantially each year. The bureaucracy, wise in the ways of resisting Presidents, was another obstacle. Faithful to his commitment to abolish the Office of Economic Opportunity, Nixon appointed an administrator dedicated to that resolve—without the required confirmation by the Senate—to liquidate the agency. Instead, thanks to legal actions brought by OEO clienteles and employees, the incumbency of the administrator was declared illegal.[23] An undeterred Nixon continued the battle, and the warfare rolled on.

The President Keeps the Balance

In working for social justice, the President must strike a balance between that element least interested in its promotion—usually business—and those elements most devoted—once known as "progressives" and now as "liberals." He must shun extremists on both sides.

Despite the caution and balance of Presidents, their administrations tend to show a predominant concern either for the advantaged or for the disadvantaged. Since the Civil War Republican Presidents have been largely disposed to favor business and Democratic Presidents labor and blacks. The Republican party of Coolidge is the party of business; the Democratic party of Franklin Roosevelt is the party of the disadvantaged groups. Roosevelt remains enshrined in business's embittered memory. He and his two Democratic successors—Harry Truman and John Kennedy—were involved in severe altercations with business. Kennedy's outcry upon discovering the steel price rise of 1962, "My father always told me that all [steel] businessmen were sons of bitches," is memorable not only for its unbridled candor but as a display of viscera not uncommon among Democratic Presidents. Equally, it is unlikely that portraits of Richard Nixon, foe of school busing and stern commentator on welfare programs, will adorn the walls of the urban poor.

The President who aspires to do things for the disadvantaged ordinarily is regarded with suspicion and even with disapproval by the progressives or liberals whose reform convictions are more advanced than his. Tension regularly prevailed between Wilson and the advanced reformers. To them he loomed as a slippery rhetorician whose heart belonged to small businessmen and manufacturers. Advanced progressives gagged over his devotion to states' rights and his simple faith that regulated competition could solve the big business evil and bring to pass a fairer distribution of wealth. Inevitably, Wilson was compared to his disadvantage with such urban-Democratic reform mayors as Tom L. Johnson of Cleveland, an apostle of Henry George, and John Purroy Mitchel of New York City, who cleansed city hall of corrupting business influence, combatted urban squalor with enlightened social services, and brought mass transportation under public ownership. Franklin Roosevelt, in his day, was widely regarded by progressives as a chameleon who spurned progressivism in 1934 and embraced it in 1935. Roosevelt, who cherished acceptance by the progressives, courted their favor with mixed success. John Kennedy, in his turn, experienced a frequent questioning of his social course by a major political organization to the left of him, the Americans for Democratic Action. Lyndon Johnson, in the eyes of his social critics, readily escalated the war in Vietnam instead of escalating the war on the urban front.

The reform President also views uneasily the rare elements of the extremists who achieve major political strength. Franklin Roosevelt's adoption of a program of old age assistance was encouraged by the rise of the Townsend movement, named for Francis Everett Townsend, an unemployed physician who, looking out his bathroom window while shaving one morning, saw in an alley below, cluttered with rubbish barrels and garbage cans, "three haggard, very old women, stooped with great age, bending over the barrels, clawing into the contents." Angered by this indignity to his generation, Townsend launched a plan for old age pensions calling for two hundred dollars a month for everyone over sixty, a sum that in those deflated days seemed outrageous. Eventually other economic lures were embroidered onto the movement. By 1935 its membership and impact had mounted so that Raymond Moley was calling it "easily the outstanding political sensation as this year ends," and Edwin Witte was writing, "The battle against the Townsend Plan has been lost, I think, in pretty nearly every state west of the Mississippi, and the entire Middle Western area is likewise badly infected." [24] With the Townsend fever burning high, Franklin Roosevelt, moving with a decisiveness he never showed for unemployment compensation, directed that an old age insurance plan be incorporated into the social security bill.

Reform as Legislation

When the President's reform proposals require legislation, they must traverse a labyrinthian course filled with obstructions and quicksands. They must run the gauntlet of committee hearings and floor debates, parliamentary motions and conference committees, where a reversal at any time may be fatal. A common ordeal for Theodore Roosevelt was the predisposed negativism of both houses. In the Senate the "Big Four" Republican leaders, all intractable conservatives, ruled with a firm hand and a granitic hostility to change. In the House a tyrannical Speaker, "Uncle Joe" Cannon, held sway. Cannon controlled committee appointments and rules of procedure and acted as a crusty, unsleeping, self-appointed watchdog over the federal treasury. He greeted every proposal of social reform with the cry, "This country is a hell of a success." Cannon and the Big Four stacked the key committees with members whose conservative instincts, they knew, would prompt them to nip Theodore Roosevelt's measures in the bud.

SUPPORTIVE LEGISLATORS   By uncommon good fortune, a President may discover a legislator whose prestige, committee assignments, parliamentary skill, and ideological convictions all harmonize with executive necessities. By these criteria, Senator George Norris' service in the cause of Franklin Roosevelt's fond dream of a Tennessee Valley Authority was almost idyllic. Prestigious progressive and chairman of the Senate Agriculture Committee, Norris for years had pushed for public power development in the Tennessee region. In 1933 Franklin Roosevelt and Norris drove through the shabby, eroded countryside along the Tennessee River in the President's open touring car, happily devising plans for a millennium of cheap electric power, flood control, soil conservation, afforestation, diversified industry, retirement of marginal farm land, and general developmental planning. Norris hailed Roosevelt's message to Congress broadly delineating the bold new idea of TVA as "the most wonderful and far-reaching humanitarian document that has ever come from the White House." [25]

THE APPROPRIATION PROCESS   One of the more formidable hazards a social measure must survive is the appropriation process, hostilely manipulated by the foes of reform. But in the Nixon era, appropriations were a busy battleground between a Democratic Congress, more generously disposed toward social programs, and a Presidential administration that beheld them with a colder eye. A standard scenario ensued: Congress appropriated sums substantially beyond administration budgetary requests. Thus Nixon, during a peak of tolerance toward social programs, approved a $5.15 billion education appropriation that was $375 million above his original request. Although Nixon budgets provided for higher overall outlays, Congress pressed to raise them even higher. In his 1970 veto of the education appropriation, Nixon noted that his budget provided for a 28 percent increase in education spending and doubled spending for HUD's urban programs above the previous year. In all, Congress appropriated $453 million more than the President requested for education and $541 million more than his request for HUD. In part, the Nixon-Congress battles over appropriations were battles over national priorities. Typically, the Democratic Congress cut the President's military, foreign aid, and space requests, and added to domestic programs, especially health, education, manpower training, and pollution control. Ford's experiences with Democratic Congresses also followed this pattern.

OPPOSITION IN THE HOUSE   John Kennedy, in his key social proposals, was bedeviled by the delaying tactics of hostile legislative committees. His plan for medical care for the aged, presented within a month after his assumption of office, was bottled up in the House Ways and Means Committee for the duration of his Presidency. Although the Committee heard a long parade of witnesses on both sides of the issue in 1961, it failed to report out the bill and chalked up a major defeat for the administration. In 1962 and 1963 the committee placed the bill behind the President's tax proposals. Since the latter received interminable review, the bill for the aged remained immobile and, like many other languishing bills, magnificently reinforced the reputation of the committee chairman, Wilbur Mills, for cautious and unhurried deliberation.

President Johnson's smashing electoral victory of 1964 was accompanied by a gain in the House of Representatives of thirty-eight more Democratic members and a more liberal outlook, which was promptly reflected in the Ways and Means Committee. When the committee was reconstituted in 1965, with more seats allotted to the Democrats because of their increased strength and with its defeated and retired members replaced, a majority of the committee supported Medicare. Chairman Wilbur Mills dropped his opposition to the bill and became its leading supporter, producing a bill more far-reaching than the administration called for, swinging other Democrats into line, and expertly managing the bill on the floor. Mills's conversion from opposition to support is not attributed to an ideological awakening but to alterations in basic political mathematics. Had he supported Medicare prior to 1965, he would have been defeated both in his committee and in the House, a disastrous blow to prestige that few committee chairman are willing to suffer. By waiting until 1965, Mills became the field marshal of an historic victory.

SUCCESS IN THE SENATE   The Senate, which earlier in the twentieth century was known as a citadel of hostility to social legislation, has undergone something of a transformation well evident in John Kennedy's and Lyndon Johnson's experiences. Kennedy enjoyed conspicuously greater success in the Senate than in the House, where measures approved by the Senate were rejected or drastically revised. Kennedy's 1961 education program was approved in the Senate only to be rejected in the House. The Senate passed his depressed areas and minimum wage bills; the House severely amended them. Johnson, to whom appropriations were vital for the progress of his Great Society program, sustained in the House drastic cuts on nearly all his requests for funds for urban measures. In the more favorable climate of the Senate, he had to push for substantially larger appropriations to strengthen his hand in the later House-Senate conference negotiations that would settle upon a final amount.

Kennedy's and Johnson's greater successes in the upper chamber than in the House are largely explained by the mounting population shifts to the cities in recent decades. The Senator, answerable to a state-wide constituency, depends increasingly upon the great mass of urban voters for election, a happy coincidence for Kennedy's and Johnson's legislative programs, which were heavily directed to the cities. The Representative, in contrast, responds to a smaller, less complex constituency. At least two types of population groupings, the suburban and the rural, are ill-disposed toward such central city problems as welfare, urban renewal, and poverty. Recent Supreme Court decisions, advancing the ideal of "one American, one vote," have prompted increased legislative representation for the suburbs. In addition, population trends are running in favor of the suburbs. In the Nixon years, the relationship of the House and Senate to social legislation was the precise opposite of that in the Kennedy-Johnson era. Nixon's more conservative stance toward social policy, in which the central city has great stakes, found readier support in the House and opposition in the Senate.

COALITIONS   Social legislation in the contemporary era faces a hostile coalition that reaches back to the Franklin Roosevelt administration. In the Eisenhower administration Southern Democrats and conservative Republicans repeatedly played a decisive part in defeating or modifying social legislation for civil rights and medical care for the aged. The same coalition flourished in Kennedy's time. (As defined by the *Congressional Quarterly Weekly Report,* the coalition exists in a house when a majority of the voting Southern Democrats and a majority of the voting Republicans oppose the position of a majority of the Northern Democrats.) In what Kennedy styled as his "Big Five" programs of 1961—medical care for the aged, aid to education, aid for housing, a higher minimum wage, and aid to depressed areas—the only item on which the coalition did not operate in the House of Representatives was housing. The coalition's single absolute victory was on federal aid to education; the medical care bill, bottled in committee, did not come to a vote. In the Senate the coalition appeared in the voting on four bills: depressed areas, minimum wage, housing, and school aid. On none of these was the coalition victorious. Despite the coalition's eclipsed influence, Kennedy was consistently wary. He withheld civil rights legislation until late in his term, anxious not to alienate Southern Democrats either simply on civil rights or on other social proposals. For the cause of social justice, the real significance of the 1964 election was that it smashed the conservative coalition. Johnson responded swiftly by moving onto the statute books the three major measures long blocked by the coalition: civil rights, education, and Medicare. When the 1966 Congressional elections restored the conservative coalition to dominance in the House, Johnson responded to the change in political atmosphere by scaling down his requests for new social legislation. Kennedy's successes against the conservative coalition and Johnson's achievements after 1966 were vitally assisted by an offsetting bipartisan liberal coalition. Most of Kennedy's victories where opposition was strong were indebted to liberal Democratic and Republican support. The Nixon period was marked by general primacy of the conservative coalition in Congress—in 1971 it prevailed in 83 percent of the votes on which it appeared, compared with a previous high of 73 percent in 1968—and its positions on social questions were frequently compatible with the President's. They disagreed on only two votes.

When Nixon undertook positive initiatives in social policy rather different coalitions appeared than the customary straight-line liberal and conservative. Since Nixon typically provided morsels for both sides in his initiatives, the resulting coalitions were a hybrid of each. To liberals, for example, he tossed the bone of raising the stipend of the guaranteed income called for by his welfare reform plan from $1600 to $2400, and to conservatives who feared that the plan would enormously inflate welfare rolls, he stiffened the "workfare" provisions, in effect requiring most able-bodied welfare recipients to work and the antifraud regulations to deal with that arch-villain of welfare critics, the welfare cheater. (Actually, those on welfare seldom conform to this stereotype. Most welfare recipients are white, somewhat fewer are black, and most are working mothers. Other major categories of recipients include the blind, the disabled, and the elderly.) Nevertheless, welfare reform, after passing the House, fell becalmed in the Senate. Liberal Senators grumbled that the plan's benefit payments were too low and its requirement that welfare recipients work, if possible, too harsh, while conservatives lamented that the total plan was too costly. Nixon and his helpers endeavored to pick up additional support from both camps, to attract, by further concessions tacked on the legislation, more liberals and conservatives to the Nixon welfare banner. But these efforts failed.[26]

Behind the hybridized Congressional coalitions on the welfare issue was a motley array of seemingly incompatible interest groups, which once again proved that ageless truism that politics makes strange bedfellows. The potential pattern was delineated in Nixon's own rhetoric when he said, in behalf of his plan, "Let us be generous to those who can't work, without increasing the burden of those who do work," a double-think formulation, palatable to both liberals and conservatives. Working together for Nixon's welfare reform plan were such improbable allies, for example, as the National Association of Manufacturers and the National Welfare Rights Organization. Though their views on what the legislation should contain were highly divergent, they were united in resolve to overcome the Congressional inactivity that had becalmed the legislation previously. Despite agreement on general objectives, the allies divided on details. NWRO's insistence on $6,500 as the minimum annual income for the poor was anathema to NAM. Other allies had different axes of self-interest to grind. The AFL-CIO wanted a $1.60 minimum hourly wage for welfare recipients who worked, and the states, counties, and cities eagerly sought relief from their own rocketing welfare budgets.[27]

The Executive Branch

The executive branch, with its abundance of talent, data, and organizations, provides the President with vital resources of social reform. His success in social enterprises depends in no small way upon his skill in exploiting these resources, particularly his cache of human talent. Within the executive branch are various specialists whose common effort is required to transmute the President's reform agenda into reality.

Presidents resort to solitary advisers and to whole teams of them like Franklin Roosevelt's Brain Trust. John Kennedy, preparing for the Presidency, recruited task forces to study and report on foreign and domestic problems. Lyndon Johnson, faced with the urgency of urban problems, appointed in 1967 several commissions to develop recommendations in specific areas of federal concern. One commission, headed by the industrialist Edgar Kaiser, was assigned to prepare a plan to lower the cost of housing for the poor through less expensive and more efficient methods of construction and financing. Another commission, led by former Senator Paul Douglas, examined local zoning laws and building codes to see how they might be altered to speed construction of low-cost housing. Both Johnson and Nixon used task forces, composed largely of distinguished private citizens with relevant expertise, to develop proposals for a wide range of social matters. Ford, confronting demands for a new federal energy policy in light of worsening shortages, was supplied a massive tome by the Federal Energy Administration, a 762-page report, backed by 30 volumes, that the FEA contended, "will form the basis for energy policy decisions for years to come." [28]

Presidential advisers hail from all sorts of nooks and crannies of the executive branch and of society at large. Andrew Jackson's principal counselor in his war upon the Bank of the United States was Amos Kendall, fourth auditor of the Treasury. The President's adviser may be a general counselor whose attention to a social justice project is but one of a host of assignments. Edward House, whose main beat was foreign policy, worked mightily in the service of Woodrow Wilson to bring about the Federal Reserve System. House harried the nation's professors of economics for the cream of their theory and data and conferred with bankers of varying viewpoints on the issue. Or again, the President's chief adviser may be, as plain logic suggests, the cabinet Secretary whose department bears most closely upon the social reform at stake. Frances Perkins, Franklin Roosevelt's Secretary of Labor, for example, made the social security program her special cause. A social worker and New York Industrial Commissioner during Roosevelt's governorship, Miss Perkins, before accepting appointment to the national cabinet, had laid out a program, including unemployment and old age assistance, that she would insist upon if she came to Washington. Franklin Roosevelt promptly invited her to come along.

EXPERTS   Since projects of social justice are founded upon the conceptualizations and data of social science's several branches, experts and technicians play leading roles in Presidential ventures. The chief expert toiling for the creation of the Social Security Act in 1935 was Edwin E. Witte, executive director of the Cabinet Committee on Economic Security. With this lordly bureaucratic title, Witte oversaw numerous outside experts, a technical board of government experts, an advisory council, and a national conference. Prior to these responsibilities, Witte had served as secretary to progressive Congressman John M. Nelson, statistician and secretary to the Wisconsin Industrial Commission, and chief of the Wisconsin Legislative Reference Library. In the last capacity he drafted pioneering social legislation for which Wisconsin is distinguished. He taught at the state's university, served as acting director of the Wisconsin unemployment compensation law and studied social insurance methods in Europe.[29]

To launch his new Washington job, Witte made a month's grand tour of the American social security world, conferring with knowledgeable Washington officialdom, professors, mayors, state legislators, business executives, and social workers. "Very contradictory advice was given me by the people consulted," he noted, "but I still regard these conferences as having been distinctly worthwhile, as they served to rapidly acquaint me with the widely varying views entertained within the Administration circle and the difficulties to be overcome."[30] At the behest of Raymond Moley, then a leading Presidential adviser, Witte prepared a lengthy statement on the problems of economic security for inclusion in Franklin Roosevelt's scheduled speech at Green Bay, Wisconsin. Although only two of Witte's sentences were eventually used, their effect was electric. The stock market dropped five points. Appalled high Treasury Department officials sprang forth to demand that social security be soft-pedaled at once.

Witte's most trying task was to find and hire social security experts willing to subordinate their professional predilections to the necessities of the executive committee and the President. Working under severe time limitations set down by Roosevelt, Witte had to badger the specialists into putting aside their accustomed standards of perfection so their reports would be finished on schedule. Witte had to shepherd the executive committee's report, which emerged from the specialists' reports, through agonizing rounds of negotiations. Several committee members refused to sign the report without having every word in it and the accompanying draft legislation scrutinized by subordinates in whom they had absolute confidence. Witte's worst hours were spent in the Treasury where two groups opposed social security, one conservative, bent upon holding down expenditures and avoiding any stir that might alarm business, the other liberal, which felt that given the deep economic morass in which the country was wallowing the proposals had little value. Witte's ordeal was topped off with four days of testimony on the technical phases of social security before the House Ways and Means Committee and three days before the Senate Finance Committee. His experience illuminates a common fate of Presidential experts. Their talents are useful at both ends of Pennsylvania Avenue.

PROMOTERS   Social justice measures, taking the form of legislation, have touched off the most violent battles that Congress has witnessed. Among the most inflamed of these scenes was the Franklin Roosevelt administration's public utility bill, with its "death sentence" provision, designed to outlaw some of the grosser abuses of the holding companies of gas and electric utilities. To guide his cherished legislation through the pending strife, the President turned to a lieutenant with proven talent for the rough and tumble of legislative politics, Thomas G. Corcoran, a youthful, cherub-faced protégé of Felix Frankfurter and former law clerk of Oliver Wendell Holmes.[31]

Nominally a counsel of the Reconstruction Finance Corporation, Corcoran, with his partner in several New Deal enterprises, Benjamin V. Cohen, the counsel of the Power Policy Committee, had drafted the utilities bill they were now promoting. To touch off his campaign, Corcoran prepared a Presidential letter of fitting exhortation to accompany the bill to Capitol Hill. He provided full-time, all-around assistance to the bill's sponsors, Senator Burton K. Wheeler of Montana and Congressman Sam Rayburn of Texas. Corcoran and Cohen coached the sponsors and a parade of government witnesses on the bill's many intricacies. For Senators and Congressmen friendly to the bill, they ghostwrote letters addressed to legislative colleagues and influential constituents, entreating their support. Corcoran negotiated compromises on hostile amendments and frantically lobbied in cloakrooms and hallways, lining up votes. The juggernaut of influence that the utilities were wheeling through Congress lifted his effort to a high and steady pitch.

The President's youthful promoter was faring tolerably well until an explosion of ominous publicity was touched off by Congressman Ralph O. Brewster of Maine. At the height of battle, Brewster rose in the House to declare,

> During the consideration of the "death sentence" clause in the Holding Company bill, Thomas G. Corcoran, Esquire . . . came to me in the lobby of the Capitol and stated to me with what he termed "brutal frankness" that, if I should vote against the death sentence for public utility companies he would find it necessary to stop construction on the Passamaquoddy dam in my district.*

Promptly after Brewster's disclosure, Corcoran was faced with two inquiries. One, a cryptic request from Franklin Roosevelt, read "Please send me as promptly as possible a complete statement of all your dealings on governmental

---

* The dam was a huge work relief project established primarily to develop public power. "Quoddy," situated across from Campobello, Franklin Roosevelt's summer home, was a pet enterprise of the President.

matters'' with Congressman Brewster.[32] The second was a House committee investigation of the incident. Corcoran passed both tests with flying colors. In putting his case before the House committee, he had the advantage of a witness, a fellow official of the executive branch, while Brewster was handicapped by having no corroborator. Meantime the utility bill was passed.

ADMINISTRATORS   A victory won in social legislation can be lost in the selection of the administrative agency to carry it out. Since the President initiates the selection of the agency's leadership, he is sometimes the perpetrator of defeat. In reality, he may yield to conservative pressures. To the newly established Federal Reserve Board, Wilson appointed an array of leading bankers and businessmen, a stroke that put the progressive community into a state of shock. ''Why, it looks as if Mr. Vanderlip [president of the National City Bank of New York] has selected them,'' sputtered one dazed progressive. When Wilson, in a similar tactic, loaded the Interstate Commerce Commission with devoted friends of American railroads, Senator Robert La Follette exclaimed, ''What an inspiring spectacle to the millions who voted for Wilson as a true Progressive.''

The cabinet of Franklin Roosevelt was, in its majority sentiment, at least middle-of-the-road and even conservative toward social questions. The state of the cabinet partly reflects the mixed sentiment of the body politic itself regarding social reform and partly the unsettled attitude of the President. Roosevelt's original Budget director, Lewis Douglas, and his Secretary of State, Cordell Hull, were devoted to sound money, fiscal orthodoxy, and tariff reduction. Old-line progressivism was embodied in Harold Ickes, a Bull Mooser, and the preferability of government-business collaboration in Raymond Moley on the right and Rexford Tugwell, Assistant Secretary of Agriculture, on the left. These and other philosophical schools scored successes, although the predominant image that emerged was of social reform. It was part of Franklin Roosevelt's administrative genius that he encouraged his diverse administrators to ride and expand their own programs vigorously and never think of sparing him. ''Thus a very energetic set of people were stimulated by their leader to develop programs of reform and action,'' Frances Perkins noted.[33]

How Presidents Resist Social Programs

Richard Nixon, exponent of the work ethic and of parsimony and prudence in social expenditure, wielded a variety of executive swords to effectuate his beliefs. Particularly after his 1972 landslide reelection, Nixon moved to implement his ascetic philosophy—for the poor, that is, not for himself, the wealthy, or others with a taste and the wherewithal for luxurious living. ''We are going to shuck off,'' he declared, ''. . . and trim down those programs that have proved simply to be failures.'' Precisely what rational tests or measurements were to be applied to warrant a program's condemnation remained unclear. Head Start, a preschool compensatory education program designed to help slum children to overcome environmental disadvantages, was marked for extinction when a White House aide announced that "Head Start is clearly a failure. It is nothing but a babysitting service for welfare mothers." [34] A possible opposite judgment that Head Start was remarkable in achieving much in little time and at little cost was dismissed out of hand.

Reform and reorganization in the name of efficiency and economy became the order of the day for many social programs, a disguise behind which lurked drastic cut-backs and outright scuttling. Nixon's most sustained "reorganization" assault was on the Office of Economic Opportunity (OEO), nerve-center of Johnson's "war on poverty." From the premise that "when programs are ineffectively administered, those hurt most . . . are the poor," the President moved to detach two key OEO programs and assign them elsewhere, relegating Head Start to HEW and the Job Corps to the Labor Department. Both quickly shrank into mere shadows of their former selves. The other major reorganization device was revenue sharing, foundation of Nixon's New Federalism, which funneled federal funds to the states and localities and was aimed at building an expanded role for them in social programs, with a corresponding reduction of federal activity. The change from federal to state and local control, as Vernon E. Jordan, Jr., director of the National Urban League, noted, meant hardship for minority citizens whose needs, historically, have evoked far more response from national than from state and local governments. Black people, said Jordan, could not "rely on some magical mixture of local good will along with a heavy dose of individual initiative." In the national government, time and again, key social programs were handed over to conservative administrators, to whom they were anathema. HEW was entrusted to Caspar Weinberger, a conservative Californian, and, to head OEO and the poverty program, Nixon designated Howard Phillips, a founder of Young Americans for Freedom, a conservative student organization. Phillips' highest duty, in his own and Nixon's eyes, was to dismantle the agency.[35]

Finally, when Congress appropriated more funds than the President requested, which it often did, Nixon employed the veto, with uncommon latitude. He vetoed appropriations for entire social program departments—HEW, Labor, and HUD—and even for such popular, long-standing social measures as the Hill-Burton program for construction and modernization of hospitals and other medical facilities. Nixon's other favorite weapon was the impoundment of funds, also brandished on a scale hitherto unknown to Presidents. Thus Nixon cut $6 billion from pollution funds for the states; $400 million in a given year was withheld from the food stamp program. Big city mayors complained that cutbacks in urban programs were "placing an added burden on already beleaguered cities." [36]

Yet it is also impressive that the President time and again was checkmated or routed into retreat by other components of the democratic political system. His impoundment of funds withered after repeated court findings that they were illegal. Howard Phillips was deposed from OEO, again by court action, because his appointment, without Senate approval, was illegal. Some Nixon social vetoes were overridden and, characteristically, the President retreated from broadly stated and firmly asserted positions when opposing political forces gathered in strength.

Early Efforts for Civil Rights

Of all social justice fields, civil rights for blacks has evoked the most various and sometimes the most enterprising executive responses. It has also been frequently ignored by Presidents.

Despite the beacon light of Lincoln's Emancipation Proclamation, Presidents have dealt gingerly with black civil rights since his time. After Lincoln, Theodore Roosevelt was the first President to act assertively, at least by the standards of his day. He was attentive to Booker T. Washington, the eminent black educator. Early in his administration, Roosevelt appointed William Crum as customs collector in Charleston and Minnie Cox as postmistress in Indianola, Alabama. Both were blacks. Although Roosevelt's moves seemingly championed the black cause, they were not unalloyed. His eye was fixed upon the 1904 Presidential nomination and his considerable rival, Mark Hanna. The latter's awesome strength at past Presidential nominating conventions was founded importantly upon unswerving Southern delegations of "lily-white" Republicans. To counterweigh Hanna, Roosevelt had to enlist the "black and tan" Republicans, and for this high enterprise Booker T. Washington was his staff and reed.

Roosevelt's good progress was suddenly jeopardized by the Brownsville affair, when black soldiers, angered at their treatment by the local folk of Brownsville, Texas, made a shooting sortie into the town, killing a citizen. Efforts to lay responsibility for the slaying failed; the soldiers would not talk. Roosevelt, the Commander-in-Chief, conscious of his duty to maintain discipline, meted out punishment by discharging "without honor" every man of three black companies. Republican politicians, mindful of the traditional black vote for their party, grew fearful, and Roosevelt redoubled his attentions.

Although Woodrow Wilson appealed openly for black support in the 1912 elections, once in office he and his principal administrators quickly exhibited the predominant Southern background of his Presidency. Civil service workers were rigidly segregated in offices, shops, restrooms, and lunchrooms. Black political appointees, including those with civil service status, were widely dismissed. Herbert Hoover, despite his Quaker roots, evidenced little interest in the black's plight. He made, said W. E. B. Du Bois, "fewer first-class appointments of Negroes to office than any President since Andrew Jackson." [37] Franklin Roosevelt accomplished the awesome feat of transferring the blacks' traditional loyalty to the Republican party, which had been cemented by Lincoln, from that party to the Democrats. The New Deal was, by contrast to the barren Democratic past, rich in its dispensations to blacks. The National Industrial Recovery Act set a single standard for black and white wage earners in the

South. Relief funds, housing projects in the wake of slum clearance, rural resettlement, land-utilization schemes providing parks, picnic grounds, and beaches for blacks, and growing federal attention to education and health were a great boon to that race, which suffered more than any other part of the population in the depression. Harry Truman created a Commission on Civil Rights whose distinguished report, *To Secure These Rights,* charted a wide ground for future action. He accepted the 1948 Presidential nomination with a fiery speech, broadcasting his future call of Congress into special session to act on civil rights. Truman tarnished his promising record by never mentioning civil rights again in his ensuing campaign until a wind-up speech in New York's Harlem. Otherwise Truman moved to establish a permanent Fair Employment Practices Commission, fought the Senate filibuster by prodding Democratic leaders to bring about an amendment of the Senate rules, attacked racial discrimination, and backed the United Nations' Declaration of Human Rights. His strong stand on civil rights was diminished by the occasional fluctuating character of his support for legislative and administrative action and by off-the-record comments that he made on several occasions after his Presidency that were hardly in keeping with his administration's record.

Black civil rights first assumed crisis proportions, in the Presidential view, in the 1957 Little Rock school episode of the Eisenhower era and boiled over into the multiple crises of the Kennedy administration. The two Presidents differed radically in their views on civil rights, particularly on public school segregation. The several Supreme Court rulings of 1954 striking down segregated public schools as a violation of the Fourteenth Amendment's requirement of equal protection of the laws were followed by widespread resistance by state and local government to the point where activity in the South toward integration came almost to a halt. President Eisenhower made little effort through federal policy to support the Supreme Court holdings, leaving the question of compliance to voluntary action and local lawsuits. He intervened personally only after Governor Orval Faubus of Arkansas defied a federal court order and employed the National Guard to prevent black school children from attending the Little Rock Central High School. In addition, after withdrawing the guard, the governor failed to prevent a mob from blocking the black children's entry to the school. Eisenhower, stung by the governor's defiance, federalized the Arkansas National Guard and called out Regular Army units to enforce the court order and protect the black children. Eisenhower, nevertheless, refused to declare that he personally favored elimination of segregation from public schools, holding that policy on the question was the province of the Supreme Court and not the President. He sometimes remarked that race relations could not be effectively regulated by law but depended upon voluntary action.

John Kennedy and Civil Rights

John Kennedy, in contrast, became the first Chief Executive to place himself at the head of the black civil rights movement. He publicly asserted his support of the Supreme Court's rulings in the school segregation cases; enforced the enrollment of James Meredith at the University of Mississippi and of Vivian Malone and James Hood at the University of Alabama; quelled the raging strife in Birmingham, Albany, Jackson, and other cities, North and South; and quietly encouraged or at least failed to discourage the 1963 march on Washington. Kennedy was faced with social revolution and had to act. That it was congenial to his own nature to act made his stand more consistent and more forceful. In meeting the civil rights issue, whether in its more subdued stage earlier in his administration or in its later critical phase, Kennedy and his aides wielded, with skill and enterprise, a variety of executive tools.

LITIGATION   The 1957 Civil Rights Act authorizes the Justice Department to sue in federal courts or to seek injunctive relief where the right to vote is denied or threatened. Kennedy's Justice Department stepped up the tempo of school segregation cases and forged a major innovation by casting itself as plaintiff in the Prince Edward County, Virginia, case. When the city of Albany, Georgia, sought an injunction banning further black protest demonstrations in that city, the Justice Department filed a friend-of-the-court brief in opposition.

THE PRESIDENTIAL CONSTABULARY   The United States Code authorizes the President to suppress domestic violence stemming from unlawful assembly or a state's inability or unwillingness to protect a constitutional right. To keep order, the President is assisted by a tripartite constabulary: the Regular Army, the federalized National Guard, and the United States marshals. Thus James Meredith's presence and safety at the University of Mississippi depended, at least in its early season, upon units of the Regular Army and the federalized Mississippi National Guard. The busiest unit of the President's constabulary was the United States marshals, called upon to protect variously the freedom riders and demonstrators in Albany, Georgia. When a mob took over the bus station in Montgomery, Alabama, six hundred marshals moved in to fill the law enforcement vacuum.

THE GOVERNMENT CONTRACT   Presidents since Franklin Roosevelt have employed the government contract as a weapon to clear pathways for civil rights advances. The one hundred largest defense contractors and their subcontractors employ approximately ten million persons. Countless other workers are employed under federal contracts or aid. From Franklin Roosevelt onward, interdepartmental committees composed of the departments contracting most heavily have existed to overcome job discrimination by private employers performing government contracts. Congress's disinclination to establish a fair employment practices commission has made reliance upon the interdepartmental committees all the heavier. Through the committees, Presidents have insisted upon antidiscrimination provisos in government contracts, heeding their implied duty as executors of the Constitution, with its affirmation of equal rights, to see that federal money is not tainted with racial prejudice.

THE CIVIL SERVICE   The United States government, as the nation's largest employer, has its own house to put in order. Legal authority to do so is abundant. The 1883 Civil Service Act established merit as the primary test for federal employment, and from 1940 onward various statutes prohibit discrimination "on account of race, creed, or color." The President's official oath and responsibility as chief administrator impart further authority. The Kennedy administration's personnel policies put new stress upon the appointment and upgrading of qualified blacks. Complaint procedures concerning discrimination were liberalized and the Committee on Equal Employment Opportunity investigated agency compliance.

ADMINISTRATIVE REGULATION   The freedom riders' visitations in Southern territory spurred the Kennedy administration to petition the Interstate Commerce Commission to desegregate facilities in terminals providing interstate bus travel. After months of delay and insistent Justice Department pressure, the desegregation order was issued. The administration lacked power to move similarly upon airports under the Civil Aeronautics Act. To foster desegregation in various Southern airport facilities, the Justice Department relied upon court action and private persuasion.

FEDERAL FUNDS   The expenditure of federal funds is a Presidential weapon of vast potency in behalf of civil rights. Few aspects of American life are untouched by the incessant outpouring of federal money. In his 1960 campaign Kennedy flayed the Eisenhower administration for not blotting out racial discrimination in federally supported housing, holding it could be achieved merely by "a stroke of the pen." After long delay and much pressure by racial groups, the President finally issued an executive order on November 21, 1962, barring discrimination in the sale or rental of housing financed through federal assistance. The executive order's seeming breadth was badly sheared by administrative interpretation. "Conventional" or private financing, houses "already built," houses that were not in commercially developed neighborhoods, and FHA-insured loans for home improvements were ruled to be not covered.

Kennedy was insistently pressed to issue a blanket order prohibiting discrimination in all federal programs. Indeed in Kennedy's efforts to enroll James Meredith in the state university, the Civil Rights Commission urged that Mississippi be barred from all federal funds. "I don't have the power to cut off the aid in a general way as was proposed by the Civil Rights Commission," Kennedy responded, adding that "I think it would probably be unwise" to grant the President that power.[38]

PUBLIC APPEALS   In the major civil rights crises, Kennedy as a regular tactic made radio and television addresses, pleading and lecturing to the nation, stressing the moral aspects and local responsibilities. In the University of Alabama episode of 1963, Governor George C. Wallace stood in the doorway of a university building to prevent the registration of two black students, Vivian Malone and James Hood. Kennedy's public expressions included an appeal to

Wallace to stay away from the university campus. The governor's plan, the President said in a published telegram, was "the only announced threat to orderly compliance with the law." The students eventually embarked upon their studies with the help of the National Guard. In his television address on the Alabama episode, Kennedy termed the rising tide of black discontent "a moral crisis," which "faces us all in every city of the North as well as the South." The problem of the black's place in American life, the President declared, "must be solved in the homes of every American across the country." [39] Kennedy's public appeals were also put to specific local communities and their key citizens. [40]

PRIVATE PERSUASION   To head off brewing civil rights crises or to steady them at a low boiling point, President Kennedy, Attorney General Robert Kennedy, and their aides counted heavily upon the arts of private persuasion. President Kennedy met at the White House with whole delegations of Southern businessmen, theater owners, and newspaper editors to present the case for voluntary desegregation and warn of the danger that black extremists might gain power should the moderates fail. Cabinet Secretaries sometimes joined the effort. Secretary of Commerce Luther Hodges, a North Carolinian, wrote letters of encouragement to fellow Southerners; the Attorney General telephoned friendly and unfriendly local officials, encouraging, persuading, or scolding, as required. The Justice Department in private, unpublicized talks helped some Southern communities desegregate their schools without incident. That department also quieted several violent intervals in Birmingham by negotiating agreements between the contending groups; as tensions mounted in Jackson, Mississippi, in June 1963, a peace-building meeting took place in the local Masonic Lodge between John Doar, Assistant Attorney General for Civil Rights, and black representatives. In its discussions with white Southern leaders, the administration stiffened its language with appeals to party loyalty and used higher and lower forms of political inducement. The administration also engaged in dialogue with black civil rights leaders, including an intensive discussion in New York at the peak of the 1963 crisis when Robert Kennedy reviewed with the leaders both what they were seeking and what the administration could do.

Like other Presidents who, because of political restraints, could give social groups only a part of what they wanted, Kennedy sustained public criticism from black civil rights leaders. In the administration's first years, when it held back civil rights legislation and shunned a futile fight to throttle the Senate filibuster, NAACP secretary Roy Wilkins sadly declared that an "atmosphere of super-caution" had "pervaded" all civil rights discussions with Kennedy and his staff since Election Day. In a television interview in June 1963, amid the demonstrations crisis, the Reverend Martin Luther King, viewing the cheerless scene, conceded that President Kennedy "may have done a little more" than President Eisenhower, "but the plight of the vast majority of Negroes remains the same."

Lyndon Johnson and Civil Rights

Like John Kennedy, Lyndon Johnson employed the substantial armory of his executive powers to advance civil rights, including public appeals, the manipulation of federal funds, and litigation. He broke precedent by bringing distinguished black citizens onto the Supreme Court and into the cabinet by his appointments of Thurgood Marshall as a justice and of Robert Weaver as Secretary of Housing and Urban Development. Johnson also appointed Carl Rowan as director of the United States Information Agency. It was in the Johnson era that civil rights legislation pressed by Kennedy before his death became law in 1964, followed by the Voting Rights Act of 1965. In 1966 Johnson labored to bring Congress to enact open housing legislation, the first civil rights bill to affect the North. But the slipping popularity of the civil rights movement and widespread white Northern hostility assured the legislation's defeat. The more conservative make-up of Congress following the 1966 elections imperiled any major legislation. Johnson, nevertheless, managed to steer through Congress the modest Civil Rights Act of 1967, making it a federal crime for anyone to interfere with another's civil rights. And finally, in 1968, following the assassination of Dr. King, President Johnson secured passage of the long-awaited open housing bill.

The several civil rights laws more or less close the chapter of the Kennedy-Johnson struggle for legal freedom and equality for blacks. In a 1965 address at Howard University, President Johnson exhorted the nation to take up a new and loftier civil rights goal, "to give twenty million Negroes the same chance as every other American to learn and grow, to work and share in society, to develop their abilities—physical, mental and spiritual—and to pursue their individual happiness." [41] The President in effect was saying that the major strides in civil rights assured blacks only the "legal right" to vote, get a job, go to unsegregated schools, and enjoy due process of law, and provided them with only "separate but equal" citizenship. Yet these legal rights, however important, are little availing if the great body of black citizens are poorly educated, confined to ghettos, and condemned to a life of poverty. The President pleaded that the black be accepted as an equal. It is, he said, "not enough to open the gates of opportunity. All our citizens must have the ability to walk through the gates."

Richard Nixon and the Black Community

Nixon was the first contemporary President to be elected without significant black voter support. He also courted and drew heavy backing from such constituencies as white suburbanites, trade union hard-hats, and the South, all largely antipathetic to white-black equality. Although political incentive was presumably lacking for Nixon to respond to the black community, he had to govern as well as win elections, and that necessity, and the continued critical proportions of black social and economic problems forced Nixon, like all other contemporary Presidents, to put black needs on his agenda.

The centerpiece of Nixon's most positive assertions in behalf of black people was the "Philadelphia Plan," consisting of minority hiring guidelines for various skilled construction crafts working on federally assisted projects in Philadelphia. Potentially, the plan could diminish the long-standing imperviousness of white trade unions to black memberships, the ticket of admission to skilled jobs. If successful, the Philadelphia Plan could spread to other cities and to other facets of private enterprise. Unfortunately, the Philadelphia Plan soon foundered from resistance by union hard-hats, a constituency that Nixon assiduously and rewardingly courted. After three years of the plan, only 200 black and Spanish-speaking workers were employed as skilled construction workers in Philadelphia, against an original Labor Department forecast that about three thousand would be working.[42]

Nixon faltered in two leading areas of black concern. In housing, after nearly a year of hesitation, he announced in a lengthy statement that he would enforce existing laws against "racial discrimination" in housing nor use federal leverage to force localities to accept low and moderate income housing against their wishes. The President's disinclination evoked an outcry from black rights groups who believed that only a deliberate policy of dispersing low- and moderate-income housing to the suburbs could break up the growing concentration of blacks in inner cities.[43]

Nixon's other hammer blow on black rights fell upon school segregation. Making ingeniously narrow interpretations of his duties according to existing court decisions, the President announced his opposition to "any compulsory busing of pupils beyond normal geographic school zones for the purpose of achieving racial balance." When subsequently a unanimous Supreme Court ruled that school busing could be ordered to end "all vestiges of state-imposed segregation," Nixon restated his opposition to busing and ordered its use restricted "to the minimum required by law." In actuality, Nixon was responding to the preferences of his suburban constituency and the necessities of his Southern strategy. He was handsomely rewarded by both sectors with a flood-tide of votes in 1972.[44]

A Ford Is Not a Lincoln

Promptly upon becoming President, Gerald Ford moved to dispel the atmosphere of manipulative hostility that marked his predecessor's stance toward the black community. Within days he met with the Congressional Black Caucus, all Democrats, fifteen of whose sixteen members had voted against his confirmation as Vice President. Some of the Representatives felt that the meeting was more symbolic than substantive, though Ford, in the course of their exchanges, promised to designate his special assistant, Stanley Scott, a black, as an adviser on domestic affairs and as a liaison between the White House and blacks. Ford also agreed to reconsider his opposition to public service employment to help ease joblessness among minorities, and he declared that the military budget, whose primacy he had earlier affirmed, "was not sacrosanct." The latter assertion provided some reassurance that the President, who was bent on fighting inflation by cutting the budget, would not concentrate his cuts on social programs that were important to blacks.[45] Subsequently Ford met with black Republicans, explored ways to enlarge black participation in the party and in his administration, and assured them they "have a friend in the White House."[46]

Black leaders seemed to breathe a unanimous sigh of relief that Ford, rather than Nixon, was President, despite the new incumbent's bleak voting record in Congress on civil rights issues. Senator Lyndon Johnson had also assumed the Presidency with a similarly poor voting record, but as President his accomplishments ranked him with Lincoln, Roosevelt, and Kennedy in black esteem.[47]

This initial optimism was suddenly chilled by Ford's responses to the 1974 school busing crisis in Boston. Following a court order, black and white students were bused to achieve racial balance. Violence erupted and a lengthy crisis commenced. State police assisted Boston's police, and when Massachusetts Governor Francis W. Sargent requested the President to send federal troops into Boston, Ford declined, holding that the step should be taken only "as a last resort," and not until the Governor had used "the full resources of the state."[48] Acting more like his predecessor than as an initiator of improved relations with blacks, Ford, in commenting on the Boston situation, urged citizens "to respect the law" but added that busing for integration was "not the best solution to quality education in Boston." Mayor Kevin White, beset by turmoil, cried that the President's remarks "fanned the flames of resistance."[49]

Like Nixon, Ford was aligning the Presidency on the side of Northern resistance to school integration. In the 1970s, accomplishment in that vital area of black civil rights contrasted unfavorably with impressive gains in the South. HEW reported that the percentage of minority group pupils in schools with enrollments more than half black in 1972 was 53.7 percent for public schools in the eleven states of the old Confederacy. The comparable figure for Northern public schools was 71.7 percent.

The Nixon-Ford posture of resistance reflected political realities in many Northern communities. Local school boards were either timid or intransigent in refusing to obey the law in the Supreme Court's historic 1954 decision in *Brown* v. *The Board of Education of Topeka*. Housing patterns also contributed to school segregation by leaving black children trapped in inferior schools in urban centers and white children concentrated in the superior schools of the suburbs.[50]

Another contributing factor was bureaucratic timidity and indifference at the national level, in the chief federal enforcement agency, the Office of Civil

Rights of HEW. The agency, according to a study by the Center for National Policy Review, was failing to enforce the law against discrimination and, consequently, permitted federal aid money to flow freely to segregated schools. HEW investigations shunned the major Northern metropolitan areas and concentrated on smaller school districts where legal issues were less complicated and court challenges easier to win.[51]

Why has the South fared better than the North in school integration? Positive efforts commenced there earlier than in the North, spurred by the Presidential leadership of Kennedy and Johnson in the 1960s. Studies of the better Southern successes underscore the favorable public attitudes of school officials, local politicians, and business leaders. In Southern small towns and rural areas, where blacks and whites often live next to one another, segregated housing patterns do not exist to provide the basis of school segregation as they do in the North. The South's less successful efforts at educational integration occur in the larger cities, where segregated housing is more prevalent.[52]

In the Nixon-Ford era, bureaucratic foot-dragging in other sectors of civil rights slowed accomplishment. The U.S. Commission on Civil Rights, a watchdog of federal performance, found that executive agencies were lax in enforcing fair housing standards and freely permitted local officials to use zoning regulations, building codes, and highway construction to keep out or remove poor and minority group families from suburban areas.[53] The Commission also found that key federal regulatory agencies were failing to carry out their responsibilities under law to eliminate employment discrimination in the industries they regulate.[54] While in the 1960s Presidential leadership challenged bureaucratic lethargy, in the 1970s a becalmed Presidency merely reinforced it.

Poor Presidential performance has, to a modest degree, been counterbalanced by the sharp rise in black office-holding in the 1970s, a harvest from seed sown in the Kennedy-Johnson years. The 1974 elections produced black lieutenant governors in California and Colorado, the highest state offices ever attained by blacks.[55] Blacks were elected mayor in such major cities as Los Angeles, Detroit, Atlanta, Cincinnati, Dayton, and Raleigh. Most black mayors have been elected in cities composed predominately of blacks and other minorities, and the most dramatic gains in the years 1970–74 were concentrated in the South. Only New York and New Jersey of Northern states matched Southern gains.[56]

Limitations of Power

The black civil rights revolution throws a sharp, unflattering glare upon the limitations of Presidential power as an instrument of social change. Johnson, in posing his new and higher goal, could envision government programs providing schools, homes, even jobs, but these, he candidly confessed, were but "part of the answer." "An understanding heart by all Americans," he added, "is also part of the answer." Further equality for blacks depends not upon federal laws, troops, and money, but upon how individual citizens behave toward one another in endless transactions that government cannot regulate. There was point to Nixon's observation that it was the private economy, both capital and labor, which, at this juncture, could determine, far more than the federal government, the advance of minority groups "into the mainstream." The President can influence the human heart, but he cannot control it.

The limitations of Presidential power are evident when the plight of blacks is reviewed in the 1970s after two decades of civil rights effort. According to 1973 Census reports, blacks remained far behind whites in most social and economic categories over a five-year period ending in 1972, and in some areas the gap was widening—for example, the median income level between black and white families of four persons. One-third of the black population lived in federally defined poverty compared with 9 percent of whites. Black unemployment in 1972 was 10 percent, compared with 5 percent for whites.[57]

As the 1974 recession and inflation settled in, blacks feared that they would suffer job lay-offs in disproportionate numbers, that independent black businessmen, especially those in new and marginal enterprises, would become unduly endangered, and that persons on welfare would be unable to purchase sufficient heating because of exorbitant prices.[58] The President, as head of the civil rights movement, in stressing legal rights and remedies, has raised black economic expectations that neither government nor private industry up to now have been able to satisfy.

To tackle the economic crisis of blacks, particularly their massive concentrations in urban ghettos, qualified testimony holds, would require outlays on the scale of a major war. The 1968 report of the President's Commission on Civil Disorders made recommendations whose costs it did not dare to estimate. Bayard Rustin, a leader of the civil rights movement, speaks of replacing the slums of New York City with public housing worth seventeen billion dollars. After the Detroit riots in the summer of 1967, Vice President Humphrey urged that a "Marshall Plan" be developed to eradicate slum areas. Humphrey contemplated a massive, long-term public-supported commitment of many billion dollars.[59] But no massive response appears on the political scene.

The effectiveness of Presidential power depends heavily upon the support of administration, which reposes in the hands of the federal departments. It is one thing for the President to issue executive orders and proclaim high policy; it is quite another to transmute policy into action and orders into compliance. In the acid test of performance, the President depends upon a vast federal bureaucracy and far-flung field organizations staffed heavily with local personnel. John Kennedy's housing order, for example, however bold and well-intentioned on its face, was softened by administrative interpretation—the sweeping exemptions and the stress upon "persuasion" rather than enforcement. The unacknowledged motivation behind such choices is the fear that vigorous executive action will alienate Southern legislators situated on strategic committees. In the Johnson era, when the Department of Health, Education and Welfare stepped up its program to desegregate Southern schools, the outcry on Capitol Hill from legislators of that region brought a quick administrative retrenchment. In another quarter, the U.S. Commission on Civil Rights found widespread discrimination against Southern Negro farmers in the administration of government farm programs, extending from education to land conservation.[60]

Since the question of black rights appears in essentially an urban context, the President must work within the confines of the federal system. His programs combatting poverty, creating "model cities," spurring urban redevelopment, and the like depend upon the quality of local administration in the cities. The urban picture, unfortunately, presents no bright landscape of efficient government. The nineteenth-century traditions of neglect and incompetence in local government still hang over us. To depend upon the cities to administer his programs, the President all too often must witness their strangulation in red tape, municipal ignorance, and the competitive chaos that occurs when one city moves to solve problems in ways that hurt its neighbors.

An Overview

Social justice brings the President, Congress, the parties, and the nation to grips with urgent and difficult choices in public affairs. It is a continuous testing of the capacity of individuals and institutions to adjust to change. It provokes struggle between those, on the one hand, whose self-interest weds them to the status quo or fills them with nostalgia for the past, and those, on the other hand, who are disadvantaged in present society or are troubled in conscience by the severe inequities dealt by economic and social forces to their fellow human beings. The exponents of social justice are not only alive in conscience; they believe progress is possible and look confidently to the future.

To compound the difficulties, social justice is itself wrapped at times in obscurity, its substance and meaning anything but clear. When does government welfare stray into paternalism; when does public authority unjustifiably intrude upon private initiative and private right? Since social justice is a human enterprise, those it involves can err. It is dispensed by no omniscient, infallible source, and the individuals, groups, and sections of the nation associated with it have no monopoly of wisdom and rectitude. A Theodore Roosevelt fights splendidly for conservation of natural resources but acts with questionable judgment and severity against the black regiments in the Brownsville episode. Franklin Roosevelt champions the New Deal, a vast mission of mercy for the downtrodden, but countenances the uprooting of Japanese-Americans in the Second World War, one of the most flagrant mass injustices in the nation's history. The South, although a locus of racial injustice, produces for the United States Senate a Lister Hill and a Claude Pepper, whose political toil played no little part in identifying the New Deal with the blacks' cause. In one of those strange ironies of history, it is the South or Southwest that produced the President who moved to the most advanced ground on black civil rights, Lyndon Johnson. The East is a stronghold of traditional business resistance to social change; yet it also produced three Presidents—the Roosevelts and Kennedy—who perceived the character of social change most acutely and acted on what they saw. The Middle West can look askance at "do-good" internationalism, but it still produced Bryan and La Follette, whose influence upon the Presidency's commitment to social reform was enormous.

The strong Presidency of the future will need to be continuously and deeply involved in furthering social justice. The ambitions and resentments of disadvantaged peoples at home and abroad have long passed the point where Presidential attention to social justice can be a part-time concern, or predominantly the pursuit of one major political party rather than the other.

Above all, the Presidency needs improvement in its resources and techniques for decision and planning. If anything, the office is over-involved in patching and piecing policy together for coping with flare-ups. It is too little engaged in long-range planning. Social-planning and decision-making must be better linked to the pluralist structure of society, with its many reference points—the cities and states, corporations and unions, professional groups and universities, minority groups, and age components. All are affected but are not linked to governmental decision structures in ways that produce the most rational outcomes. All could provide feedback on the consequences and worth of existing policies, matters concerning which remote Washington bureaucracies are prone to be deaf and dumb or to misperceive in fantasies of optimism. Lyndon Johnson well perceived that decisions about goals and programs best derive from interaction and consensus, involving governmental decision-makers with the full range of constituencies. The policy-planning task forces of Johnson, and sometimes of Nixon, at least initiated the inclusion of arrays of reference groups.

Social-planning—in the sense of selected and established goals, the measurement of distance and difficulties from the present to their future fulfillment, their periodic modification in light of experience with incremental actions—can be advanced through building on Johnson's consensus practices, on Nixon's Domestic Council, and by developing a multiyear budget. A policy-planning staff, serving the Domestic Council, could develop common premises on which planning could be based. The Council and its staff could assess problems and trends and channel its findings to the President, who in turn could place them before Congress with recommendations, his choices of goals. In the dual political arenas of the Presidency and Congress, competing goals and values could be assessed, conflicting interests resolved, and a necessary base of political support established. The nation can no long afford, as Michael Reagan has suggested, to cross bridges as it comes to them.[61]

13

POLITICAL PERSONALITY

To win and keep his office, to maximize his exploitation of its opportunities and its resources, the President functions as a political personality. "Personality" is useful as an integrative concept, a kind of union of his needs, values, and traits or style in the context of his office.[1] Far more than most offices, the Presidency is plastic and responsive to variations in the political personalities of its incumbents, a circumstance that mirrors the commonplace observation that what the Presidency is at any moment in history depends supremely upon who is occupying the office. Lesser offices can be regulated, institutionalized, and bureaucratized, but the Presidency has eluded the rigidity and servitude of impersonality.

Like other human beings, the President is apt to have certain needs that find gratification in political endeavor. As a political personality, the President may have needs that earlier office-holding has responded to and that find even more fulfillment in the larger dimensions of the post of Chief Executive. The needs a President seeks to satisfy in his office can be inferred from conduct, and they sometimes are articulated. For example, an examination of Theodore Roosevelt's political career from its state and local beginnings to the Presidential and post-Presidential phases reveals a hunger for popularity and a dread that the public might reject him. Almost invariably, he was convinced that he would lose the election for which he was campaigning. Between elections, he was certain that his support was shrinking, and even in political triumph, he remained pessimistic. After important successes in the New York legislature, he wrote, "I realize very thoroughly the absolutely ephemeral nature of the hold I have upon the people." [2]

Roosevelt used public office with enormous imagination and success to win and maintain popularity. He was blessed with a powerful personal magnetism and was astute in projecting it by exploiting the resources and opportunities of office-holding. Time and again, his specific conduct reflected his need. His craving for popularity drove him to a kind of perpetual political exhibitionism. One evidence of this phenomenon was his love of costumes. For years he struck his favorite photographic pose in his Rough Rider uniform and in his cowboy clothes, complete with pistol and rifle. Attired in a favorite cowboy suit, "I feel able to face anything," he once claimed. As New York police commissioner, he made headlines, checking up on his underlings by prowling about the streets at night in evening clothes.

The President is driven by the need to maintain his self-esteem. Woodrow Wilson, one of the more hard-driven of Presidents in this need, was goaded by Calvinistic upbringing and faith to prove to himself regularly that he was an adequate and virtuous human being. He struggled with this aspect of his ego on the ample proving grounds of the Presidency. The opportunities for assertion in the Presidency helped compensate for the damaged self-esteem of his youth sustained from an exacting father. Yet the adult Woodrow Wilson's brittle self-esteem also crippled his capacity to react objectively to the issues of his administration, a failing that reached disastrous proportions in the League of Nations fight. He needed to dominate others, such as his formidable antagonist in the League of Nations struggle, Henry Cabot Lodge, and to achieve his political objectives in order to bolster his self-esteem. Another criterion of his continuous self-evaluation was provided by his religion that stressed "good works"—the League—for which he strove and fought even to the point of his own physical collapse.[3] For Wilson, the League of Nations represented a value to which he committed his energies and his reputation unstintingly.

The reconcilability of the strong President with the requisites of democracy depends crucially upon the personality of the incumbent, upon how well his values, character, and style harmonize with democratic ways. The other two branches of government, the judiciary and the legislature, possess more built-in procedures than the executive that protect democracy, and their functions more readily synchronize with it than executive power, which bears many undemocratic or even antidemocratic elements. The executive branch is disposed to action and is judged by its capacity for positive achievement, which can make it impatient with opposition and callous in regard to civil liberties. The executive functions according to hierarchy and command and is predicated upon compliant and obedient subordinates.

Yet, like any society, democracy also needs authority; otherwise it would fall into chaos. The ideal is a strong Presidency, effective and constructive in contributing to the good life, while obeisant to democratic processes. The realization of this happy conjunction depends heavily upon the personality of the incumbent, and most particularly upon his values.

Values

Values, as Gordon W. Allport has suggested, are usually social in nature and are objects of common regard by socialized men.[4] Values may silence the President in controversy or send him roaring into the front line of combat. They may bring him eagerly to shoulder a task as altogether worthy of his administration or cause him to turn it aside.

Values have enormous variety. A President has personal values that govern his deportment toward problems, colleagues, and adversaries. Loyalty, for example, is a personal value that may control Presidential conduct. Presidents rightly prize and insist upon loyalty to themselves and their administrations, but they are as a lot somewhat spotty in the loyalty they, in turn, accord to aides and supporters. To be let down and let out is not an uncommon experience of good and faithful servants of Presidents throughout the office's history. Yet the record also carries not a few sagas of Chief Executives who were loyal to their friends well after these friends had abused their trust. Harry S. Truman's abiding loyalty to aides who were also his friends and cronies survived the severest tests. Roy Roberts of the Kansas City *Star,* who knew Truman well, catalogued his several qualities in 1945, at the outset of his sudden Presidency.[5] Near the top of Roberts' list was "loyalty, perhaps excessive loyalty that sometimes gets high officials into trouble . . . ," a prophesy that unfortunately came true when old friends among his White House aides were lured by the bait of mink coats and deep freezes into indiscretions of office. In the din of criticism that followed, Truman stood firmly behind these aides, well beyond the obligations of friendship.

The President as a rule is endowed with a hierarchy of values that is highly relevant to questions that the office churns up for him to decide. Gerald Ford, to slow inflation in 1974, resolved to cut the federal budget, but he quickly made clear that the sector of expenditure most protected against reduction was national defense. Everything else was more vulnerable. "A strong defense," he declared, "is the surest way to peace." [6] In the value scheme that President Grant applied to his decisions, education ranked high and religion low in his estimation. Education, he felt, was a boon to the republic and merited unstinting emphasis in public policy. "We are a republic," he declared, "whereof one man is as good as another before the law. . . . Hence the education of the masses becomes the first necessity for the preservation of our institutions." Grant's conviction led him to propose a constitutional amendment requiring each state to "establish and forever maintain free public schools" for all children irrespective of "sex, color, birthplace, or religion." Toward churches, however, Grant displayed a hostility as ardent as his devotion to education. He seldom let pass an opportunity to strike at churches or put them in their place. Impressed, for example, that one billion dollars worth of church property was tax free, Grant contended in a message to Congress that "so vast a sum . . . will not be looked upon acquiescently by those who have to pay the taxes." In an extraordinary step for a President, he bluntly proposed that church property be taxed.[7]

Most Presidents have a hierarchy of values that is seldom articulated but is discernible in their actions. Many a President has by his actions identified the nation's survival as the supreme value. Abraham Lincoln acknowledged that he knowingly violated provisions of the Constitution in order to assure the nation's survival. Survival, not the Constitution, was the fundamental law. In the absence of the critical national plight that Lincoln grappled with, Presidents have attached the highest value to preserving the Constitution and the integrity of their office. As Andrew Johnson's troubles boiled up furiously in Congress—to reduce the President to a figurehead, Congress had virtually deprived him of control of the army and denied him the right to remove all civil officials, including cabinet members, without consent of the Senate—he perceived his duty to be one of upholding his office and the Constitution. The means he must use for this highest of purposes, he reasoned, must also be constitutional. For all the severe unconstitutional treatment he sustained from Congress, he held himself closely to the path of legality and rejected the counsel of well-intentioned friends that he employ the Army to reorganize the legislators plus an array of less drastic, but clearly unconstitutional acts. Nor would he, to save his own job, submit to the Congressional radicals, who, to destroy him, were bent upon running a steamroller over the Constitution. If the Constitution went down, he would go down with it.[8]

The jeopardy of a superior value may bring a President to act when a lesser value cannot. President Eisenhower long maintained the detachment of himself and his office from a most dynamic issue of his time—civil rights. When asked whether he endorsed the epochal ruling of the Supreme Court in *Brown* v. *Board of Education of Topeka,* which held that separate schools for blacks, although equal in quality to white schools, violated the Constitution, or whether he merely accepted it, as the Republican platform did, he replied, "I think it makes no difference whether or not I endorse it. . . . The Constitution is as the Supreme Court interprets it. . . ." [9] In other expressions on civil rights, Eisenhower similarly abstained from committing himself on Presidential power. He observed several times that laws could not change morality or that "laws could not change men's hearts." In a news conference he declared, "I can't imagine any set of circumstances that would ever induce me to send federal troops . . . into any area to enforce the orders of a federal court, because I believe that the common sense of America will never require it . . . I would never believe that it would be a wise thing to do." [10] These several utterances constituted in a sense Eisenhower's own private dissent from the Supreme Court's decision.

Eisenhower's expressions of Presidential self-abnegation spurred Governor Orval Faubus of Arkansas to order his state troops to defy the Supreme Court's desegregation decision by blocking the entry of black children to the Little Rock high school. Faubus' defiance was, in the constitutional sense, a challenge to Presidential power and to federal authority. Quite possibly it was also founded upon a misapprehension of Eisenhower's value system. Eisenhower hesitated, then negotiated with Faubus, but in vain, and finally asserted federal authority by issuing a statement warning that he would "use the full power of the United States, including whatever force may be necessary." The Arkansas National Guard was federalized, and troops from the U.S. 101st Airborne Division were ordered to Little Rock to join in patrolling the high school. For Eisenhower, to see a cherished lesser value pushed aside by the dictates of the higher value of constitutional and Presidential authority created a bitter choice. Sending the paratroopers into Little Rock, his assistant Sherman Adams observed, was the performance by the President of "a Constitutional duty which was the most repugnant to him of all his acts in his eight years at the White House." [11]

The President may attach a higher value to a role or function in which he is skilled or experienced and a lesser value to sectors of his office with which he is little familiar. Eisenhower, for example, was more intellectually at home and more committed by personal taste to meetings of the National Security Council than to meetings of the Republican National Committee. The higher value he attached to foreign affairs, in which he was deeply experienced, was also reflected in his greater receptivity to decisions in that sphere in contrast to the more restricted record of his Presidency in domestic affairs, with which previously he had little encounter.

The arrangement of a President's hierarchy of values is determined substantially by his attitudes toward morality and power. His emphasis of one over the other will produce a strikingly different roster of values than if his choice were reversed. He may stress morality and neglect power. Andrew Johnson, conceiving of what he thought was right, pursued it with little attention to power—to the winning of allies in Congress and the parties, to the construction of compromises that might assure that at least part of what he deemed right would prevail while lesser parts might be sacrificed. Johnson's predecessor, Lincoln, viewed morality and power as complementary. He rose to the heights of moral splendor in his Gettysburg and second inaugural addresses and yet perceived that what he proposed to achieve required a bold, resourceful assertion of all available—and sometimes unavailable—power of the Constitution.

Some Presidents—Gerald Ford, for example—believe that morality is best advanced through example and practice, and they discount the capacity of legislation and executive rule-making to promote that value. When asked, at the outset of his Presidency—with the wrongdoings of Watergate in stark view—whether he planned to establish a Code of Ethics for the Executive Branch, the new President replied, "The code of ethics that will be followed will be the example that I set." [12] Likewise, Ford declined to speak out for campaign reform legislation, impressed by the superior means "of sacred scriptures to guide us on the path of personal right living and exemplary official conduct." [13]

In matters of importance or controversy, most Presidents take pains to clothe their actions in rectitude. They prefer to act or prefer to appear to act, not upon grounds of expediency, as they may seem to, but upon grounds of what is "right." Wilson liked to visualize his work as a kind of "service," an ennobling moral framework in which he fitted a remarkable variety of deeds. Andrew Johnson, faced with a decision whether to approve or veto the Freedmen's Bureau bill, which created an agency to relieve white and Negro suffering in the postwar South, was buffeted by ponderous forces, some eager to punish the South, others aiming to heal the wounds of war quickly and restore the Union. If he withheld his veto, he was promised, Senators and Representatives from his own state of Tennessee would be admitted to Congress and he could enjoy their voting support, which he badly needed. Leading members of his cabinet, Edwin M. Stanton, James Harlan, and James Speed urged him not to veto. But Johnson was unyielding to bribes or intimidation. "He could do no wrong," he told the cabinet, "to assure right." [14]

Sometimes the values Presidents articulate may be quite different from the values expressed in their actions—what they say versus what they do. In his

1968 campaign, Richard Nixon proclaimed his commitment to "an open administration—open to ideas from the people, and open in its communication with the people—an administration of open doors, open eyes and open minds." [15] Again, in outlining his plans for his second term, he declared, "we are going to have an open administration, contact with the press, and so forth." [16]

Even the most benign observer would be hard pressed to find any resemblance between these professions and the actual performance of the Nixon Presidency, which all but eliminated the news conference, was typified by long periods of the Chief Executive's withdrawal, during which he made no public comment on major issues. Nixon associated not with a wide and representative circle of "the people," but with a narrow cluster of the economically well-to-do, some with tainted reputations. One of the more gigantic chasms between actions and words opened up when revelations of the Watergate wrongdoings were appalling the nation. Nixon at that time unabashedly pledged his administration to "halt the erosion of moral fiber in American life and the denial of individual accountability for individual action." [17]

As Nixon's Presidency also demonstrated, good values can be invoked as a cover for the pursuit of values that are bad or dubious. Nixon linked his advocacy of a work requirement for welfare recipients on grounds of the "Puritan ethic," and he vetoed legislation for day-care centers, contending that such establishments would erode family life and therefore undermine basic support of American "moral and religious principles." No word came from the President's lips recognizing the needs of the poor or society's obligations to them. Time and again he affirmed his belief in hard work, competitive personal effort, a spare life style, and patriotism—a belief that other politicians have championed, but which in his advocacy seemed divisive and antiquated. [18]

Goals

The President acts not only in response to values. He also chooses goals for himself and his administration. His commitment to goals tells much of the maturity and sophistication of his Presidency and of the degree of his involvement in the tasks of the nation and the opportunities of his office. In choosing goals, he sets the tone and character of his administration, the level of its striving, and the missions to which his aides and supporters may subscribe their energy, skill, and loyalty.

Goals come in assorted shapes and sizes. They may be finely precise or general to the point of vagueness. Presidents may establish goals in several or more of the multiple roles of their office. Some goals that a President chooses to support have the attraction of guaranteeing almost universal approbation and support. Only a rare and contrary-minded member of society could reject the ringing commitment some Presidents have offered to "a better life for all" or—and sometimes almost in the same breath—to reduce taxes. Presidential roles permit the selection of goals that create an instantaneous impression of absolute high-mindedness. Time and again the President as administrative chief has proclaimed his devotion to the administrative reform of the executive branch for the sake of efficiency and economy, a goal that carries an unfailing aura of moral nobility and excites well-nigh universal support, at least so long as it stands as a broadly stated proposition.

The President may sometimes manipulate goals in one area of national interest to deflect attention from public tensions and animosities raging in another area. James Buchanan so related himself to domestic and foreign affairs. Beset by the crashing tempest of "bleeding" Kansas where the winds of Northern and Southern sectionalism converged, he chose, in composing his second annual message to Congress in December 1858, to turn the nation's attention to foreign affairs. Buchanan posed a series of goals for foreign policy worthy of the nation's united effort for years to come. He aimed to enable the United States to "attract to itself much of the trade and travel of all nations passing between Europe and Asia" and to become thereby the wealthiest nation on the globe. He proposed a string of measures that would make large claims upon the nation's resources of men and money: the purchase of Cuba to assure the United States' dominance in the Caribbean; the increase of the navy to enlarge and protect transportation routes through Panama, Nicaragua, and Mexico; the conclusion of commercial treaties with China, Japan, and other countries of the Far East; the revision of the tariff to increase revenues; the construction of a Pacific railroad. How much better, Buchanan left little doubt, for the nation to pursue these acts of self-aggrandizement than to dissipate its strength in internal strife.[19]

The President entertains personal goals, the more common of which are his reelection, a vote of confidence in a Congressional election, and the prevailing of his choice of a successor. He may aim to provide the deeds and words for the use of future historians in inscribing an admiring account of the wonders of his administration. His several goals, whether in foreign affairs, social justice, or whatever, may well reflect his underlying philosophy of life, which in actuality is his supreme personal goal. "What is your philosophy?" a young man once asked Franklin Roosevelt. "Philosophy?" Roosevelt answered. "Philosophy? I am a Christian and a Democrat—that's all." [20] Church and party implied for Roosevelt a series of commitments: respect for fellow man, nature, and freedom, or what was the very essence of his New Deal and wartime administrations.

Goals, like values, are not coins of common worth but exist in relationship to each other. There are the greater and the lesser. The greatest is a Presidential administration's central purpose, vision, or grand design. Terms like the "New Deal" or the "New Freedom" conjure up a vision of the central purposes of Franklin Roosevelt and Woodrow Wilson. A President's foreign and domestic politics may join harmoniously in support of his grand design. President Kennedy well discerned the central purpose in the administrations of several of his Democratic forebears when he declared in Ann Arbor, Michigan, in October

1960 that "because it fitted in exactly with what they were trying to do here in the United States, the Fourteen Points were the international counterpart of the New Freedom; the Four Freedoms of Franklin Roosevelt were directly tied to the aspirations of the New Deal; and the Marshall Plan, NATO, the Truman Doctrine, and Point Four were directly tied to the kind of America that President Truman was trying to build." [21]

Below the generalized grand design may stretch a great array of lesser goals that both individually and collectively may constitute the distinguishing mark of the Presidential administration. Some may be vaguely and others precisely defined. Grover Cleveland, choosing to embark on the settlement of the long simmering dispute between Britain and Venezuela over the latter's boundary with British Guiana, confided to a friend that his aim was to bring, at one sharp stroke, the whole matter into his own control, push Britain into arbitration, and put Congress in a position where it could not interfere. "My action, you see," the President said, "has been in the interests of peace—permanent peace."

Goals set the level of aspiration of an administration. John Kennedy contended, altogether plausibly, that goals should be inspiring, no matter how great the difficulties and delays in their realization.[22] Goal-setting reflects the President's instinct for the future, his understanding of the past, and his mastery of the present. It must capture the nation's needs and yearnings, perceive the potential of its resources, and grasp the directions in which the world is moving. "The President's got to set the sights," [23] Truman once said.

However, the President, if the record of his administration is to be impressive, must be able to formulate solid, possible goals. Wilson had a special knack for selecting as his political goals projects that were ripe for realization and excelled at carrying them out with shrewd political maneuver. The goal-setting President must think in terms of trends, of locating his administration and its times in the stream of events; he must be capable of developmental thinking, of conjuring up pictures of the future, of perceiving alternatives to achieve his goals, and of choosing wisely between them.[24] He must also excel in configurative thinking, visualizing each available power, tool, and project as part of the total process and keeping them in balance.[25]

Style

The President develops in the eyes of those who view his conduct over time the appearance, or impression, of a "style." The raw material, or input, of style embraces the President's gestures and flairs, his communicative acts oral and written, his enthusiasms, prejudices, and interests. Style, as an output, is a cumulative, more or less representative impression inferred from all of these elements of conduct.

Style as the product of gesture, speech, mood, and manner may tell much or little of the President's controlling impulses, attitudes, and approach to duty and decision. The cliché that appearances are misleading has special point in estimates of Presidents. Senator Robert M. La Follette, a shrewd judge of men, witnessing the passing of the Presidency from Chester Arthur to Grover Cleveland, was moved to compare the new President with the old. La Follette noted, "The contrast with Arthur, who was a fine handsome figure, was very striking. Cleveland's coarse face, his heavy inert body, his great shapeless hands, confirmed in my mind the attacks made upon him during the campaign." Before many days of the new President, however, La Follette revised his initial estimate and came "to admire the courage and conscientiousness of his character." [26]

Style also springs from the vast, diverse realm of temperament. Cleveland was at times impulsive, as in sending in troops in the Pullman strike without awaiting a request from Governor Altgeld of Illinois; Wilson was at times compulsive, rigid in dealings with others. A President's temperament, as it is manifested in private, may be wholly different from its public display. James Buchanan was known to the nation and the world as an exemplar of the quiet, flexible negotiator and compromiser. His private demeanor, according to testimony of aides, was altogether different from his public reputation. Attorney General Jeremiah S. Black voiced the general opinion of his cabinet colleagues when he said of Buchanan, "He is a stubborn old gentleman—very fond of having his own way. . . ." John B. Floyd, Buchanan's Secretary of War, who also knew Andrew Jackson well, observed, "Mr. Buchanan was different from General Jackson; . . . General Jackson could be *coaxed* from his purpose, but . . . Mr. B. could neither be coaxed nor driven." [27]

A President's private stylistic traits can serve to evoke the confidence and loyalty of his associates and to extend his influence in the executive branch. Franklin Roosevelt provided a model of such artistry. "It was part of his conception of his role," his Undersecretary of Agriculture and intimate counselor, Rexford G. Tugwell has written, "that he should never show exhaustion, boredom, or irritation." His patience, grasp of detail, his composure as emergencies fell upon him, his timing, evasiveness, and humor, his reserve, his occasional severity, his sense of office and history numbered among the rewarding stylistic administrative traits by which he held sway in the executive branch.[28]

Another style, by no means uncommon among Presidents, is that of the compromiser. "I am a compromiser and a manipulator," Lyndon Johnson said. His critics spoke of him, less flatteringly, as a "wheeler-dealer" type. The Chief Executive, in Johnson's view, dispenses the good things of life to every class and group. His perceptions of the nature of power moved him more to the backstage than to frontstage in the political drama. "In every town," he said, "there's some guy on top of the hill in a big white house who can get things done. I want to get that man on my side." [29] Johnson, then, was prone to think and act not in terms of "the people" but to carry the play to the legislative committee, the leaders of the big interest groups, and other power centers whose favor or decision could provide what he believed the country needed. The manipulator-compromiser style carried a built-in cautionary device. By the very nature of the style, nothing is ever final; everything is susceptible to accommodation and adjustment. Or, at least, the President will exercise his "options" to perpetuate as long as he can his freedom to act in a given situation. Johnson followed in an elaborate course to avoid booby traps. He consulted beyond his staff with departmental officers, private counselors, key legislators, random visitors, and labor and business leaders. The extended procedure often created delays, reversals of decisions, the impression of tentativeness, of lack of conviction and confidence.

Some expressions of style may be little more than minor excrescences of personality; others may be purposefully indulged in to facilitate the Presidential task. Franklin Roosevelt and Andrew Jackson were masters of delay, a pose they found highly valuable in politics. Thanks to delay, tumultuous political forces had more time to settle or grow distinct; the President could better weigh factors and consequences before choosing his course. Jackson also, to a degree rare among Presidents, employed the terrible rage as a standard administrative weapon. Time and again, he would break up meetings and conferences with rousing demonstrations that were shrewdly calculated and rendered so convincingly that visitors retreated in utter confusion, forgetting what they had come for. Jackson steadily preferred this volcanic method to time-consuming and perhaps inconclusive argument. Martin Van Buren, Jackson's discerning associate, perceived that the President's view of his general political strength was also an element in shaping his conduct. "The conciliation of individuals," Van Buren said of Jackson, "formed the smallest, perhaps too small a part of his policy. His strength lay with the masses, and he knew it." [30]

Presidents have stylistic traits that may become the mark of their reign and an element of their memorability in history. Benjamin Harrison is accurately remembered as frigid and intellectual. President Grant's administration was handicapped by an abysmal lack of political facility. Grant had launched his administration on a high note in an inaugural address that the New York *Tribune* hailed as "the utterance of a man of the best intentions profoundly desirous to govern wisely and justly. . . ." But the *Tribune* also sensed from the address what was to become the underlying cause of the egregious failure of the future Grant administration. Grant, the *Tribune* noted, was "profoundly ignorant of the means by which good government is secured." In a day when waves of corruption beat upon his administration, a bold statement from the President conveying his own high purpose and moral rigor would have served himself and the country well, but Grant, who was endowed with an inarticulateness that amounted to a kind of verbal lockjaw, responded feebly.[31]

Lyndon Johnson's reign was marked by a patriarchal concept of politics, which controlled his style. This concept holds that politics and its storm and stress are the preserve of the President, and from them the private citizen is spared. Except when the election campaigns of 1964 and 1966 were in progress, Johnson in public discourse tended toward a pose of serenity that exhorted good men to do good deeds, dispensed praise, and gave scant acknowledgment to problems. Doubt, defeat, and strife are repressed from view in a haze of serenity, according to the patriarchal theory. Policy must appear to evolve smoothly: It does not shift suddenly.[32] If the roof falls in, it is the sunlight that is seen. Enemies may be acknowledged, but they are not scolded. Under the patriarchal concept of the Presidency, which is utterly alien to the norms of democratic politics, the people are not privy to the President's current concerns and feelings. The concept worked both favorably and adversely in the Johnson era. In the upheaval of John Kennedy's assassination, Johnson gratified and reassured the nation by a masterful display of composure while he quickly and privately restored to normal working order the Presidential machinery. The patriarchal concept served him less well in the lengthy, tortuous, shifting war in Vietnam, with whose pressures he struggled largely in private. His course did little to promote the understanding and support of the nation.

Presidents appear divided into two schools on the question of choice of external stylistic traits. One school tends toward the model of George Washington, fitting their conduct to the intrinsic dignity of the office. In modern day, Franklin Roosevelt and Dwight Eisenhower wrapped themselves in the mantle of dignity in public appearance. Eisenhower's manly candor inspired confidence. John Kennedy veered to this school, although he tempered his proper decorum with an apposite sense of humor. At the other extreme is the warm, little inhibited manner of Andrew Johnson, Harry Truman, or Lyndon Johnson. President Truman, soon after taking office, conveyed the flavor of his style in a visit to the Pemiscot County Fair at Carhuthersville, Missouri. The new President mingled with the crowd on a "Harry" basis and discussed local problems with farmers wearing overalls. When a doddering American Legion locomotive came by, he ran into the street to toot its whistle. He played piano for the Methodist Church ladies, winking broadly as he said, "When I played this, Stalin signed the Potsdam Agreement." [33]

High-Democracy and Low-Democracy Presidential Types

A principal objective of the Framers of the Constitution was the avoidance of tyrants who would overwhelm the carefully constructed system of balanced powers. Fortunately, the many incumbents of the Presidency have numbered no tyrants in the classic sense. No Presidential personality has matched the type that has sometimes attracted wide interest among social scientists, the authoritarian personality,[34] although occasionally particular behavior has. The behavior of Presidents swings across a sufficiently wide arc of variation, in its proximity to and distance from democratic norms, that it becomes desirable, for the sake of democracy's safety, to distinguish those aspects of Presidential personality and behavior that are more akin to democracy (high-democracy type) from those that are distinctly less so (low-democracy type). The strong Presidency and the enhancement of Presidential power enlarges both tendencies. The identification of those aspects of personality and behavior that are less beneficial to

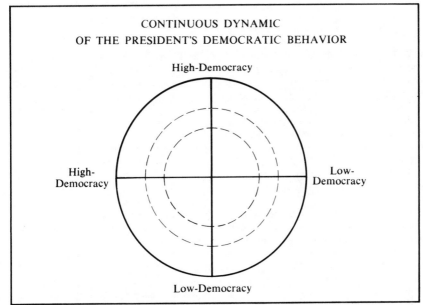

CONTINUOUS DYNAMIC
OF THE PRESIDENT'S DEMOCRATIC BEHAVIOR

High-Democracy

High-Democracy

Low-Democracy

Low-Democracy

Adapted from June L. Tapp and Fred Krinsky, *Ambivalent America:
A Psycho-political Dialogue* (Beverly Hills: Glencoe Press, 1971), p. 4.

democracy, or even antidemocratic, focuses attention on strengthening safe-guards, on deploying staff aides in ways that minimize negative behaviors, of probing, in Presidential selection, for personality characteristics inimical to democracy. Such characteristics, if serious enough, might be spotlighted, and party leaders and the public forewarned, to the point that they might halt the incipient, but clearly inappropriate, candidate.

Personality and its expression in behavior that suggests these types contains two main elements. One is content—the substance of what a President does, his programs, policies, and actions. The second is process, or how he acts. As well, the types reflect the innermost forces of personality. The low-democracy type, in attitudes and behavior, is apt to be engrossed in "externalization and ego defense." He invests substantial energies toward maintaining an inner equilibrium, toward defending the self against the often conflicting demands of impulses and conscience.[35]

No President completely fulfills either type; instead, his personality and behavior manifest both. However, he may tend markedly toward one rather than the other during particular intervals of his incumbency, or his overall performance may do so. These types suggest a continuous dynamic in which the President is engaged, a dynamic represented in the figure below.

The types and their representative elements are as follows:

THE HIGH-DEMOCRACY TYPE

1. Acts in ways that advance or enlarge the civil rights of individuals and groups. Observes the civil liberties provisions of the Bill of Rights.

THE LOW-DEMOCRACY TYPE

1. Stresses, in his political campaigns, citizen fears and irrationalities. He is a force for divisiveness rather than integration.

2. Develops and supports economic and social programs and policies responsive to the needs of many groups, not just the very powerful. Responds to the ideal of being President of all the people.

3. Is accessible to a wide variety of individuals and groups. Does not identify too emphatically with any one class or group.

4. In political campaigns, discusses important issues meaningfully and constructively.

5. Encourages his subordinates and associates to communicate with him in candor. Does not suppress or penalize criticism or dissent but respects it and profits from it, within bounds of basic loyalty, in order to comprehend the reality of the world in which he functions.

6. Manifests a sturdy socialization in democratic values and processes.

7. Responds to public problems opportunely and constructively for the common good.

2. Is inactive or regressive concerning civil rights. Is indifferent to civil liberties or readily violates them to advance a cited higher value such as national security or law and order, whose scope he interprets expansively.

3. Encroaches on the other branches of government; derogates their role; acts to promote his self-aggrandizement.

4. Is accessible to only a limited variety of groups, such as the economically powerful, and is excessively remote from other classes and groups.

5. Is overresponsive to the needs and concerns of the economically powerful and indifferent or manipulative toward those with little power.

6. Resorts readily to Presidential war, which he launches merely by his own decision; minimizes or excludes Congressional participation and conducts the war with secrecy and deception.

7. Displays weak socialization in democratic values and practices, concerning which he is ignorant or indifferent. Shows little regard for the Bill of Rights.

8. Is manipulative and secretive both toward subordinates in the executive branch and toward the public. Displays low tolerance of criticism and discredits opponents rather than confronting their contentions responsively.

9. Allows problems to drift; assures their neglect by pursuing outmoded assumptions and is unresponsive to the resulting human hardship.

In the personality and behavior of any particular President both types are represented, just as they are in any individual. Presidential roles also foster the dual pattern, with some, such as that of Commander-in-Chief, calling for low-democracy modes of behavior, while others, such as that of protecting civil liberties, virtually compel high-democracy behavior.

Studies of Richard Nixon, for example, reveal interlacings of these types and the presence of regulators within his personality whose successes or failures had much to do with whether specific behavior tended toward either extreme.[36] According to historian Bruce Mazlish, Nixon exalted strength, dreaded passivity, and projected unacceptable impulses on others; he was wracked by uncertainty concerning his courage, especially in crisis. Haunted by his father's ''failure,'' he harbored potent aggressive impulses and felt driven to avoid failure himself and redeem his parent. He identified his personal interest with the national interest; his crises were his countrymen's crises. His environment was divided into stark absolutes—''I think we can win the struggle against slavery and for freedom throughout the world''—a world of all good and all bad, slavery and freedom, aggressor and peace-lover. Ominous for the stability of democratic processes was Nixon's preoccupation with ''testing'' himself through crisis, even periodically creating them to prove himself. In justifying his 1970 invasion of Cambodia, he contended that ''our'' character was being tested, and we must not be found wanting.[37]

But in the Nixon make-up elements propitious for democracy were also present. Nixon had an ''obsession'' (his own word) with peace. In keeping with the Freudian pattern, one parent, his mother, a dedicated Quaker, was devoted to peace, in contrast to his irascible, pugnacious father. To Nixon, it was the peaceful mother who seemed strong and the competitive father ''weak,'' because of his lack of success. Nixon appears to have identified with his mother's peaceful soul as much as with his father's pugnacity, which encouraged the conclusion that the President was endowed with strong, genuine dedication to international peace. Simultaneously, his mother's influence rankled his conscience concerning his aggressiveness.[38] Accordingly, much of the time, Nixon was engaged in self-management, to resist the ''temptation'' to strike at his enemies. In Watergate and related episodes, his self-control failed and wrecked his Presidency.

What Kind of Strong President Is Most Compatible with Democracy?

A response to this question is aided by the Presidential types formulated in James David Barber's study *The Presidential Character*. After contending that Presidential personality is determined essentially by character, world view, and style, and their combination in a dynamic package, Barber notes that an incumbent's basic stance toward the office partakes of any one of four types. His classification in these types depends on how active he is and whether or not he gives the impression that he enjoys his political life.[39] Four basic character patterns emerge: the active-positive, the active-negative, the passive-positive, and the passive-negative. Only the first two—the active-positive and the active-negative—seriously respond to the needs of the strong Presidency. With their obdurate passivity, the last two fall well short of its requisites. Which of the first two is better responsive to democracy?

The active-positive type combines a high volume and fast tempo of activity with enjoyment of them. This President displays strong self-esteem and distinct success in relating to the environment. He cherishes productiveness as a value, is supple in adapting his style, stresses well-defined personal goals and rational self-mastery. Franklin Roosevelt, Harry Truman, and John Kennedy illustrate this type.

The active-negative type invests intense effort in the Presidency but derives low emotional reward. A compulsive quality permeates the effort, as though work were an escape from anxiety. This President is ambitious, aggressive toward the environment, and struggles persistently to contain his intense feelings. His self-image is vague and discontinuous and he perceives politics as a struggle to gain and keep power. Woodrow Wilson is illustrative, and one of the worst historical experiences of this type was his League of Nations defeat. Adroit political leadership was called for, but Wilson adopted a rigid commitment to his positions, viewed his senatorial opponents as "endeavoring to humiliate me," personalized and vilified his principal foe, Henry Cabot Lodge, and adamantly opposed all compromise.[40]

Clearly, the active-positive type better synchronizes with the ideal of the strong-democratic President than the active-negative. Yet the active-positive Presidents do not possess an altogether clear path to fulfilling democratic criteria. They too encounter stumbling blocks. Some have made Presidential war, with large doses of secrecy and deceit. Of contemporary active-positive Presidents, three—Roosevelt, Truman, and Kennedy—have waged war. Kennedy, and in some moments Roosevelt, supplied motifs to the strong Presidency that are dissonant with the democratic spirit. The expansive rhetoric of Kennedy's addresses bears an exalted view of "the burden and the glory" of the Presidency, sounding themes of popular sacrifice, with overtones a shade alien to the democratic conception of the high validity of the individual's own life and aspirations.[41]

Views of the Presidency

What the President does and how he behaves depend much upon his own view of the Presidency. His view is not an unsegmented monolith but a mosaic of many pieces of different sizes and hues.

A view of the Presidency embraces the attitudes of the incumbent toward the problems presented by the outside world with which he might conceivably deal. President Eisenhower began with the uncontrovertible proposition that the American people should not look to the Chief Executive to solve all their problems. This general view was supported by a more specific philosophy according to which President Eisenhower, by personal preference, chose to eliminate large sectors of problems from the purview and therefore the action of his Presidency. His expressed fear of "the menace of bankrupting waste inherent in a centralized bureaucracy . . ." lent force to his ambition to return various federal functions to the states or to private activity. For example, his views on electric power development, the "partnership" principle, as it was known, called for a larger role for state and local government and for privately owned utilities than was known in previous Presidential administrations. Or again, when pressures developed in his administration for substantial national programs to improve schools, hospitals, and other welfare services, Eisenhower stressed the responsibilities of local governments and citizens, declaring, "Here we rely not primarily upon government grant or political panacea but upon our own wisdom and industry to bring us the good and comforting things of life." [42]

A view of the Presidency includes a view of legal authority, especially the basic law of the Constitution, and of relationships with the two other branches—the legislature and the judiciary. Presidents' views of Congress, their great political competitor, range from Lincoln's, which regarded the legislature as a nuisance to be avoided if at all possible, to Buchanan's, which was deferential almost to the point of abjectness. Andrew Johnson, on the brink of launching his Reconstruction policy, took an expansive legal view of his office and, as events proved, a disastrously simplistic view of its politics. Johnson reasoned that if Lincoln inaugurated the war by deeming that the states were in rebellion and, in effect, declared war, then his successor in the Presidency had the corresponding power to say when the states were no longer in rebellion and when each was fit to return to its place in the Union. As Lincoln had, Johnson relied on the Commander-in-Chief power, his duty to take care that laws are faithfully executed, his oath of office, and the constitutional guarantee of a republican form of government to each state. [43] The boldness of this legal doctrine, Johnson's rugged tenacity, and his utter lack of political sense provided the ingredients for a struggle that came to threaten, as none ever had, the Presidency's very existence.

Above all, the President's view of his office depends upon his view of politics. To achieve policy, to use the enormous potentialities of his office, he must act by political means. The Presidents who have extracted major successes from the office—Jefferson, Jackson, Wilson, and the Roosevelts—all were eminent Presidential politicians. Politics have been notably eschewed by some Presidents, a Washington or an Eisenhower, whose extraordinary ability to symbolize the nation's intrinsic unity was little tarnished by personal political involvement. Some Presidents notably prefer certain forms of political activity to others. John Kennedy loved the arts of political management but was wary of taking his programs to the public in a nationally televised appeal. Lyndon Johnson displayed a prowess in many branches of politics that compared with the ablest political figures of any age. Yet in this strength there also lay weakness. He was so adept at politics that his mastery of that suspect art became legendary and hampered his ability, as President, to command national popular confidence. If there be a first commandment in Presidential politics, it must be this: Let the President excel at politics, but let him not be obvious about it.

An Overview

The President as a political personality, we have seen, combines, in that concept, the man, his needs, and the office. He may have personal needs that find satisfaction in political office-holding and, above all, in the Presidency. The President is a broker in values that shape his decisions and policies. He chooses between values, gives higher priority to some than others, and may over time shift his support of them. He may formulate and subscribe to goals that set the achievement levels of his administration. Above all, as a political personality, he can be seen as possessing a bundle of traits, which both separately and in combination constitute that elusive, mysterious element called ''style.''

The relation of the President, or the man, to the office is dynamic to the extent that an incumbent may come into office not particularly admired, as was the case with Lincoln and Truman, and develop and display a combination of values and traits that arouses widespread public approval and even admiration. A reverse tendency also may take place. Lyndon Johnson, confident, assertive and self-reliant, gratified the nation with the skill of his take-over in the turmoil of the Kennedy assassination. But these very qualities seemed to weaken his popular standing in the context of the Vietnam War.

On occasion it has appeared that how the President does things is more important than what he does. A President who does less may be better appreciated than one who does more. An underachiever who is blessed with a collection of traits or style that delights the public and even the historians may fare better in the public opinion of his day or in his country's annals than the overachiever whose major sin may be that he does not possess a comparably pleasing style.

The President lives in a culture in which the profession of politician has uncertain status. The values of his society emphasize private endeavor and private success. Politics is tainted as a calling less worthy than most private pursuits. To succeed in the Presidency in the largest sense, the incumbent must be a master politician. But society and the culture are reluctant that he be so. Not the least restraint upon the strong President is the distaste society is apt to have for the strong politician.

14

DECISION-MAKING

Decision-making is an area where the strong Presidency depends most upon the strong President—upon the caliber of the incumbent, his talents, prudence, and resolution. His choices point up the issues of the Presidency, give substance to its policies and effect to its purposes. Decision-making is a continuous process of the President's existence, his choices tend to be difficult, and the end-products often have great consequences. "There are no easy matters that will come to you as President," Eisenhower counseled the incoming President Kennedy. "If they are easy, they will be settled at a lower level." [1]

Varieties of Decision

Actually, the President makes all kinds of decisions: routine or programed decisions (which focus upon tasks rather than problems); adaptive decisions (the adjustment of existing policy to new circumstances); and innovative decisions (major departures from established policy). Some Chief Executives may choose to devote themselves to one kind at the expense of the others.

A President who chooses to concentrate upon routine or adaptive decisions sacrifices the opportunity to make major or innovative decisions. Franklin Pierce, in his first Presidential years, sat two hours each day with his assembled cabinet engaged in the hard business of dispensing patronage. Together they read recommendations, weighed qualifications, and estimated political consequences. He proclaimed lofty standards to guide the task: "If a man who has attained [this] high office cannot free himself from cliques and act independently, our Constitution is valueless." But a President like Pierce who concentrates so heavily upon such choices neglects the big decisions. Pierce loved detail and injected himself into an ever-shifting miscellany of petty problems. He visited the departments regularly, heeded minor matters, encouraged his Secretaries to bring him a full store of middling business; tracked down all manner of complaints pouring in from his mail; and kept his door open to the public. A disgruntled humanity, bearing paltry complaints, streamed in. The incessant puttering with trivia was, in actuality, Pierce's kind of compensation for his in-

343

ability to handle major policy. The larger problems slid by little touched by Presidential power: trouble in Cuba, Mexico, and Central America; ailing relations with England; Kansas torn and bleeding.[2]

Programed decisions, repetitive and routine, following established rules, precedents, and strategies, are part of any Chief Executive's day: the hour when he starts work, his choice of tasks, the distribution of his time, what he reads or ignores. But some Presidents are controlled by routine. Calvin Coolidge is the supreme example of Presidential subordination to programed decision. His inviolate schedule was breakfast at eight, to work at nine, lunch at twelve-thirty, back at his desk at three, and at four he called it a day. This admittedly mild routine, contrasting shockingly with the hours of the average factory worker, he clocked from minute to minute. So, in fact, did he regulate the time of his retirment at night. William Allen White, the journalist, made this discovery during a festive outing aboard the Presidential yacht, the *Mayflower*. The conversation was gay and voluble, with everyone joining in but the Chief Executive, who was proving his large reputation for silence. "Literally," noted White, "we forgot him." At the stroke of ten Coolidge rose, walked across the room to his wife, and stood in silence. Mocking his Yankee accent, she laughed, "Time tur go tew bed!" [3]

Some of the President's most important decisions are really nondecisions, or decisions to do nothing. A President's nondecisions may be as exacting as his decisions. John Kennedy, faced with Castro's refusal to permit on-the-spot inspection for the presence of missiles and launching sites in Cuba, made several protests, and then apparently relegated the thorny matter to the limbo of nondecision. But some Presidents specialize in nondecisions; Warren Harding smiled and maneuvered his way out of difficulty until his whole kingdom of neglect tumbled down upon him.

Some of the President's decisions come in response to emergencies, but more are called for automatically at established intervals by a network of fixed deadlines that he does not set and cannot change. He faces the catalysis of the electoral calendar—the next Congressional or national election. His State of the Union message, his Economic Report, his budget, which together are a massive compilation of decisions embracing the full sweep of policy, are all rendered up to Congress in January. Each of these documents has an extended subcalendar for its preparation. Budget ceilings are set in April; departments prepare their estimates in the summer; the Office of Management and Budget reviews them in the fall. His fixed schedule heightens the tyranny of events. In Monroe's day, the surge of revolutions in Latin America and the opportunistic stirrings of the imperial European powers lent special force to the President's oncoming State of the Union message. Since it would have been unthinkable for the President not to discuss in its paragraphs relations between the hemispheres, his Union message posed, in actuality, a deadline by which he was forced to formulate his historic doctrine.

Decisions vary in the risks they hold for the President's prestige and political fortunes and the nation's welfare and safety. In putting forward his Supreme Court packing plan in 1937, Franklin Roosevelt risked the prestige of his smashing electoral victory the year before that had lifted him to the crest of his influence.* In arranging the sale of wheat to the U.S.S.R. in 1963, John Kennedy risked offending sectors of American opinion and probably losing votes. His stand on civil rights appeared to alienate millions of white voters; yet to have refused to take it would have alienated millions of blacks and damaged his country in the eyes of the world. In granting a full pardon to Richard Nixon, Gerald Ford imperiled and sacrificed a substantial measure of the public approval built up during his early Presidential tenure.

Since Dwight Eisenhower's second term, Presidential risks have acquired a new and forbidding dimension. Eisenhower became the first President to live with the Soviet Union's possession of a substantial nuclear delivery capability. The mutual nuclear capacities of the United States and the U.S.S.R. give the decisions of their chief executives the quality of "irreversibility." Decisions based upon miscalculation cannot be called back nor can actions once taken be revised. Nothing that the erring chief executive might do subsequently could compensate for the costs levied upon mankind.

Sometimes a President has time to study and consider his decisions; sometimes he must act immediately. President Monroe acted on a tight time-budget at a dinner he tendered one night for the resident diplomats. Charles Vaughan, the British minister, was seated opposite Count de Serurier, the French representative, and, as always in that era, relations between their countries were edgy. So indeed was the deportment of these diplomats. Vaughan in time noticed, to his great annoyance, that whenever the French minister spoke, he bit his thumb. Finally, unable to contain his irritation any longer, Vaughan inquired, "Do you bite your thumb at me, Sir?" "I do," replied the count. Both instantly left the table, withdrew into an adjoining hall, and unsheathed their swords. Monroe, who had followed them, made a split-second decision that conceivably saved two nations from war and his own from possible involvement. With expert flourish, he forced up the ministers' crossed swords with his own, called his servants, sent the battling ministers to separate rooms, and ordered their carriages.[4]

Time is a boon when it is available. "I'd rather be slow and right," drawled Lyndon B. Johnson, "than smart and dead." He was seldom impetuous or careless in considering an important matter, preferring to appraise the big factors—"feelin', smellin', knowin'." [5] After the 1962 Cuban crisis President Kennedy expressed his thankfulness for the length of time—some fourteen

---

* In 1935 and 1936 the Supreme Court worked havoc upon Roosevelt's New Deal legislative program by declaring one measure after another unconstitutional. Roosevelt interpreted his imposing reelection victory in 1936 as a popular endorsement of his program and decided to move against the Court. In a message of February 5, 1937, he asked Congress for legislation that would add "younger blood" to the Court. A justice, upon reaching age seventy, under the President's proposal, could resign at full pay. If he did not resign, an additional judge would be appointed. The plan aroused a political furor. Roosevelt was accused of seeking to "pack" the Court, lusting for power, and undermining the sacred principle of separation of powers. Conservative and progressive legislators alike, most of the press, and distinguished lawyers, among others, rallied against the President, who had few defenders. Debate raged in Congress through the spring and summer of 1937. The bill was eventually defeated, not so much by popular opinion as by the Court's turnabout, by which it now proceeded to find New Deal legislation constitutional.

days—that the situation permitted him to take to determine the nation's response. "If we had had to act in the first twenty-four hours," Kennedy observed, "I don't think . . . we would have chosen as prudently as we finally did." [6]

The Environment

The President is driven to make decisions by the vast, dynamic environment in which he works. The environment is laden with situations and events pressing for attention; with ideas and movements; with the interests and ambitions of men and nations; with political friends and foes; with previous decisions that have failed and succeeded. The environment is the first of several elements that comprise the process of decision-making. The President maintains surveillance over the environment for developments on which to act.

The President cannot act without situations, which may develop spontaneously or which he may manage somehow to contrive. But there are limits to his inventions. If fate had wafted Franklin Roosevelt into the Presidential chair in 1880, the serenity of that age would have presented only a miniature opportunity for decision-making compared with the broad canvass of trouble on which he could leave his imprint a half-century later.

Situations may develop into events that are more focused and visible. Abraham Lincoln, considering the realities that would make the issuance of his Emancipation Proclamation a plausible act, gave great weight to a victory on the battlefield. Abolitionists and others had long urged Lincoln to deliver his proclamation and criticized his delay. He held back, fearful that border states would join the Confederacy if it were issued. He believed that without a victory the proclamation would be a hollow gesture. Finally, the battle of Antietam came, and though the Union's claim of victory was disputed, Lee had been checked. This was enough for Lincoln, and he hurried off to the quiet of the Soldiers' Home to put the finishing touches on his Emancipation Proclamation.[7] Issued September 22, 1862, the proclamation declared that slaves who were in rebellion on New Year's Day, 1863, would henceforth be free.

Situations and events are not simply physical and material things; they encompass the world of the mind. Ideas, assumptions, motives, and values abound in the President's environment. Many great Presidential decisions borrow heavily from the previous formulations of other politicians and associates. Elements of the Monroe Doctrine, for example, were provided some years prior to its appearance by the utterances of Henry Clay and Thomas Jefferson.* Of the incipient Latin-American revolts, a key event in the doctrine's development, Jefferson said in 1808, "We consider their interests the same as ours,

---

* Monroe proclaimed his doctrine in a message to Congress, December 2, 1823, of which Secretary of State John Quincy Adams was principal draftsman. The message was evoked by the revolt of the Latin-American colonies from Spain about 1815, the creation of new republics in Latin America, and the gestures of several European nations toward intervention. Monroe, in effect, threatened war against European powers that attempted to "extend their system to any portion of this hemisphere."

and the object of both must be to exclude all European influence in this hemisphere.'' The roots of the great doctrine reached back before Jefferson and Clay·· to the formative years of the republic and the pronouncements of Washington, particularly his Farewell Address. In an important sense Monroe's decision had been made for him.[8]

The President, of course, can turn anywhere for ideas: to Congress, the universities, friends, his wife, old classmates, anyone. The operative ideas of many a great Presidential decision may emerge from the researches and findings of the bureaucracy. The idea of how to pack the Court seems to have come from Roosevelt's Justice Department. The Attorney General, Homer S. Cummings, a lanky, elderly politician, had been given an important secret assignment by Roosevelt. His task was nothing less than to contrive a plan that would thwart the Court's tendency to rule unconstitutional many of the most sacred laws of the New Deal. As he mused over this delicate assignment in his lavish office, pince-nez in hand, Cummings was picking aimlessly through a pile of books one day when he came upon a volume, *Federal Justice,* that had been written by Carl McFarland, a departmental aide. The book, a study of the ills of the lower federal courts, posed a most intriguing solution. Let ''worn-out'' judges be retired on respectable pensions, the author argued. If after a reasonable interval an eligible federal judge did not retire, let the President add a judge to the court. McFarland's prescriptions for lower federal courts were joyfully taken up by Cummings for the Supreme Court. When the Attorney General spread his handiwork before the President, Roosevelt was enormously pleased. Here in essence was what quickly became the Court-packing plan.

The Presidential environment is strewn with assumptions that he and his aides fashion and entertain. Assumptions preclude certain decisions and shape and control others. In a deepening energy crisis, Gerald Ford clung to assumptions that had undergirded his lengthy earlier political career, namely, that individual self-reliance provided better answers to most social problems than the federal government. Ford spurned the urgings of Henry Ford and General Motors for a big gasoline tax to exact greater savings of fuel than voluntary action was achieving. The President drew strength from the public's sharing of his assumptions, citing an opinion poll revealing that ''81 percent of the people agree with me. . . . I think I'm on pretty solid ground.'' Meanwhile members of his cabinet, who increasingly despaired of voluntarism, openly lobbied for governmental controls.[9]

The President beholds his environment through political lenses. He knows that much of what he does faces the hostile scrutiny of the opposition party bent upon dragging him from office at the next election. Unfriendly factions in his own party may manipulate against him. In his 1803 move to purchase Louisiana, Jefferson knew full well that he was supplying the rival Federalist party with invaluable political capital.* The Federalists, who had been shouting for a

---

* Jefferson moved to purchase the vast tract known as Louisiana when Napoleon forced a weakened Spain to cede him the entire territory. War with England soon dissolved Napoleon's dream of a vast overseas empire. He suddenly decided to sell the territory to the United States for an estimated fifteen million dollars, and a treaty was signed April 30, 1803. Jefferson thus chose to add territory to the United States by purchase rather than by conquest.

war of conquest, greeted his decision with the cry that he was bankrupting the Treasury to buy a desert. But in Jefferson's own party the purchase was a huge political success. The Republican factions scrambled madly to claim credit for it. Northern Republicans, sniffing hungrily for a strong candidate to rid them once and for all of the "Virginia succession" to the Presidency, aimed to establish one of their own as the hero of the Louisiana conquest, and a lavish campaign was launched to prove that Robert Livingston of New York, who with James Monroe negotiated the purchase, deserved entire credit for its success.[10]

In choosing what to decide, the President acts as a kind of filter between his office and its environment. The state of his political fortunes, his interpretation of them, his miscalculations, and how he hopes the record of his administration will be engraved on the pages of history all may influence his choices. President Johnson's decisions, announced on March 31, 1968, to deescalate the Vietnam War and not to seek another term of office, served almost to quiet the severe attacks upon him from domestic quarters and to stake out a firm and advantageous ground upon which his eventual reputation in history might be established.

The Alternatives

Having chosen an event or situation as the occasion for a decision, the President and his aides canvass the alternative courses of action. These must be formulated and analyzed, pursuits that Herbert Simon calls "design activity." Before the alternative courses can be plotted, the raw information amassed from the environment must be studied for meaning, particularly as it foreshadows the future.

Interpretation, at its best, is a frail and inexact enterprise. At the level of the Presidency, a seemingly simple act can mean many things. When North Korean troops marched across the thirty-eighth parallel into South Korea in 1950, President Truman and his counselors started with the plausible assumption that the heavy hand of the Soviet Union was behind the venture and faced the question of the Kremlin's motive and purpose. General Omar Bradley, chairman of the Joint Chiefs of Staff, contended that the North Korean attack was a diversionary gambit preparatory to a major Soviet blow, possibly against Iran, and urged that few American troops, therefore, be committed to Korea, since they would be needed elsewhere. George Kennan, a premier authority on Soviet behavior, argued that the communists were engaging in "soft-spot probing" and advised that "situations of strength" be created wherever the Soviet thrust came, even in Korea. Others believed that the Soviets were testing the will of anticommunist nations to resist open aggression, as Hitler did when he reoccupied the Rhineland. Still other counselors advanced a "demonstration" theory stating that the U.S.S.R. expected to make Korea a show of their strength and of allied impotence, with worldwide repercussions. Finally, there was the view that the Soviet Union was promoting a general "Far Eastern strategy." [11] For example, John Foster Dulles, then negotiating the Japanese peace treaty, saw the Korean attack as a Soviet thrust to block American efforts to bring Japan into its alliances.

Once having interpreted the environment, the President and his aides advance to the next hurdle—developing alternative responses. Not infrequently, this step may be dispensed with in the face of what seems to the President a clear, convincing solution. Harry Truman, boarding his plane after violence in Korea had rudely terminated his weekend back home, came quickly and solitarily to a fundamental decision: North Korea's aggression across the thirty-eighth parallel must be countered by force. The communists had launched a challenge that could not be sidestepped: "An outlaw was terrorizing the world community"; to ignore him meant risking "a third world war." At a meeting with his military and diplomatic aides at Blair House that evening for dinner and discussion, Truman apparently did not even consider the possibility of a nonviolent response. [12] An implicit decision that American armed forces must be committed provided the operating premise. From it other necessary decisions and their alternatives would follow; what kind of force, how many men, and within what territorial confines should the Americans fight?

Alternatives may be developed by random steps over a period of time by the President and others commanding his attention. Franklin Roosevelt, vexed by the Supreme Court's mounting tendency to strike down New Deal laws as unconstitutional, developed a variety of alternatives during the exasperating months of rebuff. An earlier forceful Chief Executive, who also suffered from the judiciary, was instructively recalled. Andrew Jackson, for the moment, became Roosevelt's inspiration. When the Court weighed one important case, Roosevelt, anticipating a hostile decision, prepared an address, which borrowed Jackson's famous defiance of the Court, "You have made your law, now enforce it." But the Court's deciding in the government's favor made the address unnecessary. When, subsequently, the justices struck down the New York minimum wage law, boding ill for a great amount of national and state labor legislation, the eminent progressive, Senator George Norris, urged Roosevelt to center his approaching 1936 electoral campaign upon the Court. Of these alternatives, electoral campaigning versus packing, Roosevelt eventually chose the latter.

Alternatives are manufactured by scores of aides in the executive branch who earn their daily bread by anticipating situations and events well before they occur and preparing possible responses when they do. Some of this preparation is "contingency planning"—preparation for emergencies that might happen—a process applied since the Second World War to the world's most likely trouble spots, especially, in the Eisenhower, Kennedy, and Johnson periods, to Berlin. The planners have built up crowded files of events likely to take place in Berlin and the appropriate responses. Ironically, none of these plans anticipated the wall the East Germans threw up in 1961.

More than any other contemporary President, Eisenhower relied upon subordinates to define situations and present alternative approaches to them. The President's own contribution was largely one of choosing between alternatives in whose formulation he had had little part and with whose substance he may have been unfamiliar. The Eisenhower method placed a premium on "presentations" and "briefings," on charts and one-page summaries. Eisenhower also made heavy use of committees of Presidential aides drawn from departments and the White House staff. Such committees selected problems for study, developed alternative solutions, and chose between them, leaving the President the simple task of ratification. Critics of the committee system contend that it rewards the wrong qualities by stressing fluency and "averageness," promoting agreement but discouraging creativity. They contend that Eisenhower was often kept ignorant of alternatives that his subordinates rejected and therefore never laid before him. Eisenhower's defenders point to a considerable body of "split decisions," or alternatives that his subordinates could not decide between themselves and did lay before the President for his choice.

John Kennedy, eschewing the Eisenhower method and vowing to put himself into "the thick of things," expended great quantities of energy and time spreading himself all across the decisional spectrum. The President, he thought, should hover constantly over the quest for alternatives, and if he does not, he is a prisoner of the choices that his aides finally put before him. Kennedy consulted with many advisers both outside the executive branch and inside, at various ranks in the hierarchy, at deskside conferences and over the telephone. Hans J. Morgenthau argued that the Kennedy method exposed him to too much advice, steeping him with all shades of opinion, engendering a state of mind that makes timely and forceful decision difficult. He cited the Cuban invasion fiasco of 1961 and the delayed response to the rise of the Berlin wall as case studies of Presidential irresolution. Kennedy's reaction when the Russians built the Berlin wall in 1961 was characterized, Morgenthau noted, by a duality. Kennedy responded with a "hard" line in what he said and how he said it. His style was truly Churchillian. But what he did was something else. He acted "flexibly," or, less euphemistically, he did little, and he did it late. His deeds were reminiscent not of Churchill but of Chamberlain. The contradiction, this analysis concluded, confused the American public, the nation's allies, and probably the U.S.S.R.[13]

The gathering and weighing of alternatives may be more than a private act, reflecting the President's own necessities. The act may also bear dimensions in public relations. In 1965, Lyndon Johnson, before deciding to increase the American commitment in the Vietnam War, weighed his alternatives in a fashion evidently intended to refute critics who charged that he was given to impulsiveness in conducting foreign affairs. In preparation for the President's decision, Defense Secretary McNamara made a five-day tour of battle areas and consulted with United States and Vietnamese leaders. Upon McNamara's return, Johnson began a series of conferences with his principal advisers: McNamara, Secretary of State Dean Rusk, Undersecretary George Ball, Presidential Assistant McGeorge Bundy, CIA Chief William Raborn, Joint Chiefs of Staff Chairman Earle G. Wheeler, the newly appointed ambassador to South

Vietnam, Henry Cabot Lodge, and other officials. At the end of the second day's meeting, Bill Moyers, the President's assistant, disclosed to the press, "I think it is safe to say that a lot of the deliberation is behind the group now, and the next stage involves what to do about these recommendations and deliberations." But the discussions still continued for days and were joined by two leading Republicans experienced in foreign affairs, Arthur H. Dean and John J. McCloy. Johnson also consulted former President Eisenhower by telephone. After these discussions, Johnson ordered further special studies on "the additional strength that each military service may need in South Vietnam." These several procedures served to suggest that Johnson's decisions for Vietnam would be methodical and controlled.[14]

Choice-Making

The climactic stage of decision-making is the President's "choice activity"—selecting a particular course of action from the alternatives available. Of the several steps of decision-making, choice is the one the President is least able to escape. He can delegate the tasks of watching the environment, selecting problems for action, fashioning alternatives, and even making some choices or decisions. Yet he is expected to make the important choices or decisions as the unavoidable price of his incumbency.

Despite their monopoly of responsibility for hard choices, some Presidents excel in bringing others to make them. As revelations of the Teapot Dome corruptions of the previous Harding administration unfolded in his own young Presidency, Coolidge resisted counsel, urgently pouring upon him, that he fire his Attorney General, Harry Daugherty. Even when the prestigious progressive leader, Senator William E. Borah of Idaho, proposed the step, Coolidge demurred. "I am here to carry out the Harding policies," he said. "I am here as a Republican President. Daugherty was Harding's friend. He stands high with the Republican organization. I do not see well how I can do it." The importunities from many sides to dump Daugherty continued, but the President would not act.

At last, when a Senate resolution was introduced calling upon the President to dismiss Daugherty, Coolidge summoned Borah to the White House one night for "urgent business." After several minutes of Presidential silence, Borah was still puzzled about what the urgent business was when Daugherty came up the grand stairway to Coolidge's study, "his jaw set," according to a White House secretary, "and his eyes like flint." Coolidge tersely introduced his visitors, adding, "Well, don't let my presence embarrass you!" This instruction was superfluous. Borah and Daugherty went at it for an hour of shrill debate. Coolidge sat by, slumped in his chair smoking. In the din of the exchange, Borah exclaimed that it was not for him to tell the Attorney General to resign; it was the President's duty. Coolidge said not a word. When at last the antagonists finished, the little President, standing to hurry his parting guests, quacked, "Senator, I reckon you're right!" Daugherty, "white with rage," according to the secretary, who witnessed the encounter, stomped "angrily down the stairs and out of the White House." [15] He soon resigned. Coolidge had put upon Borah the burden of confronting Daugherty, thus forcing the decision.

The President determines what choices or decisions are possible. His choices are influenced not only by his personal ideals but by his knowledge of what has worked in the past, his estimate of the response of his adversaries, his judgment of what his publics at home and abroad will bear, of whether the bureaucracy will comply, and whether his party will go along. No one else in American government or society has a sweep of duties, and therefore of decisions, like his.

Each President has his own preferred manner of choice. Eisenhower preferred to be calm and composed. "Boy, there's just one thing I really *know*," he once said, "You *can't* decide things in a *panic*. Any decision you make when you are panicked, you can be sure of only one thing. It will be a bad one." [16]

Franklin Roosevelt's method of making choices was, as Arthur M. Schlesinger, Jr., has described it, "involved and inscrutable." Roosevelt weighed a basket of factors in a typical major decision: political timing, consequences to his personal public fortunes, interest group reactions, partisan advantage, impact on Congress and the public.[17] He permitted situations to develop and crystallize, he let competing forces pull in conflict, and then through some system of "unconscious calculation," as Rexford Tugwell termed it, the decision finally emerged. Roosevelt's method, Tugwell observed, made it seem that "no choosing had taken place" and forestalled discovery of his "governing principle." [18] Decision and policy were not thought out; rather, the President's intuitions seemed to coalesce and initiate a result. That his decisions were sometimes untidy never troubled the President. Clear-cut administrative decisions, he felt, worked only if they reflected clear-cut political realities. If they did not, the decisions would prove hollow and weak. He was devoted to final objectives and flexible means. Roosevelt, like many another President, valued procrastination. Wait long enough for clamoring forces to settle, for the momentum of events to slacken, and the imperatives of today will be gone tomorrow. Time he considered a great corrective, one that spares the President many hard choices. He loved to make minor choices in a dramatic way that shocked and surprised the public. "I'm going to spring a bombshell," he delighted to announce, and then stunned his gaping audience with a novel proposal such as changing the date of Thanksgiving or imposing national daylight-saving time the year around to aid the war effort. "He delights in surprises—clever, cunning and quick," Hugh Johnson observed. "He likes to shock friends as well as enemies with something they never expected." [19]

Often a mighty inhibiting factor in choice-making is risk-aversion, a phenomenon that is, of course, distributed unevenly among Presidents. Critical in choice-making are factors that decrease risk-aversion, such as the counsel of respected advisers and the occurrence of benign new events. Ideally, the decision-maker, faced with the task of choice under conditions of uncertainty, should choose the alternative that is consistent with his basic judgment and preferences, his strategy.[20]

That much Presidential choice-making is a rough approximation of this model is suggested by Nixon's 1970 decision to send American forces into Cambodia. The President consulted with a wide circle of advisers who rallied around two alternatives: to do nothing, and to move American troops into Cambodia to attack North Vietnamese installations there. As chief spokesman for the first alternative, Secretary of State William Rogers argued that the invasion of Cambodia meant widening the war and running the risk of entrapment in an inconclusive outcome that had befallen Johnson. Already, the President had won wide popular support for his policy of gradual withdrawal from Vietnam, and he should not hazard its loss. Further, Rogers argued, the military objectives to be sought in Cambodia could be achieved by South Vietnamese forces alone.

The Pentagon contended that a full assault, with American troops participating, was essential. Military intelligence disclosed that the enemy aimed either to overthrow the Lon Nol government or to open a supply lane to the sea in eastern Cambodia. Either development imperiled South Vietnam and American withdrawal.

After a three hour debate, Nixon withdrew to his hideaway office in the Executive Office Building and on a pad of yellow legal paper jotted down the arguments for and against an invasion, and the tenor of his notations suggests that the survival of the Nol regime was tied, in his thinking, to American success in Vietnam. In reviewing whether there should be some action in Cambodia, Nixon listed only favorable arguments—"Time running out," "Military aid" to Lon Nol could be "only symbolic." A scribble followed that inaction might tempt North Vietnam to set up a puppet regime in Phnom Penh, and, finally, a comment that inaction by both sides would leave an "ambiguous situation" that eventually would favor the communists.

Nixon then recorded the pros and cons of American action in Cambodia and for a South Vietnamese attack alone. He recognized that use of American troops would foment a "deep division" of domestic opinion, might instigate collapse of the Paris peace talks, a communist attack on Phnom Penh, or a major North Vietnamese initiative across the Demilitarized Zone. Just as Nixon was about to approve an attack with American troops, someone, probably Rogers, suggested that the military might be telling the President only what they thought he wanted to hear. Troubled, Nixon dispatched to his Vietnam field commander, General Creighton Abrams, an out-of-channels message requesting "the unvarnished truth." The participation of American troops, Abrams replied, was essential, and Nixon, after more consultations, ordered the attack.[21]

Viewed collectively over time, Presidential choices appear wavering and inconsistent. They seldom approximate neat consistent patterns like soldiers on parade. Shifting events, the alchemy of competing pressures, the President's own political sensitivities bring disarray. Franklin Roosevelt, therefore, almost alternatingly advanced upon and backed away from a progressive line. He began with an isolationist economic policy and shifted to an internationalist trade policy. He turned from cooperation with business to regulation. In reality, he was responding to changing events and situations, to the necessity of winning and holding a broad base of support.

Making the Decision Known

The President, having made his choice or decision, next makes it known. The means of promulgation are usefully varied. The President can convey his choice by simple statement or artful interference, by silence or gesture, by proclamation signed and sealed. How he communicates may be idiosyncratic. Presidents, for example, are wont to incorporate important decisions about their administrations in carefully prepared inaugural addresses. Not Franklin Pierce; despite the significant policy it had to convey, his inaugural was unwritten and extemporized without a note. Most Presidential decisions are not deliberately and systematically promulgated. As Chester Barnard observes, "most executive decisions produce no direct evidence of themselves and . . . knowledge of them can only be derived from the cumulation of indirect evidence."

Presidential decisions, when they become known, produce sensations of pleasure and pain. Some Chief Executives limit as far as possible their own acts of promulgating to the announcements of pleasurable decisions. They leave the dispensing of the hard negative to subordinates. Harry Hopkins in his day securely established himself in the craw of many a defeated decision-seeker as Franklin Roosevelt's abominable no-man. Sherman Adams excelled in the same role for Dwight Eisenhower. Indeed, Adams' eventual departure from the Presidential scene was hastened by the large and ever-growing body of the disgruntled created by his capacity to say no. Some decisions, regardless of their effect, can be communicated only by the President. It is inconceivable that President Johnson's decision not to seek reelection, which produced pain for his friends and pleasure for his foes, could have been disclosed by anyone but himself.

A President's own mood and gesture can enhance the force of his decision, just as diffidence can drain a strong decision. Lincoln added immeasurably to the force of the Emancipation Proclamation when he declared, upon signing it, "I never, in my life, felt more certain that I was doing right than I do in signing this paper." [22] Johnson's decision to halt the bombing of North Vietnam was given special force when he coupled it with his disclosure that he would not accept another term of office.

Promulgation involves timing. The decision must be revealed neither too late nor too soon. Not surprisingly, Presidents withhold their decision until the time is ripe. Lincoln had composed and firmly decided upon his Emancipation Proclamation some weeks before he finally issued it. He bided his time, waiting for a Union victory on the battlefield to enhance the historic document's importance and reception. Union victories were not easily come by at this stage in the war, and weeks passed. While he waited, one of his most formidable critics, Horace Greeley, editor of the New York *Tribune,* took him to task in a moving, widely read editorial, "The Prayer of Twenty Millions." The President's followers, Greeley charged, were "deeply pained by the policy you seem to be pursuing with regard to the slaves of rebels. . . . We think you are strangely and disastrously remiss in the discharge of your official and imperative duty with regard to the emancipating provisions of the new Confiscation Act." [23]

Some Presidents precede a statement of their choices with a subtle ritual. Franklin Roosevelt, fresh from his decision to launch the Court-packing plan, tendered the annual Presidential dinner for the judiciary. All the high court justices appeared at the White House except the aged Louis Brandeis, who never ventured out in the evening, and Harlan F. Stone, who was ill. Approximately eighty notables gathered, and those seated at the President's table presented a spectacle tinged with an irony that Roosevelt relished. At his table were all but two of the justices he was about to subjugate, and at the table also were Attorney General Cummings and several other faithful helpers who had prepared the artifacts for the subjugation. When the packing plan would be sprung, the justices would recall, and presumably with not a little awe, the President's droll finesse.[24]

The act of promulgation may require several ancillary decisions. Priority was vital to Roosevelt's Court-packing strategy, and so he directed his legislative leaders to place his judiciary bill ahead of the farm bill, the wages and hours bill, and the "little TVA" bill on the Congressional calendar. The precedence of the bill would communicate to farm and labor leaders and to liberals the loud, clear message that the quickest way to secure their cherished legislation was to put their shoulders behind the President's bill. The faster it was passed, the faster would their measures advance.

Alas for democracy, the promulgation of decisions may partake of deceit. The disclosure of key decisions increasing American involvement in the Vietnam War in the Johnson era reflected a pattern of executive manipulation of public opinion according to "the national interest," as officials defined it. Beneath that spacious umbrella they practiced concealment and half truths, which they justified to themselves in paternalistic terms, by which the American people were beheld as incapable of comprehending the day's problems and who, therefore, had to be "brought along." With the highest of motives, Johnsonian decision-makers believed that they knew best, that problems of diplomacy and national security were too subtle for unsophisticated average citizens. By shielding public opinion from information it needed to make up its minds, officials simultaneously shielded themselves from pressure.[25] All this flowered under the friendly sun of Lyndon Johnson's conviction that the President was a well-nigh omniscient, virtually irreproachable decision-maker in foreign affairs. The President was "the only President you have," who made decisions and deserved support. To question and criticize weakened the nation and aided its opponents.[26] In major decisions Gerald Ford valued secrecy, in his well-guarded plans to pardon Richard Nixon and in his earlier career. Ford's wife Betty says that after their engagement Ford cryptically notified her that their marriage must be postponed "because something was coming up that he couldn't tell me about just then." Later the mystery dissolved when Ford announced his first candidacy for Congress. "I was provoked that he would keep a secret from me," said Betty Ford, "but very happy when he confided in me a few weeks later." [27]

Consequences

Decisions are applied and implemented, and, like all acts, have consequences. For the President, decisions represent successes and losses, costs and gains. A Presidential decision of magnitude may lead to bitterness or it may touch off national exultation and create a mood rich with political promise. When a horseman rode into Washington from New Orleans on January 15, 1804, with the news that Louisiana had been peaceably delivered to the United States three weeks before, the nation rejoiced. Congress gave a great dinner, with the President and the cabinet as the honored guests, to celebrate the gain of a new empire. French representative Louis Pichon, informing his government of the jubilation, well observed that "the acquisition of Louisiana and the peaceful manner of possession have raised Jefferson and his friends to a high point of popularity and regard. His reelection must be considered as assured." [28] In great decisions it is ordinarily not the President's fate to receive the lavish approval that befell Jefferson, but mixed praise and censure.

But most Presidential decisions lead only to probable outcomes, rather than to certain consequences. Even under conditions of perfect information, the decision-maker must hazard a guess that a particular choice will lead to particular results.[29] Nixon's 1970 decision to send American troops into Cambodia reveals the possible magnitude of unanticipated consequences. In his television address explaining his decision, Nixon depicted its likely outcome in grandiose terms: the invasion would clear out communist sanctuaries that served as bases for attacks on "both Cambodia and American and South Vietnamese forces in South Vietnam as well." Wiping out these bases would get to the "heart of the trouble," bring the boys home sooner, remind the Russians and Chinese of American determination, and contribute to a just and lasting peace.

The invasion revealed, however, that the sanctuaries had been largely abandoned, yielding only a modest cache of armaments. Meanwhile, at home, an agitated Senate was spurred to new effort to clip the wings of the President's war-making power, and protests and rioting by college students, which Nixon had anticipated on a modest scale, flamed to high intensity when a sudden unexpected event exploded—the killing of demonstrating students at Kent State University by National Guardsmen.

Decisions have consequences that cannot be immediately, if ever, perceived.

A weapons system requiring seven years in passage from drawing board to operations plainly forestalls any prompt revelation of the consequences of the decisions it represents. Consequences may not be perceived because the President is blinded by prejudices and ambitions. Weeks passed in the Court-packing fight before Roosevelt regarded as credible the grim daily reports his lieutenants brought him of voting prospects on Capitol Hill. He was unaccustomed to the possibility of defeat. When his Court fight wallowed inconclusively for weeks in Congress, Thomas Corcoran and Secretary of the Interior Harold Ickes noticed a marked shrinkage in their chief's aggressive leadership. The President, Ickes noted in his diary, "has acted to me like a beaten man." [30]

Pathologies of Decision-Making:
The Case of the Vietnam War

Unfortunately, Presidential decision-making is not immune to bad choices and disastrous outcomes. A mark of the strong Presidency is the capacity to make gross errors. All contemporary Chief Executives, from Franklin Roosevelt onward, have contributed to some of the more notable failures of Presidential decision-making. Roosevelt's fiasco was his unpreparedness for the attack on Pearl Harbor. Truman erred in the invasion of North Korea, which brought Communist China into the Korean War. Lyndon Johnson was caught up in decisions escalating the Vietnam War that ultimately cost him the Presidency, and Nixon failed to check overzealous subordinates from committing the criminal folly of Watergate, which ultimately destroyed his Presidency.

One of the more involved and extended of these Presidential disasters, decision-making in the Vietnam War, has been examined for causal weakness by key participants. From their observations, caveats can be extracted that should serve as warning signs in future Presidencies.

What went wrong with the decision-making of the Vietnam War, particularly in the Johnson era, when the war's steepest escalations transpired? For one thing, as the war proceeded, the choices formulated for decision-making were loaded with false options. Memoranda to the President invariably contained three options; two of which were patently unacceptable, since they posed the extremes of humiliating defeat and total war, and the third, "Option B," which always prevailed, encompassed what nearly everyone wanted to do. Option B was a magical preserver of policy consensus and it precluded complaints from Presidential counselors that their advice was not heeded. But a consensus-type option such as Option B can bear contradictions potentially debilitating for policy. Thus, at one juncture, the United States moved both to bomb more and to negotiate seriously, though the bombing forestalled significant negotiations.[31]

In Presidential councils, tactical arguments, rather than fundamental concepts, were focused on. Fundamental assumptions were rarely, if ever, questioned. Participants argued not in terms of what they thought was right, but what they perceived would be persuasive. One participant, Leslie Gelb, organizer of the written assessment of the war subsequently known as "the Pentagon Papers," felt that the community of Presidential counselors lived in a "house without windows." With similar backgrounds in education and public service, they possessed a common view of the world, which in the context of the war was a world of dominoes, where a threat anywhere was a threat everywhere, and any adviser who challenged such assumptions was derided and discounted as "soft-headed." [32] Another constraining force was the judgment of the advisory groups that a member was "losing his effectiveness," a fate to be shunned by remaining silent, going along, or salving one's conscience with resolve to fight another day.[33]

The endless demands for Vietnam decisions brought on the malady of executive fatigue, when tired decision craftsmen from the White House and the State and Defense Departments became increasingly entrapped in their narrowing view of the world and an ever more cliché-ridden discourse. The inertia of bureaucracy, wishful thinking, took over, and there followed a weary surrender to the semantics of the military that concealed the reality of the war. For some advisers, the war's decisions were an upward-spiraling ego investment whose stakes increased with each commitment, making them less prone to question and reject.[34] Finally, the President himself. Had Johnson been more confident in foreign policy—his experience had been almost wholly in domestic politics —he could have raised the hard questions that excessive consensus submerged. Johnson had emerged from the 1964 elections with an overwhelming mandate to deescalate the war, but he failed to impose it on his advisers.

How can the strong Presidency and the country be spared from costly bad decisions? Carefully defined roles for each adviser, particularly of powers and functions, will serve as a barrier against group dominance. The establishment of operating procedures and the cultivation of traditions of workmanship that enhance critical inquiry also can help. Old assumptions need to be periodically reevaluated. Most of all, a wary President can cultivate the representation of divergent views among his counselors, competition of ideas, and freedom of argument. An alert President can be his own best insurance against big trouble.

An Overview

The President's method in decision-making has something of the quality of fire. It can serve for good or ill; it can be a virtue or a vice; at one time it can succeed, at another it leads to abysmal failure. There is no available body of absolute directives like the Ten Commandments to assure correct decision-making. "Don't put off unto tomorrow what can be done today," the adage says. But, according to another, "Sufficient unto the day is the evil thereof." A Franklin Roosevelt can long postpone a key decision, and, endowed with a kind of charmed political life, manage to get away with it. William McKinley on the eve of war with Spain, a peace-minded man eager to avoid conflict, delayed so in his bewilderment at events that war-minded legislators and the yellow press grabbed the initiative and with it the issue of war or peace.

The President does well to consult, but he does ill to consult too much. Truman and the Democratic party paid dearly for his failure to involve Congress substantially in his early Korean decisions. Later, when the Korean War became unpopular, he could not share the resulting political liabilities with a Congress shut out from his original decisions. But consultations also can be too wide and can produce such contradictory counsel and excessive information that decision is delayed and weakened. Decision is a blend of fact, thought, incisiveness, and vigor; to stress one ingredient is to diminish others.

When the occasion requires a decision, the President must communicate his will clearly and not create havoc, as Wilson did in proclaiming, "We are too proud to fight," a well-intentioned moral standard for the nation, which the Allies understandably misinterpreted as an evidence of cooling ardor toward their cause. Yet the President will also need an instinct for ambiguity in his daily grapple with petitioners and their pressures for his favor. For others to know his will too clearly and too soon may bring him political trouble and grief.

There are discernible in the world of the President several principles that seem far more often right than wrong. Above all, the President must keep the initiative in decisions that are his and not permit it to be grabbed by Congress or private groups. But neither should he preempt decisions or participation that in a democracy are rightfully theirs. For decision, as the Vietnam War makes clear, must be a continuous process of winning consent. The President should not decide in anger, or grief, or other high emotion, but only in composure. Presidents by this standard have been remarkably successful. As a lot they have not been hotheads or desk-pounders. The magnitude of the Chief Executive's power and responsibility and his need to maintain to the outside world an image of self-confidence require that he appear to be "in charge," that he speak and act with assurance, hold his subordinates in rein, and comprehend the problems they are struggling with. Decision is more than the creation of policy. It reveals the President as a person.

15

CONFLICT

Conflict is a central ingredient of the strong Presidency and democracy, and for both it can be a force for good and bad. Democratically regulated conflict is a means of confining the strong Presidency within channels that protect civil liberties and popular political processes. Conflict facilitates constructive social change, vital in a dynamic democracy. Time and again, the Presidency has engaged in conflict in initiating social policy. For example, Franklin Roosevelt's proposals for social security were greeted by the fierce resistance of interested groups and the opposition party, followed by a phase in which the policy, put into operation, gained general acceptance among its original opponents. Before long, social security was a solid plank in the platforms of both major parties.

For the Presidency and democratic society, conflict can be an integrative as well as a disintegrative force. For the Presidents of the two world wars, those conflicts blanketed domestic politics with a simple unity of will that contrasted sharply with the tumultuous prewar politics of Roosevelt's Presidency and with Wilson's disastrous postwar fight for the League of Nations. Conflict generated outside the Presidency may prod the Chief Executive into investing resources of his office into policy initiatives, which otherwise he might not do. Conflict can push more alternatives to the surface of awaiting decision than are yielded by placid routine politics.

Like the other branches of government, the Presidency and the executive departments abound with institutions and processes that regulate conflict. The President's annual budget for the executive branch is a conflict process, in which agencies and subagencies vie for limited resources. The contest is refereed by the Office of Management and Budget and major issues are decided by the President. Such bodies as the cabinet, the National Security Council, the Domestic Council, and the vast network of interdepartmental committees are arenas where conflict is waged and resolved, perhaps only tentatively, since conflict may move on to other arenas.

These and other Presidential regulators—a team-player philosophy or a policy ideology, for example—can sometimes overmanage conflict, unduly control or suppress it for the sake of a consensus that ill-serves the President and salubrious decision-making. Presidential decision-making in the Vietnam War was long plagued by excessive unity among its advisers and the withholding of dissent, the most fertile source of genuine alternatives that the President should have had available for consideration.

As one who wages conflicts, the President is regulated by the Constitution, the courts, Congress, the electoral process, and other components of the political system that require him to act within democratic confines. That he may sometimes push beyond these boundaries is evidenced by the Watergate scandals, but as those episodes also revealed, powerful back-up regulators came into play to check an errant Presidency—the intervention of federal district judge John Sirica, the televised investigation led by Senator Sam J. Ervin, Jr., the media's revelation of wrong-doing, the public opinion polls that disclosed sharp public disapproval, the constitutional processes of impeachment.

Types of Conflict

The President engages in various kinds of conflict. Some are personal, designed to protect his own political capital or enhance his reputation in the Washington political community. Others are institutional, conflicts engendered by elections, appointments, treaties, and the like. The President may be a participant in class conflicts—Franklin Roosevelt struggling for work relief projects for the unemployed, Nixon vetoing social legislation and impounding funds with argumentation that mirrored the probusiness philosophy of Calvin Coolidge. The President also faces role conflicts. Nixon, prizing détente with the Soviet Union, sold American wheat to that country at bargain prices in 1972, a step that contributed to shortages of domestic wheat in 1973 and brought down upon him consequent popular resentments. The President does battle with various types of actors—with relative equals, such as foreign leaders, Congressional chieftains, and committee chairmen, and sometimes even with subordinates who do not choose to be altogether subordinate.

Near the end of his tenure, Lyndon Johnson was caught up in a painful conflict with Secretary of Labor Willard Wirtz. The controversy centered on a reorganization order Wirtz issued, against the President's wishes, which catalyzed long-raging differences between the two men on a more serious issue, the Vietnam War. Wirtz had soured on it, and the two had exchanged bitter words on the subject in the cabinet that left Wirtz teetering on resignation. When Johnson requested that the reorganization order be withdrawn, Wirtz refused. In a spirited confrontation, Johnson requested the Secretary's resignation, and Wirtz replied that technically he already had it, adding that Johnson had the right to remove him. In a candid allusion to their differences on the war, Johnson replied that "There are those who think you have been trying to put yourself in a position to be removed for some time," a thrust for the President's theory that Wirtz was seeking removal in order to demonstrate a breakdown in the administration. Johnson suffered through an extended predicament of a subordinate who would neither obey his orders nor resign. Eventually, other cabinet and subcabinet figures intervened as emissaries with soothing ointments, and Wirtz withdrew his reorganization order and stayed on in the administration.[1]

Typically, contemporary Presidents are caught up in ideological battles between conservatives and liberals, with the President's own favor and decision as the prize. Both before and after his death, liberals vied to "adopt" John Kennedy, although for many he was not their first choice for President, and it is readily arguable that he was less liberal than his 1960 primary opponent, Hubert Humphrey, who adhered to a populist line, or his successor, Lyndon Johnson, whose programs veered more decidedly toward the liberal polarity than Kennedy's. Likewise Kennedy was courted by, and was attentive to, Congressional conservatives, whose support was necessary. With his narrow electoral victory and modest political debts in Congress that he could collect on, to secure passage of even a modest legislative program, Kennedy needed conservative support.

The President as Conflict Generator

Some Presidents and their personalities are like furnaces in which conflicts can be instantly lighted by the match of slight events or causes. In psychological make-up, these Presidents are conflict-prone and labor under special strain to manage their deportment in ways that keep conflicts at acceptable numbers and levels. Two recent Presidents seem decidedly of this genre.

Lyndon Johnson, an over-size bundle of complexities, insisted that everything within his life's reach orbit around himself. He invested little effort in controlling a quick, cutting temper, soared in crackling enthusiasm, and dropped as easily into pits of gloom; and he could plummet between these extremes within minutes, thanks to minimal effort at self-regulation.[2] On his family and staff he was relentlessly demanding. In private meeting and argument, a juggernaut style accompanied his massive presence. The visitor knew the pat on the knee, the poke of enormous fingers into his shoulder, the President hunched forward in his rocking chair, extracting from the folds of a black silk suit a printed paper with the results of the latest public opinion poll proving that "the people are for me." To some, Johnson was arrogant; to others he was engaged in a constant battle against insecurity, or so they interpreted his anger at being photographed from an unflattering angle and his endless hunger for affection, which enabled him to set something of a record among Presidents for hugging and kissing.[3]

Aggression is often triggered by anxiety, and if anxiety is the name for Johnson, conflict was the name of his foreign policy. International relations was an outer world, far distant from Texas and the White House, and he was suspicious of it. "Foreigners are not like the folks I am used to," said Johnson.[4] Domestic politics, in which he was thoroughly at home, witnessed a paucity of Johnson-initiated conflicts, but abroad, conflict was his policy's mark.

The President lives in a mental world of sentiments, values, perceptions. Conflict is generated by his sentiments, or attitudes and feelings, toward other individuals, things, events. The President's sentiments are conveyed both by verbal symbols and overt behavior—activities. There is a clue to President Nixon's sentiments toward the war protesters who jammed Washington following the incursion into Cambodia and evoked the most extensive mass arrests in American history. Through it all, Nixon watched a football game on television, a determined and publicized act of belittlement.

Like other individuals, the President has values, which, though shared with others, are shaped by his unique experience. A review of Nixon's key speeches on the Vietnam War suggests that the President regarded his personal conflict-type values as the dominant values of the United States. Vietnam policy he defended on the ground that the United States must not act "like a pitiful, helpless giant," and it must not be "impotent." If anything, Nixon's identification of self with country seemed extremely close. In one speech, for example, he asserted, "it is not our power but our will and character that are being tested tonight." [5]

A common phenomenon observable in Presidents, as in anyone, is selective perception, by which the information coming in to the recipient is sifted, with emphasis accorded to some items while others are ignored. Different kinds of distortion can sometimes affect these incoming stimuli and cause them to orient the President toward conflict. Fear or anxiety tends to increase the perceived "maliciousness" of other people, an element that may have helped trigger Nixon's lengthy and acrid conflict with the news media, culminating in his charge in a news conference, at a peak of his Watergate troubles, that the television networks engaged in "outrageous, vicious, distorted reporting." Yet when a study group, established by the Twentieth Century Fund, sought from the President's staff specific details on which these charges were based, extraordinarily few were supplied. [6]

Conflict as Political Exchange

For the President conflict is a species of political exchange. To engage in conflict is to incur likely costs and benefits. Sometimes, to engage in a conflict may entail less cost than not engaging. All too often the costs of conflicts, including major ones, cannot be anticipated, as Harry Truman discovered in choosing to resist the sudden invasion of South Korea by Communist North Korea in 1950. His resolute action was supported with acclaim and high unanimity in Congress and in public opinion. But as the struggle deepened and grew inconclusive and casualty lists lengthened, unanticipated costs mounted for Truman. From one side he was criticized as too soft on Communism and from another as too hard. Senator Joseph McCarthy launched severe attacks on Truman and his subordinates, and the crescendo of criticism broke beyond restraint when the President removed the idolized General Douglas MacArthur from his field command because of his insubordinate attempts to extend the war beyond what Truman considered prudent limits. Hereupon the President was accused of opposing victory, and the war was incorporated into the favorite anti-Truman litany of the 1952 Presidential campaign, "Communism, Cronyism, Corruption, and Korea." [7] Doubtless, as Truman would testify, conflicts, above all, wars, can be laden with risks, with low predictability of their capacity to produce an excess of costs or benefits.

Conflict can erupt from the workings of distributive justice. The President, for instance, expects to accrue to himself certain valued returns in exchange for his acts. Thus, from an appointee to a high executive post he anticipates that for the recognition and privileges conferred, loyalty and cooperation for the policies of his administration will be forthcoming. Consequently, when Henry Wallace as Secretary of Commerce and James Allen as director of the Office of Education publicly dissented from prevailing foreign policy, their respective Presidents, Truman and Nixon, forced them out. In his formulations of political distributive justice the President often acts on expectations derived from the experience of past Presidents, which may harden into practice, and his own previous dealings with individuals and institutions. From this can be derived the proposition that normally the more a President is disadvantaged when a rule of distributive justice fails of realization, the more likely he is to resort to conflict, and the stronger is his retaliatory action likely to be. [8]

The conflict over Nixon's two initial Supreme Court nominees, Clement Haynsworth and G. Harrold Carswell, supports this proposition. With rare exception, Presidential nominations for the Supreme Court elicit Senate approval, and Nixon was buoyed by the success of his first Court nominee, Warren Burger, who glided through the Senate with only three opposing votes. But both his subsequent nominations were fated to join the exceptions. In furtherance of a 1968 campaign pledge to alter the Supreme Court's philosophy through exercise of his appointing power, Nixon stipulated that his next nominee—eventually Haynsworth—must be white, Southern, a strict constructionist, experienced on the federal bench, and under age sixty. But the Senate rejected Haynsworth, with the extraordinary number of seventeen Republicans, including Republican leaders, voting against the nomination. Outraged, Nixon in the semiprivacy of the White House inveighed against the liberal press, which had built up opposition to Haynsworth, against another powerful opposing force, organized labor, and, above all, against those Republicans who had "betrayed" their President. A resolute Nixon declared that the set-back would not deter him, that he would not retreat by naming a non-Southerner. [9] After further search, Carswell emerged as the new nominee, with qualifications distinctly below Haynsworth's. Carswell's record included such bad marks as a 1948 white supremacy speech and the refusal of seven of eighteen judges of the Fifth Judicial Circuit, in which he was a judge, to endorse his nomination.

Why did Nixon choose a weaker nominee? Joseph Rauh of the Leadership Conference on Civil Rights, who opposed both nominations, noted that "The President didn't want to lose again, of course, but he wanted to win with opposition from the same people who had fought him on Haynsworth. He wanted to defeat his enemies in face-to-face combat. Lots of Southerners would have been confirmed easily, and he knew it. . . . They were willing to take all of us on because they were convinced they couldn't be beaten again." [10]

A common currency of political exchange, both of the President and those with whom he deals, is values that shape his disposition to engage in conflict or to abstain from it. As a new Chief Executive, Johnson quickly resolved, in the initial hours of his administration, that he would not preside over the loss of Vietnam, where thousands of American military "advisers," sent there by John Kennedy, were aiding the war effort. "I am not going to be the President who saw Southeast Asia go the way China went," Johnson declared.[11] For Johnson, the values implicit in this statement were a springboard to escalated conflict. Equally, values and the motivations they generate can be potent deterrents to the President's assumption of conflict. Both at home and in the Soviet Union, Richard Nixon's ascendance to the Presidency was expected to further deteriorate U.S.-U.S.S.R. relations, given the obdurate anticommunist record of his earlier career. But Nixon was resolved to prove that his reputation as a hard-liner actually provided him greater negotiating freedom with the Russians than a liberal Democrat could command. He was also eager to demonstrate to the Russians that his pledge to replace confrontation with negotiation, and the values implicit in that choice, was the most serious commitment of his foreign policy.[12]

Gradients of Conflict

For the President, as for others, conflicts vary in intensity; his determination of how much intensity to generate has important consequences for himself and his political fortunes, for the strong Presidency, and for democracy. That too many conflicts at too high intensity can be deleterious to the nation, the Presidency, and the incumbent is suggested by the Watergate crisis, which was actually a multitude of intense conflicts that depleted Nixon's capacity to provide leadership in many vital areas. Gerald Ford, after launching his Presidency with a high degree of approval, suddenly granted a full pardon to Richard Nixon, despite his earlier acknowledgment that the country would never stand for such a step. The resulting widespread outcry against Ford's action appears to have astonished the President, and he did what Presidents are wont to do in such circumstances—he moved to reduce the conflict. His tactic was the precedent-setting step of appearing personally before a House Judiciary subcommittee to explain his action and submit to questions.

The willingness or disinclination of a President to move up to the next gradient of conflict depends on the exchange factors that determined his engaging in the conflict in the first place—values, motivations, risks, costs, and benefits.[13] Gradients depend upon the goals involved in a conflict, how important they are to the President and how close he is to attaining them. Franklin Roosevelt, thwarted by a Supreme Court that struck down much of his New

Deal program as unconstitutional, launched his project to "pack" the Court with new Justices presumably favorable to his views, and with such goals he moved unflinchingly up each gradient of a long bitter conflict. In doing so, he committed what for him were rare and grave political errors in underestimating his opposition and exaggerating the depth of his support. Miscalculation lurks in the choices of gradients.

Among the goads that may draw the President up to the next rung of the ladder of conflict are the purposes of conflict management itself, whether it is to encourage the rise and spread of a given conflict or to reduce and redirect it. After the Senate's rejection of his two Supreme Court nominees, Haynsworth and Carswell, President Nixon, in a bitter public statement, declared that the Senate as "presently constituted" would not approve a Southern conservative. He contended that the South deserved "proper representation" on the Court, which the Senate had willfully denied. Nixon's bristling, conflict-escalating statement offered possibilities for serving several Presidential purposes. It reinforced his "Southern strategy" by reassuring Southern voters, whose support he courted, that he was prepared to fight and to sacrifice for the interests of their region. By expanding the fight and blaming the Democratic Senate, he could make the Senate's rejection of his nominees a future campaign issue. But there were also costs and risks in the President's action. Many Senators would resent the tone and substance of his statement and transfer their feelings into opposition to the controversial antiballistic missile program and other administration projects then afoot in Congress, and it threatened to sour even more the already bitter relations between the President and moderate Republican Senators who had voted against his nominations.[14]

Generally, the closer the relations of the individuals involved, the more intense the conflict becomes once it breaks out, as the Taft-Theodore Roosevelt split demonstrates. Roosevelt's former cabinet Secretary, political protégé, and appointed successor, Taft eventually displeased his mentor. The break was bitter and incurable, and its intensity was fed by the depth of their previous intimate political association. For Taft and Roosevelt, as well as for others, ideology and goodness of conscience can also feed the flames of conflict.

Sometimes it is beyond the President's power to reduce the gradients of conflict. Lyndon Johnson, some of whose domestic opponents to his Vietnam War policies administered some of the severest character lashings ever known in American politics, continued to be attacked even after he announced that he would not run again for President and after he halted the bombing of North Vietnam. But the bombing in domestic controversy did not cease, and Johnson never achieved the calming of the national mood that he hoped these actions would bring.[15]

Gradients of conflict are also affected by Presidential styles. Harry Truman readily resorted to fighting rhetoric, assailing the "do-nothing Eightieth Congress," Republican "bloodsuckers," and the Taft-Hartley Act, which he termed "dangerous" and "unworkable." In contrast, Lyndon Johnson employed moderate discourse, supplemented by a range of adroitly applied pressures. Addicted to what became known as "arm twisting," Johnson often displayed a dogged refusal to accept a "no," a disposition conveyed by his towering frame and his habit of leaning far out of his chair while peering intently into his listener's eyes, grasping a lapel, shoulder, or arm, and pouring into his ear a cascade of argument. But the real force behind this commanding manner was the sizeable array of political debts Johnson had built up in his favor during his years in Congress and as Senate leader—debts that he collected as President. Johnson was intricately informed about where the lines of power ran in Congress and in interest groups, of skeletons in other politicians' closets, and of hopes that were exploitable. Capable of unabashed appeals to mawkish sentiment and patriotism, he would use a standard ploy in reminding his listener that "I'm the only President you've got." Describing an encounter with Johnson, a union leader reported, "Lyndon has a flag in the corner of his office. He picked it up and ran around the room with it." [16]

CONFLICT AVOIDANCE   Like other politicians, Presidents are adept at conflict avoidance, and whether the strong Presidency and democracy are served by this skill depends on the specific situation. Clearly both are disadvantaged if avoidance becomes excessive and shields developing trouble. Why might a President shun certain conflicts? Anticipated costs may exceed likely gains or else the benefits of involvement versus abstinence may not be clear cut, and therefore the risks of conflict are deemed not worth taking. A President has a "conflict budget"—he must be selective; he cannot dissipate his limited political resources by engaging in too many fights at once.

Presidents display distinctive techniques of conflict avoidance. Franklin Roosevelt was a master of procrastination. He would often postpone action, convinced that in the meantime a conflict-laden problem would melt away, a conviction that was often justified by subsequent events. He excelled at sidetracking problems and at charming incipient opponents into quiet resignation. A standard Presidential ploy for avoiding or reducing conflict is the balancing of actions. Thus, in his 1965 State of the Union message to Congress, Johnson's call for enactment of ambitious social programs was tempered by promises of budget economies and renewed attack on crime in the streets, both promises made as concessions to likely conservative opponents of his social measures. He articulated labor's demand for repeal of Section 14b of the Taft-Hartley Act, but his move was undercut by quiet, informal assurances from the White House to opponents of the step that efforts would not be pushed too hard.[17]

Despite a solid reputation for pugnacity, Nixon displayed a broad willingness to avoid conflict on policy issues. Time and again he accepted rebuff on policy and program issues without feeling personally threatened or affronted. His commitment was not to values or principle but to himself, to the assertion and protection of his own adequacy and the preservation of his image. Anthropologist Margaret Mead observed that "The President thrives on opposition. It is a form of stimulation for him." [18] Well and good if policy issues were involved;

the burner remained at low flame. But let Nixon's self be threatened and conflict swiftly followed, sometimes with bare knuckles.

Conflict-Solving

The President's purposes are variously served by initiating, enlarging, or perpetuating conflict, on the one hand, or by avoiding, diverting, or concluding it on the other. The choices he makes are shaped by the elements of political exchange—values, risks, costs, and benefits. The natural history of conflicts has no set sequence of steps or stages, but usually junctures are reached when the President can diminish or halt a conflict.

Typically, Presidents are fertile with stratagems for slowing conflicts. A favorite move is the appointment of commissions to study and report on conflict situations, in the fashion of Presidential commissions on civil disorders and on violence that were appointed in the 1960s. Both for conflicts within his administration and in external society, the President can create new institutions to control the unwanted situations. He can invoke superordinate goals—patriotism, national honor, the duty to support "the only President you've got"—to replace conflict with cooperation between quarreling interests. The President and his helpers can formulate new rules to control a spreading conflict. In the 1973 energy crisis, as truckers, distraught by soaring fuel prices, fought back by blocking highways, White House aides, to resolve the situation, launched a stepped-up campaign of federal inspections to overcome price gouging at gasoline stations.

Far more than most Chief Executives, Lyndon Johnson felt that a central task of his Presidency was the controlling and resolving of society's conflicts. Impressed that the United States since the Second World War had wasted huge stores of energy and talent in unnecessary conflicts between labor and management, between the cities and rural regions, and between the races, he worked to develop formulas for reducing these conflicts. Above all, he was eager to terminate conflict between the North and South, and, as the first modern Southern President, to "bring the South back into the Union, not in a lot of words, but for real." [19] What Johnson sought, and what unfortunately eluded him, was a new era of good feelings.

In seeking to control conflict, Presidents face, and sometimes succumb to, great temptations to violate democratic norms. The Bill of Rights and other constitutional safeguards are violated if civilian Copperheads become subject to military arrest, steel mills are seized, and White House aides perpetrate burglaries in the name of national security in order to dominate conflict with domestic "enemies." If anything, one of the most urgent and complex problems of today's Presidency is to confine the office, in conflicts both at home and abroad, to behavior that satisfies democratic norms and that is responsive, most particularly, to the Bill of Rights and the Congressional power to declare war.

Crisis

The most intense and consequential form of conflict is crisis, a crucible in which a President and his administration are tested as nowhere else. No other condition tries so rigorously the capacity of the President for decision, perceptiveness, physical endurance, self-confidence, and prudence. Crisis is a cruel master that forces the Chief Executive to rearrange his priorities and recast his plans. If it brings him to wage war, he will do less in social policy, no matter how high his aspirations are for that endeavor, no matter how solemnly he laid his plans before the electorate and how enthusiastically they were approved. At no other time are the stakes so high as in crisis. The consequences of his actions are enormously magnified; he may find new strengths; and his weaknesses may be glaringly exposed. His decisions may determine nothing less than national survival and the preservation of the existing social order. What he does in crisis will be more remembered in history than anything else he does. If he fails, his shortcoming will be recalled, when a thousand successes he may have won in quieter times are long forgotten.

Most great Presidents have been crisis Presidents. Lincoln brought the nation through the holocaust of civil war, Wilson through the First World War, and Franklin Roosevelt through the depression and toward victory in the Second World War. But the brilliant success of Presidents in crisis cannot blind us to the debit side of the balance sheet, to the substantial failures. James Madison, administrator of the War of 1812, suffered defeats and retreats and the ignominy of having the White House burned from under him. Lincoln was preceded by Buchanan's administration, which failed to stay the onrush of civil war.

Contemporary Presidents face crises of a scale unknown to their predecessors. Since the end of the American nuclear monopoly, the Presidency has existed in a state of perpetual crisis in its enforced vigil to prevent some incident or issue from escalating into general war. Presidents since the Second World War have chronically been caught up in multiple crises, thanks to the capacity of communist nations to strike on many fronts and domestic society's capacity to churn up big trouble. For John Kennedy, 1962 was a year of crisis. The Soviets placed missiles in Cuba. Civil rights crises exploded in Mississippi and Alabama, and a price rise in steel threatened to smother the administration's foremost economic goals: curbing inflation, bettering the balance of payments, speeding economic growth, and relieving unemployment. Fortunately, Kennedy resolved the missile crisis, the first confrontation between the U.S. and the U.S.S.R. as nuclear powers. Because of the uniqueness and success of Kennedy's approach, it qualifies automatically as a model for future Presidents should they have the misfortune to face a similar conflict situation.

JOHN KENNEDY AND THE CUBAN MISSILE CRISIS The Cuban crisis of 1962 began in the whirring camera of an Air Force U-2 reconnaissance plane high over San Cristobal on October 14. Analysis of the developed films the next day struck the Kennedy administration with massive impact. Soviet medium-range missiles, a mobile type used by the Red Army, were in place near San Cristobal, one hundred miles west of Havana. Every American city was potentially only a few minutes away from them. The revelation set off fourteen days of diplomatic maneuver and military buildup that brought the United States to the threshold of nuclear war. The buildup contradicted assertions by Soviet leader Nikita Khrushchev, made after the disastrous attempt to land a brigade of American-trained Cuban exiles in the Bay of Pigs. In one note to Kennedy, following the episode, the Soviet Premier warned that Cuba could count on Soviet support in "beating back" any future armed attack, but in a second, he reassured the United States that his government had no bases in Cuba and did not intend to establish any.[20]

The U-2's October discovery was the climax of a Soviet buildup commencing in July. Soviet technicians and instructors, surface-to-air missiles, patrol boats with missiles, and MIG-2 fighters, according to U.S. intelligence sources, were pouring into Cuba. The executive branch was not alone in its watch. Republican and Democratic legislators alike followed and exclaimed upon the ominous developments.[21]

A frequent Republican critic of Kennedy's Cuban course was Senator Kenneth B. Keating of New York. On September 2 he urged that an Organization of American States mission investigate reports of Cuban missile bases. If the OAS failed to act, the United States should blockade Western Hemispheric waters against vessels carrying armed forces personnel or material.[22] In early September, at the instigation of Democratic Senator Richard B. Russell of Georgia, chairman of the Armed Services Committee, Congress passed a resolution invoking the Monroe Doctrine against foreign intervention in the Western Hemisphere and the 1947 Rio pact for joint Western Hemispheric defense. The United States, the resolution declared, was determined to prevent, by "use of arms" if necessary, any Cuban military buildup threatening American security. The resolution's backers, who hailed from both parties, had a double purpose: to warn Khrushchev and Castro, and to invigorate certain administration policy-makers who seemed to them to be taking too detached a view of the Cuban developments.[23]

The administration appeared to accept Khrushchev's characterization of the weapons imported into Cuba as "defensive," although the President stated publicly on September 4 that "were it otherwise the gravest issues would arise." The close surveillance the United States intelligence community was simultaneously maintaining upon Cuba was spurred by reports from Cuban refugees in Florida that surface-to-surface missiles with nuclear warheads capable of reaching American cities were on the island. But Kennedy, having been burnt by inaccurate intelligence that led to the Bay of Pigs fiasco, adopted a "twice-shy" attitude. In a speech at Albuquerque, New Mexico, on October 6, Vice President Johnson brushed aside the critics' proposal of a blockade by declaring that "the stopping of a Russian ship is an act of war." Answering a call by Senator Homer Capehart, Republican of Indiana, for more action on Cuba, President Kennedy in a campaign speech at Louisville, on October 13, hit at those "self-appointed generals and admirals who want to send someone else's sons to war."

The momentous news of the U-2 discovery was conveyed to the President at 8:45 A.M. October 16 by his special assistant for national security affairs, McGeorge Bundy, who had learned of it the night before. Bundy later explained, when Kennedy himself inquired, that nothing could have been done that night and that to call advisers in from dinners about town would have touched off alarmed public speculation. The possibility remains, however, that the President could have been informed personally, without disturbance of his aides at their dinners. The question lingers whether Bundy had such a right of choice, and whether in making it he was not, in a limited way, superseding the President. Kennedy was immediately aware of the atomic danger, and was outraged at Khrushchev's barefaced duplicity. The President ticked off to Bundy a list of officials he wished to see. These included his brother, Attorney General Robert Kennedy, and Treasury Secretary C. Douglas Dillon, upon whose judgment he often relied.[24]

The implications of the Soviet move were clear enough. By placing medium- and intermediate-range missiles in Cuba, Russia was narrowing its gap with the United States. Missiles of such range in Cuba would provide the Russians with immediate power without the long wait necessary for equivalent increases in its intercontinental missiles arsenal. A missile fired from Cuba promised far more accuracy than an ICBM from Russia. Cuba-based missiles would reduce the United States' attack-warning time virtually to seconds. The Strategic Air Command would have to be dispersed on a more or less permanent basis.

At 11:45 A.M. on October 16 Kennedy met with a group later known as the Executive Committee (Ex Com) of the National Security Council. The President presided, and his fellow conferees included Vice President Johnson, Secretary of State Rusk, Secretary of Defense McNamara, Dillon, Robert Kennedy, Undersecretary of State George Ball, Deputy Secretary of Defense Gilpatric, CIA Deputy Director Carter (CIA Director McCone was away from Washington in the crisis's first days), Assistant Secretary of State for Inter-American Affairs Martin, General Maxwell Taylor (chairman of the Joint Chiefs of Staff), and Theodore Sorensen, Presidential counsel and principal speech-writer.

The atmosphere of crisis hung thickly over the group as they canvassed the possible responses to the Soviet thrust. If the United States did nothing, it would have to live with communist missiles at its doorstep, its prestige would tumble, and the credibility of its pledges would be destroyed. Latin America might fall into the Soviet basket. If, as a second possibility, the United States bombed or invaded Cuba, its moral position would be tainted, its alliances would be disarrayed, the neutral nations would burst into great cry, and the Russians might make a countermove in Berlin or elsewhere. A third possibility was a blockade, but it too might stir a Soviet response and offend our allies, particularly the maritime powers. On the other hand, a blockade would provide the opportunity both for the United States to prepare and the Soviets to recede.[25] The meeting produced two immediate decisions. One was that air surveillance over Cuba should be intensified and the other that any action the United States took should as nearly as possible coincide with United States' public disclosure of the Russian bases.[26]

The vast departmental machinery began to turn. The Defense Department estimated the kinds of units, numbers of men, and time factors necessary for various military actions. The State Department explored the possibilities of Latin-American and European support, and its most sophisticated analysts of Soviet behavior began mulling over the probable effects of various actions on the Russians. United Nations Ambassador Adlai Stevenson was brought into the discussions.

The President had other commitments in addition to the crisis. The Congressional electoral campaign was in full swing, and Kennedy set out for Connecticut to honor long-established speaking dates. The discussions on Cuba were to be kept secret—Khrushchev did not know that Kennedy knew about the offensive missiles, and the secret could best be kept by maintaining a normal Presidential schedule. During his absence, the Ex Com met day and night in Undersecretary of State Ball's conference room, or "think tank" as it was dubbed, a windowless chamber furnished with a long table, pumpkin leather chairs, prosaic water decanters, and Dixie cups. The meetings were informal, the participants wandering in and out to keep up simultaneously with their regular duties. Further incoming U-2 reports of new discoveries of medium- and intermediate-range missile sites compounded the situation's urgency. Former Secretary of State Dean Acheson was brought into the meetings.[27]

Upon returning to Washington from the Connecticut campaigning, the President took up a varied schedule of regular business, ceremonial duties, and crisis management. He met often with the Ex Com, brought former Defense Secretary Robert Lovett into the discussions, and deliberately absented himself to encourage his aides to express their views uninhibitedly. In moments away from the Ex Com, Kennedy received the Crown Prince of Libya, conferred with a former Finance Minister of Japan, discussed a new threat to Berlin with the West German Foreign Minister, lunched at the Libyan embassy, vetoed a Tariff Commission recommendation to raise duties of self-closing coin purses, and rejected a proposal for the exclusion of foreign-made nails. Although poised on the knife's edge of incipient decision that could long determine the fate of the nation, the West, and mankind, Kennedy bore up with his accustomed composure even in his severest test, a White House meeting with Andrei A. Gromyko. The visit of the Soviet Foreign Minister had been arranged prior to the crisis. In his two hours and fifteen minutes with Kennedy, Gromyko reaffirmed previous assurances that Soviet activity in Cuba was defensive only. Kennedy repeated to Gromyko his belief that the Soviet effort in Cuba was defensive and his warning that any change in this estimate would have grave consequences. The President refrained from confronting Gromyko with the damning truth because the administration had not yet decided what action to take, and the Russians, faced with exposure, might resort to an evasive counterthrust to blunt the eventual decision.

Gromyko dined that evening with Secretary of State Rusk and other officials on the eighth floor of the department. On the floor below, in the "think tank," the planning group continued its crisis discussions. In midevening they piled into a single limousine, sacrificing comfort for security, and journeyed to the White House. In this meeting the President seemed to be moving toward a blockade. Ambassador-at-large Llewellyn Thompson, Jr., stressed the need for the solid legality of any action taken. The Russians, he said, had a feeling for "legality," and well-grounded legal action would impress world opinion. The State and Justice Departments began work on the legal justification for a blockade.

On October 19 Kennedy resumed his political campaigning, partly to quiet press suspicions that great happenings were afoot, with stops at Cleveland, Chicago, and at Springfield to lay flowers on Lincoln's tomb. Before departing, he expressed approval to the Ex Com of the trend of decision toward a blockade. In the continuing Ex Com discussions, advocates of an offensive air attack vigorously pressed their case, but the blockade attracted the dominant support, even with its admitted danger that, in Vice President Johnson's words, "stopping a Russian ship is an act of war." Staff work proceeded on each alternative to preserve the President's choices to the very moment of decision.

The next day a telephone call from Robert Kennedy brought the President back from Chicago to Washington. Time was running out and secrecy was crumbling, said the Attorney General. The White House informed the press that the President was forced to return by a slight infection of the upper respiratory tract, with one degree of fever. In actuality, the President's cold, which was mild, did not require his return, but it was considered necessary to mislead the reporters by some contrivance in the interest of security. Kennedy, arriving at 1:37 P.M., went over a speech Sorensen had prepared upon the assumption that a blockade would be imposed. The final speech emerged after five drafts. The President all but clinched the decision for blockade and directed the relevant operations to proceed, subject only to his final word the next day. The State and Defense Departments drafted a blockade proclamation, the chief of Naval Operations made the plans necessary to enforce it, the State Department laid out an approach to the Organization of American States, Acheson prepared to embark for Paris to confer with De Gaulle and the NATO council, and Alexis Johnson, Deputy Undersecretary of State for Political Affairs, worked up a "master scenario" depicting every necessary preparation prior to the President's speech; briefings, orders to embassies, ship movements, and the like. A military helicopter picked up former President Eisenhower at his Gettysburg farm and flew him to Washington for a briefing by the CIA. Vice President Johnson dropped his election campaigning in Hawaii and flew back to Washington.

The next day, October 21, the scenario was converted into action. Kennedy, after conferring again with numerous key officials, definitely decided upon the blockade. In the afternoon he met with the statutory National Security Council. The State Department drafted forty-three Presidential letters to the heads of government of all the alliances and to Willy Brandt, mayor of West Berlin. A Kennedy-to-Khrushchev letter was prepared to accompany a copy of the TV speech announcing the blockade. Instructions were readied for distributing the speech to sixty embassies. On October 22 Lawrence O'Brien, the President's Congressional liaison assistant, telephoned twenty Congressional leaders of both parties for a meeting with Kennedy. The Soviet ambassador to Washington, Anatoly Dobrynin, was called to the State Department. General Lauris Norstad, the NATO commander, was alerted. In the meeting with Congressional leaders, Senator Russell, supported by Senator Fulbright, the Foreign Relations Committee chairman, who had opposed the Bay of Pigs attack, bluntly asserted that a blockade was too slow and therefore involved great risk, but the President was not to be dissuaded.[28] At the State Department, Undersecretary Ball and Intelligence and Research Director Roger Hilsman briefed forty-six allied ambassadors in the State Department's International Conference Room.

At 7 P.M. in a calm but intense and blunt eighteen-minute television report, the President delivered his speech alerting the public for the first time. He blamed not Cuba but the Soviet Union for the crisis, which, he said, had violated its leaders' most solemn assurances that only defensive weapons were going to Cuba. The President said he had ordered a "quarantine"—a word he had substituted for "blockade"—on all offensive weapons for Cuba. Ships carrying them would be turned back. Furthermore, he said, the preparation of the missile sites must cease, and if it did not, "further action" would be taken. He was ordering the surveillance continued, and he called upon Khrushchev to withdraw "all offensive weapons" from Cuba.[29]

While the President was speaking, his vast administrative machinery was in full motion. At the State Department the forty-six allied ambassadors watched the speech on a large screen, Assistant Secretary Martin gave a further private briefing to Latin-American ambassadors, Secretary Rusk and Director Hilsman briefed the neutral nations, including Yugoslavia, Undersecretary Ball briefed the diplomatic correspondents, and Defense Secretary McNamara the military correspondents. "Whatever force is required"—even striking—said McNamara, would be employed to enforce the blockade. At the United Nations, Ambassador Adlai Stevenson requested a special meeting of the Security Council.

Thirteen hours after Kennedy's speech came the Soviet's first reaction, a long, rambling, published statement of accusations and warnings of thermonuclear war, plus a letter from Khrushchev to Kennedy. These the administration interpreted as betraying that the Kremlin was caught off guard and playing for time to think out its moves. Developments elsewhere were encouraging despite protest marches in various world capitals. In Paris marchers carried placards reading "Kennedy the Assassin" and "Peace in Cuba," and in London two thousand demonstrators screamed "Long Live Castro" and "Down with Kennedy." British Prime Minister Harold Macmillan telephoned his full support. In a meeting with Acheson, West German Chancellor Konrad Adenauer was equally positive. At the United Nations the NATO countries supported a United States resolution calling upon the Soviet Union to withdraw the missiles and dismantle the sites under United Nations verification, after which the United

States would end the quarantine. Citing the Rio pact of 1947, Secretary Rusk offered the Organization of American States a resolution authorizing the use of force, individually or collectively, to enforce the blockade. The OAS Council adopted the resolution nineteen to zero. The NATO and OAS unanimity surprised both the United States and the Soviet Union and apparently added to the latter's confusion.

There were less gratifying developments, however. U Thant, Acting Secretary General of the United Nations, urged several weeks' suspension of the blockade and arms shipments to Cuba while negotiations were held. Khrushchev accepted with alacrity, but Kennedy, anticipating the disarming of his powerful diplomatic and military initiative and doubting that they could ever regain momentum if negotiations failed, as they were expected to, turned down Thant's request. "The existing threat," the President replied, "was created by the secret introduction of offensive weapons into Cuba, and the answer lies in the removal of such weapons." [30]

A nearly two-day lapse between the announcement of the blockade and its imposition permitted the Soviets to redirect any ships headed for Cuba. On October 25, twenty hours after the blockade began, the United States Navy made its first interception, stopping a Soviet tanker, the *Bucharest*. It was allowed to proceed without search because the Navy was satisfied it carried only petroleum. Kennedy and his associates agreed that in the interests of establishing the principle of the blockade without humiliating the Russians the first ship to be boarded should not be a Soviet ship but a vessel of a neutral nation.[31] Two days later the Lebanese freighter *Marucia* was stopped, boarded, and searched by a five-man party from the destroyers *Joseph P. Kennedy, Jr.,* and *John R. Pierce.* The *Marucia* was also allowed to proceed after it was ascertained that she carried nothing but peaceful cargo.

On October 26 and 27 Khrushchev dispatched two letters to Kennedy. Embedded in the first, although not explicitly stated, was an offer to withdraw the offensive weapons under United Nations supervision if the United States would lift the blockade and promise not to invade the island. The President heard the transcription of this letter with great relief. Then a second Khrushchev letter came clattering over the wires bearing another catch. The Soviet Union would trade its bases in Cuba for the NATO missile base in Turkey. In a National Broadcasting Company telecast of February 9, 1964, McGeorge Bundy stated that the Soviet offer also proposed that the United States pull its missiles out of Greece as well. As Kennedy and his aides pondered a reply, incoming intelligence reports disclosed that Soviet technicians were building away furiously at the Cuban sites. It was estimated that the sites would be ready for missile launchings within a mere five days. Kennedy decided to write again to Khrushchev, saying that if he understood the Premier correctly—that the offensive weapons would be removed in return for an end of the blockade and a promise of no American invasion of Cuba—then it was a deal. It could now go "either way," the President remarked grimly.[32]

If it should go the bad way, the United States armed forces were ready. The Tactical Air Command's 19th Air Force had moved into the sprawling base outside of Homestead, Florida. By October 23 nearly one thousand attack-fighter and fighter-bomber aircraft were poised in Florida, with a conventional airborne firepower rivaling that of the Allied forces in England prior to the Normandy invasion in 1944. Army divisions from Fort Bragg, North Carolina; Fort Campbell, Kentucky; Fort Riley, Kansas; and Fort Benning, Georgia, were on full alert. These divisions plus marines at sea, in Florida, and at Guantánamo, formed a one hundred thousand-man force the United States stood ready to hurl into Cuba. Drop-zones in the Cuban interior had been carefully designated for paratroopers of the 82nd and 101st Airborne Divisions. Globemaster transports poured into the Key West naval base with soldiers, sailors, marines, mobile radar units, photographic gear, trucks and jeeps, and weapons of all types. The Association of American Railroads was alerted, and 2,418 flatcars and 299 equipment cars from as far distant as Denver and Minneapolis began rolling to Fort Hood, Texas, to take on Honest John Rockets and rocket-launcher vehicles, Patton tanks, self-propelled howitzers, and other cargo. Bases at Miami, Canaveral, Orlando, and Homestead were mushrooming with fighter and fighter-bomber aircraft.

The United States military preparations indeed were proceeding on a global scale. U.S. Navy ships and submarines in the European Atlantic, Pacific, and Mediterranean were hurrying out to sea. Three Polaris-firing submarines scurried to sea from their berths at Holy Loch, Scotland. The Strategic Air Command was on Defcon 2, or full war footing, from which it needed but one signal to go to Defcon 1, which puts it at war. For the first time in history, SAC's medium-range bomber force of B-47's were ordered to disperse. ICBM firing crews, spread in complexes throughout the United States, were brought to full alert and missiles were raised. The Navy's Fleet Ballistic Missile submarines were on station, carrying 128 Polaris missiles, within range of major Soviet targets. The United States had made full preparations to lay the explosive equivalent of more than thirty billion tons of TNT upon the Soviet Union.

The United States was also maintaining close air surveillance over Cuba. On October 27 Major Rudolf Anderson, Jr., one of two U-2 pilots whose photographs touched off the crisis, was shot down over Cuba.[33] In cryptic comment during a speech at Columbia, South Carolina, on April 25, 1963, six months after the crisis, Attorney General Robert Kennedy said that Major Anderson's death "led the President to notify Mr. Khrushchev that strong and overwhelming retaliatory action would have been taken unless he received immediate notice that the missiles would be withdrawn." United States officials connected with the crisis believe that this Presidential message, the text of which was not revealed, coupled with the open movement of American military power were the factors that really brought Khrushchev around to his ultimate decision in the immediate crisis. "What got the message through to Khrushchev was action," one official said. "The message was clear that something was going to happen and happen soon."[34]

October 28 brought Khrushchev's answer, the fifth Premier-President exchange in seven days. Khrushchev said that he had ordered work on the bases stopped and the missiles crated and returned to the Soviet Union. Representatives of the United Nations, he promised, would "verify the dismantling." In return, the President's no-invasion pledge would be trusted. After hurried consultations with his aides, the President issued a statement welcoming Khrushchev's "statesmanlike decision," and the blockade was lifted.[35]

In the months following the crisis, the United States and the Soviet Union handled the Cuban question with high caution, neither side appearing to contemplate any drastic action so long as the other kept the October "gentlemen's agreement." Senator Keating remained attentive to Cuba, declaring on the Senate floor on January 31, 1963, that "there is continuing, absolutely confirmed and undeniable evidence that the Soviets are maintaining the medium-range sites they had previously constructed in Cuba. . . . Without on-site inspection, it is hard to see how we will ever know for sure the true missile situation in Cuba." In a press interview, Keating said he would be glad to disclose his information, but not his sources, to the President.[36] Senator Strom Thurmond, Democrat of South Carolina, made similar charges. But intelligence estimates one year after the crisis disclosed that the Soviet force in Cuba was down to ten thousand from twenty-two thousand at the peak of the crisis. The remaining personnel were believed to be devoted to training the Cuban armed forces.

In a 1966 interview Premier Castro, asked if he could "state unequivocally" that there were no offensive ground-to-air nuclear missiles in Cuba, replied that he had "no objection to declaring that those weapons do not exist in Cuba" and added that "unfortunately, there are none." In the same interview, Castro also remarked, mysteriously and without elaboration, that "one day, perhaps, it will be known that the United States made some other concessions in relation to the October crisis besides those that were made public." [37]

In 1970 Richard Nixon neared the brink of a second confrontation when the Soviet Union began building facilities for nuclear submarines in the Cuban port of Cienfuegos, with a submarine tender and other Soviet vessels standing by. To cope with this ominous situation, Nixon and his aides resorted to processes of quiet diplomacy, in which was cited the Kennedy-Khrushchev agreement to keep Soviet nuclear weapons out of the Western Hemisphere. What the U.S.S.R sought to do in 1970 was the equivalent of what it had failed to do in 1962. With facilities in Cuba, Russian nuclear submarines could operate in the Atlantic and avoid the 8,000-mile round trip back to their Soviet base. This time assertive Presidential diplomacy produced an unwritten Soviet pledge not to base missile-carrying nuclear submarines, store nuclear weapons, or install repair and servicing facilities anywhere in the Western Hemisphere. In return, the United States would closely watch, but not obstruct, periodic visits by the Soviet fleet to Cuban and other Western Hemispheric ports for crew shore leave and routine ship maintenance.[38] The incipient crisis dissolved, although how fully the agreement is adhered to remains obscure, and crisis can flame anew simply with the embarking of a Soviet tender for Cuban waters.[39] Kennedy's success established a standard for future Presidents to maintain, a task that will become more difficult to accomplish as it becomes more difficult to define.

THE ART OF CRISIS MANAGEMENT   The Cuban crisis was the first confrontation of its kind since the onset of the age in which the two great nuclear powers possessed the capacity to destroy each other and much of the world. The decisions that Kennedy was called upon to make were therefore the most delicate and the most perilous that any President has ever faced. Not only the welfare of the American public, but the fate of peoples everywhere who had no voice in his selection, of unborn generations, of western civilization itself depended upon his choices.

The stressful decision-making of the Cuban crisis—the pattern of action by which the President mastered the tangled skein of intense events—was a nightmarish experience. The President is often spoken of, to the point of cliché, as a lonely figure. He has never appeared more solitary than in nuclear confrontation. Surrounded though he is by aides and data and counsel, he must decide alone. His choice cannot be delegated. It is a cruel test of self-confidence that has undeniably removed the Presidency for all time as a refuge for the faint-hearted.

Kennedy followed several elementary procedures in facing the nuclear showdown. He rightly insisted that before publicly according the Cuban events the status of crisis, he needed "hard intelligence" and could not act simply upon rumor and report. He held to his course despite the revelations and criticisms of legislators of both his own and the opposition party and despite the hostile Congressional resolutions. To be careful and responsible, as Kennedy had to be, is neither easy nor popular. Political outcry was perhaps not the worst of the afflictions he had to bear. The atmosphere in which the President acted was charged with danger and uncertainty, with inexorable climax and with scores of opportunities for surprise. For all their knowledge of the Soviet Union, American officials could not predict what the Soviet leader would decide to do—especially since he delighted in surprise as a source of strength in foreign affairs. The Russians took advantage of seasonal flunctuations in our political system, launching their gambit during an election campaign. They expected that the President would be eager to postpone the prickly Cuban issue until after the election, and by that time it would be too late.

In the Cuban crisis the President sought always to leave Khrushchev with an option or choice. Above all, the aim of Kennedy and his advisers was to avoid backing him into a corner, where his only recourse would be military. A military attack of any kind upon Cuba, a communist power, would have posed to the Soviet Union the necessity of either a military response or a humiliating surrender, badly damaging to its prestige around the world. The blockade afforded the advantage of giving Khrushchev a choice. He did not need to have his ships approach the blockade and be stopped and searched but could divert them, as he did. The blockade, therefore, left an acceptable way out for the Soviet Union, a cardinal principle of decision-making in the nuclear confrontation. Equally important, Kennedy carefully preserved the United States' own options; that is, he did not rely wholly upon the blockade but simultaneously speeded the full-scale alert of American forces, a procedure that many felt finally prodded Khrushchev to agree to remove the missiles from Cuba.[40]

Another cardinal principle was evident in the effort of the President and his aides to slow down the escalation of the crisis to permit Khrushchev time to consider his next moves. Deliberation, it was hoped, might produce a more measured and less drastic response than fast-moving exchanges—hence the value of notes and ambassadorial visits and the preferability of a blockade, a relatively gradual procedure compared with the precipitous engagement of an invasion or an air strike.

Kennedy took the fullest precautions to keep the decisions in his own hands, both the initial decision settling upon the blockade and the further critical decisions required to implement it. When a United States Navy reconnaissance plane spotted the *Marucia* headed for Cuba, the information was sped to the President, and it was he who gave the order to board and search it. Other procedures assured that control of the blockade operation remained in his hands. Kennedy was resolved that the issue of peace or war should not turn upon the decision of a local commander.

In making his choices, the President must be mindful of several constituencies but still keep decision in his grasp. He must be willing to act, as Kennedy was, notwithstanding the express disapproval of certain of these constituents. Kennedy accordingly convened members of his legislative constituency, leaders of both parties. Paradoxically, his party's leading legislators in the fields of foreign affairs and national security held that his decision was inadequate for the situation and urged him to do more. The House Republican leader, however, Congressman Halleck, declared, "I'm standing with the President." The dissent of several of his own party leaders did not deter the President. He won the approval of another great constituency: the leaders of the nation's major allies—Macmillan, De Gaulle, and Adenauer—and the member countries of the principal alliances, NATO and the OAS. Kennedy was fortunate enough to win an approval from his foreign constituency extending well beyond his expectations. But it is also clear that he was prepared, as a President in a nuclear confrontation may need to be, to carry forward his decision even without allied endorsement. In choosing his course, the President must weigh and balance factors that no ally can know or perceive, owing to the simple circumstance that only he occupies his Presidential place, and only he, therefore, holds the responsibility.

Nuclear crisis is more than an intensive exercise in decision-making. Equally, if not more important, it is an enterprise in communication. The evidence is impressive that a major cause of the crisis was a misreading by Khrushchev and his colleagues of the Kennedy administration's attitude and intentions. In their June 1961 Vienna meeting, Khrushchev reportedly found Kennedy somewhat deferential, which the Soviet leader apparently interpreted as weakness. The fiasco of the Bay of Pigs and Kennedy's restrained response to the Berlin wall may well have encouraged a Soviet impression of American softness. The strength of this impression was conveyed in Khrushchev's remark to Robert Frost that the United States was "too liberal to fight."

A nuclear confrontation involves a desperate resort to various communications channels and an intensive scrutiny of the opponent's act and word for clues of his intent and meaning. Kennedy and his counselors were heavily occupied in the dangerous and difficult task of estimating the probable Soviet reaction to possible United States moves. Equally to be anticipated was the effect upon our allies, upon trouble spots around the world, whether Berlin or Turkey, which held our bases that the Soviet Union was discussing, or the Formosa straits, where the Chinese were preparing for belligerent action. Likewise the effect upon Latin America: If the United States responded strongly, would the Latin countries become alarmed? Would they be even more alarmed if we did too little? For Kennedy and his aides, the crisis was a rigorous introspective experience in determining American purposes, in anticipating what our reaction might be to the Soviet reaction, and so on, until each possible course that might be chosen was followed to its ultimate conclusion. From the highly consequential endeavors of the Ex Com, public opinion and the individual citizen were shut out. Robert Kennedy was impressed with the necessity of adhering to this undemocratic scenario, evocative of the handful of kings and emissaries who in olden days decided man's fate. "If our deliberations had been publicized," he wrote, ". . . I believe the course that we ultimately would have taken would have been quite different and filled with far greater risks. The fact that we were able to talk, debate, argue, disagree, and then debate some more was essential in choosing our ultimate course." [41] Paradoxically, the putting aside of external democratic norms enhanced the internal democratic processes of the decision-makers. Kennedy's preference for secrecy was assisted by the successful handling of the missile crisis. But in an earlier episode, the fiasco of the Bay of Pigs invasion, secrecy also prevailed, for which John Kennedy subsequently voiced regret. To preserve that secrecy, he personally intervened to forestall publication of reports in the press that deliberations on launching the enterprise were proceeding. But after the disaster he ruefully acknowledged that he might have been spared the debacle if public discussion and opinion had accompanied Executive deliberations.

Although Kennedy was an action-oriented, strong President, he was not, in any degree, a creature of impulse. The latter type, installed in the contemporary Presidency, would be disastrous for the nation and mankind. An activist President triggered by emotion, who neither consulted advisers nor pondered consequences, would be both decisive and wrong-headed, a type who would keep the nation, so long as it survived, quaking in high alarm. Chief Executives such as Kennedy root their actions in thought and validated evidence. They are decisive and forceful only in response to reason tested by qualified opinion. Here the strong President and the President who abides by democratic norms coincide.

16

THE PRESIDENCY COMPARED

Comparisons, we are often warned, are odious. But comparisons have a special usefulness in the study of political institutions. We can better estimate the value of one political institution if we measure its performance against other institutions. We can better perceive what the American Presidency has been and what it might become if we compare it with other relevant institutions of our own and other political societies. The comparisons may illuminate those aspects of the Presidency that reflect our deepest traditions and most tightly held values and those aspects, as well, that represent large and clear exceptions to the established ways of our political community. In other political systems may be discovered democracy-enhancing practices that may be adapted to the American system.

The American President invites comparison with the other members of the nation's family of political executives: the state governor and the local chief executive. As with most families, the several executives bear certain resemblances to each other, and any one of them has influenced the development of all. They have imitated and inspired one another and have felt the brunt of common historical forces. The governor and the mayor can rightfully be viewed as Presidential-type executives, having the contours and much of the power and function of the national executive.

The Governor

In shaping the Presidency, the Founding Fathers were influenced to a large degree by the New York governorship; weaknesses in other governorships warned them of mistakes to avoid. The state governorship was influenced by experience with the colonial governorship, which was commonly viewed as the agency of monarchic tyranny. Thus, state constitution-makers in the Revolutionary era tended to look askance at the strong executive, and they chose to concentrate power in the state legislatures, which during the colonial crisis acquired a reputation as defenders of the popular interest. But the abuses that state legislatures made of their powers caused the Founding Fathers to resolve to create a Presidency of substantial strength.

Although the Presidency and the governorship have swelled in influence and power since the eighteenth century, the latter has always been the substantially weaker of the two executive offices. The change was slow-building for the governor. In the early state constitutions, legislative supremacy was firmly established. According to many constitutions, the legislature appointed the governor, and the governor lacked a veto power over legislation. Leadership in public policy reposed with the legislature. Unlike the President, whose power derived from general constitutional provisions permitting generous interpretation and enlargement, the governor had to struggle for the increase of power through the rewriting of state constitutions and by wringing out concessions of power from the legislature. The Jacksonian era caused more governors and their fellow executive officials (including, sometimes, even prison superintendents) to be popularly elected and entrusted more power to their care, but all through the nineteenth century, while Jackson, Lincoln, and Cleveland demonstrated the primacy of the Presidency, the legislature endured as the dominant instrument of state policy-making.

It is in the twentieth century that the governor comes into his own, through forces in that era that served to enlarge the President's influence and power. The increase of government's social and economic tasks, especially from the First World War onward, and the ever-broadening base of democratic government profited both the governor and the President. In addition, the governor gained from new constitutions and executive reorganizations that imitated the Presidential model. As well, the clear inadequacy of the state legislature in an era of positive government contributed to the governor's growth in function and power. Yet there remains an ambiguity about the role of the states, and therefore of the governor, in public affairs. The states fall somewhere between local government, with its natural responsibility for urban or local problems, and the national government, which most naturally deals with foreign affairs and problems incident to a grand-scale economy. The states lack any comparable natural jurisdictions enjoyed by the other governments.

If a typical early governor were compared with a typical contemporary governor, the influence of the Presidency upon gubernational change would become evident. Most contemporary governors enjoy a four-year term rather than the one- or two-year span of their predecessors. A little more than half the governors can be reelected to the office indefinitely, while in earlier times a one-term limitation was commonplace. Early governors shared the exercise of their veto power with a council, on which legislators might be represented, yet the present-day governor enjoys a veto power over his legislature fully equal to the President's. Indeed four-fifths of the governors enjoy an advantage that the President lacks, except by the questionable exercise of impoundment—an item veto over individual appropriations in general revenue bills. The governor's power to appoint his administrative colleagues, long a source of weakness because these key figures might be popularly elected or chosen by the legislature, has improved to the point where more than half the governors can appoint, with or without the consent of their senates, the heads of the chief departments and the budget and tax officers. A major source of the President's power in the executive branch is his strong appointing power.

In the general layout of his functions and powers, in the relationship of the incumbent's personality to the office, the governor resembles the President, although with important variations springing from differences between the nation and the states and the imprint of historic forces and tradition. Like the Presidency, the governorship provides a spacious arena for the play of personality. Just as the Presidency has developed under the touch of creative incumbents, the governorship developed strength and resilience in the tenures of Robert M. La Follette in Wisconsin, Hiram Johnson and Earl Warren in California, Charles Evans Hughes and Alfred E. Smith in New York, Gifford Pinchot in Pennsylvania, to mention a few. Some governors, such as Woodrow Wilson of New Jersey and Franklin Roosevelt of New York, displayed skills and indulged in techniques of leadership that they later applied with marked success in the Presidency. In the 1970s, the energy crisis, revenue sharing, and the scaled-down domestic priorities of the Nixon Presidency as well as its extended enfeeblement following Watergate and the conservative tendencies of the Ford Presidency have shunted more burdens upon and spurred more innovative policies from the governors. Gasoline rationing was first instituted by Governor Tom McCall of Oregon, who also rallied his state to antigrowth policies by illuminating the dangers of Oregon's unchecked expansion of population and industry. In Pennsylvania, Governor Milton J. Shapp advanced a comprehensive, state-wide plan to regulate and administer health services in seeking to contain "skyrocketing medical costs." [1]

Just as the President tends to be the outstanding political leader in the nation, the governor enjoys the same distinction in the smaller domain of the state. The governor, more than other political personalities in the state, is identified with the "general public good." Whatever he does makes news in the local press. Radio and television can command him a state-wide audience; he travels frequently about the state, makes numerous personal appearances, handles a high volume of correspondence and telephone calls, and receives large quantities of visitors. Many governors keep their doors open to one and all who wish to interview them. Coleman B. Ransone, Jr., in his study of the governorship, concluded that public relations is the most time-consuming role of the state executive. [2] As with the President, much of the governor's success turns upon his skill as a party and legislative leader. His party role most resembles the President's in states that are populous and where a genuine two-party system flourishes. The interparty competition fosters a discipline that the governor can exploit as party leader. In some states, particularly in the South and Middle West, there is a steady one-party dominance that casts the governor in a role as the leader of a party faction or a coalition of factions whose support he manages to attract. In the factional structure, state politics may become highly responsive to the governor's personality. Georgia, therefore, in the era of its colorful Governor Gene "Red Suspenders" Talmadge, was dominated by Talmadge and anti-Talmadge factions, and Louisiana, in the heyday of Huey

Long, by Long and anti-Long factions. A governor is less apt than the President to be the acknowledged leader of his party because he may have rivals for the role in one or both of the United States Senators of his state.

The governor, like the President, is heavily judged by his success as legislative leader. Increasingly most of the important policies that the legislature considers come from the governor or the executive departments. As legislative leader, the governor enjoys political means that are fully comparable to the President's. He reports to the legislature on the conditions of the state and recommends legislation. Much turns upon his ability to persuade legislators of both major parties to support his proposals. He has the inducements of patronage and public works construction—nothing can be more eloquent than building a new highway in a legislator's district; he can speak in support of a legislator's candidacy; or he can grant a pardon to one of his constituents. The governor's power is also buttressed by substantial formal authority. He gains leverage from budget-making powers if he has them, which enables him to include or omit the favorite projects of legislators.

Most governors can also gain leverage with the item veto. Legislators, however, may blunt the effect of the item veto by combining objectionable and unobjectionable items in the same clause. The item veto also invites buckpassing, by which legislators vote appropriations with the expectation that the governor will bear the political blame for disallowing them.[3] In four states— Alabama, Massachusetts, New Jersey, and Virginia—the governor has an "amendatory" veto. He can return a bill without his signature to the house where it originated, with suggestions for change that would make it acceptable to him. The legislature first considers the question of accepting the changes before deciding whether to pass the bill over his veto or return it to him for final consideration. The device has strengthened the governor's hand in shaping legislation. Like the President, the governor can call the legislature into special session, and, unlike the President, he can, in about half the states, specify the matters to be considered, thus increasing executive authority over the legislative agenda.

But even more than the President, the governor faces a formidable legislative power structure. In most state legislatures, the speaker of the house, the presiding officer of the senate, and the chairmen of the leading standing committees, enjoy authority and influence that overshadow the substantial power of their counterparts in Congress. In the states, the rules of seniority, geographical distribution, and party representation are often far less well established than in Congress, thus enhancing the leaders' influence. The leaders, that is, can be more arbitrary in the selecting of committee slates and committee chairmen. Further, the general body of legislators are more dependent upon the personal favor of the legislative leaders and more pressed to win and keep their approval than in the national Congress where these matters are more regularized. The actions of state legislative leaders are, in addition, less covered by official written records and the press. The resulting obscurity increases the power of legislative leaders to manipulate against the governor.

The governor is also an administrative chief whose powers are more qualified than the President's. In nearly four-fifths of the states, he shares administrative power with other elected executives: the secretary of state, the attorney general, the treasurer, the controller, and others who already are or will be his political competitors. A heavy trend in the states toward the creation of independent agencies, authorities, and commissions, endowed with their own fiscal powers, represents incursions into the governor's administrative primacy on a scale well exceeding the President's difficulties with the independent commissions. Frequently the governor lacks power to appoint or remove a department head, and many departments may not be subject to the executive budget and other fiscal controls. Not surprisingly, governors tend to feel that administration should receive no heavy portion of their time and that success in that endeavor contributes little to their reelection.

For the rest, the governorship reflects the Presidential system, although on a smaller scale and with milder strength. The governor is commander-in-chief of the state military forces, a capacity of special importance in the Revolutionary era, when not a few governors commanded in the field. The governor may enter into industrial and civil rights disputes, under his duty to assist local officials in maintaining public order. The governor conducts various external relationships that more or less parallel the President's activity in foreign affairs. He is the official organ of communications between his state and other states and with the national government. He certifies election results in his state for national officers; the state's participation in federal-state cooperative programs may turn upon his approval; he may make "good will" visits abroad.

The Mayor

Of the several types of local executives, the one most deeply rooted in the American tradition—the mayor—also fits most securely into the Presidential pattern. Two other forms of the local executive that first appeared in the twentieth century—the city manager, who is a professional and appointed executive, and the commission, in reality a plural executive—constitute sharp departures from the Presidential format and therefore will not concern us here.

Like the governor, the mayor has long been engaged in a struggle to convert insubstantial powers into strength. Of the two general types of mayor plans, the older is the "weak mayor," widely prevalent in the nineteenth century and still the predominant plan in middle-size and smaller cities. Under that plan, various executive and administrative officers are either popularly elected or are appointed by the city council or legislature. Budget-making powers and powers of administrative supervision are reserved to the council. Los Angeles and Atlanta are the principal cities employing the "weak mayor" plan.

In the twentieth century the nation's largest cities have been veering sharply to the second type of mayor plan—the "strong mayor"—which bears greater resemblances to the Presidential model. In theory, at least, the plan seeks to establish the mayor as the chief executive with the fullest possible control over departments and agencies; it empowers him to prepare a comprehensive executive budget and to propose legislation. He possesses a strong veto power and enjoys broad powers of appointment and removal. Practice is some steps removed from theory. Of the largest cities, only Boston and Cleveland make the mayor the sole elected incumbent of the principal executive offices; in New York, Chicago, and Detroit, the mayor shares budget and administrative powers with other governmental organs that he does not direct or control. In Chicago, for example, a council committee prepares the budget.

It is useful for students of the Presidency to examine the strong, big city mayor type because it illuminates dependence and weakness at the local level of government that could conceivably appear in a later day at the Presidential level. The big city mayor is the front-line soldier who deals with the most urgent problems of American domestic politics located as they are in the urban sector. The problems of health, education, civil rights, housing, and the others that stand high on the President's agenda are the daily grist of the big city mayor. The mayor meets close up, and in the most concentrated form, problems from which the President enjoys a greater distance and whose priority he can balance and juggle with his nonurban concerns, especially those in foreign affairs. Despite the resemblances of his formal powers to the President's, the mayor's actual power to deal with the problems is only a fraction of the national executive's substantial capacity to act.

The gap between what the mayor can do and what the President can do is all the more striking since both officers have been buffeted by common historic social forces. Both the President and the mayor are affected by the radical change in the urban environment of late decades. The radical alteration of the composition of its population, the ever-enlarging bureaucratization of government, and the almost infinite appetite for government services are the common lot of mayors and Presidents. Faced with these common pressures, the President, on the whole, has been able to respond—if he chooses to—with greater initiative and force than the mayor. The explanation does not lie wholly in the superiority of federal resources. Especially important are essential differences in the political environments of the mayor and the President.

The mayors of the great cities, as Scott Greer has suggested, reign but do not rule.[4] Big city mayors often assume heroic or Presidential poses and work hard at constructing images of vigorous creative leadership that are some distance removed from the record of actual achievement. The watchword with big city mayors is caution. They preside over routine, caretaker governments and struggle with the most urgent and complex problems on the domestic scene without the capacity to mount major offensives or launch bold initiatives. Meanwhile the problems and the forces producing them work their havoc. Industry continues its move to the suburbs; the differentiation between the central city and the suburban populations becomes ever sharper; the predominance of city groups who suffer most from economic depression grows apace. The strong mayor must endure several handicaps from his political environment. His governmental jurisdiction, although large, is not large enough. His city is one among a number of governmental divisions of a metropolis, which consists of numerous municipalities, counties, and special districts, each empowered to do certain tasks and to withhold cooperation from other local governments.

Big city government is largely one-party government, or in reality nonpartisan government. The big city mayor tends to be the dominant political personality in the metropolitain area. Yet for all of his prominence, his ability to achieve political results is modest. One-party government frees the mayor from many pressures, but the freedom he enjoys is negative rather than positive. He is free from partisan limitations, but not free to make new and radical departures. With the evaporation of the threat of electoral defeat that the one-party system affords, the party structure loses its discipline, on which the mayor, or any executive, depends to push his program through the legislature. In the one-party arrangement, the central city electorate becomes a captive electorate of the Democratic party, which dominates the big cities. There is no effective alternative party to turn to, and the electorate tends toward passivity. The mayor must cope with factional leaders who have substantial personal and political power, wielded in the legislature and in appointed and elected executive posts.

The big city mayor must also cope with a huge bureaucracy that easily eludes his control. New York City, for example, has a bureaucracy of 350,000. There and elsewhere, the bureaucracy may cling to established ways and resist innovation, which is viewed as a threat to the existing distribution of power and privilege. In the cities, the indulgence in independent agencies and authorities is even greater than in the states, which further bolsters the autonomy of municipal bureaucracies.

Above all, the big city is hobbled by political segregation, by the separation of numbers and wealth, by the concentration of population in the central city and resources in the suburbs, by the separation of need from means. In effect, government is segregated by social class, with the middle class on the one hand, and the lower classes on the other, each having its own local government. Relations between the central city and the suburb are ruled by mutual suspicion, an attitude that can be profitably exaggerated by candidates for office.

Finally, in the conservative Nixon Presidency, big city mayors felt shortchanged in the distribution of federal largess. In 1973, when the Nixon administration set forth new ground rules for revenue sharing, Mayor Theodore M. Berry of Cincinnati remarked that the generally pro-Nixon suburban counties of the 1972 elections would do especially well and that revenue sharing was becoming "another form of patronage." Subsequently, in 1973, when the President imposed budget cuts on city programs despite earlier promises of no cuts, a large city mayor viewed the step as consistent with the perception of the cities "as repositories for the poor, the black, the Latin, the elderly—those who are relatively powerless against the interests of stronger and more affluent elements of our society." [5]

Foreign Executives: Selection and Tenure

The strengths and weaknesses of the American Presidency and the possible linkings of Executive power with democratic norms also may be better perceived if we examine the chief executives of other major nations. We may find in the experience of others clues for eliminating flaws from our own system and for keeping up better in the race every nation is running against the forces of change. Possibly, too, we may take some small comfort if we find that weaknesses that afflict the American Chief Executive are also bedeviling other nations.

The period 1973–74, which brought Watergate and Richard Nixon's resignation, was a period of general instability for the leaderships of major western political systems. In Britain, Edward Heath was deposed by a national election, and the ministry of his successor, Harold Wilson, was tarnished by a land-buying scandal that touched his personal staff. In France, after the death of President Georges Pompidou, his Gaullist party failed in the national elections to prevail in the selection of his successor. Willy Brandt, seemingly popular and enduring in the West German chancellorship, was suddenly ejected from office when it was revealed that an East German spy occupied a principal position on his staff. In the Middle East, Israel witnessed a shift of leadership, as did Japan in the Far East.

Why this sudden general political "decline of the West"? A pervasive factor is the frailty of leaders and their associates, physically and judgmentally. Another is the juggernaut of problems that democratic governments seem incapable of solving or even slowing—unemployment and inflation as well as shortages of food, energy, and other life essentials. Still other forces beset leadership. Enhanced education levels that have fostered rising expectations and a greater willingness to sharply question institutions and to reject leadership; the media's capacity for instant global communication as well as the availability of a limitless canvass more than sufficient to support the journalistic penchant for bad news rather than good news; and the rapidity and severity of change that befalls the individual and with which government constantly demonstrates it cannot cope.[6] The nations yearn for leaders who will achieve, but they seldom appear.

Even when they offer themselves, no major nation can boast a method of selecting its chief executive that assures a choice from among the proverbial "best men available" by means that are assuredly democratic. Because of the enormous stakes, the contest is almost universally a great scramble to which the arts of pressure and maneuver are fully committed. It is an enterprise in which democratic values and procedures are vulnerable. The United States prefers its Presidents from large states and therefore arbitrarily excludes worthy contenders from the small. It requires long primary campaigns, thus loading the dice for the candidate with money. The creaky electoral college machinery is a standing invitation to disaster in opening wide the gates of chance that a Presidential candidate with a minority of popular votes may be elected. And as mention of Agnew, Nixon, and Watergate suggests, the machinery, in an unprecedented lapse after nearly two centuries of functioning, can produce a criminal and an incumbent whose most generous ethical self-appraisal enables him to declare only, ''I am not a crook.''

In Great Britain the selection of the Prime Minister after a national election follows a well-regulated routine. The voters elect a new House of Commons, and the leader of the majority party is automatically made the new Prime Minister. Following the election, the Queen requests the leader of the winning party to form a government, in effect ratifying the electorate's choice. But the selection of the party leader in the first place, prior to his appearance before the electorate, is largely a matter of intraparty maneuver. The magic key is the building of support among the factions. Harold Wilson bested George Brown in their contest for the Labor leadership in 1963 as a kind of middle-of-the-roader who had least offended the factions whose support was vital. When Labor won the national elections the following year, it was only a formality for the Queen to summon Wilson to form a new government. Wilson's successor as Prime Minister, Edward Heath, outpaced his chief rival in the Conservative party, Reginald Maulding, an achievement that was enormously aided by the previous Conservative Prime Minister, Sir Alec Douglas-Home, who meted out to Heath the choice ministerial appointments, assignments, and other preferences.[7] And party leaders were impressed that in a potentially close election some of Heath's personal qualities might provide the margin of victory—his possession of Wilson's most attractive attributes: humble origins, drive, comprehension of technical economics, and commitment to efficiency and modernization.

The American President, once elected, enjoys extraordinary stability of tenure, decidedly greater than the British Prime Minister's and rather less than that of the President of the French Fifth Republic. The sole legitimate means of removing the American President—impeachment—is constructed to operate only in the utmost extremity. Presidents as unpopular as Buchanan and Hoover persisted in office until the next inauguration even though the majority of public opinion was set against them.

For more than a year, until he resigned in the face of his certain impeachment, Nixon endured despite widespread public belief that he was guilty of criminal acts, and the severe drain that this shadowed status inflicted upon his effectiveness. In Britain, Nixon would have been ejected from office in a matter of weeks by the pressures of his parliamentary party responding to hostile public opinion.

But Britain's built-in eventuality of interrupted tenure has an underside. The fact that the possibility exists that a Prime Minister can be pulled down by fiat of his party in the House of Commons makes him vulnerable to plots against his political security, particularly in seasons when policy may go awry and the country's fortunes dip, common occurrences in the present stage of Britain's historical experience. Nineteen forty-seven was just such a bad year for the Prime Minister. A general economic decline was aggravated by the ill luck of a terrible winter, the worst since 1880, which touched off a fuel crisis and temporarily brought all industry to a stop. Stafford Cripps, a member of the cabinet, let it become known that in the sudden crisis the country required greater inspiration than the mild-mannered Prime Minister Clement Attlee could possibly provide. Cripps proposed that Attlee step down and permit the Prime Ministership to be handed over to Ernest Bevin, whose toughness he admired. Attlee nevertheless held fast by several adroit maneuvers, including a sudden reshuffling of his cabinet, not the least part of which was the installation of Cripps in the new post of Minister of Economic Affairs with more extensive powers over the economy than any minister in peacetime had ever before possessed.[8]

The tenure of Soviet leadership is vulnerable to palace revolution. Premier Nikita Khrushchev was challenged in two known and severe tests, one of which he narrowly survived; the other he failed, and was quickly swept into the limbo of political disgrace. In his first crisis of June 1957, Khrushchev seemed doomed when the majority of the party Presidium called an extraordinary session and by a vote of seven to four elected to remove him from his party post as First Secretary. The anti-Khrushchev majority comprised the older members and former associates of Stalin: Voroshilov, Molotov, Kaganovich, Bulganin, and Malenkov; and, from the newer generation of leadership, Pervuklin and Saburov. The hazardous maneuver was apparently born of fear of Khrushchev's ambition and growing doubts of his capacity to rule. But the power of the rebelling group was limited. Khrushchev controlled the parent body of the Presidium, the Central Committee. He dominated the vast party apparatus across the Soviet Union, and his impregnable influence blocked his foes' access to the means of physical force—the political police and the armed forces. Backed by such enormous strength, Khrushchev could counter with swift and bold measures. He quickly mobilized the Central Committee members who were then in Moscow, summoning them into a meeting where they reversed the Presidium's decision and expelled the anti-Khrushchev factions from both the Presidium and the Central Committee.

Seven years later, in 1964, Russia experienced another October revolution, this time a palace revolution resulting in Khrushchev's overthrow. The initial external signs of that event were placid but lethal. First, Khrushchev had not spoken to the cosmonauts after their landing, contrary to custom, which reserves proud national ceremonies to the top leader. As it happened, he could not, since he was flying to Moscow at that joyous moment under heavy escort. In the press, his name was not mentioned, as normally it would be, in an article in *Izvestia* commemorating the twenty-fifth anniversary of the liberation of the Ukraine in the Second World War. Indeed, his name had suddenly vanished everywhere, as though a blue pencil had deleted all references to him from every Soviet newspaper on the first evening of his apprehension. Thus began the plunge of Khruschev, the leader who had presided over the country's fortunes for a decade, into the ignominy of an unperson.[9] Where before his friends of the Central Committee had saved him, they now forsook him. The committee replaced Khrushchev as First Secretary of the party with his own protégé of many years, Leonid Brezhnev, and delivered the crowning blow of disgrace by taking away Khrushchev's seat on the party Presidium. He next was stripped of his governmental position as Premier, and that post was handed to his successor, Alexei Kosygin.[10]

Succession Compared

When the Vice Presidency is filled, the American Presidency clearly holds the advantage over other chief executives in handling the problem of succession. John Kennedy's assassination, for all its rending tragedy, was also the occasion of a remarkable demonstration of the velocity and assurance with which executive power can be transferred in the American system. Less than two hours after Kennedy's death the Presidential oath was administered to Vice President Johnson, with Mrs. Kennedy by his side, herself a brave witness to the continuity of the American system. With Nixon ousted, Ford immediately succeeded him.

Nearly a month before the catastrophe in Texas, a succession occurred in the British Prime Ministership. The procedure of deciding who the new Prime Minister should be took all of eleven days to consummate, with lengthy passages of farce and satire. Through much of this anguished interlude, the effort to find a successor to the ill and hospitalized Prime Minister Harold Macmillan foundered upon the deadlock of two intractable and opposed groups in the Conservative party. To the left were the liberal revisionists, headed by R. A. Butler, Deputy Prime Minister in the Macmillan cabinet and the man who, according to party and public opinion polls, enjoyed the greatest backing. Prime Minister Macmillan reportedly wished above all else to bar Butler's succession. A second major contender was Viscount Hailsham of the Conservative right wing. Several lesser contenders made up the field. Early in his quest for an heir, Macmillan pressed Alec Douglas-Home, the Foreign Secretary, to enter the lists, but Home declined.

A polling that Macmillan ordered taken of the cabinet revealed that Home was running strong as a second and third choice. Soundings were likewise made among the 50 junior ministers, the 350 M.P.'s, and the active Conservative peers. The party whips were instructed to gather answers to three questions: 1. Whom would you like to see in office? 2. Do you want to choose *possible* runners-up? 3. Is there anybody you would rather *not* see in office? Home emerged with a slight majority of first preferences and a clear margin of second choices, but the column most in his favor was "against"; few opposed him. Martin Redmayne, chief whip and poll supervisor, also weighted the votes according to each M.P.'s status in the party, a process that Home's opponents later disputed. A Butler man said, "Redmayne could have weighted Home's votes and tied little balloons to Rab's."

Buttonholing and telephoning proceeded intensively. Hailsham's candidacy began to sag with Home's advance, although Butler's held strong. Meanwhile

Home, notwithstanding heavy pressure from Macmillan, would not declare his candidacy. With more time, he told Macmillan, either Butler, Hailsham, or a third candidate, Reginald Maudling, might come through. Maudling, who might have thrown in with Butler, thereby establishing a majority for the latter, made no move. Macmillan, bound to his sickbed, dreaded a deadlock that would entitle the monarch to send for Harold Wilson, leader of the opposition Labor Party, who would have then formed a government, dissolved Parliament, and called an election. Macmillan again appealed to Home, who now acquiesced. The Prime Minister called the polltakers to his bedside to arrange an updated tabulation of Conservative Parliamentary opinion. Butler was now revealed to have gained strength, although he was outnumbered by combined Hailsham and Home first preferences. The blackball again provided the clearest impression. So many interviewees opposed Butler and Hailsham that the double negative in a sense produced Home as a positive. Macmillan wrote out a lengthy, complex assessment of the balance of opinion.

Hours before Macmillan resigned and presented Home's name to the Queen, an emergency cabal led by Ian Macleod, cochairman of the Conservative party and leader of the House of Commons, and Enoch Powell, Minister of Health, met with Redmayne, who was requested to inform Macmillan that both Hailsham and Maudling were prepared to support Butler. Michael Adeane, the Queen's link with the party, was telephoned and told that, irrespective of what Macmillan might say, Butler could now form a government. Butler telephoned Macmillan at King Edward VII's Hospital, but the call was not accepted. Macmillan resigned, presented his written estimate to the Queen, with supplementary oral comment. The Queen sent for the Earl of Home. In the aftermath, critics assailed Home's elevation "on the heap of blackballs cast against his three rivals" and the "tricky maneuverings" of Macmillan and Redmayne and called for "modernization" of the selection procedure.[11] More typically, succession in the Prime Ministership is simple and assured. The Parliamentary Party of both the Conservative and Labor parties elect a leader, and he normally is tapped for the Prime Minister post if his party attains a majority. Consequently, Harold Wilson won election as Labor Leader in 1963 on the second ballot against his rivals George Brown and James Callaghan and was summoned to form a government the following year when Labor won the national elections. In 1974, even when a national election produced no party majority in the House of Commons, for the first time in nearly forty-five years, the succession machinery promptly produced a new Labor government, headed by Wilson, capable of evoking Parliamentary support for a full-sized program.[12]

Soviet Russia, like all dictatorships, cannot solve the problem of succession. The transfer of power, for which the Soviet constitution makes no provision, can be the occasion of numbing uncertainty, subterfuge, terror, and violence. One or more of those elements attended the successions to Lenin, Stalin, and Khrushchev. Stalin's death and its aftermath disclose the jagged course of dictatorial succession. The announcement of his demise was withheld for six hours and ten minutes. A statement accompanying the eventual disclosure declared that the "most important task of the party and the government is to insure uninterrupted and correct leadership . . . the greatest unity of leadership and the prevention of any kind of disorder and panic." As Bertram D. Wolfe has well observed, admonitions against "disorder and panic" are inconceivable in an American transfer.[13] When power passed from Roosevelt to Truman and from Kennedy to Johnson, there were, needless to say, no comparable warnings from high places.

With Stalin's passing, a reshuffling of state and party positions proceeded, with Malenkov, in the intrafactional bargaining, emerging as the head of government and First Secretary of the party. But the bargain did not stick. After nine days Malenkov "asked to be relieved" of his duties as party First Secretary. Two years later, again at his own request, he abandoned the Premiership as well. Malenkov's degradation continued in the Soviet manner when he confessed to "errors" in agricultural policy that could only have been committed by his rival Khrushchev. Another major figure, Lavrenti Beria, head of the secret police, was arrested, shot, and made an "unperson." Meanwhile Khrushchev took over the post of First Secretary and consolidated his power to the point where, in an extraordinary address to the Twentieth Party Congress, he denounced the memory of Stalin, depicting him as a tyrant, a sadist, and a glutton for adulation. Among the interpretations placed upon this grotesque performance is one that Khrushchev, in effect, was pledging not to employ his newly won power according to Stalin's example.

But in time, Khrushchev too veered toward the Stalinist prototype of personalized leadership, which with his ill-regarded management of the Cuban missile crisis, plus other policy lapses, produced his overthrow. As before, in the obscure turnings of the succession machinery the identity of his successor emerged slowly. Again an interval of "collective leadership" set in, and then, by deft maneuver, Leonid Brezhnev emerged head and shoulders above such fellow sharers of leadership as Kosygin, Shelepin, and Podgorny. By mid-1965 undeniable external signs attested to Brezhnev's succession. Once the First Secretary of the party, he was now its "Secretary General"; at victory celebrations he monopolized the prime roles; in foreign relations he became the sole authoritative spokesman, and took over the range of accessory functions that once belonged to Khrushchev.[14] Increasingly his face beamed benignly from posters and his deeds were acclaimed, more than any other figure's, on Soviet television. Yet, even in 1973, occasional traces of ambiguity pockmarked Brezhnev's pretensions as successor. Sporadic indications of collective leadership confined Brezhnev to what at most was a minor cult of personality. To counterbalance the attention being showered upon Brezhnev, Premier Aleksei N. Kosygin and Mikhail A. Suslov, chief party ideologist, made well-publicized domestic political trips. A more subtle but positive assertion of collective leadership occurred in the obituary for General of the Army and Deputy Defense Minister Aleksandr N. Komarovsky. Ordinarily such statements are signed by the Politburo in alphabetical order, but with Brezhnev appearing first. On this occasion, the entire top triumvirate—Brezhnev, Podgorny, and Kosygin—were placed first, instead of just Brezhnev, and then the usual alphabetical order was observed. This subtly amended protocol appeared designed to prevent Brezhnev's rising eminence from escalating into a solid trend toward one-man rule at the expense of the "collective leadership" that toppled Khrushchev in 1964.[15] Even after eight years following that event, the question whether Brezhnev would succeed to the amplitude of Khrushchev's powers had not been decisively answered.

The British Parliamentary System

Many a critic of the Presidency gazes admiringly upon the British Parliamentary system and proposes to graft upon the American structure some of the better elements of the British. Woodrow Wilson, both as a youthful political scientist and as a practicing President, longed to introduce the British method into American politics. He would greatly have preferred to have been a Prime Minister rather than a President and indeed tried manfully during his incumbency to nudge the office into the ways of the British model. Such legislators as George Pendleton of the nineteenth century and Estes Kefauver of the twentieth doggedly proposed to borrow from British practice to bring executive and legislative effort into purposeful cooperation. A study committee of the American Political Science Association in 1950 emerged with an ingenious plan for adapting the British party system to the circumstances of American parties.[16]

In Canada, where the parliamentary system closely resembles that of the British, the chairman of the House of Commons committee engaged in assessing a key parliamentary institution, the daily question period, asserted: "Looking at the United States, there's a lot of feeling that the whole Watergate thing might not have gone along so far if the members of the President's Cabinet had been required to spend 40 minutes in Congress every day answering questions." [17] Is the British Parliamentary system better for the United States than the existing Presidential system? The leading attractions of the Parliamentary system are unity and coherence of policy. It encourages the executive to tackle the major problems of the day, to propose bold plans and broad programs. The British executive has every assurance that every major thing he asks for will be enacted, not the 40 or 50 percent of the important measures that the American President is likely to secure but 100 percent. The secret weapon of the Parliamentary system is tight party discipline.

The Prime Minister's party, be it Conservative or Labor, provides him with a majority of legislators whose obedience, with few exceptions, is granitic, "solid masses of steady votes," Walter Bagehot put it, for policy and program. The party leader, who is ordinarily either the Prime Minister or leader of the opposition, possesses powers that are well-nigh autocratic and against which the American President's party powers are limp and pallid. The Prime Minister has the sole ultimate responsibility for formulating policy and an electoral program. The party secretariat or central office is his personal machine. He appoints the principal officers and thereby controls propaganda, research, and finance. He is vested with lordly power over his party followers in Parliament. An M.P. can ill afford to incur his dread wrath by challenging, criticizing, or publicly differing with his party. No M.P. who has crossed the floor, or aligned himself with the opposition, on a major issue has won reelection since 1945.[18] All this, needless to say, is a far cry from the American President's circumstances. Franklin Roosevelt was the only President to launch a substantial purge upon recalcitrant Democrats, with results so inglorious that no successor has dared repeat the venture.

In the selection of candidates for American national legislative office, state and local organizations and primaries dominate the decisions. The result is a goodly crop of Senators and Congressmen opposed to the President of their own party on principal policy questions. In Britain the local choice of the candidate must win central approval. The Labor party's constitution provides that a candidate's selection "shall not be regarded as completed until the name of the person has been placed before a meeting of the National Executive Committee, and his or her selection has been duly endorsed." The Labor constitution clearly stipulates the conditions of approval: The candidate must conform to "the Constitution, Program, Principles and Policy of the Party" and "act in harmony with the Standing Orders of the Parliamentary Labor Party." [19] Even if a rebel is backed by his own constituency, the Labor party will enter a candidate against him, thus dividing the party's usual vote and making almost certain his defeat.

British party discipline depends not simply on organization and gadgetry. It also reflects the lesser role of pressure groups in national life. The United States, in contrast, is a land where pressure groups flourish, where regional differences are vast, and their influence is divisive, preventing the tight integration of opinion and leadership in the major parties. Above all, differences between the British and American peoples are an influence, the latter's heterogeneity forcing the parties to be broad and flexible in method. British party methods in the areas of finance, selection of candidates, and platform-development, however, deserve close study for possible borrowings and adaptations to the United States.

The British Prime Minister

Whereas the American President's weakness as party leader earns him unreliable Congressional support for his program—once when the House of Representatives overrode his veto, Gerald Ford mustered only seven votes, most of them from lame-duck Republicans [20]—the British Prime Minister knows the luxury of enduring legislative backing. The President, viewing the British executive, across the Atlantic, must see him as abiding in a political utopia that assures that whatever he asks for, the legislature will provide.

In theory, the President is more powerful than the Prime Minister in legislation. Head of the executive branch, he is the coequal of Congress. He is not responsible to Congress in the sense that the Prime Minister is to Parliament. To become Prime Minister, Harold Wilson had to be elected to the House of Commons, where he answers daily for the actions of his government. In British constitutional theory he, his cabinet, and other ministers are a committee of the House of Commons.

Although in theory the Prime Minister and his government are the servants of the House of Commons, they are in fact its masters. The government, not the House, legislates. The government plans and controls the House's time. The introduction of legislation is almost completely the government's monopoly. A rule requiring that all legislation involving expenditure bear the crown's, or in actuality the government's, approval invests the government with a sweeping control, since virtually all legislation of significance requires money. This order of things is supported by an implicit democratic rationalization: Parties contest elections on platforms; upon winning a popular, and therefore a legislative, majority a party should command priority for its program in the House.

Normally, the British government is certain that any important bill it introduces will pass without significant change, in good time. Although the cannonade of brilliant oratory and merciless jibes may beat upon its program in House debate, the government ultimately prevails. It knows no evil like the committee bottleneck and the crippling amendment that kills or damages beyond recognition the President's requests. At most, Parliament can only influence the government's future course. Flaws exposed in legislative debate presumably will not be prolonged or repeated.

In his daily legislative life the Prime Minister sails a smooth sea compared with the American President. Harold Wilson squeaked through the national elections of 1964 with a four-seat margin in the House of Commons. Despite this slim margin, he announced that the bold program promised in his campaign would be fully presented to the House. "Nothing could be worse," Wilson declared, "than failing both at home and abroad because of the Parliamentary balance of power." He brought forward his program, and it proceeded with assurance through Parliament, even when, through attrition, his margin fell to one vote. But Wilson still moved ahead, and the country approved and rewarded his effort by returning him to office in 1966 by a landslide.

In 1974, although the national elections gave Wilson's party only a minority of House seats with which to govern, he was again undeterred in advancing a substantial (by American standards) national program, including the nationalization of new industries. But Britain's severe economic plight of inflation, falling productivity, rising unemployment, and general decline in the quality of life exposed Wilson increasingly to factional attack within his party. Labor's left wing assailed Wilson's budget, criticized his government for providing excessive help to industry, and objected to his cautious pace in nationalizing the shipbuilding and aircraft industries. Wilson was not endangered, but the political bickering reinforced the atmosphere of decline and futility afflicting British society.[21]

The Prime Minister, also unlike the President, shares power with fellow executives, the ministers, and particularly those who comprise the cabinet. The Prime Minister, however, enjoys powers his fellow ministers do not have. In constitutional practice all ministerial offices derive from him and depend upon him, since he can make and unmake ministers. The Prime Minister can prompt the dissolution of the entire government simply by resigning, as Edward Heath did in 1974 to force a general election. No minister has such power. The Prime Minister alone can make certain great decisions without cabinet approval. His fellow ministers have small choice but to back him. To repudiate him is to split the party and deliver the government to the enemy.

Yet, in choosing his cabinet, the Prime Minister faces ground rules far more restrictive than any confronting the President. The Prime Minister is literally forced to work with certain associates; the President is not. John Kennedy could choose a cabinet in which not a single major legislative figure of his party was represented, and in Richard Nixon's original cabinet there was only one. The President, it is true, must pay heed to some customary limitations in constituting his cabinet: Give Interior to a Westerner, and Labor, Agriculture, and perhaps Commerce to appointees acceptable to the clienteles of those departments. But these are generalized frameworks within which the President can select among scores, if not hundreds, of individuals. "It is important," Prime Minister Harold Macmillan has written of cabinet-forming, that "different groups of opinion within the party should be represented." [22] The Prime Minister's choices, on the other hand, are definite and particular. To form a government, the Prime Minister must build upon the support of the principal factions of his party. Factional allegiance requires a *quid pro quo,* a seat for the factional leader in the cabinet. Accordingly, Edward Heath, in constructing his cabinet, had no choice but to bring his principal opponent, Reginald Maudling, into a leading post. This Heath did by selecting Maudling as Home Secretary.

It is a commonplace of Anglo-American comparison to suggest that the British Prime Minister is coming to resemble more and more the American President. Impetus for the observation is provided especially by the growing involvement of the Prime Minister in television activity, projecting, as the President is prone to, the image of the leader in a mass democracy. Increasingly, British elections are contests between rival leaders, and one, the incumbent Prime Minister, easily dominates the news with the bountiful resources of his office. As his power and impact flourish, that of other institutions has diminished, whether the Monarch, the houses of Parliament, or the cabinet. Nonetheless, differences between the President and the Prime Minister remain substantial. For the active, assertive President, for example, the American system provides no substitute. Eisenhower, felled by illness, and Nixon, wounded by Watergate, were not replaced in their enfeeblement by any other locus of effective executive power. But in Britain, when Prime Minister Sir Alec Douglas-Home lapsed into semiretirement by choosing to function modestly and to withdraw from making initiatives and from steering and maneuvering, his ministers solidified working relations with each other, united in common action, and produced a viable government position that they guided through the cabinet and the House of Commons.[23] And the inconclusive 1974 elections, which produced a minority government headed by Harold Wilson, moved the Prime Minister to share power more with his fellow ministers. "Harold is acting very much like the chairman of the board," said a senior minister, ". . . After all that talk about Presidential-style government in England, it's back to the cabinet system." [24]

The Parliamentary System Evaluated

The supreme attractiveness of the Parliamentary system is the ease and assurance with which it produces policy. The executive has charge of legislation, guided by public opinion as it is expressed by interest groups, the press, and in the House of Commons. Administration, whether it concern organizational structure, program, finance, or personnel, is the secure province of the executive. The House votes the funds that the cabinet requests. The House lacks constitutional power to vote more money for any purpose than the cabinet asks for, a situation that is the bane of budget-minded Presidents. Thanks to iron party discipline, the cabinet can count not only on a majority but regularly on the same majority. Lyndon Johnson, who knew the luxury of large Congressional majorities for his party, never ceased to marvel at Harold Wilson's ability to act decisively in domestic and international affairs with merely a paper-thin legislative margin. [25] Parliament's orientation, like the cabinet's, is national rather than local. The lack of a tradition that the legislator reside in his own district, the common incident of an M.P. elected from a district he has never visited, the party's intolerance of any local deviation from national policy, give Parliament an orientation as resolutely national as the consciousness of Congress, and particularly of the House of Representatives, is local.

But the Parliamentary system, for all its undeniable excellence as a vehicle of national policy, also carries weakness. It is immediately suspect because of Britain's own decline in power and place in the family of nations, which, although a product of many factors, strongly suggests that the Parliamentary method smacks excessively of the past and has not adjusted sufficiently to modern change. There is indeed much that is anachronistic in the British Parliamentary model, much that once was meaningful but that time and change have reduced to hollow pretense. What was constitutional political fact in that nation in the nineteenth century, as Don K. Price has put it, has become constitutional fiction in the twentieth. The House of Commons in bygone days did control the government and could, when it chose, dismiss it. Nowadays, however, public opinion rather than the House determines cabinet tenure. [26]

The House of Commons has been reduced to a passivity that even the most resolute critic of Congress would not wish upon it. In its tightly restricted capacity, the House resembles the American electoral college, registering the popular will in choosing a government and then automatically ratifying its program and voting the funds it asks for. The House lacks means of initiating policy; unlike Congress, it has no standing committees to investigate and recommend, deprivations that preclude any legislative capacity to take an independent line and exercise meaningful control. More than three decades ago Stanley Baldwin rightly observed that House members widely felt they had "nothing much to do of a responsible nature." [27]

Nowadays outcries are rising in Britain against Parliament's general ineffectuality. Brian Chapman of Manchester University voiced the wide concern of responsible Britons when he wrote, "We need a state in which Parliament is an effective partner in the process of government, and not simply an ineffectual appendage employed to make noises of approval or discontent." Seeking a rearranged governmental structure enabling Parliament to "play a vital role in the formulation of policy," Chapman looked admiringly upon the American Congress, with its subject matter and joint committees and urged that the House of Lords be reconstituted by regions.[28]

The administrative features of the Parliamentary system are also questionable. The minister, the equivalent of the American departmental Secretary, is primarily a legislative leader and not an administrator. He is chosen not so much for administrative ability as for his command of House support and his skill in defending party policy. He makes his way by shining in debate and by leadership in party affairs. Accordingly, if Henry Kissinger, the extraordinarily effective Secretary of State, were to live and work as a Briton, chances are less that he would achieve the place and make the contribution permitted him in American public affairs.

Finally, much of the criticism that Britons themselves have levied against their governmental system has fallen upon the civil service. Long and rightly hailed as a model career system for other nations, including the United States, to emulate, the British civil service is handled roughly by its present-day critics. It is viewed as ingrown, uninspired, uncreative, and out of step with the swift pace of Britain's problems. In essence, the administrative class, or policy-making career service, is recruited at a youthful age, when its members complete their university education, after which they pass all their working lives in governmental service. Except for specialized employment, it is difficult to bring into the civil service those midway and beyond in a business, academic, or professional career.[29]

The British ministerial system reinforces the tendency of large bureaucratic organizations to be cautious and safe, and therefore unenterprising. A minister progresses in his political career if the civil service keeps him out of trouble. The civil service reads the handwriting on the wall, which instructs that they will gain more by caution (which avoids trouble) than by initiative (which invites it). Furthermore, the civil servant figures that even if the initiative succeeds, the minister will receive most of the credit. Some Britons looking for reform take their cues from American practice. They propose a generous use of a "brain trust" to be attached to the Prime Minster's and each minister's office, an injection of new blood into the civil service at many levels from the untapped talent of the professions, business, and local government.

Changes have transpired. In 1971 the several personnel classes, including the administrative class, were merged into a single structure, and the interview procedure that is used in recruitment and that facilitates indulgence of class and educational biases was overhauled to enhance its objectivity. A Civil Service College was established for postentry training and a reform study has urged at least a year's experience in banking or industry for the young recruit. Whether these changes are enough to produce variety and vitality remains to be seen. Both Wilson and Heath abandoned traditionally exclusive reliance on the civil service for developing policy and imported several private economists into the government. Heath also recruited a cadre of business executives to enhance civil service management and to effect savings, a high commitment of his Conservative government.[30]

The Administrative State

All nations have donned increasingly the trappings of the administrative state. Managing the economy, providing welfare services, and maintaining the military force and weaponry have compounded executive tasks, resources, and power in society. In most of the nations of the world, administration has gained in power and autonomy at the expense of the legislature. The United States, however, for all the expansion of its governmental responsibilities displays far less of a shift of power from the legislature to the executive. The American Congress exerts controls over administration that other legislatures do not possess. Its legislation is more detailed, its controls over administrative structure, finance, program, and personnel are far tighter than those exercised by other legislatures of the world.

In Great Britain Parliament practices a relationship with the executive in matters of administration that, were it followed in the United States, would immeasurably strengthen the President's position as administrative chief. Although Britain has a unified political system, with both legislative and executive power concentrated in Parliament, administration is treated altogether differently. Administration is accorded the full benefit of the doctrine of separation of powers. Paradoxically, the United States claims to observe a separation of powers, but Congress freely breaches it in matters of administration. The British, applying separation of powers, leave to executive discretion the employment of the basic means of administration. The organizational structure of departments, which Congress provides for in close detail, Parliament delegates to executive decision. Personnel policy, for which Congress has compiled a thick volume of close legislation, the British leave to the executive. The executive budget, which Congress can deal roughly with when it chooses, remains fully intact in the hands of Parliament. If even one of these instances of legislative self-denial were adopted by Congress, the President's prowess as administrative chief would be vastly strengthened.

But here the claims of the strong Presidency clash with the requisites of democracy. In the abuses of executive power that surfaced in the Watergate scandals, the departmental bureaus sometimes provided the most effective resistance to the overweening demands of the White House staff. A potent ingredient of the bureaus' capacity to resist was the actual or potential backing of Congressional power centers—committees, leaders, and individual legislators—whose availability stemmed from Congress's traditional involvement all along the broad front of administration.

The Fifth French Republic is the ultimate in the democratic administrative state, veering as it does in certain seasons into constitutional dictatorship.[31] As a model of the continuously strong chief executive in a more or less democratic setting, it is too extreme for adaptation to the United States. In the Fourth Republic a well-nigh powerless executive was subordinate to an all-powerful lower legislative house, the Chamber of Deputies. In the Fifth Republic much of the Deputies' power has been transferred to the executive, chiefly to the President and, to a much lesser degree, to the Prime Minister in subordination to the President. The President controls policy-making in foreign affairs and national security, and he can, when he chooses, extend his powers by revising constitutional practice at will and ruling under emergency powers for periods extending well beyond the actual emergency. The Prime Minister and his cabinet wield so many powers not subject to the approval of the Assembly, the lower legislative house of the Fifth Republic, that they can confidently anticipate the enactment of most of their vital policies for the low price of occasional minor changes in program and personnel shifts. Parliament's lawmaking powers are limited to specific subjects set out chiefly by the constitution. The administration, in turn, wields a rule-making power over all matters not specifically reserved to Parliament.

French Parliamentary lawmaking is subordinate to administrative necessity. Article XXXVIII of the constitution provides that "for the execution of its program" the executive may ask Parliament for power temporarily to take measures by ordinance that constitutionally are among the subjects reserved to the legislature. The French Senate, which belongs to the administrative tradition of French politics works as an ally of the executive. A Constitutional Council tests the constitutionality of laws enacted by Parliament. The Council, too, is an auxiliary of executive dominance, watchful that Parliament remains within the confines of its inferior position. De Gaulle conducted his Presidential office as a crisis executive, and under Article XVI, which provides unlimited emergency powers in external and internal crisis, he enjoyed authority that largely subjected the government and its policies to Presidential control. His Presidential successor, Georges Pompidou, former premier, professor, and banker, governed with the same sweep of power, but unlike DeGaulle, who disdained administration, Pompidou directly and personally supervised all the business of government except a small domain of social and economic affairs allotted to the Premier. In 1974 incoming President Giscard d'Estaing recruited a cabinet whose strength was more administrative than political. Generally, the Ministers were highly qualified in technical fields, having been drawn substantially from the professions and the civil service, including the key incumbencies for foreign affairs and finance.[32]

Both the French President and the British Prime Minister have personal staffs, but they are far less numerous than the American President's. These staffs, though they play a significant role in policy development, have generally less impact than their American counterparts. Particularly in France, the personal staffs are enlarging their influence on policy. Pompidou's initial Secretary General of the Elysée Palace, a kind of chief of staff, Michel Jobert, was known as the "French Kissinger." Matters in both foreign and domestic affairs filtered through Jobert as they moved toward Pompidou, and the Secretary General, like Kissinger as national security assistant, was entrusted with crucial diplomatic negotiations, including some with Kissinger himself.[33] The parallelism persisted when both moved subsequently to cabinet posts, Kissinger as Secretary of State and Jobert as Foreign Minister.

In France and Britain, the top executive's use of personal staff is regulated by forces that are less prevalent, or even nonexistent, in the United States, with the consequent danger of excesses by the White House staff. While a British Prime Minister looks to his personal staff and the cabinet secretariat for political advice, he is, unlike the American President, constrained by the likely resentment of senior ministers if they suspect that the counsel of nonelected persons—the staff—is preferred to theirs. In both France and Britain, irritation and conflict between the staff on the one hand and the ministers and civil service on the other is diminished by the practice of constituting the staffs heavily, if not entirely, with civil servants. In light of the misdeeds of the White House staff in Watergate, a possible safeguard against future aberrations might be to draw more of the Presidential staff from the departmental civil service and to move more toward the British conception of a loyal staff that will serve succeeding Presidents or Prime Ministers, with the right to return to departmental duty protected.

The United States, an executive-legislative state, faces in its competitor, the Soviet Union, a monolithic administrative state. The Soviet Union is in the hands of party administrators, a political bureaucracy or "new class," as Milovan Djilas terms it. The governmental and economic apparatuses are part of the party organism, but each has its separate structure, caste characteristics, and narrower self-interests. The new class members enjoy special privileges and economic preferences derived from their administrative monopoly. Unlike bureaucracies in the noncommunist world, which are subject to political authorities, "the Communists," as Djilas has written, "have neither masters nor owners over them." [34]

The Soviet Union's top leadership is produced by the party administrative system. Stalin was himself the epitome of the party administrator, rising not as a charismatic leader but as one skilled in the ways of the party apparatus, who outdid competitors who excelled as orators or theoreticians. Stalin neither preached nor inspired but made decisions, spoke without ardor or color, and stressed the concrete administrative tasks of industrializing the Soviet Union and collectivizing its agriculture. To retain power, he incorporated a system of relentless terror into the administrative apparatus.[35]

Stalin's successors, Malenkov and Khrushchev, and their successors, Kosygin and Brezhnev, all were party administrators who climbed the career ladder. The ascent to the top is by apolitical means, accomplished without a struggle for votes or an assertion of new ideas for program and policy but dependent rather upon one's usefulness to the incumbent leadership and upon choosing the right protectors. Conservatism is the dominant characterisitic of the Soviet new class, which, while enormously capable of maintaining itself, is little capable of creating change and is apprehensive of it as a threat to its position and privilege. Hence the bureaucratic oligarchy is locked in its ideology and fears debate and free opinion as threats to its power. The banishment of novelist Alexander Solzhenitsyn illustrates the problem.

Such a posture chills the hopes of those who look for increasing convergence of the Soviet and American systems, which might diminish the incidence of violence in international affairs, and therefore the American Presidency's preoccupation with national security pursuits and their consequent strains on the compatibility of the office's acts with democracy. As yet, the most promising possibilities for convergence center upon Soviet-American approaches to common problems like those of outer space and control of nuclear armaments. Among the more formidable roadblocks are the Soviet's bureaucratic rigidities and political conformities. Although political freedom occasionally sprouts and external developments are eroding traditional Russian isolation, little prospect appears of disturbing the entrenched bureaucratic oligarchy in the near future. For the Soviet and American systems to converge, a drastic change of direction must occur in the path of development of one of them. But healthy political systems change only gradually, and there is little spur to change on a drastic scale, since the Soviet and American systems, each in their own way, are highly successful.[36]

Decision-Making Compared

Lyndon Johnson's commitment to an eighteen-hour workday, Eisenhower's extensive overhaul of his top-level staff machinery, Kennedy's overhaul of Eisenhower's overhaul, Nixon's aberrations, and Ford's correctives evidence a restless dissatisfaction with the means and processes of decision-making. Is the Soviet leadership similarly troubled? Does internal, top-level executive decision-making differ substantially in method in the monolithic Soviet system from that in the normally pluralistic American system? Is Soviet experience at all relevant and instructive for American needs?

After Khrushchev was overthrown in October 1964, the Soviet Union was governed by a "collective leadership," in which Kosygin as Premier was teamed with Brezhnev, the party's General Secretary. In 1965 Brezhnev added a state post to his party capacity by becoming a member of the Presidium of the Supreme Soviet, or legislature. By serving in the party's Politburo, Kosygin too combines state and party posts. In the 1970s, collective leadership became somewhat tattered by Brezhnev's clear emergence as head of the Soviet political machinery. But his ascendance was constrained by his apparent judgment that he must follow a consensus course, and according to the evidence of Soviet decision-making, Brezhnev's voice, while persuasive, is not necessarily conclusive.

The top policy organ, over which Brezhnev presides, is the Politburo of the party, which since 1971 has comprised fifteen full, or voting, members and a handful of candidate members, who participate to varying degrees in decision-making. Djilas provided insight into the functioning of a top-level communist policy group when he wrote, "In the Communist system, exclusive groups are established around political leaders and forums. All policy-making is reduced to wrangling in these exclusive groups, in which familiarity and cliquishness flower. The highest group is generally the most intimate." [37] The Politburo and the huge party Central Committee are packed with Brezhnev's protégés, enabling him to push through his policies when he chooses, and diminishing the indecision of Soviet policy-making that was characteristic in earlier stages of the Brezhnev-Kosygin take-over.

But even in the full sun of his power, Brezhnev sometimes falters. The Politburo was divided on whether he should proceed with his summit talks with Nixon after the United States mined North Vietnam's ports. Some Politburo members appear to have favored challenging the American blockade of North Vietnam, or at least cancelling Nixon's impending visit, to protest the mining of Haiphong harbor. Just before Nixon's arrival, one Politburo member, Pyotr Y. Shelest, long a hard-liner toward the West, was demoted by appointment to a less important post, and, as is customary, the announcement was made without public explanation. [38]

All members and candidate members of the Politburo are either officials or deputies of the Supreme Soviet. Thus the highest policy decisions are made in a relatively small group bearing governmental and party authority. The Politburo appears to meet frequently and to work out many decisions on the spot. [39] The American President does not work with any single group as regularly as the Soviet leadership does. The President distributes his consultations among large groups such as the cabinet, the National Security Council, and *ad hoc* groups thrown together for such critical situations as Cuba in 1962 and Panama in 1964. The President, unlike Soviet leaders, may feel behooved to touch base with figures outside the executive branch, such as legislators, private group leaders, and former Presidents. The Politburo seems to have nothing of the elaborately prepared and negotiated papers that characterized Eisenhower's National Security Council. Yet Soviet departments have access to the Politburo through its members and the Secretariat, the party's principal administrative apparatus, over which Brezhnev presides. Agencies like the Ministry of Foreign Affairs report to the Politburo directly.

In actual decision-making, the American President is rather more apt to employ competing sources of information and advice than the Soviet leadership. Brezhnev has revealed that an inner cabinet of four members—himself, Kosygin, Suslov, and Podgorny—maintain continual discussions of major policy issues. The other members of the Politburo carry responsibilities for overseeing departments and bring to the Politburo information and recommendations from their departments. The Politburo receives regular reports on scientific and military developments, the economy, and foreign policy.

The Soviet administrative system is an elaborate mechanism of control from the top. There are no departmental bureaus with the autonomy of an FBI and an Army Corps of Engineers. In Soviet practice the party, which dominates the government apparatus from top to bottom, leaves nothing undone to assure that the orders of the top command are carried out. The Soviet leader can act with a rigor toward his administrators and ministers that no American President would dare consider even in his fondest dreams. The top leadership must appear infallible despite the treachery of events and human error. If it falters, others must bear the blame.

The Presidency Abroad

The Presidency is America's foremost political export. The Philippines and most of all Latin America have grafted onto their governments elements of the American Presidential model. At one time or another all the Latin American countries have adopted the strong Presidency. It is instructive to study what they have borrowed, added, or left out in their adaptation of the American prototype because it reveals what they believe to be the strengths and shortcomings of the Presidential institution.

The powers of the Latin American President invariably exceed those of the United States Chief Executive.[40] The Latin American President's appointment power is stronger. He can fill most offices on his own authority, referring relatively few for senatorial or congressional approval. He sends messages and appears personally before congress to request action. In Venezuela he can even introduce bills, a power treated somewhat ambiguously in several other constitutions, which assertive presidents have interpreted to their own advantage. He presents the budget in the form of an appropriation bill, enjoys a broad and strong veto power, including an item veto for appropriations, and has a sweeping power to issue decrees and administrative orders. Laws are passed in far more general terms than the American Congress would ever tolerate, affording the President broad discretion. He enjoys extraordinary powers to cope with civil disorder, invasion, or other crisis and to intervene in the provincial governments.

Latin American experience abundantly demonstrates, however, that in spite of all his impressive power the President must dominate the army and build a political party or following of "interests," especially the organized urban workers, if he is to succeed.

Even the best Latin American presidents have indulged in what is termed "exaggerated presidentialism," by which they assume dictatorial powers for brief or substantial periods. Simón Bolívar, for one, was convinced that exceptional executive powers must be readily available to counter the demagogic exploitation of racial-cultural tensions. The spectacle of the presidency transformed into an outright military dictatorship is all too common. Although the United States' transplant has not proved to be the means to good government, it is reassuring that each departure from legitimate government for some variant of dictatorship has been marked by an eventual return to the presidential form.

As is the fate of merchandise, not every potential foreign buyer who has looked at the American Presidential system has bought it. Charles de Gaulle, beholding the American Presidency in 1964, turned aside clamors in certain domestic quarters that France repattern its own presidency along American lines. De Gaulle would have nothing of it. The American system, he declared in a press conference, was functioning in a limping way, and if it were applied in France he foresaw only "a chronic opposition" between the executive and the legislature that would lead to "general paralysis." Presumably De Gaulle had in mind the breakdowns in Presidential-Congressional cooperation that provide the American nation with a frequent diet of political futility. The American Presidential system, De Gaulle contended, had thrived in the peculiarly favorable environment of the United States:

> it is in a country which because of its technical make-up, its economic riches, its geographical position, never knew invasion, and which for a century has known no revolution; in a country where, moreover, there are only two parties that are divided by nothing essential in any field, national, social, moral, international; in a federal country where the Government assumes only general tasks—defenses, diplomacy, finance—while the 50 states of the union are entrusted with all the rest.[41]

The American Presidency was not transferable, at least not to France.

EPILOGUE:
THE FUTURE
OF THE
AMERICAN
PRESIDENCY

For reasons different from De Gaulle's, the American Presidency has come to be questioned and doubted in many quarters of domestic opinion. The danger is that the worth and future of the office will be judged chiefly on the basis of the worst hours of the Nixon incumbency, a caldron of overflowing trouble for democratic government. It is submitted, however, that the Nixon Presidency was, fortunately, one of a kind. His conduct of the office bore little resemblance to the performances of his 35 predecessors and the likely deportment of Gerald Ford and other successors.

Richard Nixon was engaged in nothing less than remaking the Presidency, in imposing his own design—a Gaullist-Mafia concoction, if you please—upon the historic office. The Presidency of Nixon was not the Presidency of Jefferson, McKinley, Taft, Ford, or of any one else. It was a solitary aberration, a radical, indeed a revolutionary, reformulation of the Presidency, with pretensions to powers that no previous incumbent ever claimed. Nixon and his associates did nothing less than resurrect the doctrine of the Divine Right of Kings, restated as the Divine Right of the President. The President can do no wrong; he can authorize or perpetrate illegal acts, including crimes, suppress civil liberties, spy on citizens, burglarize their offices, do anything to anyone in the name of national security. This is the Presidency that, with its inflated conception of its powers, claimed competence to disregard the law to achieve its objectives. It refused to implement programs that Congress established, declined to spend funds that Congress appropriated, and violated Congressional prohibitions on war-making in Laos and Cambodia.

This errant Presidency was checked and eventually terminated by mechanisms the Founding Fathers provided for such an extremity: the courts, Congress, and that ultimate recourse, impeachment. But though the system worked, the democratic order had a close call, a brush with extinction. That order was saved by the alertness of a federal district judge and the fortuitous bunglings of the would-be tyrants. Common sense requires a reexamination of the constraints the political system provides against abuse, and, if possible, their strengthening; next time the special factors that saved the democratic order may not be operative.

Essentially, the future Presidency will face the problem of the past Presidency—how best to effect an equilibrium between Presidential power, on the one hand, and democracy on the other. Both components of the equation are indispensable for modern government. Presidential power is necessary for the accomplishment of programs, the maintenance of security, and the betterment of the social order. But these accomplishments must be achieved without the violation of democratic limitations, constitutional requirements, and civil liberties. Presidential power can be tolerated in substantial quantity—the strong Presidency—only if the assorted democratic constraints are working effectively. Presidential power can be safely increased to meet new problems and crises only if the efficiency of democratic safeguards is correspondingly increased. The task of democratic politics is to respond simultaneously to both sides of the equation.

The Presidency of strength, competence, and good will has been historically, and can be in the future, an office of good works. As the repository of the resources of governmental action, the Presidency constitutes the accomplishing side of government. The other branches express goals, resolves, and principles, but their effectuation depends on the Executive. If, in reaction to Watergate, the Presidency is weakened, problems at home and abroad—whether crime in American cities or hunger in Africa—won't simply vanish, but will, most likely, grow worse if they are neglected. By most forecasts, crises are looming for energy, food, housing, and a host of other matters, and the chief alternative to letting the general citizenry flounder and suffer with their onset is adequate provision beforehand in Presidential planning. Nor is there a viable alternative in the current vogue of discounting some Presidential programs as not working, with the implication that the problems they respond to should either be left to drift or to the care of some other agency that is vaguely, if at all, defined. It has long been evident that such problems as unemployment, inflation, and health care cannot be managed acceptably by private, state, or local action. These and other national problems can be dealt with on a sufficient scale only by the national government.

The strong Presidency is tolerable, the Framers of the Constitution perceived, only if the other branches of government—the Congress and the judiciary—are also strong. In the checking of Richard Nixon and in his eventual expulsion from the Presidency, the other two branches functioned precisely as the Framers intended. The principle of three strong branches is a necessary and prudent guide for the future Presidency. A strong Presidency needs to be counterbalanced by a thoroughly modern Congress, an objective toward which an encouraging momentum has lately developed. Among the most innovative and promising of the recently adopted reforms are the new powers and resources Congress has endowed itself with for evaluating the President's budget and for formulating and asserting its own judgments concerning priorities and policies. For too long, Congress has forfeited television to the President, and that medium has provided the lever of an enormous shift of power in his favor. But the 1974 impeachment hearings of the House Judiciary Committee, a belated and highly successful trial run for legislative television, demonstrated the compatibility of Congressional proceedings with the medium. The more normal business of Congress contains abundant drama, and its selective and imaginative presentation on television should enable the legislature to become an effective competitor to the President in the use of that medium to gain the attention of the public.

The relationship between the President and his party, which has been declining dangerously, must be restored. The President's personal party organization, run exclusively for the benefit and at the whim of the Chief Executive, has been a burgeoning phenomenon for nearly three decades. But such an organization is a negation of democratic practice. Contemporary Presidents, endowed with personal parties of money and workers committed to their election or reelection, can treat as they please the traditional party whose nomination they win, which means that invariably they treat it badly. A major argument in favor of complete public financing of Presidential elections is that it would press the Chief Executive to conduct his campaigns within the regular party structure, which, according to the historical record, is capable of preventing such lawlessness as was rampant in Nixon's personal campaign organization in 1972, the Committee for the Reelection of the President. Likewise, it will be salutary for the strong President if his party conducts an annual or at least a biennial national party conference to develop and review positions on policies and issues. The 1974 Democratic mini-convention was a stride in this direction. The annual party convention would expose the President to a greater diversity of opinions and range of interests than he might confront in the usual workings of his office. Great power is used more safely if it is shared in processes of consultation.

The future President must give practical effect to the boast of many a predecessor that he is President "of all the people." He governs neither well nor democratically if he favors excessively a single class or group. A President who, like a Coolidge or a Nixon, fashions economic policies on the assumption that what is good for General Motors is good for the country will not be tolerated in a future of economic interdependence and an increasingly educated and politically sophisticated citizenry. Neither can a President succeed if he is indifferent, as incumbents of the 1960s sometimes were, to the wants and fears of the middle class, suburbanites, and, most of all, the lower middle class. The lower middle class bears a disproportionate tax burden, is treated niggardly in the distribution of government benefits, and is engaged in front-line confrontation with urban blight and decay. To govern democratically, the President and his policies and programs must respond to all the segments of American society—the powerful, the not-so-powerful, the powerless. "President of all the people" is more than a boast; it is an apt formulation of what the Presidency's overriding operating principle should be in a democratic government whose workings are designed to reflect distributive justice.

Of the future Presidency, the nation must insist, as it did in its ejection of

Richard Nixon from the office, that the Chief Executive satisfy the requisites of democratic decorum. In Nixon's case, it was simply the enforcement of the modest but basic stipulation that the incumbent must not engage in criminal conduct. But democratic standards embrace other elements—observance of the Constitution and civil liberties, tolerance of political opposition, regard for the other branches of government and for private organs of opinion, especially the news media, and concern for people, for the welfare of the general body of one's fellow human beings. The workings of the Presidential selection process must be reexamined to assure that it does not again produce a Chief Executive who embodies the indifference of a stone wall toward democratic values and practices.

Above all, in a democracy, the President must conduct himself on an elevated moral plane. If he slips or falters, the price is citizen rejection and alienation, with his tenure drained of credibility and effectiveness. Any future President would do well to paste beside his mirror a comment made many years ago by Walter Lippmann:

> Those in high places are more than administrators of government bureaus. They are more than the writers of the laws. They are the custodians of the nation's ideals, of the beliefs it cherishes, of its permanent hopes, of the faith which makes a nation out of a mere aggregation of individuals. They are unfaithful to that trust when by word and example they promote a spirit that is complacent, evasive and acquisitive. . . .

NOTES

1 Perspectives on Presidential Power

1 Peregrine Worsthorne, "Suggestions of a Banana Republic," *New York Times,* April 23, 1973.
2 The text of the address is in *New York Times,* August 10, 1974.
3 James David Barber, *The Presidential Character: Predicting Performance in the White House* (Englewood Cliffs, N.J., 1972), pp. 6–9.
4 For elaboration, see Louis W. Koenig, *The Presidency and the Crisis: Powers of the Office from the Invasion of Poland to Pearl Harbor* (New York, 1944). See also W. C. Langer and S. E. Gleason, *The Challenge to Isolation* (New York, 1952).
5 The most extended analysis of Presidential abuses is in Arthur M. Schlesinger, Jr., *The Imperial Presidency* (Boston, 1973).
6 Ibid., p. 184, 190–92; see also John Norton Moore, *Law and the Indo-China War* (Princeton, 1972), p. 603.
7 George E. Reedy, *The Twilight of the Presidency* (New York, 1970), p. 4.
8 Philip Shabecoff, "Congress Weighs Curb on President's Spending," *New York Times,* January 1, 1974.
9 In Thomas L. Hughes, "Foreign Policy: Men or Measures?" *The Atlantic Monthly* (October 1974), p. 53.
10 Reedy, *Twilight of the Presidency,* p. 1.
11 Schlesinger, *Imperial Presidency,* pp. 222–23.
12 Russell Baker, "Can Say-So Make It So," *New York Times,* March 8, 1973.
13 News conference, August 28, 1974; see transcript in *New York Times,* August 29, 1974.
14 *New York Times,* September 9, 1974.
15 *New York Times,* July 25, 1973.
16 *New York Times,* May 24, 1973 and December 22, 1974.
17 Les Brown, "The Administration vs. TV," *New York Times,* December 17, 1973.
18 *New York Times,* January 22, 1973.
19 Stewart Alsop, "War, Not Politics," *Newsweek,* May 14, 1973.
20 Thedore M. Hesburgh, "The Hucksters," *New York Times,* May 24, 1973; Paul Leventhal, "The Most Successful Americans," *New York Times,* December 19, 1973. For a more optimistic view, see Henry Fairlie, "Common Denominators, High and Low," *New York Times,* December 11, 1973.
21 In Schlesinger, *Imperial Presidency,* pp. 404–05.
22 Stewart Alsop, "The Presidency in Danger," *Newsweek,* November 12, 1973.
23 John Herbers, "Since Watergate, Major Shifts in Power Have Given the Presidency Gains and Losses," *New York Times,* January 28, 1974.
24 Barbara W. Tuchman, "Should We Abolish the Presidency?" *New York Times,* February 13, 1973.
25 Richard E. Neustadt, *Presidential Power* (New York, 1960), pp. 10–12.
26 Woodrow Wilson, *Constitutional Government in the United States* (New York, 1911), p. 59.
27 George Washington to Catherine Macauley Graham, January 9, 1790, in J. C. Fitzpatrick, ed., *The Diaries of George Washington,* vol. 293 (Washington, D.C., 1931–44), p. 495.
28 Herbert Hoover, *The Memoirs of Herbert Hoover,* vol. 2 (New York, 1952), p. 293.
29 Neustadt, *Presidential Power,* p. 34.
30 Allan Nevins, *Grover Cleveland: A Study in Courage* (New York, 1932), p. 510.
31 Ibid., p. 308.
32 William Howard Taft, *Our Chief Magistrate and His Powers* (New York, 1915), p. 144.
33 Philip Shriver Klein, *President James Buchanan* (University Park, Pa., 1962), p. 337.
34 Dwight D. Eisenhower, *Mandate for Change* (Garden City, N.Y., 1963), p. 193.
35 James Bryce, *The American Commonwealth,* vol. 1 (New York, 1907), p. 58.
36 Taft, *Chief Magistrate,* p. 13.
37 William Henry Harbaugh, *Power and Responsibility: The Life and Times of Theodore Roosevelt* (New York, 1961), p. 282.
38 In James MacGregor Burns, "The One Test for the Presidency," *New York Times Magazine* (May 1, 1960), p. 102.
39 Theodore Roosevelt, *An Autobiography* (New York, 1920), p. 406.

2 Creation of the Presidency

1 In Charles C. Thach, *The Creation of the Presidency,* Johns Hopkins University Studies in Historical and Political Science, ser. 40, no. 4 (Baltimore, 1922), p. 22.
2 Evarts Boutell Greene, *The Provincial Governor in the English Colonies of North America* (New York, 1898).
3 Thach, *Creation of the Presidency,* p. 29.
4 Ibid., p. 30.
5 Ibid., pp. 34–40.

6 E. Wilder Spaulding, *His Excellency George Clinton* (New York, 1938), pp. 95–138.

7 George Bancroft, *History of the Formation of the Constitution of the United States of America* (New York, 1885), pp. 326–28.

8 Carl Van Doren, *The Great Rehearsal* (New York, 1948), pp. 88–90, 272–73.

9 Ibid., pp. 91–94.

10 Max Farrand, ed., *The Records of the Federal Convention of 1787,* vol. 2 (New Haven, Conn., 1921), p. 135; Max Farrand, *The Framing of the Constitution of the United States* (New Haven, Conn., 1913), p. 129.

11 Farrand, *Framing the Constitution,* p. 77.

12 Van Doren, *Great Rehearsal,* pp. 59–60.

13 Ibid., p. 145.

14 Farrand, *Records,* vol. 2, p. 318.

15 Ibid., pp. 59, 100, 105.

16 Ibid., pp. 335, 537.

17 Farrand, *Framing the Constitution,* p. 166.

18 Farrand, *Records,* vol. 2, pp. 538–39.

19 Ibid., pp. 318, 427, 535.

20 Ibid., p. 318.

21 Van Doren, *Great Rehearsal,* pp. 139–42.

22 Ibid., pp. 292–94.

23 Farrand, *Records,* vol. 2, p. 568.

24 Bancroft, *Formation of the Constitution,* p. 208.

25 Douglas Southall Freeman, *Patriot and President,* vol. 6 of *George Washington* (New York, 1943), p. 117.

26 Farrand, *Records,* vol. 1, p. 140.

27 Ibid., p. 100.

28 Ibid., p. 82.

29 Thach, *Creation of the Presidency,* p. 169.

30 Ibid., pp. 191–95.

31 Ibid., p. 252.

32 Leonard D. White, *The Federalists: A Study in Administrative History* (New York, 1948), p. 103.

33 J. C. Fitzpatrick, ed., *The Diaries of George Washington,* vol. 4 (Boston, 1925), p. 82.

34 Freeman, *Patriot and President,* p. 265.

35 John A. Carroll and Mary W. Ashworth, *First in Peace,* vol. 7 of *George Washington* (New York, 1957), pp. 353–57.

36 In Saul K. Padover, ed., *The Complete Jefferson* (New York, 1943), pp. 138–39.

37 Jared Sparks, *The Writings of George Washington,* vol. 10 (Boston, 1836), p. 186.

38 Edward S. Corwin, *The President's Control of Foreign Relations* (Princeton, 1917), Chapter 1.

39 Carroll and Ashworth, *First in Peace,* p. xxiii.

3 Selection

1 Paul T. David, Ralph M. Goldman, and Richard C. Bain, *The Politics of National Party Conventions* (Washington, 1960), p. 311.

2 Theodore H. White, *The Making of the President, 1960* (New York, 1961), p. 50.

3 Arthur S. Link, *Wilson: The Road to the White House* (Princeton, N.J., 1947), p. 405.

4 James A. Farley, *Behind the Ballots* (New York, 1938), p. 101.

5 Ibid., p. 89.

6 Margaret Leech, *In the Days of McKinley* (New York, 1959), pp. 55–57.

7 *Congressional Quarterly Weekly Reports,* July 8, 1972, p. 1650.

8 Ibid.

9 Malcolm Moos and Stephen Hess, *The Making of Presidential Candidates* (New York, 1960).

10 *New York Times,* May 14 and 28, 1972; *Congressional Quarterly Weekly Reports,* February 19, 1972, p. 231.

11 Frank Freidel, *Franklin D. Roosevelt: The Triumph* (Boston, 1956), p. 294.

12 Ibid.

13 White, *Making of the President, 1960,* pp. 155–57.

14 Freidel, *Franklin D. Roosevelt,* pp. 291–93.

15 *New York Times,* August 24, 1972.

16 Freidel, *Franklin D. Roosevelt,* pp. 308–09.

17 *New York Times,* October 22, 1971 and October 35, 1972.

18 Link, *Wilson,* p. 462.

19 White, *Making of the President, 1960,* pp. 248, 324–25.

20 *New York Times,* August 11, 1968.

21 *New York Times,* May 17, 1968.

22 Theodore H. White, *The Making of the President, 1972* (New York, 1973), pp. 49–50.

23 Ibid., pp. 276–77.

24 *Congressional Quarterly Weekly Reports,* August 12, 1972, pp. 1984–85.

25 White, *Making of the President, 1972,* p. 224.

26 James Reston, "Nixon's Campaign Strategy," *New York Times,* August 18, 1972.

27 Alfred Steinberg, *The Man from Missouri: The Life and Times of Harry S Truman* (New York, 1962), pp. 322–24.

28 *Congressional Quarterly Weekly Reports,* April 15, 1972.

29 Ibid.

30 *New York Times,* October 4, 1972.

31 Herbert E. Alexander, "Communications and Politics: The Media and the Message," *Law and Contemporary Problems* (Spring 1969), pp. 257–58.

32 *New York Times,* November 28, 1971.

33 *New York Times,* September 23, 1972.

34 *New York Times,* August 20, 1972.

35 *New York Times,* May 28, 1973.

36 Ibid.

37 Lucius Wilmerding, Jr., *The Electoral College* (New Brunswick, N.J., 1958), pp. 46–59.

38 Ibid., pp. 38–42. The most careful evaluation of the present electoral system and its alterna-

tives is found in Wallace S. Sayre and Judith Parris, *Voting for President* (Washington, 1970).

39 Ibid., p. xi.

40 Ibid., p. 89.

41 *New York Times,* January 2, 1975.

42 *New York Times,* June 7, 1973.

4 Tenure

1 Joseph E. Kallenbach, "Constitutional Limitations on Reeligibility of National and State Executives," *American Political Science Review* 46 (June 1952): 443.

2 Fred Rodell, *Democracy and the Third Term* (New York, 1940), pp. 13–28.

3 Richard L. Strout, "The Twenty-second Amendment: A Second Look," *New York Times Magazine,* July 28, 1957, p. 5.

4 R. S. Baker, *Woodrow Wilson,* vol. 6 (Garden City, N.Y., 1927–39), pp. 438–52.

5 *New York Tribune,* November 5, 1920.

6 Concerning the resignation, see *New York Times,* August 9, 1974.

7 Concerning impeachment, see Raoul Berger, *Impeachment: The Constitutional Problems* (Cambridge, 1973) and Charles L. Black, Jr., *Impeachment: A Handbook* (New Haven, 1974).

8 Gideon Welles, *Diary of Gideon Welles,* vol. 3 (Boston, 1911), p. 292.

9 Eric McKitrick, *Andrew Johnson and Reconstruction* (Chicago, 1960), p. 318.

10 Ibid., p. 309.

11 In John F. Kennedy, *Profiles in Courage* (New York, 1955), pp. 168–69. For a revisionist view, see M. L. Benedict, *The Impeachment and Trial of Andrew Johnson* (New York, 1973).

12 David E. Rosenbaum, "A Catalogue of Matters Involving the President," *New York Times,* February 10, 1974.

13 *New York Times,* June 5, 1974.

14 *New York Times,* June 10, 1974. For discussions of Nixon's abuses, see *The Impeachment Report* (New York, 1974); Leonard Lurie, *The Impeachment of Richard Nixon* (New York, 1973); Jerry Voorhis, *The Strange Case of Richard Nixon* (New York, 1973); and Lewis Chester et al., *Watergate* (New York, 1973).

15 Lesley Oelsner, "The President's Strategy," *New York Times,* March 10, 1974.

16 *New York Times,* March 7, 1974.

17 *New York Times,* June 4, 1974.

18 *New York Times,* April 18, 1974.

19 *New York Times,* May 17, 1974.

20 Concerning the articles of impeachment, see *New York Times,* July 22–August 1, 1974. For the House Judiciary Committee's final report, see *New York Times,* August 26, 1974.

21 The text of the Supreme Court's ruling in *Nixon v. United States* is in *New York Times,* July 25, 1974.

22 *New York Times,* March 12, 1974.

23 *New York Times,* June 12 and July 25, 1974.

24 The text of the President's declination is in *New York Times,* February 27, 1974.

25 *New York Times,* February 26, 1974.

26 For excerpts of the court's opinion, see *New York Times,* October 13, 1973.

27 The text of the Supreme Court's ruling is in *New York Times,* July 25, 1974.

28 The text of the President's letter is in *New York Times,* June 11, 1974.

29 The texts of the Proclamation of Pardon and accompanying statements by Ford and Nixon are in *New York Times,* September 9, 1974.

30 For extended treatment of disability and succession problems see John D. Feerick, *From Failing Hands: The Story of Presidential Succession* (New York, 1965); Richard Hansen, *The Year We Had No President* (Lincoln, Neb., 1962); and Ruth Silva, *Presidential Succession* (Ann Arbor, Mich., 1951).

31 Robert G. Caldwell, *James A. Garfield: Party Chieftain* (New York, 1931), pp. 350–52; Theodore Clarke Smith, *The Life and Letters of James Abram Garfield,* vol. 2 (New Haven, Conn., 1935), pp. 1194–97.

32 George F. Howe, *Chester A. Arthur: A Quarter-Century of Machine Politics* (New York, 1935), p. 152; David S. Muzzey, *James G. Blaine: A Political Idol of Other Days* (New York, 1934), p. 197.

33 Howe, *Chester A. Arthur,* pp. 150–53.

34 Ibid., p. 53.

35 Cary T. Grayson, *Woodrow Wilson: An Intimate Memoir* (New York, 1960), p. 99.

36 Joseph Tumulty, *Woodrow Wilson as I Know Him* (New York, 1921), pp. 446–48.

37 Grayson, *Woodrow Wilson,* p. 52.

38 Edith Boling Wilson, *My Memoir* (Indianapolis, Ind., 1939), pp. 289–90.

39 Ibid., p. 290.

40 Tumulty, *Woodrow Wilson,* p. 443.

41 Herbert Hoover, *The Ordeal of Woodrow Wilson* (New York, 1958), p. 275.

42 See Sherman Adams, *First-Hand Report* (New York, 1961), pp. 181–87; Richard M. Nixon, *Six Crises* (Garden City, N.Y., 1962), pp. 144–51.

43 U.S. Senate Subcommittee on Constitutional Amendments, Judiciary Committee, *Hearings,* 88th Congress, 2nd Session (Washington, D.C., 1964), p. 22.

44 In Clinton Rossiter, *The American Presidency,* rev. ed. (New York, 1960), p. 214.

45 Nixon, *Six Crises,* p. 168.

46 *New York Times,* February 11, 1967.

47 *New York Herald Tribune,* June 9, 1964.

48 Louis W. Koenig, *The Truman Administration* (New York, 1956), p. 43.

49 *New York Times,* October 13, 1973.
50 Laurin L. Henry, *Presidential Transitions* (Washington, D.C., 1960), pp. 474–76.
51 David T. Stanley, *Changing Administrations* (Washington, D.C., 1965), p. 6.
52 *New York Times,* August 16, 1972.
53 *New York Times,* August 13, 1974.
54 *New York Times,* August 25, 1974.
55 *New York Times,* January 4, 1961.

5 Publics

1   The leading general work is Elmer E. Cornwell, Jr., *Presidential Leadership of Public Opinion* (Bloomington, Ind., 1964).
2   Fred I. Greenstein, "Popular Images of the President," *American Journal of Psychiatry* 22 (November 1965): 525–26.
3   *New York Times,* October 13, 1974.
4   For discussion of these studies, see Martha Wolfenstein and Gilbert Kliman, eds., *Children and the Death of a President* (Garden City, 1965), pp. 33–40.
5   Ibid., pp. 184–88.
6   Louis Harris, *The Anguish of Change* (New York, 1973), pp. 231–32.
7   Nadine Brozan, "Between Parent and Child, What Does Watergate Mean?" *New York Times,* November 23, 1973.
8   John E. Mueller, "Trends in Popular Support for the Wars in Korea and Vietnam," *American Political Science Review* 65 (June 1971): 371.
9   Ibid., pp. 371–72.
10 John P. Robinson, "Public Reaction to Political Protest: Chicago 1968," *Public Opinion Quarterly* 34 (Spring 1970): 9.
11 Sidney Verba et al., "Public Opinion and the War in Vietnam," *American Political Science Review* 61 (June 1967): 319–21.
12 Harris, *Anguish of Change,* pp. 250–52.
13 Lady Bird Johnson, *A White House Diary* (New York, 1970), p. 472.
14 Ibid., pp. 592–93.
15 Rowland Evans, Jr., and Robert D. Novak, *Nixon in the White House* (New York, 1971), p. 58.
16 Eric F. Goldman, *The Tragedy of Lyndon Johnson* (New York, 1969), p. 184.
17 Harry McPherson, *A Political Education* (Boston, 1972), pp. 443–45.
18 *New York Times,* March 24, 1974.
19 For background on concepts, see James T. Tedeschi, ed., *The Social Influence Process* (Chicago, 1972), pp. 51–53.
20 *New York Times,* October 9, 1974.
21 William S. White, *The Responsibles* (New York, 1972), pp. 178–79.
22 Goldman, *Tragedy of Lyndon Johnson,* p. 416.
23 James Reston, "Washington: On the Art of

24 Backing into the Future," *New York Times,* March 11, 1970.
24 For discussions of roles, see Luigi Petrullo and Bernard M. Bass, eds., *Leaderships and Interpersonal Behavior* (New York, 1961), pp. 17–75; and Erving Goffman, *Encounters: Two Studies in the Sociology of Interaction* (Indianapolis, 1961), pp. 85–88.
25 Newton N. Minow, John Bartlow Martin, and Lee M. Mitchell, *Presidential Television* (New York, 1973), pp. 5–6. See also Stewart Alsop, *The Center* (New York, 1969); and Douglass Cater, *The Fourth Branch of Government* (Boston, 1959).
26 George Christian, *The President Steps Down* (New York, 1970), p. 188. Concerning the problem of the credibility gap, see David Wise, *The Politics of Lying* (New York, 1971); and Bruce Ladd, The *Crisis of Credibility* (New York, 1968).
27 McPherson, *Political Education,* pp. 261–67.
28 Ibid., p. 265.
29 *New York Times,* August 29, 1974.
30 Leo Rosten, *The Washington Correspondents* (New York, 1937), p. 47.
31 See Cornwell, *Presidential Leadership,* pp. 189–90.
32 *New York Times,* April 27, 1969.
33 *New York Times,* June 19, 1972.
34 *New York Times,* August 29, 1974.
35 Arthur Krock, "Mr. Kennedy's Management of the News," *Fortune* 67 (March 1963), p. 82.
36 Ibid.
37 George F. Howe, *Chester A. Arthur: A Quarter-Century of Machine Politics* (New York, 1934), p. 173.
38 Minow et al., *Presidential Television,* pp. 55–56.
39 *New York Times,* November 16, 1969.
40 Arthur Schlesinger, Jr., "Freedom of the Press in the United States," *New York Times,* December 27, 1972.
41 *New York Times,* November 1, 1973.
42 See James Reston, *The Artillery of the Press* (New York, 1967), pp. 20–21.
43 James G. Randall and Richard N. Current, *Lincoln the President: Last Full Measure* (New York, 1955), pp. 42–44.
44 Transcript of news conference, *New York Times,* November 14, 1966.
45 For fuller statement of these proposals, see Minow et al., *Presidential Television,* pp. 161–62.
46 Robert Reinhold, "Experts Ask Changes to Ease Flow of Information to the Public," *New York Times,* November 20, 1973.

6 Party Chief

1   In Clinton Rossiter, *Parties and Politics in America* (Ithaca, N.Y., 1960), p. 15.

2 In James A. Farley, *Behind the Ballots* (New York, 1938), p. 293.
3 Allan Nevins, *Grover Cleveland: A Study in Courage* (New York, 1932), p. 401.
4 Sherman Adams, *First-Hand Report* (New York, 1961), p. 167.
5 Ibid.
6 In George F. Howe, *Chester A. Arthur: A Quarter-Century of Machine Politics* (New York, 1957), p. 254.
7 Ibid., pp. 255–64.
8 Cabell Phillips, *The Truman Presidency* (New York, 1966), p. 195.
9 Hugh Bone, *Party Committees and National Politics* (Seattle, 1958), pp. 167–68.
10 Carl R. Fish, *The Civil Service and the Patronage* (Boston, 1904), p. 82.
11 Nevins, *Grover Cleveland*, p. 219.
12 Farley, *Behind the Ballots*, p. 267.
13 Martin and Susan Tolchin, *To the Victor* (New York, 1971), pp. 283–88.
14 Bone, *Party Committees*, p. 219.
15 *New York Times*, October 1, 1972.
16 In Nathan Schachner, *Thomas Jefferson: A Biography* (New York, 1951), p. 703.
17 Ibid., p. 704.
18 Ibid., pp. 709, 810.
19 William Cabell Bruce, *John Randolph of Roanoke* (New York, 1922), p. 265.
20 Bennett Champ Clark, *John Quincy Adams* (Boston, 1932), pp. 242–46.
21 Ibid., pp. 252–53.
22 Oliver Perry Chitwood, *John Tyler: Champion of the Old South* (New York, 1939), p. 217.
23 Ibid., p. 317.
24 Ibid.
25 Ibid.
26 Farley, *Behind the Ballots*, p. 231.
27 James A. Farley, *Jim Farley's Story* (New York, 1948), p. 96.
28 Ibid., pp. 122–33.
29 Ibid., p. 133.
30 The most extended analysis of Presidential abuses is in Arthur M. Schlesinger, Jr., *The Imperial Presidency* (Boston, 1973), pp. 409–23.
31 Ibid., pp. 598–99.
32 Adams, *First-Hand Report*, pp. 25–26.
33 Ibid., p. 21.
34 Dwight D. Eisenhower, *Mandate for Change* (New York, 1963), p. 431.
35 Robert J. Donovan, *Eisenhower: The Inside Story* (New York, 1956), p. 272.
36 Adams, *First-Hand Report*, p. 166.
37 Ibid., p. 287.
38 *New York Times*, May 1, 1963.
39 *New York Times*, January 30, 1961.
40 *New York Times*, July 26, 1962.
41 Ibid.
42 *Christian Science Monitor*, February 14, 1963.
43 *New York Times*, December 26, 1966.
44 *New York Times*, April 3, 1966.
45 *New York Times*, June 8, 1967; London *Economist*, July 30, 1967.
46 Theodore H. White, *The Making of the President, 1972* (New York, 1973), pp. 49–50; Philip Shabecoff, "Hard Hats Spurred Nixon Labor Bid," *New York Times*, October 12, 1972.
47 Kevin P. Phillips, *The Emerging Republican Majority* (New Rochelle, N.Y., 1969), 437–40.
48 *Congressional Quarterly Almanac*, 1969, p. 114. Concerning Nixon's Southern strategy, see Leon Panetta and Peter Call, *Bring Us Together* (Philadelphia, 1971); and Reg Murphy and Hal Gullever, *The Southern Strategy* (New York, 1971).
49 White, *Making of the President, 1972*, 49.
50 Clayton Fritchey, "Nixon Isn't the GOP's Man Any More," *Newsday*, January 17, 1973.
51 Robert Bendiner, "Election 'Bible' Re-examined," *New York Times*, November 9, 1970.
52 Louis Harris, *The Anguish of Change* (New York, 1973), p. 250.
53 Richard E. Neustadt, "The Presidency after Watergate," *New York Times Magazine*, October 13, 1973.
54 *New York Times*, October 25, 1973; Newton N. Minow, John Bartlow Martin, and Lee M. Mitchell, *Presidential Television* (New York, 1973), pp. 126–58.

7 Legislative Leader

1 *New York Times*, October 10, 14, and 19, 1974.
2 Dwight D. Eisenhower, *Mandate for Change* (Garden City, N.Y., 1963), p. 502.
3 Ibid., pp. 194–95.
4 *Congressional Quarterly Weekly Reports*, August 12, 1972, pp. 2002–004.
5 *Congressional Quarterly Almanac*, 1965, vol. 21 (Washington, D.C., 1966), p. 67.
6 For thoughtful elaboration, see Louis Fisher, *Presidency and Congress* (New York, 1972), pp. 122–27; and for critiques of Nixon's impoundments, see *New York Times*, June 8, 1972 and February 12, 1973.
7 See *New York Times*, March 5, 13, and July 23, 1973. The leading work on executive privilege is Rauol Berger, *Executive Privilege: A Constitutional Myth* (Cambridge, Mass., 1974). A valuable collection of materials is in U.S. Senate Subcommittee on Separation of Powers, Committee on the Judiciary, *Executive Privilege: The Withholding of Information by the Executive* (Washington, D.C., 1971).
8 For excerpts from the court's opinion, see *New York Times*, October 13, 1973.

9 For Ford's testimony, see *New York Times*, October 25, 1974.

10 In *Congressional Quarterly Weekly Reports*, June 10, 1972, p. 1369.

11 *In Congressional Quarterly Almanac, 1970*, p. 154.

12 Ibid., pp. 89, 154–56.

13 *New York Times*, October 31, 1972.

14 In Ralph K. Huitt, "Democratic Party Leadership in the Senate," *American Political Science Review* 55 (June 1961): 353.

15 See *Congressional Quarterly Weekly Reports*, January 11, 1963, pp. 31–32.

16 *Congressional Quarterly Weekly Reports*, January 4, 1963.

17 See Richard E. Neustadt, "Presidency and Legislation: Planning the President's Program," *American Political Review* 49 (December 1955): 980.

18 Robert Donovan, *Eisenhower: The Inside Story* (New York, 1956), p. 83.

19 Richard M. Scammon and Ben J. Wattenberg, *The Real Majority* (New York, 1970), p. 59.

20 *New York Times*, January 11, 1967.

21 *Congressional Quarterly Weekly Reports*, January 15, 1972, pp. 74–75.

22 *Congressional Quarterly Almanac, 1973*, p. 946.

23 Sherman Adams, *First-Hand Report* (New York, 1961), pp. 25–26.

24 Huitt, "Democratic Party Leadership," p. 353.

25 Louis W. Koenig, *The Truman Administration* (New York, 1956), pp. 240–46.

26 Arthur S. Link, *Wilson: The New Freedom* (Princeton, N.J., 1956), pp. 146–49.

27 Ibid., p. 151; Arthur W. Macmahon, "Woodrow Wilson as Legislative Leader and Administrator," *American Political Science Review* 50 (September 1956): 656.

28 In Tom Wicker, "The Johnson Way with Congress," *New York Times Magazine*, March 8, 1964, p. 103.

29 See Marshall E. Dimock, "Wilson the Domestic Reformer," *Virginia Quarterly Review* 32 (Autumn 1956): 549–50.

30 Helen Fuller, *Year of Trial: Kennedy's Crucial Decisions* (New York, 1962), pp. 255–57.

31 Marjorie Hunter, "President Seeks Congress Accord," *New York Times*, August 13, 1974.

32 Ibid., p. 97.

33 Koenig, *Truman Administration*, pp. 246–47.

34 Neustadt, "Presidency and Legislation," 980.

35 *New York Times*, May 15, 1966.

36 Koenig, *Truman Administration*, 148–76.

37 Link, *Wilson*, pp. 146–57.

38 Macmahon, "Woodrow Wilson," pp. 651–56.

39 *New York Times*, July 12, 1965.

40 Ibid.

41 Ibid.

42 In James MacGregor Burns, "The One Test for the Presidency," *New York Times Magazine*, May 1, 1960, p. 102.

43 Eisenhower, *Mandate for Change*, p. 286.

44 Adams, *First-Hand Report*, pp. 25–27.

45 Ibid., p. 9.

46 *New York Times*, March 23, 1966.

47 News conference, *New York Times*, November 14, 1966.

48 Macmahon, "Woodrow Wilson," pp. 652–56.

49 See Edward S. Corwin, *The President: Office and Powers*, 4th ed. (New York, 1957), pp. 250–52.

50 Philip S. Klein, *President James Buchanan* (University Park, Pa., 1962), pp. 396–97.

51 *Congressional Quarterly Weekly Reports*, June 15, 1974, pp. 1590–94.

52 For discussion of the 1974 House reforms, see David E. Rosenbaum, "Reform vs. Legislation," *New York Times*, December 6, 1974.

53 *New York Times*, February 22, 1973.

54 *New York Times*, February 23, 1973.

8 Administrative Chief

1 William D. Carey, "Presidential Staffing in the Sixties and Seventies," *Public Administration Review* 29 (September-October 1969): 450–52. See also Norman C. Thomas, "Presidential Advice and Information," *Law and Contemporary Problems* 35 (Summer 1970): 540–72; and Alex B. Lacy, "The White House Staff Bureaucracy," *Trans-Action* 6 (January 1969): 50.

2 William Hillman, *Mr. President* (New York, 1952), p. 14.

3 Lecture, "Training for the Presidency," delivered at New York University, May 2, 1957. For a cogent discussion of the President's relations with the departments, see Thomas Cronin, "Everybody Believes in Democracy Until He Gets to the White House," *Law and Contemporary Problems* 35 (Summer 1970): 573–625.

4 Leonard White, *The Jacksonians: A Study in Administrative History, 1829–1861* (New York, 1954), p. 141.

5 Richard Fenno, Jr., *The President's Cabinet* (New York, 1959), p. 5.

6 *New York Times*, November 29, 1969.

7 *New York Times*, March 13, 1972; December 11, 1971; and December 15, 1972.

8 White, *Jacksonians*, p. 83. For extended discussions of recent Vice Presidents, see Donald Young, *American Roulette* (New York, 1974); Leonard Baker, *The Eclipse of Lyndon Johnson* (New York, 1966); concerning Hubert Humphrey, see Allan B. Ryskind, *Hubert* (New Rochelle, 1968); concerning Spiro

Agnew, see Theodore Lippman, *Spiro Agnew's America* (New York, 1972), and Richard M. Cohen and Jules Witcover, *A Heartbeat Away* (New York, 1974). The case for abolishing the Vice Presidency is found in Arthur M. Schlesinger, Jr., "Is the Vice Presidency Necessary?" *Atlantic* 234 (May 1974), pp. 37–44.

9   James Reston, "Spiro Agnew v. the Republican Party," *New York Times*, October 2, 1970; Arthur Schlesinger, Jr., "The Amazing Success Story of 'Spiro Who?'," *New York Times Magazine*, July 26, 1970.

10 *New York Times*, August 23, 1974. For Ford's initial announcement of Rockefeller's assignments, see *New York Times*, December 22, 1974.

11 In Louis Koenig, *The Invisible Presidency* (New York, 1960), p. 308.

12 *New York Times*, December 21, 1940.

13 See Harold L. Ickes, *The First Thousand Days*, vol. 1 of *The Secret Diary of Harold L. Ickes* (New York, 1954), p. 111.

14 Rexford G. Tugwell, *The Democratic Roosevelt* (Garden City, N.Y., 1957), p. 14.

15 Dwight D. Eisenhower, *Mandate for Change* (Garden City, N.Y., 1963), p. 87.

16 Ibid., p. 135.

17 Sherman Adams, *First-Hand Report* (New York, 1961), p. 51.

18 Koenig, *Invisible Presidency*, p. 338.

19 Ezra Taft Benson, *Cross Fire: The Eight Years with Eisenhower* (Garden City, N.Y., 1962), pp. 386–89.

20 See Aaron Wildavsky, *Dixon-Yates: A Study in Power Politics* (New Haven, Conn., 1962).

21 *Christian Science Monitor*, January 12, 1963.

22 Joseph Kraft, "Kennedy's Working Staff," *Harper's Magazine* (December 1962), p. 33.

23 U.S. Senate Subcommittee on National Security Staffing and Operations, Committee on Government Operations, *Administration of National Security: Basic Issues* (Washington, D.C., 1963), p. 6.

24 *New York Times*, June 19, 1962.

25 Kraft, "Kennedy's Working Staff," p. 33.

26 Ibid., p. 31.

27 Ibid., p. 36.

28 See Charles Roberts, *L. B. J.'s Inner Circle* (New York, 1965), and Joseph Kraft, "Kennedy's Working Staff," p. 32.

29 James Reston, "Washington: A 'Small' Staff in an Open Administration," *New York Times*, June 17, 1970; *New York Times*, May 10, 1970. For a critique of the Nixon staff, see Richard Whalen, *Catch the Falling Flag* (Boston, 1972).

30 R. W. Apple, Jr., "Haldeman the Fierce, Haldeman the Faithful, Haldeman the Fallen," *New York Times Magazine*, May 6, 1973; Mary McCarthy, *The Mask of State: Watergate Portraits* (New York, 1974), pp. 108–15.

31 In J. Anthony Lukas, "The Story So Far," *New York Times Magazine*, July 22, 1973, p. 13; McCarthy, *Mask of State*, pp. 108–09.

32 John Pierson, "Right-Hand Man," *Wall Street Journal*, January 22, 1970. For an insider's account, see Jeb Stuart Magruder, *An American Life: One Man's Road to Watergate* (New York, 1974).

33 William V. Shannon, "The Sad Young Men," *New York Times*, July 25, 1973.

34 *New York Times*, June 22, 1970. For extended treatment of the Nixon staff's misdeeds, see Bob Woodward and Carl Bernstein, *All the King's Men* (New York, 1974).

35 In Lukas, "Story So Far," p. 13.

36 Robert G. Cox, "The Open Door Boss and the Other Kind," *New York Times*, July 1, 1973.

37 *New York Times*, July 8, 1973.

38 *New York Times*, July 28, 1970.

39 *New York Times*, March 26, 1971.

40 Joseph A. Califano, "The Nixon Plan Makes Sense," *New York Times*, January 29, 1971; *New York Times*, March 26, 1971.

41 John Herbers, "Revision of the Presidency," *New York Times*, August 28, 1974.

42 Jerry Landay, "Right Next to Mr. Ford is Mr. Hartmann," *New York Times*, October 6, 1974.

43 *New York Times*, September 4, 1974.

44 Leslie H. Gelb, "Ford's Unchanged Style," *New York Times*, October 24, 1974.

9 Chief Diplomat

1   In Clinton Rossiter, *The American Presidency*, rev. ed. (New York, 1960), p. 10.

2   Ibid.

3   Edward S. Corwin, *The President: Office and Powers*, 4th ed. (New York, 1957), p. 180.

4   Ibid., 185.

5   Arthur Schlesinger, Jr., "Presidential War: 'See if you can fix any limit to his power,' " *New York Times Magazine*, January 10, 1974, pp. 12ff; Arthur M. Schlesinger, Jr., *The Imperial Presidency* (Boston, 1973), passim. Additional valuable discussions are found in L. C. Ratner, "The Coordinated Warmaking Power—Legislative, Executive, and Judicial Roles," *Southern California Law Review* 44 (December 1971): 461–89; Charles A. Lofgren, "War-Making Under the Constitution: The Original Understanding," *Yale Law Journal* 81 (March 1972): 672; James Grafton Rogers, *World Policing and the Constitution* (Boston, 1945); Louis Henkin, *Foreign Affairs and the Constitution* (New York, 1972); and

John N. Moore, *Law and the Indo-China War* (Princeton, 1972).

6 *New York Times,* July 24, 1973.

7 Ibid.

8 See Louis W. Koenig, *The Invisible Presidency* (New York, 1960), p. 14.

9 *New York Times,* September 12, 1963.

10 *New York Times,* October 19, 1972. On Congress's power, see Jacob K. Javits, "The Congressional Presence in Foreign Relations," *Foreign Relations* 48 (January 1970): 232; Jacob K. Javits, *Who Makes War: The President Versus Congress* (New York, 1973); and Louis Fisher, *President and Congress* (New York, 1972), pp. 225–28.

11 Sherman Adams, *First-Hand Report* (New York, 1961), pp. 93–94.

12 *New York Times,* September 5, 1974.

13 For extended discussion see *Congressional Quarterly Guide to American Government* (Washington, D.C., Autumn 1966), pp. 4–5.

14 In James Grafton Rogers, *World Policing and the Constitution* (Boston, 1945), p. 36.

15 Dwight D. Eisenhower, *Mandate for Change* (Garden City, N.Y., 1963), pp. 129–30.

16 Ibid., p. 271.

17 David Halberstam, *The Best and the Brightest* (New York, 1972), p. 419.

18 *New York Times,* May 9, 1972.

19 For details of the truce and Nixon's address concerning it, see *New York Times,* January 29, 1973.

20 *New York Times,* January 28, 1973.

21 Jacob K. Javits, "The Balance in the War Powers Bill," *New York Times,* February 14, 1972.

22 *New York Times,* November 8, 1973.

23 Leslie H. Gelb, "The Foreign Aid Fight," *New York York Times,* October 12, 1974. For general discussion of the Presidency and foreign aid, see Michael O'Leary, *The Politics of American Foreign Aid* (New York, 1967).

24 *New York Times,* October 18, 1974.

25 *New York Times,* March 24 and September 22, 1972.

26 Eleanor Lansing Dulles, *John Foster Dulles: The Last Year* (New York, 1963). For an account by journalists who observed Kissinger at first hand, see Marvin Kalb and Bernard Kalb, *Kissinger* (Boston, 1974).

27 Adams, *First-Hand Report,* pp. 89–90.

28 In Commission on Organization of the Executive Branch of the Government, *Task Force Report on Foreign Affairs* (Washington, D.C., 1949), p. 83.

29 Ibid., p. 266.

30 Harry S. Truman, *Year of Decisions,* vol. 1 of *Memoirs* (Garden City, N.Y., 1955), pp. 22–23.

31 For studies of Kissinger, see David Landau,

Kissinger: The Uses of Power (Boston, 1972), and Stephen R. Graubard, *Kissinger: Portrait of a Mind* (New York, 1973).

32 Landau, *Kissinger,* p. 92; Richard M. Nixon, "Asia after Viet Nam," *Foreign Affairs* 46 (October 1967): 111.

33 Subcommittee on Separation of Powers, Senate Juduciary Committee, "Executive Privilege: The Withholding of Information by the Executive" (Washington, D.C., 1971), p. 270.

34 *New York Times,* March 3, 1971.

35 Joseph Kraft, "Secretary Henry," *New York Times Magazine,* October 28, 1973, p. 82.

36 Frederick C. Thayer, "Presidential Policy Processes and 'New Administration': A Search for Revised Paradigms," *Public Administration Review* 31 (September–October 1971): 555–56.

37 Edward A. Kolodziej, "The National Security Council: Innovations and Implications," *Public Administration Review* 29 (November–December 1969): 578–81.

38 Charles W. Yost, "The Instruments of American Foreign Policy," *Foreign Affairs,* 50 (October 1971): 64.

39 John Robinson Beal, *John Foster Dulles* (New York, 1957), p. 279.

40 Lyndon Baines Johnson, *The Vantage Point: Perspectives on the Presidency, 1963–1969* (New York, 1971).

41 Chester L. Cooper, "The CIA and Decision-Making," *Foreign Affairs* 50 (January 1972): 223–36. For comprehensive treatment of the CIA, see Victor Marchetti and John D. Marks, *The CIA and the Cult of Intelligence* (New York, 1974).

42 For details concerning the CIA and Chile, see *New York Times,* September 8 and 23, 1974.

43 *New York Times,* October 23, 1974.

44 David Binder, "CIA's Cover Role," *New York Times,* October 23, 1974; Harry Rostzke, "Controlling Secret Operations," *New York Times,* October 7, 1974; and Ray S. Cline, "The Value of the CIA," *New York Times,* November 1, 1974.

45 *New York Times,* May 21, 1961.

46 In I. M. Destler, *Presidents, Bureaucrats, and Foreign Policy* (Princeton, 1972), pp. 87–88.

47 *New York Times,* October 8, 1972.

48 *New York Times,* November 17, 1970. Concerning Nixon's foreign policy generally, see Robert Osgood, ed., *Retreat from Empire* (Baltimore, 1973).

49 *New York Times,* January 7, 1972.

50 *New York Times,* August 4, 1971.

51 *New York Times,* October 30, 1973.

52 *New York Times,* November 8, 1973.

53 *New York Times,* November 14, 1973.

54 Max Frankel, "Behind the Cold Print," *New York Times,* February 29, 1972; *Newsweek,*

"First Steps of a Long March," March 6, 1972, pp. 14–23.

55 For details, see *New York Times,* May 24–May 30, 1972.

56 Max Frankel, "To Force Two Great Powers to Live in Peace," *New York Times,* May 28, 1972. For the U.S.-U.S.S.R. accords, see *New York Times,* May 25 and 30, 1972 and June 25, 1973.

57 *New York Times,* November 25 and 26, 1974.

58 *New York Times,* May 8, 1972.

59 *New York Times,* May 22, 1974.

60 *New York Times,* July 26, 1972.

61 *New York Times,* February 11, 1962.

62 *New York Times,* September 21, 1963.

63 *New York Times,* November 6, 1974.

64 *New York Times,* December 3, 1970.

65 Alexander M. George, "The Case of Multiple Advocacy in Making Foreign Policy," *American Political Science Review* 66 (September 1972): 751–91.

10 Commander-in-Chief

1 Adam Yarmolinsky, *The Military Establishment* (New York, 1971), pp. 381–91. McNamara's budget and systems analysis innovations are examined in Leonard Merewitz and Stephen Sosnick, *The Budget's New Clothes* (Chicago, 1971).

2 David Halberstam, *The Best and the Brightest* (New York, 1972), p. 405; Yarmolinsky, *Military Establishment,* p. 91.

3 Neil Sheehan, "Influence of Joint Chiefs Is Reported Rising," *New York Times,* June 30, 1969.

4 *New York Times,* July 24, 1962.

5 Morton H. Halperin, "The President and the Military," *Foreign Affairs* 50 (January 1972): 310–12.

6 Ibid.; *New York Times,* July 29, 1970.

7 Allan Nevins, *The War for the Union* (New York, 1960), pp. 133–59.

8 Ibid., p. 330.

9 Harry S. Truman, *Years of Trial and Hope,* vol. 2 of *Memoirs* (Garden City, N.Y., 1956), p. 354.

10 Ibid., pp. 365–83.

11 Ibid., pp. 384–85.

12 Ibid., p. 445; Richard H. Rovere and Arthur M. Schlesinger, Jr., *The General and the President* (New York, 1951), p. 169.

13 Truman, *Years of Trial and Hope,* p. 356; Walter Millis, *Arms and the State* (New York, 1958), pp. 319–20.

14 Edward S. Corwin, *The President: Office and Powers,* rev. ed. (New York, 1957), pp. 229–32; J. G. Randall, *The President: Midstream* (New York, 1952), pp. 152–53.

15 Seymour M. Hersh, "National Security: A

Nixon Rationale," *New York Times,* January 17, 1974.

16 *New York Times,* March 9, 1962.

17 Randall, *President,* pp. 132–34.

18 Ibid., p. 186.

19 *New York Times,* July 26, 1973 and April 16, 1974.

20 *New York Times,* June 14, 1972.

21 *New York Times,* May 9, 1972.

22 Dwight D. Eisenhower, *Mandate for Change* (Garden City, N.Y., 1963), p. 168.

23 *New York Times,* December 6, 1962.

24 *New York Times,* January 12, 1972.

25 *New York Times,* November 30, 1973.

26 C. L. Sulzberger, "Three for the Seesaw," *New York Times,* May 24, 1972, and "The Non-Allied Alliance," *New York Times,* June 2, 1972.

27 Eisenhower, *Mandate for Change,* p. 181.

28 *New York Times,* October 27, 1973.

29 See Peter Wyden, "The Chances of Accidental War," *Saturday Evening Post* (June 3, 1961), p. 58.

30 *New York Times,* July 6, 1962.

31 *New York Times,* December 10, 1966.

32 *New York Times,* July 22, 1973.

33 *New York Times,* May 27, 1972.

34 John W. Finney, "Soviet Arms Data Raise Suspicions," *New York Times,* November 6, 1974.

35 *New York Times,* August 5, 1972.

36 Robert Gilpin, *American Scientists and Nuclear Weapons Policy* (Princeton, N.J., 1962), p. 132.

37 *New York Times,* December 3, 1963.

38 Gilpin, *American Scientists,* pp. 174–264.

39 C. P. Snow, *Science and Government* (Cambridge, Mass.: 1961), p. 1. For discussion of the Office of Science and Technology, see Michael D. Reagan, *Science and the Federal Patron* (New York, 1969).

40 Yarmolinsky, *Military Establishment,* p. 297.

41 Halperin, "The President and the Military," pp. 319–22.

42 Ibid., pp. 323–24.

43 Yarmolinsky, *Military Establishment,* pp. 51–52.

44 Ibid.

11 The Economy

1 *New York Times,* August 19, 1974.

2 Frances Perkins, *The Roosevelt I Knew* (New York, 1946), p. 330.

3 Arthur M. Schlesinger, Jr., *The Coming of the New Deal,* vol. 2 of *The Age of Roosevelt* (Boston, 1959), p. 567.

4 Ibid., pp. 425, 431.

5 *New York Times,* March 20, 1972.

6 Arthur S. Link, *Woodrow Wilson and the Progressive Era* (New York, 1954), p. 236.

7   Robert H. Wiebe, *Businessmen and Reform: A Study of the Progressive Movement* (Cambridge, Mass., 1962), pp. 45–47.

8   Edward S. Corwin, *The President: Office and Powers*, 3rd ed. (New York, 1948), pp. 297–98.

9   See Grant McConnell, *Steel and the Presidency, 1962* (New York, 1963). Concerning Kennedy and business generally, see James F. Heath, *John F. Kennedy and the Business Community* (Chicago, 1969).

10 *New York Times,* November 11, 1965. Concerning Kennedy's economic policies, see E. Ray Canterberg, *Economics on a New Frontier* (Belmont, Calif., 1968), Chapter 11.

11 *New York Times,* August 13, 1974. For analysis of Nixon's 1971 economic decisions, see Leonard Silk, *Nixonomics* (New York, 1972); Rowland Evans, Jr., and Robert D. Novak, *Nixon in the White House* (New York, 1971), Chapter 7; and Roger Miller and Raburn Williams, *The New Economics of Richard Nixon* (New York, 1972).

12 *New York Times,* January 27, 1967.

13 *New York Times,* March 24, 1971.

14 The text of Ford's address to Congress is in *New York Times,* October 9, 1974.

15 Ibid.

16 *New York Times,* November 29 and December 20, 1974.

17 George E. Mowry, *The Era of Theodore Roosevelt, 1900–1912* (New York, 1958), p. 178.

18 *New York Times,* June 13, 1973.

19 Robert Donovan, *Eisenhower: The Inside Story* (New York, 1956), pp. 35, 171.

20 Mowry, *Theodore Roosevelt,* p. 173.

21 Matthew Josephson, *Sidney Hillman: Statesman of American Labor* (Garden City, N.Y., 1952), p. 431.

22 Ibid., p. 404.

23 Saul Alinsky, *John L. Lewis: An Unauthorized Biography* (New York, 1949), p. 165.

24 Josephson, *Sidney Hillman,* p. 474.

25 Alinsky, *John L. Lewis,* p. 189.

26 *New York Times,* May 3, 1965.

27 *New York Times,* September 7, 1970; A. H. Raskin, "George Meany's Way Isn't the President's," *New York Times Magazine,* January 23, 1972, p. 10ff.

28 Raskin, "George Meany," p. 33; *New York Times,* November 25, 1971.

29 In *New York Times,* November 24, 1971.

30 *New York Times,* September 1 and 12, 1974.

31 Alinsky, *John L. Lewis,* p. 162.

32 Josephson, *Sidney Hillman,* p. 447.

33 *Congressional Quarterly Almanac,* 1971, vol. 27 (Washington, D.C., 1972), p. 804.

34 *New York Times,* March 16, 1966.

35 *New York Times,* February 24, 1973.

36 James Tracy Crown, "Organized Labor in American Politics: A Look Ahead," *Proceedings of the Fourteenth Annual New York University Conference on Labor* (New York, 1961), p. 261.

37 In *New York Times,* November 24, 1971.

38 Josephson, *Sidney Hillman,* p. 618.

39 Crown, "Organized Labor," p. 265.

40 Josephson, *Sidney Hillman,* p. 399.

41 John M. Blum, *The Republican Roosevelt* (Cambridge, Mass., 1961), p. 59.

42 Perkins, *Roosevelt,* pp. 324–26.

43 *New York Times,* February 4, 1971.

44 In A. H. Raskin, "Organized Labor: Awaiting the Crash," *New York Times,* September 2, 1974.

45 Haynes Johnson and Nick Kotz, "Hard Times in the House of Labor," *Newsday,* April 18, 1972.

12   Social Justice

1   William D. Carey, "Presidential Staffing in the Sixties and Seventies," *Public Administration Review* 29 (September–October 1969): 450–51.

2   *New York Times,* October 27, 1974. Concerning Nixon's welfare proposals, see Daniel P. Moynihan, *The Politics of a Guaranteed Income* (New York, 1973).

3   *New York Times,* August 23, 1974.

4   *New York Times,* October 10, 1974.

5   *New York Times,* August 23 and October 30, 1974.

6   *New York Times,* August 14, 1974.

7   Edward Cowan, "Energy-Policy Search: Sawhill vs. Morton," *New York Times,* October 31, 1974.

8   *New York Times,* November 13 and 24, 1974.

9   *New York Times,* November 16, 1974.

10 Louis W. Koenig, *The Invisible Presidency* (New York, 1960), p. 215.

11 John M. Blum, *The Republican Roosevelt* (Cambridge, Mass., 1961), p. 60.

12 Rexford G. Tugwell, *The Democratic Roosevelt* (Garden City, N.Y., 1957), p. 153.

13 Ibid., p. 54.

14 Ibid., pp. 153, 215.

15 Blum, *Republican Roosevelt,* p. 107.

16 James Reston, "Washington: Roosevelt, Nixon and 'The Forgotten Man,' " *New York Times,* September 8, 1968.

17 Richard Scammon and Ben J. Wattenberg, *The Real Majority* (New York, 1970), p. 21.

18 Tugwell, *Democratic Roosevelt,* p. 151.

19 Ibid., p. 231. Concerning the impact of coalitions on domestic programs, see James L. Sunquist, *Politics and Policy* (Washington, D.C., 1968).

20 George E. Mowry, *The Era of Theodore Roosevelt, 1900–1912* (New York, 1958), p. xii.

21 Henry F. Pringle, *Theodore Roosevelt* (New York, 1931), p. 427.

22 *Congressional Quarterly Almanac, 1971,* p. 714; *New York Times,* January 2, April 16 and June 6, 1970.

23 *Congressional Quarterly Weekly Reports,* June 3, 1972, pp. 1271–72; *New York Times,* July 21, 1973.

24 Arthur M. Schlesinger, Jr., *The Politics of Upheaval,* vol. 3 of *The Age of Roosevelt* (Boston, 1960), p. 29.

25 Arthur M. Schlesinger, Jr., *The Coming of the New Deal,* vol. 2 of *The Age of Roosevelt* (Boston, 1959), p. 322.

26 *Congressional Quarterly Almanac,* 1970, p. 1030; *New York Times,* January 14, 1971.

27 *Congressional Quarterly Almanac,* 1971, pp. 521–22.

28 Leonard Silk, "Missing: Energy Policy," *New York Times,* November 13, 1974.

29 See Edwin E. Witte, *The Development of the Social Security Act* (Madison, Wis., 1962).

30 Ibid., p. 45.

31 Koenig, *Invisible Presidency,* p. 260.

32 Arthur S. Link, *Woodrow Wilson and the Progressive Era* (New York, 1954), p. 20.

33 Frances Perkins, *The Roosevelt I Knew* (New York, 1946), p. 197.

34 *New York Times,* January 29, 1973.

35 *New York Times,* February 20, 1969 and February 17, 1973.

36 *New York Times,* March 4, 1971.

37 Schlesinger, *Politics of Upheaval,* p. 428.

38 *New York Times,* October 1, 1962.

39 *New York Times,* June 12, 1963.

40 *New York Times,* October 1, 1962.

41 *New York Times,* June 5, 1965.

42 *New York Times,* September 24, 1969, September 19, 1972, and January 17, 1973.

43 *New York Times,* June 12, 1971.

44 *New York Times,* May 26, 1972.

45 *New York Times,* August 22, 1974.

46 *New York Times,* September 1, 1974.

47 Ibid.

48 *New York Times,* October 16, 1974.

49 *New York Times,* October 11, 1974.

50 William E. Farrell, "School Integration Resisted in Cities of North," *New York Times,* May 13, 1974.

51 *New York Times,* September 13, 1974.

52 B. Drummon Ayres, Jr., "Desegregation of Southern Schools Since '54," *New York Times,* May 13, 1974.

53 *New York Times,* August 13, 1974.

54 *New York Times,* November 12, 1974.

55 *New York Times,* November 7, 1974.

56 *New York Times,* April 23, 1974.

57 *New York Times,* July 23, 1973.

58 William E. Farrell, "Blacks Fear Layoffs and Rising Costs," *New York Times,* January 26, 1974.

59 *New York Times,* August 20, 1967.

60 Ibid.

61 Michael D. Reagan, "Toward Improving Presidential Level Policy Planning," *Public Administration Review* 23 (March–April 1963): 177–86; William D. Carey, "Presidential Staffing," pp. 456–58.

13 Political Personality

1 For extended studies of Presidential and related personalities see Alexander L. George and Juliette L. George, *Woodrow Wilson and Colonel House: A Personality Study* (New York, 1956); Erwin C. Hargrove, *Presidential Leadership: Personality and Political Style* (New York, 1966); Arnold Rogow, *James Forrestal* (New York, 1964).

2 Hargrove, *Presidential Leadership,* pp. 12–13.

3 George and George, *Woodrow Wilson,* passim.

4 Gordon W. Allport, *Personality: A Psychological Interpretation* (New York, 1937), p. 229. See also his *The Nature of Personality: Selected Papers* (Cambridge, Mass., 1950).

5 Alfred Steinberg, *The Man from Missouri: The Life and Times of Harry S. Truman* (New York, 1962), p. 238.

6 Address to Congress, August 12, 1974; see transcript in *New York Times,* August 13, 1974.

7 William B. Hesseltine, *Ulysses S. Grant, Politician* (New York, 1935), p. 392.

8 Robert W. Winston, *Andrew Johnson: Plebian and Patriot* (New York, 1928), p. 373.

9 Marquis Childs, *Eisenhower: Captive Hero* (New York, 1958), p. 245.

10 Ibid., p. 247.

11 Emmet John Hughes, *The Ordeal of Power* (New York, 1963), pp. 268–69.

12 News Conference, August 28, 1974; see transcript in *New York Times,* August 29, 1974.

13 Address to Congress, August 12, 1974; see transcript in *New York Times,* August 13, 1974.

14 Winston, p. 342.

15 *New York Times,* September 20, 1968.

16 *New York Times,* November 10, 1972.

17 Tom Wicker, "What Kind of Moral Fiber?" *New York Times,* November 17, 1972.

18 Charles P. Henderson, Jr., "Mr. Nixon's Theology," *New York Times,* July 3, 1972.

19 Philip S. Klein, *President James Buchanan* (University Park, Pa., 1962), p. 331.

20 Arthur M. Schlesinger, Jr., *The Coming of the New Deal,* vol. 2 of the *The Age of Roosevelt* (Boston, 1959), p. 585.

21 James MacGregor Burns, "The Four Kennedys of the First Year," *New York Times Magazine,* January 14, 1962, p. 72.

22 Ibid., p. 70.

23 Steinberg, *Man from Missouri,* p. 250.

24 Harold D. Laswell, *Power and Personality* (New York, 1948), p. 203.
25 Ibid.
26 Allan Nevins, *Grover Cleveland: A Study in Courage* (New York, 1932), p. 206.
27 Klein, *James Buchanan*, p. 285.
28 Schlesinger, *The Coming of the New Deal*, p. 575.
29 In Max Frankel, "Why the Gap Between L. B. J. and the Nation," *New York Times Magazine*, January 7, 1968, p. 37.
30 John S. Bassett, *The Life of Andrew Jackson* (New York, 1925), p. 702.
31 Hesseltine, *Ulysses S. Grant*, pp. 315–16.
32 Frankel, "Why the Gap Between L. B. J. and the Nation," p. 37.
33 Steinberg, *Man from Missouri*, p. 256.
34 T. W. Adorno, et al., *The Authoritarian Personality* (New York, 1950).
35 For elaboration, see Fred I. Greenstein, *Personality and Politics* (Chicago, 1969), pp. 108–10.
36 Bruce Mazlish, *In Search of Nixon: A Psychological Inquiry* (New York, 1972), pp. 142–43.
37 Ibid., p. 132.
38 Ibid., pp. 153–54.
39 James David Barber, *The Presidential Character: Predicting Performance in the White House* (Englewood Cliffs, N.J., 1972), pp. 362–63.
40 Ibid., pp. 13–24.
41 Henry Fairlie, *The Kennedy Promise: The Politics of Expectation* (Garden City, N.Y., 1973), p. 107.
42 Childs, *Eisenhower*, p. 4.
43 Winston, *Andrew Johnson*, pp. 329–30.

14 Decision-Making

1 Interview, televised December 17, 1962.
2 Roy F. Nichols, *Franklin Pierce: Young Hickory from the Granite Hills* (Philadelphia, 1931), p. 251.
3 William Allen White, *A Puritan in Babylon* (New York, 1938), p. 260.
4 William Cresson, *James Monroe* (Chapel Hill, N.C., 1946), p. 346.
5 In Eric F. Goldman, *The Tragedy of Lyndon Johnson* (New York, 1969), p. 23.
6 Interview, televised December 17, 1962.
7 John Hope Franklin, *The Emancipation Proclamation* (Garden City, N.Y., 1963), p. 26.
8 Cresson, *James Monroe*, pp. 449–50.
9 Joseph Alsop and Turner Catledge, *The 168 Days* (Garden City, N.Y., 1938), pp. 33–35. J. F. ter Horst, *Gerald Ford and the Future of the Presidency* (New York, 1974), p. 58; James Reston, "Nice-Guy Leadership," *New York Times*, December 4, 1974.
10 Cresson, *James Monroe*, pp. 185–86.
11 Albert L. Warner, "How the Korea Decision Was Made," *Harper's Magazine* (June 1951), p. 99; Richard C. Snyder and Glenn D. Paige, "The United States Decision to Resist Aggression in Korea," *Administrative Science Quarterly*, vol. 3 (December 1958), p. 348. The most comprehensive study is Glenn Paige, ed., *1950: Truman's Decision—The United States Enters the Korean War* (New York, 1970).
12 Harry S. Truman, *Years of Trial and Hope*, vol. 2 of *Memoirs* (Garden City, N.Y., 1956), pp. 185–86.
13 Hans J. Morgenthau, "The Trouble with Kennedy," *Commentary* (January 1962), p. 51.
14 *Newsweek*, August 2, 1965, p. 15.
15 White, *Puritan in Babylon*, pp. 267–69.
16 Sherman Adams, *First-Hand Report* (New York, 1961), p. 252.
17 Arthur M. Schlesinger, Jr., *The Coming of the New Deal*, vol. 2 of *The Age of Roosevelt* (Boston, 1959), pp. 528–31.
18 Rexford G. Tugwell, *The Democratic Roosevelt* (Garden City, N.Y., 1957), p. 546.
19 Schlesinger, *New Deal*, p. 531.
20 Howard Raiffa, *Decision Analysis* (Reading, Mass., 1968), pp. 128–29.
21 "Reconstruction of Cambodia Decision," *New York Times*, June 30, 1970.
22 Franklin, *Emancipation Proclamation*, p. 95.
23 Ibid., p. 26.
24 Alsop and Catledge, *The 168 Days*, p. 63.
25 Leslie H. Gelb, "Today's Lessons from the Pentagon Papers," *Life*, September 17, 1971, p. 35.
26 Goldman, *Lyndon Johnson*, pp. 413–14.
27 Interview with Garret D. Horner, Washington *Star-News*, November 9, 1972, and *New York Times*, November 10, 1972.
28 Cresson, p. 445.
29 James T. Tedeschi, ed., *The Social Influence Process* (Chicago, 1972), pp. 352–53.
30 Harold L. Ickes, *The Inside Struggle*, vol. 2 of *The Secret Diary of Harold Ickes* (New York, 1954), p. 339.
31 Gelb, "Pentagon Papers," pp. 34–35.
32 Ibid., pp. 35–36.
33 James C. Thomson, Jr., "How Could Vietnam Happen?" *The Atlantic Monthly* (April 1968), p. 47.
34 Ibid., pp. 49–52; Irving L. Janis, *Victims of Groupthink* (Boston, 1972); Irving L. Janis, "Groupthink in Washington," *New York Times*, May 28, 1973.

15 Conflict

1 George Christian, *The President Steps Down* (New York, 1970), pp. 71 and 237–38.

2 Eric F. Goldman, *The Tragedy of Lyndon Johnson* (New York, 1969), pp. 348–49.

3 Timothy G. Smith, ed., *Merriman Smith's Book of Presidents* (New York, 1972), pp. 36–37.

4 Goldman, *Lyndon Johnson,* p. 378.

5 Bruce Mazlish, *In Search of Nixon: A Psychohistorical Inquiry* (New York, 1972), p. 117.

6 *New York Times,* January 29, 1974.

7 William S. White, *The Responsibles* (New York, 1972), pp. 67–68.

8 For a sociological view of conflict and distributive justice, see George C. Homans, *Social Behavior* (New York, 1961), pp. 74–75. See also Elton B. McNeil, ed., *The Nature of Human Conflict* (Englewood Cliffs, N.J., 1965).

9 Rowland Evans, Jr., and Robert D. Novak, *Nixon in the White House* (New York, 1971), pp. 163–64.

10 In Richard Harris, *Decision* (New York, 1971), pp. 28–29.

11 In David Halberstam, *The Best and the Brightest* (New York, 1972), p. 298.

12 Evans and Novak, *Nixon in the White House,* p. 257.

13 For useful allied studies in psychology and sociology, see Homans, *Social Behavior;* Judson S. Brown, "Gradients of Approach and Their Relation to Level of Motivation," *Journal of Comparative and Physiological Psychology* 41 (December, 1948): 450–65; Roger Barker, "An Experimental Study of the Resolutions of Conflict by Children," in Quinn McNemas and Maud A. Merrills, eds., *Studies in Personality* (New York, 1942).

14 *New York Times,* April 10, 1970.

15 White, *Responsibles,* pp. 243–45.

16 Goldman, *Lyndon Johnson,* p. 91.

17 Ibid., pp. 281–82.

18 In James David Barber, *The Presidential Character* (Englewood Cliffs, N.J., 1972), p. 442.

19 In Goldman, *Lyndon Johnson,* pp. 170–01.

20 Elie Abel, *The Missile Crisis* (Philadelphia, 1966), p. 16.

21 For discussions of the crisis see Henry M. Pachter, *Collision Course: The Cuban Missile Crisis and Coexistence* (New York, 1963); Abel, *Missile Crisis;* James Daniel and John Hubbell, *Strike in the West: The Complete Story of the Cuban Missile Crisis* (New York, 1963); Arthur M. Schlesinger, Jr., *A Thousand Days: John F. Kennedy in the White House* (Boston, 1965); Theodore C. Sorensen, *Kennedy* (New York, 1965); David L. Larson, *The "Cuban Crisis" of 1962: Selected Documents and Chronology* (Boston, 1963); Robert F. Kennedy, *Thirteen Days: A Memoir of the Cuban Missile Crisis* (New York, 1969). For conceptual models applicable to the missile crisis, see Graham T. Allison, *Essence of Decision: Explaining the Cuban Missile Crisis* (Boston, 1971).

22 Kenneth Keating, *Cuba Chronology, 1962* (Washington, D.C., 1962), mimeographed.

23 Daniel and Hubbell, *Strike in the West,* p. 88.

24 For Bundy's own reasons, see "Cuba: The Missile Crisis," *NBC White Paper* (NBC broadcast, February 9, 1964), mimeographed transcript, pp. 13–14.

25 Robert F. Kennedy, *Thirteen Days,* p. 111.

26 Daniel and Hubbell, *Strike in the West,* pp. 64–67.

27 For a detailed chronology of the crisis see "The Cuban Crisis: Fourteen Days That Shook the World," *New York Times,* reprint, November 3, 1962 (includes texts appearing in the *Times,* October 23–November 3, 1962).

28 Daniel and Hubbell, *Strike in the West,* pp. 92–93.

29 *New York Times,* October 22, 1962.

30 *New York Times,* October 25, 1962.

31 Abel, *Missile Crisis,* p. 168.

32 *New York Times,* October 27, 1962.

33 Daniel and Hubbell, *Strike in the West,* pp. 95–125.

34 *New York Times,* April 26, 1963.

35 *New York Times,* October 28, 1962; Daniel and Hubbell, *Strike in the West,* pp. 150–53.

36 Kenneth Keating, news release, January 31, 1963, mimeographed.

37 *New York Times,* November 12, 1966.

38 *New York Times,* November 15, 1970.

39 For distinctions between the 1962 and 1970 situations, see George G. Quester, "Missiles in Cuba, 1970," *Foreign Affairs* 49 (April 1971): 493–506.

40 See comment by Theodore Sorensen, *NBC White Paper,* p. 22.

41 Robert F. Kennedy, *Thirteen Days,* p. 111.

16 The Presidency Compared

1 *New York Times,* April 27 and May 7, 1973.

2 Coleman B. Ransone, Jr., *The Office of Governor in the United States* (University, Ala., 1956), pp. 116–17.

3 Joseph E. Kallenbach, *The American Chief Executive: The Presidency and the Governorship* (New York, 1966), pp. 364–65.

4 See Scott Greer, *Governing the Metropolis* (New York, 1962).

5 In John A. Hamilton, "Mayors on the March," *New York Times,* June 26, 1973, and *New York Times,* February 22, 1973.

6 See James Reston, "The Crisis of Democracy," *New York Times,* March 3, 1974; Theodore C. Achilles, letter to the editor, *New York Times,* May 24, 1974.

7 Anthony King, ed., *The British Prime Minister* (London, 1969), pp. 56–57.

8 Francis Williams, ed., *Twilight of Empire: Memoirs of Prime Minister Clement Attlee* (New York, 1962), pp. 223–25.

9 Michel Tatu, *Power in the Kremlin from Khrushchev to Kosygin* (New York, 1969), p. 413.

10 *New York Times,* October 16, 1964.

11 *London Times,* October 22, 1963.

12 Alvin Shuster, "Low-Profile: Harold Wilson's First 100 Days," *New York Times,* June 13, 1974.

13 Bertram D. Wolfe, *Khrushchev and Stalin's Ghost* (New York, 1957), pp. 22–25.

14 Tatu, *Power in the Kremlin,* pp. 511–25.

15 *New York Times,* December 2, 1973; Hedrick Smith, "Brezhnev at Crest of His Prestige," *New York Times,* June 25, 1974.

16 American Political Science Association, Committee on Political Parties, *Toward a More Responsible Party System* (New York, 1950).

17 *New York Times,* December 22, 1973.

18 R. T. McKenzie, *British Political Parties* (London, 1955), pp. 297–99.

19 In Samuel H. Beer et al., *Patterns of Government: The Major Political Systems of Europe,* rev. ed. (New York, 1962), pp. 183–84.

20 *New York Times,* November 21, 1974.

21 Alvin Shuster, "British in Crisis. Losing Faith in 'Muddling Through'," *New York Times,* November 22, 1974.

22 Harold Macmillan, *Riding the Storm 1956–1959* (New York, 1971), p. 191.

23 Richard E. Neustadt, "White House and Whitehall," in King, *British Prime Minister,* p. 140.

24 *New York Times,* June 13, 1974.

25 Harold Wilson, *A Personal Record: the Labour Government 1964–1970* (Boston, 1971), p. 47.

26 Don K. Price, "The Parliamentary and Presidential Systems," *Public Administration Review* 3 (Winter 1941): 360.

27 Ibid., p. 322.

28 *London Times,* October 22, 1963.

29 Ibid.

30 Gwendolen M. Carter and John H. Herz, *Major Foreign Governments,* 6th ed. (New York, 1972), pp. 175–80.

31 See Roy C. Macridis and Bernard E. Brown, *The De Gaulle Republic* (Homewood, Ill., 1960). For an analysis of democracy and administration, see Emmette Redford, *Democracy in the Administrative State* (New York, 1969).

32 *New York Times,* May 29, 1974.

33 C. L. Sulzberger, " 'Kissinger' and Kissinger," *New York Times,* June 24, 1973.

34 Milovan Djilas, *The New Class* (New York, 1957), pp. 44–47.

35 Boris Souvarine, *Stalin* (New York, 1939), pp. 407–09.

36 Milovan Djilas, "The 'New Class'—Faceless, Fearful," *New York Times,* January 7, 1971; Zbigniew Brzezinski and Samuel Huntington, *Political Power: USA/USSR* (New York, 1965), p. 436.

37 Djilas, "The 'New Class'," p. 82.

38 Bernard Gwertzman, "Brezhnev's Future Priorities," *New York Times,* April 12, 1971, and *New York Times,* June 16, 1972.

39 U.S. Senate Subcommittee on National Policy Machinery, Committee on Government Operations, *National Policy Machinery in the Soviet Union,* 86th Congress, 2nd Session (Washington, D.C., 1960), pp. 36–42.

40 See Charles O. Porter and Robert J. Alexander, *The Struggle for Democracy in Latin America* (New York, 1961).

41 *New York Times,* February 1, 1964.

PRESIDENTS OF THE UNITED STATES

	PARTY	TERM
1. George Washington (1732–99)	Federalist	1789–1797
2. John Adams (1735–1826)	Federalist	1797–1801
3. Thomas Jefferson (1743–1826)	Democratic-Republican	1801–1809
4. James Madison (1751–1836)	Democratic-Republican	1809–1817
5. James Monroe (1758–1831)	Democratic-Republican	1817–1825
6. John Quincy Adams (1767–1848)	Democratic-Republican	1825–1829
7. Andrew Jackson (1767–1845)	Democratic	1829–1837
8. Martin Van Buren (1782–1862)	Democratic	1837–1841
9. William Henry Harrison (1773–1841)	Whig	1841
10. John Tyler (1790–1862)	Whig	1841–1845
11. James K. Polk (1795–1849)	Democratic	1845–1849
12. Zachary Taylor (1784–1850)	Whig	1849–1850
13. Millard Fillmore (1800–74)	Whig	1850–1853
14. Franklin Pierce (1804–69)	Democratic	1853–1857
15. James Buchanan (1791–1868)	Democratic	1857–1861
16. Abraham Lincoln (1809–65)	Republican	1861–1865
17. Andrew Johnson (1808–75)	Union	1865–1869
18. Ulysses S. Grant (1822–85)	Republican	1869–1877
19. Rutherford B. Hayes (1822–93)	Republican	1877–1881
20. James A. Garfield (1831–81)	Republican	1881
21. Chester A. Arthur (1830–86)	Republican	1881–1885
22. Grover Cleveland (1837–1908)	Democratic	1885–1889
23. Benjamin Harrison (1833–1901)	Republican	1889–1893
24. Grover Cleveland (1837–1908)	Democratic	1893–1897
25. William McKinley (1843–1901)	Republican	1897–1901
26. Theodore Roosevelt (1858–1919)	Republican	1901–1909
27. William Howard Taft (1857–1930)	Republican	1909–1913
28. Woodrow Wilson (1856–1924)	Democratic	1913–1921
29. Warren G. Harding (1865–1923)	Republican	1921–1923
30. Calvin Coolidge (1872–1933)	Republican	1923–1929
31. Herbert Hoover (1874–1964)	Republican	1929–1933
32. Franklin Delano Roosevelt (1882–1945)	Democratic	1933–1945
33. Harry S Truman (1884–1972)	Democratic	1945–1953
34. Dwight D. Eisenhower (1890–1969)	Republican	1953–1961
35. John F. Kennedy (1917–63)	Democratic	1961–1963
36. Lyndon B. Johnson (1908–73)	Democratic	1963–1969
37. Richard M. Nixon (b. 1913)	Republican	1969–1974
38. Gerald R. Ford (b. 1913)	Republican	1974–

CONSTITUTIONAL PROVISIONS RELATING TO THE PRESIDENCY

SECTION 3

6. The Senate shall have the sole power to try all impeachments. When sitting for that purpose, they shall be on oath or affirmation. When the President of the United States is tried, the Chief Justice shall preside; and no person shall be convicted without the concurrence of two-thirds of the members present.

7. Judgment in cases of impeachment shall not extend further than to removal from office, and disqualification to hold and enjoy any office of honor, trust, or profit under the United States; but the party convicted shall, nevertheless, be liable and subject to indictment, trial, judgment, and punishment, according to law.

SECTION 7

2. Every bill which shall have passed the House of Representatives and the Senate shall, before it becomes a law, be presented to the President of the United States; if he approve he shall sign it, but if not he shall return it, with his objections, to that house in which it shall have originated, who shall enter the objections at large on their journal and proceed to reconsider it. If after such reconsideration two-thirds of that house shall agree to pass the bill, it shall be sent, together with the objections, to the other house, by which it shall likewise be reconsidered, and if approved by two-thirds of that house it shall become a law. But in all such cases the votes of both houses shall be determined by yeas and nays, and the names of the persons voting for and against the bill shall be entered on the journal of each house respectively. If any bill shall not be returned by the President within ten days (Sundays excepted) after it shall have been presented to him, the same shall be a law, in like manner as if he had signed it unless the Congress by their adjournment prevent its return, in which case it shall not be a law.

3. Every order, resolution, or vote to which the concurrence of the Senate and House of Representatives may be necessary (except on a question of adjournment) shall be presented to the President of the United States; and before the same shall take effect, shall be approved by him, or being disapproved by him, shall be repassed by two-thirds of the Senate and House of Representatives, according to the rules and limitations prescribed in the case of a bill.

ARTICLE II

SECTION 1

1. The executive power shall be vested in a President of the United States of America. He shall hold his office during the term of four years, and, together with the Vice President, chosen for the same term, be elected as follows:

2. Each state shall appoint, in such manner as the legislature thereof may direct, a number of electors, equal to the whole number of Senators and Representatives to which the State may be entitled in the Congress; but no Senator or Representative, or person holding an office of trust or profit under the United States, shall be appointed an elector.

3.* The electors shall meet in their respective states and vote by ballot for two persons, of whom one at least shall not be an inhabitant of the same state with themselves. And they shall make a list of all the persons voted for, and of the number of votes for each; which list they shall sign and certify, and transmit sealed to the seat of the government of the United States, directed to the President of the Senate. The President of the Senate shall, in the presence of the Senate and House of Representatives, open all the certificates, and the votes shall then be counted. The person having the greatest number of votes shall be the President, if such a number be a majority of the whole number of electors appointed; and if there be more than one who have such majority, and have an equal number of votes, then the House of Representatives shall immediately choose by ballot one of them for President; and if no person have a majority, then from the five highest on the list the said House shall in like manner choose the President. But in choosing the President the votes shall be taken by states, the representation from each state having one vote; a quorum for this purpose shall consist of a member or members from two-thirds of the states, and a majority of all the states shall be necessary to a choice. In every case, after the choice of the President, the person having the greatest number of votes of the electors shall be the Vice President. But if there should remain two or more who have equal votes, the Senate shall choose from them by ballot the Vice President.

4. The Congress may determine the time of choosing the electors and the day on which they shall give their votes, which day shall be the same throughout the United States.

5. No person except a natural born citizen, or a citizen of the United States at the time of the adoption of this Constitution, shall be eligible to the office of President; neither shall any person be eligible to that office who shall not have attained to the age of thirty-five years, and been fourteen years a resident within the United States.

6.* In case of the removal of the President from office, or of his death, resignation, or inability to discharge the powers and duties of the said office, the same shall devolve on the Vice President, and the Congress may by law provide for the case of removal, death, resignation, or inability, both of the President and Vice President, declaring what officer shall then act as President, and such officer shall act accordingly until the disability be removed or a President shall be elected.

7. The President shall, at stated times, receive for his services a compensation, which shall neither be increased nor diminished during the period for which he shall have been elected, and he shall not receive within that period any other emolument from the United States or any of them.

8. Before he enter on the execution of his office he shall take the following oath or affirmation:

> I do solemnly swear (or affirm) that I will faithfully execute
> the office of President of the United States, and will to the best of
> my ability preserve, protect, and defend the Constitution of the
> United States.

SECTION 2

1. The President shall be Commander-in-Chief of the Army and Navy of the United States, and of the militia of the several states when called into the actual service of the United States; he may require the opinion, in writing, of the principal officer in

* This paragraph was superseded by the Twelfth Amendment.
* This paragraph was modified by the Twenty-fifth Amendment.

each of the executive departments, upon any subject relating to the duties of their respective offices, and he shall have power to grant reprieves and pardons for offenses against the United States, except in cases of impeachment.

2. He shall have power, by and with the advice and consent of the Senate, to make treaties, provided two-thirds of the Senators present concur; and he shall nominate, and, by and with the advice and consent of the Senate, shall appoint ambassadors, other public ministers and consuls, judges of the Supreme Court, and all other officers of the United States, whose appointments are not herein otherwise provided for, and which shall be established by law; but the Congress may by law vest the appointment of such inferior officers, as they think proper, in the President alone, in the courts of law, or in the heads of departments.

3. The President shall have power to fill up all vacancies that may happen during the recess of the Senate, by granting commissions which shall expire at the end of their next session.

SECTION 3

He shall from time to time give to the Congress information of the state of the union, and recommend to their consideration such measures as he shall judge necessary and expedient; he may, on extraordinary occasions, convene both houses, or either of them, and in case of disagreement between them with respect to the time of adjournment, he may adjourn them to such time as he shall think proper; he shall receive ambassadors and other public ministers; he shall take care that the laws be faithfully executed, and shall commission all the officers of the United States.

SECTION 4

The President, Vice President, and all civil officers of the United States shall be removed from office on impeachment for and conviction of treason, bribery, or other high crimes and misdemeanors.

AMENDMENT XII

The electors shall meet in their respective states and vote by ballot for President and Vice President, one of whom, at least, shall not be an inhabitant of the same state with themselves; they shall name in their ballots the person voted for as President, and in distinct ballots the person voted for as Vice President, and they shall make distinct lists of all persons voted for as President and of all persons voted for as Vice President, and of the number of votes for each; which lists they shall sign and certify, and transmit sealed to the seat of the government of the United States, directed to the President of the Senate. The President of the Senate shall, in the presence of the Senate and House of Representatives, open all the certificates and the votes shall then be counted. The person having the greatest number of votes for President shall be the President, if such number be a majority of the whole number of electors appointed; and if no person have such majority, then from the persons having the highest numbers not exceeding three on the list of those voted for as President, the House of Representatives shall choose immediately, by ballot, the President. But in choosing the President the votes shall be taken by states, the representation from each state having one vote; a quorum for this purpose shall consist of a member or members from two-thirds of the states, and a majority of all states shall be necessary to a choice. And if the House of Representatives shall not choose a President whenever the right of choice shall devolve upon them, before the fourth day of

March next following, then the Vice President shall act as President, as in the case of the death or other constitutional disability of the President.

The person having the greatest number of votes as Vice President shall be the Vice President, if such number be a majority of the whole number of electors appointed; and if no person have a majority, then from the two highest numbers on the list the Senate shall choose the Vice President; a quorum for the purpose shall consist of two-thirds of the whole number of Senators, and a majority of the whole number shall be necessary to a choice. But no person constitutionally ineligible to the office of President shall be eligible to that of Vice President of the United States.

AMENDMENT XX

SECTION 1

The terms of the President and Vice President shall end at noon on the 20th day of January, and the terms of Senators and Representatives at noon on the 3rd day of January, of the years in which such terms would have ended if this article had not been ratified; and the terms of their successors shall then begin.

SECTION 2

The Congress shall assemble at least once in every year, and such meeting shall begin at noon on the 3rd day of January, unless they shall by law appoint a different day.

SECTION 3

If, at the time fixed for the beginning of the term of the President, the President elect shall have died, the Vice President elect shall become President. If a President shall not have been chosen before the time fixed for the beginning of his term, or if the President elect shall have failed to qualify, then the Vice President elect shall act as President until a President shall have qualified; and the Congress may by law provide for the case wherein neither a President elect nor a Vice President elect shall have qualified, declaring who shall then act as President, or the manner in which one who is to act shall be selected, and such person shall act accordingly until a President or Vice President shall have qualified.

SECTION 4

The Congress may by law provide for the case of the death of any of the persons from whom the House of Representatives may choose a President whenever the right of choice shall have devolved upon them, and for the case of the death of any of the persons from whom the Senate may choose a Vice President whenever the right of choice shall have devolved upon them.

AMENDMENT XXII

No person shall be elected to the office of the President more than twice, and no person who has held the office of President, or acted as President, for more than two years of a term to which some other person was elected President shall be elected to the office of the President more than once. But this article shall not apply to any person holding the office of President when this article was proposed by the Congress, and shall not prevent any person who may be holding the office of President, or acting as President, during the term within which this article becomes operative from holding the office of President or acting as President during the remainder of such term.

AMENDMENT XXV

SECTION 1

In case of the removal of the President from office or of his death or resignation, the Vice President shall become President.

SECTION 2

Whenever there is a vacancy in the office of the Vice President, the President shall nominate a Vice President who shall take office upon confirmation by a majority vote of both Houses of Congress.

SECTION 3

Whenever the President transmits to the President pro tempore of the Senate and the Speaker of the House of Representatives his written declaration that he is unable to discharge the powers and duties of his office, and until he transmits to them a written declaration to the contrary, such powers and duties shall be discharged by the Vice President as Acting President.

SECTION 4

Whenever the Vice President and a majority of either the principal officers of the executive department or of such other body as Congress may by law provide, transmit to the President pro tempore of the Senate and the Speaker of the House of Representatives their written declaration that the President is unable to discharge the powers and duties of his office, the Vice President shall immediately assume the powers and duties of the office as Acting President.

Thereafter, when the President transmits to the President pro tempore of the Senate and the Speaker of the House of Representatives his written declaration that no inability exists, he shall resume the powers and duties of his office unless the Vice President and a majority of either the principal officers of the executive department or of such other body as Congress may by law provide, transmit within four days to the President pro tempore of the Senate and the Speaker of the House of Representatives their written declaration that the President is unable to discharge the powers and duties of his office. Thereupon Congress shall decide the issue, assembling within forty-eight hours for that purpose if not in session. If the Congress, within twenty-one days after receipt of the latter written declaration, or, if Congress is not in session, within twenty-one days after Congress is required to assemble, determines by two-thirds vote of both Houses that the President is unable to discharge the powers and duties of his office, the Vice President shall continue to discharge the same as Acting President; otherwise, the President shall resume the powers and duties of his office.

SOURCES

Note: Asterisk denotes a book available in a paperback edition.

General Works on the American Presidency

Bailey, Thomas A., *Presidential Greatness* (New York, 1966).*
Barber, James David, *The Presidential Character* (Englewood Cliffs, N.J., 1972).*
Brown, Stuart Gerry, *The American Presidency: Leadership, Partisanship, and Popularity* (New York, 1966).
Brownlow, Louis, *The President and the Presidency* (Chicago, 1949).
Burns, James MacGregor, *Presidential Government* (Boston, 1965).*
Corwin, Edward S., *The President: Office and Powers,* 4th ed. (New York, 1957).*
————, and Louis W. Koenig, *The Presidency Today* (New York, 1956).
Finer, Herman, *The Presidency: Crisis and Regeneration* (Chicago, 1960).
Hardin, Charles M., *Presidential Power and Accountability* (Chicago, 1974).
Hargrove, Erwin C., *The Power of the Modern Presidency* (New York, 1974).*
————, *Presidential Leadership: Personality and Political Style* (New York, 1966).*
Heller, Francis, *The Presidency: A Modern Perspective* (New York, 1960).*
Herring, E. Pendleton, *Presidential Leadership* (New York, 1940).
Hoxie, R. Gordon, *The Presidency of the 1970's* (New York, 1973).
Hughes, Emmet John, *The Living Presidency* (New York, 1973).
Hyman, Sidney, *The American President* (New York, 1954).
James, Dorothy, *The Contemporary Presidency* (New York, 1972).*
Kallenbach, Joseph, *The American Chief Executive* (New York, 1966).
Laski, Harold, *The American Presidency* (New York, 1940).*
McConnell, Grant, *The Modern Presidency* (New York, 1967).*
Milton, George F., *The Use of Presidential Power, 1789–1943* (Boston, 1944).
Murphy, John F., *The Pinnacle: The Contemporary American Presidency* (Philadelphia, 1974).
Neustadt, Richard E., *Presidential Power* (New York, 1960).*
Orban, Edmond, *La Présidence Moderne Aux États-Unis* (Montreal, 1974).*
Patterson, C. P., *Presidential Government in the United States* (Chapel Hill, N.C., 1947).
Reedy, George, *The Presidency in Flux* (New York, 1973).
————, *The Twilight of the Presidency* (New York, 1970).
Rienow, Robert, and Leona T. Rienow, *The Lonely Quest: The Evolution of Presidential Leadership* (Chicago, 1966).
Rossiter, Clinton, *The American Presidency,* rev. ed. (New York, 1960).*
Schlesinger, Arthur M., Jr., *The Imperial Presidency* (Boston, 1973).*
Stanwood, Edward, *History of the Presidency* (Boston, 1928).
Strum, Philippa, *Presidential Power and American Democracy* (Pacific Palisades, Calif., 1972).*
Taft, William H., *Our Chief Magistrate and His Powers* (New York, 1916).
Tugwell, Rexford G., *The Enlargement of the Presidency* (New York, 1960).
U.S. National Archives, *Public Papers of the Presidents of the United States* (Washington, D.C., 1957 and after).
Vinyard, Dale, *The Presidency* (New York, 1971).

Specialized Works

Abraham, Henry, *Justices and Presidents: A Political History of Appointments to the Supreme Court* (New York, 1974).
Anderson, Patrick, *The President's Men* (Garden City, 1968).*

Barber, James David, ed., *Choosing the President* (Englewood Cliffs, N.J., 1974).*

Berdahl, C. A., *War Powers of the Executive in the United States* (Urbana, Ill., 1921).

Berger, Raoul, *Executive Privilege: A Constitutional Myth* (Cambridge, Mass., 1974).

———, *Impeachment: The Constitutional Problems* (Cambridge, Mass., 1973).*

Binkley, Wilfred, *President and Congress* (New York, 1947).*

Black, Charles L., Jr., *Impeachment: A Handbook* (New Haven, Conn., 1974).*

Brown, Stuart Gerry, *The Presidency on Trial: Robert Kennedy's 1968 Campaign and Afterwards* (Honolulu, 1972).

Chamberlain, Lawrence H., *The President, Congress, and Legislation* (New York, 1946).

Commission on Organization of the Executive Branch of the Government (Hoover Commission), *Reports* (Washington, D.C., 1949 and 1953).

Committee on Government Operations, Senate Subcommittee on National Policy Machinery, *Reports* (Washington, D.C., 1959 and after).

Cornwell, Elmer E., Jr., *Presidential Leadership of Public Opinion* (Bloomington, Ind., 1965).

Cronin, Thomas E., and Sanford D. Greenberg, *The Presidential Advisory System* (New York, 1969).

David, Paul, Malcolm Moos, and R. M. Goldman, *Presidential Nominating Politics,* 5 vols. (Baltimore, 1954).

Davis, James, *Presidential Primaries: Road to the White House* (New York, 1967).

Destler, I. M., *Presidents, Bureaucrats, and Foreign Policy* (Princeton, N.J., 1972).*

Feerick, John D., *From Failing Hands: The Story of Presidential Succession* (New York, 1965).

Fenno, Richard F., Jr., *The President's Cabinet* (Cambridge, Mass., 1959).*

Fersh, Seymour H., *The View from the White House: A Study of the Presidential State of the Union Message* (Washington, D.C., 1961).

Fisher, Louis, *President and Congress* (New York, 1972).*

Flash, Edward S., *Economic Advice and Presidential Leadership* (New York, 1965).

Goebel, Dorothy B., *Generals in the White House* (New York, 1945).

Graff, Henry, *The Tuesday Cabinet* (Englewood Cliffs, N.J., 1970).

Hansen, Richard, *The Year We Had No President* (Lincoln, Neb., 1962).*

Hart, James, *The American Presidency in Action* (New York, 1948).

Hatch, L. C., and E. L. Shoup, *A History of the Vice Presidency* (New York, 1934).

Henry, Laurin L., *Presidential Transitions* (Washington, D.C., 1960).

Hess, Stephen, *The Presidential Campaign: The Leadership Selection Process after Watergate* (Washington, D.C., 1974).*

Hinsdale, Mary L., *A History of the President's Cabinet* (Ann Arbor, Mich., 1911).

Hobbs, Edward H., *Behind the President: A Study of Executive Office Agencies* (Washington, D.C., 1954).

Holtzman, Abraham, *Legislative Liaison: Executive Leadership in Congress* (Chicago, 1970).

Hoxie, R. Gordon, ed., *The White House: Organization and Operations* (New York, 1971).

Humbert, W. H., *The Pardoning Power of the President* (Washington, D.C., 1941).

Javits, Jacob, *Who Makes War?* (New York, 1973).

Johnson, Richard, *Managing the White House* (New York, 1974).

Koenig, Louis W., *The Invisible Presidency* (New York, 1960).

———, *The Presidency and the Crisis: Powers of the Office from the Invasion of Poland to Pearl Harbor* (New York, 1944).

Learned, H. B., *The President's Cabinet* (New Haven, Conn., 1912).

Longaker, Richard, *The Presidency and Individual Liberties* (Ithaca, N.Y., 1961).

McClure, Wallace, M., *International Executive Agreements* (New York, 1941).

McConnell, Grant, *Steel and the Presidency* (New York, 1963).*

McGinniss, Joe, *The Selling of the President 1968* (New York, 1969).

Marcy, Carl M., *Presidential Commissions* (New York, 1945).

Matthews, Donald R., ed., *Perspectives on Presidential Selection* (Washington, D.C., 1973).*

Minow, Newton, et al., *Presidential Television* (New York, 1973).

Moos, Malcolm, *Politics, Presidents, and Coattails* (Baltimore, 1950).

Morgan, Ruth, *The President and Civil Rights* (New York, 1970).*

Morris, Richard B., *Great Presidential Decisions* (New York, 1969).*

Mueller, John, *War, Presidents, and Public Opinion* (New York, 1973).*

Nash, Bradley D., *Staffing the Presidency* (Washington, D.C., 1952).

Overacker, Louise, *Presidential Campaign Funds* (Boston, 1946).

————, *The Presidential Primary* (New York, 1926).

Pollard, J. E., *The Presidents and the Press* (New York, 1947).

Polsby, Nelson W., and Aaron Wildavsky, *Presidential Elections,* 3rd ed. (New York, 1971).

Pomper, Gerald, *Nominating the President* (Evanston, Ill., 1963).*

President's Committee on Administrative Management (Brownlow Committee), *Report with Special Studies* (Washington, D.C., 1937).

Rich, Bennett M., *The Presidents and Civil Disorder* (Washington, D.C., 1941).

Roseboom, Eugene H., *A History of Presidential Elections,* rev. ed. (New York, 1964).*

Rossiter, Clinton, *The Supreme Court and the Commander-in-Chief* (Ithaca, N.Y., 1951).

Sayre, Wallace S., and Judith H. Parris, *Voting for President: The Electoral College and the American Political System* (Washington, D.C., 1970).*

Schlesinger, Arthur M., Jr., and Alfred de Grazia, *Congress and the Presidency* (New York, 1967).*

Schubert, Glendon, *The Presidency in the Courts* (Minneapolis, 1957).

Sickels, Robert J., *Presidential Transactions* (Englewood Cliffs, N.J., 1974).*

Silva, Ruth, *Presidential Succession* (Ann Arbor, Mich., 1951).

Silverman, Corinne, *The President's Economic Advisers* (University, Ala., 1959).

Small, Norman J., *Some Presidential Interpretations of the Presidency* (Baltimore, 1930).

Somers, Herman M., *Presidential Agency: OWMR* (Cambridge, Mass., 1954).

Sorensen, Theodore C., *Decision-Making in the White House* (New York, 1963).*

Sparks, Will, *Who Talked to the President Last?* (New York, 1971).

Stanley, David T., *Changing Administrations* (Washington, D.C., 1965).

Stein, Charles W., *The Third Term Tradition* (New York, 1946).

Thomas, Norman C., and Hans W. Baade, eds., *The Institutionalized Presidency* (Dobbs Ferry, N.Y., 1972).

Tolchin, Martin, and Susan Tolchin, *To the Victor: Political Patronage from the Clubhouse to the White House* (New York, 1971).

Tugwell, Rexford G., *How They Became President* (New York, 1965).*

Warren, Sidney, *The President as World Leader* (New York, 1964).

Waugh, Edgar W., *Second Consul* (Indianapolis, 1956).

Weinbaum, Marvin G., and Louis H. Gold, *Presidential Election: A Simulation with Readings,* 2nd ed. (Hinsdale, Ill., 1974).

White, Theodore, *The Making of the President, 1960* (New York, 1961).* See further volumes of *The Making of the President* for *1964,* * *1968,* * and *1972.* *

Williams, Irving G., *The Rise of the Vice-Presidency* (Washington, D.C., 1956).

Wilmerding, Lucius, Jr., *The Electoral College* (New Brunswick, N.J., 1958).

Young, Donald, *American Roulette: The History and Dilemma of the Vice Presidency* (New York, 1965).

Biographies, Papers, Memoirs, and Studies of Presidents

1. GEORGE WASHINGTON

Flexner, James Thomas, *George Washington and the New Nation* (1783–1793), and *George Washington: Anguish and Farewell* (1793–1799), Vols. III and IV (Boston, 1969–1972).

Freeman, Douglas Southall, *George Washington: A Biography,* 7 vols. (New York, 1948–1957). Volume VI is *Patriot and President* (1954).

2. JOHN ADAMS

Chinard, Gilbert, *Honest John Adams* (Boston, 1933).

Smith, Page, *John Adams,* 2 vols. (Garden City, N.Y., 1962).

3. THOMAS JEFFERSON

Malone, Dumas, *Jefferson and His Time,* 5 vols. (Boston, 1948–1974).* Volume V is *Jefferson
    the President, 1805–1809* (1974).
Peterson, Merrill D., *Thomas Jefferson and the New Nation* (New York, 1970).
Schachner, Nathan, *Thomas Jefferson: A Biography* (New York, 1951).

4. JAMES MADISON

Brant, Irving, *Madison the President* (Indianapolis, 1970).
Ketcham, Ralph, *James Madison: A Biography* (New York, 1971).

5. JAMES MONROE

Ammon, Henry, *James Monroe: The Quest for National Identity* (New York, 1971).
Brown, Stuart Gerry, *The Autobiography of James Monroe* (Syracuse, 1959).
Cresson, William P., *James Monroe* (Chapel Hill, 1946).
Dangerfield, George, *The Era of Good Feelings* (New York, 1962).*

6. JOHN QUINCY ADAMS

Adams, Charles Francis, ed., *Memoirs of John Quincy Adams,* 12 vols. (Philadelphia, 1875).
Bemis, Samuel Flagg, *John Quincy Adams and the Foundations of American Foreign Policy* (New
    York, 1949).
————, *John Quincy Adams and the Union* (New York, 1956).

7. ANDREW JACKSON

James, Marquis, *Andrew Jackson: Portrait of a President* (Indianapolis, 1937).*
Schlesinger, Arthur M., Jr., *The Age of Jackson* (Boston, 1945).*

8. MARTIN VAN BUREN

Curtis, James C., *The Fox at Bay: Martin Van Buren and the Presidency, 1837–1841* (Lexington,
    Ky., 1970).
Remini, Robert V., *Martin Van Buren and the Making of the Democratic Party* (New York,
    1959).*
Van Deusen, Glyndon G., *The Jacksonian Era, 1828–1848* (New York, 1950).

9. WILLIAM HENRY HARRISON

Cleaves, Freeman, *Old Tippecanoe: William Henry Harrison and His Time* (New York, 1939).
Gunderson, Robert Gray, *The Log-Cabin Campaign* (Lexington, Ky., 1957).

10. JOHN TYLER

Chitwood, Oliver Perry, *John Tyler: Champion of the Old South* (New York, 1939).
Seager, Robert, *And Tyler Too* (New York, 1963).

11. JAMES K. POLK

McCormac, Eugene Irving, *James K. Polk, A Political Biography* (Berkeley, Calif., 1922).
Quaife, Milo M., ed., *The Diary of James K. Polk,* 4 vols. (Chicago, 1910).
Sellers, Charles Grier, *James K. Polk, Jacksonian, 1795–1843* and *James K. Polk, Continentalist,
    1843–1846* (Princeton, N.J., 1957–1966).

12. ZACHARY TAYLOR

Dyer, Brainerd, *Zachary Taylor* (Baton Rouge, 1946).
Hamilton, Holman, *Zachary Taylor,* 2 vols. (Indianapolis, 1941–1951).

13. MILLARD FILLMORE

Rayback, Robert J., *Millard Fillmore: Biography of a President* (Buffalo, N.Y., 1959).

14. FRANKLIN PIERCE

Nichols, Roy F., *Franklin Pierce, Young Hickory of the Granite Hills,* 2nd ed. (Philadelphia, 1958).

15. JAMES BUCHANAN

Klein, Philip Shriver, *President James Buchanan, A Biography* (University Park, Pa., 1962).
Nichols, Roy F., *The Disruption of American Democracy* (New York, 1948).*

16. ABRAHAM LINCOLN

Randall, James G., *Constitutional Problems under Lincoln* (New York, 1926).*
————, *Lincoln the President,* 2 vols. (New York, 1945 and 1955).*
Sandberg, Carl, *Abraham Lincoln: The War Years,* 4 vols. (New York, 1939).*
Thomas, Benjamin P., *Abraham Lincoln, A Biography* (New York, 1952).*

17. ANDREW JOHNSON

Lomask, Milton, *Andrew Johnson: President on Trial* (New York, 1960).
McKitrick, Eric L., *Andrew Johnson and Reconstruction* (Chicago, 1960).*

18. ULYSSES S. GRANT

Hesseltine, William B., *Ulysses S. Grant, Politician* (New York, 1935).
Nevins, Allan, *Hamilton Fish: The Inner History of the Grant Administration* (New York, 1936).

19. RUTHERFORD B. HAYES

Barnard, Harry, *Rutherford B. Hayes and His America* (Indianapolis, 1954).
Davison, Kenneth E., *The Presidency of Rutherford B. Hayes* (Westport, Conn., 1972).
Williams, Charles Richard, ed., *Diary and Letters of Rutherford B. Hayes* (Columbus, Ohio: 1924).

20. JAMES A. GARFIELD

Caldwell, Robert G., *James A. Garfield, Party Chieftain* (New York, 1931).
Smith, Theodore Clarke, *The Life and Letters of James Abram Garfield,* 2 vols. (New Haven, Conn., 1925).

21. CHESTER A. ARTHUR

Howe, George Frederick, *Chester A. Arthur: A Quarter-Century of Machine Politics* (New York, 1934).
Reeves, Thomas C., *Gentleman Boss: Chester Allen Arthur* (New York, 1975).

22. GROVER CLEVELAND

Merrill, Horace S., *Bourbon Leader: Grover Cleveland and the Democratic Party* (Boston, 1957).*
Nevins, Allan, *Grover Cleveland, A Study in Courage* (New York, 1932).

23. BENJAMIN HARRISON

Sievers, S. J., and Harry J. Sievers, *Benjamin Harrison: Hoosier Warrior, 1833–1865* (Chicago, 1952); *Benjamin Harrison: Hoosier Statesman, 1865–1888* (New York, 1959); *Benjamin Harrison, Hoosier President, 1888–1901* (Indianapolis, 1968).

24. WILLIAM McKINLEY

Leech, Margaret, *In the Days of McKinley* (New York, 1959).
Morgan, H. Wayne, *William McKinley and His America* (Syracuse, N.Y., 1963).

25. THEODORE ROOSEVELT

Blum, John Morton, *The Republican Roosevelt* (Cambridge, Mass., 1954).*
Gatewood, Willard B., Jr., *Theodore Roosevelt and the Art of Controversy* (Baton Rouge, La., 1970).
Harbaugh, William Henry, *The Life and Times of Theodore Roosevelt,* rev. ed. (New York, 1963).*
Mowery, George F., *The Era of Theodore Roosevelt, 1900–1912* (New York, 1958).*
Pringle, Henry F., *Theodore Roosevelt: A Biography* (New York, 1931).*
Roosevelt, Theodore, *Autobiography* (New York, 1931).

26. WILLIAM HOWARD TAFT

Anderson, Donald F., *William Howard Taft: A Conservative's Conception of the Presidency* (Ithaca, N.Y., 1973).

27. WOODROW WILSON

Bailey, Thomas A., *Woodrow Wilson and the Lost Peace* (New York, 1944).*
————, *Woodrow Wilson and the Great Betrayal* (New York, 1945).*
Baker, Ray Stannard, *Woodrow Wilson: Life and Letters,* 8 vols. (Garden City, N.Y., 1927–1939).
Blum, John Morton, *Woodrow Wilson and the Politics of Morality* (Boston, 1956).*
George, Alexander, and Juliette L. George, *Woodrow Wilson and Colonel House: A Personality Study* (New York, 1956).*
Link, Arthur S., *Woodrow Wilson,* 5 vols. (Princeton, N.J., 1947–1955).*
Smith, Gene, *When the Cheering Stopped: The Last Years of Woodrow Wilson* (New York, 1964).*

28. WARREN G. HARDING

Downes, Randolph C., *The Rise of Warren Gamaliel Harding, 1865–1920* (New York, 1970).
Murray, Robert, *The Harding Era: Warren G. Harding and His Administration* (Minneapolis, 1969).
Russell, Francis, *The Shadow of Blooming Grove* (New York, 1968).

29. CALVIN COOLIDGE

Fuess, Claude, *Calvin Coolidge, The Man from Vermont* (Boston, 1940).
McCoy, Donald R., *Calvin Coolidge: The Quiet President* (New York, 1967).
Quint, Howard H., and Robert H. Ferrell, eds., *The Talkative President: The Off-the-Record Press Conferences of Calvin Coolidge* (Amherst, Mass., 1964).

30. HERBERT HOOVER

Hoover, Herbert, *The Memoirs of Herbert Hoover,* 3 vols. (New York, 1951–1952).
Romasco, Albert U., *The Poverty of Abundance: Hoover, the Nation, the Depression* (New York, 1965).*
Warren, Harris G., *Herbert Hoover and the Great Depression* (New York, 1959).*

31. FRANKLIN D. ROOSEVELT

Burns, James MacGregor, *Roosevelt: The Lion and the Fox* (New York, 1956) * and *Roosevelt: The Soldier of Freedom* (New York, 1970).*
Freidel, Frank, *Franklin D. Roosevelt,* 4 vols. (Boston, 1952–1973).
Leuchtenburg, William E., *Franklin D. Roosevelt and the New Deal, 1932–1940* (New York, 1963).*

Schlesinger, Arthur M., Jr., *The Age of Roosevelt,* 3 vols. (Boston, 1957–1960).*
Tugwell, Rexford G., *The Democratic Roosevelt* (Garden City, N.Y., 1957).

32. HARRY S TRUMAN

Cochran, Bertram, *Crisis and the Truman Presidency* (New York, 1973).
Phillips, Cabell, *The Truman Presidency* (New York, 1966).*
Rudoni, Dorothy, *Harry S Truman: A Study in Presidential Perspective* (Ann Arbor, Mich., 1969).
Steinberg, Alfred, *The Man from Missouri: The Life and Times of Harry S Truman* (New York, 1962).
Truman, Harry S, *Memoirs,* 2 vols. (Garden City, N.Y., 1955 and 1956).
Truman, Margaret, *Harry S Truman* (New York, 1972).*

33. DWIGHT D. EISENHOWER

Adams, Sherman, *First-Hand Report: The Story of the Eisenhower Administration* (New York, 1961).
Donovan, Robert J., *Eisenhower: The Inside Story* (New York, 1956).
Eisenhower, Dwight D., *The White House Years, 1953–1961,* 2 vols. (Garden City, N.Y., 1963–1965).*
Hughes, Emmet John, *The Ordeal of Power* (New York, 1963).
Lyon, Peter, *Eisenhower: Portrait of a Hero* (Boston, 1974).
Parmet, Herbert S., *Eisenhower and the American Crusades* (New York, 1972).

34. JOHN F. KENNEDY

Burns, James MacGregor, *John Kennedy: A Political Profile* (New York, 1960).*
Fairlie, Henry, *The Kennedy Promise: The Politics of Expectation* (Garden City, N.Y., 1973).
Latham, Earl, *J. F. Kennedy and Presidential Power* (Lexington, Mass., 1972).*
Manchester, William R., *Portrait of a President: John F. Kennedy in Profile,* rev. ed. (Boston, 1967).*
Schlesinger, Arthur M., Jr., *A Thousand Days: John F. Kennedy in the White House* (Boston, 1965).*
Sorensen, Theodore C., *Kennedy* (New York, 1965).*

35. LYNDON B. JOHNSON

Goldman, Eric, *The Tragedy of Lyndon Johnson* (New York, 1969).*
Heren, Louis, *No Hail, No Farewell* (New York, 1970).
Johnson, Lady Bird, *A White House Diary* (New York, 1970).*
Johnson, Lyndon B., *The Vantage Point: Perspectives of the Presidency 1963–1969* (New York, 1971).
Steinberg, Alfred, *Sam Johnson's Boy: A Close-Up of the President from Texas* (New York, 1968).
White, William S., *The Professional: Lyndon B. Johnson* (Boston, 1964).

36. RICHARD M. NIXON

Evans, Rowland, and Robert D. Novak, *Nixon in the White House* (New York, 1971).*
Mazlish, Bruce, *In Search of Nixon: A Psychohistorical Inquiry* (Baltimore, 1973).
Mazo, Earl, and Stephen Hess, *Nixon: A Political Portrait* (New York, 1968).*
Nixon, Richard M., *Six Crises* (Garden City, N.Y., 1962).
Wills, Garry, *Nixon Agonistes* (Boston, 1970).*
Witcover, Jules, *The Resurrection of Richard Nixon* (New York, 1970).

37. GERALD R. FORD

ter Horst, J. F., *Gerald Ford and the Future of the Presidency* (New York, 1974).
Vestal, Bud, *Jerry Ford Up Close* (New York, 1974).

Court Cases

In re Debs (158 U.S. 564, 1895).
Ducan v. *Kahanamoku, Sheriff* (327 U.S. 304, 1946).
Ex parte Grossman (267 U.S., 1925).
Hirabayashi v. *United States* (320 U.S. 81, 1943).
Humphrey v. *United States* (295 U.S. 602, 1935).
Korematsu v. *United States* (323 U.S. 214, 1944).
Ex parte Milligan (4 Wall 2, 1866).
Mississippi v. *Johnson* (4 Wall 475, 1867).
Myers v. *United States* (271 U.S., 1926).
In re Neagle (135 U.S. 1, 1890).
Ex parte Quirin (317 U.S. 1, 1942).
Ray v. *Blaire* (343 U.S. 214, 1952).
United States v. *Curtiss-Wright Export Corp.* (299 U.S. 304, 1936).
United States v. *Montgomery Ward and Co.* (58 Fed. Supp. 408, N.D., Ill., 1945; 150 Fed. [2d.] 369, C.C.A. 7th, 1945).
United States v. *Nixon* (44 Sup. Ct. 3090, 1974).
Yakus v. *United States* (321 U.S. 414, 1944).
Youngstown Sheet and Tube Co. v. *Sawyer* (343 U.S. 579, 1952).

Chief Executives of Other Countries

GREAT BRITAIN

Alexander, Andrew, and Alan Watkins, *The Making of the Prime Minister 1970* (London, 1970).
Beer, Samuel H., *British Politics in the Collectivist Age* (New York, 1965).*
Carter, Byrum E., *The Office of Prime Minister* (Princeton, N.J., 1956).
Eden, Anthony (Earl of Avon), *Memoirs,* 2 vols. (Boston, 1960 and 1965).
Jennings, Sir Ivor, *Cabinet Government,* 3rd ed. (London, 1959).
King, Anthony, ed., *The British Prime Minister* (London, 1969).*
Mackintosh, John P., *The British Cabinet,* 2nd ed. (London, 1968).
————, *The Government and Politics of Britain,* 3rd ed. (London, 1974).
Macmillan, Harold, *Memoirs,* 4 vols. (New York, 1966–71).
Walker, Patrick Gordon, *The Cabinet* (London, 1972).*
Wilson, Harold, *A Personal Record: The Labour Government, 1964–1970* (Boston, 1971).

FRANCE

Anderson, Malcolm, *Government in France: An Introduction to the Executive Power* (London, 1970).
Aron, Robert, *An Explanation of de Gaulle* (New York, 1966).
Colliard, Jean Claude, *Les Républicains Indépendants: Valérie Giscard d'Estaing* (Paris, 1971).
Grégoire, Roger, *The French Civil Service* (Brussels, 1965).
Mauriac, François, *De Gaulle* (Garden City, N.Y., 1966).
Suleiman, Ezra N., *Politics, Power, and Bureaucracy in France* (Princeton, N.J., 1974).
Viansson-Ponte, *The King and His Court (Les Gaullistes)* (Boston, 1965).

THE SOVIET UNION

Crankshaw, Edward, *Khrushchev Remembers* (Boston, 1970).
Deutscher, Isaac, *Stalin: A Political Biography,* 2nd ed. (New York, 1967).
Djilas, Milovan, *The New Class* (New York, 1957).
Juviler, Peter H., and Henry W. Morton, *Soviet Policy Making* (New York, 1967).
Rush, Myron, *Political Succession in the USSR,* 2nd ed. (New York, 1968).
Schapiro, Leonard, *The Communist Party of the Soviet Union* (New York, 1971).

Strong, John W., ed., *The Soviet Union under Brezhnev and Kosygin* (New York, 1971).
Tatu, Michel, *Power in the Kremlin, from Khrushchev to Kosygin* (New York, 1969).*

The American Governor and Mayor

Banfield, Edward C., and James Q. Wilson, *City Politics* (Cambridge, Mass., 1963).*
Greer, Scott, *Governing the Metropolis* (New York, 1962).*
Jacob, Herbert, and Kenneth N. Vines, eds., *Politics in the American States,* 2nd ed. (Boston, 1971).
Jewell, Malcolm E., *The State Legislature* (New York, 1962).*
Kammerer, Gladys, *et al., The Urban Political Community* (Boston, 1963).*
Key, V. O., Jr., *American State Politics* (New York, 1956).
Lockard, Duane, *The Politics of State and Local Government,* 2nd ed. (New York, 1969).
Ransone, Coleman B., Jr., *The Office of Governor in the United States* (University, Ala., 1956).
Sayre, Wallace S., and Herbert Kaufman, *Governing New York City* (New York, 1960).*

INDEX

Abrams, Creighton, 353
Acheson, Dean, 372–73
Adams, Alva, 132
Adams, John
  on checks and balances, 28
  Presidency of, 33–34
Adams, John Quincy
  and 1824 election, 56
  party chief, 129–30
Adams, Sherman, 80–81, 170, 173, 193–94, 354
Adenauer, Konrad, 230, 374
Administrative chief, President as, 181–212
  and bureaucracy, 184–85
  and Congress, 183–84
  Eisenhower, 192–96
  Ford, 208–10
  L. B. Johnson, 200–02
  Kennedy, 196–200
  Nixon, 202–10
  and Presidential staff, 185–89
  proposals for, 210–12
  F. D. Roosevelt, 189–92
AFL-CIO, 285–87, 309
Agnew, Spiro, 46, 86, 121, 126, 188
Aiken, George, 219
Albert, Carl, 179–80
Aldrich, Nelson W., 278
Alien and Sedition Acts, 34
Allen, George E., 268
Allen, James E., Jr., 206, 364
Allende Gossens, Salvador, 227
Alliances, U.S., 233–35, 254–56
  see also specific alliances
Allison, William B., 278
Allport, Gordon W., 327
Aluminium Company of America (Alcoa), 274
Ambassadors, 216–17
American Medical Association, 112
Americans for Democratic Action, 304
Anderson, George W., 241–42
Anderson, Rudolf, Jr., 376
Appointing power, 24, 156–57
Appropriations, 237, 306
Armas, Carlos Castillo, 254
Arms control, 233
Arthur, Chester A., 334
  and Garfield's disability, 77
  and news management, 109
  renomination attempt of, 121–22
Arvey, Jacob M., 122
Ash, Roy L., 185, 209
Atomic Energy Commission, 260

Baer, George, 288
Bailey, John, 37
Ball, George, 350, 374
Banks, Nathaniel P., 249

Barber, James David, 339
Barkley, Alben, 43, 132, 187
Barnard, Chester, 354
Bates, Edward, 249
Bay of Pigs, invasion of, 241
Bayard, James A., 128
Bayh, Birch, 81
Beam, Jacob D., 228–29
Beard, Charles A., 176
Beecher, Henry Ward, 122
Beria, Lavrenti, 393
Berle, Adolf A., 300
Berlin, 236, 349–50, 372, 379
Berry, Theodore M., 387
Bethlehem Steel Corporation, 273–74
Black, Jeremiah S., 334
Black caucus, Congressional, 320–21
Blackmun, Harry, 157
Blacks
  office-holding by, 322
  and poverty, 323
  and Presidential nomination, 45
Blackstone, William, 28
Blaine, James G., 77, 122
Blum, John M., 299
Bohlen, Charles, 162, 206
Borah, William E., 13, 39, 351
Borden, William L., 260
Boston, school busing crisis, 321
Bowles, Chester, 122
Bradley, Omar, 348
Brain Trust, 309
Brandeis, Louis, 191, 355
Brandt, Willy, 63, 373, 388
Brennan, Peter, 186, 286
Brewster, Ralph O., 311–12
Brezhnev, Leonid, 390, 393–94, 403–05
Brown, George, 389, 392
Brown v. Board of Education of Topeka, 321, 329
Brownlow Committee, 183
Bruce, David E. K., 217
Bryan, William Jennings, 223, 295–96, 302
Bryant, Farris, 143
Bryce, James, 15
Buchanan, James, 176
  goals of, 332
  personality of, 334
  view of the Presidency, 15, 341
Buchen, Philip, 88
Buckley, Charles A., 138–39
Budget and Accounting Act of 1921, 165, 182, 187
Bundy, McGeorge, 198, 224, 350, 371, 375
Bureaucracy, executive branch, 10, 184–85
  and cities, 387
  constrains the President, 191

Burleson, Albert S., 45, 172
Burr, Aaron, 56, 74
Burton, Phillip, 179
Bush, George, 217
Business and the President, 265–70
Business Council, 51, 268
Busing, school, 157, 320–21
Butler, Pierce, 27
Butler, R. A., 391
Butz, Earl, 72, 209
Byrd, Harry F., 55
Byrnes, James F., 85, 223–24, 287

Cabinet, 185–86
  beginnings of, 32
  Eisenhower's, 186, 194
  Kennedy's, 186, 199
  Wilson's, 79–80
Calhoun, John, 129
Callaghan, James, 392
Cambodia, 3, 70
  decision-making concerning, 353, 356
  secret air war over, 214, 218, 252
Camp, Lawrence S., 133
Campaign financing, 51–53
  public subsidy for, 62
Cannon, Joseph ("Uncle Joe"), 305
Capehart, Homer, 370
Carmichael, Gil, 126
Carswell, G. Harrold, 157, 282, 364
Case, Clifford, 237
Castro, Fidel, 370, 377
Cater, Douglass, 201
Caucus, House Democratic, 179
Central Intelligence Agency, 6, 227–28
  and South Vietnam, 235
  and Watergate, 69
Chandler, Albert ("Happy"), 132
Chase, Salmon, 67, 128
Checks and balances, 27–29
Chiang Kai-shek, 244
Chief diplomat, President as, 213–38
  advisory systems of, 237–38
  and alliances, 233–35
  and ambassadors, 216
  autonomy of, 213–14
  and Congress, 214–15, 220–21, 237
  executive agreements of, 216
  foreign aid program, 221
  and foreign leaders, 229–31
  personal staff of, 224–29
  proposals for, 236–38
  recognition of governments, 216–17
  and Secretary of State, 222–24
  and summit conferences, 231–33
  and treaties, 215–16
  and United Nations, 235–36
  and war, 217–20
China, Communist, 217, 244
China, Nationalist, 244
Chotiner, Murray, 204

Christian, George, 105
Church, Frank, 125
Citizens' Research Foundation, 51
Civil rights, of blacks, 314–24
Civil Rights Act
  of 1957, 316
  of 1967, 319
Civil Rights Commission, 317
Civil service, British, 399–400
Civil Service Act of 1883, 124
Clark, Bennett C., 132
Clark, Joseph S., 139, 179
Clay, Henry, 129–30, 346
Clayton Act, 172
Cleveland, Grover, 14
  election of (1888), 56
  goals of, 333
  and labor, 288
  personality of, 334
  platform of (1888), 119
  and sense of right, 14
  and the tariff, 125–26
Clifford, Clark, 226
Clinton, De Witt, 130
Clinton, George, 20
Coal strike of 1902, 288–89
Coalitions, Congressional, 163, 307–09
Cohen, Benjamin V., 311
Colmer, William M., 160
Colson, Charles W., 204
Commander-in-Chief, President as, 239–63
  and alliances, 254–56
  authority of, 245–46
  and Communist war-making, 253
  and courts, 248–52
  and Defense Department, 240–42
  and field generals, 242–45
  and Indochina war, 218–19
  and Joint Chiefs of Staff, 241–42
  limitations on, 239–40
  and nuclear weapons, 256–59
  proposals for, 261–63
  and Presidential war, 3, 215
  and scientists, 259–61
  and war, 217–20
  and War Powers Act of 1973, 219–20
Commission on Civil Disorders, 323
Commission on Civil Rights, 322, 324
Committee for the Reelection of the President, 9
  and fund raising, 52, 278
  organization of, 47, 51
  and political sabotage, 53
  and the Republican party, 145
Committee of Detail, 25
Committee of Style, 25
Common Cause, 180, 292
Computers, in Presidential campaigns, 49–50
Conflict, Presidential, 360–80
  crisis, 369–80
  gradients of, 365–68
  initiation of, 362–63

Conflict, Presidential (*Continued*)
  as political exchange, 363–65
  solution of, 368
  types of, 361–62
Congress, 150–80
  administrative powers of, 183–84
  committees of, 159–61
  constrains the President, 150, 177
  and foreign affairs, 214–15, 221, 237
  majorities in, 161–62
  military powers of, 247, 263
  party management, 120
  reorganization of, 178–80
  term of, 177
Congressional caucus, 127
Connally, John B., Jr., 86, 142
Connally, Tom, 132, 215
Constitutional Convention, 20–26
Consumer Federation of America, 298
Convention, miniconvention, *1974,* 148
Convention, national nominating, 40–45
Convention reform, *1972,* 41
Coolidge, Calvin, 57
  and business, 265, 269
  as decision-maker, 344, 351–52
  view of Congress, 10
Cooper, John Sherman, 121, 196
Corcoran, Thomas G., 132, 191, 311–12, 357
Cortelyou, George B., 277
Corwin, Edward S., 246
Council of Economic Advisers, 187, 264,
  273, 275
Council on Environmental Quality, 187
Court-packing plan, 345, 347, 355
Courts, and military power, 248–52
Cox, Archibald, 11, 46, 69
Cox, Eugene E., 132
Cox, Minnie, 314
Cripps, Stafford, 389–90
Crisis, 369–80
  and decision-making, 377–80
  Kennedy and, 369–80
Crotty, Peter J., 139
Crown, James Tracy, 286
Crum, William, 314
Cuba
  1961 invasion of, 374, 380
  1962 missile crisis, 217, 226, 345–46,
    369–80
  1970 nuclear submarines negotiation, 377
Cummings, Homer S., 347, 355
Curtis, George William, 121
Cutler, Robert, 238
Cyprus war, 150, 221

Daugherty, Harry, 351–52
Davis, John W., 57
Dean, Arthur H., 351
Dean, John, 205
Debs, Eugene, 302
Debs, In re, 288

Decision-making, Presidential, 343–59
  alternatives in, 348–51
  choice-making, step of, 351–54
  consequences of, 356–57
  environment of, 346–48
  kinds of, 343–46
  making the decision known, 354–56
  pathologies of, 357–58
Decision-making, Soviet, 404–05
Defense Department, 240–42
De Gaulle, Charles, 401
  on U.S. Presidency, 406
Democracy
  and administration, 181, 190
  and conflict, 360, 368
  and decision-making, 355
  and the economy, 265
  and ethics, 9
  and executive reorganization, 207–08
  groundrules of, 8–9
  and military power, 239
  Nixon and, 6–7
  parties and, 147
  and personality, 327, 336–40
  and political sabotage, 53
  proposed commission for, 212
  and selection, Presidential, 35–36
  and tenure, Presidential, 63
  and the White House staff, 210
Democratic Steering and Policy Committee, 124,
  179
Democratic Study Group, 180
Dent, Harry S., 145, 204
Dercum, Francis X., 78–79
De Sapio, Carmine, 139
Dewey, Thomas E., 122
De Witt, J. L., 250
Dickinson, John, 23, 25, 27
Diem, Ngo Dinh, 235
Dillon, C. Douglas, 167, 371
Dirksen, Everett, 116, 126, 164
Disability, Presidential, 76–84
Dixon-Yates contract, 196
Djilas, Milovan, 402
Doar, John, 318
Dobrynin, Anatoly, 229, 374
Dole, Robert, 145
Domestic Council, 206, 325, 360
Donahue, Richard, 46
Douglas, Lewis, 191, 268, 312
Douglas, Paul, 309
Douglas, William O., 123
Dubinsky, David, 281
Du Bois, W. E. B., 314
Dulles, John Foster, 135, 193, 223, 349
Duncan v. *Kahanamoku, Sheriff,* 251
Dungan, Ralph, 46
Durkin, Martin, 186, 286

Eagleton, Thomas F., 220
Eastland, James O., 126, 160

Economy and the President, 264–92
  business, 265–70
  labor, 279–88
  labor-management disputes, 288–91
  "New Economics," 274–77
  proposals for, 291–92
Education Act of 1965, 111
Ehrlichman, John, 6, 203–05
Eisenhower, Dwight D., 285
  administrative methods of, 192–96
  and black civil rights, 315
  and business, 268
  cabinet of, 278
  and Congress, 161–62
  and Cuban missile crisis, 373
  as decision-maker, 343, 345, 349–50, 352
  and executive privilege, 155
  and Guatemala take-over, 254
  illnesses of, 80–81
  and Joint Chiefs of Staff, 241
  and labor, 290
  legislative methods of, 170, 173–74
  and National Security Council, 195
  news conferences of, 106
  and nuclear weapons, 256
  party chief, 135–38
  and party platforms, 151
  personality of, 329–30
  as possible Democratic nominee, 123
  Presidential nomination of, 1952, 44
  and Secretaries of State, 223
  and social justice, 296
  style of, 336
  and test ban treaty, 260
  view of the Presidency, 340–41
  war resolutions of, 217–18
Electoral College, 54–58
  alternatives to, 58–61
Ellsberg, Daniel, 6, 70
Ellsworth, Oliver, 23–24
Emancipation Proclamation, 246, 294, 346, 354–55
Emergency Price Control Act, 1942, 175
Employment Act of 1946, 265
Energy crisis, 297–98
Environmental Protection Agency, 209
Equal Rights amendment, 297
Ervin, Sam J., Jr., 361
Espionage, electoral, 7
Evans, Joe L., 125
Executive agreements, 216, 237
Executive privilege, 155–56
  Nixon and, 155

Fair Campaign Practices Committee, 53
Fair Deal program, 296
Fair Labor Standards Act of 1938, 283
Faisal, King, 72
Fall, Albert B., 79
Farbstein, Leonard, 139–40
Farley, James, 42–43, 125, 139
Faubus, Orval, 315, 329

Federal Bureau of Investigation, 6, 69, 181
Federal Election Campaign Act of 1971, 52
Federal Energy Administration, 309
Federal Reserve System, 276, 309
Federal Trade Commission, 273
Felknor, Bruce, 53
Fenno, Richard F., 185
Filibuster, 161
Finnegan, James A., 119
Fitzgerald, A. Ernest, 156
Fitzhugh Commission, 242
Flanigan, Peter M., 269–70
Floyd, John B., 334
Flynn, Ed., 42
Food crisis, 298
Ford, Gerald R.
  as administrator, 208–10
  and black civil rights, 320–22
  and business, 266, 274
  and campaign organization, 48
  and the C.I.A., 227
  and Communist China, 217
  and conflict, 365
  and Congressional elections, 121
  and Congressional leaders, 164
  and Cyprus war, 226, 233–34
  as decision-maker, 345, 356
  economic policies of, 276–77
  and energy crisis, 297–98, 309, 347
  and ethics, post-Watergate, 330
  and food shortages, 298
  and foreign aid, 221
  inaugural address of, 1
  and inflation, 276–77
  and Kissinger, 223
  and labor, 282–84, 291
  legislative methods of, 168–69
  media coverage of, 4
  news conferences of, 107
  and pardon of Nixon, 5, 75, 156, 365
  personality of, 328, 330
  Presidential candidacy of, 37
  and public opinion polls, 93
  and recession, 277
  and regal style, 5
  and social justice, 297
  transition into Presidency, 88
  and the United Nations, 236
  Vice President, 86, 188
  and Vladivostok conference, 233, 258
Ford, Mrs. Gerald R., 356
Ford, Henry, Jr., 347
Formosa resolution, 218
Foster, Charles, 122
Fowler, Henry, 226
Frankfurter, Felix, 191
Franklin, Benjamin, 24, 27
Frelinghuysen, Peter H. B., 173
Friends of the Earth, 298
Frost, Robert, 379
Fulbright, J. William, 96, 223, 227, 237, 374

Gallatin, Albert, 127
Garfield, James A., 76–77, 122
Garfield, James R., 271
Garland, Ex parte, 75
Garner, John N., 44
Gary, Elbert, 271
Gelb, Leslie, 358
General Motors Corporation, 274, 289, 347
General ticket system, 54–55, 57
George III, 18, 24
George, Henry, 304
George, Walter F., 132–33
Gerry, Elbridge, 23, 25
Gibson, Andrew E., 298
Giles, William B., 129
Gillette, Guy M., 132
Giscard d'Estaing, Valéry, 401
Glass, Carter, 159, 172
Glassboro conference, 232
Goals, Presidential, 331–33
Goldberg, Arthur, 286
Goldwater, Barry, 55, 66
Gompers, Samuel, 279
Goodpaster, Andrew, 242
Goodwin, Richard, 46
Gore, Albert, 83
Governor, 381–85
  colonial, 18
  in early state constitutions, 19
Granger, Francis, 130
Grant, Ulysses S., 64, 335
Gray, Gordon, 195, 260
Grayson, Cary T., 78–80
Great Society program, 296
Greeley, Horace, 355
Green, William, Jr., 139
Greer, Scott, 386
Gromyko, Andrei, 229, 372
Guidelines, 274–75

Habeas corpus, 246, 248–49
Hagerty, James, 80–81
Haig, Alexander M., Jr., 66
Haldeman, H. R., 73, 202–05
Halleck, Charles, 174, 379
Hamilton, Alexander, 24, 56
  as party leader, 31
  plan of, for Presidency, 21
  and war power, 217
Hanna, Mark, 39, 277, 279, 314
Hannegan, Robert E., 287
Harding, Warren G.
  as administrator, 182
  and business, 269
  as decision-maker, 344
  and the Secretary of State, 223
Harlan, James, 330
Harriman, Averell, 244
Harriman, E. H., 267
Harris, Louis, 37, 46, 94–95, 146

Harrison, Benjamin, 56, 335
Hartmann, Robert T., 208–09
Hawaii, 251
Hay, John, 223
Hayes, Rutherford B., 56, 288
Haynsworth, Clement, 107, 157, 282, 364
Head Start, 313
Health insurance, 297
Hearst, William Randolph, 38–39
Heath, Edward, 388, 397
Helms, Richard, 226
Henderson, Leon, 123, 134
Henry, Laurin, 88
Hickel, Walter J., 206
High, Stanley, 134
Hill, James J., 267
Hill, Lister, 324
Hillman, Sidney, 190, 280, 284, 287
Hilsman, Roger, 374
Hirabayashi v. *U.S.,* 251
Hitchcock, Gilbert, 79
Hodges, Luther, 318
Hoffa, James, 144
Hoffman, Paul G., 222
Home, Alec Douglas-, 389, 391–92
Hood, James, 316–17
Hoover, Herbert
  and black civil rights, 314
  and business, 269
  and the economy, 264
  practical politics of, 13
Hoover, J. Edgar, 6, 184, 204
Hopkins, Harry, 132, 190–92, 354
House, Edward M., 39, 309
House of Commons, 396, 398–99
House of Representatives
  and Presidential programs, 162
  and Presidential selection, 54
  reforms, *1974,* 179
Housing
  and civil rights, 320–21, 323
Housing Act of *1974,* 297
Howe, Louis, 39
Hughes, Charles Evans, 57, 65, 182, 383
Hughes, Howard, 70
Hull, Cordell, 312
Humphrey's Executor v. *U.S.,* 182
Humphrey, Hubert, 39, 122, 125, 187–88, 323, 362

Ickes, Harold, 134, 190, 312, 357
Impeachment, 66–73
Impoundment, 154–55
Indochina war, 218–19
  as Presidential war, 2
Inflation, 291
Interest groups, 238
Internal Revenue Service, 69, 72, 181
International Telephone and Telegraph Company (ITT), 70, 156, 270

Jackson, Andrew
  and *1824* election, 56
  legislative methods of, 165
  majoritarian leader, 112
  and social justice, 294
  style of, 335
Jackson, Henry, 303
Jackson State University, 204
Japanese-Americans, 7
Javits, Jacob K., 220
Jaworski, Leon, 11, 69, 74–75
Jay, John, 18, 31–32
Jay treaty, 155
Jefferson, Thomas
  and *1800* election, 56
  and foreign policy making, 213
  legislative methods of, 154
  and Louisiana Purchase, 347–48, 356
  party leader, 126–29
  simplicity of, 4
  subpoena of, 74–75
  and Washington, 33
Jobert, Michel, 402
Johnson, Andrew
  impeachment of, 66–68
  personality of, 328–29
  style of, 336
  view of the Presidency, 341
Johnson, Hiram, 383
Johnson, Hugh, 134
Johnson, Lyndon B.
  as administrator, 183, 200–02, 205
  and antiwar activists, 97
  and black civil rights, 319, 322
  and business, 266, 273–74
  and conflict, 361–62, 365–68
  and Congressional coalitions, 163
  and Congressional elections, 120
  consensus leader, 111–12, 211, 325
  and Cuban missile crisis, 373
  as decision-maker, 345, 350–51, 355–56, 358
  and external reality, 4
  and Glassboro conference, 232
  and Israel, 230
  and labor, 286, 290
  legislative methods of, 152, 166–67, 169–73
  and the media, 104
  news conferences of, 106–07
  party leader, 141–43
  and patronage, 125
  personality of, 334
  and Presidential war, 2
  and F. D. Roosevelt, 132
  as Senate leader, 164, 174
  and social justice, 296, 304, 307–08
  and the Soviet Union, 221
  style of, 335–36
  as Vice President, 187
  and Vietnam War, 239, 243
Johnson, Mrs. Lyndon B., 96
Johnson, Tom L., 304

Joint Chiefs of Staff, 241–42, 257, 261–62
Joint Committee on the Conduct of the War, 248
Jones, Jesse H., 267
Jordan, Vernon E., Jr., 313
Judiciary Committee, House, 69, 71–73, 75

Kaiser, Edgar, 309
Kassal, Bentley, 139
Keating, Kenneth B., 81, 370, 377
Kefauver, Estes, 273, 394
Kendall, Amos, 309
Kennan, George, 348
Kennedy, Edward M., 297
Kennedy, John F.,
  administrative methods of, 196–200
  assassination of, 93
  and black civil rights, 315–18
  and business, 268, 304
  and cabinet, 199
  campaign organization of, 36–37, 119–20
  and conflict, 362
  and Congressional coalitions, 163
  and Cuban missile crisis, 2
  as decision-maker, 344–46, 350
  foreign aid, 222
  and goals, 333
  and Khrushchev, 229, 232
  and labor, 281, 285, 287
  legislative methods of, 151–53, 160–61, 166–67, 169, 171, 175
  and National Security Council, 199
  and NATO, 254
  news conferences of, 106
  as news manager, 108
  nomination of, 42–43
  and nuclear weapons, 256, 258
  party chief, 38–41
  personality of, 339
  Presidential campaign of, 46
  Presidential candidacy of, 49
  and RS-70 bomber, 247
  and Skybolt, 255
  and social justice, 296, 306–07
  and State Department, 228
  and steel price conflict, 272–73
  and test-ban treaty, 215, 261
  and United Nations, 235–36
Kennedy, Joseph P., 134
Kennedy, Robert F., 36, 46, 96, 138, 143, 228, 318, 371, 373, 376, 380
  and South Vietnam, 235
Kent State University, 204, 356
Khrushchev, Nikita, 372, 374
  and Cuban missile crisis, 229, 370, 376, 378
  tenure of, 390, 393
Killian, James, 260
King, Martin Luther, 238, 318
Kissinger, Henry, 187, 209
  and Arab-Israeli war (*1973*), 72
  and Congress, 225
  and diplomacy, 228–29

Kissinger, Henry (*Continued*)
  and Ford, 223, 225–26
  national security assistant, 224–26
  and the National Security Council, 227
  and Nixon, 224–25
  and resignation of Nixon, 66
  and wiretaps, 214
Klein, Herbert G., 109
Kleindienst, Richard G., 157
Knowland, William F., 116, 123, 136, 164, 174
Knox, Henry, 32
Knudsen, William, 190
Korean War, 218, 348–49, 363–64
Korematsu v. *U.S.*, 251
Kosygin, Alexei, 391, 393, 403
Kremer, Bruce, 43
Krogh, Egil, Jr., 8

Labor, 279–88
Labor-management disputes, 288–91
La Follette, Robert, 312, 334, 383
La Follette, Robert, Jr., 124
Laird, Melvin R., 241
Landis, James M., 134
Lansing, Robert, 65, 79–80
Laos, 70
  war in, 3
Latin America, 405–06
Lawrence, David, 126
League of Nations, 327
Legislative leader, President as, 150–80
  accomplishment, intervals of, 151–53
  and coalitions, 163
  imbalances, interbranch, 153–57
  messages of, 170–71
  methods of, 168–76
  obstacles of, 158–61
  popular appeals by, 165–66
  proposals for, 176–80
  veto by, 165
Lehman, Herbert H., 139
Le May, Curtis E., 241–42
Lemnitzer, Lyman, 241
Lend Lease Act, 247
Lerner, Max, 281
Lever Act of *1917,* 247
Lewis, John L., 280–81, 283–84
Lincoln, Abraham
  cabinet of, 190
  as Commander-in-Chief, 245–46
  as decision-maker, 346, 354
  and generals, 243–44
  and habeas corpus, 248–49
  legislative methods of, 176
  personality of, 328
  and Secretary of State, 223
  and social justice, 294
  view of the Presidency, 341
  and war investigating committee, 248
Lincoln, Franklin B., Jr., 87
Lippmann, Walter, 39
Lipset, Seymour Martin, 97

Little Rock school crisis, 315, 329
Livingston, Robert, 29, 348
Locke, John, 27–28
Lodge, Henry Cabot, 78, 327, 340
Lodge, Henry Cabot, Jr., 235, 351
Lombardi, Vince, 9
Lonergan, Augustine, 132
Long, Huey, 383–84
Louisiana Purchase, 347–48, 356
Lovett, Robert, 372
Luce, Henry, 104

MacArthur, Douglas, 244–45, 363
McCall, Tom, 383
McCarran, Pat, 132, 165, 216
McCarthy, Eugene, 12, 50
McCarthy, Joseph R., 162, 216, 363
Maclay, William, 31, 215
McClellan, George B., 243–44
McCloy, John J., 351
McCombs, William F., 37
McCormack, John W., 123
McFarland, Carl, 347
McGovern, George, 8, 12, 40–41, 87, 303
  Presidential nomination of, *1972,* 44
McGregor, Clark, 47
Macmillan, Harold, 137, 255, 374, 391–92
Macon, Nathaniel, 128
McKinley, William
  as decision-maker, 359
  Presidential candidacy of, 39
McNamara, Robert, 96, 186, 200, 224, 240, 273, 350, 374
Madison, James, 21, 24–25, 29, 32
Malone, Vivian, 316–17
Mansfield, Mike, 123–24
Marsh, John O., 208
Marshall, Thomas, 65
Marshall, Thurgood, 319
Martin, Edward, 373–74
Martin, Joseph ("Joe"), 85, 174, 244
Mason, George, 24
Mathias, Charles, 5
Maudling, Reginald, 389, 397
Maverick, Maury, 132
Mayor, 385–87
Mazlish, Bruce, 338
Mead, Margaret, 367
Meany, George, 157, 281–83
Media, mass, 103–04
Medicare, 306
Meir, Golda, 230–31
Mellon, Andrew, 269
Mencken, H. L., 40
Meredith, James, 316
Merryman, John, 249
Merryman, Ex parte, 249
Metcalf, Victor H., 271
Metzger, Delbert E., 251
Michelson, Charles, 43
Middle East resolution, 218

Middle East war, *1973,* 230–31, 236
Middle East war, *1967,* 226
Milligan, Ex parte, 249
Mills, Wilbur D., 160, 179, 306
Miniconvention, Democratic, *1974,* 148
Minow, Newton, 103
Minuteman, 255
Mitchell, John, 47, 97
Mitchell, John Purroy, 304
Moley, Raymond, 191, 300, 305, 310, 312
Mondale, Walter F., 62
Monroe, James
  as decision-maker, 344–45
  subpoena of, 74
Monroe Doctrine, 346–47
Monroney, Mike, 124
Monroney-Madden Committee, 178
Montesquieu, 28
Moorer, Thomas H., 256
Moos, Malcolm, 114
Morgan, J. Pierpont, 267, 270, 288.
Morgan v. *TVA,* 182
Morgenthau, Hans J., 350
Morgenthau, Henry, Jr., 134, 190, 268
Morris, Gouverneur, 20, 23, 26, 29
Mowry, George, 302
Moyers, Bill, 105, 201, 351
Moynihan, Daniel P., 303
Murphy, Frank, 289
Murray, Philip, 281
Murray, W. Vans, 34
Muskie, Edmund, 40, 53, 303
Myers v. *U.S.,* 182

Nader, Ralph, 292
National Association of Manufacturers, 308–09
National Catholic Welfare Council, 111
National Education Association, 111
National Industrial Recovery Act, 280–81,
  283, 314
National Labor Relations Act of *1935,* 283
National Security Act of *1947,* 186
National Security Council, 186, 195, 199, 224–25,
  360, 371
National Science Foundation, 261
National War Labor Board, 247
National Welfare Rights Organization, 238, 308–09
Neustadt, Richard, 13
New Deal program, 295, 314
"New Economics," 274–77
New Federalism, of Nixon, 313
New Frontier program, 296
"New American Majority," Nixon's, 144–46
New Jersey plan, 21
New York constitution, 19–20
News conference, Presidential, 105–08
News management, 108–10
Nhu, Ngo Dinh, 235
Nhu, Mme. Ngo Dinh, 235
Nicholas, William Cary, 129
Nicolay, John, 243

Nicholson, Joseph, 128
Nixon, Richard M.
  abodes of, 4
  as administrator, 202–10
  and allies of U.S., 255
  and appointment power, 156–57
  and black civil rights, 319–20
  and bombing of Laos, 3
  and bombing of North Vietnam, 253
  and Brezhnev, 233
  and bureaucracy, 206
  and business, 265
  campaign of, *1972,* 48
  and China, 217, 230, 232–33, 255–56
  and conflict, 363–64, 366–68
  and Congressional coalitions, 163–64
  and Congressional elections, 120–21
  and Congressional reform, 180
  and Cuba, 377
  as decision-maker, 353, 356
  "enemies list" of, 7
  and executive privilege, 74–75
  and foreign policy making, 234
  impeachment of, 68–73
  and impoundments, 313
  and invasion of Cambodia, 3
  and Israel, 230
  and Japan, 230
  and Kissinger, 224–26
  and labor, 282, 285, 291
  legislative methods of, 151, 153–57
  and mayors, 387
  and "national security" concept, 246
  and National Security Council, 186–87, 241, 262
  and "new American majority," 46–47, 144–46
  "new American Revolution" of, 297
  and "New Economics," 275–76
  news conferences of, 107
  and news media, 7, 101, 109
  and nuclear weapons, 257–59
  and "Opponents List," 204
  pardon of, 5, 75, 365
  party leader, 144–46
  and patronage, 125
  personal campaign organization of, 119–20
  personality of, 331, 338–39
  Presidential aberrations of, 1
  Presidential candidacy of, *1960,* 49
  Presidential nomination of, *1972,* 44
  and Presidential war, 2
  as radical, 5–7
  and regulatory commissions, 278–79
  resignation of, 66
  and school busing, 99
  seclusiveness of, 5
  and social justice, 296–97, 300–03, 306–08,
    312–14
  "Southern strategy" of, 46
  and Soviet detente, 255–56
  and the Soviet Union, 232–35
  subpoena of, 74
  and summit conferences, 232–33

Nixon, Richard (*Continued*)
  Supreme Court nominations of, 157, 364–66
  unindicted coconspirator, 74
  vetoes by, 313
  Vice President, 80–81, 187
  and Vice Presidential vacancy, *1973,* 86
  and Vietnam truce, 219
  weakens Presidency, 11–12
  and wiretaps, 214
  and withdrawal from Vietnam, 243
Nixon Doctrine, 234
Nixon v. *U.S.,* 74
Norris, George, 159, 305, 349
Norris-LaGuardia Act of *1932,* 283
Norstad, Lauris, 374
North Atlantic Treaty Organization (NATO), 234–35, 254–55, 374–75
North Vietnam, Nixon's bombing of, 218–19
Nuclear arms limitations agreements, 258
Nuclear weapons, 256–59

O'Brien, Lawrence F., 36, 46, 53, 138, 172, 198, 202, 374
O'Connor, Frank, 142
O'Connor, John J., 132–33
O'Donnell, Kenneth, 37, 46, 138, 198
Office of Economic Opportunity (OEO), 206, 303, 313
Office of Management and Budget (OMB), 187, 206, 242, 264, 360
Office of Price Administration, 247
Old age assistance, 304–05
O'Neill, Thomas P., Jr., 179–80
Oppenheimer, J. Robert, 260
Organization of American States (OAS), 374–75
Otis, Samuel, 29

Pardon, Nixon's, 5
Park, Chung Hee, 256
Parker, Alton, 277–78
Parliamentary system, British, 394–95
  evaluated, 398–400
Parties, British, 395
Party chief, President as, 115–49
  J. Q. Adams, 129–30
  and Congressional party, 120–21, 123–26
  Eisenhower, 135–38
  Jefferson, 126–29
  L. B. Johnson, 141–43
  Kennedy, 138–41
  Nixon, 144–46
  as nominee, 119–23
  and patronage, 124–25
  President's party, 115–18
  proposals for, 146–49
  and renomination, 121–23
  F. D. Roosevelt, 131–35
  Tyler, 130–31
Passman, Otto E., 167, 222
Paterson, William, 21
Patman, Wright, 179

Patronage, 124–25, 167
Pegler, Westbrook, 287
Pendleton, George, 394
Pentagon Papers, 227, 358
Pepper, Claude, 324
Percy, Charles H., 109
Perkins, Frances, 281, 299–300, 310
Perkins, George W., 271
Personality, Presidential, 326–42
  and democracy, 336–40
  goals, 331–33
  style, 333–36
  values, 327–31
  views of the Presidency, 340–41
Peurifoy, John, 254
Philadelphia Plan, 144, 320
Phillips, Howard, 313
Phillips, William, 191
Pichon, Louis, 356
Pierce, Franklin
  as decision-maker, 343–44, 354
Pinchot, Gifford, 299, 383
Pinckney, Charles, 22
Platt, Orville, 278
Platt, Tom ("Boss"), 39, 122
"Plumbers," White House, 70, 204
Plumer, William, 31, 55, 128
Pluralism, 211, 291, 298
Poindexter, J. B., 251
Polaris, 255
Policy committees, Congressional, 124
Politburo, 404
Polk, James, 75
  as administrator, 182
Polls, public opinion, *see* Public opinion polls
Pompidou, Georges, 388, 401
Poverty program, 296
Powell, Enoch, 392
Powell, Lewis, 157
Presidency
  beginnings of, 18–34
  compared to other systems, 381–406
  conflict regulators of, 360–61
  and democratic ground rules, 8–9
  excessive powers of, 1–3
  imagined v. real, 11
  imperiled, 10–12
  monarchic aspects of, 3
  structural concepts of, 27–29
  see also President *and individual functions*
President
  as administrative chief, 181–212, *see also* Administrative chief, President as;
  as chief diplomat, 213–38, *see also* Chief diplomat, President as;
  as Commander-in-Chief, 239–63, *see also* Commander-in-Chief, President as;
  and conflict, 360–80, *see also* Conflict, Presidential;
  and decision-making, 343–59, *see also* Decision–making, Presidential;

disability of, 76–84, *see also* Disability, Presidential;

and the economy, 264–92, *see also* Economy and the President;

impeachment of, 66–73

and legal processes, 73–75

as legislative leader, 150–80, *see also* Legislative leader, President as;

"literalist," 14–15

as party chief, 115–49, *see also* Party chief, President as;

political personality of, 326–42, *see also* Personality, Presidential;

and publics, 92–114, *see also* Publics, Presidential;

selection of, 35–61, *see also* Selection of President;

and social justice, 293–325, *see also* Social justice;

"strong," 9–10, 16

tenure of, 63–91, *see also* Tenure, Presidential

President, French Fifth Republic, 401–02

Presidential power

excesses of, 1–3

Presidential staff, 185–89

Presidential war, 2, 214, 217–20

President's Club, 142

Press secretary, Presidential, 105

Preston, Francis, 31

Price, Don K., 398

Primaries, Presidential, 39–40

Prime Minister, British

administrative powers of, 400

cabinet of, 397

legislative powers of, 305–06

as party leader, 394–95

selection of, 388–89

staff of, 402

and succession, 391–92

tenure of, 389–90

Public opinion, 92–95

Public opinion polls, 51

Publics, Presidential, 92–114

communications experts, 104–05

constituencies, 95–98

influence process, 98–102

leadership patterns, 111–13

and the media, 103–04

news conferences, 105–08

news management, 108–10

proposals concerning, 113–14

public opinion, 92–95

roles, 102–03

Pueblo, 236

Purge, by F. D. Roosevelt, 131–33

Quay, Matt, 39

Quirin, Ex parte, 250

Raborn, William, 350

Radford, Arthur W., 226, 241

Rail Passenger Service Act of *1970,* 285

Randall, Samuel J., 124–25

Randolph, Edmund, 22

Randolph, John, 127

Ransone, Coleman B., 383

Rauh, Joseph, 364

Ray v. *Blair,* 55

Rayburn, Sam, 44, 85, 161, 174, 311

Reagan, Michael, 325

Rebozo, Bebe, 70

Reconstruction Finance Corporation, 267

Redmayne, Martin, 391–92

Reed, Daniel A., 162

Reedy, George, 3, 105

Rehnquist, William, 3, 157

Reid, Whitelaw, 122

Reorganization Act of *1939,* 183

Resignation, Presidential, 65–66

Revenue-sharing, 387

Richardson, Elliott, 11

Richardson, Robert C., 251

Richberg, Donald, 134, 284

Ripley, W. Z., 300

Rivers, E. D., 133

Rives, William C., 130

Roberts, Clifford G., 268

Roberts, Roy, 328

Robinson, William E., 268

Rockefeller, Nelson A., 142, 188, 283

Roddan, Edward L., 134

Rodino, Peter, 69, 75

Rodney, Caesar A., 128

Rogers, William P., 80–81, 226, 353

Roles, Presidential, 102–03

Roosevelt, Elliott, 122

Roosevelt, Franklin D.

administrative methods of, 189–92

and black civil rights, 314

and business, 266–68

as Commander-in-Chief, 246–47

and conflict, 365–66

and Congressional elections, 120

as decision-maker, 344–45, 349, 352, 355

and Democratic coalition, 133–34

first nomination of, 42–44

first Presidential candidacy of, 38

goals of, 332

governor, 383

and Japanese-Americans, 7, 250

and labor, 279–81, 283–84, 287, 289

legislative methods of, 165, 169, 175

party chief, 131–35

personality of, 334, 339

Presidential campaign of, *1932,* 45–46

and Presidential war, 2

press conferences of, 106

property seizures by, 252

and seizure power, 272

and social justice, 295, 301–02, 304–05

style of, 335

and third term, 64

Roosevelt, Mrs. Franklin D., 280, 300
Roosevelt, James, 122
Roosevelt, Theodore
    and black civil rights, 314
    and business, 267, 270, 279
    and coal strike of *1902*, 288
    and conflict, 366
    and Congressional leaders, 278
    as decision-maker, 354
    and labor, 283
    legislative methods of, 152, 165, 171
    personality of, 326–27
    and Secretaries of State, 223
    and social justice, 294–95, 299–300, 302, 305
    "stewardship" theory of, 16
    and third term, 64
Root, Elihu, 223, 279, 288
Roper, Daniel, 284
Rosenman, Samuel, 114, 300
Rostow, Walt W., 202
Rowan, Carl, 319
Rule, Gordon W., 185
Rules Committee, House, 160
Rumsfeld, Donald, 208–09
Rusk, Dean, 186, 200, 350, 372, 375
Russell, Richard B., 370, 374
Rustin, Bayard, 323

Sabotage, political, 7, 53, 62
Sadat, Anwar, 72
St. Clair, James D., 71
Salinger, Pierre, 37, 46, 105, 198
Sargent, Francis W., 321
Sato, Eisaku, 230
Sawhill, John C., 298
Schlesinger, Arthur M., Jr., 352
Schlesinger, James R., 88, 256–57
Schneiderman, Rose, 300
School busing, 157, 320–21
School integration, 322
Schwartz, Maude, 300
Science adviser, 261
Scientists, 259–61
Scott, Stanley, 321
Seamans, Robert C., Jr., 156
Seidman, William, 208
Seizure power, 272
Selection of President, 35–61
    electoral college, 54–58
    national nominating convention, 40–45
    postconvention campaign, 45–54
    preconvention phase, 36–40
    Presidential candidates, sources of, 37
    proposals for, 61–62
Selective Service system, 252
Seniority, Congressional, 159–60
Separation of powers, 27–28
Seward, William H., 223
Shapp, Milton J., 383
Sharkey, Joseph T., 139
Shay's Rebellion, 18

Shelest, Pyotr Y., 404
Shouse, Jowett, 43
Simmons, F. M., 175
Simon, Herbert, 348
Simpson, Richard M., 120
Sirica, John, 73, 75, 361
Skybolt, 255
Sloan, Alfred, 289
Smith, Alfred E., 383
Smith, "Cotton Ed," 132
Smith, Howard W., 132
Smith, Hulett C., 142
Smith, James, Jr., 300
Smith, Stephen, 37, 138–39
Smoot, Reed, 13
Snow, C. P., 164, 261
Social justice, 293–325
    and civil rights, 314–24
    and the executive branch, 309–12
    history of, 293–98
    legislation, 305–09
    and political constraints, 301–05
    and Presidential personality, 299
    Presidential resistance to, 312–14
Social Security program, 360
Socialization, democratic, 92–94, 212
Sorensen, Theodore C., 37, 46, 114, 198, 373
Souers, Sidney, 238
South Carolina, 176
South Vietnam, 234
Southeast Asia Treaty Organization (SEATO), 234
"Southern strategy," Nixon's, 144
Soviet Union
    as arms supplier, 253
    succession in, 392
Sparling, James M., Jr., 72
Special agents in foreign affairs, 228–29
Special Prosecutor, Watergate, 11, 69
Speed, James, 330
Spingarn, J. E., 134
Spooner, John C., 278
Sprague, O. M. W., 300
Sputnik, 260
Staff, Presidential, *see* Presidential staff
Stalin, Joseph, 393, 402
Stans, Maurice H., 278
Stanton, Edwin M., 67, 330
Star Route frauds, 76–77
State Department, 228
Steelman, John R., 289
Stettinius, Edward M., Jr., 85
Stevenson, Adlai, 119, 372
Stockpiles, government, 273
Stone, Harlan F., 355
Strategic Air Command, 257
Strauss, Robert S., 286
Style, Presidential, 333–36
Suburbs, 307
Succession Act of *1886,* 65
Succession Act of *1947,* 85
Succession, Presidential, 84–86

Summit conferences, 231–33
Supreme Court
    and executive privilege, 73, 75
    see also specific cases
Supreme Soviet, 404
Suslov, Mikhail A., 393
Symington, Stuart, 225

Taber, John, 162
Taft, Robert A., 44, 118, 123, 136, 164, 216
Taft, William Howard, 14–15
    and conflict, 366
    on patronage, 125
Taft-Hartley Act, 167–69, 252, 272, 285–86, 288, 290
Tallmadge, James, 130
Talmadge, Eugene, 383
Taney, Roger B., 249
Tapes, Watergate, 73
Task forces, Presidential, 197–98, 309
Taylor, Maxwell, 241–42
Taylor, Zachary, 135
Technology, in Presidential campaigns, 49–50
Television debates, 49, 62, 113
Television
    and parties, 149
    and the Presidency, 113
    in Presidential campaigns, 49–50
Tennessee Valley Authority (TVA), 305
Tenure, Presidential, 63–91
    disability, 76–84
    impeachment, 66–73
    and legal processes, 73–75
    proposals for, 89–91
    resignation, 65–66
    succession, 84–86
    term of office, 63–65
    transitions, 86–89
Tenure of Office Act of *1867,* 67
Ter Horst, J. F., 105
Test ban treaty, 260
Thach, Charles C., 28
Thant, U, 375
Thomas, Elmer, 132
Thomas, Lorenzo, 67
Thompson, Llewellyn, Jr., 373
Thompson, Sir Robert G. K., 242
Thrasher, Wilkes T., Jr., 139
Thurmond, Strom, 46, 282, 377
Tilden, Samuel J., 56
Tobin, Dan, 280
Tonkin, Gulf of, resolution, 3, 218
Townsend, Francis Everett, 304
Trade Expansion Act of *1962,* 269
Train, Russell E., 209
Transitions, Presidential, 86–89
Treaty power, 24, 215–16
Truman, Harry S
    and atomic bombs, use of, 256
    and black civil rights, 315
    and conflict, 363–64, 366

coordination of executive branch by, 182
    as decision-maker, 349
    and defense investigating committee, 248
    and foreign policy making, 213
    and Joint Chiefs of Staff, 241
    and Korean War, 2, 218, 239
    and labor, 285, 287, 289–90
    legislative methods of, 154, 169, 171
    and MacArthur, 244–45
    majoritarian leader, 112
    and NATO, 234
    and nuclear weapons, 257
    personality of, 328, 339
    on Presidential power, 13
    renomination of, 122–23
    and scientists, 259
    and Secretaries of State, 223–24
    and social justice, 296
    and steel seizure, 252, 272
    style of, 336
    and succession, 85
    and Truman-Attlee-King Declaration, 259
    "whistle-stop" campaigner, 48
Trumbull, Lyman, 68
Tuck, Dick, 54
Tugwell, Rexford G., 191, 300, 312, 352
Tully, Grace, 191
Twain, Mark, 122
Twelfth Amendment, 56, 60
Twentieth Amendment, 89
Twenty-fifth Amendment, 81–84
Twenty-second Amendment, 64–65, 276
Two-term tradition, 64
Tydings, Millard, 132
Tyler, John, 130–31

Udall, Morris, 40
Underwood, Oscar, 175
United Nations, 235–36, 375
    Charter, 217
United States Steel Corporation, 267–68, 271–72
United States v. *Curtiss-Wright Corp.,* 216
Unruh, Jesse M., 138

Van Buren, Martin, 130, 264
Vallandigham, Clement L., 249
Vallandigham, Ex parte, 249
Values, Presidential, 327–31
Vandenberg, Arthur, 215
Van Nuys, Frederick, 132
Veto, 154, 165
    item, 384
Vice President
    administrative role of, 187
    nomination of, 45
Vietnam War
    decision-making concerning, 357–58
    escalation of, 218
    and Great Society program, 296
    and public opinion, 94–95

Vietnam War (*Continued*)
  truce, 219
  withdrawal from, 243
Vinson, Carl, 248
Virginia plan, 21
Vladivostok conference, 233, 258
Voting Rights Act of *1965*, 319

Wade, Ben, 67
Wagner, Robert F., 284
Wallace, George, 6, 55, 317
Wallace, Henry A., 112, 122, 134, 187, 364
Walsh, Thomas J., 43
War, power concerning
  Founding Fathers' views, 24–25
  Hamilton, 33
  Madison, 33
War Manpower Commission, 252
War Powers Act of *1973*, 219–20, 245
War Relocation Authority, 251
Warnke, Paul C., 87
Warren, Earl, 383
Washington, Booker T., 314
Washington, George
  and executive privilege, 155
  influence on creation of Presidency, 26–27
  legislative methods of, 173
  and partisanship, 135
  practical politics of, 13
  Presidency of, 29–33
  on reeligibility, 63–64
  style of, 336
  and treaty power, 215
Watergate
  burglaries, 69
  cover-up, 69
  and executive privilege, 156
  and "national security," 246
  and socialization, 94
  Special Prosecutor, *see* Special Prosecutor,
    Watergate tapes, 73
  and White House staff, 205–06
Watterson, Henry, 119
Ways and Means Committee, House, 128, 159, 179
Webster, Daniel, 130
Weinberger, Caspar W., 206–07, 313
Welfare reform, 151, 163, 296–97, 308
Welles, Gideon, 67
Wenzell, Adolphe, 196
West Germany (German Federal Republic), 230–31
Westwood, Jean, 286

Wheeler, Burton K., 311
Wheeler, Earle G., 350
White, Byron, 46
White, Kevin, 321
White, William Allen, 344
Whitehead, Clay T., 88, 109
White House staff, 194, 200, 202–05, 208–12,
    224–26
Wilkins, Roy, 318
Williamson, Hugh, 23
Willkie, Wendell, 281
Wilmerding, Lucius, 57–58
Wilson, Harold, 388–89, 392, 396, 398
Wilson, James, 22–24
Wilson, William B., 286
Wilson, Woodrow
  and black civil rights, 314
  and business, 270
  as Commander-in-Chief, 246
  and Congressional elections, 120
  disability of, 77–80
  goals of, 332–33
  as governor, 383
  and labor, 286
  legislative methods of, 165, 172, 175
  New Freedom program of, 295
  personality of, 327, 340
  Presidential candidacy of, 37
  on Presidential power, 13
  press conferences of, 106
  resignation plan of, 65–66
  and Secretaries of State, 223
  and social justice, 299–300, 304, 312
  and Vice Presidential nomination, 45
Wilson, Mrs. Woodrow, 78–79
Winant, John, 134
Wiretaps, 214
Wirtz, Willard, 361
Witte, Edwin E., 310–11
Wolfe, Bertram D., 393
Woodin, Will, 191
Women
  and Presidential nomination, 45
World Food Conference, *1974*, 298

Yalta conference, 216
Youngstown Sheet and Tube Co. v. *Sawyer*, 252, 272

Zarb, Frank G., 298
Ziegler, Ronald, 105